Creativity, Trauma, and Resilience

Creativity, Trauma, and Resilience

Paula Thomson and S. Victoria Jaque

LEXINGTON BOOKS
Lanham • Boulder • New York • London

Published by Lexington Books
An imprint of The Rowman & Littlefield Publishing Group, Inc.
4501 Forbes Boulevard, Suite 200, Lanham, Maryland 20706
www.rowman.com

6 Tinworth Street, London SE11 5AL, United Kingdom

Copyright © 2019 by The Rowman & Littlefield Publishing Group, Inc.

All rights reserved. No part of this book may be reproduced in any form or by any electronic or mechanical means, including information storage and retrieval systems, without written permission from the publisher, except by a reviewer who may quote passages in a review.

British Library Cataloguing in Publication Information Available

The hardback edition of this book was previously catalogued by the Library of Congress as follows:

Library of Congress Cataloging-in-Publication Data

ISBN: 978-1-4985-6020-7 (cloth : alk. paper)
ISBN: 978-1-4985-6022-1 (pbk : alk. paper)
ISBN: 978-1-4985-6021-4 (electronic)

∞™ The paper used in this publication meets the minimum requirements of American National Standard for Information Sciences—Permanence of Paper for Printed Library Materials, ANSI/NISO Z39.48-1992.

Printed in the United States of America

Contents

Acknowledgments		vii
Introduction		ix
SECTION I: CREATIVITY		**1**
1	Theories of Creativity	3
2	Talent and Giftedness	23
3	Creative Process	45
4	Fantasy and Pathology	67
5	Neurobiological and Physiologic Components of Creativity	85
SECTION II: TRAUMA		**109**
6	Childhood Adversity	111
7	Attachment	135
8	Trauma and Loss	163
9	Neurobiological and Psychophysiological Effects of Childhood Adversity, Trauma, and Loss Experiences	203
10	Shame	219
11	Dissociation	231
SECTION III: RESILIENCE		**247**
12	Regulation and Resilience: Psychosocial and Biological	249

13	Hardiness and Post-traumatic Growth	267
14	Constricting and Fostering Creative Resilience: A Complex Relationship	279
References		297
Index		421
About the Authors		429

Acknowledgments

Thank you to the Department of Kinesiology at California State University, Northridge, which supports our research efforts; Maurice Godin, who offered suggestions during the writing of this book; members of the International Society for the Study of Trauma and Dissociation, who shared their insight on complex trauma; colleagues in the American Psychological Association's Division 10, who offered their expertise in creativity research; and Mary Main and Erik Hesse, who continually mentor our research findings in the field of attachment. We are indebted to our many mentors over the years, some of whom include Jim Healy, Maria Jaque, Allen Schore, Daniel Siegel, Marion Solomon, Stan Tatkin, and Bessel van der Kolk. Lastly, special thanks to all the artists and athletes who joined our ongoing research study that is designed to investigate the positive and negative psychophysiological effects of stress on performance.

Introduction

Creative expression can be a powerful response to traumatic events. Leonard Bernstein stated: "This will be our reply to violence: to make music more intensely, more beautifully, more devotedly than ever before" (Speech at John F. Kennedy Memorial, 1963). It is estimated that exposure to traumatic events ranges between 40.5 percent (Lukasheck, 2013) to 89.7 percent (Elhai et al., 2012; Kilpatrick et al., 2013). This high exposure rate to trauma directly, and indirectly, influences the act of engaging in creativity. For example, many traumatized individuals avoid nurturing their creative potential in an effort to reduce states of vulnerability. A phobic response to any situation that renders them vulnerable may develop and soon avoidance strategies become the solution to diminish vulnerability. This avoidance has far-reaching effects, including an increase in the risk of morbidity and mortality. It also constrains creative productivity, which is potentially a profound loss for society.

In general, engaging in the creative process increases uncertainty and vulnerability; however, it also increases exploratory problem-solving behaviors. The combination of these and other factors all converge when creating a product. However, if creativity is constrained as a result of unresolved trauma or loss, then great works of art or scientific discoveries may never exist. Nurturing creativity, along with healing the wounds of past trauma, might offer increased resilience to the individual as well as increased resilience to communities and cultures. Ultimately, creative resourcefulness enhances effective problem-solving solutions and coping strategies and promotes resilience and hardiness. The positive interface between creativity and trauma is powerful and vital.

PURPOSE OF THE BOOK

This book is written for researchers, undergraduate and graduate students, and individuals interested in promoting creativity despite a history of adversity. The book incorporates research findings from diverse fields of study in an effort to present the complex interactions between creativity, trauma/loss, and factors that promote resilience. The content of this book covers general theories of creativity as they apply along the continuum from everyday creative activities to eminent creativity. Primarily, this book looks at the person rather than the creative product. It presents information about the psychobiological processes that are amplified within creativity, including the capacity to achieve flow (optimal) states. The long-lasting effects of childhood adversity and early attachment are examined in relationship to the effects they have on creative achievement. The psychological and neurobiological nature of trauma is outlined along with an in-depth discussion on shame and dissociation. Strategies related to self-regulation are discussed, including hardiness, resilience, and post-traumatic growth. Lastly, the book explores the constriction and fostering of creativity and well-being. The overarching focus of the book is on integrating two diverse fields, creativity and traumatology. Adapting to adversity is essential for survival. All species must adapt if they are to continue to exist. What may be uniquely human is the need to create; this is embedded in our adaptive instincts and has been evidenced since the beginning of recorded human history. Unfortunately, the history of the human condition is also marked by horrific exposure to traumatic events. Often these events alter the trajectory of individuals, families, or communities forever. By bringing the fields of creativity and traumatology closer together, it is hoped that responses to horrific trauma may be viewed less from a deficit model and more from a model of creative resilience, and ideally this creative resilience may foster a sense of meaning and purpose in those who have endured unimaginable trauma.

ORGANIZATION

The book is divided into three sections. Section One, Creativity, focuses on creativity theories as they relate to everyday creativity and to eminent creativity across all domains. Chapter 1 addresses integrative theories and models of creativity, types of creativity, and research methodologies to explore creativity. Chapter 2 examines the differences between giftedness and talent and the current theories and models associated with talent development, talent identification, and talent nurturance. Chapter 3 explores the creative process, including the values and motivation to engage in creative activities, flow states and dimensions, and creative factors operating during the creative experience. Chapter 4 examines the concepts of fantasy, daydreams, imagination, and awe, and how these processes exacerbate or alleviate pathology. Chapter 5 outlines the psycho-neurobiological findings related to creativity and flow experiences, including cognitive and physiologic processing, neuroaesthetics, and mystical experiences.

In Section Two, Trauma, attention is directed to trauma and loss across the lifespan. Chapter 6 discusses the different forms of childhood adversity, prevalence rates, signs of adversity, and the complex consequences resulting from cumulative childhood adversity. Chapter 7 focuses on attachment patterns, including secure, insecure, and disorganized/unresolved attachment patterns of behavior. Infant and adult attachment research studies are outlined (self-report, interview, and narrative methodologies). In Chapter 8, trauma and loss events are explored through the lens of diagnosis, prevalence rates, types of traumatic exposure, symptom patterns, comorbidity, and secondary traumatization. Chapter 9 addresses the psychophysiological and neurobiological responses that typify exposure to childhood adversity, trauma, and loss experiences. Chapter 10 explores shame, including the neurobiology of shame, and the relationship of shame to childhood adversity, PTSD, dissociation, and eating disorders. Chapter 11 explores the complex array of dissociative processing such as peritraumatic dissociation, depersonalization, childhood and adult dissociative responses, self-harming behaviors, and neurobiological factors.

In Section Three, Resilience, the focus is directed toward regulation, resilience, and post-traumatic growth. Chapter 12 presents theories on self-regulation and resilience, coping strategies, and vicarious resilience. Chapter 13 explores the concepts of hardiness and post-traumatic growth, as well as factors contributing to post-traumatic growth and secondary growth. Chapter 14 is the concluding chapter; it discusses the constriction and fostering of creative resilience, as well as factors such as limiting and expanding a sense of self, self-efficacy, passion, courage, and hope.

CONCLUSION

It is our hope that this book will add to the field of creativity and traumatology. This book presents a unique integrative overview on this topic, incorporating recent research in the fields of creativity and traumatology, with recommendations for future studies. Educators, students, and researchers can benefit from a greater understanding of the interacting effects of creativity, trauma, and resilience. Many talented and gifted individuals struggle with unresolved mourning; they falter in their attempts to realize their potential. By examining creativity through the lens of vulnerability and resilience, more specific strategies to optimize creative potential may be mobilized to support the countless number of individuals who are exposed to adversity.

Section I

CREATIVITY

Chapter 1

Theories of Creativity

Creativity is a concept that all children and adults acknowledge, although the ubiquitous nature of creativity makes it challenging to define, measure, and quantify. It is often resistant to scientific examination (Pinheiro and Cruz, 2014). Theories have been developed, specific variables have been isolated and probed, and creative individuals have been analyzed, and yet the phenomenon of creativity eludes definitive constructs; consequently, investigating creativity is never a straightforward process. Even determining a consensual agreement regarding an operational definition is fraught with debate and disagreement (Weisberg, 2015). This line of research unleashes a quagmire of challenges for those who study it. One of the key challenges is teasing out conscious from unconscious assumptions regarding creativity and how these assumptions bias research designs and findings (Smith, 2005; Sternberg, 2005). Navigating these assumptions requires creativity researchers to adopt a meta-creative stance; like metacognition (thinking about thinking), meta-creativity is "being creative about research on creativity" (Runco, 2015).

Questions persist in the creativity field, such as the following (Cropley, Kaufman, and Cropley, 2008):

1. Does creativity only exist in the preeminent few who are deemed titans in their respective fields?
2. Do creative studies promote hero identification or self-glorification?
3. Is the aesthetic creation of an artwork more creative than the diagnosis and repair of a motor engine?
4. Are specific domains (i.e., arts, sciences, technology) regarded as more creative or do they operate with different creative functions?

5. Is creativity identified in the product or in the person(s) who produced the product?
6. Is the existence of a product essential before someone can be selected as a viable participant in creativity research?
7. Did the creative process produce something that was unique, useful, and valued?
8. Was the product an eccentric manifestation of something concocted by the mind of a psychotic individual or something presented by an individual who is highly creative?
9. Is creativity a response from individuals who are sane or insane? Is creativity benevolent or malevolent?
10. Do criminals and terrorists share similar traits and engage in similar processes as scientists, artists, innovators, or entrepreneurs?
11. Despite being motivated by very different intentions, is creativity an a priori factor that is shaped by social context and psycho-neurobiological processes?

All these, and many more, questions are embedded in the field of creativity. Despite all these questions, ultimately, creating individuals, along with the environment in which they reside, are the primary sources for understanding factors that contribute to the creative process (Smith, 2005). Consequently, the complexity contained in this line of research makes it challenging to quantify and operationalize (Sternberg, 2005). Creativity is a multifaceted construct that requires a multifaceted investigation (Fryer, 2012; McKay, Karwowski, and Kaufman, 2017).

CREATIVITY: CHALLENGES ASSOCIATED WITH OPERATIONALIZING DEFINITIONS

Despite these difficulties, definitions do exist for creativity; however, a simple definition listed in the Merriam-Webster dictionary illustrates the lack of specificity that is often present (Merriam-webster.com). According to the Merriam-Webster dictionary, creativity is defined as "the ability to create" and create is defined as "to bring into existence." These are extremely vague definitions. Amongst creativity researchers, there is more specificity. Generally, they define a creative product; it must contain novelty (originality, uniqueness) and usefulness (effectiveness, value) (Sternberg, 2001). Most research studies deem novelty to be the primary ingredient in creativity (Corazza, 2016; Diedrich, Benedek, Jaunk, and Neubauer, 2015). Unlike usefulness, novelty is more easily recognized (Acar, Burnett, and Cabra, 1017), although both criteria are vulnerable to the test of time (Weisberg,

2015), as evidenced by creative works such as Stravinsky's Rite of Spring, which was initially rejected because it was too novel. Also the uniqueness of the product must not be viewed as "crazy," "insane," or "banal." This raises the question of who is actually evaluating uniqueness (novelty) (Weisberg, 2015). Usefulness is an equally difficult factor to assess, especially because something may initially be regarded as relevant (valued) or irrelevant, but this may change over time. Consequently, research investigators attempt to situate the effectiveness of a creative product within a shared understanding of reality, with the full awareness that this shared reality can change later (Diedrich et al., 2015).

Beyond novelty and utility (value), Kharkhurin (2014) proposed a four-dimensional matrix for evaluating creative work. He proposed that aesthetics and authenticity should be included as criteria to define creativity. Incorporating factors of aesthetics and authenticity differentiates the appraisal level of the creative product, process, and person. The term aesthetics goes beyond the implied sense of beauty and pleasure and includes inherent truthfulness and simple eloquence. Whether the work is artistic, scientific, mathematical, or economic, assessing the aesthetic element adds to the evaluative matrix of creative work. Likewise, when the person who created the new product incorporates values and beliefs that express the inner self of the person, the product often reflects the authentic nature of the creator. Certainly, integrating a sense of authenticity into the process yields meaning and value for the person who created the work, and, hopefully, for others who enjoy the benefits of the creative product (Nelson and Rawlings, 2009).

Despite the richness of the four-dimensional matrix for evaluating creative work (Kharkhurin, 2014), many argue that the four-dimensional model is really part of the two-dimensional model. It is argued that aesthetic appeal is integral to artistic novelty and authenticity is a component of both novelty and usefulness (Corazza, 2016). On the other hand, Weisberg (2015) claims that the criteria for creativity should only be one single dimension, intentional novelty. He suggests that the two-dimension definition of creativity (novelty and usefulness/value) is inadequate. He views value as a difficult and unstable factor to assess in creativity and recommends that it be excluded from the definition. He adds that including intentionality eliminates the bizarre random responses that are sometimes identified as creative products. Weisberg (2015) proposes that all creative products must have an intentional goal-directed component that operates during the creative process.

This need to recognize a creative product, although problematic, has persisted over the ages (Diedrich et al., 2015). Currently, the Consensual Assessment Technique is regarded as the gold standard for recognizing whether a product is creative (Amabile, 1996; Kaufman and Baer, 2012). A panel of qualified experts is deemed to be the best judge of creativity. To be regarded as an expert judge usually requires that the individual gained mastery over a minimum period of ten years, followed by working within the field for ten years (Ericsson, Roring, and Nandagopal, 2007; Kaufman and Kaufman, 2007). Consensual assessment requires that the judges have a record of accomplishment in their field (Kaufman and Baer, 2012). This consensual assessment method of identifying a creative product, although biased, establishes consistent responses related to product novelty and usefulness. It is argued that the experts in their field understand the breadth and depth of their field and can recognize when a new product exhibits creative features that make it stand out against other products (Amabile, 1996). Regardless of the field, whether artistic, scientific, technological, economic, military, or political, and the nature of the product, whether benevolent or malevolent, experts can be identified and their opinions sought out.

The need to identify a product as creative remains important; however, most researchers focus on investigating the creative process and/or the creative person (including the development and social context of the person) (Smith, 2005). By examining both the process and person, motivation and intentionality can be included in the factors of novelty and value (Weisberg, 2015). According to researchers who are oriented to a systems view, creative products exist within a cyclic process that must include a person (with creative potential), an environment within which he or she works, and a domain that is situated within the environment (field) (Csikszentmihalyi, 1999). A systems view also relies on consensual assessment; the importance of a positive evaluation by others in the field and domain remains. All three factors directly influence the appraisal of a creative product. This systems view opens the path toward a more dynamic definition. The emergence of a product results from a dynamic interplay of variables that reflect a more inclusive orientation toward the creative process (Corazza, 2016).

The limiting factors of defining creativity are also exposed when researchers take a cross-cultural perspective. For example, when viewing creative activities, Western views tend to endorse individualism, whereas Eastern views regard the creative enterprise as a collective process. Like all studies in creativity, this binary East/West view is routinely challenged or unsupported (Paletz, Peng, and Li, 2011). Likewise, dividing novelty and value into an external orientation (i.e., collectivism, holistic) and an internal orientation (i.e., individualistic, analytic) or as practical or impractical may increase understanding of the creative product, but the binary nature of these categorizations precludes the inherent complexity that resides within the person, process, and product. Ultimately, including the person, process, and product enables a deeper cross-cultural investigation into how creativity operates and what may be valued within specific cultures (Paletz et al., 2011).

Expanding the study of creativity allows pervasive myths to be explored and challenged. Three of the most common myths that persist within creativity research fields are the notions (1) that creativity is "heaven-sent," (2) that it predominantly manifests within aesthetic-artistic domains, and (3) that it is a momentary flash of creative brilliance described as the "aha moment" (Cropley, 2016). Currently, research attention is directed beyond the study of aesthetic creativity and of individuals who are deemed as preeminently talented. Creativity actually operates on a continuum from understated humbleness to overly aggrandized glitter. Because of this continuum, researchers must attempt to differentiate subtle markers of creativity and separate these markers from the current media practice of heralding potentially derivative, mediocre works as seemingly creative works (Cropley, 2016). The researcher's challenge is to examine creativity without trivializing or reifying it. Ideally, identifying factors that promote creative output might benefit everyone. This need to identify and promote creativity is even more important given the reality that, despite increased IQ scores, creativity has diminished in the United States since the 1990s (Kim, 2011).

GENERAL FACTORS ASSESSED IN CREATIVITY

According to the Torrance Tests of Creative Thinking (TTCT), six factors are involved in creative output (Kim, 2011). These factors remain as stable longitudinal predictors of creative aptitude, a fact that increases their importance when attempting to evaluate creative potential in students from culturally diverse and lower socio-economic backgrounds (Cramond, Matthews-Morgan, and Bandolos, 2005):

1. Fluency (ability to produce ideas)
2. Originality (ability to produce unique and unusual ideas)
3. Creative strengths (emotionally expressive, energetic, humorous, lively, passionate, unconventional, imaginative, perceptive, interactive)
4. Elaboration (ability to think in a detailed and reflective manner)
5. Abstraction (ability to synthesize and organize thinking)
6. Resistance to premature closure (intellectually curious and open-minded).

The importance of these factors is that they can be readily trained and enhanced throughout childhood and adolescent development (Cramond et al., 2005). Currently, these factors are strongly embraced and promoted in Chinese education, whereas in the United States, the educational focus has shifted away from creative fluency and toward concrete standardized testing (Hartley and Plucker, 2014). This may account for the significant decrement in creativity in the United States of America, especially fluency, creative strengths, elaboration, and resistance to premature closure. American students are now less engaged in creative thought (Florida, 2004; Kim, 2011), a finding that is strongly associated with increased psychopathology and suicidal ideation (Mraz and Runco, 1994). Without an ability to generate an array of possibilities, problem solving becomes constrained and creative thought becomes impoverished.

An overlapping pattern of Torrance factors emerged when creative individuals were asked to define features that enhanced their creativity (Gluck, Ernst, and Unger, 2002). These individuals added talent, risk-taking, assertiveness, and, most importantly, hard work. According to eminent creative individuals, creative output is always the result of hard work (Gluck et al., 2002). This finding runs counter to another myth that posits that creativity is an easy activity bestowed on the gifted few. The myth of the struggling artist who suffers for the sake of art is closer to that suggested by the artists in the Gluck et al. (2002) study. In this study, strong findings indicate that the domain of creativity (aesthetic, scientific, constrained versus free) influences the importance of specific creativity factors. Creative individuals readily identify the unique domain-specific talents and skills necessary to achieve expertise in their field, although domain-general traits (i.e., problem recognition, problem solving) are also recognized by individuals engaged in domain-specific fields (i.e., scholarly, performance, scientific, entrepreneurial, technological, artistic) (McKay et al., 2017).

These results fuel efforts of researchers to isolate factors that reside only in the domain-general versus domain-specific creative processing (Baer, 2015; Baer, 2010b; Silvia, Kaufman, and Pretz, 2009; Sternberg, 2005). Despite the unique factors that are identified by individuals who operate in domain-specific disciplines, study findings suggest that the task itself typically evokes domain-general creative factors required to complete the task (Reiter-Palmon, Illes, Buboltz, Cross, and Nimps, 2009), such as resistance to task closure and creative strengths needed to meet the demands of the task. Some studies suggest that individuals who are recognized within different creative domains, such as engineers and composers, may actually use similar processes during creative problem solving (Charyton and Snelbecker, 2007). Creative problem solving involves the generation of viable solutions needed to address novel, ill-defined, and ambiguous problems (Treffinger, Selby, and Isaksen, 2008). A combination of knowledge, skill, ability, and cognition (problem defining, conceptual formation, information gathering, idea generation, idea evaluation, and idea application) operate during creative problem solving (Watts, Steele, and Song, 2017). These factors are some of the more readily identified multifaceted variables that operate during creative problem solving.

Creative individuals, regardless of domain, must spend substantial time learning the field within which they interact (Ericsson et al., 2007; Gardner, 1993; Simonton, 1999). Creative individuals spend years gaining skills and preparing to engage in the critical tasks that enable the manifestation of the creative product. Studies indicate that creative productivity is fundamentally contingent on adequate preparation (Simonton, 1999). During the creative process, the "magical" moments of illumination are always recycled back into more preparation (Cropley, 2016). The hard work of creating involves taking action, generating a product, verifying to see if it works, communicating, and then validating the creative work with other experts in the field and within the larger general population. Even when an inherently creative person is engaged in everyday activities such as riding the bus, washing dishes, or reading, new knowledge is gained and new understandings unfold (Cropley, 2016). The creative product is ultimately directly related to hard work that takes place over time (Cropley, 2016). Knowledge, skill acquisition, and repeated practice in problem identification and problem solving are the ingredients that facilitate creative output, whether the output is benevolent or malevolent (Cropley et al., 2008).

CREATIVE THEORIES AND MODELS

Multiple theories have been proposed to describe the creative process. Many of the theories have endured over time, although they are challenged and debated with regularity (Fryer, 2012). Generally, creative models that endure reflect the multifaceted nature of creativity. They incorporate dynamics that can cross all domains and cultures (Sternberg, 2005). Ultimately, the ingredients to work creatively are fundamentally pragmatic factors, even though some individuals may work with more creative ease and facility (Cropley, 2016). Including these pragmatic factors, while differentiating the nature and quality of creativity, inevitably informs all theories and models proposed by creativity researchers.

The Four Cs of Creativity

Originally, creativity research, and the models that emerged, focused on creative greatness, genius, or eminence (Smith, 2001). This focus was known as "Big-C" creativity (Kaufman and Beghetto, 2009). Attention was directed toward the production of eminent creative works, the personalities of the creative titans (including mental well-being or illness), and cognitive processes that were employed (divergent, convergent). The other line of research addressed everyday creativity, in particular, research in educational policy and curriculum, and in corporate settings. Defining everyday creativity expanded the scope of creativity research. It enabled inclusion of average people who participate in crafts, culinary activities, or even simple daily problem-solving tasks (Hennessey and Amabile, 2010). This line of research became known as "little-c" creativity.

Gradually, the need to disambiguate the dichotomous classifications of Big-C versus little-c creativity led to the inclusion of two more classifications (Beghetto and Kaufman, 2015). Creative output operates on a continuum and so the inclusion of two more categories helped define this continuum (Kaufman and Beghetto, 2009). The third category, "Pro-C," describes creative individuals who have achieved a certain professional expertise within their domain. For example, they may be highly skilled performers, artists, scientists, or entrepreneurs who implement creative processes to sustain their work, but they are not necessarily producing eminent creative products. The inclusion of the fourth category, "mini-c" creativity helps differentiate Pro-C from everyday creativity (little-c). The mini-c category identifies individuals who routinely engage in personally meaningful activities that involve dynamic interpretations and understandings. For example, a doctor or car mechanic may incorporate mini-c creativity to formulate a diagnosis. Such individuals use knowledge and experience to construct novel applications of their knowledge. Mini-c is a more subjective form of creativity and is a key component to achieving Pro-C levels of creativity (Kaufman and Beghetto, 2013). Creative insight manifests in mini-c activities, just as it operates in Big-C, Pro-C, and little-c activities. The expansion of the two-category model to a four C model incorporates the natural fluidity of these creative dimensions. A Big-C creator most certainly partakes in all the other levels of creativity, although the average person may only interact at the mini-c and little-c levels. It is important to acknowledge that this model was never intended to limit classification of creative studies; rather, it was formulated to emphasize the overlapping degrees of creativity (Beghetto and Kaufman, 2015).

Distinguishing between these four levels of creativity implies awareness of the fifth and opposite category, "Not Creative." Both lay people and experts can readily recognize when someone is engaging in a non-creative process or if the resulting product is not creative (i.e., has no value or novelty) (Kaufman and Beghetto, 2013). The ability to perceive levels of creativity reinforces a developmental appreciation of creativity; for example, recognizing that a small child is creatively engaged enables appreciation that this child may eventually move from mini-c to Pro-C or Big-C (Kaufman and Beghetto, 2009). Likewise, engaging in different types of creativity reveals creative behavior, in particular, an openness to new experiences (Ivcevic and Mayer, 2006–2007). Individuals can effectively engage in creative activities or just as easily disengage into non-creative activities. Further, the ability to perceive creativity, and all its levels, is greatly influenced by personality traits (Kaufman and Beghetto, 2013). People who are generally more open to experiences, hence more likely to be exposed to creative diversity, tend to recognize and appreciate creative behavior across the continuum (Ivcevic, 2007), whereas individuals who are closed to experiences tend to overlook creativity and are unable to differentiate creativity levels in general. Further, individuals who are oriented toward more contrary or oppositional attitudes may overtly reject activities or products as non-creative (Kaufman and Beghetto, 2013).

Investment Theory

Theories that attempt to explain why an individual invests in creative enterprises have been devised, especially when individuals strive for Pro-C or Big-C creative levels. According to suggestions by Sternberg and Lubart (1992), such individuals "buy low and sell high." They refer to buying low as engaging in activities that are unknown or not valued. The creative individual identifies a need and persists in engaging in the activity until it is recognized and valued. He or she must tolerate resistance and ambiguity and maintain his or her belief in the value of the activity. The validity of this investment theory is reinforced when the six creativity resources of those who "bought low and sold high" are identified and examined (Zhang and Sternberg, 2011). These resources include the following (Sternberg, 2012):

1. The confluence of three types of intelligence: (a) synthetic intelligence (seeing problems from different perspectives and incorporating remote ideas), (b) analytical intelligence (recognizing and discerning which idea should be explored), (c) practical intelligence (knowledge related to how to persuade others to invest in the creative plan).
2. Knowledge (the creative person must have knowledge about the field within which he or she is working and the needs of the field).
3. Intellectual style (preferred ways of using one's intelligence such as global associations, inclusive acceptance of ideas, and adhering to individual uniqueness while exploring creative ideas).
4. Personality (tolerating ambiguity, risk taking, openness to new experiences, self-belief, persistence, and determination).
5. Motivation (having intrinsic motivation to pursue the task as well as a passion for the work).
6. Environmental support (having a place to work and resources to complete the task).

Sternberg and Lubart elaborated on their initial investment theory, suggesting that multiple styles of creative thinking are engaged during the creative process (Sternberg, 2012). Ultimately, the individual must determine when a current paradigm needs to be expanded or replaced. Once this has been determined, a sequence of creative thought is deployed to meet the challenge. Some of these styles of thinking include replicating, redefining, redirecting, reconstructing, and reinitiating. If no paradigm exists, then a new one must be created by synthesizing information into a new constructed paradigm (Sternberg, 2005).

EIGHT COMPONENTS WITHIN THE CREATIVE PROCESS

Mumford and colleagues (1991) elaborated on the six factors identified by Torrance (Kim, 2011). They outlined eight key components within the creative process:

1. problem construction (identifying and recognizing the problem)
2. information gathering (retrieving relevant information)
3. category search (reorganizing the material and carefully selecting search criteria)
4. selection of best-fitting categories (via reorganizing and recombining information)
5. combining and reorganizing category information
6. idea evaluation
7. idea implementation (applying to problem solution)
8. monitoring (checking to make sure the solution remains effective) (Mumford, Mobley, Uhlman, Reiter-Poman, and Doares, 1991).

These eight factors amplify the creative cognitive process during all problem-solving tasks. By applying these factors, a preeminent creative product or a modification of an existing product may be produced (Gill, Horgan, Hunter, and Cushenbery, 2013).

Stage-Based Models

Stage-based models have also been promoted with varying degrees of success (Lubart, 2001). Wallas' four-stage model of creativity (preparation, incubation, illumination, and verification) is one of the most prominent models in the creativity field (Bourgeois-Bougrine, Botella, Glaveanu, Guillou, De Biasi, and Lubart, 2014; Wallas, 1926). This model grew from Poincairé's introspective reflections and descriptions of his mathematical creative problem-solving process (Lubart, 2001; Wallas, 1926/1976). In Wallas' model, the first stage, preparation, includes years of prior training along with specific details directly related to the task at hand. In the preparation phase, the problem is clearly defined or the need is directly identified and information is gathered to solve the problem or resolve the need. The information gathering is drawn from a rich educational history, direct experience within the field, and inquiry-based skills essential to explore the problem (Sadler-Smith, 2015).

According to Wallas (1926), the second stage, incubation, may take minutes or years. During this phase, the unconscious mind explores the problem and accesses remote memories associated with the problem or need. The unconscious mind may work while the individual is engaged in mental distractions (actively working on another mental task) or mental relaxation (i.e., exercise, meditation, sleep). The third stage, illumination, begins when part or whole memories are retrieved that are associated with the problem or desire. This stage is often termed the "aha" moment or a "flash" of insight. Ideas seemingly emerge from nowhere. They are brief rushes of insight that may last moments or hours. Also contained within the illumination stage is a slower and longer process, one that is marked by a rising series of associations that converge into a coherent solution (Sadler-Smith, 2015).

The final stage is verification; during this stage, individuals must demonstrate that the information garnered from the illumination stage answers the problem or satisfies the need. This stage resembles the initial preparation phase because the solution must be tested based on background knowledge, experience, and validation garnered from respectable sociocultural resources (Sadler-Smith, 2015). Wallas also posited that a more mercurial factor operates throughout all four stages. This intuitive mercurial factor was also gleaned from Poincaré's writings. Poincaré described "sensibilité" as a feeling that guided him forward during his explorations. This term describes the "felt" knowing that unconsciously guides the creative process. Today, increased attention is directed toward creative intuition, including ways to measure it through the lens of phenomenology and neurobiology (Sadler-Smith, 2015). Wallas' four-stage model describes a process that takes years before all the variables, even the sudden moment of illumination, ultimately converge into a new work (Fryer, 2012; Cropley, 2016).

Unlike the four-stage model, the two-stage model of creativity was derived from a neurocognitive approach. For example, the geneplore model describes the generative phase and the exploratory phase (Sternberg, 2005). During the generative phase, mental representations are consciously or unconsciously constructed to solve the creative problem, whereas the exploratory phase intentionally or unintentionally embraces all forms of emerging creative ideas that are related to the properties of the pre-inventive structure (Tang and Gero, 2002). The geneplore model is a cognitive model that provides a circular process of generating and exploring possibilities. During both phases, divergent and convergent cognitive processes can be implemented, just as chaotic unstructured or organized structured idea generation can manifest during the process (Finke, 1996). This biphasic model shares features of the psychodynamic model of primary (unconscious) and secondary (pre-conscious and conscious) processing (Dijksterhuis and Meurs, 2006; Holt, 2002; Lubart, 2001). According to this psychodynamic model, illumination or "aha" awareness springs from the primary creative unconscious, one that is differentiated from the primal "Id" impulses that typify the primary unconscious described in psychodynamic theory (Holt, 2002). The creative primary unconscious (Holt, 2002) shares processing features with mysticism and mystical practices (Brown, 2008). Whether actively or passively practiced, inward reflective mysticism promotes metaphoric and symbolic thought, as well as the emergence of novel associations that are often endowed with a profound sense of expansive unity. The practice of mysticism is an ancient doorway to acquire insight and illumination (Brown, 2008), although introspective practices are also promoted in the geneplore and psychodynamic models.

Component Model of Creativity

Differing from the models above, Amabile (1996) suggests that an individual must first be motivated to engage in a task. He or she must recognize the potential need for creative responses and intentionally address the task. She created the Principle Component Model of Creativity (1996), which includes motivation, expertise, and creativity skills. The model proposes that creativity can only take place when enough expertise has been cultivated to meet the challenges of the task. Specific creative skills such as level of intelligence, divergent thinking, memory retrieval, and cognitive/physical abilities must be mastered and applied to the task (Zhang, Zhang, Yu, and Zhao, 2015). She describes the creative process as a series of phases: (1) problem identification, (2) preparation (gathering information and materials), (3) response generation, and (4) response validation (Lubart, 2001). Unlike the four-stage model, the Componential Model is a recursive model that operates as a set of feedback loops; these phases can also occur simultaneously. Within each phase, multiple sub-phases are also embedded (Amabile, 1996; Lubart, 2001). Amabile's research and the inherent complexity of her model have paved the way for other more dynamic creativity models. They all share the recursive nature of her model (Weisberg, 2006).

Distributed Creativity

One example of a dynamic creativity model is the distributed creativity model. It approaches the creative process not from the standpoint of a single individual engaged in the creative act; rather, it describes a dynamic social network involved in creating something novel (Sawyer and DeZutter, 2009).

Jazz performers or improvisational theater performers are two examples that typify this form of creative process; however, scientists, entrepreneurs, and all organizations that devise new products, policies, or procedures are included in this model (Perry-Smith and Shalley, 2003). Ultimately, effective collaboration is the bedrock of this creative model (Sawyer and DeZutter, 2009). These groups intentionally or unintentionally form to address a specific problem (task) or collection of problems. A collaborative emergence of novel ideas or products manifests as the group works together. The group also collaboratively evaluates the validity of the product and determines the future of the product as well as the continuation of the collaborative group (Sawyer, 2000, 2006).

Large organizational groups also adhere to the concept of distributed creativity, especially when they intend to promote creative processes designed to produce innovative products (Hennessey and Amabile, 2010). Educational work environments are examples of distributed creativity (Sawyer, 2006). Collectively, the administrators, teachers, and students can cultivate creative exploration and strengthen creative problem-solving skills. Likewise, industrial and entrepreneurial work environments and community organizations can enhance collaborative creative enterprises by providing opportunities to produce novel products and acknowledge their value. Ensuring that these organizations are successful requires that they face the challenge of balancing the positive and negative effects of diversity. Including diversity ensures innovation and increases competitiveness in the work environment. It also requires organizations to manage potential workplace conflicts that are often associated with diversity (Bassett-Jones, 2005). Ultimately, diversity is essential for collaborative creativity (Uzzi and Spiro, 2005). When a workplace or school environment provides a sense of security and affiliation, the members of the organization work with a feeling of freedom to explore, even though they must still work with real constraints that exist in the external environment (Hennessey and Amabile, 2010; Stokes, 2001). In fact, studies have demonstrated that the paradoxical nature of freedom and constraint may actually promote creative productivity (Haught, 2015; Kristensen, 2004). Large groups and organizations have the potential to ensure positive or negative creative productivity; the innovative productivity may benefit the individual and community or subjugate them to criminal or terrorist behaviors (James and Drown, 2008).

TYPES OF CREATIVITY

Dividing creativity into types of creativity is far different from examining different domains and models. Domain-based research explores a specific field, as well as potentially multiple sub-disciplines within the field. For example, research studies may focus on the arts in general or sub-divisions within the arts such as writing, performing arts, or painting, and these fields can be further subdivided. Dividing creativity into types involves organizing the field into radical versus incremental creativity or into malevolent versus benevolent creativity (Jaussi and Randel, 2014; Lee and Dow, 2011). Identifying the specific type of creativity is particularly useful to organizational enterprises, especially since cultivating creative strategies ensures that we manage our rapidly changing environment (Jaussi and Randel, 2014). Understanding types of creativity (incremental versus radical and benevolent versus malevolent) can help facilitate adaptation.

It is posited that incremental creativity includes small adaptive creative responses that provide small changes to existing products, processes, or policies. Radical creativity completely changes existing products, processes, or policies (Janussi and Randel, 2014). Both forms are appropriate depending on the conditions and needs of the environment. Key components associated with each type can be identified and encouraged depending on the demands of the organization. For example, when an individual has strong self-efficacy, radical creativity is more likely to occur, whereas those with lower self-efficacy may be ideally suited to continue working on the incremental creative changes that need to take place, especially in the aftermath of a radical creative change. Radical changes are also more likely to occur when individuals employ cognitive strategies that involve scanning for information within the organization as well as outside the organization. Individual openness to experience and a strong sense of self-efficacy tend to promote radical creativity. Incremental and radical change occurs via internal and external scanning during knowledge retrieval (Janussi and Randel, 2014). Cultivating networking ties increases diversity and collaboration and ensures both incremental and radical creative types (Janussi and Randel, 2014; Uzzi and Spiro, 2005).

Another type of creativity is benevolent and malevolent creativity. The challenge of differentiating malevolent from benevolent creativity is fundamentally determined by who is harmed and who benefits from the creative product (Cropley et al., 2008). This is not a clear-cut distinction as is evident when discussing terrorist bombings; the political or religious affiliation of those evaluating this act determines whether it is benevolent or malevolent creativity. One side gains while the other side loses; consequently, one side views the act as benevolent while the other side regards it as malevolent (Cropley et al., 2008). Further, the use of a product can inform benevolent or malevolent results; for example, the creation of a drug can be used to heal but it can also be used to kill if mishandled (Eisenman, 2008). Engaging in this level of analysis inevitably includes the degree of functionality of the product. Novelty and, even more importantly, usefulness (relevance and effectiveness) are criteria that determine whether an act or product is creative. Certainly, the intentionality of the individual is fully manifested during these acts (Eisenman, 2008).

Determining if an individual is antisocial becomes a fuzzy parameter. The person may be diagnosed as antisocial or proclaimed a national hero (Cropley et al., 2008). Many individuals lack emotional intelligence, which may facilitate participation in malevolent creativity (Harris, Reiter-Palmon, and Kaufman, 2013). Along with deficits in emotional intelligence, physical aggressive traits are associated with malevolent creativity (Lee and Dow, 2011), but again, the effects of the aggressive act biases the appraisal of whether aggressive features are positive or negative. Aggression, when considered a malevolent trait, is associated with intent to cause harm to an individual or organization (Gill et al., 2013). Including aggression as a feature of creativity raises many questions that remain fundamentally unanswered; however, in one study that investigated criminals, the level of creativity was generally low. A few criminals in this study did score very high on creative measures, especially when they discussed criminality (Eisenman, 2008). These gifted few could be described as exhibiting creative talent in the field of criminality, a notion that may include aggressive behaviors and the intent to cause harm.

Understanding the mind and strategies of a terrorist, as well as of the counterterrorist, can shed light on the creative process employed by these groups and the individuals who are engaged in these practices (James and Drown, 2008). Terrorist organizations ultimately incorporate imitative as well as innovative creative behaviors. Like the criminal study, many terrorists operate in imitative behaviors (low creativity); however, some are truly innovative and creative (Gill et al., 2013). The practices of these organizations are no different from those described in the four-stage model of creativity, the six Torrance factors of creativity, the six creative resources described by Sternberg and Lubart, and the eight problem-solving strategies outlined by Mumford and colleagues (Gill et al., 2013). They produce a novel product that has usefulness and value, and they operate with clear intention and motivation. They have talent and have cultivated strong skills and expertise. Their target audience is surprised by the attack and their message is delivered in an innovative and creative, although deadly, manner. The goal of counterterrorism is to stop the surprise attack, although the counterterrorists in turn implement a surprise attack on the terrorist organization. In both terrorist and counter-terrorist organizations, the creative factors of novelty and value are clearly evident, as well as the simple elegance of their deadly plan (Cropley et al., 2008; Gill et al., 2013).

Both criminal and terrorist organizations operate with incremental and radical types of creativity. They operate as both collaborative organizations with distributed creative processing, and hierarchical structures that are guided by the creativity of their leadership. Dissatisfaction with the community motivates these organizations. Within these communities, moral standards are inherently understood (Gutworth and Hunter, 2017). When these moral values are malleable or if there is a dissonance between the moral values of the group and the needs of an individual or subgroup, then deviance from group norms often follows. These responses may promote growth and adaptation in the organization or it may collapse because of a rigid adherence to organizational demands (Gill et al., 2013). Organizational psychology, and its vast wealth of information related to effective organizational structures, could be directly applied to understanding criminal, terrorist, and counter-terrorist organizations. Factors such as group size, leadership traits, extrinsic/intrinsic rewards, flexibility to adapt to changing conditions, available resources (foreign and local financial support, cultural beliefs, and geographical conditions) all predict longevity and creative effectiveness of the organization (Cropely et al., 2008; Gill et al., 2013). Skills of the members and leaders ensure the actualization of creative products that are produced within these organizations (Gill et al., 2013).

CREATIVITY RESEARCH METHODOLOGIES

Empirical studies in creativity incorporate multiple research design methodologies. These empirical studies have enhanced the examination and evaluation of theories and models designed to explain creativity. According to Long's study (2014), the research field of creativity primarily utilizes quantitative designs. Experimental and cross-sectional studies are the primary approach and all utilize psychometric measurements. In many studies, consensual judges are included to determine degree of creativity. Qualitative methodology is predominately a case study or grounded theory approach, and many of these studies include a mixed-method design. There are fewer longitudinal studies, although when they are conducted they fundamentally address child development and the importance of creativity for future achievement (Russ and Wallace, 2013; Gajda, Karwowski, and Beghetto, 2017).

According to study findings that implemented a network analysis technique, multiple measures to assess creativity should be included in all creativity research studies. The measures should include cognitive processes employed during a creative task, attitudes and personality traits of the creative individual, and consensual agreement on product novelty and value (Pinheiro and Cruz, 2014). Understanding creativity is derived from multiple intersecting fields such as psychology, neuroscience, physiology, sociology, economics, and culture. Factors such as positive or negative affect, quality of social leadership, developmental history, motivation, and achievement all influence how creativity is assessed. The challenges for creativity researchers include integrating these complex factors via cluster analyses or network analyses. The limitations of the research tools also limit study findings and conclusions (Pinheiro and Cruz, 2014).

In general, the nature of the research design, although providing empirical evidence, also reflects social truths and assumptions that operate in the background (Long, 2014). This fact is evident in creativity research, although attempts to counter these limitations are being addressed by utilizing more powerful statistical analyses (i.e., latent growth modeling, multilevel modeling, and Item Response Theory). The need to include multiple factors to investigate the complex dynamic of creativity is generally reflected in the field (Mumford, 2003). Five primary lines of research have been identified in the body of creativity research. The dominant line of research investigates creativity applications in specific domain areas (i.e., geographical region, specialty field, activity status such as risk factors, evolution, and influence) (Zhang et al., 2015). Other lines of research include psychopathology and physiology, individual level of creativity, organizational level of creativity, and basic theories and methodologies at the core of creativity research (Zhang et al., 2015).

The expansion into new fields is just beginning to emerge (i.e., sport, traumatology, negotiation, therapeutic interventions). Beyond identifying what is creative, the theory of creative functioning, including experiential possibilities, needs further exploration. This approach necessitates new ways to study the deeply subjective functioning of creativity such as the notions of embodied knowing (Gibbs, 2003; Smith, 2001; Sullivan and McCarthy, 2009). Explorations into subjectivity may also promote a return to the often-abandoned examination of aesthetics. This topic once resided within the field of philosophy, then in literature and the arts, and to a lesser degree in the early psychodynamic psychological writings about the unconscious (Martindale, 2007). With the implementation of new research measures and designs, understanding creative aesthetics may once again flourish. An increasing number of studies that are rooted in cross-cultural investigations are now expanding, including more international collaborations. The creativity field continues to expand and the goal of gaining more scientific diversity and rigor is evident in emerging research studies (Long, 2014). Ultimately, the identification of creative individuals and promoting more creative productivity will be enhanced when interdisciplinary approaches to constructing research designs are implemented. Likewise, moving beyond, the implicit view that creativity is a positive moral expression of humanity is changing. Establishing research instruments that can accurately assess values, intentions, and positive or negative (malevolent) responses are still needed. The burgeoning field of valence now extends beyond previous studies that examined emotional valence of the creative person; it is now moving into the creative product and environment (Kapoor and Khan, 2016).

CONCLUSION

The complex nature of creativity research requires researchers to continually practice perspective shifting (Runco, 2015). For example, if studies investigate divergent thinking as a major component in creativity, then other studies need to examine the role of convergent thinking in creativity (Tan, 2015). Likewise, when studies demonstrate that a positive mood promotes the creative process, other studies might demonstrate how negative or neutral moods influence creativity (Davis, 2009; Kaufman, 2003; Kaufmann and Vosberg, 1997). Understanding creativity through a narrow lens often intensifies debates that may distract researchers from effectively addressing its inherent complexity. For example, researchers continue to argue that creativity is associated with madness, possession, an evolutionary necessity, incubation and illumination, divergent thinking, or boundary breaking (McKerracher, 2016). The focus of these arguments reveals the metaphoric nature of creativity as well as the reality that it is a complex construct that requires both discrete study designs and integrative investigations that incorporate multiple disciplines (McKerracher, 2016; Sternberg, 2005).

Researchers primarily investigate one or several of the four major fronts, often named the four Ps: person, product, process, and press (environmental and social contexts) (Csikszentmihalyi, 1999; Rhodes, 1961; Runco, 2004; Simonton, 2000). The need to integrate the four Ps has been suggested in several matrix models. For example, one matrix includes the actual measurement approaches that influence the findings and assumptions in the field of creativity. In this proposed matrix model, creativity is assessed on the basis of level (individual, team, organization, culture), facet (the four Ps), and measurement design (objectives, self versus other ratings) (Batey, 2012). Although assessing all these variables is important, finding ways to examine the underlying heuristics of creativity remains critical (Vessey and Mumford, 2012). For example, the challenge for researchers is to devise models that account for the reality that creativity fundamentally operates at the intersection of all fronts (Batey, 2012). It is dynamic and complex. The ability to examine these underlying factors will shape future assessments of creative training programs and innovative organizational systems. To move beyond what already exists, the creativity field must improve assessments of creative output as well as ways to effectively train others to create (Vessey and Mumford, 2012).

Investigating creativity and promoting it within organizations is an evolutionary necessity (Hennessey and Amabile, 2010). The persistent myths and stereotypes that surround creativity need to be challenged and changed. As discussed earlier, creativity is in crisis; conceptualizing and defining creativity is vital (Kimbell, 2000). Perceiving creativity along a continuum increases knowledge at the individual and group level. The major components that operate during the creative process can be recognized, trained, and supported. Educational and organizational psychologists can maximize the practice of creativity; they may also maximize innovative practices that promote future adaptability and survival (Plucker, Beghetto, and Dow, 2004).

Chapter 2

Talent and Giftedness

The creativity continuum, from everyday to eminent levels, acknowledges that some individuals are deemed gifted or talented whereas others are not endowed with this potential. The problem for researchers who investigate talent/giftedness is that these terms are often contentiously debated, especially because of an implied inequality that resides within these words (Morelock, 1996; Renzulli, 1978). To claim that someone is gifted suggests that he or she is ranked higher than others. One of the many challenges to this concept is the possibility that his or her elevated ranking may not reflect his or her innate abilities, but, rather, his or her sociocultural advantages. Problems also exist when differentiating intellectual giftedness from domain-specific talents such as athletics, arts, or technology. Determining that someone is talented or gifted is ultimately informed by socially constructed values (Pfeiffer, 2012). Another limitation when determining talent/giftedness is related to retrospective evaluations; identification is based on the value placed on the products produced by the individual in adulthood rather than the talents exhibited during development (Subotnik, Olszewski-Kubilius, and Worrell, 2011).

Establishing operational definitions to differentiate the terms gifted and talented has received great attention (Morelock, 1996; Renzulli, 2002, 2005). Often these terms are used interchangeably, which has added further confusion to research studies that investigate giftedness/talent. Although different viewpoints persist, three pathways now dominate the field. First, giftedness, as originally defined, assesses intelligence level as measured by standardized IQ tests, with scores over 180 considered to be in the gifted range (Renzulli, 2002). Second, driven by Gardner's proposal of multiple intelligences (1983, 1993), the concept of giftedness expanded to include the top one per cent of the population who manifest prodigious talent(s) (i.e., academic, athletic, artistic, scientific, IQ) (Renzulli, 2002). Third, the talent development perspective defines talent/intelligence as profound ability in childhood, but it must actuate as outstanding performance in adulthood (Pfeiffer, 2012). In the talent development perspective, talent/giftedness is not an immutable fact; rather, it can change during development in response to multiple factors that influence maturation (Pfeiffer, 2012). To date, the terms gifted and talented are still used interchangeably, although most researchers and educators accept the criteria that people are deemed gifted when their abilities place them in the top one percent of the population (Renzulli, 2002; Subotnik et al., 2011).

INTELLIGENCE AND CREATIVITY

Determining the interacting variables of intelligence and creativity has sparked robust research in the fields of both giftedness and creativity (Preckel, Holling, and Wiese, 2006). Previous studies suggest that an IQ of 120 determines the threshold for creative giftedness; simply stated, IQ scores above 120 do not increase creativity (Lubart, 1994). Later studies demonstrate that this threshold relationship is not accurate. Intelligence (divergent thinking and reasoning ability) and creativity are directly relational, without a threshold effect in evidence (Preckel et al., 2006). Other studies have presented a more complex relationship: Intelligence and creativity are not linked to an IQ threshold or tied in a linear trajectory; rather, the age and gender of the individual influences this relationship, with varying alterations throughout development (Welter, Jaarsveld, van Leeuwen, and Lachmann, 2016).

Divergent thinking has been a long-standing focus of study in creativity research (Moore et al., 2009). The ability to explore widely in order to find novel relationships is the hallmark of divergent thinking. This form of cognitive processing is associated with heightened creativity in young children (Wallace and Russ, 2015), as well as the elderly (Melendez, Alfonso-Benlliure, Mayordomo, and Sales, 2016). Divergent thinking is also associated with attentional flexibility, although not necessarily with creative achievement per se (Siegel and Bugg, 2016). However, divergent thinking is not the only form of thinking when assessing intelligence, especially in gifted individuals. Studies have also investigated convergent thinking: a process of executive functioning that narrows associations (Dietrich, 2007; Gute and Gute, 2015). In a latent factor study, the bipolar investigations of divergent versus convergent thinking as well as intelligence versus creativity were discounted (Nusbaum and Silvia, 2011). In this study, multiple variables were found that influence creativity, such as crystallized intelligence, visualization, openness to experience, domain knowledge, and motivation. In an earlier latent factor analysis, three lower-order intelligence factors that included fluid reasoning, verbal fluency, and strategy generation, when combined, formed one higher-order intelligence factor that was strongly associated with increased outcomes on creativity tasks (Silvia, 2008). The major conclusion of these studies suggests that differentiating intelligence from creativity might not be an accurate line of investigation for the future, unless intelligence is examined via higher-order models (Nusbaum and Silvia, 2011; Silvia, 2008).

Emotional intelligence is less often evaluated in relationship to giftedness; however, there are multiple studies that investigate emotional aptitude and regulation in creative individuals (Morelock, 1996). Emotional giftedness, in contrast to general intelligence, includes heightened ability (1) to perceive emotions, (2) to access, generate, and use emotions to assist thoughts, (3) to understand emotional knowledge, and (4) to regulate emotions to augment emotional and intellectual growth (Mayer, Perkins, Caruso, and Salovey, 2001). Including emotional giftedness in studies of talent and giftedness expands the investigative field and may provide students who possess these abilities opportunities to extend their gifts (Ivcevic, Mayer, and Brackett, 2007). Further, many gifted students may possess both emotional and mental giftedness. One significant by-product gained by including emotional intelligence may be associated with the promotion of greater prosocial interactions. Valuing these innate socializing aptitudes in emotionally gifted individuals may potentially help identify future leaders (Mayer et al., 2001).

Motor creativity and motor intelligence has received even less empirical study when compared to general intelligence, emotional intelligence, and artistic or scientific talents (Bournelli, Makri, and Mylonas, 2009). Motor creativity actually reinforces divergent thinking. Both motor activities and divergent thinking rely on feedback-feedforward processes, including oscillating patterns of inhibitory and activating neural networks (Scibinetti, Tocci, and Pesce, 2011; Siedler, Noll, and Thiers, 2004). By encouraging motor giftedness, children may excel in domain-specific talents and cultivate a healthy self-concept (Bournelli et al., 2009). Self-concept is even further enhanced when children experience maternal acceptance of their motor creativity (Bournelli et al., 2009). Further, when motor intelligence/ creativity is encouraged in childhood, it tends to persist into adulthood. It remains a stable trait and is associated with improved academic achievement throughout child and adolescent development (Pagona and Costas, 2008). Motor creative ability is further amplified when children are exposed to both structured and unstructured activities within a sport or performance activity (Bowers, Green, Hemme, and Chalip, 2014). Ultimately, the opportunity to participate in sport/performance activities is directly associated with the promotion of creativity. Expanding research investigations that examine motor intelligence will expand the intelligence-creativity paradigm, especially when neuroscience measures are included in these studies (Jackson and Decety, 2004).

As stated, intelligence (general, emotional, motor) is a predictor of talent, giftedness, and creativity; however, personality traits are even stronger predictors (Furnham and Bachtiar, 2008). Personality traits also influence cognitive flexibility and adaptability, heightened creative performance (Meneely and Portillo, 2005), and cognitive processing, including divergent thinking (Furnham and Bachtiar, 2008; von Stumm, Chung, and Furnham, 2011). Like motor intelligence/creativity (Pagona and Costas, 2008), personality traits tend to endure over the life span and powerfully influence the productivity and expression of creativity (Feist and Barron, 2003; Helson, 1999). Based on multiple studies, it can be stated that general intelligence is not the lynchpin for generating creative thought; in fact, creative thought is a complex construct that involves a diverse array of factors (cognitive, emotional, motor, personality), and these factors are even more complexly distributed within talented and gifted individuals (Sawyer, 2006).

MODELS OF TALENT DEVELOPMENT

Stable models have been developed to account for giftedness and talent. These models reinforce the essential requirement: Children must receive developmental support. With this support it is easier to identify their gifts and talents (Morelock, 1996). Once talent is identified, enrichment programs and accelerated programs are designed to promote optimal development. Investigation continues amongst scholars, educators, and policymakers. They are constantly seeking ways to cultivate skills that will ensure future accomplishments in gifted students (Subotnik et al., 2011). Talent models isolate key components and elaborate on these components in order to provide a coherent and systematic platform that influences educational policymaking for gifted/talented/creative students.

Talent-Development Model

Tannenbaum (2003) developed the talent-development model as a way to describe talent development from childhood to adulthood. According to Tannenbaum (2003), five components must be operational if talent is to transform from potential to eminence. These five components include (1) general, (2) domain-specific, (3) psychosocial abilities, (4) external support, and (5) the mercurial variable of chance. Individuals who have intellectual and domain-specific abilities must also have the perseverance to acquire skill-mastery and to have the support of others who are willing to invest in their talent trajectory. Delay of gratification and hard work, including deliberate practice, all enhance self-discipline, a key component to ensure talent development

(Pfeiffer, 2012). All of these factors are paramount to realize talent; however, chance opportunities must manifest if these talents are to be fully realized (Tannenbaum, 1992).

Enrichment Triad Model (Three-Ring Talent Model)

Renzulli (2002) proposed a model to identify and train children and adolescents. This model focused on gifted behaviors rather than on gifted abilities; the behaviors are promoted within educational programs, as well as in outside experiences that foster talent (Subotnik et al., 2011). Beyond above average ability, which is a prerequisite, task commitment and creative behaviors must be present. According to Renzulli (2002), above average ability includes a general capacity to think abstractly, adapt to novel situations, and rapidly and accurately retrieve knowledge. The facility to apply these abilities to specific areas of knowledge as well as to differentiate and acquire knowledge to promote expertise within these specific domains further defines an individual with giftedness. Committing to the task involves hard work, determination, perseverance, strong interest and desire, and an unwillingness to accept average or mundane standards. The essential components inherent in creativity such as fluency, flexibility, openness to experiences, curiosity, aesthetic awareness, and a willingness to take risks complete the three-rings of gifted behavior. All these behaviors must be present simultaneously and consistently in order to realize giftedness (Renzulli, 2002).

Talent-Search Model

Beyond motivation, task commitment, and perseverance, Stanley and colleagues suggested that talented individuals must be given challenges that meet their abilities and skills (Stanley and Benbow, 1986; Swiatek, 2007). An appropriate level of challenge helps augment talented individuals' interests, values, and desires. These challenges must consistently change to meet the growing skills of the individual. In this talent-search model, testing was designed to assess gifted students via presenting them with developmentally more advanced tests. Gifted students learn at an accelerated rate and often require testing that far exceeds educational grade-level tests (Assouline and Lupkowski-Shoplik, 2012). According to Stanley's model, students who scored in the top 3 to 5 percent on standardized testing should be invited to participate in tests designed for older students. Along with intelligence testing, the inclusion of creativity tests further helps in identifying students who possess creative giftedness (Kaufman, Plucker, and Russell, 2012). This first phase was coined the discovery phase. Once talented students were identified, their talents needed to be described and then developed. Research studies have demonstrated that providing opportunities to engage in accelerated programs promotes student interest and enhances their academic achievement (Swiatek, 2007). According to Stanley and colleagues, the challenge for school districts is to provide these enrichment programs once students have been accurately assessed as gifted (Swiatek, 2007). Enrichment programs must also tailor educational goals that match the domain-specific talents of the child rather than just providing general all-round gifted classes (Assouline and Lupkowski-Shoplik, 2012). When the talent-search model is accurately applied, the results are impressive, a fact that intensifies the need for such programs. In fact, some have coined these results the "Julian Stanley Effect" (Assouline and Lupkowski-Shoplik, 2012).

Pyramid Model

Piirto (1995, 1998) proposed the pyramid model to illustrate the levels of individual and community engagement necessary to develop talent. The base of the pyramid model includes personality traits that have been identified in gifted and talented individuals (i.e., aggressiveness, androgyny, curiosity, imagination, flexibility, overexcitability, persistence, perfectionism, passion, perceptiveness, tolerance for ambiguity, risk-taking) (Piirto and Fraas, 2012). The next level is considered the essential ingredient for giftedness, general ability. The top level incorporates all specific abilities associated with the talent domain. According to Piirto (1995, 1998), at a minimum, the gifted individual must have above average intelligence coupled with superb aptitude in at least one domain. The "suns" that shine over the pyramid all help foster talent development such as (a) home and family stability and support, (b) school and community programming and promotion, and (c) cultural acceptance and recognition. Genetic inheritance and chance opportunities complete the "sun" nurturance for talent development (Piirto, 1995, 1998).

Theory of Positive Disintegration (TPD)

Dabrowski proposed the theory of positive disintegration (TPD) to describe the developmental trajectory of gifted and talented individuals (Ackerman, 2009). According to the TPD, three sets of factors influence development. They are inheritance (special abilities), positive environmental conditions, and autonomous factors that will transform ability into talent development. These autonomous factors, also described as "dynamisms," influence the developmental trajectory of positive disintegration, a recursive process that oscillates between integration, disintegration, and reintegration (Mendaglio and Tiller, 2006). Factors such as inner conflict, self-awareness, and efforts to attain personal growth shape positive disintegration. Dabrowski believed individuals were born with a capacity for developmental potential, although this potential could easily fail or it could be realized at any point throughout the life span (Ackerman, 2009; Mendaglio and Tiller, 2006).

In talent development, five levels of positive integration-disintegration must occur; they are marked by a series of progressions and regressions until talent potential, and the personality structure required to realize talent, are fully expressed. The first level, a *primary or primitive level of integration*, reveals the personality forming without inner conflict and self-reflection. For talented individuals, a clear presentation of innate talents and drives are sensed during this level. Dabrowski claimed that average or "normal" individuals never develop beyond level one (Ackerman, 2009). They lack the innate push to progress through the other four levels of talent development. Level 2, *unilevel disintegration*, is the first evidence of inner ambivalences and discomfort. The talented individual experiences intense internal pressure to seek change. Distrust for authority and personal oscillations in beliefs and desires provoke their efforts to seek more complex solutions. During level 3, *multilevel disintegration* arises. The individual is forced to self-evaluate and explore options that differ significantly from the family and community. Internal and external conflict is pronounced during this level of talent development. A vision of a potential self emerges and propels the talented individual to explore and find new paths. It is a time of internal reflection, including an acute awareness of distress. The *fourth level of disintegration* takes on a more organized or directed resonance. A growing sense of autonomy emerges as a result of the intense distress and inner conflicts experienced during level 3. Many individuals seek counselors or mentors to guide them through the distress of the third level and these interactions help facilitate the organized multilevel process of disintegration in the fourth level. The fifth and final stage, *secondary integration*, is achieved once the personality structure has undergone substantial conflict and resolution. Autonomy at this stage of development is marked by cognitive and emotional flexibility and adaptability. According to Dabrowski, the capacity to fully realize talent is now feasible during this fifth stage (Ackerman, 2009).

One of the basic personality structures that Dabrowski highlighted, overexcitability, has received robust research once it was operationalized (Falk, Lind, Miller, Piechowski, and Silverman, 1999). The concept of overexcitability was developed in an effort to explain talented and gifted individuals' heightened internal awareness of internal and external stimuli (Mendaglio and Tiller, 2006). Overexcitabilities are regarded as mental functions or perceptual "channels" (Ackerman, 2009). The five overexcitabilities (OE) are as follows (Ackerman, 2009; Mika, 2005; Falk et al., 1999; Piechowki and Cunningham, 1985; Piirto and Fraas, 2012):

1. *Psychomotor Overexcitability*—This describes heightened physical energy that can often manifest as restless, hyperactive, and even agitated behaviors. Individuals with psychomotor OE are motivated to pursue physical activities and readily excel in them. They can easily be misdiagnosed with attention deficit hyperactivity disorder (ADHD), but once they are given opportunities to channel their psychomotor OE they are able to focus, attend, and rapidly master physical skills.
2. *Sensual Overexcitability*—Heightened sensitivity to smells, textures, tastes, or other sensory pleasures drive individuals who have high sensual OE. As children they manifest as active seekers of physical touch and contact. They may be picky eaters and may express a hypersensitivity to textures and smells, experiences that may override their ability to self-regulate. Ideally, individuals with this OE should be given opportunities and situations that will engage their heightened awareness of sensual perceptions. For example, acquiring culinary or design skills often helps them manage their sensual OE. Without these positive avenues of expression, negative behaviors such as excessive eating, sex, or substance use may increase distress.
3. *Imaginative Overexcitability*—The hallmark of this OE is the desire to escape boredom via engaging in internal imaginative constructs. These individuals can engage their imagination on all sensory domains and can sustain long elaborate imaginative narratives that may evolve over years. Like worldplay or paracosms (Root-Bernstein and Root-Bernstein, 2006; Taylor, Mottweiler, Naylor, and Levernier, 2015), individuals who have an innate imaginative OE readily retreat to the excitement of their own imagination.
4. *Intellectual Overexcitability*—This OE is not defined by a high IQ; rather, it is marked by an urge to engage in problem-solving activities. Children with high intellectual OE love to ponder intellectual problems and they will persist in seeking solutions for long periods of time. Paranormal visions, quantum physics, and existential meaning-making are common themes that occupy their minds. They love to think about thinking, a trait that may enhance theory of mind capacities (Shahaeian, Peterson, Slaughter, and Wellman, 2011). They present as independent thinkers who intuitively integrate ideas that may seem remote and disparate.
5. *Emotional Overexcitability*—According to Dabrowski, this is the most important OE for personality growth and talent development (Ackerman, 2009). Individuals who possess this OE are motivated to understand relationships and reflect on the emotional origins of these relationships. Although this OE may drive psychological understanding, it can also increase anxiety, shame, and self-criticism. Fear of rejection and increased distrust as well as sensitivity to potential betrayal or abandonment may

occupy the thoughts and feelings of individuals with high emotional OE. When directed toward positive expression, this OE may lead individuals into careers in the performing arts or mental health. Like the other OEs, emotional OE can manifest as a global manifestation or as a narrow self-absorbed neurosis.

Talented and gifted individuals may possess none, one, several, or all of the OEs, although approximately 80 percent of gifted students endorse at least one of the OEs (Alias, Rahman, Majid, and Yassin, 2013; Piechowski, Silverman, Cunningham, and Falk, 1982). During development, OEs become more integrated; they operate as a dynamic force that propels talented individuals to engage in their innate abilities (Ackerman, 2009). This dynamic process can also increase distress; many individuals with high levels of OE have difficulty regulating them (Mika, 2005). For example, children may be ostracized from social groups because they are not able to modulate the intensity of their OEs and as a result they have difficulty understanding and interacting with other children. They may be described as nervous, anxious, mentally unstable, or overly sensitive. They frequently have sleep difficulties, death anxieties, and may present with features of obsessive-compulsive disorder (Harrison and van Haneghan, 2011). Fortunately, gifted children can be provided skills to manage their OEs and will then present as psychologically stable and physically healthy individuals (Mika, 2005).

Research findings have supported the identification of OE profiles, in particular, differentiating intellectually gifted from artistic talents (Piechowski and Cunningham, 1985: Piechowski et al., 1982; Piirto and Fraas, 2012), as well as differentiating performing artists from athletes (Thomson and Jaque, 2016a, 2016b). Examining OE profiles helps to individualize gifted students who are often grouped as one generic class of high IQ scorers. With this knowledge, more targeted educational programs can be offered along with specific skills to manage the intensity of the individual OEs (Alias et al., 2013). The effect of OE profiles and their influence on self-esteem in gifted and talented adolescents have also been demonstrated. For example, teens with low psychomotor OE tended to manifest poor self-concept and required counseling to help them manage the imbalance between higher imaginational OE and lower psychomotor OE (Rinn, Mendaglio, Rudasill, and McQueen, 2010). OE profiles also differ between gender in addition to influencing gender identity (van den Broeck, Hofmans, Cooremans, and Staels, 2014), with higher OE scores endorsed by gifted students who were rated as more androgynous (Miller, Falk, and Huang, 2009). OE profiles have also been demonstrated in cross-cultural studies (Chang and Kuo, 2009; Falk, Manzanero, and Miller, 1997). Lastly, there are significant associations between OE profiles and the Big Five personality traits; in particular, higher intellectual, sensual, and imaginational OEs were associated with gifted students who were ranked higher for openness to experience and lower for neuroticism. The gifted students with higher psychomotor OE also displayed more extraversion (Limont, Dreszer-Drogorob, Bedynska, Sliwinska, and Jastrzebska, 2014).

Although robust research has been conducted on OEs, this is only one aspect of the theory of positive disintegration. More research is needed to further understand the unique model proposed by Dabrowski. Qualitative case study work demonstrates strong support for this theory, and educators who work in enrichment educational programs are well positioned to perceive the developmental struggles of their gifted and talented students through this lens (Mika, 2005). The value of assessing OE profiles may reduce the psychopathology diagnoses that are often associated with these gifted and talented individuals. Helping individuals achieve the fifth level of positive integration may promote the realization of their potential (Ackerman, 2009).

Mega-Model of Talent Development (MMTD)

The mega-model of talent development (MMTD) was constructed to identify common factors that persist across all talent domains (Olszewski-Kubilius, Subotnik, and Worrell, 2015; Subotnik et al., 2011). These factors are described as follows:

1. Developmental trajectories operate in all talent domains (beginning, peak, and end points). Certain domains require earlier talent recognition and skill acquisition (i.e., sports, dance, music), whereas other talent domains can be identified later in development (i.e., psychology, culinary arts, medicine).
2. All domains have the same pathway that leads to achievement (identification of talent, skill acquisition, and skill expertise).
3. Creativity factors such as independent thinking, openness to experience, persistence, and problem-solving skills help propel the development of talent from novice to expert levels.
4. Psychosocial skills, coupled with motivation and persistence, support talent development.
5. Opportunities to receive training and to work within the talent domain are also required.

In this model, talent identification and talent education are vital. Those with high abilities will not achieve eminence without the socioeconomic support of others; consequently, talent development is dependent on the values of the community in which the individual resides and the opportunities that are available to the individual (Subotnik et al., 2011).

According to the MMDT model, talented individuals must seize opportunities to realize their talent. Without optimal motivation to achieve eminence they will remain as underachievers who fail to realize their potential (Olszewski-Kubilius, Subotnik, and Worrell, 2015). According to the MMDT, motivation is nurtured and cultivated over time; it is part of several psychosocial skills (i.e., persistence, self-knowledge, interpersonal skills, self-regulation) essential to developing talent. Gifted and talented students need to train all these psychosocial skills, including motivation to optimize their gifts (Olszewski-Kubilius et al., 2015). This model emphasizes training in areas such as learning methods, emotional regulation, coping skills to manage stress, enhancing personal meaning in the talent domain, social skills to support engagement within the talent domain, concrete methods to build a supportive social network, and the means to assess and enhance strengths while minimizing weaknesses (Olszewski-Kubilius et al., 2015). Although adequate education and opportunity must be given to nurturing the identified talent, acquiring these psychosocial skills is an essential ingredient in the MMDT model.

IDENTIFYING TALENT

The opportunity to acquire skill, even before talent is assessed, is paramount. Without exposure to a specific domain a child will never demonstrate talent, and this includes gaining some skill development so that he or she can then exhibit his or her accelerated learning aptitudes (Rostan, Pariser, and Gruber, 2002). This exposure also includes opportunities to engage in creative problem-solving tasks; children who are given these opportunities can enhance their competence, especially in artistic expressivity. Talent identification emerges when they demonstrate motivation, persistence, frustration tolerance, and expressivity that manifests in the creation of a novel work (Rostan, 1997). Gifted parents tend to recognize talent in their children and will parent them differently; in particular, they will engage in more creative problem-solving activities and dialogue in more complex and elaborative modes of communication (Perrone, Ksiazak, Wright, Vannatter, Crane, and Tarrney, 2010). The fact that giftedness tends to be multigenerational may suggest a genetic component to giftedness (Piffer and Hur, 2014), although behaviors and skills that promote talent are equally essential (Olszewski-Kubilius et al., 2015). Classifying behaviors associated with talent, especially creative aptitude, offers clear parameters to distinguish creative giftedness. Behaviors such as curiosity, sensation seeking, preference for novelty, reflective thinking, persistence, task commitment, imagination, multi-tasking, insight, and visionary perspective all influence creative productivity. Rigorous verification and maintenance of high standards further ensures productivity (Kirschenbaum, 1998). These traits may emerge at any time during childhood; the essential step is to guide students toward their innate talent so that they can apply their creative aptitude to achieve eminence (Winner, 2000a).

Despite the clear trait markers that have been discussed above, identifying talent remains a challenge, in part because talented individuals respond in diverse ways and not in stereotypical patterns (Rasmussen and Rasmussen, 2015). For example, students readily describe themselves as talented based on feedback from their peers and teachers. Typically, students who display versatility across domains are often regarded as innately talented and these students then self-identify as gifted. However, students who are identified as "gifted" on testing assessments often fail to describe themselves as talented. They adopt stereotyped assumptions gathered within their school setting and they believe that they do not match these stereotypes. Likewise, quiet shy students and industrious students who work diligently tend to underestimate their talent and are often overlooked by teachers and fellow students (Rasmussen and Rasmussen, 2015). The assumption that talent and giftedness can only exist when achievement is effortless and easy undermines the reality that achieving expertise requires hard work and persistent efforts to cultivate mastery (Subotnik et al., 2011).

Without external support, realizing talent in gifted individuals will falter. External support is even more important when talented individuals grow up in harsh environments. Underserved communities, economic disparity, racial diversity, and recent immigration are all factors that can prohibit talent recognition and talent development (Gaztambide-Fernandez, Saifer, and Desai, 2013). Educational efforts need to expand to identify children from these populations. Identifying talented children in these underserved communities can only occur when students are provided opportunities for their talent to be revealed. Testing protocols must move beyond assessing for giftedness and talent; they must also capture the multifaceted traits of creativity (Lemons, 2011). To date, children who are raised in two-parent homes represent the majority of students enrolled in gifted programs; usually their parents have sufficient financial and emotional means to promote the talents of their children (Rasmussen and Rasmussen, 2015). Educators and members of the community can offset this uneven distribution; they can recognize the quiet child who works diligently at school tasks or the child who displays one-dimensional or multi-dimensional talents and direct them into after-school community-based programs. Informing children of their talent will augment their self-identification as "talented" and may spark intrinsic motivation to pursue their talent (Rasmussen and Rasmussen, 2015). Ideally, the experience of being mentored in gifted programs (or ordinary classrooms) can be transferred so that talented individuals who are supported can then embrace opportunities in which they can engender the talent of others in their community (Miller and Cohen, 2012).

Engendering creativity and promoting talent is vital to ensuring the realization of talent. Although most studies examine the attributes of the gifted, fewer studies actually investigate the traits of those who promote these gifted individuals (Miller and Cohen, 2012). The act of nurturing the talents of others could easily be described as a creative act in itself. The supportive individuals such as family members, mentors, teachers, coaches, counselors, or agents share in the actualization of the talented individual. Like all creative problem-solving processes, they must identify the developmental tasks of the child, find solutions, evaluate these solutions, and maintain the exploratory and evaluative process throughout the nurturance of the talented individual. Those who support and engender talent must first accept their role and they must gain sufficient knowledge about the talent domain in order to identify what is missing or what is going wrong (Chua, 2015). Finding individuals who will assume the role of engendering talent, especially within underserved communities, can greatly diminish the disparity in talent recognition and talent development (Gaztambide-Fernandez et al., 2013). The commitment and resources provided by those who engender talent may become models for the gifted; they can internalize the commitment of others into self-commitment (Baker and Cote, 2003). Likewise, recognizing and valuing the tremendous creative output of those who engender talent may encourage others to assume responsibility to nurture the hidden talents of children who struggle in environments that are dominated by adversity (Gaztambide-Fernandez et al., 2013; Miller and Cohen, 2012).

PERSONALITY TRAITS IN THE CREATIVELY GIFTED AND TALENTED

Examining gifted and talented personality traits poses many challenges. In fact, Smith (2008) argued that examining traits is foolhardy; creative personality should be understood as an experiential process and not a set of static traits (Smith, 2008). Traditionally, personality research examines (1) individual differences and similarities, (2) dispositional traits (temperament), (3) characteristic adaptations during development, and (4) self-defining narratives that endure throughout the life span (McAdams and Pals, 2006). Given the scope of these topics, the field of personality research is vast, and often unwieldy (Eysenck, 1997). For example, some of the major areas in personality studies include cognitive processes, emotions, motivation, social interaction behaviors, self-regulation, and whole personality traits (Ivcevic and Brackett, 2015; Ivcevic and Mayer, 2006–2007). Ultimately, personality psychologists focus on models to explain the whole person, although this is also one of the most difficult tasks to accomplish (McAdams and Pals, 2006).

The early pioneering work of researchers led to the identification of strong factors associated with highly gifted and talented individuals. Typical traits included hard work, a wide range of interests, high self-confidence, and love of novelty (Martindale, 2001). Drawing from many different branches of psychology (i.e., psychoanalytic, psychodynamic, positivist, self-growth), a long list of attributes associated with highly creative personalities grew. Not only were traits identified, they were also influenced by dispositional temperament, environmental adaptations, cultural norms, and personal self-narratives (McAdams and Pals, 2006). Traits that commonly appeared in the early personality studies were often contradictory or overlapping. Individuals regarded as creatively talented or gifted could easily be described as fantasy-prone, sensitive to problems, rebellious, aggressive, reflective, energetic, unsociable, risk-taking, intuitive, adaptable, persistent, self-disciplined, having an internal locus of control, defiant, neurotic, curious, conscientious, playful, tenacious, independent, hardworking, tolerant of ambiguity, and/or overly emotional (Selby, Shaw, and Houtz, 2005).

Examining creative individuals through the lens of psychoanalytic defense structures raises even more contradictions, including attributes that are often fundamentally negative. Some of these ego defense mechanisms include schizoid fantasy, dissociation, acting out, displacement, intellectualizing, sublimation, suppression, humor, and reaction formations (Domino, Short, Evans, and Romano, 2002). Adding to the complication of this list, multiple differing lists of personality traits and cognitive thinking styles are identified in talented and gifted individuals who work in different domains (i.e., scientists, visual artists, writers, musicians, architects) (Feist, 1998; Haller and Courvoisier, 2010). These different talent abilities may be the driving force behind differences in personality and ego defense mechanisms, or the differences may actually be a response to the working conditions within these specific talent domains (Lee and Min, 2016).

Csikszentmihalyi (1996) and Barron (1969/1976) suggested that these seemingly contradictory traits operate in highly creative individuals, but at different times. People with prodigious talent can easily work with great physical energy and intense interpersonal interactions and then remain alone and quiet for long periods of time. They can present as introverts in some settings and extroverts in other settings. Likewise, they can be highly passionate and overly sensitive and yet equally rational and objective. Despite the variance in these traits, studies have demonstrated that many of these traits stay stable over the life span, especially psychological mindedness (Feist, 1998; Feist and Barron, 2003; Helson, 1999). The interplay of temperament, environment, and developmental maturation may modify personality traits, in particular, conscientiousness and agreeableness; however, in general, according to personality research, personality structures remain stable throughout adulthood (McAdams and Olson, 2010).

Personality Factor Models

The need to organize all these personality variables into larger clusters propelled the creation of integrative models. For example, Jung's personality typology was absorbed into the Myers-Briggs assessment; it has yielded relevant information associated with talent, giftedness, and creativity (Chavez-Eakle, Eakle, and Cruz-Fuentes, 2012). The three factor (Eysenck and Eysenck, 1991) and five factor models (McCrae and Costa, 1987) are clustered models that integrate multiple traits into a few overarching factors. Along with the desire to identify whole personality traits, these models were designed to identify psychopathology predispositions, including in individuals who are regarded as talented and gifted. Likewise, personality studies examine the ego strengths of the individual. Essentially, personality studies attempt to reveal differences and predict potential outcomes (Eysenck, 1997).

The *Myers-Briggs Type Indicator* is based on Jung's four psychological functions (sensation, thinking, intuition, feeling). Jung (1923) proposed that two functions were associated with rational or judging traits. He claimed that the psychological functions, thinking and feeling, promote decision-making. The other two functions are associated with irrational or perceiving traits. Jung named these information gathering types sensation and intuition (Jung, 1923). The Myers-Briggs Type Indicator is an assessment tool that isolates sixteen types (Isaksen, Lauer, and Wilson, 2003); these types are based on a combination of the four psychological functions as well as Jung's concepts of extraversion (turning outward) and introversion (turning inward). This instrument has yielded novel information regarding creative individuals; for example, in one study highly creative individuals were classified as intuitive and perceptive types. This typology profile was associated with innovative thinking, willingness to explore a wide array of possibilities, and being unconstrained by rules (Isaksen et al., 2003).

Eysenck and colleagues created another important integrative model, the *Three Factor Model* (Eysenck and Eysenck, 1991). According to Eysenck, developing a model with fewer personality factors would yield more effective information (Eysenck and Eysenck, 1991). The Three Factor Model incorporates biological and behavioral factors and identifies three major traits, Extraversion (Introversion), Neuroticism (Stability), and Psychoticism

(Socialization) (Eysenck and Eysenck, 1991). *Extraversion* is marked by traits such as energetic, exhibitionistic, hypomanic, high tolerance for arousal, sensation seeking, ambitious, and assertive. Introversion is basically the inversion of extraversion in this model; thus someone who scores low on the extraversion scale could be identified as being more introverted. *Neuroticism* captures features such as anxiety, depression, emotional volatility, hypochondria, insecurity, worry, and excitability. Lastly, *psychoticism* (i.e., aggressive, egocentric, unsympathetic, manipulative, dogmatic) addresses the prodromal susceptibility to develop psychotic disorders. Eysenck also suggested that if individuals score high on the psychoticism scale, they may not be prone to psychopathology, but they do engage in overinclusive thinking (loose associations) and creativity. As with extraversion, when scores are low in neuroticism or psychoticism, then personality features are manifested in the opposite direction.

The third integrative model that is consistently implemented when studying gifted and talented creative individuals is the *Five Factor Model (FFM)*, also described as the Big Five Model (McAdams and Pals, 2006). Like the Three Factor Model, high and low scores determine whether the personality trait is strongly or weakly manifested (McCrae and Costa, 1987). These five factors are as follows (Feist, 1998; McCrea and Costa, 1987):

1. Neuroticism: Anxious, defensive, depressed, excitable, guilty, hypochondriacal, insecure, neurotic, shrewd, tense, worrying, and emotionally volatile.
2. Extraversion: adventurous, ambitious, assertive, autonomous, confident, cyclothymic, dominant, energetic, enthusiastic, exhibitionistic, gregarious, hypomanic, impulsive, independent, positive, self-assertive, sensation seeking, and sociable.
3. Openness: creative, curious, flexible, imaginative, intelligent, open-minded, original, sensitive, and having wide interests.
4. Agreeableness: agreeable, communal, cooperative, easygoing, empathic, friendly, generous, nurturing, peaceful, supportive, and warm.
5. Conscientiousness: careful, cautious, conscientious, orderly, reliable, responsible, and self-controlled.

These five personality traits remain stable over the life span in creative individuals (Feist, 1998). Recurring factors in creatively gifted individuals include extraverted, neurotic, and open to experience (Feist, 1998). Openness to experience has received the most positive findings regarding creative talent and giftedness, and it has been associated with better emotion regulation (Ivcevic and Brackett, 2015). In addition, extraversion and openness to experience are strongly associated with divergent thinking skills and creativity

(Furnham and Bachtiar, 2008). Hypomania, a criterion within the extraversion factor, was also identified in a latent class study (von Stumm, Chung, and Furnham, 2011). Hypomania is associated with creative achievement, although it is not known whether hypomania increases creative achievement or if the pressure to achieve creative output increases risk for hypomania (Siegel and Bugg, 2016). The von Stumm et al. (2011) study claimed that extraversion was a stable predictor for creative achievement. Along with openness to experience, extraversion illustrates the importance of energetic expression associated with creative achievement and creative personality (von Stumm et al., 2011). The other notable factor, agreeableness, was strongly associated with psychologically minded individuals (Kaufman, Pumaccahua, and Holt, 2013).

Perfectionism and Creative Personality Profiles

Perfectionism has long been associated with creative achievement (Hewett and Flett, 2004), perhaps because perfectionistic attentional rigidity, as opposed to attentional flexibility, promotes task persistence (Siegel and Bugg, 2016). Talented and gifted individuals tend to manifest strong perfectionistic tendencies, a trait that is associated with the Big Five conscientiousness factor. Unlike measuring creative achievement, perfectionism often runs counter to creative thinking; in particular, it is often a more rigid style of thinking that hampers cognitive flexibility and exploration (Ahmetoglu, Harding, Akhtar, and Chamorro-Premuzic, 2015). The multidimensional nature of perfectionism indicates that this personality trait can positively or negatively influence appraisals about the self, others, and perceptions related to how others may appraise the self (Ahmetoglu et al., 2015; Hewett and Flett, 2004). Although perfectionism can drive talented individuals to reach eminence, it can also increase risk for injury, burnout, and intense feelings of shame and failure (Eusanio, Thomson, and Jaque, 2014; Krasnow, Mainwaring, and Kerr, 1999; Sagar and Stoeber, 2009). Helping highly talented and gifted individuals manage perfectionistic traits is essential during their training and mentoring experiences (Stoeber, Harris, and Moon, 2007; Stoeber and Otto, 2006). Creating environments that promote entrepreneurial exploration may promote creative achievement, even if an individual is predisposed to high perfectionistic tendencies (Ahmetoglu et al., 2015).

The *creative personality profile (CPP)* was developed to specifically identify personality features that are shared amongst creative individuals (Martinsen, 2011). This profile identified seven overarching factors: (1) instability, (2) motivation (achievement, persistence, goal-oriented), (3) ambition (need for attention, desire to seek position of influence), (4) associative orientation (ideational productivity), (5) agreeableness (friendliness, ethical), (6) flexibility (restructuring or redefining situations), and (7) need for originality (preference for complexity). Many of these factors overlap with the FFM. For example, associative orientation, the strongest factor identified in the factor analysis, was associated with the FFM, open to experience. This factor indicated high levels of fantasy, ideational productivity, playfulness, and absorption. In Martinsen's study (2011), the profile of creative people included high levels of emotional instability, associative orientation, and originality, moderate levels of motivation, and lower levels of agreeableness, ambition, and flexibility. The factor findings at the lower level are somewhat surprising, given that one of the essential features of creativity is cognitive flexibility (Kim, 2011).

When creative behaviors are strongly displayed in childhood, the likelihood that they will persist into old age is high. Creative engagement and productivity, although it may take on different forms of expression, tends to persist longitudinally (Helson, 1999). However, early interaction between innate talent and the environment in which the gifted are nurtured dictates which personality traits will become dominant. For example, supportive versus hostile environments will amplify or modify traits such as agreeableness, conscientiousness, autonomy, or rebelliousness (Chavez-Eakle, Eakle, and Cruz-Fuentes, 2012). Likewise, changes in educational practices can influence personality structures, especially in children and adolescents (Chavez-Eakle, Lara, and Cruz, 2006).

NURTURING TALENT

The developmental theorist Vygotsky suggested that creative giftedness is cultivated in early development through optimal play settings (Newman and Newman, 2015). According to Vygotsky, play settings reveal the maturation of creative cognitive processing. For example, during adolescence, play exploration matures into more abstract reasoning and conceptualizing. Vygotsky believed that creative ability is only fully integrated in adulthood (Ayman-Nolley, 1992; Newman and Newman, 2015). He also observed that many highly imaginative child prodigies do not continue their gifts into adulthood, in part because some children fail to meet the challenges of different developmental creative tasks, such as acquiring abilities to integrate imagination and reason (Ayman-Nolley, 1992). Vygotsky also described how successful parenting of gifted children occurs as a result of scaffolding (Newman and Newman, 2015), a concept he proposed to optimize child development. Scaffolding involves a parent or teacher who sensitively guides a child through tasks that are slightly more advanced than their developmental ability. Parents of gifted children who scaffold their children foster creativity and self-esteem. Scaffolding can include acting as a mediator between teachers and the child, encouraging exploratory play behavior, demonstrating flexible disciplinary control, and exhibiting low levels of frustration (Snowden and Christian, 1999).

The application of principles derived from complexity theory greatly helps explain the nurturance of creative talent and giftedness. Complexity theory describes how complex systems (i.e., biological, familial, societal) move toward differentiation, as well as integration, via flexible adaptation to changing conditions (Lewis and Granic, 2000). The operation of complex systems features a simultaneous seeking of novelty and order, stability and a broadening of attention, and integration-disintegration. These complex patterns are evident within families that nurture talent. Likewise, the complexity of the family system is internalized and translated during the creative process. A balance of seemingly opposite variables emerges in complex family systems that nurture talented children (Gute, Gute, Nakamura, and Csikszentmihalyi, 2008). For example, complex families provide ethical modeling while encouraging novel exploration, facilitate opportunities to explore alone and with family members, and hold high standards while accepting exploratory failures. An authoritative parenting style directly influences complex family environments. This type of parenting style provides a balance of encouraging independence while maintaining a sensitive awareness of the child's needs. Authoritative parenting and complex family systems promote optimal development for gifted children (Milevsky, Schlecter, Netter, and Keehn, 2007). Parents who provide a complex family environment directly influence maturational experiences in addition to pushing talented children into situations that may initially be deregulating (disintegrating) until they successfully gain mastery (Gute et al., 2008).

Nurturing psychological resilience and vulnerability in gifted children is contingent on many factors, and all need to be monitored while helping talented individuals achieve their potential (Cross, 2014). For example, helping gifted and talented students manage obsessive tendencies, traits that are common in this population, will promote psychological resilience. Without adequate awareness and regulation, obsessive tendencies can increase anxiety and constrain creative flexibility (Cross, 2014). The intense desire to explore interests, even if it seems obsessive, can function as positive motivation during skill mastery; helping gifted children regulate obsessive behavior is a key factor in promoting their resilience (Cross, 2014). In addition, parental acceptance of the unique needs of a talented child is a major factor in nurturing creativity. For example, talented children require protracted periods to engage in solitary exploration. They are not lonely when they know their parents accept and support their need for isolation (Lim and Smith, 2008). The delicate balance of cultivating resilience and vulnerability is reinforced by other key factors such as personality traits, self-perceptions, and educational fit (Neihart, 1999). Unique biological factors influence talent realization and talent vulnerability (Winner, 2000a). The balance (and imbalance) between resilience and vulnerability is often demonstrated in studies that suggest some gifted people may suffer more mental illness whereas others are stable and well regulated (Neihart, 1999). Resilience and vulnerability were clearly identified in the early work of Frank Barron. He deduced from his research findings that creative individuals "appear to be both sicker and healthier psychologically than people in general" (Barron, 1969/1976, p. 197).

The knowledge that some children manifest "precocious" gifts has been the driving force behind the need for special educational programs that are designed to nurture these children. Gifted children often display asynchronous development, with accelerated understanding and skill mastery within their domain-specific talent(s) (Morelock, 1996; Subotnik et al., 2011). The very nature of being gifted includes uneven development of these talents, as well as uneven development across the full range of developmental tasks during childhood and adolescents (Claxton, Pannells, and Rhoads, 2005; Winner, 2000a, 2000b; Urban, 1991). Further, variance in development occurs within and across subjects; some gifted children show no lag in development whereas other gifted children may have uneven bursts in their ability (Charles and Runco, 2000–2001). Multiple factors play an integral role in the emergence of talent and talent achievement (Olszewski-Kubilius et al., 2015). These factors go far beyond the individual who demonstrates precocious abilities. For example, parental values, including the unconscious cultural values that parents impart to their children, strongly influence creative achievement, with clear differences identified in American and Chinese talented students, such as autonomy versus collectivism (Deng, Wang, and Zhao, 2016). Ultimately, early attachment experiences, parental caregiving, disciplinary styles, complex family systems, economic opportunities, and cultural values all influence the nurturance of talent (Wellisch and Brown, 2013).

CONCLUSION

Nurturing creativity and talent is directly enhanced by educational policies that identify and provide opportunities to cultivate them. Unfortunately, most school districts fail to adequately assess intellectual giftedness, and exhibit even less ability to assess artistic and athletic talent (Oreck, Owen, and Baum, 2003; Tranckle and Cushion, 2006). One of the major problems impeding accurate talent assessment is the fact that most assessment tools are English language-dependent. Developing assessment tools that are sensitive to cultural diversity can greatly alleviate this problem (Deng et al., 2016).

Students are typically evaluated based on their writing skills, and not on their domain-specific talents. Talent can only be assessed after students are initially exposed to a wide range of domain-specific activities (Gaztambide-Fernandez et al., 2013). Once exposed to diverse activities, their natural proclivities will influence preferences. Allowing students to actively engage in multiple activities facilitates their participation; they readily identify their interests and acknowledge their burgeoning talents. These talents are typically not reflected in their reading ability and academic grades (Oreck et al., 2003).

Educating intellectually gifted and domain-specific talented students remains at the margins of educational attention (Oreck et al., 2013). It is often believed that "gifted students will make it on their own"; their prodigious abilities will prevail despite their being neglected or ignored (Subotnik et al., 2011). These children are typically not an educational priority, especially given insufficient financial resources and the educational demands of current standardized testing (Subotnik et al., 2011). The missed opportunity to adequately educate these talented students increases the likelihood of academic underachievement and school dropout (Kim, 2008). Unfortunately, many gifted children are considered gifted underachievers. They are easily deterred when forced to learn in highly structured conforming school environments. Because they are often sensitive to negative social feedback (from peers, parents, teachers), many children withdraw from their natural giftedness. Underachieving behavior often masks their giftedness and so they are not identified as gifted or challenged appropriately. However, once they are accurately recognized and provided opportunities to explore without negative judgment, then underachievement behavior reverses (Kim, 2008). These students have the potential to change the future trajectory of society; losing them will prove too costly for society (Oreck et al., 2013).

Psychologists, politicians, and educators must draw attention to the negative stereotypes associated with giftedness programs. Many talented students remain unrecognized, while others live in communities that do not promote opportunities to realize their talent. Transforming giftedness and talent from innate abilities to competence, and then expertise, remains problematic. Many individuals whose talents are recognized early, fail to reach their potential (Wellisch and Brown, 2013). Without intrinsic motivation and substantial skills to regulate emotional intensity, high levels of achievement will not occur (Olszewski-Kubilius et al., 2015). The need for sensitive assessment policies and procedures remains; subjective bias and underexposure limit the development of talent and giftedness (Tranckle and Cushion, 2006). Research investigation is needed to understand the unique needs of these individuals, including ways to identify, educate, and support growth from novice to expert levels (Piirto, 1995, 1998).

Chapter 3

Creative Process

Engaging in the creative process implies valuing creativity, deriving pleasure or meaning from this activity, and being motivated to create (Csikszentmihalyi, 1996). Values reflect a general orientation to life and provide a foundation for evaluating actions of self and others (Kasof, Chen, Himsel, and Greenberger, 2007). They shape intrinsic and extrinsic motivational behaviors and propel individuals to establish a lifestyle that facilitates the maintenance of their values (Schwartz, 1992). According to Schwartz and colleagues, ten value types are consistently identified in all cultures and religions (Schwartz and Bardi, 2001). They consist of power (social status and prestige), achievement (personal success, expertise), stimulation (novelty, change), hedonism (self-pleasure and gratification), benevolence (enhance the welfare of others), conformity (adhere to social norms), tradition (commitment to established customs), security (stability, harmony), self-direction (independent thought and action), and universalism (tolerate, accept, and protect the welfare of nature and humanity) (Kasof et al., 2007). According to Schwartz and colleagues, these values tend to operate in opposing directions, for example, someone who values tradition and conformity would not tolerate stimulation and self-direction as highly (Schwartz and Bardi, 2001).

Although Schwartz did not list creativity as a value, values such as self-direction, stimulation, and universalism relate to creativity. Further, a desire to break from tradition and conformity also reinforces creative "values." Consequently, creativity could readily be included as a value that informs life orientation (Dollinger, Burke, and Gump, 2007). This was demonstrated in a study that did include creativity as a value. The study determined a relationship between creativity and values of self-determination, universalism, and stimulation. Creative accomplishments and products were negatively associated with the values of tradition, security, and power (Dollinger et al.,

2007). Researchers argue the importance of including creativity as the eleventh value in a value typology (Kasof et al., 2007; Pryor, Hurtado, Saenz, Londholm, Korn, and Mahoney, 2006). They also observe that creativity is not highly valued or prioritized by Americans, a finding that is troubling given how essential creativity is for future innovation and survival (Kasof et al., 2007; Pryor et al., 2006).

MOTIVATION

Values are also evident in motivational characteristics that propel individuals to participate in activities and achieve goals. Motivation is strongly influenced by a complex array of factors such as individual opportunities, family support and values, educational programs, peer interactions, and social norms (Hallam, 2002). Three types of motivational patterns have received robust research: they are intrinsic, extrinsic, and synergistic motivation (Collins and Amabile, 1999). *Intrinsic motivation*, the internally generated desire to engage in an activity for its own sake, is strongly associated with creative productivity (Collins and Amabile, 1999; de Jesus, Rus, Lens, and Imaginario, 2013). This form of motivation directly influences positive performance and shapes clear goal-setting behaviors (Lacaille, Kostener, and Gaudreau, 2007), including deriving enjoyment when the challenges are perceived as both internally goal-directed and desired (Abuhamdeh and Csikszentmihalyi, 202). In organizational settings, individuals who are driven by intrinsic motivation often engage in activities with even more optimism and view their work settings as fairer than participants who lack intrinsic motivation (Hannam and Narayan, 2015). Perceptions of justice within the workplace, including fair interpersonal treatment, consistent and appropriate application of rules and procedures, and work demands matching work output all positively influence creative output and reinforce worker intrinsic motivation (Hannam and Narayam, 2015).

Extrinsic motivation is generally regarded as being contingent on external rewards and punishers. This form of motivation has received less support as a motivating factor in creativity, although all individuals who engage in creative activities are aware of the potential rewards or punishers that may follow any creative output (Collins and Amabile, 1999; de Jesus et al., 2013). Extrinsic motivation can be subdivided into three factors. The first factor is defined as the actual *external benefits* that accompany a creative product (financial rewards, fame, approval). The second factor, *introjected motivation*, informs behavior (sense of duty, obligation). For example, obligation is a strong extrinsic motivator that may drive group productivity (Cooper and Jayatilaka, 2006). Over time, extrinsic introjected obligation may actually convert to intrinsic motivation. The group members may begin to internalize a desire to engage in an activity for its own sake, even though the initial impetus was to not disappoint group members (Cooper and Jayatilaka, 2006). The third extrinsic factor, *identified motivation*, includes a process in which internalized social values are then identified as personal values (Deci and Ryan, 1991; Kasof et al., 2007). This motivation pattern is strongly associated with personal self-direction. The individual welcomes stimulation and strives for a sense of universalism (Kasof et al., 2007). Identified motivation shares features with intrinsic motivation such as a sense of autonomous direction; however, according to Deci and Ryan (1991), identified motivation expands intrinsic motivation so that higher values can be consciously identified and promoted; these higher values are viewed as operating outside the individual, which make them extrinsic in nature.

As well, a positive bi-product of internal and/or external motivation is self-efficacy; it is derived from creative (innovative) experiences that enhance creative output (Prabhu et al., 2008). Both motivational types also directly influence individual and group identity/productivity, especially when the group or individual possesses an autonomous awareness of variables that may facilitate or inhibit productivity (Kosaf et al., 2007). Given the interplay between these seemingly opposite forms of motivation, a model was proposed to integrate them. *Synergistic motivation* is a model that incorporates the undeniable relationship between intrinsic and extrinsic factors (Collins and Amabile, 1999). Optimally, the synergistic effects resulting from interactions between intrinsic and extrinsic motivation promote skill mastery, problem solving, and self-esteem (Prabhu, Sutton, and Sauser, 2008). These effects ensure a willingness to persist with a creative activity despite challenges, including fatigue, despair, anxiety, and fear (Elliot and Thrash, 2001, 2002). Synergistic motivation is colored by early socialization experiences. For example, self-guides are internalized factors that inform individual motivation. "Ideal self-guides" reflect socialized moral development and ethical principles, whereas, "ought self-guides" become internalized motivators to promote duty and social responsibility. Like benevolent and malevolent forms of creativity, these "ideal" and "ought" self-guides may promote or deter creative expression, exploratory behavior, and creative problem solving (Zabelina, Felps, and Blanton, 2013).

When working conditions are based on competition, such as in sports, the competitive environment naturally evokes a synergistic interplay between intrinsic and extrinsic motivation (Eisenberg and Thompson, 2011). These synergistic motivating factors directly influence perception of stress, including success and failure beliefs (Eisenberg and Thompson, 2011). Relational interactions, environmental conditions, cultural values, emotional support, and encouragement are all colored by the dynamic interplay between intrinsic and extrinsic motivation (Hassandra, Goudas, and Chroni, 2003). For example, approach and avoidant behaviors are powerfully influenced by beliefs related to failure and success. Approaching failure may enhance skill development just as avoiding success might curtail growth; these behaviors are ultimately influenced by a synergistic interaction of motivating factors (Elliot and Covington, 2001).

Motivation behaviors are also encapsulated in models such as the *achievement-motivation model* (Alexander and Schnick, 2008). This model describes motivation as a factor that promotes meeting realistic goals and receiving appropriate feedback, which ideally culminates in a sense of accomplishment and self-efficacy (Alexander and Schnick, 2008). The *self-determination* model elaborates on intrinsic and extrinsic motivational types as well as social and cultural factors that support or undermine initiative and achievement. It is a model that offers explanations about human success. More importantly, it provides concepts that can enhance motivation in talented individuals as well as within those who are regarded as "underachievers" (Deci and Ryan, 1991, 2000). Vroom's *expectancy motivation theory* is embedded in his model of valence, instrumentality, and expectancy (VIE) (Ilgen, Nebeker, and Pritchard, 1981; Vroom, 1964). The concept underpinning expectancy motivation is the belief that an individual's effort will lead to the achievement of good results, and these results will earn secondary rewards or recognition (instrumentality). Expectancy motivation is enhanced when individuals sustain positive optimistic feelings (valence) that then propel them to exert more effort to succeed (Erez and Isen, 2002). The expectancy model integrates cognitive and emotional evaluations about the abilities of the self, the desired goal, and the subsequent primary and secondary results gained when the goal is achieved (Erez and Isen, 2002). Other integrative motivation theories (Naylor, Pritchard, and Ilgen, 1980) also describe achievement as a solid relationship between ability, motivation, and factors (individual and environmental) that strengthen or weaken accomplishments (Subotnik et al., 2011).

Research investigating motivational factors continues to expand to even more remote or atypical variables; they often coexist as intrinsic and extrinsic motivators. For example, one study examined the influence of romantic motivation and its influence on creative effort (Griskevicius, Cialdini, and Kenrick, 2006). In this experimental study, desires for sexual intimacy and the possibility of attracting a mate promoted increased creative exploration and output. Gender differences were found in this study, with males generating more creative work when either short-term or long-term mating relationships were available; whereas, females produced more creative work only when long-term mating was possible. These sexual motivational factors support biological behaviors of all animal species; specifically, greater mating success is associated with more esthetic appeal. The colorful display of peacocks attracting a mate is not dissimilar to human displays of creativity. The creative act may be regarded as a means to attract a mate; however, attractive mates may also serve as a muse for those who create. This was certainly evident in the life and work of the eminent artist, Picasso (Griskevicius et al., 2006).

As demonstrated above, passion is a powerful motivating factor in creative expression, and this passion can extend beyond the desire for a romantic partner (Vallerand, Mageau, Elliot, Dumais, Demers, and Rousseau, 2008). Passion for an activity strongly influences efforts to excel within the activity; however, sometimes a passionate desire becomes inextricably linked with self-identity (St-Louis and Vallerand, 2015). For example, an individual with a passionate love of playing music can easily convert into a delimiting self-identity of being a musician. This is not problematic if the individual can also include other self-identifying factors. Researchers have developed the Dualist Model of Passion (St-Louis and Vallerand, 2015); obsessive and harmonious passions are regarded as two distinct motivating forces (Luh and Lu, 2012; Magu et al., 2009; St-Louis and Vallerand, 2015). *Obsessive passion* manifests as a controlled effort to engage in an activity in order to shape identity, receive social approval and validation. This form of passion is associated with internal conflict and pressure, and is often related to more injuries (Rip, Fortin, and Vallerand, 2006), increased burnout rates (Trepanier, Fernet, Austin, Forrest, and Vallerand, 2014), negative emotions, ruminating behavior, and poor relationships (St-Louis and Vallerand, 2015). The second type, *harmonious passion*, is associated with an autonomous internalization of the activity and self-identity. Free will, positive emotions, and pleasurable interests are hallmark features of this form of passion. Harmonious passion positively influences self-esteem, well-being, excellence, innovative thinking, and creative achievement: factors that promote success within the workplace (Bonnevillle-Roussy, Lavigne, and Vallerand, 2010; Luh and Lu, 2012; Pradham and Aujla, 2014).

MOOD AND AFFECT

Mood and affect are major factors influencing creative output and motivation (Kaufmann, 2003); in fact, emotion and motivation have profound effects on each other (Ryan, 2007). Affect, emotion, and mood all influence behavioral and cognitive processing (Gross and Thompson, 2007); they are the bedrock of most decision-making including influencing intuition and gut feelings. The somatic marker hypothesis was developed to explain this physiologic-based gut-feeling decision-making experience (Bechara and Damasio, 2005). The somatic marker hypothesis opens the door to acknowledge how bodily states also influence mood. This reciprocal relationship between mood and bodily states necessitates the acquisition and daily implementation of effective self-regulatory skills (Critchley, 2005, 2012; Critchley, Wiens, Rotshtein, Ohman, and Dolan, 2004). Optimally, it is a process that integrates motivation, physiologic states, and emotional states that promote creative output.

The examination of affect, mood, emotion, and feeling necessitates the acceptance of several key concepts (Damasio, 1999). First, these words describe four different ideas (Panksepp, 1998). The term *affect* describes basic (primitive) biological states such anger, fear, sadness, and happiness. The term *emotion* incorporates the basic biological affective states as well as a broader range of socially induced states such as shame, guilt, and pride. *Feeling* is the subjective awareness of emotions; all three terms describe immediate responses to situations. Mood, on the other hand, is generally not associated with an immediate external event and tends to persist much longer. When a mood or emotion persists for long periods of time, they may become personality traits or dispositions (Davis, 2009; Gross and Thompson, 2007). The second major concept involves differentiating between valence (hedonic positive or negative tone) and intensity (activation level) (Baas, De Dreu, and Nijstad, 2008; De Dreu, Baas, and Nihstad, 2008; Schimmack and Diener, 1997). It is important to identify the hedonic tone, a practice that is commonly followed in mood-creativity research (To, Fisher, Ashkanasy, and Rowe, 2011); however, the intensity of the valence may have greater effect during the creative experience. Emotion and mood intensity are driven by psychological subjective appraisals as well as physiologic changes. Examining emotion/mood intensity necessitates observing and quantifying activation and deactivation patterns (To et al., 2011). This can be observed by measuring within-person cardiovascular reactivity, such as when individuals are confronted with difficult tasks and they are approaching these tasks in a negative mood state. Likewise, positive moods may enhance approach behavior even when task difficulty is great and this will reduce physiologic reactivity. These interactional patterns are described in the mood-behavior model (Silvestrini and Gendolla, 2009).

Engaging in creativity increases a capacity to tolerate negative emotions such as the morally repellent emotion of disgust. Although disgust generally inhibits behavior, it does not constrain aesthetic interest or creative judgment (Rabb, Nissel, Alecci, Magid, Ambrosoli, and Winner, 2016). In general, all creative experiences are influenced by mood, whether induced or naturally occurring (Boerner and Jobst, 2013; Hunter, Schellenberg, and Schimmack, 2010). For example, listening to music can evoke a particular mood that is then translated into subjective feelings of sadness or happiness (Morinville, Miranda, and Gaudreau, 2013); unfortunately music can also induce or intensify dysphoria (Verhaeghen, Khan, and Joorman, 2005). Likewise, when in a particular mood, listeners generally select music that is congruent with their mood, which further intensifies their mood (DeMarco, Taylor, and Friedman, 2015).

During the creative process, mood can directly influence self-reflection and provoke ruminating behavior (Verghaeghen, Joormann, and Aikman, 2014). The convergence of a congruent mood with a creative activity may evoke a persistent state of conscious thought that revolves around one activity or idea. When individuals enter a state of rumination, their thoughts are directed toward self-reflection regarding the creative project. New insights and solutions may emerge while in this state; however, if rumination becomes brooding the thoughts and focus are negatively biased. Brooding is a form of perseveration; negative thoughts about the self-become fixated, which constricts creativity. Ultimately, creative experiences are enhanced by self-reflective ruminating moods; whereas, they are crippled by brooding rumination (Verghaeghen et al., 2014).

Unfortunately, current research findings are inconclusive regarding the mood-creativity equation (Kaufmann, 2003). For example, negative moods have consistently been linked to artistic creativity (Akinola and Mendes, 2008). On the other hand, positive mood has been identified with fostering intrinsic motivation, which then enhances enjoyment and responsibility for task completion (Isen and Reeve, 2005). Another example of mixed emotional findings is evidenced in early and late idea formation. Positive emotions are associated with promoting divergent thinking and early idea production (Kaufmann and Vosburg, 2002); creative possibilities are expanded and broadened (Rathunde, 2000). However, negative emotions actually encourage a narrowing of thought, which facilitates creative decision-making (Kaufmann and Vosburg, 1997; Rathunde, 2000). Other studies have demonstrated that positive and negative moods can evoke more creative fluency compared to when individuals work in a neutral mood. Increased tolerance for unusual ideas has been associated with a combination of feeling happy as well as tired. The combination of fatigue and happiness lowers the rejection threshold; consequently, unusual ideas are more readily accepted. The problem with this happy-fatigued state is that accepting novel ideas also indicates poor discriminating abilities, in particular, determining whether unusual ideas are beneficial or harmful (Middlewood, Gallegos, and Gasper, 2016). When not fatigued, positive mood is related to more cognitive fluency; however, negative mood is associated with greater creative persistence (De Dreu et al., 2008).

The effect of positive and negative mood was also investigated in a study that examined work setting productivity. Results suggest that positive moods increase worker confidence that the task is going well; however, negative moods signal uncertainty, which actually increases worker effort to seek novel approaches to complete the task. This study demonstrates how positive moods might actually compromise employees' self-evaluation of creative efforts and their subjective appraisal of creative success (George and Zhou, 2002; Montgomery, Hodges, and Kaufman, 2004). Based on results from this study, the corporate organization actually integrated the findings and encouraged workers to induce specific mood states that enhanced productivity. They recognized when positive or negative moods were most appropriate and rewarded employees when they engaged in these mood states (George and Zhou, 2002). Given the current mood-creativity equation findings, one that suggests both positive and negative emotional states are important for creativity, it has been recommended that encouraging only happy feelings during the creative experience is insufficient (Rathunde, 2000).

Although mixed findings remain and despite the recommendation to not exclusively encourage happy feelings, research attention continues to shift toward the value of positive mood states. For example, Fredrickson (2004) claimed that when individuals nurture positive emotional states, they build personal resources (physical, intellectual, psychological) and increase their ability to manage stress. In general, happy people seldom experience negative moods and engage in more positive interpersonal relationships (Diener and Seligman, 2002). The relational component associated with positive mood suggests that this mood state will induce increased creative effort. For example, when supervisory expectations and support are both high, greater creative output results in the workers. However, even when these workers are in a positive mood, without a combination of clear goals and the encouragement of a supervisor, creative efforts are less successful (To et al., 2011). In the workplace, positive mood has also been associated with the promotion of ideas, self-affirmation, creative idea selection, and increased effort (Buisonje, Ritter, de Bruin, Horst, and Meeldijk, 2017). By investigating positive mood in the workplace, researchers have been able to identify the relationship between creative effort, supervisory support, and positive affect in workers as strong predictors of organizational success, both in productivity and employee satisfaction (Amabile, Barsade, Mueller, and Staw, 2006; Montgomery, Brodersen, and Eisenberg, 2004).

Researchers also investigate whether emotions activate or deactivate creative engagement (Baas et al., 2008). This is clearly evident when surprising moments arise while individuals engage in creative tasks; the positive feelings induced by surprise spark more creative effort (Filipowicz, 2006). This line of research is critical when studying complex social emotions such as shame; an emotional state that may activate approach or withdrawal behavior or it may deactivate and immobilize the person completely (Turner and Schallert, 2001). The need for further exploration into the emotion-creativity equation remains. Minimal research has focused on complex emotions and even less on cultural perspectives associated with emotion/mood. Every culture has different acceptance levels of emotional states, including during the creative process. Similarly, different cultures and subcultures may be biased to accept or reject a creative product based solely on an emotional aesthetic (Averill, Chon, and Hahn, 2001). For example, the heavy metal rock subculture openly expresses hostility toward authority; consequently, they reject creative products that reflect "mainstream" cultural emotional values. Likewise they endorse a strong need to portray a unique identity, one that may simultaneously increase aesthetic rejection from other subcultures (Swami, Malpass, Havard, Benford, Costescu, Sofitiki, and Taylor, 2013).

Investigating the emotion-creativity equation is further complicated by individual differences. In general, emotional activation levels are often considered dispositional traits, thus each individual will respond with different intensity and hedonic tone when exposed to a creative product or engaged in the creative process (Kring, Smith, and Neale, 1994). Intensity of arousal in positive and negative emotions also influences individual differences in attentional processes, specifically broad or focused attention. Changes in attentional processes directly influences creative output (Tidikis, Ash, and Collier, 2017). Given this variance, research that attempts to induce emotional states may be flawed simply based on individual differences in emotional intensity and expressivity.

One line of research that explores individual difference as it relates to the emotion-creativity equation is the study of empathy. Heightened empathy intensifies sensory and emotional responses, including increasing pain perceptions in response to others' pain (Jackson, Meltzoff, and Decty, 2005; Loggia, Mogil, and Bushnell, 2008). Because empathy is strongly linked with bodily sensations, highly empathic individuals also have an increased ability to recognize somatic markers to guide decision-making (Critchley et al., 2004). This also augments aesthetic appreciation and the ability to discern aesthetic value in a creative work (Freedberg and Gallese, 2007). High empathy individuals are easily absorbed in aesthetic experiences and often gravitate to music or artwork that evokes sadness; these experiences are paradoxically pleasurable to them even though they feel negative emotions more intensely (Garrido and Schubert, 2011). Empathy may also promote efforts to gain skills required to engage successfully in creative experiences. It can augment perceptual-motor performances, essential factors that operate in creative experiences (Sevdalis and Raab, 2014).

EXPERIENTIAL CREATIVE PROCESSES

Flow Experiences

Flow is a term coined by Csikszentmihalyi (1990). It is an experience that is described as optimal, positive, joyful, and meaningful. Initially, flow studies began as qualitative phenomenological investigations. Countless interviews were conducted with elite artists, athletes, surgeons, scientists, and entrepreneurs. The descriptions of entering into flow states or "being in the zone" were consistently similar across domains and between participants. Researchers determined that flow states tend to occur whenever individuals personally seek situations that they value and desire (Csikszentmihalyi, 1990). The conditions associated with flow states are universally endorsed, although some cultural variations exist among some of the flow elements (Moneta, 2004), and some learning-based activities may incorporate slightly different features of flow, especially if students are combating boredom (Ainley, Enger, and Kennedy, 2008).

Csikszentmihalyi theorized and outlined elements that contribute to flow experiences. The elements were then operationalized and included in two self-report measures that investigate participant responses immediately following the engagement in a physical activity (state) or general appraisal of the activity (dispositional/trait) (Jackson and Eklund, 2002, 2004; Jackson, Martin, and Eklund, 2008). The multidimensional dispositional and state flow scales evaluate nine flow elements (Csikszentmihalyi, 1996; Jackson, and Eklund, 2004; Kawabata and Mallett, 2011; Peterson and Greenleaf, 2014).

1. *Challenge-skill balance*—Flow states always involve a balance between the skills an individual possesses and the challenge of the task that they are fulfilling. Establishing opportunities to participate in an activity must include determining if the individual has sufficient skill acquisition to succeed in the task. Whether beginner or expert, flow is optimized when the challenge inherent in the activity is met with adequate technical skills that have been trained and practiced. If the task is not challenging for an individual, boredom will result and flow will not be fostered. Similarly, when the task is too difficult, feelings of inadequacy are evoked and opportunities for flow experiences are lost.
2. *Merging of action and awareness*—Heightened awareness during the activity ensures success when it is focused on the actions that are being executed. For example, attending to any task requires physical and mental engagement, and in flow experiences this engagement is directed fully toward the activity.
3. *Clear goals*—Once participants consciously decide to engage in an activity, they usually know what is expected of them during the activity. When goals are clearly identified, even if they are ambiguous such as during creative acts, the intention of the individual is understood and accepted. To reach major goals, years of preparation may be required. Ensuring that this process remains positive, a series of short-term goals must be identified

in order to reach long-term goals. The results gained during participation in an activity are then measured against the established goals and these results inform subsequent short-term goal setting.

4. *Immediate and unambiguous feedback*—Feedback while engaging in a task helps guide the execution of the task. This flow factor is evident in all activities that are successfully accomplished. For example, while climbing a rock face, the climber must notice any potential crevice to secure a handhold and immediately evaluate the accuracy of this decision when reaching into the crevice. Continual unambiguous feedback occurs in all flow experiences and helps ensure success.

5. *Concentration on the task at hand and ability to exclude distractions*— Absorption in the task is the hallmark of flow states. The ability to become fully engrossed in the task along with the ability to filter out all irrelevant distraction promotes flow. If the task is too easy or too difficult, concentration will waiver. Ultimately, all negative self-talk and extraneous worries must be muted in order to concentrate completely.

6. *Sense of control*—While engaging in activities that balance skill with challenge, individuals identify a feeling that they are in control of their actions and they can direct their energy toward realizing their goals. They experience a positive and pleasurable feeling of efficacy, which will persist as long as concentration is maintained throughout the activity.

7. *Loss of self-consciousness*—Individuals who enter flow states describe experiences in which they feel a union with the activity that extends beyond the limits of self-consciousness. They no longer scrutinize themselves or anticipate potential shame or rejection. They do not lose a sense of self; rather the self is expanded into a more universal connection.

8. *Transformation of time*—During flow states, time is distorted. The subjective experience of engaging in an activity may be fleeting or forever. During the activity, time may slow down such as when individuals successfully receive and respond to external and internal stimuli or it may evaporate and be experienced as a dream-state. Clock time is expanded or contracted. After the event is completed, pleasant feelings of disbelief about temporality may emerge.

9. *Autotelic experience*—According to Csikszentmihalyi (1990), autotelic experiences are the desired goal. The activity is an end in itself. The activity has meaning and purpose and fosters feelings of confidence, resilience, and involvement. It may have an addictive quality, which drives individuals to pursue their chosen activities. There is a passion to repeatedly engage in these activities. It is speculated that this flow factor is strongly linked to personality traits, and has actually been coined the autotelic personality (a propensity to experience flow).

In the self-report assessment, these nine factors are all examined during the activity; however, one, several, or all may be strongly present during a flow state. The individual does not have to experience all of these factors during a positive flow-like activity, nor do the nine factors operate in an additive manner (Jackson and Eklund, 2002). Researchers who examine the nine factors as individual dimensions suggest that balance of challenge and skill, clear goals, and unambiguous feedback are the three key proximal components involved when achieving flow states (Kawabata and Mallett, 2011). Confirmatory factor analysis and structural equation modeling indicate that the existence of these three proximal components will increase the likelihood that the other six flow factors will emerge during flow activities (Kawabata and Mallett, 2011). It is important to note, however, that two other ingredients must operate even before the three key proximal flow components. Without intrinsic motivation and a positive perception that skills were sufficient to meet the challenge of the task, flow is unlikely to result (Engeser and Rheinberg, 2008).

Research studies have identified different intensities and flow factors in divergent populations. Some of the populations that have been studied include students and employees in work settings (Martin and Jackson, 2008; Mills and Fullagar, 2008), performing artists, athletes, and participants engaging in recreational and leisure activities (Havitz and Mannell, 2005; Peterson and Greenleaf, 2014; Robb and Davies, 2015; Thomson and Jaque, 2011–2012, 2016a). In all samples, multiple flow factors were strongly endorsed although individuals who were ranked at the elite level tended to endorse lower flow states, perhaps due to their high goal setting level and heightened appraisal of their performance skills (Peterson and Greenleaf, 2014; Thomson and Jaque, 2011–2012, 2016a). In studies that examined performing artists, flow states were associated with transcendent experiences, especially when music or storytelling was involved (Chirico, Serino, Cipresso, Gaggioli, and Riva, 2015; Fritz and Avsec, 2007; Heffron and Ollis, 2006; Robb and Davies, 2015). The examination of practitioners of mindfulness suggested that highly competent practitioners of mindfulness are able to increase four flow factors while engaging in any activity. They employ their mindfulness skills to increase concentration, sense of control, loss of self-consciousness, and establish clear goals (Kee and Wang, 2008).

Moving beyond the examination of different populations, studies have explored the relationship between flow and psychological factors such as anxiety, well-being, and motivation. For example, study findings indicate that heightened flow is associated with decreased anxiety (Kirchner, Bloom and Skutnick-Henley, 2008; Thomson and Jaque, 2011–2012), less pathological dissociation (Thomson and Jaque, 2012a), diminished self-doubt (de Manzano, Theorell, Harmat, and Ullen, 2010), and increased subjective well-being

(Fritz and Avsec, 2007). Self-determination is strongly associated with flow, in particular, positive perceptions of autonomy, competence, and relatedness (Kowal and Fortier, 1999). Intrinsic and extrinsic motivating variables are inherent in self-determination and they are associated with flow; however, consistent findings suggest that the primary motivator in flow experience is intrinsic motivation (Martin and Cutler, 2002; Mills and Fullagar, 2008). Participants' perceptions of their skill competence in relationship to the task demand are positively associated with achieving a flow state and directly increase intrinsic motivation to engage in the task (Keller and Bless, 2008). This pattern is particularly strong for individuals who are action-oriented because they tend to pursue an activity with intense focus (Keller and Bless, 2008). In comparison, individuals who are more volatile are less likely to sustain intrinsic motivation; they are easily distracted and lose concentration, which inevitably diminishes their flow experiences (Keller and Bless, 2008).

Personality traits have also been aligned with greater flow experiences; in particular, novelty seeking, persistence, and self-transcendence are all associated with flow states (Mosing, Magnusson, Pedersen, Nakamura, Madison, and Ullen, 2012; Teng, 2011; Ullen et al., 2012). Neuroticism is negatively associated with flow whereas conscientiousness is positively associated (Ullen et al., 2012). When including intelligence as a factor in dispositional flow studies, no significant relationship is found (Ullen et al., 2012); however, the lack of association between intelligence and flow is more complicated when investigations involve intellectually gifted samples. Generally, highly gifted people desire flow experiences but they have difficulty finding and sustaining tasks that offer challenge. For highly gifted individuals, they consistently seek creative activities as a source of flow; creativity tends to alleviate their boredom problem (Heylighen, 2006).

Flow proneness is a clearly identified trait; it is recognized as an epigenetic phenomenon. For example, individuals with increased genetic flow heritability combined with opportunities to engage in preferred activities manifest decreased behavioral inhibition and anxiety. As well, the genetic trait of flow-proneness increases a sense of being in control of future events (internal locus of control) (Mosing, Magnusson et al., 2012; Mosing, Pedersen et al., 2012). Csikszentmihalyi (1990) described this flow proneness as the autotelic personality, literally a flow personality. These individuals actively seek challenges and inevitably experience heightened flow. They have a strong ability to direct attention and strive for goals (Busch, Hofer, Chasiotis, and Campos, 2013). Some of the Big Five personality factors associated with autotelic personality include heightened extraversion and conscientiousness as well as diminished neuroticism and agreeableness (Ross and Keiser, 2014). Unlike personality traits associated with creativity, openness to experience was not included in an autotelic personality structure, a finding that was surprising, even though it may help differentiate overlapping variables associated with flow and creative experiences (Ross and Keiser, 2014).

Examining the effects of a flow personality has yielded some important findings. For example, individuals who are considered to possess an autotelic personality are generally actively engaged in personal growth and self-advancement. This positively influences time management and goal directedness in everyday activities as well as in more skill demanding activities (Ishimura and Kodama, 2009). Flow proneness is directly associated with long-term academic success across cultures (Asakawa, 2004; Busch et al., 2013). Other positive factors related to autotelic personality include higher quality of life and greater sense of coherence, even when experiencing stressors such as unemployment (Hirao and Kobayashi, 2013). These individuals also manifest greater optimism during career searches and express a stronger sense of daily fulfillment (Asakawa, 2010). Individuals with autotelic personality traits also engage in more personal innovations as well as experience a stronger sense of self-efficacy and control while exploring. As well, they have a playfulness that can be observed when seeking mobile information and entertainment services (Tan and Chou, 2011). Individuals with autotelic personalities engage in all activities with a sense of adventure and resilience (Csikszentmihalyi, 1990).

Maintaining flow experiences into later life is solidly associated with increased daily happiness (Collins, Sarkisian, and Winner, 2009). In younger years, both teachers and students can share in flow experiences; there is a potential for an emotional contagion that is cultivated between teachers and students who work intensely together (Bakker, 2005). Both can share flow factors such as skill-challenge balance, clear goals, concentration, and unambiguous feedback. As well, both are often driven by intrinsic motivation, a factor that propels the effort required to achieve flow states (Bakker, 2005; Fritz and Avsec, 2007). Engaging in activities that can promote flow experiences are also directly linked to effective leadership, especially within stressful work environments (Lovelace, Manz, and Alves, 2007). Creating effective environments that promote flow states have the potential to enhance individual well-being and improve performance levels. This potential exists within settings such as sport, performing arts, education, entrepreneurial organizations, and corporations (Bakker, Oerlemans, Demerouti, Slot, and Ali, 2011). Flow experiences and performance improvement can occur when physical fitness is encouraged (Lovelace et al., 2007), music is included (Pates, Karageorghis, Fryer, and Maynard, 2003), positive reinforcement is implemented, and skills to reduce anxiety and promote performance are taught (Harmison, 2006; Jackson, Kimiecik, Ford, and Marsh, 1998; Jackson,

Thomas, Marsh, and Smethurst, 2001; Kirchner et al., 2008; Klein, Rossin, Guo, and Ro, 2010; Riggs, 2006).

Creative Experiences: A Phenomenological View

Investigating the criteria to determine talent, personality traits, or motivational behaviors of the creative person is important; equally important is the examination of the subjective experience of creating (Nelson and Rawlings, 2007). Studying the phenomenology of how creative people experience the creative process can help identify key elements in the creative experience (Nelson and Rawlings, 2007; Reinders, 1992). Inherent in phenomenological studies is the intersubjective concept of being-in-the-world; phenomenology examines a relational field that incorporates interactions with the self, the world, and the lived meaning derived from all lived experiences (Heidegger, 1962; Stolorow, Atwood, and Orange, 2002). Consequently, phenomenological analyses can address the nature of being-in-the-world during creative experiences. What has been identified in the phenomenological study conducted by Nelson and Rawlings (2009) is that individuals experience a heightened sense of unity within the self, they operate in "flow" states that are guided by intuition, and they tolerate a paradoxical sense of certainty and uncertainty (Csikszentmihalyi, 1996; Nelson and Rawlings, 2007). Like the "Janusian" concept, creative experiences are marked by a physical and psychological tension that is activated when individuals simultaneously look in multiple directions while creating (Rothenberg, 1990). Fundamentally, phenomenological studies identify creative experiences as a dynamic engagement with the self.

Nelson and Rawlings identified clear themes in their qualitative phenomenological studies and incorporated these themes into the Experience of Creativity Questionnaire. The purpose of this self-report measurement is to give creative people an opportunity to report on their own creative experience. Two major dimensions are identified: the experiential dimension describes the ways creativity is experienced, and the existential dimension refers to the meaning derived from the creative experience (Nelson and Rawlings, 2009). Multiple factors are included within each dimension. The experiential factors are listed as follows (Nelson and Rawlings, 2009, 2010):

1. *Distinct experience*—The distinct experience factor differentiates everyday experiences from creativity. There is a loss of self-awareness, a breakdown of boundaries, and greater emotional intensity during the creative experience. A heightened sense of emotional stability is combined with a

sense of contact with a force beyond the individual, a sense of confidence and effortlessness during the creative experience, plus potential heightened spiritual dimension. Primarily, distinct creative experiences include increased technical and expressive abilities.
2. *Anxiety*—Anxiety is identified before, during, and after the creative process; greater vulnerability is experienced in the creative process.
3. *Absorption*—The individual feels inspired and becomes deeply absorbed in the creative action, while feeling a strong sense of coherence. Feelings of freedom, discovery, receptivity, and openness prevail when the individual is connected with the creative work. The oscillating distancing process of critical awareness counters intense absorption during the creative experience; however, absorption is essential before critical awareness occurs.
4. *Power/pleasure*—During the creative process, this factor is expressed as profound pleasure, coupled with internal power and a feeling of ultimate control. Like absorption, analytic control (power) is an integral part of the creative experience.
5. *Clarity/preparation*—A simultaneous feeling of certainty and clarity informs the direction, meaning, and purpose of the creative work. During the creative experience an appropriate mood, whether pleasurable or painful, is evoked that sustains the creative process.

The existential dimension contains factors that are directly related to the meaning derived from "being-in-the-world." The existential dimension, even more than the experiential dimension, discriminates participants who are engaged in artistic versus athletic activities; in particular, dancers report more existential meaning during the creative experience compared to athletes (Thomson and Jaque, 2016a). These factors are also strongly endorsed by professional performing artists who were exposed to substantial childhood adversity (Thomson and Jaque, 2018). The existential variables include (Nelson and Rawlings, 2009):

1. *Transformation*—This existential variable describes how the creative experience deepens an engagement with the self and the world. Awareness is broadened, confidence increases, and a strong healing component is felt during the subjective experience of creating.
2. *Centrality*—Individuals who experience centrality report a need to engage in a creative activity; their primary motivation is self-discovery and the by-product is joy. This need to create is a central element in their lives. They feel purpose and meaning while creating and anxiety when they are not engaged in creative experiences. For many creative individuals, the creative experience has an addictive quality; it offers a sense of healing and a deeper connection to spirituality.

3. *Beyond the personal*—This factor is closely aligned with the intersubjective concept of being-in-the-world. The creative experience transcends the personal and offers deeper connections with others. The creative experience facilitates opportunities to create works that will help others.

Many features identified in the phenomenological study of creativity overlap with the concept of flow; however, a few variables are not part of flow. Some of the factors unique to the creative experience, and not flow experiences, include movement between intuitive and analytic mental processes, along with an attitude of exploration, and a sense of discovery (Nelson and Rawlings, 2007). Creativity has a very different sense of time compared to flow experiences. Time is not narrow in the creative process, especially given the reality that many ideas germinate for years or decades before they begin to take form. Flow experiences, on the other hand, tend to exist during a single activity. Likewise, creative experiences often evoke a sense of spirituality. Individuals engaged in the creative process often describe a unity of self and the universe (Csikszentmihalyi, 1996; Nelson and Rawlings, 2007, 2009). Flow experiences may evoke similar transcendent states, especially when engaging in artistic activities (Bernard, 2009), although most activities that elicit flow are described as profound enjoyment (Csikszentmihalyi, 1990). The transcendent quality shared in both creative and flow experiences necessitate embodied engagement during the execution of a task (Robb and Davies, 2015). Many posit that these transcendent experiences resemble meditative states, a comparison that has some legitimacy. However, during meditative states mental focus takes precedent whereas creative and flow activities require both physical and mental attention. This phenomenological difference between meditation and flow/creative experiences is important (Hunter and Csikszentmihalyi, 2008). Creative, flow, and meditative experiences are slightly different; however, the value the individual places on the quality of the experience is similar, and the ability to transfer skills gained in all three modalities can augment all of them (Nelson and Rawlings, 2007; Kee and Wang, 2008).

OTHER INFLUENCING FACTORS DURING THE CREATIVE PROCESS

The creative process necessitates high arousal states, including high energy to achieve results, as well as a high desire to engage in creative cognition (Watts, Steele, and Song, 2017). Although *passion* functions as an intrinsic motivating factor, it also directly influences the creative process. Harmonious passion, compared to obsessive passion, is a positive influence. It helps reinforce positive emotions and increases cognitive flexibility during the process of creating (St-Louis and Vallerand, 2015). During development, harmonious passion can be cultivated by environmental influences that support autonomy; whereas, children who experience parental and adult pressure-to-achieve often develop obsessional passion (Mageau et al., 2009). Obsessive passion directly influences job burnout and rigid work behavior (Trepanier, Fernet, Austin, Forrest, and Vallerand, 2014); however, when creative output results from harmonious passion, there is an integration of corporeal creativity (felt-body knowing), situational adaptability, and fluent generation of ideas to meet the creative challenges (Julmi and Scherm, 2015). Ultimately, harmonious passion is a bidirectional factor that shapes the "structure" of creative experiences (Julmi and Scherm, 2015; Mageau et al., 2009).

In addition to the above stated factors that shape creative experiences, *constraints* play an equally major role in the generation of creativity (Stokes, 2007). Ultimately, creative productivity within the sciences and arts is dependent on constraints (Haught, 2015). It has been speculated that the more constraints in the awareness of the individual the more creative the response, a finding that is in direct opposition to the notion that creativity is fostered within free and unfettered conditions (Haught, 2015; Martin, Ric, and Hirstovski, 2015). Examples of constraints include limitations in time, finances, personnel, opportunities, and resources. Although constraints can promote creative productivity, when there are too few or too many then the problem solving and creative productivity falters (Medeiros, Partlow, and Mumford, 2014). Individual appraisal also influences the consequences of constraint. For example, people respond individually to physical environments such as to noise level and light quality. Some may feel constrained while others believe that the constraints enhance their creative freedom (Kristensen, 2004). Individual emotional responses to the environment also positively or negatively determine creative success. All physical contexts influence a feeling of embodied creativity. Ideally, providing settings that enhance imagination and promote the materialization of a creative product can coexist despite inevitable constraints (Kristensen, 2004).

The *working climate* can also operate as a constraint that augments or hampers creativity. Perceptions of the work environment, including subjective feelings of being positively supported, influence creative productivity (Hunter, Bedell, and Mumford, 2007). An optimal balance between challenge, intellectual stimulation, and relational support encourages creative achievement, especially in highly competitive environments where production pressure is the norm (Hunter et al., 2007). Ultimately, the work environment culture can either promote or prevent innovation and exploration (Friedman and Foster, 2011). Specifically, promotion cues are designed to encourage risky cognitive processing styles; whereas, prevention cues provoke risk-aversive and vigilant cognitive styles. Ideally, promotion cues within the environment will increase creative exploration, although prevention cues may propel the creation of solutions that will increase security and shelter from harm (Friedman and Forster, 2001). The *"small-world" network model* adds to an understanding about constraint in the work environment (Schilling, 2005). Knowledge sharing and increased productivity occur when small groups form networks; this model can be applied to social and neurobiological networks (people and cells). "Small-worlds" are highly clustered although sparse when compared to the entire population; they may be constrained by the weakness within some of the members or strengthened by the skills of some of the members of the small-world network. Understanding how "small worlds" interact sheds light on how to foster creative insight and innovation, for example, within all "small-world "networks, promotion and prevention cues, challenge, support, and autonomy are all operating (Schilling, 2005). Individuals who work in "small-world" networks are able to generate ideas, develop them, and ultimately finalize and evaluate the idea (Nemiro, 2002). Within "small-world" network environments the group may simultaneously or sequentially constrain or augment creative work.

A *competitive environment*, one that encourages exploration and risk-taking, has a direct influence on creative output (Simmons and Ren, 2009). Cultural diversity in the workplace helps sharpen this competitive edge (Florida, 2004). Without new minds and new perspectives, creative innovation declines (Florida, 2004). Differences in individual problem solving styles are essential to promote creativity; cultural diversity is directly associated with problem solving diversity. Unfortunately, the United States is falling behind in immigration rates, while other countries continue to welcome immigrants and consequently are gaining more of an international competitive edge (Florida, 2004). Beyond the immediate gains derived from a diverse workforce, cultivating variations in problem-solving styles requires policies and working environments that foster creativity. These conditions must meet the needs of a wide range of ages and cultural backgrounds. Schools and corporate settings should encourage person-focused and task-focused engagement, internal and external orientation to change, peak performance skills to meet the challenges associated with change and competition, as well as selecting individuals who are either explorers, developers, or both (Hallet and Hoffman, 2014; Treffinger et al., 2008). Recognizing these dimensions and implementing effective programs that support individual work and collaborative group dynamics will promote effective and diverse problem solving styles. This diversity also influences the ability to manage stressful situations (Carson and Runco, 1999). With more successful opportunities to meet stressful demands, action-oriented coping strategies tend to dominate. Individuals who do not cope well often collapse under the demands of creative competition.

Ultimately, optimal problem solving and problem finding abilities are recognized factors to achieve success when working under stressful conditions (Carson and Runco, 1999).

Under any working condition when individuals set unrealistic and rigid goals of perfection, then the success falters (Hewitt and Flett, 2004). *Maladaptive perfectionism* undermines motivation and impairs performance. It constrains productivity by intense fear of failure and uncompromising standards that cripple creative exploration (Hall and Hill, 2012). Like perfectionism, *excessive self-judgment* also cripples creativity (Zabelina and Robinson, 2010). Despite a desire to succeed, self-judgmental individuals compromise success by self-imposed restrictions that deter productivity. As well, negative self-judgment may contain features of brooding rumination. In this state, individuals present as self-immersed, indecisive, and passive; they lack the capacity to self-distance, a capacity that operates during self-reflective rumination as well as during a self-compassionate mindset (Copeland, 2016; Jones, Roy, and Verkuilen, 2014; Zabelina and Robinson, 2010). The ability to distinguish and then shift from states of brooding, maladaptive perfectionistic, and negative self-judgment to states of self-reflective rumination and self-compassion are key ingredients to augment creative output (Copeland, 2016; Hewitt and Flett, 2004; Trapnell and Campbell, 1999).

CONCLUSION

The creative process is a multidimensional dynamic process (Peilloux and Botella, 2016). Individual, group, and multi-level organizations must all adapt to constraints during this process (Watson, 2007). Complexity is essential for adaptability; many factors help foster creative experiences. For example, self-compassion is a significant factor that directs and promotes creative output, including originality (Zabelina and Robinson, 2010). Encouraging growth mindsets, literally maintaining a belief that learning is possible, may promote the expansion of creative abilities and creative self-efficacy (Hass, Katz-Buonincontro, and Reiter-Palmon, 2016). In fact, both fixed and growth mindsets may best be applied to individuals while engaging in the creative process, especially when they are redefined as creative mindsets (Hass et al., 2016). Another factor that enhances creative potential is physical activity, including aerobic exercise. Following bouts of exercise, creative output increases, as well as a positive sense of well-being (Blanchette, Ramocki, O'del, and Casey, 2005; Kim, 2015; Steinberg, Sykes, Moss, Lowery, LeBoutillier, and Dewey, 1997).

Recognizing and respecting individual preferred learning and creative styles, whether working independently or within a collaborative group, is critical to nurturing creative output. Accommodating these learning styles also promotes enjoyment and self-efficacy (Sitar, Cerne, Aleksic, and Mihelic, 2016). Even within "small-world" networks, preferred learning styles can be accommodated during the creative process, especially since most people recognize that the creative process includes periods of independent and collaborative engagement (Schilling, 2005; Sitar et al., 2016). One key ingredient within these "small-world" networks is effective communication (Peilloux and Botella, 2016). Likewise, emotional responsiveness during the creative output varies according to task demands. Individuals who work in creative fields that require emotional engagement learn to tolerate and regulate emotional intensity while creating (Trnka, Zahradnik, and Kuska, 2016). Appreciating the need to differentiate emotional creativity from emotional intelligence helps normalize artistic creative processes, including greater fantasy proneness and emotional expressivity (Fuchs, Kumar, and Porter, 2007). Students and professionals who must engage emotional creativity require working climates that accept these fundamental needs (Thomson and Jaque, 2017; Trinka et al., 2016).

The creative process is also enhanced in environments that foster engagement in multiple knowledge structures, literally integrating *schematic knowledge* (abstracted concepts developed from past experiences) and *associational knowledge* (immediate associations that form in response to a problem or situation). These knowledge structures are built from general and domain specific stimuli. For example, musicians cultivate a vast array of sound schemas that are integrated into schematic knowledge and they then inform how stimuli are heard and appraised (Woodward and Sikes, 2015). Complex interactions between fast, spontaneous thought and effortful, purposeful thought are invariant elements in all creative thinking (Allen and Thomas, 2011). During the entire creative experience these bipolar thought processes are mobilized. Ultimately, all these forms of knowledge structures operate with great variance during idea generation and problem solving (Hunter, Bedell-Avers, Hunsicker, Mumford, and Ligon, 2008), factors that are always assumed in creative experiences (Nelson and Rawlings, 2009).

Incorporating multiple factors to construct a *creative knowledge environment* may further individual, group, and corporate productivity and innovation (Hemlin, Allwood, Martin, 2008). General work situations, the physical working environment, group dynamics, leadership styles, domain specific needs, individual talent, knowledge, and skills, and the emotional, social, financial, and physical resources are all aspects of a creative knowledge environment. Although intended to exert a positive influence, these conditions can easily be directed toward malevolent intentions (James and Drown, 2008). Regardless of intent, fostering this environment can directly influence performance level, with a clear possibility of achieving world-leading innovations (Hemlin et al., 2008). All shape the creative experience, one that is embedded within an intricate relational field (Nelson and Rawlings, 2009).

Chapter 4

Fantasy and Pathology

Creativity is dependent on an ability to imagine something that does not yet exist or to perceive common objects in novel ways (Taylor, Pham, Rivkin, and Armor, 1998). Becoming absorbed in a fantasy, daydream, or imaginative world are all terms that portray the creative process; they also describe processes to escape boring or troubling situations. Fundamentally, all describe mental constructs that are internally generated. Because these three terms share overlapping features it is often challenging to disambiguate them. Typically, fantasy is regarded as a mental creation of improbable or unrealistic settings, characters or events; these fantasies may range from terrifying and horrific to sublime and beautiful (Coleridge, 1817/1976; Merriam-Webster.com). Daydreams share features with fantasy; however, they are usually pleasant wishful creations of the mind. Daydreams are less fantastical in nature and provide pleasurable sojourns for the daydreamer (Merriam-Webster.com). Unlike fantasy and daydreams, imagination has a more intangible definition. It is an ability to construct mental images of something that is not present to the senses or was never fully perceived in reality (Merriam-Webster.com). Although imagination includes the capacity to evoke images it is also much more than imagery (Lin, Chang, and Liang, 2015). Theoretically, imagery is an everyday cognitive process; for example, the ability to construct images of future activities or scenarios provides ongoing opportunities to plan and rehearse (Le Boutillier and Marks, 2003). On the other hand, imagination, whether expressive or instrumental in nature, is closely aligned with the emergent properties of creativity (Feng, Logan, Cupchik, Ritterfeld, and Gaffin, 2017). Although imagination is often highly romanticized, it is highly valued across all cultures and is directly implicated when constructing complex or novel products (Feng et al., 2017; Frye, 1963; Thomas, 1999).

Gaining a deeper understanding about these profoundly human activities has posed many problems. First, researchers tend to employ these terms interchangeably without operationalizing them; although they have operationalized terms such as creativity and cognitive imagery. The more illusive terms of imagination and fantasy remain less clearly defined. Consequently, substantial research has been conducted on creativity and imagery, less on fantasy, and even less on daydreaming. Despite this imbalance, psychopathology research has addressed these concepts (imagination, fantasy, daydreaming) (Somer, 2002). For example, psychotic delusions, hallucinations, and visions all share features with fantasy, daydreams, and imagination. Unfortunately, these shared features have reinforced the notion that creativity is related to insanity and mental illness (Klinger, Henning, and Janssen, 2009). Likewise, psychopathology studies have included the examination of paranormal experiences. For example, investigators have examined the nature and origin of a paranormal event, including studies that explored children who suffered trauma (Gow, Lang, and Chant, 2004; Parra, 2006; Watt, Watson, and Wilson, 2007). To date, questions related to fantasy, imagination, and the paranormal still reside on the outer edge of creativity research, and yet they remain relevant avenues to explore.

FANTASY AND DAYDREAMS

Fantasy Proneness

While investigating behaviors in individuals who were considered highly hypnotizable, Wilson and Barber (1983) discovered a group of women who were not only highly hypnotizable but also experienced intense fantasies. These women described their fantasies with the full intensity of reality and they engaged in their fantasy for protracted periods of time. Wilson and Barber (1983) labeled this small group of women (approximately 4% of the population) as fantasy prone personalities; their intense capacity to fantasize separated them from the moderate and low fantasizing groups. Interestingly, the fantasy prone group shared similar past experiences and personality traits. Common features of their childhood included experiencing a significant adult who encouraged fantasy activities, exposure to performing arts classes that helped nurture their natural abilities to fantasize, spending time isolated and alone (often in a single child household), growing up in bad environments (home and/or community), and some suffered traumatic or loss experiences. As adults they described vivid fantasies that extended for hours, days, or weeks. These fantasies were fully realized on all sensory dimensions, for example, when imagining a sexual fantasy they felt physical sensations including reaching an orgasm. The high fantasy prone individuals maintained their fantasies even while doing mundane activities; perhaps their fantasies provided pleasant escape while engaging in unpleasant tasks.

High fantasy proneness does not alter the ability to recognize items during memory tasks (Horselenberg, Merckelbach, van Breukelen, and Wessel, 2004); however, a different level of recognition may manifest when generating fantasies. For many fantasy prone individuals, fantasy life is so intense that they confuse memories of real events with fantasized events (Merckelbach, 2004; Merckelbach and van de Ven, 2001; Somer, 2002; Wilson and Barber, 1983). It is not uncommon for fantasy prone individuals to imagine illnesses or pregnancies with such intensity that they will experience most of the symptoms without being ill or pregnant (Candel and Merckelbach, 2003). For example, they may fail to menstruate for months during a false pregnancy. Also, personal past memories (pleasurable and painful) can be recovered with the full sensory and physical intensity of the original experience. Many high fantasy prone individuals also report more paranormal events such as out-of-body experiences, telepathy, precognition, automatic writing, and religious or apparitional visions. Another common feature in high fantasy prone individuals is a tendency to hide their experiences from others. And for some, they avoid social occasions and work activities in order to disappear into their fantasy life. When this trait begins to compromise functioning, it is described as pathological fantasy proneness or maladaptive daydreaming. Once fantasizing and daydreaming becomes addictive, high fantasy prone individuals may experience more psychological and social problems including an increased risk for psychopathology disorders (Lynn and Rhue, 1988; Rauschenberger and Lynn, 2002/2003; Rhue and Lynn, 1987; Somer, 2002; Wilson and Barber, 1983).

Individuals who are classified with fantasy prone personalities (high fantasy prone) also demonstrate personality traits of neuroticism, openness to experience, and agreeableness, plus they score lower on conscientiousness (Sanchez-Bernardos and Avis, 2004; Sanchez-Bernardos, Lloreda, Avia, and Bragado-Alvarez, 2015). In these personality studies, age was not a factor, however more women were identified with fantasy prone personality (Sanchez-Bernardos and Avis, 2004). This personality type is also strongly associated with creativity, including intellectual giftedness (Dunn, Corn, and Morelock, 2004). When examining MMPI scores in individuals classified as fantasy prone personality, they manifest increased vulnerability for schizophrenia spectrum disorders as well as personality disorders, in particular schizotypy (Merritt and Waldo, 2000; Sanchez-Bernardos and Avia, 2006). In the Merritt and Waldo (2000) study, more fantasy prone individuals were identified with a pathological disorder compared to the lower rate in the earlier study by Rhue and Lynn (1987). Like the findings in Rauschenberger and Lynn's study (2002/2003), the fantasy prone individuals had more current or past histories of major depression, generalized anxiety, and poorer self-regulation. They also had more disturbed sleep due to their increased awareness of dreaming (Giesbrecht and Merckelbach, 2006).

The association with fantasy prone personality and psychopathology also includes higher rates of dissociative disorders as well as more Axis-II personality disorders (Waldo and Merritt, 2000). Both fantasy proneness and dissociation share features of heightened absorption, although the quality of absorption is generally quite different between the two conditions, with fantasy absorption associated with creativity and dissociative absorption related to psychopathology (Klinger et al., 2009; Thomson, Keehn, and Gumpel, 2009). It is important to note that dissociation is not a unidimensional condition: it can be divided into non-pathological dissociative absorption as well as dissociative pathology (Levin and Spei, 2003; Thomson and Jaque, 2011). When these two dimensions are examined, fantasy remains strongly related to the non-pathological absorption scale and not the pathological scale (Levin and Spei, 2003). When dissociative pathology is sub-divided into dimensions of depersonalization, amnesia, and identity confusion, fantasy is strongly related to depersonalization, a disorder that is marked by profound absorption and perceptual distortions (Levin, Simeon, and Guralnick, 2004; Wolfradt and Engelmann, 2003). Dissociation, in general, is also strongly associated with childhood abuse (Dalenberg et al., 2012). Given these studies, the relationship between fantasy proneness and dissociation remains strong (Giesbrecht, Merckelbach, and Geraerts, 2007; Pekala, Angelini, and Kumar, 2001).

Frequently, fantasy prone individuals report intense paranormal experiences. They often engage in practices to offset superstitious beliefs, such as knocking on wood to dispel evil thoughts from becoming reality (Lack, Kumar, and Arevalo, 2003). High fantasy prone individuals tend to identify with traditional religious concepts as well as witchcraft, spiritualism, precognition, and extraordinary life forms (Irwin, 1990). Those who express more paranormal beliefs also experience more somatoform disorders, as well as out-of-body experiences (Gow et al., 2004). Congruent with their abilities to fully evoke real or imagined events with full sensory embodied engagement, they often blur fantasy experiences with paranormal beliefs and experiences (Blanke and Arzy, 2005). It is important to note that both paranormal and religious beliefs offset anxiety; when fantasy is directed toward these spiritual beliefs anxiety is reduced, despite the fact that seeing and feeling apparitions increases (Parra, 2006; Watt et al., 2007). Although high fantasy prone individuals manifest these beliefs, the majority of the population, worldwide, also endorses spiritual beliefs of a life after death. These beliefs are deeply embedded into our social cognition; they provide comfort and order to life that is fundamentally unsettling and chaotic (Bering, 2006), a reality that indicates the essential role of fantasy in our lives.

Fantasy proneness can also be employed as a coping skill (Levin and Fireman, 2001/2002). In a study that examined emotionally unstable patients, those with higher fantasy prone traits were less troubled by intense nightmares (Levin and Fireman, 2001/2002). This trait was also linked to more behavioral self-regulation, including higher creative aptitude (Lack et al., 2003). Fantasy proneness has also served to buffer the troubling effects of childhood sexual and physical abuse (Perkins and Allen, 2006; Irwin, 1990). Although not a marker of behavioral self-regulation, fantasy proneness has also been associated with extreme celebrity worship, perhaps because these individuals can happily disappear into a full sensory fantasy about a romantic life with the chosen celebrity figure (Maltby, Day, McCutcheon, Houran, and Ashe, 2006). Fantasy prone individuals are also gifted storytellers, in part, because they can depict situations in more elaborate linguistic style and with vivid clarity and emotional intensity, factors that enhance creative experiences (Marinelli, Bindi, Marchi, Castellani, Carli, and Santarcangelo, 2012; Merckelbach, 2004).

Daydreaming

Daydreaming shares many features with mind wandering and fantasy. Mind wandering is a common daily occurrence that happens multiple times in the day, whereas, daydreaming involves complete inward focus. Fantasy is an inward activity that is consciously elaborated and continuous; whereas, daydreaming is experienced as an ongoing series of brief associated thoughts (Bulter, 2006). While daydreaming, attention is fully removed from external stimuli for brief or protracted periods of time. It often takes place when individuals are bored or they are doing an activity that requires minimal attention (Langens, 2003). According to Singer and colleagues (Huba, Aneshensel, and Singer, 1981), daydreaming is not a unidimensional construct. Daydreams can be grouped into three clusters: (1) positive constructive daydreaming (wishful or intentional thoughts associated with creativity and future planning), (2) Guilt/fear-of-failure daydreams (negative emotions and thoughts dominate), (3) Poor attentional control (inability to sustain focus on tasks or problem solving) (Williams and Vess, 2016). The quality of daydreaming can reveal the inner core beliefs of the individual, in particular, positive constructive daydreaming is associated with an authentic self; whereas, the other two daydream constructs reveal more self-alienation and distress (Williams and Vess, 2016).

Positive daydreams are important factors for individuals who are highly motivated; they commit to their goals and usually achieve them. For these individuals, positive daydreaming increases goal achievement; however, if individuals are not highly motivated to achieve their goals, positive daydreaming has no influence (Langens, 2003). Future studies may shed light on this discrepancy. Perhaps highly motivated people employ positive daydreams that are more reality-based; whereas, low motivated people may be less realistic in their goals (Langens, 2003). Another possibility is that positive as well as guilt/fear-of-failure and poor attentional control daydreams may vary in their dreamlike quality. For example, heightened emotions tend to make daydreams more dreamlike; the expression of the emotion intensifies a symbolic and dreamlike quality. This can make daydreams, whether positive or negative, more bizarre and more intense (Hartmann et al., 2002/2003).

When daydreaming becomes compulsive and excessive, regardless of the type of daydream, daily activities are severely compromised. These individuals self-identify as *maladaptive daydreamers*, a term that was originally introduced in a study conducted by Somer (2002). These addictive daydreamers make their presence known in online support forums; to date, researchers are just beginning to examine this population (Bigelsen and Schupak, 2011; Schupak and Rosenthal, 2009). Unlike the fantasy prone personality individuals, maladaptive daydreamers describe addictive and compulsive qualities to their daydreaming. Their daydreams are filled with excessive detail, they usually need to rock, sway, or pace to sustain their daydreaming, they avoid social and work activities in order to continue daydreaming, they hide their daydreaming activities from others, and they are fully aware that they cannot stop their uncontrollable urge to daydream (Somer, Somer, and Jopp, 2016). Maladaptive daydreamers have no difficulty distinguishing their daydreams from reality, nor do they endorse paranormal experiences (Bigelsen and Schupak, 2011). The Maladaptive Daydreaming Scale captures three maladaptive clusters: (1) Affective Qualities (joy while daydreaming and distress associated with lack of opportunity to daydream), (2) Behavioral Qualities (compulsive behavioral urges), and (3) Impaired Functioning (distress associated with uncontrollable and excessive daydreaming) (Somer, Lehrfeld, Bigelsen, and Jopp, 2016). Maladaptive daydreaming has been associated with obsessive-compulsive behaviors, attention-deficit disorder, and dissociative absorption but not with psychotic symptoms (Somer et al., 2016). This syndrome may overlap with individuals who suffer Internet addictions, although Internet images are generated from external sources whereas maladaptive daydreaming is internally generated.

CHILDHOOD IMAGINING

The development of fantasy begins in early childhood. Small children often create an imaginary companion; this companion offers support, friendship, mentoring, entertainment, and promotes self-regulation (Hoff, 2004/2005). Imaginary companions may take the form of animal, fantasy creature, or same-age children and they are often modeled from siblings, friends, or media figures (Hoff, 2004/2005). The creation of imaginary companions is primarily a healthy and adaptive activity during development. Although children with childhood abuse histories may engage in this creation more frequently, it is not a necessary condition for the existence of imaginary companions (Aguiar, Mottweilier, Taylor, and Fisher, 2017). Children with imaginary companions tend to be more creative; however, these children also lack a strong self-image and psychological well-being (Hoff, 2005). They view themselves as different from other children, an experience that is also strongly associated with creatively talented children (Hoff, 2005; Wellisch and Brown, 2013). Despite the intense relationships that are cultivated with imaginary companions, autobiographical memories are not confused with imaginary play memories. Again, this is a feature of highly creative individuals (Firth, Alderson-Day, Woods, and Fernyhough, 2015).

During development, children use their imagination to reinforce social relationships and to explore skills required in adulthood. Imaginary social relationships provide stronger social networks that offer support to both the young and the old (Gleason, 2002). Pretend play and pretend friends provide exploratory opportunities that facilitate the formation of self-identity and self-regulatory skills, and these skills indirectly enhance academic success (Wallace and Russ, 2015). Objects, such as dolls and stuffed animals, provide supportive exploratory relational experiences. Children project meaning and feelings onto these objects, a pattern that can persist into adulthood such as when adults endow their cars with personalities and develop relationships with the car (Gleason, 2002).

A more elaborate form of imaginary companions is *imaginary worldplays*, also termed *paracosm* (Root-Bernstein and Root-Bernstein, 2006). The invention of imaginary worlds extends beyond a single relationship. Entire worlds are constructed that persist and remain consistent over time. These worlds grow and change throughout development and may continue into adulthood. At the most extreme end of the imaginary continuum, worldplays incorporate imagined languages, geographic regions, and elaborate social and cultural events. Highly gifted individuals have reported inventing worldplays in childhood, adolescence, and for some, into adulthood. Intense absorption, persistence, and synthesis of ideas are required to construct worldplays; these are all factors that are part of the creative process (Root-Bernstein and Root-Bernstein, 2006). The construction of worldplays is completely volitional and lacks the compulsive addictive quality of maladaptive daydreaming. Individuals who create paracosms can disengage from their imaginative worldplay in order to attend to other activities; they have confidence that they can return later. Their self-regulatory abilities are evident in their daily activities as well as in their fantasy worldplay (Taylor et al., 2015).

IMAGINATION AND IMAGERY

Imagination is a difficult construct to measure, in part, because the word is deeply value laden. This term tends to encapsulate the higher creative functions of humanity (Thomas, 1999). It contains all theories developed regarding imagery and goes beyond them. In research studies, this term is seldom used, whereas the operationally defined terms, creativity and innovation, are commonly employed (Forgeard and Kaufman, 2015). Imagination was idealized during the Romantic era; it captured the divine connections between humanity and God (Thomas, 1999). Given its historical origins, imagination is still employed when discussing artistic creativity, as well as childhood explorations during play (Thomas, 1999). Many theorists working in the arts frequently employ the term *imagination*, for example, enhancing musical imagination is a clear directive in music education (Hargreaves, 2012). According to the Scottish philosopher, David Hume, metaphysical, artistic, and scientific imagination was central to product realization (Streminger, 1980). Imagination is fundamentally a mental process rather than a reified state (Feng et al., 2017). It is both expressive and instrumental in its purpose; literally it incorporates episodic nonlinear narratives as well as pragmatic problem solving. The continuum between reality and imagination is often blurred, both constructs overlap during the process of engaging the imagination (Feng et al., 2017).

Imagery is a mental construct. Imagery involves perceptual experiences that are internally, rather than externally, generated. Mental imagery, especially during the creative process, has been examined in relationship to individual and group differences, divergent thinking processes, and image generation (LeBoutillier and Marks, 2003). Research findings reinforce the notion that mental imagery manifests in different styles, forms, contents, and contexts, as well, they emerge spontaneously or deliberately. Other criteria that are examined in imagery studies include vividness, duration, and imagery stimulus (i.e., emotions, guided suggestions, shifting perspectives, mental practice employed during skill improvement) (Krasnow and Willmerding, 2015; LeBoutillier and Marks, 2003). Imagery studies explore who employs imagery, what types of imagery are generated, why imagery is used, when and where imagery practices are implemented, and how images are generated (training effect and imagery ability) (Pavlik and Nordin-Bates, 2016). Lastly, investigations have focused on determining ideal conditions for implementing imagery, such as performance improvement in sport, performing arts, healing arts, academics, and career planning (Pavlik and Nordin-Bates, 2016).

Three theories of imagery have been proposed (Thomas, 1999). The first, *description theory*, describes images that are internally generated based on memory retrieval or the invention of new constructs to meet demands of current situations. The second imagery construct, the *picture theory*, is the most commonly understood theory. The ability to intentionally form mental pictures reflects the notion that the mind can form pictures about future events. Constructing mental mnemonics enhances memory retrieval (Thomas, 1999). Mental pictures can be transformed or manipulated such as rotating an image, increasing or decreasing size, or adding/changing details. The third construct, *perceptual activity theory*, captures sensory-motor images that guide real and imagined performances (Thomas, 1999).

Perceptual imagery is directly related to domain-specific aptitudes. This is clearly evident in musicians who are readily able to vividly and clearly imagine auditory stimuli. They can use auditory imagery to mentally practice and to create new musical compositions (Campos and Fuentes, 2016). When recalling childhood and adult events imagery engagement differs; specifically, imaginational inflation is greater when discussing adult memories compared to childhood memories (Sharman and Barnier, 2008). Further, *guided imagery* (a process that encourages adding detail) and *prompted imagery* (request to retrieve a memory without encouraging details) evoke different memory imagery constructs. Guided imagery increases the likelihood of false memories or inaccurate memory embellishment compared to prompted imagery (Bays, Zabrucky, and Foley, 2015).

Acquiring imagery skills such as *mental simulation* coupled with self-regulation during the generation of images can enhance more effective visions of future prospects (Taylor et al., 1998). Engaging mental simulations involves constructing mental scenarios to explore potential outcomes. It helps intensify potential problem solving solutions before any actual event transpires. Employing mental simulation also amplifies potential sources of distress and provides opportunities to implement self-regulating strategies to cope with these future situations. Successful outcome when implementing mental simulation requires the elimination of wishful thinking; ideally, realistic self-regulating mental simulation promotes effective problem solving for future events (Taylor et al., 1998). Teachers, coaches, leaders (corporate, religious, political), and health practitioners can engage in mental imagery skills to improve their performance as well as encourage their students, athletes, followers, and patients to implement imagery to improve their performance and/or healing (Hanrahan and Verger, 2000/2001; Overby, Hall, and Haslam, 1997/1998).

AWE AND TRANSCENDENCE

What is surprising is that very few researchers venture into the field of *awe* (Darbor, Lench, Davis, and Hicks, 2016; Keltner and Haidt, 2003). Currently, three clusters of psychophysiological variables have been identified; they are emotional, cognitive, and sensory (physiologic) (Bonner and Friedman, 2011). Fundamentally, the phenomenological experience of awe is immediately recognized and may be potentially life altering. Awe resides on the upper emotional boundary of joy and fear and can be evoked by a vast array of events or objects (Keltner and Haidt, 2003). The emotional state of awe, including a feeling of inspiration or wonder, is outwardly directed and away from self-awareness, unlike the typical emotional states that are inwardly focused experiences. Awe-provoking events challenge our sense of possibility and expectation and promote transcendence from our usual sense of self (Shiota, Thrash, Danvers, and Dombrowski, 2016). Efforts to understand, often described as wonderment, are mobilized (Darbor et al., 2016) and attention is directed outwardly to absorb the awe experience.

The experience of awe involves perceived vastness. Understanding this vastness requires altering (accommodating) previous cognitive and emotional schemas (Keltner and Haidt, 2003). The concept of vastness incorporates size of an object, power and social importance of an event, and complex sensory breadth and detail of an artistic work (Shiota et al., 2016). Awe also requires an unexpected element of surprise (Keltner and Haidt, 2003; Shiota et al., 2016). Experiencing an awe-inspiring moment inevitably involves a subjective perception of the self as smaller and more inconsequential while in the presence of something that is greater than the self (Piff, Dietze, Feinberg, Stancato, and Keltner, 2015). Moments such as witnessing natural landscapes like the Grand Canyon or Mount Everest, listening to the speech of a great leader, aesthetic chills while observing or listening to an artistic work, or experiencing the devastation caused by earthquakes, hurricanes, or the human atrocities of war or terrorist attacks all necessitate alterations of cognitive and emotional schemas. These events, although usually positive in nature, disrupt our everyday expectations. They elicit strong feelings of rapture, love, or horror.

Awe is an intense physiologic experience as well. Universal physical changes emerge during awe experiences. Heart rate increases and piloerection ("goose bumps" or hair rising up) appears, indicating intense sympathetic autonomic nervous system activation (Keltner and Haidt, 2003; Schurtz, Blincoe, Smith, Powell, Combs, and Kim, 2012). Facial expressions include wide-eyed openness, raised eyebrows, and open mouth. When conducting facial analyses on individuals during an awe moment, researchers demonstrated that awe is a compound emotion. It is a mixture of surprise and fear, with surprise dominating the facial expression; however, fear coexists within the facial musculature (Du, Tao, and Martinez, 2014). Body posture inevitably shifts; individuals physically lean into the awe experience (regardless of its positive or negative valence) (Keltner and Haidt, 2003).

Aesthetic chills (goose bumps), a factor that is often associated with awe, occurs unexpectedly and is generally transient. Aesthetic chills are very different than the chills induced during fearful events or in extreme cold temperature changes (McCrae, 2007; Schurtz et al., 2012). One of the most common aesthetic chill inducing events occurs while listening to music, as is evident when listening closely to self-selected musical choices while in happy or sad emotional states, but not worry. These conditions can increase aesthetic chills (Nusbam, Silvia, Burgin, Hodges, and Kwapil, 2014). Nature is another awe inducing experience, and again, individuals who report aesthetic chills are generally more open to experiences (Silvia, Fayn, Nusbaum, and Beaty, 2015).

Awe also influences perception of time by decreasing impatience and increasing the awareness of the present moment (Shiota et al., 2016). Prior to such a profound experience, time is viewed as fleeting; there is a perceived insufficiency of time to complete task demands. During an awe moment, a sense of time expansion is evoked.

This elongation of the present moment can then be integrated into new cognitive schemas related to the self in time (Rudd, Bohs, and Aaker, 2012). The by-products of altering time perception to one that is more expansive include increasing well-being, decreasing stress, enhancing self-regulation, positively influencing decision-making, and changing behaviors such as aggressive driving. Given these positive benefits, researchers recommend increasing opportunities for awe-inspiring moments (Rudd et al., 2012).

Studies have demonstrated that some individuals are more prone to experience awe. It has been suggested that the personality trait, openness to experience could be termed *awe proneness*; literally some individuals are more likely to be awe-inspired (Silvia, Fayn et al., 201) and to experience aesthetic chills (McCrae, 2007). Dispositional awe is associated with traits that include increased focus on external stimulus and diminished self-focus, greater cognitive schema adaptations, and identification with shared values of a larger group (Shiota, Keltner, and Mossman, 2007). Awe proneness, and in particular, awareness that the self is part of a greater whole, decreases anxiety, increases adaptability, and promotes positive moods (Shiota et al., 2007).

Also, awe proneness has a strong relationship with beliefs in the supernatural and paranormal experiences (Van Cappellen and Saroglou, 2012). Giving agency and intentionality to something larger than the self is concordant with subjective awe experiences; thus awe may increase the possibility of mystical experiences. As well, responses to metaphoric language, sounds, and images are received with more emotional intensity and appreciation (Brown, 2008). These visceral experiences may activate religious and spiritual feelings. Reciprocally, for deeply religious or spiritual individuals, awe enhances heightened positive emotions and self-transcendence. A feeling of oneness with others and with spirituality intensifies (Van Cappellen and Saroglou, 2012). Ascribing non-human agency to events such as awe experiences reduces uncertainty, heightens acceptance, and promotes cognitive and emotional adaptation (Valdesolo and Graham, 2014).

Essentially, inspiration and transcendence give a sense of purpose and meaning. As described earlier, this existential experience is possible during the creative process (Nelson and Rawlings, 2009). Inspiration is deeply intertwined with motivation; it can be a mobilizing factor to embody and give expression to the feeling of inspiration such as during activities like writing, painting, singing, dancing, or praying (Shiota et al., 2016). Thrash and Elliot (2003) created an inspiration scale to assess intensity and frequency of being inspired by something and being inspired to do something. According to them, inspiration is always a dual process of either "by" or "to." Personality traits correspond to this dual inspiration process, with openness to experience associated with "inspired by" and extraversion related to "inspired to" (Thrash and Elliot, 2003; Thrash, Elliot, Maruskin, and Cassidy, 2010). When inspiration is induced by awe experiences, the subjective experience that the self is smaller has the potential to mobilize prosocial altruistic behaviors. Awe experiences may increase awareness that people are situated within broader social contexts with more existential collective concerns; this pattern is even more pronounced within individuals who display dispositional tendencies to experience awe (Piff et al., 2015). A similar experience unfolds during aesthetic awe; literally individuals feel a subjective sense of being moved. Exposure to stimuli that are sublime, grand, rare, or exquisite can indelibly alter perceptions of self, others, objects, and places; ideally they may be converted into aesthetic altruism and transpersonal experiences (Ayers, Beaton, and Hunt, 1999; Konecni, 2005).

Given these powerful findings, along with an ongoing need to examine fantasy proneness and autotelic personality traits, future studies should investigate awe proneness. Many questions remain unanswered such as: Is awe proneness a dispositional trait that is related to resilience? Is it a trait that can be strengthened with development? Is it an underlying factor for religious and spiritual beliefs? Beyond investigating the three cluster groups of cognition, emotion, and sensory (physiology) (Bonner and Friedman, 2011), understanding awe proneness may be augmented by neuroscience and epigenetic research methods. This field remains in its early infancy.

PATHOLOGY, FANTASY, AND CREATIVITY

The "mad genius" hypothesis has persisted for centuries and continues to be debated (Schlesinger, 2009). Robust research demonstrates relationships between highly creative people and higher incidences of mental illnesses. These findings may be biased by the nature of self-report methodology. For example, some creative people affirm this relationship, not because they are mentally ill, rather because they don't want to be viewed as ordinary; likewise, mentally ill patients prefer to view their illness as a feature of their creativity (Kaufman, Bromley, and Cole, 2006/2007). Beyond self-report biases, examining creativity as a binary concept, one that either pathologizes or celebrates it (Schlesinger, 2009), undermines the complexity of creativity, including the complexity of creative individuals who may display features of psychopathology and resilience (Ayers et al., 1999; Barron, 1969/1976). In order to avoid this either-or dilemma, researchers have proposed a *shared vulnerability model* (Carson, 2011). Elements of the shared vulnerability (creativity and pathology) include cognitive disinhibition (neurobiological sensory-motor process of allowing more stimulus into awareness), neural hyper-connectivity that is associated with increased divergent thinking, and attentional bias toward novel signals. Protective factors from psychopathology may include high IQ, cognitive flexibility, and enhanced working memory (retention and retrieval). There are strong indicators that shared vulnerability to pathology and creativity are associated with genetic inheritance, consequently, if protective factors are insufficient then pathology may be more likely (Carson, 2011; Richards, 1993). This shared vulnerability is expressed more within populations of highly creative people, regardless if they are working within the arts or sciences (Ludwig, 1998; Richards, 1993).

Eysenck's (1997) personality traits include psychoticism, a trait that indicates an over-inclusive cognitive style. This personality trait is strongly associated with psychotic disorders as well as creativity (Joy, 2008). Broad associative thinking, less cognitive inhibition, and decreased goal-directed thinking are features of both psychoticism and creativity (Abraham, Windmann, Daum, and Gunturkun, 2005). Perhaps psychoticism may moderate creative contribution, even though it also may increase psychopathology vulnerability (Ko and Kim, 2008). Of note, openness to experience, a personality trait strongly associated with creativity (Puryear, Kettler, and Rinn, 2016), is not a trait that is identified with psychotic pathology (Ko and Kim, 2008). This personality difference indicates that creative individuals, although more vulnerable to psychopathology, are also able to sustain cognitive flexibility and motivation, essential features in creative achievement (Crabtree and Green, 2016).

Schizotypy

Like schizophrenia, schizotypy has positive and negative symptoms; hence, this disorder is considered a risk factor for schizophrenia (APA, 2013; Fisher,

Mohanty, Herrington, Koven, Miller, and Heller, 2004). Positive symptoms include hallucinations, delusions, magical thinking, and perceptual aberrations. Negative symptoms involve social and physical anhedonia (Michalica and Hunt, 2013). A third cluster, social impairment (impulsive nonconformity, suspiciousness), has also been identified (Michalica and Hunt, 2013; Venables and Rector, 2000). A fourth cluster, disorganization, is often presented as a separate cluster (anxiety, attentional difficulties, distractibility) or is folded into the positive symptom cluster (Michalica and Hunt, 2013; Venables and Rector, 2000). According to the fifth edition of the Diagnostic and Statistical Manual Mental Disorders (APA, 2013), traits of schizotypy include reduced capacity for close relationships, cognitive and perceptual distortions, odd beliefs, thoughts and speech patterns, eccentric/bizarre behavior, inappropriate or flattened affect, social anxiety, and suspicious or paranoid beliefs (APA, 2013).

When these schizotypy traits are related to creative individuals, determination related to health or disease (distress) must be assessed, especially given the reality that divergent thinking and cognitive inhibition may produce odd or bizarre ideas (Fisher et al., 2004). Positive schizoptypy symptoms and creative health may share features such as odd beliefs or thoughts, and cognitive/perceptual distortions (Acar and Sen, 2013; Fink et al., 2014; Parra, 2006). One means of differentiating schizoptypy as a creative feature or a disorder is to assess deficits in cognitive-perceptual and interpersonal functioning as well as degree of disorganization caused by traits of schizoptypy (Burch et al., 2006). In general, creative individuals do not demonstrate behavior that impairs their ability to function. Those with a diagnosis of schizoptypy do display significant impairments and deficits, especially caused by antisocial and disorganized traits (Armstrong, 2012; Burch et al., 2006; Nettle and Clegg, 2006; Parra, 2006).

Despite these key differences between individuals who are deemed creative versus those diagnosed with schizotypy, substantial studies demonstrate a relationship between creativity and schizotypy personality disorder. Personality features of healthy schizoptypy include openness to experience and neuroticism; these features also enhance flow-like experiences and creativity (Nelson and Rawlings, 2010). Because schizotypy has multiple dimensions, there is an uneven relationship between schizotypy and creativity. For example, unusual experiences are associated with both creativity and schizotypy; whereas, the schizotypy trait, introverted anhedonia, is negatively related to creativity (LeBoutillier, Barry, and Westley, 2016). Fantasy proneness and schizotypy often share similar traits such as magical ideation and unusual cognitive-perceptual experiences (Sanchez-Bernardos and Avia, 2006). Divergent thinking, reduced cognitive inhibition, along with more impulsive thoughts and behaviors further add to the association between schizoptypy and creativity (Burch, Pavelis, Hemsley, and Corr, 2006; Green and Williams, 1999). Likewise, drugs may amplify some schizotypy traits and creativity. Polner and colleagues (2015) discovered that patients with Parkinson's disease, during treatment with dopamine agonist medication, exhibited schizotypy features (positive and disorganized symptoms) along with increased scores on creativity measures (verbal divergent thinking). These results suggest that elevated dopamine may influence schizotypy and creativity (Polner, Nagy, Takats, and Keri, 2015).

Mood Disorders and Attention-Deficit/Hyperactivity Disorder

Investigating the association between personality traits and other psychopathology disorders has revealed a similar pattern as found in schizotypy. Openness to experience and neuroticism remain the two dominant personality traits that were related to the disorders of cyclothymia and dysthymia (Strong, Nowakowska, Santosa, Wang, Kraemer, and Ketter, 2007). These disorders are less extreme variants of bipolar and major depressive disorders, respectively. The presence of dysthymia/neuroticism may increase access to negative emotions, a factor that can increase creative exploration (Strong et al., 2007). Heightened cyclothymia, a disorder noted for its emotional changeability, may promote creative exploration. It may enhance the creative process by amplifying anxiety and intensify pleasure (Nelson and Rawlings, 2009; Vellante et al., 2011). Likewise, hypomanic episodes coupled with positive schizotypy behaviors may support creative exploration, along with productivity (Rawlings and Locarnini, 2008); however, hypomania may also increase suicidal ideation in creative individuals (Drapeau and DeBrule, 2013).

Exploring how bipolar spectrum disorders influence creativity has yielded some important findings. The relationship between bipolar disorder, openness to experience, and intuition indicates that individuals with bipolar disorder employ more complex creative cognitive styles (Srivastava et al., 2010). Although this correlational finding remains consistent across studies, there are newer studies that do not show this positive link between creativity and bipolar disorder (Johnson, Tharp, and Holmes, 2015). Only a small group of bipolar individuals, with exceptional creativity, were able to accomplish creative success. In a unique study, how individuals with bipolar disorder engaged in creative activities over time was examined. The study demonstrated that children with bipolar disorder (or with a high risk for bipolar) expressed disfavor for simple and symmetric images (Simeonova, Chang, Strong, and Ketter, 2005). This aversion increased their desire for more complex images. As well, they could easily access negative affect that could be positively channeled into creative expression; however, their negative affect compromised interpersonal relationships, which then intensified depressive symptoms. Unfortunately, the longer they suffered bipolar symptoms, including successive manic episodes, the less they were able to function creatively. This attenuation pattern occurred regardless if they were treated with medication or not (Simeonova et al., 2005). This finding reinforces the need to differentiate creative engagement from creative achievement, as well as the effects of disease duration and the progressive deterioration over time. Future research is needed to determine whether introducing strategies to reinforce creative achievement may not only foster more creative works but also more symptom stability (White and Shah, 2006).

Attention-deficit/hyperactivity disorder (ADHD) has also been examined in relationship with creativity. Similar to the other psychiatric disorders, individuals with ADHD often score higher on creativity measures such as divergent thinking tasks; however, the ability to engage in convergent thinking to complete tasks and to produce creative products is attenuated (White and Shah, 2006). This attenuation is worsened when individuals have both ADHD and a bipolar spectrum disorder (Simeonova et al., 2005). Creative individuals with ADHD may be more readily able to generate novel ideas; with the acquisition of skills that promote sustained creative engagement that leads to creative achievement, these individuals may not suffer the progressive deterioration that typifies mood disorders and the personality insufficiencies inherent in schizotypy (Simeonova et al., 2005).

The above discussion demonstrates that vulnerability to psychopathology in creative individuals is greater, including mood disorders, psychosis, substance abuse disorders, sleep disorders, attention-deficit disorder, and dissociative disorders (Preti and Vellante, 2007). Suicide risk is also elevated in highly creative populations (Preti and Miotto, 1999). This risk increases when hypomanic symptoms are present, and when domain-specific talents are factored into the equation (Drapeau and DeBrule, 2013). For example, authors had the highest incidence of schizophrenia, bipolar disorder, unipolar disorder, anxiety disorders, substance abuse disorders, and suicidal ideation (Kaufman, 2001, 2003, 2005; Kyaga et al., 2013). Architects had higher rates of suicidal ideation compared to other artistic domains (Drapeau and DeBrule, 2013). In the group of architects that were studied, hypomania, creative achievement, and divergent thinking increased suicidal ideation. Musicians are also known to struggle with mental illness, despite their sustained ability to produce creative products (Barbar, Crippa, and Osorio, 2014; Wills, 2003). Creative professionals also have a higher rate of first-degree relatives who are diagnosed with disorders such as schizophrenia, bipolar disorder, eating disorders, and autism (Kyaga, Landen, Boman, Hultman, Langstrom, and Lichtenstein, 2013; Kyaga, Lichtenstein, Borman, Hultman, Langstrom and Landen, 2011). They also have a response bias to negative information and negative emotional content. This response bias is associated with greater rumination and slower repair of unpleasant feelings, all features of psychopathology. However, the negative response bias and protracted period of time experiencing this information also translates into more creative output (Drus, Kozbelt, and Hughes, 2014). Unlike mentally ill patients, these creatively successful people still remain motivated, sustain their creative engagement, and are able to achieve their goals (Dru et al., 2014; Neihart, 1998; Preti and Miotto, 1999).

CONCLUSION

The positive relationship between creativity, profound experiences of awe, and psychopathology remain significant in most research studies (Michalica and Hunt, 2013), especially when fantasy proneness and daydreaming are frequently employed and for protracted periods of time (Schupak and Rosenthal, 2009). Differentiating psychopathology symptoms as either healthy or a disorder may shift some assumptions. An important factor to help determine health versus pathology is the ability to achieve creative goals and products (Dru et al., 2014). Cognitive and emotional flexibility and adaptability are key elements in successful creativity. When mood disorders and schizoptypy symptoms interfere with goal accomplishment and daily functioning, then creativity is compromised, regardless of high scores on creative testing measures. Sadly, research studies have demonstrated that bipolar spectrum disorders are not only associated with greater creative engagement but also less creative achievement; this is an extremely important distinction when assessing creative health, and when discussing the relationship between creativity and psychopathology (Johnson et al., 2015; Vellante et al., 2011).

Dabrowski's model of positive disintegration may shed light on this topic (Fraser, 2010). The five overexcitability dimensions share symptom clusters with psychopathology, and may even indicate more traits of anxiety and depression (Thomson and Jaque, 2016b). The major factor in Dabrowski's model is that highly gifted/talented individuals must achieve complex self-regulating abilities in order to achieve creative autonomy; mental illness is an indicator that these abilities have collapsed (Mika, 2005). This differential pattern is evident when comparing mentally ill patients and artists. Both may share heightened mystical experiences and endorse more bizarre associations; however, unlike the patients, the artists had better spatial orientation skills, physical balance, and more embodied sensorimotor awareness (Michalica and Hunt, 2013). When regarded from the lens of Dabrowski's model, psychiatric symptoms may actually operate as positive features of giftedness, especially when creative individuals gain self-regulatory skills to manage positive and negative stimuli (Fraser, 2010; Michalica and Hunt, 2013; Mika, 2005; Thomson and Jaque, 2016d). Perhaps individuals with schizophrenia and mood disorders, who also demonstrate high creative abilities, may be helped by acquiring skills to promote creative achievement. These skills may enhance their well-being and increase a sense of autonomy and meaning (Taylor, Fletcher, and Lobban, 2015).

Further research is needed to parse out the overlapping features of creativity and pathology. Biological studies suggest that creativity and psychosis may share genetic roots. Given this finding, creativity may increase risk for psychopathology; however, in healthy creative individuals there may be other neuro-protective genetic factors that facilitate creative expression and sustain mental health. These genetic factors may stop the transcription process that leads to a genetic expression of mental illness (Power et al., 2015). In an effort to dispel the binary view of pathology and creativity, implementing other statistical approaches may reveal the inherent complexity that underlies both. For example, exploring the interacting effects of creative cognition, creative accomplishments, and creative self-concepts may add more complexity to this either/or stance (Silvia and Kimbrel, 2010). Cultivating models that embrace the complexity of creativity and psychopathology will demonstrate the dynamic nature of these two concepts, including how they dynamically operate within the individual (Schuldberg, 2000, 2001).

Including imagination into research studies may increase understanding about how fantasy proneness, excessive daydreaming, and the ability to create paracosms operate. Currently, creativity and innovation are more readily embraced as legitimate fields of study; imagination still waits to be explored (Forgeard and Kaufman, 2015). Hopefully, the inclusion of imagination (as well as awe) into creativity studies will expand the field of creativity. For example, neurobiological studies may help explain the processes of the imagination. Despite this lack of research attention, studies demonstrate the importance individuals place on their imagination (Bille, Fjaellegaard, Frey, and Steiner, 2013). They report that engaging their imaginative abilities within employment settings enhances their job satisfaction compared to employees who do not incorporate imaginative processes. Ultimately, providing any creative opportunity promotes greater autonomy and enhances well-being in the work environment (Bille et al., 2013).

Chapter 5

Neurobiological and Physiologic Components of Creativity

Discussing the complex interactions between the brain and body often encourages Cartesian thought (Damasio, 1994). A Cartesian paradigm parcels out the mind and the brain as two different concepts; for example, the mind describes the functioning of the brain and the brain is the biological ingredient that supports the mind (Damasio, 1999). Likewise, the body and the brain are often divided. This division is evident in discussions on mental processes; the implication is that mental processes occur within the brain and information gathered from the body is discounted. Dualism is also present when discussing the self as a separate isolated entity (Stolorow et al., 2002). The fact is that the physical environment and interpersonal relationships all shape and change the mind, brain, body, and self; they are inextricably linked. Life exists within a complex interconnected web. The body, brain, mind, and self are sustained by multiple biological and social systems. With new advances in cognitive neuroscience, complex concepts such as creativity, including distributed creativity, can be examined. Although studies do examine unitary variables as well as isolated regions of the brain and body, most researchers in creativity assume an integrative approach (Abraham and Windmann, 2007).

THE BRAIN, NEURAL NETWORKS, AND CREATIVITY

Creative processes in general, and creative cognition in particular, have received substantial investigation, via neuropsychological testing and neuroimaging. Because creativity and brain functioning are complex, results to date have minimal overlap. This makes it difficult to interpret findings and formulate coherent models that capture the neurobiological essence of creativity (Arden, Chavez, Grazioplene, and Jung, 2010). Even when creative assessment is reduced to two forms of cognitive processing, divergent and convergent thinking, the results remain inconsistent (Fink, Benedek, Grabner, Staudt, and Neubauer, 2007). Worse, many of the neurobiological ideas that describe creativity and cognition are outdated, too simplistic, and/or factually inaccurate (Dietrich, 2007). Some of the earlier neurobiological theories associated with creativity can now be discounted completely or integrated into a much larger cognitive neural construct. According to Dietrich (2007), four of these early theories need revision: (1) creativity is divergent thinking (multiple cognitive styles operate during the creative process besides divergent thinking), (2) creativity is a right hemisphere activity (both hemispheres work in complex patterns all the time), (3) the creative process occurs in a state of defocused attention (cognition requires an array of attentional and focused processes), and (4) altered states of consciousness enhance creativity (taking drugs to alter consciousness does not guarantee that an individual will become creative). These theories imply that creativity is a unitary construct when it is actually one of the most complex constructs.

Imaging the brain during creative activities is currently problematic. The largest challenge when imaging the brain is the assumption that creativity can be fully measured based on creative cognition. However, creativity is an embodied activity, even when a new idea first begins in the mind (Deitrich, 2008). The implicit motor feedback system powerfully informs emotional, cognitive, and intuitive processes and these all influence creativity (Dietrich, 2008). Domain-specific enterprises reflect the degree of motor imagery operating during the creative process; this is particularly evident in activities such as composing music, painting, or choreographing (Arden et al., 2010). Because of the limitations of neural imaging, in particular, the need to remain still, it is impossible to accurately measure the essential component of motor imagery (Arden et al., 2010). In fact, multiple neurophysiological factors are employed which heightens the need to improve measurement instruments and research designs (Arden et al., 2010). Despite these very real limitations, simple experimental creative thinking tasks have yielded useful information suggesting possible neurological behaviors (Fink et al., 2007). The current information, although limited, provides a glimpse into the neurobiological and physiologic patterns engaged during the creative process.

Geneplore Model and Neurobiology

The geneplore creative model contains two phases that operate during the creative process, the generative and exploratory (evaluative) phases (Tang and Gero, 2002; Sternberg, 2005). In neurobiological terms, creative *generation* is related to activation of medial temporal regions, and *exploratory/*

evaluative processes involve a complex array of regions and networks, such as the executive and default mode networks, rostrolateral prefrontal cortex, insula, and temporopolar cortex (Ellamil, Dobson, Beeman, and Christoff, 2012). The geneplore model functions in a recursive manner; it is reflected in the activation-deactivation-reactivation of multiple neural networks while generating and evaluating creative ideas. By observing these neural networks at play during creative thought, more detailed information is derived about the complexity of creativity.

Engagement of the *medial temporal regions* during the *generative phase* indicates that memory retrieval occurs. This larger region contains key brain structures that encode, store, and retrieve memory, in particular, the hippocampus and parahippocampus. Part of memory retrieval involves associative processing; information cannot be retrieved unless it is associated with something else. Novel ideas are generated from a recombination of associative and retrieval processing (Ellami et al., 2012). These regions are also activated during future planning as well as constructing fictitious scenarios (Hassabis, Kumaran, and Maguire, 2007). Depending on the domain, the generative phase may also involve the action-oriented neural network. This network is comprised of sensory-motor regions of the brain that operate during motor idea generation such as during the creation of music or dance, or possibly during the development of innovative technologies (Christensen and Calvo-Merino, 2013; Dietrich, 2008).

The *exploratory/evaluative* process recruits many more regions and networks in the brain. The *executive network* is comprised of the prefrontal cortex (dorsolateral, orbitofrontal, frontopolar), the dorsal anterior cingulate cortex, and the frontoparietal regions. These regions operate during idea evaluation; they are directly engaged in problem solving, reasoning, decision-making, task flexibility, and working memory (Alvarez, Emory, and Emory, 2006; Koechlin and Summerfield, 2007). The *default mode network* is equally involved during the evaluative process, a finding that demonstrates the high correlation between the two networks during task activities (Ellamil et al., 2012). The default mode network operates during internally focused tasks related to daydreaming, future planning, or reminiscing. It provides information related to the self (autobiographical, emotional awareness) and others (moral reasoning, empathy, social evaluation) (Andrews-Hanna, Smallwood, and Spreng, 2014; Beatty, 2015; Mayseless, Eran, and Shamay-Tsoory, 2015). This complex network includes midline and posterior structures such as the dorsal medial prefrontal cortex, posterior cingulate cortex, temporoparietal cortex, anterior and lateral temporal cortex, precuneus, angular gyrus, hippocampal and parahippocampal regions, retrosplenial cortex, and posterior inferior parietal cortex (Andrews-Hanna et al., 2014; Beaty and Schacter, 2017; Ellamil et al., 2012).

The evaluative/exploratory phase also engages networks that are deeply involved in somatosensory, motor, emotional, and integrative processing. For example, the *cerebellum* is extensively activated during creative evaluation, suggesting its role in integrating and transmitting information from the executive and default networks (Ellamil et al., 2012). Likewise, the *salience network* is associated with creative analytic processing. Not surprising, this network is deeply interconnected with the default mode network; it provides sensory and affective information, integrates internal and external stimuli related to the self and others, and offers "gut" or embodied decision-making (Critchley et al., 2004; Seeley et al., 2007). The salience network includes regions such as the anterior cingulate cortex, anterior insula, amygdala, temporopolar cortex, hypothalamus, somatosensory cortex, and autonomic nervous system (ANS) (Ellamil et al., 2012).

Depending on domain-specific tasks, the *action-oriented network* and the *reward circuit* may also be recruited during the evaluative phase, although the action-oriented network may also operate during the generation phase (Christensen and Calvo-Merino, 2013; Dietrich, 2008). The reward network is also deeply involved in conflict recognition and resolution as well as determining potential pain or pleasure (valence) (Brattico and Pearce, 2013; Nadal and Skol, 2013). Regions in the action-oriented network include motor (premotor, supplementary motor, basal ganglia), sensory (parietal cortex), cerebellum, thalamus, and lower brain centers (Chrsitensen and Calvo-Merino, 2013). The reward circuit contains an array of cortical and subcortical structures that are also associated with the executive, default mode, and salience networks (Brattico and Pearce, 2013).

Examining the generative and evaluative stages of the geneplore model provides a fine-grained analysis of neural networks and the complex feedback and feedforward processes that occur between these networks. Multiple regions are coactivated and deactivated during the creative process. No network operates independently, although task demands continually activate or suppress multiple brain regions (Ellamil et al., 2012). Task demands directly influence neural engagement, including when a task is just being learned versus when a task is fully mastered. The difference in familiarity and skill level influences cognitive set shifting, literally the brain must accommodate new information while formulating novel ideas versus generating novel ideas that are drawn from highly practiced skills (Newman, Carpenter, Varma, and Just, 2003).

Incubation and Insight

Incubation of ideas that leads to new insights is part of the creative process. According to neurobiological findings, *working memory* plays an integral role. Working memory is generally conceived as a limited neurological event that temporarily maintains information to support human thought. There are two "storage" systems, the phonological loop and the visuospatial sketchpad (Baddeley, 2003). These systems are aligned with the executive network, default mode network, and salience network respectively; they engage a mixture of short-term and long-term memories required to formulate ideas and to communicate with others. Working memory is a cognitive activity that influences decision-making and reasoning processes (Baddeley, 2003). Another significant brain region that is strongly implicated in both the incubation and insight phases of creativity is the cerebellum. It enhances integration and speed of processing and is directly influenced by working memory (Chevez-Eakle, 2007).

Insight, in general, is a very difficult concept to operationalize, even though subjective reports are abundant. The subjective experience of an "aha" moment is instantly recognized and usually remembered. Engaging in a problem often requires deliberate and methodical analysis; whereas, insight is a sudden recognition of the solution or answer. Neurobiological findings are currently conflicting, although across multiple studies, the engagement of the superior-temporal gyrus and the anterior cingulate cortex are evident (Dietrich and Kanso, 2010). These findings support the roles of these regions; the superior-temporal gyrus enhances remote associations and the anterior cingulate cortex allows detection of cognitive conflict, as well as initiating solutions to address the conflict. Decreased alpha power is also identified during an "aha" moment, perhaps because the more activating gamma power propels aha moments (Dietrich and Kanso, 2010). Other studies have indicated that raising the theta-alpha ratio increases creative responsiveness while simultaneously decreasing depression and anxiety (Gruzelier, 2009, 2014). It is suggested that achieving this ratio may also promote insight experiences (Gruzelier, 2014).

Latent Inhibition and Divergent Thinking

Latent inhibition is a neurobiological process in which irrelevant stimulus is blocked out of conscious awareness (Carson, Peterson, and Higgins, 2003). When inhibition is decreased more stimuli enters into consciousness. This reduction has been associated with psychosis as well as creativity. Eminently creative individuals acknowledge significantly diminished inhibition, and this is even more pronounced in individuals with high IQ. They also recognize a reduction in inhibition during the early phase of creativity; however, when controlled selection is required more inhibitory attentional processes are employed (Benedek, Franz, Heene, and Neubauer, 2012; Carson et al., 2003). In general, reduced inhibition promotes fluency of ideas while intelligence influences depth and degree of originality of ideas (Benedek et al., 2012). Latent inhibition suggests that specific regions of the brain are activated to filter out stimulus. Viewed from a different perspective more interhemispheric connection occurs as a result of momentary inhibition of hemispheric independence. This may occur by increased corpus callosum (bridge between the right and left hemisphere) connectivity or by smaller corpus callosum volume (Moore et al., 2009). Enhanced hemispheric connectivity decreases hemispheric specialization; this may facilitate insight, illumination, and divergent thinking during the creative process (Moore et al., 2009).

Collectively, neurobiological studies that examine *divergent thinking* as a separate concept have yielded preliminary findings that suggest different sub-stages of divergent thinking engage different regions and different hemispheres (Dietrich and Kanso, 2010). The generation of remote associations relies on cooperation between these neural regions. Because of this complexity, theories such as low arousal or defocused attention are not substantiated across research studies. Again sub-stages of creativity may reveal low arousal (i.e., EEG alpha wave patterns) or global focus of attention (greater interhemispheric connections); however, the complex process of idea generation and evaluation demands complex activation and deactivation patterns. The lack of consensus in study findings may also be related to study designs that implement different divergent thinking tasks or neuroimaging/EEG protocols (Dietrich and Kanso, 2010). When studies examine specific aspects of divergent thinking, more cohesion emerges. For example, examining the location of associative thinking reveals activation in the default mode network and increased originality is associated with even more interconnectivity within brain regions that extend beyond the default mode network (Mayseless et al., 2015). Likewise, examining creativity within specific domains such as music demonstrates more overlap between studies (Gibson, Folley, and Park, 2009).

Laterality and Interconnectivity

As stated above, interconnectivity is essential for creativity. Early studies suggested that creative people engaged more right hemispheric laterality; they were described as right brain thinkers (Ornstein, 1997). Although this is a simple explanation to situate creativity in the brain, the complex nature of creativity necessitates a less lateralized model (Lindell, 2011). Greater interhemispheric communication and integration must occur during the creative process. For example, the slower fine-grained processes of the left hemisphere balances the rapid coarse-grained analysis occurring in the right hemisphere. Cross-hemisphere analysis provides elaboration and expansion of creative meaning. Less creative individuals lack this interhemispheric interplay, relying more on left hemisphere domination when giving meaning to a creative problem (Whitman, Holcomb, and Zanes, 2010). Despite sold evidence demonstrating interhemispheric activation, reports of right hemispheric dominance still persist. For example, Shen and colleagues reported right hemispheric dominance during creative insight (Shen et al., 2013). There is also evidence that right hemisphere global analysis facilitates figurative (visual) creativity, in part, because the fine-grained left hemispheric processing slows the ability to rapidly surmise original images (Razumnikova and Volf, 2015). Perhaps these right hemisphere dominance findings reflect the activity being examined. Studies on musicians do not show this hemispheric bias; rather musicians have unusually high symmetry in hemispheric activation (Patston, Kirk, Rolfe, Corballis, and Tippett, 2007).

Interconnectivity also occurs between cortical and subcortical regions. This pattern was demonstrated in high achieving scientists (Li et al., 2015). Their creative output was based on publication count, citations, and grants. Managing this scientific creative achievement requires motivation, goal-directed behavior, adaptive learning, anticipation of rewards and punishers, self-regulation, along with action planning. These complex tasks require higher cortical structures such as the executive network and the default network, along with substantial subcortical basal ganglia (putamen, lentiform nucleus) activation. The inclusion of the basal ganglia is associated with action planning, motor preparation and control, reward expectation, and motivation achievement (Di Martino et al., 2008). The ANS is also a key system that helps support self-regulation during creative activities (Li et al., 2015). As well as cortical and subcortical interactions, there are contralateral connections between the cerebellum and cortical regions during creative cognitive tasks. These feedback and feedforward interactions enhance working memory, and coordinate the changing cognitive demands that arise over time during task initiation and completion (Chen and Desmond, 2005).

Implicit and Explicit Functions

Examining neural activity based on *explicit conscious and implicit unconscious* (non-conscious) awareness provides a layered understanding about neurological functioning (Dietrich, 2008; Karabanov, Cervenka, de Manzano, Forssberg, Farde, and Ullen, 2010). The value of conceptualizing neural functioning as explicit and implicit processing offers clear explanations for all the complex conscious and non-conscious activities that occur at every moment of life (Dietrich, 2008). For example, the sensorimotor and autonomic systems primarily operate at implicit levels; whereas, verbal content and communication presents as explicit processing. Both implicit and explicit processes must interact; the difference is in degree of awareness. This is evident in motor behaviors such as walking or sitting; they are implicit neural activities. They can also be processed at explicit levels such as when a performing artist performs or when someone must rehabilitate from an injury (Thomson and Jaque, 2017). Engaging in mental imagery is also an explicit activity, including the construction of motor imagery (even though motor behavior usually operates at the implicit level).

The *explicit system* is responsible for higher-order management of communication: functions that are primarily handled by the executive network, especially the prefrontal cortex and the hippocampus (responsible for consolidating, storing, and retrieving information) (Dietrich, 2008). The explicit system is largely unaware of activities operating at the implicit level. This allows the explicit system to process higher-order content without the distraction of lower-order processing that occurs simultaneously. Explicit functioning also allows for future planning, including the establishment of goals. This system has the potential for great cognitive flexibility, even though it is also limited by the capacity of working memory. Complex mental processing is directed to future-oriented tasks as well as daydreaming or imagining possibilities that may never manifest in real time.

The *implicit system* relies on deeper neurological structures that are responsible for more evolutionary life-sustaining functioning. Autonomic and sensorimotor processing enable daily performance, as well as complex and sophisticated motor skills that have been deliberately practiced for long periods of time (i.e., playing a musical instrument or sporting activities) (Ericsson, 2007, 2013, 2014; Krampe and Ericsson, 1996). The implicit system is highly efficient and requires less brain structures to organize and sustain behavior. There is also great overlap in the lower brain structures to ensure that basic functioning is supported; for example, regions in the basal ganglia and cerebellum can equally coordinate daily motor activities (Barnes, Kubota, Hu, Jin, and Graybiel, 2005; Dietrich, 2008). Implicit systems contain memories, thus they are not designed to evaluate abstract thought; rather implicit responses tend to be inflexible and predictable. Only explicit systems can shed awareness on implicit activities, even though implicit systems support the work of the explicit system (Ericcsson, 2007).

Sensory-Motor Systems and Creativity

The sensory and motor systems directly and indirectly engage most regions within the brain. Together, these two systems support the most complex behaviors, even though the executive network may generate more complex ideas (Dietrich, 2008). The interconnections within the sensory regions are vast; these structures must receive and process information from internal and external stimuli. The motor system, in turn, must rapidly mobilize highly coordinated responses to this sensory information. Fine motor and gross motor behavior operate simultaneously to complete tasks that occur outside conscious awareness. The efficiency of these systems necessitates both real-time engagement as well as a complex integration of anticipatory responses. These regions continually predict outcomes and mobilize responses so that real-time behavior is efficient and accurate (Seidler, Noll, and Thiers, 2004). For example, a jazz ensemble must perform in real time while also anticipating the trajectory of the improvisational musical work. This allows jazz musicians to work in a highly coordinated manner while collectively creating new performances (Matare, 2009). To date, neuroscience research that employs neuroimaging is not able to fully capture complex interactions, such as jazz improvisation (McPherson and Limb, 2013). Because of the movement constraints during imaging, the findings are limited to explicit systems with minimal implicit system engagement revealed (Dietrich, 2008). In general, consistent findings suggest that creative improvisation requires increased functional connectivity between the sensory, motor, and executive regions of the brain (Beaty, 2015; Pinho, de Manzano, Fransson, Eriksson, and Ullen, 2014).

Beyond the incredible complexity of these two systems and their primary importance in the creative process, they also support perceptions of our own movements and the ability to differentiate movements of self and others. Perceiving self-movement requires fine-grained temporal information to be analyzed, modulated, and mobilized. Such fine-grained temporal responses take place within the cerebellum, along with cooperation from multiple sensorimotor structures. The individual must continually recognize self-generated actions; without this recognition, moving body parts are regarded as alien entities that do not belong to the self (Leube, Knoblich, Erb, Grodd, Bartels, and Kircher, 2003). Movement that is generated in response to an external stimulus is monitored by different feedforward and feedback loops compared to when movement is self-initiated without external sensory stimuli promoting it. These neural patterns, although distinct, are brief and transient. Ultimately, complex interconnecting activation and deactivation patterns must transpire during all sensorimotor movement, whether self-generated or in response to an external event. Likewise, perceiving temporal versus spatial features of the self in motion provides specific neural signals that mobilize unique motor coordination behaviors. When sensory or motor signals are misconstrued, whether transient or persistent, alterations in a sense of self occur. This is evidenced in disorders such as schizophrenia, depersonalization, or hemi-neglect; the coordinated interconnective feedforward-feedback loops are disrupted in these disorders (Leube et al., 2003).

Motor cognition is a slightly different way of conceptualizing the interaction between implicit and explicit systems. This term suggests that cognition is also embodied action; intentionality is a major factor in motor cognition

(Freeman, 2000; Jackson and Decety, 2004). Motor cognition is dependent on neurodynamic processes that integrate action and perception, key factors in agency (Jackson and Decety, 2004). Regions such as the insula and inferior parietal cortex influence a sense of agency. *Proprioception*, the sensory awareness of our body positions within space (Moore, 2007) is an essential component of motor cognition. It is considered part of the sensory system; but unlike the other senses, proprioception directly influences motor coordination and integration. Large regions such as the premotor and parietal cortices are key players in proprioception (Jackson and Decety, 2004). Some argued that it is also part of our motor aesthetic system (Montero, 2006). This is evident when performing artists and athletes enhance their proprioceptive awareness, which results in increased creative responsiveness and performance expertise (Jola, Davis, and Haggard, 2011; Smitt and Bird, 2013).

The functioning of proprioception and motor action share neural network systems, including sharing feedback from the *mirror neuron system* (Iacoboni, 2009). These neurons have the ability to perceive movements performed by others while simultaneously sending tiny signals to muscles within the body that would be engaged if the self were performing the activity (Jackson and Decety, 2004; Rizzolatti and Craighero, 2004). This ability to viscerally experience another person's movement, while maintaining a separation of self and other, enhances complex motor skill learning. Working within ensembles such as in sport or the performing arts necessitates mirror neuron signaling to coordinate sensorimotor stimuli among the players or performers (Jeffers, 2009; Molner-Szakacs and Overy, 2006).

Interoceptive awareness may involve proprioception and mirror neuron signaling; however, it is also a separate internal awareness about our physiologic states (Critchley et al., 2004; Tsakiris, Tajadura-Jimenez, and Costantini, 2011). Major regions that generate interoception include the operculum, insula, parietal and somatomotor cortices, the supplementary motor, and anterior cingulate cortices, as well as regions in the executive and default mode networks (prefrontal cortices). These regions are engaged in physiologically monitoring and regulating the body at higher-order processing levels. When interoceptive awareness is heightened, it shifts awareness from implicit to explicit. At extremely high levels, interoception can cause dysregulation; it is associated with increased anxiety, pain, and psychosomatic disorders. Likewise, heightened interoceptive awareness can increase pleasure and reward signals, features that may promote the return to creative activities (Critchley et al., 2004). Whether awareness is amplified toward negative or positive states, interoception increases self-identity; it heightens internal sensations and shifts the balance from external to internal focus (Tsakiris et al., 2011). This awareness is more acute in some individuals, which suggests that it may operate like a personality trait, especially in neuroticism personality structures (Stewart, Buffett-Jerrott, and Kokaram, 2001).

Motor Skill Acquisition and Embodied Experiences

Learning new movement skills require both implicit and explicit systems. Literally, motor learning occurs via doing the movement as well as thinking about the movement (Nyberg, Eriksson, Larsson, and Marklund, 2006). Training practices that implement mental practice (sometimes referred to as mental imagery) have positive effects, even though they engage less intense signals from the motor systems. Mental images tend to engage more explicit associational regions of the brain, as well as strong dominance in the visual regions (Kosslyn, 2005). Unfortunately, mental practice alone will not develop strong neural motor signaling; physical activity must occur, and at intensity levels appropriate for developing skill mastery (Nyberg et al., 2006). When learning a new skill multiple regions of the brain are recruited; whereas, once expert levels are achieved, reduced cortical and subcortical activation is required (Lotz, Scheler, Tan, Braun, and Birbaumer, 2003; Meister et al., 2004). Once developed, even with minimal practice later, strong motor networks are sustained as evidenced when someone learns to play a musical instrument as a child and can relearn this skill after years of hiatus (Lotz et al., 2003). Engaging in complex motor activities such as dancing also diminishes the negative effects of aging; older dancers sustain cognitive flexibility and enhanced memory (Coubard, Duretz, Lefebrve, Lapalus, and Ferrufino, 2011; Kattenstroth, Kalish, Holt, Tegenthoff, and Dinse, 2013; Kattenstroth, Kolankowska, Kalisch, and Dinse, 2010). While developing strong motor skills, neural processing is also enhanced for other tasks. For example, skill acquisition for speech and music is enhanced in musicians; they develop more efficient neural networks in the subcortical auditory and audiovisual processing regions (Musacchia, Sams, Skoe, and Kraus, 2007). Early music training enhances interconnectivity in the brain, which results in greater cognitive gains during development (Schlaug, Norton, Overy and Winner, 2005). These finding suggest that attaining mastery in one skill may augment transfer of learning across other tasks; this may explain the neuroprotective factors in aging that are derived from dancing and music.

Embodied experiences that are derived from somatosensory systems not only give a sense of self-identity, but they also enrich memory and linguistic meaning (Gibbs, 2003). This interrelationship is evidenced in common language phrases that exist across all cultures. For example, statements such as "to stand the test of time," "my heart aches for you," "blowing off steam," or "blew up at me" all reflect an embodied knowledge of these emotional or cognitive states (Gibbs, 2003). Fundamentally, language is the product of sensorimotor systems; speech and gesture share the same neurobiological systems. This is evident in neuroscience studies that capture the simultaneous motion of the body and hands while speaking. Both the speaker and listener understand these closely paired response patterns during communication (Bernardis and Gentilucci, 2006).

Memories are also encoded during specific body posturing; consequently memory retrieval is enhanced when assuming body posturing that resembles the initial body posture (Dijkstra, Kaschak, and Zwaan, 2007). This neurobiological reality demonstrates how memory can be embodied, a fact that is even more pronounced in traumatic memories (Culbertson, 1995). Along with physical gesture, rhythmic structures help reinforce memory. Both physical actions and rhythmic patterns enhance the visceral sensation of what is being communicated and when this communication or event is retrieved, a sensorimotor state may be induced (Jakobson, Cuddy, and Kilgour, 2003). Sound and pitch recognition are also encoded as embodied memories and facilitate verbal memory abilities (Franklin, Moore, Yip, Jonides, Rattray, and Moher, 2008). Again, musicians have a heightened ability to tag events based on time, sensory perceptions, and motor action (Jakobson et al., 2003).

Emotion, Neuroscience, and Creativity

Emotional intensity and valence spring from deeply interconnected cortical and subcortical structures. Emotions have their own neural network pathways that influence behavior and cognition; they operate as both discrete systems and can blend to create complex emotional states (Panksepp, 2003). As previously discussed, enhanced interoception also increases emotional awareness, in particular, heightened activation in the insula. Heightened awareness is augmented by interconnections between the insula, executive network, default mode network, brainstem-hypothalamus, and the thalamo-cortical pathways (Craig, 2004). When all these systems interact to give emotion a visceral intensity, individuals receive strong "gut" feelings. According to Damasio's *somatic-marker hypothesis model*, this gut feeling helps decision-making processes (Damasio, 1994, 1999). These systems are also engaged during empathic pain experiences (Logia et al., 2008). Reading emotions in others and communicating emotional states involve both the most primitive and the most sophisticated neural network systems in the brain. Reflexive signals are interpreted and expressed within the amygdala, basal ganglia (striatum), midbrain, and brainstem. Awareness within the body transpires in the insula, somatosensory cortex, anterior cingulate, and ventromedial prefrontal cortex. Perceptions of emotional states in self and others involve multiple sensory regions of the brain (occipital cortex, superior-temporal sulcus, intraparietal gyrus, fusiform gyrus, amygdala, as well as the premotor cortex). All these hierarchically organized structures provide coarse and fine-grained information about the emotional state of self and others (de Gelder, 2006).

Emotional regulation also engages all these brain regions, with higher structures regulating lower subcortical structures (LeDoux, 1996, 2002). The feedforward and feedback loops between these structures ensure emotional coping behaviors. Emotional coping strategies may be either activating or deactivating. For example, under specific conditions, activating strategies of confrontation, fight, or flight behaviors are essential; whereas, under other conditions, deactivating strategies such as quiescence, immobility, and decreased responsiveness are required. Midbrain regions such as the periaqueductal gray are critical in mobilizing or immobilizing behaviors, consequently the midbrain has vast extensions into higher cortical regions, regulating centers such as the hypothalamus, and all regions within the motor system (Bernard and Bandler, 1998). Higher cortical structures help formulate understanding related to contextual situations; they can provide new perspectives which will augment or calm emotional responses and ideally provide greater emotional regulatory flexibility (Bonanno and Burton, 2013); whereas, lower subcortical structures ensure rapid survival behaviors (LeDoux, 2002).

Neurotransmitters, Neuropeptides, and Creativity

Substantial research has been directed toward understanding the role *neurotransmitters and neuropeptides* play in emotional activation and emotional regulation, with less focus on creativity. One of the key neurotransmitters associated with creativity is dopamine, although there are paradoxical effects with this neurotransmitter. Dopamine within the reward circuit, especially in the substantia nigra and ventral tegmental area, promotes memory associations and the anticipation of novel or pleasurable stimuli (Wittmann, Bunzeck, Dolan, and Duzel, 2007). Dopamine in this circuit also has extensions into the frontal cortex as well as other structures in the basal ganglia; consequently it influences the encoding of reward prediction, facilitates the scanning for potential errors in acquiring the reward, and reinforces learning associated with the reward (Glimcher, 2011). Because there are many dopamine receptors, there is great complexity when investigating the effects of this neurotransmitter. For example, fewer dopamine D2 receptors located in the thalamus are associated with lower thalamic gating thresholds, a factor that promotes divergent thinking (de Manzano, Cervenka, Karabanov, Farde, and Ullen, 2010). Dopamine D2 receptor density in the limbic system is related to implicit learning and not explicit sequential learning, a fact that may indicate the joys derived from performing a learned skill versus the struggles learning a new skill (Karabanov et al., 2010). This finding also suggests that implicit movement that is coordinated by dopamine D2 receptor activation interacts with deeper subcortical structures within the basal ganglia and less within higher cortical structures (Karabanov et al., 2010). Similar to the D2 receptor, the DRD4 gene influences creativity and cognitive flexibility, and when dysfunctions arise in this dopamine system more pathology arises along with diminished creativity (Maysless, Uzefovsky, Shalev, Ebstein, and Shamay-Tsoory, 2013). The DRD4 gene operates in higher cortical regions of the brain and interacts with the reward circuit and pleasure; this response is strongly associated with creativity and may serve as a trait marker for creativity (Chavez-Eakle and Eakle, 2012).

The bonding that is experienced when people engage in meaningful activities also has positive effects on creativity. Activities such as choral singing increase levels of oxytocin, a response that is both pleasurable and bonding. As oxytocin levels increase, stress hormones decrease, which makes this activity even more desired (Keeler, Roth, Nesuer, Spitsbergen, Waters, and Vianney, 2015). Likewise, increased levels of serotonin improve memories of safety and activate safety signals, which promotes exploratory behavior (Foilb and Christianson, 2016). In highly creative individuals, the serotonin transporter gene (5'SLC6A4) is associated with harm avoidance and novelty seeking traits, factors that may support creative engagement in some individuals (Chavez-Eakle and Eakle, 2012). A genetic predisposition to encode and synthesize serotonin (tryptophan hydroxylase—TPH) has been identified with increased creative potential (Zhang and Zhang, 2017). The GABAergic system is equally powerful during creativity, especially the need for emotional regulation during the creative process. It modulates and regulates the hormones released by the endocrine system, as well as supports the efficient operation of the ANS (Gladkevich, Korf, Hakobyan, and Melkonyan, 2006).

THE BODY AND PHYSIOLOGY

Understanding the regulation of the body along with the complex interplay between sensory and motor signaling underscores the multifactorial complexity when discussing the physiologic process of creativity. For the purposes of this chapter, only the ANS will be examined in relationship to creativity. The somatic nervous system, as well as all the other physiologic systems in the body (i.e., digestive, cardiovascular, endocrine, lymphatic, reproductive, respiratory, integumentary) will not be discussed. The authors are acutely aware that the efficient functioning of these systems is essential for sustaining life. In physiologic terms, the notion of homeostasis still dominates the field; however, the physiologic response to moment-to-moment changes actually requires a *homeodynamic* process (Berntson and Cacioppo, 2007).

This homeodynamic term describes the adaptive responses essential to manage the stress of living. The physiologic concept of stress refers to the actual process of biological functioning; it is not just relegated to extreme situations (Sherwood, 2010). The physiologic capacity to respond to change determines individual resilience. Macro systems such as the ANS, the central nervous system (brain and spine), neuroendocrine system, and the immune system all manage daily functioning (Sherwood, 2010). Human physiology is also regulated at the micro (cells and biochemistry) systems level. They all continually manage and alter the homeodynamic status (Sherwood, 2010). Life is sustained by a perpetual partnership at the macro and micro level; each influences the other.

The ANS directly interfaces with the body and the brain. Examining responses within the ANS provides information related to emotional arousal intensity as well as neurobiological regulation at the larger physiologic systems level. The ANS is directly regulated by the hypothalamus, insula, and anterior cingulate. It is part of the salience network as well as the reward network (Salimpoor and Zatorre, 2013). It could be argued that it also influences and is influenced by the default mode network. Identifying autonomic balance and autonomic regulation requires examining the interplay of the two branches of the ANS (Berntson, Norman, Hawkley, and Cacioppo, 2008a). Traditional classification of the two branches portrays the *sympathetic* branch as the activating system whereas the *parasympathetic* branch as the calming system. Despite the utilitarian efforts to simplify these two branches, once again, complexity within the ANS must be recognized. In actuality, the two branches operate in rapid activating and deactivating patterns. The more variance between these two branches the more adaptable the system. These systems are also directly influenced by genetic variance and daily activities; for example, individuals who are deeply engaged in spiritual practices tend to have more resilient ANS control (Berntson, Norman, Hawkley, and Cacioppo, 2008).

Observing and measuring responses in the ANS is contingent on capturing cardiorespiratory responses as well as galvanic skin conductance. Sympathetic nervous system activation is evidenced by increased heart rate, respiratory patterns, and skin temperature; parasympathetic nervous system activation displays decreased activation. Heart rate variability is an indirect method to measure ANS patterns; it is the time period between R-to-R intervals of the heart beat (Kleiger, Stein, and Bigger, 2005; Porges, 1995). The more variance between R-to-R intervals indicates more resilience in the physiologic systems. Along with heart rate variability assessment, determining the rate of physiologic ANS recovery after a stressor indicates degree of resilience. Highly creative individuals demonstrate a faster rate of recovery after a stressor; a finding that suggests creativity may be a factor in psychophysiological resilience (Razumnkkova, Kovtun, and Krivoshchekov, 2013). It also indirectly suggests that the individual has enough metabolic energy to meet task demands. This capacity to meet metabolic demands ensures ongoing functioning and is usually associated with physiologic and psychological well-being (Friedman, 2007). Autonomic variance also reinforces establishing goals and meeting them, key factors in successful creative productivity (Kreibig, Gendolla, and Scherer, 2012).

During creative activities, even when they are subjectively appraised as positive and meaningful, the physiologic demands on the body are high. The capacity to tolerate higher sympathetic arousal directly promotes creativity and cognitive flexibility; when parasympathetic vagal tone is too great then cognitive flexibility and creativity are compromised (Ghacibeh, Shenker, Shenal, Uthman, and Heilman, 2006). With increased training, as well as fitness, the ability to regulate ANS responses supports creative stress and decreases negative mood symptoms (Blanchette et al., 2005; Weinstein, Deuster, and Kop, 2007). For example, the parasympathetic branch may be deactivated to accommodate the sympathetic demands of creating. A nonsynergistic pattern of uncoupling, co-activating, or co-inhibiting the two ANS branches, enables more variance when meeting creative demands. The variance in ANS patterning reflects the resilience in the ANS system. Ultimately, optimal creative flow experiences require a complex interaction of the two branches. Too high or too low activation-deactivation patterns will sabotage creative flow (Peifer, Schulz, Schachinger, Bauman, and Antoni, 2014). Likewise, the emotional intensity during the creative process directly influences ANS responsiveness. Anger, sadness, pride, guilt, fear, and joy all operate in specific ANS behaviors; these affective states inhibit or excite one or both branches and either increase heart rate variability (a marker of ANS resilience) or diminish it (Fourie, Rauch, Morgan, Ellis, Jordaan, and Thomas, 2011; Golland, Keissar, and Levit-Binnun, 2014; Rochman and Diamond, 2008). These unique emotional responses may operate as physiologic stressors, especially during the creative process when emotional states are imaginatively induced and amplified (Faulkner and Leaver, 2016; Foster, Webster, and Williamson, 2003); however, with experience and familiarity more physiologic regulation can be cultivated.

NEUROAESTHETICS

The study of neuroaesthetics has existed for several hundred years; writers and researchers described the physiologic responses to beauty and the appreciation of objects or landscapes that had aesthetic appeal. However, only in 1999 was the term *neuroaesthetics* coined. Zeki (1999) used this term to describe the inner working of the brain while observing art. Neuroaesthetics can be examined by narrowing the parameters such as investigating neural activation while observing the beauty in art work or by broadening the parameters to observe neural activation of intense feelings that are evoked when witnessing or listening to something that is aesthetically pleasing (Brattico and Pearce, 2013; Nadal and Skov, 2013). With the advances in neuroimaging, researchers are now able to detect and describe the neurological origins of aesthetic appreciation (Nadal and Skov, 2013). Ultimately, this new field is well situated to examine aesthetic cognition, aesthetic emotions, aesthetic embodiment, and aesthetic movement (Chrsitensen and Calvo-Merino, 2013; Cinzia and Vittorio, 2009; Nadal and Skov, 2013). For example, examining the neuroaesthetics of dance and movement provides a deeper understanding about motion and pleasure and its relationship to aesthetic beauty (Cross and Ticini, 2012). Inherent in neuroaesthetics is the subjective appraisal and evaluation that underpins aesthetic experiences. Like the experience of awe, perhaps some people are more prone to aesthetic appreciation. The new field of neuroaesthetics is well situated to determine how the brains of those prone to appreciate aesthetics respond compared to those with less affinity (Silvia et al., 2015).

One major finding is the role of the reward circuit; it is a major contributor in aesthetic experience, in particular, pleasure. Regions such as the anterior cingulate, orbitofrontal cortex, ventromedial prefrontal cortex, caudate nucleus, substantia nigra, and nucleus accumbens, as well as the regulating regions of the amygdala, hypothalamus, thalamus, and hippocampus are all activated during aesthetic events (Blood and Zatorre, 2001; Salimpoor, Benovoy, Larcher, Dagher, and Zatorre, 2011). These regions are even more strongly engaged when emotional arousal is intensified during events such as listening to music (Salimpoor, Benovoy, Longo, Cooperstock, and Zatorre, 2009). Ultimately, study findings suggest that aesthetic appreciation involves brain regions responsible for reward, autonomic regulation, emotional arousal, and cognitive processing (Menon and Levitin, 2005).

Other networks involved in aesthetic appreciation include regions involved in evaluation, as well as regions that process auditory, visual, and somatosensory stimuli (Nadal and Skov, 2013). Specific studies that investigate dance have added to an understanding about sensorimotor aesthetics. Strong convergence within the somatosensory regions is involved to integrate emotional expressivity communicated via movement in the body and face. Auditory signals merge with the movement being performed, which intensifies the aesthetic response to dance (Christensen and Calvo-Merino, 2013). Although this preliminary study has opened awareness of dance aesthetics, the complexity of this field necessitates much more research (Calvo-Merino, Jola, Glaser, and Haggard, 2008). More advanced imaging measures, along with more sophisticated research designs that move beyond the laboratory, are still needed to fully understand kinesthetic neuroaesthetics (Christensen and Calvo-Merino, 2013).

Aesthetic emotional engagement is directly linked with physiologic responses; the insula and ANS interact with the reward circuit to increase sensations of pleasure (Salimpoor and Zatorre, 2013). Individual preferences add to the pleasure-displeasure valence. For example, some individuals love to listen to music that is slow and melancholy while others find it boring and irritating. Likewise, some find aesthetic pleasure listening to heavy metal and others become enraged (Swami et al., 2013). Although neuroaesthetics is biased toward exploring positive experiences, future studies need to address the aesthetic power of negative emotional responses (Salimpoor and Zatorre, 2013). Examining aesthetic emotions (awe, nostalgia, enjoyment) opens up the potential for even more complex array of neural network interactions.

Aesthetic preferences, familiarity, attentional acuity, and expectations directly influence the intensity of aesthetic experiences. These factors have been examined in music and dance appreciation; individual responses vary over time and across settings, which makes it difficult to make definitive statements related to neural processing (Braticco and Pearce, 2013; Christensen and Calvo-Merino, 2013). For example, over the past twenty years, aesthetic preferences have changed relative to dancers' body positions, the designs created in space, and the speed of execution. Today, audiences prefer more vertical lines and faster movement compared to previous generations of dancers (Christensen and Calvo-Merino, 2013). Whether these aesthetic preferences have changed in response to socioeconomic values, increased technical prowess in today's dancers, or media images and stereotyping is unknown.

The field of neuroaesthetics is growing. Ultimately, greater integration must occur between disciplines if progress is to continue. Ideally, psychological, neuroscientific, and evolutionary approaches should be integrated in order to understand the complexity of this deeply human experience (Cinzia and Vittorio, 2009; Nadal and Skov, 2013). Neuroaesthetics is well situated to not only reveal brain regions that are engaged during aesthetic experiences, but also the rapid time sequencing processes that underscore these events. The interplay between implicit and explicit neural networks has a unique time sequencing pattern. Gaining understanding of these processes will influence the creation of new aesthetic models and will promote new lines of research (Leder, 2013). Although no aesthetic neural center is likely to be identified, individual differences lend further diversity in neural activation patterns. The top-down cortical influences of anticipating, evaluating, and appreciating aesthetic experiences may dominate neuroaesthetic activation for those who are viewing or listening to something that evokes an aesthetic appreciation (Salimpoor and Zatorre, 2013); however, for those who are actively engaged in the creative process, micro moments of aesthetic pleasure may be provoked by body-up stimuli. The physiologic, ANS, as well as subcortical and cortical systems may share in these subjective aesthetic moments (Ellis and Thayer, 2010; Thayer, Ahs, Fredrikson, Sollers, and Wager, 2012).

MYSTICAL EXPERIENCES, MEDITATION, AND ANOMALOUS BRAINS

Although neuroaesthetics investigates aesthetic experiences, other associated experiences are often excluded from this field of study. For example, awe, transcendent, and anomalous experiences share features with aesthetic appreciation. Likewise, meditation may evoke deep states of happiness and acceptance. One overlapping variable that is generally included in neuroaesthetic studies is aesthetic chills, a feature that also appears during experiences of awe. Chills have been associated with dopamine release in the ventral striatum and subsequent activation in the nucleus accumbens. The caudate nucleus also plays a role in evoking chills; this region anticipates the moment when chills will be induced which actually amplifies the pleasurable experience (Salimpoor et al., 2011). The ANS, in conjunction with the insula, anterior cingulate, and supplementary motor system, is directly responsible for the physiologic activation during chills. Piloerection and changes in heart rate and breathing patterns signal a sensation of chills and aesthetic pleasure (Braticco and Pearce, 2013; Keltner and Haidt, 2003; Schurtz et al., 2012).

Highly creative people often report out-of-body experiences, and these experiences are typically associated with highly pleasurable feelings (Gow et al., 2004). In these states, transient disturbances in self-processing result due to a lack of integration of multisensory stimuli (proprioception, vestibular, tactile, visual) in the temporo-parietal junction (Blanke and Arzy, 2005). When integration of stimuli in this junction occurs, a unified sense of self is perceived as operating in time and space; however, when a failure to integrate sensorimotor information occurs, then altered sensations of the self arise such as feeling as if the self is located outside the body. Illusory visual experiences transpire to enable seeing the self outside the body or failing to recognize body parts as connected (i.e., phantom limb). As well, vestibular sensations are altered which induce feelings of floating or levitating. The integrative processing within the temporoparietal junction supports self-processing, including visuo-spatial perspective, vestibular perception, mental imagery of one's own body, monitoring of motion by self and others, as well as self and other agency (Blanke and Azzy, 2005). Any alterations, whether transient or persistent, provokes altered awareness. During creative work, these alterations may provide significant insight; however, they can also be intensely disturbing if they occur outside creative explorations (Bunning and Blannke, 2005).

Transliminal experiences, literally crossing thresholds of consciousness, evoke profound sensations of awe. Transliminality may be marked by magical ideation, mystical experiences, or intense fantasies. It is hypothesized that the gating of information decreases in the temporal region of the brain (Thalbourne, Crawley, and Houran, 2003), as well as decreased connections to the anterior cingulate (Szechtman, Woody, Bowers, and Nahmias, 1998). This instability of information processing may be at the root of transliminal experiences, and may induce mystical sensations such as feeling the presence of ghosts, religious or spiritual visions, or auditory hallucinations of being called or commanded. Like experiences of awe, post-transliminal experiences typically evoke elevated states of happiness but they can also engender intense depression when the sensations contain morbid themes or images (Thalbourne et al., 2003). For individuals who possess more temporal lobe labiality, they also risk greater psychopathology as well as the potential for greater enlightenment (Thalbourne et al., 2003). Beyond the temporal lobe, when widespread activation across multiple brain regions occurs, rapid transmission of information increases. This collaborative interaction ultimately means that no single region is inhibiting other regions and dominating in cognitive-affective processing; consequently sensations and images can emerge without censorship. Not only is creativity enhanced but also an increased vulnerability for psychopathological disorders such as schizoptypy is potentiated (Park, Kirk, and Waldie, 2015).

Creative processing can also be enhanced via mediation practices, a less extreme form of transliminality. Experienced long-time meditation practitioners literally change brain structures. Increased cortical thickness in brain regions associated with attention, interoception, and sensory processing are observed in these practitioners. Specifically, the prefrontal cortex and insula were thicker, a finding that persists in elderly meditators (Lazar et al., 2005). The practice of meditation can enhance the creative phases of incubation and illumination (Houran, 2009). Attentional processing, inherent in meditation practices, also promotes transcendence and integration. Studies have demonstrated that increased interhemispheric EEG synchronization (coherence/integration of several frequency bands) occurs during meditation (Houran, 2009). Integration of information is derived from long neural networks that connect distant cortical regions. These connections, along with shifting patterns of alpha, theta, beta, and gamma wave lengths, augment integration while simultaneously heightening awareness that extends beyond the self, thus diminishing a sense of self (Houran, 2009). Specifically, increases in the alpha wave length band are associated with low cortical arousal thus enhancing remote associations. Theta activation promotes awareness of novelty and increases pleasure and fulfillment. Delta waves are associated with increased motivation and intention and the high frequency gamma waves enhance spatial and temporal binding of information necessary for insight problem solving (Houran, 2009). Meditation, via these neural processes, enables a detachment from personal daily problems and offers more expansive possibilities and connections (Lazar et al., 2005). Achieving these transcendent states opens the possibility to experience heightened transliminality and offers a deeper connection with the creative self (Karwowski and Kaufman, 2017).

FLOW

The vital subjective experience of flow reveals a specific pattern of neurological and physiologic responses. The task demands associated with flow activities demonstrate the need for more sympathetic and less parasympathetic activation (de Manzano et al., 2010). Study findings suggest that engaging in flow activities is regarded as stressful to the body despite increased perceptions of well-being (Peifer et al., 2014; Thomson and Jaque, 2011a; Vickhoff et al., 2013). Within the brain, temporal and spatial movement sequencing during creative flow activities engage complex feedback and feedforward cortical and subcortical systems, especially between the pre-supplementary motor region, dorsal premotor region, and the cerebellum (de Manzano and Ullen, 2012a). The executive and default mode networks are also integrated within the action-oriented motor network during free response creative engagement (de Manzano and Ullen, 2012). The training effect that is essential for skill mastery influences response patterns, in particular, less executive network activation, which enhances flexible idea generation and exploration during creative flow experiences (Pinho et al., 2014). At the neurotransmitter level, more norepinephrine activation occurs due to increased activation of the locus coeruleus. These responses mobilize more prefrontal activity, especially in the orbital frontal cortex and the anterior cingulate; regions that are responsible for optimizing task performance (Aston-Jones and Cohen, 2005).

As discussed earlier, some individuals are more prone to experience flow. Their ability has been associated with increased availability of dopamine (D2-receptor) in the dorsal striatum. When dopamine is increased more positive affect is engendered, a classic response in all flow experiences (de Manzano, Cervenka, Jucaite, Hellenas, Farde, and Ullen, 2013). These individuals are also able to temporarily suspend prefrontal activation of the executive explicit network (transient hypofrontality) while engaging more implicit neural networks (Dietrich, 2004). At a genetic level, flow prone individuals demonstrate less behavioral inhibition, although they also feel more control during flow activities. It is suggested that these are traits of a more activated dopaminergic system, as well as more engagement in the default mode network and the implicit sensorimotor systems (Mosing, Pedersen et al., 2012).

Concurrent with these response patterns, decreased engagement of the amygdala has been observed, suggesting that flow states are earmarked as positive and nonthreatening (Ulrich, Keller, Hoenig, Waller, and Gron, 2014). The deactivation of the amygdala may also explain why increased physiologic sympathetic activation, a typical marker of stress, does not mobilize the neurological alarm (stress) network (Ulrich et al., 2014). Despite the stressful physiologic demands, flow is ultimately pleasurable, and not surprising, along with increased dopamine response, flow powerfully engages the reward circuits in the brain (Klasen, Weber, Kircher, Mathiak, and Mathiak, 2012). Both neuroscience and psychophysiology reveal a unique pattern of stress and pleasure in flow prone individuals.

CONCLUSION

The current neuroscience research on creativity provides strong evidence that the entire brain is engaged, although in different neural patterns, during the creative process. Each phase of the creative process draws upon multiple regions of the brain; activities such as recognizing insight, idea generation, incubation, remote associations, decision-making, and set shifting all require complex neural activation and deactivation patterns (Sawyer, 2011). The complex feedback and feedforward loops between brain regions and hemispheres reflect the complex nature of creativity. It is a neurodynamic activity (Jackson and Decety, 2004); however, engaging in other everyday tasks may also activate similar neural network patterns (Sawyer, 2010). Despite shared activation patterns across tasks, domain-specific tasks do engage specific neural profiles, as evidenced when comparing novice and expert musicians or artists (Schlaug et al., 2005; Schlaug, Forgeard, Zhu, Norton, Norton, and Winner, 2009). These differences are strongly evident during neuroimaging that measures motor imaging and motor skills (Milton, Small, and Solodkin, 2008). Remote associations, incubation, and unconscious influences during the creative process are consistently identified and neural activation/deactivation networks are profiled (Sawyer, 2011). Despite solid research findings, major limitations still exist in moving neuroscience research forward; they are associated with current testing capacities. Brain imaging such as PET, EEG, and fMRI only reveal a small window into the brain (Dietrich and Kanso, 2010). Laboratory settings also hamper real-time creative experiences, while distributed creativity (collaborative group activities) still remains a challenge to measure with these instruments (Sawyer, 2011).

Physiologic investigations are equally complex and equally difficult to measure. The current studies on flow do offer some insight into how the body responds to flow demands. Despite indicators that it is stressful to the body, flow and creative experiences are subjectively evaluated as pleasurable (Peifer et al., 2014). Increased fitness, both physical and psychological, enhances creative adaptability. More energy is available to meet the metabolic demands exerted during the creative process (Blanchette et al., 2005; Weinstein et al., 2007). Likewise, more variance within the physiologic systems augments adaptive strategies, including expressing, amplifying, and regulating emotional intensity and valence (Friedman, 2007; Kreibig et al., 2012). Task demand and task difficulty also influence physiologic responses; the ANS and the somatosensory systems are engaged and interconnected during these conditions (Silvestrini and Gendolla, 2009). Indirect measures of physiologic responsiveness can be achieved by measuring heart rate variability, a measurement that is derived from the cardiovascular systems and their inferred association with the ANS (Kleiger et al., 2005; Berntson et al., 2008). To date, this method of measuring creativity is the most efficient way to assess creative responses outside the laboratory (Dietrich, 2008).

One consistent finding across physiologic and neuroscientific studies is the limitations of the current operational criteria that defines creativity. Examining usefulness via observing the body and brain processes is not helpful because all activities are useful for daily functioning. Likewise, examining novelty in the brain and body is only identified by more activation or arousal. These two key components in creativity are still best understood via subjective assessment. A reductionistic hope to isolate the neural pathway for creativity or to identify the optimal physiologic state within which to create is foolhardy (Sawyer, 2011). Emergent complexity theories and measurements that can capture emergent complexity may yield more relevant information in the future (Faust and Kenett, 2014; Lewis and Granic, 2000; Sternberg, 2005). Currently these explorations are still in their infancy (Dietrich and Kanso, 2010; Sawyer, 2011).

With more advanced scientific tools and sophisticated research designs, increased neurobiological understanding about the potential resilience factors that reside within creativity may provide information that can be integrated into programming that will directly target creativity enhancement. As well, this knowledge may hopefully migrate into fields of traumatology and psychopathology. For example, emerging research indicates that despite histories of substantial exposure to childhood adversity, engaging in the creative process offers a sense of purpose, healing, and meaning in performing artists (Thomson and Jaque, 2018b). Higher childhood exposure to trauma and loss was also associated with increased achievement and optimal performance among elite athletes (Hardy et al., 2017; Rees et al., 2016). By gaining in depth knowledge about the physiologic and neurobiological factors underlying creativity and flow, it is hoped that understanding may increase about resilience despite substantial exposure to adversity.

Section II

TRAUMA

Chapter 6

Childhood Adversity

Childhood adversity is a term that incorporates multiple forms of abuse, neglect, and family challenges that pose a threat to optimal development (Felitti and Anda, 2010). The term *maltreatment* is commonly employed to describe abuse and/or neglect (Child Trends Data Bank, 2016). Maltreatment and adversity both indicate that normal child development is compromised; injury and/or damage may occur at the neurological, physical, emotional, and/or psychological level (Child Trends Data Bank, 2016). At the extreme, these experiences may lead to death. Childhood maltreatment is often provoked by one or several factors such as poor knowledge about child development, generational transmission of parental childhood abuse and neglect to the offspring, and/or situational stressors such as poverty, domestic violence, substance abuse, mental illness, or criminal activity (Child Trends Data Bank, 2016). National reporting of child maltreatment is highly structured in most countries; many people are identified as mandated reporters (legal and law enforcement personnel, educators, social service workers, medical, and mental health professionals) (U.S. Department of Health and Human Services, 2015). Prevalence rates and statistical profiles are generated based on these official reports; however, many maltreated children remain undetected or are not reported. Adding to inadequate data collection is the reality that each child is identified and recorded as a single case despite the possibility that they may have experienced multiple maltreatment events or suffered polyvictimization by multiple perpetrators (Child Trends Data Bank, 2016). These reporting practices and statistical analyses add to the under-reporting of childhood maltreatment (Crimes against Children Research Center, 2017).

Beyond maltreatment within the family, children are at increased risk of victimization outside the family such as assault, robbery, kidnapping, trafficking, and bullying. Institutional abuse is also pervasive (i.e., church, military, trafficking, genital mutilation, orphaned, and abandoned children) (Middleton et al., 2014). Despite a high rate of under-reporting, the current prevalence rate of all forms of maltreatment internationally raises grave concerns. It has reached epidemic proportions (Crimes against Children Research Center, 2017). What is not known is whether the negative effect of child exposure to adversity is now better understood, consequently receiving more attention than in the past, or if child maltreatment is growing worldwide. Countering the devastating long-term consequences of this epidemic, local communities, national governments, and international organizations must actively investigate and educate. Early interventions and preventive programs can greatly diminish this epidemic (Evans, Garner, and Honig, 2014).

TYPES OF MALTREATMENT

Maltreatment of a child under the age of eighteen years manifests in multiple types, and all types vary in frequency and intensity (CDC, 2014). Most states within the United States adhere to Federal Law standards that identify physical and sexual abuse, neglect, and psychological maltreatment; these may occur separately or in any combination (U.S. Department of Health and Human Services, 2015). Any abuse to a minor is considered a crime and must be reported by all mandated reporters (law enforcement personnel, school administrators and educators, health professionals, legal professionals) (U.S. Statistics on Child Abuse, 2017). Reporting complications include the reality that many forms of childhood maltreatment are interrelated; for example, a child who is sexually abused is also more likely to be emotionally abused and experience household dysfunctions such as mental illness or substance abuse. This same co-occurrence can be applied to all forms of childhood maltreatment, thus it is unusual for a mandated reporter and the investigation that follows to identify a single form of maltreatment (Dong, Anda et al., 2004).

Physical Abuse

According to the U.S. Child Welfare Department (2016), physical abuse is defined as bruising caused by punching, beating, kicking, biting, as well as, burning, breaking bones, hair pulling, and/or shaking an infant. Physical abuse occurs as a result of any intentional or unintentional act that is not deemed an accident. It also includes unlawful corporal punishment that may be experienced as a traumatic event. Willful cruelty or unjustifiable punishment is also considered physical and/or emotional abuse. It involves physical or mental suffering and may endanger the child's health (U.S. Department of Health and Human Services, Administration on Children, Youth and

Families, 2016). Children who are victims of physical violence are more likely to manifest internalizing (depression, anxiety, withdrawal) and externalizing (aggressive and delinquent) behaviors. These behavioral problems may be trauma-related posttraumatic stress disorder (PTSD) symptoms (Yoon, Steigerwald, Holms, and Perzynski, 2016). During development, exposure to physical abuse is frequently coupled with witnessing interparental violence. The combined experience of physical abuse and witnessing domestic violence increases the long-term likelihood that these children will experience more physical assaults in adulthood, as well as perpetrate more aggression within adult relationships (Milletich, Kelley, Doane, and Pearson, 2010).

Sexual Abuse

Sexual abuse is considered any sexual assault or exploitation of a minor. It includes intentional masturbation in the presence of a minor, molestation, exploitation such as preparing, selling, or distributing pornographic material, and child prostitution. These sexual acts or assaults are conducted by any individual who is eighteen years of age or older, or by another minor who is five years older than the sexually abused minor (Child Welfare Department, 2016; Douglas and Finkelhor, 2005a). According to the adverse childhood experience (ACE) studies, it is rare that sexual abuse occurs in a vacuum; typically other forms of maltreatment are also present which increases the damaging effects of this form of abuse (Dong, Anda, Dube, Giles, and Felitti, 2003). Investigations suggest that *sexual violence* is a stronger term to describe sexual abuse (Summer et al., 2015). The term *sexual violence* is generally reserved for oral, vaginal, or anal penetration, whether by a penis, finger, hand, mouth, or object, although some countries limit this term to penis penetration only. The nature of sexual violence implies that it is unwanted and forced (Summer et al., 2015). Other terms for sexual violence include rape (forced sexual intercourse), attempted rape (perpetrator intent to rape but unsuccessfully penetrates vaginally, anally, or orally), sexual assault (unwanted sexual contact, either directly or on top of clothes), attempted sexual assault (failure to make contact but intend is clearly unwanted sexuality), force or attempted force (grabbing, pushing, restraining, chasing with the intent to remove victim's clothing), and noncontact sex-related crimes (exhibitionism, voyeurism) (Finkelhor, Hammer, and Sedlak, 2008). Many of these violent sexual acts are perpetrated by someone known to the victim, with the majority of victims being females who were attacked by males (Finkelhor et al., 2008). Internationally, rates of sexual violence are high, with minimal services available to treat these victims who are at increased risk of sexually transmitted diseases including HIV (Summer et al., 2015).

Emotional Abuse

Emotional abuse and emotional neglect may present as less overt signs of maltreatment compared to physical or sexual abuse. They are more difficult to define and identify; however, the effects have devastating long-term effects, especially in relationship with self and others because emotional abuse and neglect must occur within the child-parent/caregiver relationship (Glaser, 2002). Emotional abuse includes inappropriate or inconsistent interactions with the child, failure to recognize the individuality of the child, and failure to promote the child's socializing needs (Glaser, 2002). Emotional abuse is a failure to provide a supportive environment as well as a high probability of damaging the child's physical, mental, spiritual, and moral health (Butchart et al., 2006). Emotional abuse often underlies more extreme maltreatment exposure; it is also associated with higher incidence of parental/caregiver difficulties such as alcohol and substance abuse, mental illness, and other family dysfunction (Wright, Crawford, and Del Castillo, 2009). Emotional abuse is a more chronic exposure compared to acute bouts of physical and sexual abuse, which makes this form of maltreatment more insidious (Taillieu, Brownridge, Sareen, and Afifi, 2016). It often leads to increased shame, anger, depression, anxiety, and personality disorders in the child (Taillieu et al., 2016; Wright et al., 2009). Perhaps even more problematic, emotional abuse is internalized as a negative self-concept that influences all cognitive schemes about the self and interactions with others (Wright et al., 2009). Increased vulnerability to self-harm, including eating disorders and borderline personality disorder are strongly associated with this form of maltreatment (Afifi et al., 2011; Hund and Espelage, 2006). Although both emotional abuse and emotional neglect are problematic, emotional abuse compared to the passive act of emotional neglect is associated with even more psychopathology (Taillieu et al., 2016). In general, adults with a history of emotional abuse and neglect tend to avoid or withdraw from interpersonal relationships. Profound feelings of not being loved coupled with intense fears of rejection and failure persist (Taillieu et al., 2016).

Neglect

Physical neglect includes both acts and omissions that result in harm or threat to the child's welfare. Criteria such as inadequate nutrition, clothing, and hygiene, medical neglect, left unattended, and/or abandoned by an adult who is responsible for the child's welfare are considered acts of neglect. Neglect is considered severe when intentional failure to care for a child occurs and the neglect places the child in danger (mental and physical health) (Child Welfare Department, 2016). Child neglect is the most commonly reported form of child maltreatment and is often pervasive throughout childhood, although under extreme periods of stress, parents may inadvertently neglect their children (Hildyard andWolfe, 2002). Emotional and physical neglect have profound negative developmental effects; fundamentally these children do not cultivate adaptive skills to manage daily challenges, consequently they are poorly prepared to meet normal developmental tasks (Hildyard and Wolfe, 2002).

Abuse of Children with Disabilities

Abuse of children with disabilities is particularly problematic. Disabled children are three times more likely to be victims of sexual abuse, especially if the disability is intellectual or mental health related (Gotby, Lichtenstein, Langstrom, and Pettersson, 2018; Smith and Harrell, 2013). Despite increased frequency, these children are less likely to receive services and support, plus the abuse incidents are less likely to be reported. Increased vulnerability is associated with increased discrimination and devaluation of these children. They are more dependent on caregivers, which can increase the potential for abuse. Stereotypes of disabled individuals include a belief that they are asexual; consequently they would not be targets of sexual violence. This biased view increases the likelihood that perpetrators would remain undetected, especially if they are also the ones administering intimate personal care to these children (Sullivan and Knutson, 2000). Currently, there are inadequate policies and procedures, including policies to monitor the behavior of personal care attendants. Many disabled children are unable to communicate abuse events, and symptoms that are rooted in traumatic exposure are often misinterpreted as distress associated with their disability. The convergence of these factors increases the "silent epidemic" of abuse in children with disabilities (Smith and Harrell, 2013; Sullivan and Knutson, 2000).

Bullying

Bullying, whether by peers or siblings, is defined as a child exposed repeatedly over time to negative actions (verbal, physical, relational) by one or more individuals. Bullying always involves a power differential, with the aggressor physically, emotionally, or psychologically attacking the victim (Turner, Finkelhor, Shattuck, Hamby, and Mitchell, 2015). The victims present as weaker and more vulnerable and may display depression, loneliness, avoidance of school or social activities, and increased suicidal ideation. Bullies often manifest behavioral, emotional, or learning problems, as well as experiencing increased physical discipline by parents or caregivers. According to national surveys, approximately 30 percent of children and adolescents experience some form of bullying, with girls experiencing more social exclusion and boys more physical attacks (Crimes against Children Research Center, 2017). Although education programs have increased awareness, current findings indicate that receiving positive support from bystanders and confiding in adults about experiences of bully victimization (online and in-person) do not ameliorate the psychological damage. On the other hand, negative bystander reactions such as taunting or humiliating the victim intensifies emotional distress (Jones, Mitchell, and Turner, 2015), especially if the victim is bullied both in-person and online (Mitchell, 2016). The current state of bullying indicates that the term may not capture the extreme violence that is often inflicted on the victim, such as date rape, robbery, assault, and extreme forms of cruelty and torture. Bullying, or more appropriately, peer victimization occurs in all settings and not just within schools (Turner et al., 2015). Many of these forms are better classified as hate crimes, especially when victimization is motivated by discrimination that is based on race, ethnicity, sexual orientation, religion, or disability (Turner et al., 2015). As violent victimization increases, more traumatic symptomatology emerges. Often medical and legal aid is required to halt these extreme behaviors. Bullying has received substantial attention; however, more awareness must be directed toward the degree of violence that is inflicted on the victims (Crimes against Children Research Center, 2017).

Sextortion

Sextortion is a term that describes online threats to expose sexual images, including coercive actions to gain sexual images from unwilling victims (Wolak and Finkelhor, 2016). These actions are often conducted for revenge or to humiliate another. The target victims are usually adolescents or young adult females (83%). Sextortion may occur after a romantic relationship has ended. The rejected partner then threatens to disseminate sexually explicit images with the goal to force reconciliation or to humiliate the former partner. It can also occur in online relationships when sexual images are exchanged and then displayed in order to force commitment to the online relationship or to exploit the victim. Sextortion can escalate into serious incidents that involve stalking, as well as physical and sexual assault. Usually sextortion persists for six months or longer. Many victims require medical help to address psychological trauma symptoms. Very few victims of sextortion report these incidents, and when reports are filed the majority believe that the help is insufficient, especially in relationship to efforts to remove online images. Currently, criminal law and policies established by technology companies remain insufficient to address the range of sextortion episodes. Lack of viable avenues to stop sextortion increases victim distress. Often law enforcement and family members blame the victim for submitting to sextortion, which further compounds their psychological vulnerability (Wolak and Finkelhor, 2016).

Exposure to Violence

Rate of exposure to violence, including domestic violence and general crimes, is high in children. These are regarded as the "unseen crimes" in the home and few are publically acknowledged and reported (Crimes against Children Research Center, 2017). The Office of Juvenile Justice and Delinquency Prevention and the Centers for Disease Control and Protection currently conduct surveys to investigate exposure to violence among minors. Exposure to firearms is particularly problematic, with firearm-related deaths classified as one of the ten leading causes of death in minors (Mitchell, Hamby, Turner, Shattuck, and Jones, 2015). Typically, law enforcement personnel are the first responders to such events; however, minors receive considerably less attention compared to crimes against adults. Sadly, more resources are directed toward juvenile delinquency compared to juveniles who are victims of domestic violence and violent crimes outside the home (Crimes against Children Research Center, 2017). This disparity reinforces the negative outcomes related to childhood exposure to violence.

Prostitution and Sex Trafficking

Prostitution and sex trafficking is sadly not a new phenomenon. It remains a difficult area to research primarily because it is poorly reported and documented, especially within different regions of the country (Stansky and Finkelhor, 2008). Adding to the difficulty in gathering statistics on prostitution rates among minors is the limiting criteria to classify prostitution; it is determined based on an exchange of sex for financial remuneration. Many minors may receive drugs or presents in exchange for sex, which muddies the reporting criteria (Stansky and Finkelhor, 2008). The more covert sex trafficking rings make gathering statistical data even more difficult. Law enforcement personnel may have the most accurate reporting figures, but this information is limited to actual arrests of youth who were working as prostitutes. The role of the Internet has increased access to sex trafficking and prostitution and has compounded the difficulty to regulate and report this form of child abuse (Crimes against Children Research Center, 2017).

Missing or Abducted Children

Another adversity factor is missing or abducted children (Crimes against Children Research Center, 2017). Like child abuse and neglect reports, missing children incidents have decreased since 1999 (Sedlak, Finkelhor, and Brick, 2017). There is a vast array of reasons a child can be categorized as missing. The five major categories include (1) abducted by a family member, (2) abducted by a nonfamily member, (3) the minor ran away or was thrown out of the household, (4) they were lost, stranded, or injured, and (5) benign reasons such as misunderstandings and miscommunications (Sedlak et al., 2017). In the first category, a family member may take or fail to return a child and is in violation with custody rights. In order to abduct older children use of physical force or threat is required. Nonfamily abduction, an event that is always without permission from parental or legal guardians, inevitably requires force with older children and coercion with younger children. Criteria such as taking a child at least twenty feet away from the pre-abduction place or into a vehicle or building, detaining the minor including prohibiting the child from leaving for at least one hour, concealing the minor's location, demanding ransom, and/or indicating an intent to keep the child permanently are all part of nonfamily abduction. The third category involves a child leaving home without parental or legal guardian permission and stays away overnight (two or more nights in adolescents over fifteen) or fails to return from a setting that was permitted. To be thrown away requires a family member to tell a minor to leave home or blocks the minor from returning home. In this situation, the parent fails to arrange adequate care for at least one night. The fourth and fifth categories are not intentional acts and usually involve caregiver concern as well as their lack of knowledge regarding the whereabouts of the minor (Sedlak et al., 2017).

Stereotypical Kidnapping

A subtype of nonfamily abduction, stereotypical kidnapping, involves a stranger or someone who is slightly known to the family. The perpetrator detains the child overnight or longer, removes the child at least fifty miles from home, demands a ransom, intends to keep the child permanently, and/ or murders the child. Stereotypical kidnapping events usually occur with a single child who is alone (Wolak, Finkelhor, and Sedlak, 2016). The use of deception or nonthreatening pretext begins the initial phase of the kidnapping, including via the Internet. Detainment is often in buildings, and in the majority of cases, the perpetrator commits a sexual crime. Approximately 35 percent of the victim cases are physically assaulted, 24 percent suffer extreme neglect, and 20 percent are threatened with weapons, as well as messages related to threatening family members or pets. Approximately 16 percent are kidnapped into sex trafficking organizations. To date, these events are relatively rare and each case is uniquely different, although the physical and psychological damage to the minor is similarly extensive. The use of technology has reduced the lag time from moment of abduction to recovery, and most offenders have previous criminal records prior to the kidnapping (Wolak et al., 2016).

Polyvictimization

Polyvictimization is a term that describes multiple forms of victimization by many different perpetrators. This may last for a short period of time or over years; however, it is usually severe, chronic, and multifaceted (Grasso, Petitclerc, Henry, McCarthy, Wakschlag, and Briggs-Gowan, 2016). These children frequently experience maltreatment by caregivers, bullying by siblings or peers, assault (sexual or non-sexual) by family members and/or strangers, exposure to domestic violence, and high likelihood of violence within their communities (Crimes against Children Research Center, 2017). Polyvictims are also frequently exposed to weapon violence, a factor that is often linked with exposure to gangs, drug trafficking, and extreme domestic violence (Mitchell et al., 2015). The strong association between weapon violence and polyvictimization suggests that identifying youth exposed to weapon violence may help determine the occurrence of multiple forms of maltreatment by multiple perpetrators (Mitchell et al., 2015). Polyvictim children are at increased risk of mental illnesses, including PTSD, depression, anxiety, dissociation, and suicidality (Finkelhor, Shattuck, Turner, Ormrod, and Hamby, 2011). Children who experience polyvictimization are highly vulnerable to revictimization in childhood and adulthood (Grasso et al., 2016; Turner, Finkelhor, and Ormrod, 2010).

Maltreatment Fatalities

Maltreatment fatalities include all deaths of minors that are directly related to abuse or neglect, as well as when abuse and neglect contributed to the fatality (Douglas and Finkelhor, 2005). It is difficult to gather accurate data related to this form of extreme maltreatment, especially if the families are not registered with a social service organization. Based on the limited data available, neglect is the largest cause of fatalities, primarily due to caregivers' lack of provisions that are essential for sustaining life (Bonner, Crow, and Logue, 1999). Recent findings also indicate that one in four children are exposed to weapon-involved violence, a factor that increases risk of mental illness, suicidality, polyvictimization, and increased lethality risk (Mitchell et al., 2015). Increased risk of child fatalities are associated with families who are under extra stress such as moving, unemployment, the birth or death of a family member, living in crowded homes, homeless, single-parent families, or instability in parental relationships (Douglas and Finkelhor, 2005). Child fatalities are also associated with younger age of caregivers, and in the greater majority of cases, the perpetrators of child fatalities are living with the child at the time of death (Douglas and Finkelhor, 2005).

PREVALENCE RATES

Prior to 2001, incidence of maltreatment reporting rose. This was followed by a five-year decline in incidence reporting, and as of 2014 rates have remained relatively unchanged, with the exception of child neglect, which declined the least (Child Trends Data Bank, 2016). Approximately 1,500 children died in 2014 due to child maltreatment with approximately 702,000 (9.4 child victims per 1,000 children) child maltreatment cases reported that same year (U.S. Department of Health and Human Services, 2015). The national rate is determined based on an average of reported incidents in each state. State reporting rates vary between 22.9 child victims per 1,000 children and 1.2 child victims per 1,000 children (U.S. Department of Health and Human Services, 2015). The highest rate of maltreatment occurred in children under the age of three years (i.e., 24.4 children per 1,000 children under one year of age), with a steady decrease in cases between the ages of four and seven, eight and eleven, twelve and fifteen, and sixteen and seventeen years old (U.S. Department of Health and Human Services, 2016). Gender differences are evident and this varies by age groupings. Boys between the ages of one and five years have higher victimization rates, whereas, girls between the ages of eleven and seventeen have higher rates (OVC, 2017). Ethnicity also influences prevalence rates. Higher maltreatment cases are reported among multiple race, African American, Native Alaskan, and American Indian populations, and lower incidence among Hispanic, Pacific Islander, and Caucasian children. The lowest rates are among Asian children (U.S. Department of Health and Human Services, 2016).

Children placed in foster care face challenges such as length of time in foster care, risk of further maltreatment while in foster care, reunification process with family of origin, and/or adoption into a new family. Again there is a large difference among states, ranging from 1.5 children per 1,000 children to 9.8 children per 1,000 children placed in foster care (U.S. Department of Health and Human Services, 2015). Overall, twenty-two states reduced child maltreatment incidences between 2010 and 2014; however, sixteen states had increased reported incidences during the same time period. Nationally, the time period increased between foster care placement and reunification or adoption. Likewise, multiple foster care placement rates increased, and length of stay within foster care also increased. These trends reflect a need for improvement in effectively managing maltreated children once they are identified (U.S. Department of Health and Human Services, 2015). For example, preschool children in foster care who are also diagnosed with PTSD (11.7–15.4%) typically have higher exposure rate to interpersonal trauma coupled with the negative influence of unregulated stress-response behaviors with their foster care parents (Vasileva and Petermann, 2017). Foster care parents need more education related to managing traumatized children, including better self-regulating strategies for themselves (Vasileva and Petermann, 2017). Children with disabilities tend to be placed in residential treatment centers, in part because of increased medical needs. These children have even less likelihood of permanent placement (U.S. Department of Health and Human Services, 2015). Older children are also less likely to receive permanent placement, which contributes to higher risk behavior in this population. Often these older children actively initiate and seek connection with their birth parents despite maltreatment histories (U.S. Department of Health and Human Services, 2015). Internationally, a similar foster care pattern is evident. In general, most children who are placed in foster care have experienced multiple forms of victimization, and foster care experiences themselves frequently add to the dosing of psychological abuse (Seiler, Kohler, Ruf-Leuschner, and Landolt, 2016). The cumulative effects are associated with higher rates of all forms of psychopathology, including personality disorders, depression, anxiety, dissociation, somatization, and PTSD (Lueger-Schuster et al., 2018).

Types of maltreatment reporting varied during 2014, with incidence of neglect the highest (75%) followed by physical abuse (17%). Frequently a reported child case includes multiple forms of maltreatment (U.S. Department of Health and Human Services, 2015). Among maltreatment type, in 2014, "7.1 per thousand children were reported victims of neglect, compared with 1.6 for physical abuse, 0.8 for sexual abuse, and 0.6 for psychological or emotional abuse" (Child Trends Data Bank, 2016). It is important to note that these statistic numbers vary greatly depending on the data source that gathered the information. For example, many minors who were sexually abused do not report abuse until they are adults and often these reports are given in anonymous surveys (Douglas and Finkelhor, 2005a). An estimated 6.3 children per 1,000 children were considered missing in 2013, including family and nonfamily abduction, runaway or thrown away children, or more benign causes for children missing to their caretakers. This estimated number has also decreased since the 9.2 per 1,000 children in 1999 (Sedlak et al., 2017).

Child fatalities are typically associated with both abuse and neglect. According to older statistics, 36 percent of victims died as a result of neglect, 28 percent died from abuse (beaten, shot, strangled, hanged, smothered), and another 29 percent died from a combination of neglect and abuse (United States Administration for Children and Families, 2005). The greatest rate of fatalities occurred in children under three years of age, with the most fatalities under the age of one year (Douglas and Finkelhor, 2005). There is a higher incidence of boys dying compared to girls, as well, more Caucasian (43%), African American (30.3%), and Hispanic (15.1%) children die compared to other ethnicity groupings. Of these fatalities, 79.3 percent of the fatalities were caused by at least one parent, with mothers causing 28 percent of the fatalities, fathers committing 15 percent of the fatalities, and both parents committing 22 percent of the fatalities (OVC, 2017). In terms of perpetrators, 54.1 percent were female and the greater majority of victims were between the ages of eighteen and forty-four years (U.S. Department of Health and Human Services, 2015).

When maltreatment expands to include child violent victimization, 69.7 percent of children and adolescents were physically assaulted, physically intimidated, bullied, robbed, or assaulted with a weapon (OVC, 2016). Juveniles experience substantially more property crimes than adults, with higher rates of robbery that are unreported to law enforcement (i.e., stolen clothes, bikes, electronic devices) (Crimes against Children Research Center, 2017). Unlike most maltreatment categories that have remained stable for reported incidents, rates of exposure to violence (i.e., bullying) and witnessing violence are significantly higher. Sexual violence remains extremely high in some parts of the world, with figures ranging between 37.6 percent in Swaziland and 5.6 percent in Cambodia (Summer et al., 2015). The average across most countries is approximately 25 percent of children experiencing sexual violence (Summer et al., 2015). Homicide rates are highest among adolescents between the ages of fifteen and twenty-four years, with the next highest among children from birth to four years of age (Crimes against Children Research Center, 2017). Frequently adolescents are murdered in large urban settings and killed by other young adults or teens, whereas, young children are typically murdered by a family member, most often by a female offender (Crimes against Children Research Center, 2017). Growing rates of online victimization continue, including degree of harassment, distress, and threat (OVC, 2017; Turner et al., 2015). This growth may be related to increased access to the Internet, reduced inhibition due to online anonymity, and increased violence in school settings (OVC, 2016, 2017). Cyber-bullying may also be growing because the power differential between aggressor and victim has been removed. Even those who may be targeted as victims at school can retaliate via technology now. To date, this form of peer harassment is less physically and psychological devastating compared to violent peer victimization; however, it still remains a serious and harmful experience (Mitchell; 2016; Mitchell, Jones, Turner, Shattuck, and Wolak, 2016).

Polyvictimization usually involves some of the most extreme cases of maltreatment and exposure to violence (OVC, 2016). Factors such as growing up in a violent or chaotic home, increased life-stress such as poverty, and/or living in a violent neighborhood increase the likelihood of polyvictimization (Klest, 2012; OVC, 2016). Severe polyvictimization of children typically involves high levels of exposure to violence as well as impaired caregiving. Impaired caregiving usually involves high rates of domestic violence between partners as well as physical and sexual abuse directed at the child (Grasso et al., 2016). Maternal depression, anxiety, and PTSD compromise adequate parenting. Children raised in households with harsh physical discipline are also at increased risk of polyvictimization. Without positive parenting, polyvictimized children are more likely to manifest poorer behavioral and emotional regulation, with a higher likelihood of PTSD symptoms (Grasso et al., 2016). Other factors associated with higher risk of polyvictimization include being a boy, an African American youth, children raised in single-parent households, or children growing up in households with stepparents (OVC, 2016). These children have heightened vulnerability to mental illness as well as revictimization in adulthood (Klest, 2012; OVC, 2016; Wilkins, Tsao, Hertz, Davis, and Klevens, 2014). They are also more likely to behave violently; either the violence is directed outwardly toward others or inwardly via self-injurious behaviors (Wilkins et al., 2014). Often a single maltreatment type is reported in these high-risk children, without identifying the other types of victimization that occurs in the lives of these children. Approximately 10 percent of children each year suffer at least four or more types of maltreatment, which may account for their increased risk of further victimization (Crimes against Children Research Center, 2017). Adding to the complications of polyvictimization is the fact that posttraumatic stress symptoms remain unrecognized and untreated in these children (Wilkins et al., 2014).

SIGNS OF ADVERSITY

Risk factors associated with childhood adversity are consistent across communities and cultures (Wilkins et al., 2014). Family and peer relationships that are fraught with conflict are strong predictors. The likelihood of child maltreatment increases in neighborhoods that lack support and trust, especially when higher rates of domestic and community violence occur. Poor economic opportunities and unemployment increase despair and emotional volatility, and this instability is likely to be expressed violently against partners, children, and the elderly. Adolescents are more likely to act in sexually and physically violent behavior under these conditions. This reinforces community norms that are more aggressive and coercive, which further increases bullying and perpetrating behavior as well as witnessing violence (Wilkins et al., 2014). Without adequate role models, skills to resolve problems in non-violent ways are not learned; consequently coping strategies under stress frequently escalate to violent behavior (Wilkins et al., 2014).

In rural United States, risk factors vary somewhat compared to urban communities. For example, single-parent families are associated with increased risk of maltreatment (Mattingly and Walsh, 2010). Most maltreatment cases that are reported in rural communities come from Caucasian families (80%) compared to urban areas (41%). Like urban communities, poverty is a major factor associated with rural maltreatment reports. Childhood poverty is associated with increased chronic family stress, compromised physiologic stress systems within all family members, and disrupted self-regulating coping strategies (Evans and Kim, 2012; Mattingly and Walsh, 2010). Maternal mental illness, low social support, history of prior maltreatment reporting, imprisonment, substance abuse, domestic violence, and caregivers' personal maltreatment history are all associated with risk factors in rural and urban communities (Mattingly and Walsh, 2010). However, unlike urban communities, rural community risk factors include more family chronic stress such as difficulty meeting basic financial needs. They also have fewer services available to offset their stress, for example, fewer mental health providers and educators who can assist in improving parenting skill acquisition (Mattingly and Walsh, 2010).

ACE STUDY

The ACE study is a combined study between Kaiser Permanente's Department of Preventive Medicine (San Diego) and the Centers for Disease Control and Prevention (CDC). It began in 1985 as an obesity program to help patients lose weight. Dr. Felitti (Kaiser Permanente) inadvertently discovered that patients who failed to lose weight, or who lost weight and then rapidly regained it reported more childhood experiences of physical and sexual abuse. Upon closer examination, these patients identified a host of dysfunctional childhood household experiences. Concurrently, Dr. Anda (CDC) was examining multiple medical and public health problems (i.e., smoking and alcohol abuse in relationship to chronic diseases). Both Felitti and Anda realized that early childhood adversity was the common thread in all these cases. They joined forces and developed the ACE study, one of the largest studies in existence, and a study that is ongoing. Via a series of interviews and screening measures they created the ACE questionnaire (Felitti et al., 1998). It contains ten yes/no items that probe for abuse (emotional, physical, sexual), neglect (emotional, physical), and family dysfunction (mental illness, substance abuse, household member imprisoned, divorce/separation, domestic violence). A total score of yes items yields the ACE score, regardless of frequency and intensity. They found that ACEs are common. In the original ACE study and subsequent studies, approximately two-thirds of study participants are exposed to at least one ACE (Felitti et al., 1998; Murphy et al., 2014; Thomson and Jaque, 2017a). The effects of ACEs are cumulative; literally the more ACE items endorsed the more likely psychological and physical pathology will exist (Felitti and Anda, 2010).

Vast numbers of studies have been generated to determine the ACE predictive strengths for diseases such as ischemic heart disease (Dong, Giles et al., 2004), stroke and asthma, as well as increased risk of illicit drug use (Dube, Felitti, Dong, Chapman, Giles, and Anda, 2003). In the original study, ACE exposure was determined to be the leading cause of adult death, with four or more ACE items associated with increased risk of smoking, sexually transmitted diseases, obesity, cancer, chronic lung disease, liver disease, skeletal fractures, depression, and suicide (Felitti et al., 1998). ACEs have also been linked to increased frequency and severity of non-suicidal self-injury (Kaess et al., 2013), as well as more psychiatric disorders such as major depressive disorder, borderline personality disorder, and schizophrenia (Pietrek, Elbert, Weierstall, Muller, and Rockstroh, 2013). In all studies, a dose effect is demonstrated; the higher the ACE score (maximum of ten) the more risk of mental illness, especially when it occurs earlier in childhood (Pietrek et al., 2013). This dose effect is further pronounced when emotionally abusive family environments are reported, notably in association with increased mental illness in a family member (Edwards, Holden, Felitti, and Anda, 2003). ACE studies have also demonstrated that high parental ACE exposure is strongly associated with generational transmission, a pattern that perpetuates negative outcomes on morbidity and mortality in parents and their offspring (Randell, O'Malley, and Dowd, 2015).

Based on multiple study findings, when ACEs are four or more, the odds ratio for adult psychopathology is extremely high, hence cut off scores of four or more ACEs are often used to differentiate the additive and multiplicative synergistic effects for increasing the probability of acquiring adult disorders (Putnam, Harris, and Putnam, 2013). Many research programs include other items that are not addressed in the original ACE studies such as peer rejection, bullying, low socioeconomic status, and discrimination. These events are also strong adversity factors with significant negative consequences associated with them (Finkelhor, 2017). Given the robust findings that demonstrate long-term consequences of childhood adversity, there is a strong push to standardize ACE assessments in health-care settings. Gathering cumulative ACE scores may help identify individuals who are at high risk of increased morbidity and mortality. Greater efforts to address adversity during childhood may reduce these health risks that tend to increase in adulthood. Maltreated children manifest a myriad of symptoms; if left unaddressed they may develop into severe psychological and physical disorders and diseases (Finkelhor, 2017).

LONG-TERM CONSEQUENCES

The long-term consequences of ACEs influence emotional, physical, psychological, social, academic, and workplace functioning. For example, parents with maltreatment histories and their maltreated children tend to display great difficulty with emotion regulation (Gratz and Roemer, 2004). Emotional dysregulation is associated with difficulties identifying, interpreting, and responding to social-emotional experiences. These difficulties increase behavioral patterns of avoidance, misappraisal, and escalation, which then increase anxiety and relational difficulties (Mennin, Heimberg, Turk, and Fresco, 2002). Emotional dysregulation alters perceptions of self and others. Individuals with histories of childhood adversity and emotional dysregulation perceive themselves as lacking control over external events. They regard their environment as uncertain and unreliable. These beliefs (and lived experiences) compromise their willingness to tackle challenging tasks, and if such tasks are attempted the likelihood of quitting sooner is greater (Mittal and Griskevicius, 2014).

Physiologic dysregulation further intensifies emotional dysregulation. Most abused children and adults who were maltreated report poor quality of sleep, digestive disorders, cardiorespiratory abnormalities, and chronic pain. They cannot trust that their bodies will adapt and respond to internal and/or external stress. They struggle with difficulties concentrating, problem solving, and sustaining a task: signs indicating deficits in cognitive processing, (Mittal, Griskevicius, Simpson, Sung, and Young, 2015). All these factors lead to lower levels of physical, social, work/school, and interpersonal functioning (Springer, Sheridan, Kuo, and Carnes, 2003). This reality is clearly demonstrated in a recent study that examined data on the relationship between childhood adversity and adult socioeconomic status (education, employment, income). The study analyzed data from ten states and the District of Columbia. A strong pattern emerged; individuals with higher ACE scores were more likely to live in poverty, have greater rates of unemployment, and less likely to complete a high school education (Metzler, Merrick, Klevens, Ports, and Ford, 2017).

Specific types of childhood adversity are also associated with problematic behavior and pathology. For example, in a study that examined college student dating, the transmission of physical abuse and domestic violence experiences was clearly evident in undergraduate dating relationships (Milletich et al., 2010). Women who were physically abused were more likely to behave aggressively during dating, and this behavior increased if these women also witnessed mother's acting aggressively toward their fathers. A similar pattern was evident in males. Witnessing father's aggression to their mother influenced greater dating aggression; however, mother-to-father aggression decreased dating aggression in male students, in part because these males tended to select more passive partners to date (Milletich et al., 2010). Experiencing emotional abuse changed this profile. Women who experienced physical and emotional abuse as well as witnessing domestic violence were less likely to act aggressively during dating relationships; whereas, males with a similar background were more likely to perpetrate aggressive behavior, especially if they were shamed or rejected (Milletich et al., 2010). These findings demonstrate the powerful modeling effect that is internalized during child development.

Physical abuse, in general, is linked to substantial physiologic complications such as chronic fatigue syndrome as well as multiple chemical sensitivities and fibromyalgia (Fuller-Thomson, Sulman, Brennenstuhl, and Merchant, 2011). Even more sobering, the relationship between childhood physical abuse and adult heart disease is strong, a finding that indicates a lifetime of compromised health and well-being (Fuller-Thomson, Brennenstuhl, and Frank, 2010). Sexual abuse has received substantial investigation. For example, sleep problems and dissociation begin when sexual victimization occurs and these symptoms persist into adulthood (Hebert, Langevin, Guidi, Bernard-Bronnin, and Allard-Dansereau, 2017; Lind, Aggen, Kendler, York, and Amstadter, 2016). Even with treatment, sexual concerns and dissociative symptoms tend to remain chronic; this finding is evident across ethnicity groups (African American, Latino, Caucasian) and among older children and adolescents (Ruiz, 2016). Sexual preoccupation, a marker that predicts future sexual revictimization, is strongly evident in African American children (Ruiz, 2016).

When examining the effects on gender, sexual abuse is associated with increased mental disorders in males compared to females who are exposed to similar maltreatment, although females often display more sexual distress than male children (Ruiz, 2016; Turner, Taillieu, Cheung, and Afifi, 2017). Research findings do not often include male sexual abuse consequences, primarily because males tend to hide this form of abuse, and clinicians and researchers often fail to inquire about childhood sexual abuse in male samples (Turner et al., 2017). As a result, males are seldom treated and often go undetected until suicidal attempts are identified. As well, male victims of sexual abuse tend to have increased rates of shame, anxiety, depression, PTSD, substance abuse, and personality disorders. Although other types of childhood adversity exposure may co-occur with sexual abuse, many cases of male victimization only involve sexual abuse, a reality that often intensifies secrecy and humiliation in the male victims (Turner et al., 2017). Importantly, childhood sexual abuse in both genders is strongly associated with severe long-term mental disorders in adulthood (Ruiz, 2016; Turner et al., 2017).

Psychological (emotional) abuse has equally long-term effects, in part because it co-occurs with other forms of child maltreatment. Seldom it is absent when children are raised in environments with physical and sexual abuse. Likewise, periods of emotional and physical neglect, role reversing, inappropriate discipline, and hostility are usually present in these households. Emotionally abused children are at increased risk of further psychological abuse by others (i.e., teachers, peers) (MacArthur, 2011). Psychological abuse often transforms into chronic and recurrent adult depression and suicidal behavior (Bifulco, Moran, Baines, Bunn, and Stanford, 2002). Childhood maladaptive schemas form in these environments and persist into adulthood, such as beliefs that they are more vulnerable to harm and they must sacrifice themselves rather than defend themselves. They internalize toxic levels of shame that are often managed by dissociative cognitive processing (Wright et al., 2009). Often coping strategies to ameliorate these distressing thoughts and beliefs take the form of substance use, including alcohol and illicit drugs. The likelihood for traumatic exposure increases along with subsequent problems associated with substance use (Mandavia, Robinson, Bradley, Ressler, and Powers, 2016).

The sequelae of childhood neglect (physical and/or emotional) include anxiety, depression, and somatic symptoms, as well as increased vulnerability to trauma exposure and PTSD (Spertus, Yehuda, Wong, Halligan, and Seremetis, 2003). Childhood neglect is strongly associated with substance abuse within the family, as well as substance abuse later in adulthood (Dunn, Tarter, Mezzich, Vanyukov, Kirisci, and Kirillova, 2002). Parents who are addicted to substances are less aware of the activities of their children, including when their children begin to engage in substance abuse (Dunn et al., 2002). These children are less likely to succeed academically, and are more likely to experience poverty and domestic violence in adulthood. A history of childhood emotional and physical neglect is also associated with later adolescent and adult eating disorders, a finding that is deeply troubling given the probability that eating disorders tend to persist throughout the lifespan (Pignatelli, Wampers, Loriedo, Biondi, and Vanderlinden, 2017). These pathology patterns are insidious, unlike the clear onset of symptoms following sexual and physical abuse.

Collectively, cumulative non-sexual abuse and neglect is associated with later development of drug use, suicide attempts, sexually transmitted infections, and risky sexual behavior (Norman, Byambaa, De, Butchart, Scott, and Vos, 2012). Mental illness such as depression is also linked with cumulative psychological maltreatment. Increased rates of deliberate self-harm among young adults are directly associated with these experiences (Gratz and Chapman, 2007). An inability to monitor and regulate difficult emotions that stem from past maltreatment indicates emotional dysregulation. Efforts to regulate distressing emotions may manifest in high sensation seeking behavior; however, this is countered by depressive episodes that then provoke more high-risk behavior such as illicit drug seeking or other self-harm behaviors (Goldstein, Flett, Wekerle, and Wall, 2009; Gratz and Chapman, 2007). Childhood non-sexual abuse and neglect histories also have profound negative effects on health. For example, early onset and increased frequency and severity of migraine and/or disabling severe headaches are associated with emotional abuse (Tietjen et al., 2010). These early experiences directly influence psychological and physiologic dysregulation.

The above findings, although not directly part of the ACE study, demonstrate the same outcome profiles as found in countless ACE studies. For example, in a World Mental Health organization international study, maladaptive family functioning, including family caregiver mental illness and parental violence, were the strongest predictors for adult physical and psychological disorders (Kessler et al., 2010). A large sample drawn from across the United States demonstrated that a higher frequency of adults with four or more ACEs did not complete high school, had unemployment histories, and lived in poverty. The trajectory of long-term consequences is evident in early childhood and these physical, psychological, cognitive, and social deficits continue throughout the lifespan (Green et al., 2017). Adult adversity adds to poor physical and mental health in this population (Metzler, Merrick, Klevens, Ports, and Ford, 2017). The reality that different study methodologies reveal the same negative consequences raises grave concerns and increases the need for effective intervention and treatment programs to protect children and to heal them before they reach adulthood (Norman et al., 2012; Teitjen et al., 2010).

RESILIENCE AND PROTECTIVE FACTORS

Factors that operate as protection from adversity are considered resilience or protective factors (Wilkins et al., 2014). Many children, despite exposure to maltreatment, manifest remarkable resilience, although this is less likely in high-risk environments where exposure to violence and neglect are elevated (Miller-Graff and Howell, 2015). In a sample of severely abused and neglected children, only 22 percent were deemed resilient (McGloin and Widom, 2001). To be considered resilient these children had to demonstrate an absence of psychiatric disorders, stable functioning in schools, and no behavioral difficulties. Ultimately, stable family environments are powerful protective factors (Wilkins et al., 2014). When a child is maltreated, either at home or outside home, parental emotional regulation can increase or decrease childhood symptoms. For example, parents who are able to manage intense feelings of betrayal when they learn of abuse events greatly facilitate optimal healing in their children; whereas, parents who become emotionally dysregulated increase distress in their children (Langevin, Hebert, Allard-Dansereau, and Bernard-Bonnin, 2016).

By increasing community services and resources, including access to mental health care and substance abuse counseling, the risk of community violence decreases (Wilkins et al., 2014). Community and school programs can offer stress management skills that will help reduce escalation of violent behaviors. Greater external supports from parents, teachers, and mentors can decrease the potential to be bullied, rejected, or isolated (Wilkins et al., 2014). Providing and sustaining integrative approaches in communities and social service organizations can strengthen protective factors (Wilkins et al., 2014). When a concerted effort by all members of the community is directed toward decreasing violence, more stability can be nurtured which directly enhances the development of children who are growing up in these neighborhoods. Providing opportunities to cultivate skill mastery and social supports during skill acquisition as well as during stressful times greatly promotes resilience and ameliorates the potential negative consequences of ACEs (Lee, Phinney, Watkins, and Zamorski, 2016). As well, identifying and helping high-risk mothers supports both parents and their children. Intervention programs can increase meaning via expressive arts therapy and trauma-informed care; such programs can greatly reduce the negative consequences of ACEs (Davis, 2010; Grossman, Sorsoli, and Kia-Keating, 2006).

Children also develop coping strategies to enhance resilience. For example, some children cultivate strong relationships with imaginary companions, including when they are placed in foster care homes. Imaginary companions provide positive sources of entertainment, friendship, and social support (Aguiar et al., 2017). Many abused children endorse paranormal experiences and supernatural beliefs; these beliefs and experiences provide a sense of control (Perkins and Allen, 2006). For maltreated children who are more fantasy prone, engaging in imaginative worlds becomes a refuge (Lynn and Rhue, 1988; Taylor et al., 2015). Some of these highly creative children may construct elaborate parascosms that can be cultivated over the course of child development (Taylor et al., 2015). When alternative realities are powerful and meaningful, anxiety diminishes and hopes increase. Children create a positive antidote to the negative experiences endured in their dysfunctional households (Watt et al., 2007).

Despite these protective factors, it remains challenging to alter the trajectory of generational maltreatment behavior, even when high-risk new mothers who have their own abuse history are provided intervention treatment programs (Levey, Gelaye, Bain, Rondon, Borba, Henderson, and Williams, 2017). Intervention programs are essential, with home visitations demonstrating the most significant positive effect; however, much more work is needed in this field. To date, providing interventions starting in pregnancy and continuing throughout the first two years of infant life decreases post-partum depression and promotes better caregiving behavior. Assessing pregnant women for current PTSD also raises awareness about increased risk of prenatal morbidity and obstetric outcomes. For example, pregnant women living in war zones are at very high risk of both PTSD and obstetric complications (Punamaki, Diab, Isosavi, Kuittinen, and Qouta, 2018). As well, many pregnant women with PTSD symptoms have histories of childhood abuse, poverty, lower education levels, and living in higher crime areas (Seng, Low, Sperlich, Ronis, and Liberzon, 2009). Unfortunately, despite greater anxiety about their role as a mother, young mothers with abuse histories tend to avoid seeking help. Consequently, they are at increased risk to be isolated emotionally and physically and to have more difficulty raising their infants and toddlers (Levey et al., 2017).

CONCLUSION

Child maltreatment remains problematic. It is estimated that $124 billion dollars is spent each year on child abuse and neglect, whether it is costs incurred to provide care for minors or the cumulative costs that are incurred over a maltreated child's lifetime (U.S. Department of Health and Human Services, 2015). When factoring in lost productivity, criminal justice services, teen pregnancies, substance abuse, and direct health-care costs this number grows to 5.9 trillion dollars (CAN, 2015; Perryman Group, 2014). The average lifetime cost per maltreated individual is approximately $1,272,900 U.S. dollars. This includes medical costs in childhood and adulthood, child welfare costs, special education needs, and lost productivity (Fang, Brown, Florence, and Mercy, 2012).

When child maltreatment is left untreated, the likelihood of child maltreatment transmitted across generations is strong. Factors such as school dropout, mental illness, and substance abuse all contribute to poor caregiving that is visited onto the next generation of children (CAN, 2015). Increased exposure to child maltreatment increases risk of a complex array of adult disorders such as anxiety, depression, PTSD, substance abuse, conduct disorder, heart disease, obesity, diabetes, metabolic disorders, asthma, smoking related diseases, sleep disorders, premature births, sexually transmitted diseases (CAN, 2015; Miller-Graff and Cheng, 2017), as well as cancer (Fuller-Thomson and Brennenstuhl, 2009). Negative social problems are also associated with increased ACEs, including homelessness, unemployment or unstable employment, academic instability, criminal behavior, prostitution, parenting problems, and interpersonal violence (Miller-Graff and Cheng, 2017; Thompson et al., 2012). Incarcerated violent offenders report extremely high rates of ACEs; experiencing pervasive emotional abuse, impoverishment, and increased contact with child protective services intensified their deviant behavior and may contribute to their lack of empathy, inability to mentalize, emotional labiality, and impulsivity (Asberg and Renk, 2013; Schimmenti, Di Carlo, Passanisi, and Caretti, 2015). Unfortunately, the direct and indirect costs incurred by violent offenders are seldom included in reports on child maltreatment costs. Despite this lack of inclusion, the cumulative effects of ACEs often lead to high utilization of health-care services and a shortened lifespan (CAN, 2015). These deleterious costs (financial, personal, and societal) can be reduced if preventive programs are implemented, including widespread screening for ACEs and integrating treatment programs across settings such as within schools, community projects, health-care programs, and faith-based organizations (CAN, 2015; Evans et al., 2014).

Although the most rigorous reporting is conducted by Child Protective Services, with documentation of investigated and confirmed cases of abuse and neglect listed in the reports, unofficial estimates that are based on national surveys suggest that one in four children experience some form of child maltreatment (Crimes against Children Research Center, 2017). National surveys also indicate that 9–32 percent of women and 5–10 percent of men were victims of assault (sexual and/or non-sexual) during childhood. In early childcare settings, designed to address family-based mental health care, it was estimated that 72 percent of young children had already been exposed to at least one type of traumatic event; these children also had greater behavioral and emotional regulation challenges (Snyder et al., 2012). It is difficult to gather accurate numbers of abuse and neglect cases, in part because people are often reticent to report these incidents or they may normalize or minimize these events (Crimes against Children Research Center, 2017). Statistical studies do suggest that the trend for child abuse and neglect has declined since 2001 (Child Trends Data Bank, 2016); however, identifying cases of maltreatment continues to remain challenging, with many cases remaining unreported. This is even more problematic when attempting to discern the rate and extent of institutional abuse that may still remain hidden (Middleton et al., 2014).

The sobering statistics reported in the U.S. Child Abuse Statistics Report indicates that every ten seconds a child is abused or raped. It also claims that most abusers know the child well, every race and religion has child abuse, and that at least seven children will die each day (murdered or suicide) as a result of abuse (Crimes against Children Research Center, 2017). A similar profile is evidenced internationally with statistical reports claiming at least forty million children are abused each year (Crimes against Children Research Center, 2017). These abuse rates identify the need for significant integrative preventive programs as well as treatment programs. A comprehensive approach is mandatory to effectively alter the long-term consequences of childhood maltreatment (Springer et al., 2003). Unfortunately, conducting widespread screening for childhood adversity experiences may not help the victims without equal efforts to implement trauma-informed care programs among professionals such as law enforcement personnel, educators, and medical providers (Finkelhor, 2017). Programs that strengthen the resources of children and their caregivers may help ameliorate the devastating long-term consequences of cumulative trauma. For example, offering creative play experiences to maltreated children may enhance healing and foster hope and resilience (Dalebroux, Goldstein, and Winner, 2008; Russ and Wallace, 2013). Childhood development is powerfully shaped by all environmental interactions; hopefully positive experiences might counter some of the adversity experiences.

Chapter 7

Attachment

ATTACHMENT THEORY

Attachment forms during repeated interactions between infants and caregivers. These early experiences are embedded into the neurobiology of the infant; *internal working models* of the self, other, and the world are established (Bowlby, 1988). The nature of these relationships influences the development of emotional regulation and relational behaviors. Internalized attachment working models, also known as mental representations, tend to remain relatively stable throughout the lifespan, acting as filters for future relationships and experiences (Bowlby, 1988; Carlson, Sroufe, and Egeland, 2004; Sroufe, Egeland, Carlson, and Collins, 2005; Waters and Waters, 2006). During stressful situations, attachment working models are activated even more; they influence appraisals, behaviors, and beliefs (Mikulincer, Gillath, and Shaver, 2002). Early attachment experiences are also significantly associated with psychopathology vulnerability or resilience (Caspers, Yucuis, Troutman, and Spinks, 2006). Research studies suggest that these attachment representations are often transmitted to the next generation (Carlson et al., 2004; Fleming et al., 2002; Walters, Merrick, Treboux, Crowell, and Albersheim, 2000); however, because attachment representations are shaped via relational interactions with caregivers, changes within these relationships can alter these mental representations. Fundamentally, attachment relationships are both stable and yet malleable (Groh, Fearon, van IJzendoorn, Bakermans-Kranenburg, and Roisman, 2017; Madigan et al., 2006; Weinfield, Whaley, and Egeland, 2004).

During infancy, babies form attachment relationships with their primary caregivers (Bowlby, 1988). These attachment figures may be mothers, fathers, grandparents, nannies, adopted parents, or even older siblings (Sroufe et al., 2005; Stams, Juffer, and van IJzendoorn, 2002). The infant manifests behavioral responses that are unique to each infant-caregiver interaction; hence, the primary caregiver is determined based on the infant's preference during moments of needing safety and security. Other members of the family may be important in their own specific ways but there is always a hierarchical order in attachment preference (Sroufe et al., 2005). Attachment formations are evident across all cultures, including within institutional orphanages and between caregivers and developmentally atypical infants (Tomlinson, Cooper, and Murray, 2005; Zeanah, Smyke, Koga, and Carlson, 2005).

Based on observational and laboratory studies, Mary Ainsworth and her colleagues identified three infant organized attachment strategies that are deployed after separation from a primary caregiving (Ainsworth, Blehar, Waters, and Wall, 1978; Main, 2000). During the Strange Situation Laboratory experiment, infants with a *secure attachment* strategy show signs of distress (protest) during separation and they actively seek direct engagement with the primary caregiver upon reunion. This infant-caregiver relationship provides rapid soothing; hence, securely attached infants are able to quickly recover from distress and once again explore the environment in the presence of the primary caregiver. Maternal sensitive attunement to the infant's needs directly reinforces secure attachment in the infant (Main, 2000). The two other infant organized attachment strategies are the *anxious avoidant* and the *ambivalent-resistant* patterns. Infants who are classified as *avoidant* do not actively seek comfort from their caregiver after brief separations despite the fact that elevated cortisol levels indicate increased stress in the infants (Main, 2000). These infants actually turn away from their caregiver during the reunion and their play prior to separation, during separation, and after the reunion is impoverished. The *ambivalent-resistant* infants exhibit great distress during separation and even more distress during the reunion. They are not soothed by the presence of their caregiver and are not able to explore their environment (Main, 2000).

A fourth infant classification is not considered an organized attachment strategy (Hesse and Main, 2000). This classification is termed *disorganized/ disoriented*. It is marked by brief or prolonged anomalous behaviors that emerge while in the presence of the caregiver. Under moments of distress, the usual organized interactive strategies (secure, avoidant, ambivalent-resistant) between caregiver and infant collapse. A desire to seek or avoid soothing from the caregiver is compromised by disorganized behaviors of approaching and retreating simultaneously. More overt disorganized markers of fear are evident in freeze behavior, apprehension, mistimed and misdirected movements, and overt spatial disorientation and confusion. Infants who are classified as disorganized/disoriented are at increased risk of developmental difficulties (internalizing and externalizing behaviors) and later psychopathology (dissociation, anxiety, depression) (Sroufe et al., 2005).

Attachment formations during infancy are minimally associated with infant temperament, especially for secure and avoidant attachment (Groh, Narayan et al., 2017). Ambivalent-resistant attachment is modestly associated with temperament, perhaps because heightened anxiety and difficulty to be soothed may be genetically inherited, which is then present in infant-caregiver interactions (Groh, Narayan et al., 2017). Child temperament does affect the quality and frequency of interactions between parents and infants/toddlers; however, these interactional needs generally do not influence attachment patterns (Laible, Panfile, and Makariev, 2008). For example, parenting sensitivity, a strong predictor for attachment security, greatly diminishes the negative effects of a difficult temperament, and this is even more pronounced when children enter into elementary school (Stright, Gallagher, and Kelley, 2008). Their attachment security buffers the challenges associated with a difficult temperament.

Assessing early attachment experiences in adults presents many problems; however, the Adult Attachment Interview opens a window into these attachment representations. It was developed based on findings from the Strange Situation Laboratory experiments (Main, 2000). Rather than observing behavioral responses during separation and reunion episodes, the adult classifications are derived from narrative discourse about childhood attachment experiences (Main, Goldwyn, and Hesse, 2003). The attachment mental representations are observed in the form of the narrative and not within the content. Informed by the infant attachment classifications, the adult attachment classifications are based on the states-of-mind revealed during the interview. The secure state-of-mind is also termed the *autonomous state-of-mind*. This narrative discourse is marked by a clear collaborative awareness between the interviewer and the interviewee. There is a sense of openness, balance, humor, compassion, and coherence. The *dismissing* classification resembles infant avoidant attachment behaviors. During the interview, dismissing speakers often provide brief and poorly elaborated answers, with many claiming a lack of memory for childhood events. There is a tendency to portray childhood attachment experiences as positive and yet no memories or contradictory memories are offered as examples. The *preoccupied* speaker resembles the ambivalent-resistant infant attachment classification. Memories of childhood attachment experiences are typically presented in long answers that are filled with angry detail, confusion of self-other pronouns, vague or nonsensical speech, and a loss of awareness of the collaborative relationship with the interviewer. Both dismissing and preoccupied adult state-of-mind patterns lack coherence (Main et al., 2003).

Like the infant disorganized/disoriented classification, adults can be identified with similar disorganization when speaking about past traumatic or loss events (Hesse and Main, 2000). Indices of narrative disorganization/disorientation include lapses of monitoring in reason (i.e., anomalous beliefs, disorientation in space and time), monitoring discourse (i.e., tense confusion, eulogistic tone, long disconnected pauses), or reporting significant behavioral disorganization (i.e., self-injurious behavior or suicide attempt after the loss of a significant other or major traumatic event(s) that involve attachment figures). Adults who are deemed disorganized for trauma or loss events are classified as *Unresolved*. When the disorganization is pervasive and is evident throughout the interview then the individual is described as *Cannot Classify*. These individuals manifest global disorganization; their narrative lacks coherence and collaboration (Hesse, 1996; Main et al., 2003).

In the adult, attachment states-of-mind directly influences behavioral responses and emotional regulation under stress (Main et al., 2003). As described above, secure-autonomous adults describe regret, compassion and openly recognize difficulties encountered during stressful conditions. The two organized but insecure attachment adult classifications are employed under threat conditions, especially threats that are associated with close relationships. Dismissing adults avoid, distance, or minimize the effects of threat (dismissing classification) and preoccupied adults are entangled by thoughts and feelings related to distressing situations. Both dismissing and preoccupied adults are unable to respond effectively (Main et al., 2003).

CHILDHOOD AND ADULT LOSS

The loss of attachment figures during early childhood leads to profound distress in the surviving partner and their children. For example, in a study by Bahm and colleagues (2016), parents who suffered significant loss two years prior to the birth of their offspring directly influenced attachment attentional strategies in their offspring. As young adults, increased mental absorption was evident, a behavioral pattern that was exhibited by their parents during their infancy (Bahm, Duschinsky, and Hesse, 2016). The National Child Traumatic Stress Network, a federally funded organization that provides mental health care for children and families, stated that the two most frequently reported childhood traumatic events were parental loss/separation and domestic violence (Briggs et al., 2013). In this data bank, children with parental loss/separation had greater exposure to three or more traumatic types (59%) and 31 percent were exposed to more than five types. These findings indicate a significant need for increased awareness associated with childhood loss; mental health workers need to provide bereavement support as well as trauma-informed care (Briggs et al., 2013). This need is intensified in children who are abandoned by parents and institutionalized. Attachment difficulties increase with many children diagnosed with an inhibited attachment disorder, a disorder that is associated with persistent social and emotional difficulties (Corval et al., 2017).

In adults, the loss of attachment figures or the loss of their own children is initially associated with intense grief (Albuquerque, Narciso, and Pereira, 2018), especially for individuals with secure or preoccupied attachment formations. Attachment-related avoidance may buffer the pain of loss. By dismissing the importance of the deceased person, adults who are avoidant/dismissing manifest features of resilience to loss (Fraley and Bonanno, 2004). Regardless of attachment orientation, as internalized models of the deceased attachment figure are revised more resolution may emerge (Shear and Shair, 2005). Developing continuing bonds with the deceased may help ease complicated grief (Albuquerque et al., 2018); however, individuals with attachment-preoccupied insecurity often struggle to establish continuing bonds (Stroebe, Schut, and Stroebe, 2005). Although attachment orientation influences bereavement, adults with depression are at increased risk of complicated grief. They struggle to find meaning in loss and feel hopeless in their ability to manage the loss of a close loved one (Bonanno et al., 2002; Bonanno, Wortman, and Nesse, 2004). Adults without a history of depression may also develop depression following the loss of a significant loved one. In studies by Bonanno and colleagues, conditions of loss influence the trajectory of bereavement. For example, unlike the chronic depressed group, the non-depressed group who lost a healthy spouse (or family member) struggled to adjust their pre-loss cognitive beliefs. They had difficulty finding emotional resources. The circumstances surrounding the loss directly influenced their level of distress and depressive symptoms. Both pre-loss depressed individuals and those who suddenly lost healthy family members took substantially longer than the majority of bereaved individuals to find meaning (Bonanno et al., 2002; Bonanno, Wortman et al., 2004). Attachment security may provide some resilience despite some lack of resolution for the loss (Shear and Shair, 2005).

INFANT ATTACHMENT STUDIES

Infant attachment assessment that is based on the Strange Situation Protocol provides reliable attachment classifications. This procedure has been applied in cross-sectional and longitudinal studies and has demonstrated robust attachment stability across the lifespan (Sroufe et al., 2005). Generally, maternal sensitivity is associated with greater attachment security and it tends to persist into adulthood (Schoenmaker et al., 2015). Likewise, maternal insensitivity is associated with increased infant attachment insecurity. Often maternal insensitivity is associated with parental lack of resolution for past loss and/or trauma. In a study that examined refugee parent-child dyads, parental PTSD and unresolved classification on the Adult Attachment Interview was significantly associated with disorganized infant attachment (van Ee, Kleber, Jongmans, Mooren, and Out, 2016). As well, infants that are deemed "failure-to-thrive" are more likely to be classified as disorganized and their mothers more likely to be unresolved for loss or trauma. It is important to note that attachment security is not fully protective. A small percentage of infants who are securely attached are also classified as "failure-to-thrive," which suggests other factors are involved beyond attachment formation (Ward, Lee, and Lipper, 2000). In the above studies, infant disorganization and failure-to-thrive are not associated with parental maltreatment behavior, although child abuse and neglect are strongly associated with infant disorganization (van Ee et al., 2016).

Examining infant attachment behaviors and how they relate to early development adds a unique perspective on normal development, especially the examination of parenting style and attachment patterns. For example, in a study that examined toddler levels of conflict, typical toddler and caregiver engagement involved a high frequency of conflict, with reports ranging between four and fifty-five per hour. Conflict occurred regardless of attachment classification (Laible et al., 2008). Frequency of conflict was associated with child temperament and a capacity to self-regulate. Attachment behaviors directly influenced the quality of the conflict. Securely attached children and mothers engaged in conflict that was marked by a lack of escalation or aggravation. These dyads actively found solutions and compromises, which reduced destructive and aggressive behavior. Insecurely attached toddlers were more aggressive and the dyadic exchange during conflict was more argumentative. Poor self-regulation strategies by both mothers and their toddlers were present (Laible et al., 2008). In another study, attachment insecurity was associated with greater dyadic struggles, and by four years of age children exhibited greater developmental behavioral difficulties. As infants, attachment insecurity was related to parental power assertions, which later resulted in greater resentment and antisocial behavior in the children (Kochanska, Barry, Stellern, and O'Bleness, 2009).

Findings from the Strange Situation procedure demonstrate a strong relationship between infant attachment insecurity and sleep difficulties. Specifically, disorganized infants have lower duration of sleep cycles, shorter periods of uninterrupted sleep, shorter periods of time in bed, and more awakenings (Pennestri et al., 2015). Examining caregivers' level of distress reveals a cyclic pattern of infant difficulties with sleep that intensifies caregiver distress, which further stresses the infant (Pennestri et al., 2015; Simard et al., 2017). The Q-sort offers a different means to measure infant attachment. It is a continuous scoring process that differentiates security via infants actively seeking contact and proximity versus difficulties with contact and proximity (resistance) (Waters and Deane, 1985). Continuous scoring allows more freedom in statistical analyses and resembles findings derived from the Strange Situation Protocol. In a meta-analysis study, continuous scoring yielded results related to infant sleep behaviors (Simard, Chevalier, and Bedard, 2017). Compared to infants with more security, infants with attachment resistance had much greater sleep problems based on sleep quality and quantity. These sleep problems reflect the strained relationships between infants and their caregivers (Simard et al., 2017).

As children move from infancy to early and middle childhood, attachment patterns tend to continue to influence behavior. For example, sleep patterns in toddlers resemble early infancy patterns. Toddlers who are securely attached are able to relax and fall asleep compared to toddlers who are avoidant or ambivalent/resistant (Belanger, Bernier, Simard, Bordeleau, and Carrier, 2015). Maternal sensitivity is one of the strongest predictors for secure attachment stability over time (Bernier, Matte-Gagne, Belanger, and Whipple, 2014; Stams et al., 2002). The trust that is established enables securely attached children to seek parental support during high conflict situations; whereas, avoidant children do not rely on parental support and ambivalent-resistant children seek even more reassurance from parents (Corriveau et al., 2009). Likewise, global maternal insensitivity is a strong predictor of infant disorganized attachment, even more than overt maternal maltreatment behavior. This pattern of maternal insensitivity transcends race and socioeconomic status (Gedaly and Leerkes, 2016). Children with disorganized attachment have increased negative mood and poorer emotion regulation that persists throughout development (Kerns, Abraham, Schlegelmilch, and Morgan, 2007; Weinfield et al., 2004). They also display more externalizing behavioral problems (Wang, Willoughby, Mills-Koonce, and Cox, 2016). A similar profile is found in children classified as ambivalent-resistant (Kerns et al., 2007). These attachment behaviors are even more pronounced when children have insecure attachment formations with both parents compared to children who establish a secure attachment with one parent despite insecurity with the other (Kochansk and Kim, 2013). When examining adolescents, these patterns tend to persist. Adolescents who are classified with disorganized attachment as infants continue to exhibit greater rates of psychopathology and more difficulties in partner relationships, including more partner abuse (Obsuth, Hennighausen, Brumariu, and Lyons-Ruth, 2014).

Insecure attachment is more prevalent in maltreated infants and toddlers; the combination of maltreatment and attachment insecurity increases difficulties during childhood development (Baer and Martinez, 2006). As adults, caregivers who remain unresolved for childhood trauma and loss are more likely to transmit attachment insecurity to their offspring and these children are more likely to manifest behavioral problems in middle childhood and adulthood. This negative pattern emerges even when unresolved parents do not abuse or neglect their children (Zajac and Kobak, 2009). The effect of unresolved states-of-mind in the caregiver accounts for more variance than caregiver depression or dissociation in the transmission of attachment insecurity (Zajac and Kobak, 2009).

FINDINGS FROM ADULT ATTACHMENT INTERVIEW STUDIES

Research studies that use the Adult Attachment Interview (AAI) yield important findings that add to infant attachment findings. The AAI captures states-of-mind regarding attachment experiences that are more likely to endure throughout the lifespan (Main et al., 2003). The AAI provides a lens to categorize attachment states-of-mind; under attachment-related stress individuals may demonstrate an autonomous coherent state-of-mind (secure), dismiss relational stress, intensify it (preoccupied), and/or be resolved/unresolved for past trauma or loss events. Using the AAI provides researchers categorical information regarding attachment classification as well as continuous scores on inferred childhood experiences (maternal and paternal loving, rejecting, neglecting, role reversing, pressure-to-achieve) and specific states-of-mind (idealizing, preoccupied anger, passivity, lack of memory, derogation, degree of resolution for trauma or loss events, coherence of mind, and coherence of discourse). This instrument also enables researchers to determine degree of security as well as categorical secure versus insecure groupings.

A unique feature of the AAI is that it offers a process to determine whether the speaker is resolved or unresolved for past trauma and/or loss experiences. It reveals a collapse in mental processing as evidenced by a lapse in narrative coherence. Determining degree of resolution enriches research findings that examine psychological processing related to trauma or loss. For example, an AAI study demonstrated that individuals classified as unresolved endorsed more paranormal beliefs (Thomson and Jaque, 2014). This finding reinforces models that propose a relationship between conditions of stress and increased paranormal beliefs, even for rational thinkers (Lasikiewicz, 2016). Increased paranormal beliefs are also found in children who are maltreated (Irwin, 1990; Parra, 2006). Correlational studies suggest that belief in spiritual possession is a substantial indicator that trauma-related symptoms are present, especially disorders such as PTSD, depression, somatic complaints, psychosis, and feelings of shame and guilt (Hecker, Barnewitz, Stenmark, and Iversen, 2016). Robust study findings demonstrate that a classification of unresolved mourning is a significant measure to evaluate trauma-related symptoms and beliefs.

The AAI can also reveal mentalizing processes, also known as reflective functioning or metacognition (Bouchard et al., 2008; Main et al., 2003). There is a strong relationship between high reflective functioning and attachment security; this indicates more sensitive caregiving and better mental health (Bouchard et al., 2008). As well, other psychological factors can be assessed to determine their relationship to attachment security/insecurity as measured by the AAI. For example, in a study that examined perceptual processing of emotional stimuli associated with social interactions, dismissing and to a lesser extent, preoccupied individuals attended to signs of distress more than secure individuals (Maier et al., 2005). Insecurely attached individuals must sustain increased vigilance in order to mobilize their respective attachment-related deactivating or hyperactivating coping strategies (Maier et al., 2005). According to computer linguistic analyses (Buchheim and Mergenthaler, 2000) and AAI reliable coders (Main et al., 2003), deactivating responses of dismissing speakers is characterized by the shortest interviews (least words), substantial lack of emotional abstraction, emotionally distancing language, and reduced emotional vulnerability. A higher proportion of emotionally negative words, longest interviews, and greater emotional conflict mark the hyperactivating strategy of the preoccupied speaker. The secure speakers reside in the middle of this continuum. The computer analyses matched the trained attachment interview coders, although the trained coders are able to assess more fine-grained detail that exceeds other forms of analyses (Beijers-bergen, Bakermans-Kranenburg, and van IJzendoorn, 2006).

The AAI analysis can retrospectively capture continuous attachment security versus earned-security (Main et al., 2003; Roisman, Padron, Sroufe, and Egeland, 2002). Continuous-secure-autonomous individuals were raised by parents who provided sensitive caregiving compared to earned-secure individuals who were exposed to high levels of rejection, role reversing, neglect, pressure-to-achieve, and low levels of active loving during infancy or childhood (Roisman, Fortuna, and Holland, 2006; Roisman et al., 2002). An AAI earned-secure classification often results from stable intimate adult relationships, meaningful supportive relationships with others during childhood, or therapeutic relationships during childhood or adulthood (Saunders, Jacobvitz, Zaccagnino, Beverung, and Hazen, 2011). Compared to insecure and continuous-secure individuals, earned-secure individuals tend to spend more time in therapy (Saunders et al., 2011). Despite increased exposure to childhood adversity, earned-secure individuals can shift toward more autonomy and resilience (Main et al., 2003). The capacity to move toward adult security is then transmitted to the offspring during pregnancy and during the early years of childrearing (Roisman et al., 2007; Sexton, Davis, Menke, Raggio, and Muzik, 2017). The earned-secure group is likely to raise children who are securely attached (Phelps, Belsky, and Crnic, 1998; Saunders et al., 2011); however, the effects of their own childhood adversity emerge in later adult pathology. They have a greater bias toward more sadness and difficulties in self-regulation (Caspers et al., 2006; Roisman et al., 2006). In a study that examined substance use patients, those who were deemed earned-secure as well as individuals with insecure attachment classifications (dismissing and preoccupied) had higher rates of substance use. Unlike earned-secure individuals, dismissing individuals were less likely to seek treatment or withdrew from treatment prematurely; this behavior reinforced their internal working model to minimize or withdraw from support (Caspers et al., 2006).

Mothers and caregivers who provide sensitive attunement are often described as providing continuous active loving experiences, which increases attachment security (Main et al., 2002). In a longitudinal study that followed adopted infants into adulthood, maternal sensitivity was the strongest predictor of attachment security and it persisted into adulthood (Schoenmaker et al., 2015). A similar finding was evidenced in parents exposed to ongoing military violence and stressful life events. Parental sensitive attunement ameliorated later development of depression, PTSD, and poor quality of life in their children (Qouta et al., 2007). Despite exposure to childhood trauma, sensitive caregiving can influence resilience (Sexton, Hamilton, McGinnis, Rosenblum, and Muzik, 2015). On the other hand, harsh-intrusive parenting and maltreatment increase rates of insecure attachment (both dismissing and preoccupied classifications) (Brown, Gustafsson, Mills-Koonce, and Cox, 2017; Roisman et al., 2017). For example, childhood sexual and physical abuse are associated with preoccupied states-of-mind (Roisman et al., 2017). In the Roisman et al. study, all maltreated adolescent participants were identified via Department of Childhood Protective Services. These adolescents reported higher frequency of (inferred) negative maternal and paternal experiences (Roisman et al., 2017). Similar findings were found in a longitudinal study that investigated a high-risk sample. In this study, abuse and neglect was associated with an unresolved and preoccupied classification (Raby, Labella, Martin, Carlson, and Roisman, 2017).

The effects of generational transmission of attachment insecurity and maltreatment can readily be assessed when AAI and Strange Situation protocols are concurrently administered to parents and their offspring. Bailey and colleagues (2017) identified clear attachment transmission patterns between mothers and their infants. Specifically, maternal sensitivity and an autonomous state-of-mind determined infant secure attachment, whereas maternal insensitivity and unresolved trauma predicted disorganized infant attachment.

Likewise, dismissing maternal attachment and insensitive caregiving predicted avoidant attachment in infants. All these negative generational transmission patterns were more pronounced in adolescent mothers compared to adult mothers (Bailey, Tarabulsy, Moran, Pederson, and Bento, 2017). The analysis of the AAI based on hostile and helpless states-of-mind also demonstrated a similar transmission pattern. Mothers classified as hostile/helpless have more disrupted mother-infant communication and their infants are more frequently deemed disorganized (Lyons-Ruth, Yellin, Melnick, and Atwood, 2003; Lyons-Ruth, Yellin, Melnick, and Atwood, 2005).

As posited by Hesse and Main (2006), primary caregivers who remain unresolved (disorganized) for past trauma and loss often transmit disorganized attachment behavior to their offspring. For infants, parental disorganization induces a fear response, which increases dissociation that persists into adolescents and adulthood (Carlson, 1998). Multiple studies have demonstrated a relationship between a classification of unresolved mourning and dissociative processes in adults (Thomson and Jaque, 2012b, 2012c, 2014). As well, mothers with disorganized infants have higher rates of unresolved mourning; they were also diagnosed with factitious illness by proxy or Munchhausen syndrome by proxy. These mothers transmitted their own disorganization onto their infants (Adshead and Blueglass, 2005). When differentiating unresolved loss from unresolved trauma and its affects on parenting, unresolved loss was associated with atypical caregiving behaviors (i.e., frightened or frightening behavior) (Ballen, Demers, and Bernier, 2006). Other parental disorganized behaviors are associated with unresolved loss as well. For example, the combination of unresolved loss and childhood sexual abuse increased parental interactions of passivity and withdrawn behaviors; whereas, unresolved loss and a history of physical abuse was associated with increased negative and hostile parenting (Ballen et al., 2006). Collectively, these unresolved mourning behavioral responses negatively influence parent-infant relationships (Hesse and Main, 2006).

AAI analyses can reveal coping strategies related to memory retrieval. For example, dismissing adults engage a deactivating strategy; consequently memory retrieval for emotional childhood events is reduced compared to preoccupied adults who have a hyperactivating strategy and report heightened memories for emotional childhood events (Dykas, Woodhouse, Jones, and Cassidy, 2014). In a study that examined adolescents, an unresolved classification was associated with increased cognitive processing difficulties, including poor attention, working memory, and cognitive efficiency. Difficulties with mind wandering and poor attentional control is associated with unresolved status in adults who experienced childhood trauma (Marcusson-Clavertz, Gusic, Bengtsson, Jacobsen, and Cardena, 2017). These results suggest that a dismissing and/or unresolved classification indicate significant difficulties with memory retrieval and cognitive processing (Dykas et al., 2014; Webster, Hackett, and Joubert, 2009).

Perceptions of social support are also associated with attachment classification. Perceived social support powerfully buffers the negative effects of stress and encourages greater resilience during natural disasters or traumatic events (Arnberg, Hultman, Michel, and Lundin, 2012). Perceived safety is also a significant factor that ameliorates PTSD symptoms (Cai, Ding, Tang, Wu, and Yang, 2014). Secure attachment experiences in childhood operate as relational working models in adulthood; they reinforce positive perceptions related to social support (Main, 2000). When securely attached individuals experience hyperarousal symptoms, they are more likely to approach others for support and to appraise instrumental aid as a source of stress reduction; whereas, dismissing individuals who employ more avoidance and numbing are less likely to draw comfort from others. They continue to perceive threat and danger despite offers of instrumental safety (Cai et al., 2014). Unfortunately, study findings have demonstrated that unresolved women who were sexually abused in childhood have great difficulty with social support; they have a much higher incidence of revictimization by multiple partners in adulthood (Alexander, 2009).

In traumatized population samples, more attachment security is associated with fewer PTSD symptoms (Benoit, Boutillier, Moss, Rousseau, and Brunet, 2010). For example, adult veterans with secure attachment status are more resilient and less likely to suffer PTSD symptoms and substance use disorders compared to those with disorganized, preoccupied, or dismissing attachment (Currier, Holland, and Allen, 2012). Attachment security enabled veterans to maintain or cultivate support systems; they gained emotional stability, conscientiousness, and reduced attachment-related anxiety or avoidance (Clark and Owens, 2012). In a longitudinal study of World War II veterans, those who recalled family cohesion during childhood also recalled greater cohesion in their combat units. Long after the war, they continued to nurture friendships established in childhood and during the war and they had fewer trauma-related symptoms compared to those who did not endorse secure attachment experiences (Nevarez, Yee, and Waldinger, 2017). This secure attachment pattern was found in Israeli mothers and their children who were subjected to ongoing missile attacks (Besser and Neira, 2012). Their resilient responses remained stable over time; resilience factors associated with this group included family adaptability, patterns of communication (ability to discuss ongoing conflict in their daily environment), emotional responsiveness and involvement, and behavioral control. In another Israeli study, securely attached Israeli adolescents who entered the military were able to cope better and cultivate more mature intimacy with others. These positive factors did not override normal adolescent developmental tasks; they were still developing an autonomous adult individuated identity (Scharf, Mayseless, and Kivenson-Baron, 2004). This study finding highlights the potential for optimal individuation as they enter adulthood despite military challenges (Scharf et al., 2004).

Unlike attachment security, insecure attachment classifications are associated with deficits in adaptive resilience. For example, women with a history of childhood abuse have a higher distribution of insecure attachment, which is associated with poor emotion regulation, reduced expectations of social support, and higher rates of psychiatric impairment (Cloitre, Stoval-McClough, Zorbas, and Charuvastra, 2008). In a different sample, women with a history of childhood abuse were more likely to be classified with unresolved attachment, PTSD, and more avoidant trauma-related symptoms (Stovall-McClough and Cloitre, 2006). Across multiple studies, a classification of unresolved mourning and cumulative early childhood abuse coexist (Bailey, Moran, Pederson, 2007; Murphy et al., 2014; Thomson and Jaque, 2017a). These studies demonstrate the power of the AAI to detect the deleterious effects of early abuse and attachment states-of-mind.

AAI assessments also identify emotional and attentional flexibility (Pat-Horenczyk et al., 2017). The hallmark of securely attached individuals is their increased capacity to engage attentional flexibility in order to solve problems under stressful situations (Main, 2000). They are more readily able to explore novel situations and interact with curiosity (Johnston, 1999). They do not minimize distress nor do they exaggerate emotional responses (Main, 2000; Main et al., 2003). Likewise, adults who experienced childhood maltreatment plus parental sensitive care demonstrate more emotional and attentional flexibility despite their early adversity (Sexton et al., 2015). These attachment experiences facilitate an increased capacity to assess and accept support from peers and establish secure adult romantic relationships. Emotional and attentional flexibility operate as protective factors for mental illness; whereas, adults who experience the same type and frequency of childhood maltreatment without secure attachment experiences have substantial rates of psychopathology. They lack the capacity to problem solve and flexibly employ different coping strategies to manage childhood adversities (Collishaw et al., 2007).

Psychopathology is clearly associated with AAI insecure classifications (preoccupied, dismissing, or unresolved). In a sample that investigated mother-infant interactions, 32 percent of women classified as dismissing, 100 percent classified as preoccupied, and 65 percent classified as unresolved also received a psychiatric diagnosis. The lower rate in the unresolved classification was attributed to the secondary secure classification. Women who were unresolved but had an underlying secure attachment were at lower risk of psychiatric disorders (Ward, Lee, and Polan, 2006). A combined classification of unresolved loss and trauma (unresolved mourning) and attachment insecurity was associated with a higher rate of personality disorders (Chiesa, Cirasola, Williams, Nassisi, and Fonagy, 2017; Cirasola, 2017); in particular, schizotypy, borderline (Riggs et al., 2007), paranoid, and avoidant personality disorders (Cirasola, Hillman, Fonagy, and Chiesa, 2017). A high percentage of adolescents in a psychiatric residential setting had a classification of unresolved mourning (59%) or attachment insecurity (51% dismissing and 28% preoccupied) (Wallis and Steele, 2001). A similar attachment distribution was found in a clinical sample of borderline personality disordered patients (Barone, 2003). These high rates suggest that some of the psychiatric struggles may be related to histories of childhood maltreatment that remain unresolved and/or negative attachment experiences that manifest in dismissing or preoccupied attachment patterns (Barone, 2003; Wallis and Steele, 2001). In all these studies, attachment insecurity indicates higher risk of psychiatric distress (Cirasola et al., 2017).

A diagnosis of PTSD is significantly associated with unresolved mourning classification. Likewise, an unresolved classification for trauma strongly predicts pathological dissociation and PTSD (Riggs et al., 2007). In a veteran sample with PTSD, there was a higher rate of unresolved mourning along with more trauma-related anxiety and avoidance/numbing symptoms (Nye et al., 2008; Harari et al., 2009). In a sample of Arabic-speaking refugees with PTSD, 67 percent were classified as unresolved, with only 14 percent classified with secure attachment (Riber, 2016). Likewise, a psychiatric clinical sample had a similar prevalence of unresolved mourning classification (Murphy et al., 2014).

AAI studies that investigate levels of suicidality and attachment insecurity, including unresolved mourning, have yielded mixed findings. For example, suicidal narratives in adolescents demonstrate attachment insecurity and low expectations that a caregiver is available to support or comfort them (Zisk, Abbott, Ewing, Diamond, and Kobak, 2017). In a veteran sample study (Nye et al., 2009), an unresolved mourning classification was actually associated with lower levels of suicidality; whereas, a classification of secure attachment was significantly associated with elevated suicidal ideation (Nye et al., 2009). Contrary to findings that suggest attachment security operates as a protective factor, this study demonstrated the opposite effect (Nye et al., 2009). Further studies need to be conducted to see if these results are replicated.

Difficulties with emotion regulation are identified via the AAI. For example, women with unresolved and/or preoccupied classifications have greater difficulty with emotion regulation and they display increased negative mood (Creasey, 2002). Non-suicidal self-injury behavior is also increased in individuals with preoccupied attachment classifications (Martin, Raby, Labella, and Roisman, 2017). As well, adolescents who are classified as preoccupied manifest the highest level of truancy and disruptive externalizing behavior (Zegers, Schuengel, van IJzendoorn, and Janssens, 2008). In this study, adolescents with a dismissing or autonomous classification behaved with more violence toward staff at the treatment center compared to adolescents who were unresolved for past trauma or loss events. In a study that examined binge eating disorder with a co-morbid overweight factor, the AAI analysis of reflective functioning revealed that this group of eating disordered individuals had lower reflective functioning, a marker of poor emotional regulation (Kuipers, van Loenhout, van der Ark, and Bekker, 2016; Maxwell et al., 2017). Eating disordered patients also had a higher rate of attachment insecurity and unresolved mourning (Kuipers et al., 2016). Based on substantial findings that link attachment insecurity and emotional dysregulation, the need to recognize different attachment strategies during treatment may enhance positive outcomes in residential treatment center programs (Zegers et al., 2008).

Religious beliefs are also influenced by attachment states-of-mind. For example, in a sample of lay Catholics and priests, greater attachment security was associated with a loving God and a stronger faith (Cassibba, Granqvist, Costantini, and Gatto, 2008). Individuals with higher scores on the AAI loving scales tend to regard God as loving; whereas, individuals with inferred negative childhood experiences of role reversing and rejection have increased prevalence rates of New Age spiritual beliefs (Granqvist, Ivarsson, Broberg, and Hagekull, 2007). Likewise, individuals with a classifications in the disorganized unresolved/cannot classify attachment grouping are more likely to endorse more supernatural and paranormal experiences and claim more New Age beliefs (Granqvist et al., 2007; Granqvist, Fransson, and Hagekull, 2009; Granqvist, Hagekull, and Ivasson, 2012; Marcusson-Clavertz et al., 2017; Thomson and Jaque, 2014). Insecure attachment, especially unresolved mourning, is strongly associated with rapid religious conversions. In a study that examined adolescents, the more securely attached group reported a gradual conversion compared to the sudden conversion in the insecurely attached group (Schnitker, Porter, Emmons, and Barrett, 2012). Religious beliefs do add to coping success under stressful situations, especially when faith is strongly endorsed (Schottenbauer et al., 2006). However, these beliefs may also reinforce unresolved mourning including associated behaviors such as absorption, mind wandering, spatial and temporal disorientation, and an inability to name painful events (Marcusson-Clavertz et al., 2017; Thomson and Jaque, 2014).

The Current Relationship Interview (CRI) was developed from the AAI. It examines romantic relationships (Haydon, Collins, Salvatore, Simpson, and Roisman, 2012). Both the AAI and the CRI demonstrate strong influences of early attachment experiences; however, study findings indicate that adult romantic relationships are also influenced by ego resilience that is cultivated during childhood and adolescence (Hayden et al., 2012). Overall, the AAI is a better predictor for core attachment-relevant behaviors that exist across relationship types, although specific romantic relationships may evoke more distress that is not buffered by secure-autonomous classifications on the AAI (Haydon et al., 2012). In general, attachment security is enhanced within secure romantic relationships. In a study, individuals who were secure on both the AAI and the CRI were better able to manage conflict in general, and romantic conflict specifically (Hayden et al., 2012). This was also demonstrated in a study that examined newlywed couples over the course of two years (Crowell, Treboux, and Waters, 2002). AAI attachment classifications generally remained stable (78% of the sample). Change in AAI classification occurred for some members of the dyad who actually moved toward security, and almost half the sample who were initially assessed as unresolved found more resolution for past trauma and loss experiences (Crowell et al., 2002).

SELF-REPORT ATTACHMENT CLASSIFICATIONS AND FINDINGS

Attachment classification originally began with infant behavioral observations. With the introduction of the AAI, adult states-of-mind related to attachment experiences were organized into discrete classifications; these classifications were highly predictive of infant attachment formations with their caregiver (Roisman, 2009). The cost and time demands inherent in AAI studies make this research approach challenging (Waters and Waters, 2006). Implementing self-report measures offers opportunities to examine large population samples more rapidly and less costly. Social psychology researchers who created self-report measures approached the field from the lens of two patterns of attachment, secure and insecure (Steele, Steele, and Murphy, 2009). The introduction of self-report attachment measures was welcomed; however, the association between self-report and interview methodologies in adult samples has remained non-significant (Jacobvitz, Curran, and Moller, 2002; Riggs et al., 2007). Self-report measures yield substantial findings but the relationship to infant attachment classifications is low (Roisman et al., 2007). Although both approaches address attachment, the AAI assesses adult psychological appraisals of attachment experiences; whereas, self-report measures focus on subjective felt security and degree of confidence that others will provide security and support (Roisman, 2009).

Unlike the AAI that follows infant classification status, self-report measures provide slight variations on these four classifications. For example, in some self-report measures, attachment orientations are divided into two major dimensions, avoidance and anxiety (Mikulincer et al., 2002). Some argue that self-report measures are best served to discriminate three groupings: low insecurity (secure), moderate insecurity (avoidant and anxious), and extremely insecure (disorganized) (Stein et al., 2002). Self-report measures also provide two categories of avoidance: a dismissing category that describes individuals who do not value attachment and consequently avoid it and a fearful category that describes individuals who are afraid of intimacy (Bartholomew; 1990). Self-report studies may also collapse findings into four discrete groupings: secure, dismissing, fearful, and anxious (preoccupied) (Bartholomew and Horowitz, 1991). How they are organized yields different results. Despite these differences most self-report attachment studies demonstrate that these are strong measures to predict psychopathology (Stein et al., 2002).

In the *two-group model*, the avoidance orientation is described as a deactivating strategy to protect emotional vulnerability (Mikulincer et al., 2002). This strategy helps reduce emotional distress and is often associated with satisfactory adult romantic relationships (Godbout et al., 2017). Despite seeming success in romantic relationships, avoidance-oriented dismissing adults have great difficulty responding congruently to angry facial expressions. They tend to smile when seeing an angry expression; this strategy may be unconsciously employed as a form of repression of negative feelings (Sonnby-Borgstrom and Jonsson, 2004). The second dimension, anxiety orientation, is a hyperactivating strategy that is marked by a preoccupation of attachment relationships and high anxiety. This strategy propels the individual to move toward others but they are not able to derive a feeling of safety or support (Mikulincer et al., 2002). They perceive the other as unavailable; it intensifies their fears and exaggerates perceptions of threat. Individuals who are attachment anxious are more likely to enter relationships that are violent (Godbout et al., 2017).

The two-group model has yielded important information about rates of PTSD and the effects of childhood adversity. For example, attachment-avoidance and attachment-anxiety are both associated with higher rates of PTSD; however, attachment-anxiety intensifies PTSD symptoms more (Currier, Holland, and Allen, 2012). In a PTSD sample, the hyperactivating strategy of attachment-anxiety elevates intrusive thoughts and re-experiencing of trauma (Ferrajao, Badoud, and Oliveira, 2017). A study that examined separation effects due to wildfires in Australia found that individuals with attachment-anxiety had higher rates of PTSD and depression; whereas, individuals with attachment-avoidance had much lower rates of PTSD and depression (Gallagher et al., 2016). A similar finding in a college sample demonstrated attachment-avoidance operated as a protective factor for PTSD, especially for those who were victims of childhood maltreatment (Sandberg, 2010). On the other hand, attachment-anxiety is a significant factor associated with trauma-related symptoms. Attachment-anxiety was related to secondary traumatization in wives of ex-prisoner of war veterans. There attachment insecurity increased vulnerability to acquire posttraumatic stress symptoms (Lahav, Kanat-Maymon, and Solomon, 2016). In an older adult sample, attachment-anxiety was also strongly associated with chronic PTSD (Ogle, Rubin, and Siegler, 2015). In this study, early childhood trauma and maltreatment directly influenced the severity of PTSD symptoms rather than adult onset traumatic events. This finding suggests that early childhood trauma may have disrupted attachment security and intensified attachment-anxiety. These early experiences heighten vulnerability to PTSD. The older adults also expressed more physical responsiveness when recounting trauma memories. They also struggled with more frequent intrusions of trauma memories and more emotional distress with these intrusions (Ogle et al., 2015).

Under threat, such as political evacuation, attachment-avoidant adults withdrew from social support; whereas, the attachment-anxious adults had higher levels of PTSD and they perceived that social support was inadequate (Besser and Neira, 2012). Anxious hyperactivating individuals have greater PTSD symptoms and they also view traumatic events as more severe and ascribe feelings that the traumatic event deeply influences their sense of identity (Ogle, Rubin, and Siegler, 2016). The hypoactivating strategy of avoidant adults does not increase appraisal severity of the traumatic event nor does it shape their sense of self-identity; however, contrary to other study findings, this study found that they suffer similar rates of PTSD symptoms (Ogle et al., 2016). The anxious (hyperactivating) and avoidant (hypoactivating) adults were less resilient under stressful conditions (Ogle et al., 2016). These coping strategies inhibit an ability to adequately draw support from interpersonal relationships; hence it increases PTSD symptoms (Besser and Neira, 2012). Many trauma survivors describe loneliness years after the event (Itzhaky, Stein, Levin, and Solomon, 2017). This feeling is amplified when trauma survivors determine that important relationships are unfulfilling. This pattern is most prevalent in individuals with insecure attachment-anxiety or attachment-avoidance (Mikulincer et al., 2002; Mikulincer and Shaver, 2007). The inability to derive support from important relationships and feelings of loneliness significantly intensifies PTSD symptoms (Itzhaky et al., 2017) and predicts higher rates of depression and suicidal ideation (Teo et al., 2018).

Self-report measures are included in many studies that examine emotion regulation problems and parenting style. When parents are extremely negligent, children have greater difficulty establishing a sense of autonomy and emotional regulation compared to securely attached children raised by authoritative warm parenting (Karavasikis, Doyle, and Markieqicz, 2003). Authoritative parenting enhances secure attachment as well as promotes greater emotional adjustment strategies during socializing interactions and stressful situations (Doinita and Maria, 2015). In a sample of trauma-exposed veterans, insecurely attached veterans lacked emotion regulation and skills to effectively communicate with others (Cox, Bakker, and Naifeh, 2017). They were unable to use social support as a way to reduce PTSD; rather they avoided managing trauma-related symptoms and remained emotionally dysregulated (Cox et al., 2017). Likewise, in a sample of veterans from Iraq and Afghanistan, individuals with attachment insecurity were more likely to experience PTSD; they had more difficulty managing negative emotions, more emotional instability, greater avoidance of intimate relationships, more fear associated with abandonment, and an excessive need for approval (Clark and Owen, 2012; Currier et al., 2012). Similar findings were found in an adolescent inpatient psychiatric sample (Venta, Hatkevich, Mellick, Vanwoerden, and Sharp, 2017). Insecure attachment negatively compromised social-cognitive abilities and social-emotional regulation. These adolescents were unable to adequately think about, perceive, represent, or understand social relationships. Baseline attachment-anxiety predicted impoverished social-cognitions and increased PTSD symptoms (Venta et al., 2017).

Emotional attention is also influenced by attachment, as assessed by self-report studies. In a study that examined facial expressions during neutral and distressing movie scenes, fearfully attached individuals recognized emotional changes more rapidly than individuals who were secure, anxious or dismissing during neutral scenes but during distressing scenes this group was the slowest to react (Niedenthal, Brauer, Robin, and Innes-Ker, 2002). During both conditions, the dismissing and anxious individuals recognized emotional changes slower than securely attached individuals (Niedenthal et al., 2002). Attachment-anxiety is generally associated with a bias toward feeling more negative affect compared to secure attachment styles; whereas, avoidant attachment styles are associated with minimal emotional responses to positive, negative, or neutral stimuli (Mikulincer and Sheffi, 2000). In general, insecure attachment is associated with a bias toward negative cognitive style and more negative life events (Hankin, 2005). Conversely, security is associated with better creative performance on problem-solving tasks; a marker that suggests heightened access to the creative process (Mikulincer and Sheffi, 2000).

Applying self-report measures when investigating the quality of relationship to a partner and the self are key areas of research. Attachment-avoidance is associated with increased self-criticism, which further adds to deficits in developing adult romantic attachments (Lassri, Luyten, Cohen, and Shahar, 2016). Self-criticism behaviors are marked by elevated self-standards that are accompanied by shame, self-blame, and self-punishment when these standards are not met. Self-criticism is strongly associated with attachment-avoidance; the effort to turn away from attachment needs intensifies a need for independence and control (Mikulincer and Shaver, 2007). Self-criticism also intensifies dissociative processes; it is a psychological strategy to avoid painful feelings (Lassri and Shahar, 2012). Both attachment-avoidance and self-criticism are strongly associated with histories of childhood maltreatment, especially emotional abuse (Lassri et al., 2016). Child efforts to understand emotional abuse influences the construction of negative beliefs about the self. Emotionally abused individuals internalize a self-critical stance and it tends to persist throughout development. The perpetrator's emotional hostility is transformed into self-blame as well as increased distrust for others (Lassri et al., 2016). This pattern diminishes opportunities for successful adult romantic relationships; engaging in such relationships activates more self-blame and distrust. Consequently attachment needs reactivate attachment-avoidance behavior, which reduces opportunities for further emotional abuse. For adults with attachment-anxiety and histories of childhood emotional abuse many enter into revictimizing adult romantic relationships. These relationships usually end, which increases patterns of self-criticism, self-blame, and less trust of others (Lassri et al., 2016; Messman-Moore and Long, 2003). Increased self-criticism is associated with depression. The association between emotional abuse, depression, and insecure attachment is strong, with insecure attachment mediating emotional abuse and later onset depression (Hankin, 2005).

Self-report attachment studies also examine relationships within a work environment (Richards and Schat, 2010). As expected, insecure attachment styles were associated with more workplace difficulties. Specifically, individuals with anxious attachment had increased intention to quit, greater support seeking behaviors at both the instrumental and emotional levels, and lower valuing of the organization. Attachment-avoidant individuals had lower levels of support seeking at both the instrumental and emotional level and they maintained more superficial interactions across all organizational settings. These opposing attachment styles add predictive strength to studies that investigate individual behavioral and emotional responses during job stress and employment stability (Richards and Schat, 2010).

NEUROBIOLOGICAL FINDINGS AND DEVELOPMENTAL ATTACHMENT PATTERNS

Attachment is a biological necessity (Bowlby, 1988). It is informed by primitive structures within the brain; the experience-dependent nature of attachment experiences influences the developing brain of the infant (Schore, 1994). Physiologic studies have demonstrated clear autonomic nervous system patterns. For example, securely attached children acquire greater vagal regulation under stress. This physiologic regulation was evident in a research study that assessed six and seven years old children during exposure to threatening stimuli (Stupica, Brett, Woodhouse, and Cassidy, 2017). Securely attached children display decreased sympathetic arousal, increased parasympathetic activation, and decreased fearful responses during threat stimuli, and this physiologic response was more pronounced when attachment needs were primed (Stupica et al., 2017). Importantly, they were also able to withdraw vagal activation from baseline conditions to meet the physiologic needs of a stressor compared to ambivalent-attached children who demonstrated no vagal withdrawal (Paret, Bailey, Roche, Bureau, and Moran, 2015). Further, ambivalent children manifested less engagement of the parasympathetic branch after a stressor; this provides evidence that they have more difficulty with physiologic regulation (Abtahi and Kerns, 2017). Likewise, in a study that examined child attachment narratives, ambivalent children had higher levels of vagal tone during the narrative, a finding that demonstrates vagal braking to manage distress (Borelli, Somers, West, Coffey, and Shmueli-Goetz, 2016). Study findings demonstrated that dismissing adolescents have diminished ANS responses during the AAI (Beijersbergen, Bakermans-Kranenburg, van IJzendoorn, and Juffer, 2008); however, they also have increased electrodermal activity, a study finding that suggests emotional suppression while they respond to attachment-related questions (Roisman, Tsai, and Chiang, 2004). Contrary to emotional suppression during the attachment interview, the adolescents were unable to regulate arousal during real-time conflict interactions with their attachment figures (Beijersbergen et al., 2008). This finding illustrates their psychophysiological disengagement strategy when reflecting on attachment memories and the diminished capacity to emotionally and physiologically regulate under immediate stressful conditions (Beijersbergen et al., 2008). Unlike dismissing individuals, those who were classified as preoccupied had greater physiologic and emotional intensity while discussing attachment relationships; whereas, individuals classified as securely attached had congruent physiologic and emotional responses relative to the childhood events discussed (Roisman et al., 2004).

Maternal support is translated into optimal neurobiological development (Luby et al., 2012). For example, in a sample that investigated children in South Africa who grew up in poverty and adversity, securely attached children had effective stress system responses as evidenced by their cortisol levels. The children without secure attachment had blunted or elevated cortisol responses; in particular, under stress, boys had blunted cortisol responses and girls had heightened cortisol responses (Fearon et al., 2017). Mothers with insecure attachment representations can be biologically supported via the administration of intranasal oxytocin. Enhancing oxytocin decreases amygdala activation especially while listening to a crying infant. Deactivating maternal stress responses may encourage greater attachment security in their infants (Riem, Bakermans-Kranenburg, and van IJzendoorn, 2016). When primary caregivers provide adequate support, children develop greater hippocampal volume and this persists into later childhood (Luby et al., 2012). Even in children with early onset depression, although to a lesser degree, secure attachment derived from maternal support was associated with greater hippocampal volume. Both non-depressed and depressed groups had significant growth in the hippocampal region compared to children who did not receive maternal support; hippocampal growth is associated with enhanced memory and better stress modulation (Luby et al., 2012).

Attachment experiences are also expressed at the genetic level. These changes are part of epigenetics. Epigenetic alterations occur as a result of DNA methylation; these changes are encoded at the genomic memory level (Lutz et al., 2017). Epigenetic studies still need to be conducted, especially because current findings are often contradictory. For example, novel genes have been associated with attachment disorganization, specifically HDAC1, ZNF675, and BSCD1 (Pappa et al., 2015). These genes influence synaptic transmission. In an earlier study, findings suggested a relationship between DRD2, DRD4, COMT, 5HttlPR, OXTR, and attachment security, insecurity, and disorganization; however, in a recent study no evidence was found for these genetic factors and attachment groupings (Leerkes et al., 2017).

TRAUMA AND LOSS NARRATIVES

Trauma and loss narrative tasks, including the AAI, are invaluable tools to assess degree of resolution for previous trauma and loss experiences. Narrative implies a first-person account of lived experiences (Grysman and Mansfield, 2017). Narratives are openings to understand cognitions or personality and they reveal developmental processes related to the construction of the self and the memories and understandings associated with the self (Grysman and Mansfield, 2017). Narratives are socially shared; they offer opportunities to form meanings of selfhood (Grysman and Mansfield, 2017). Narrative analysis focuses on the manner of what is spoken or written and not on the content that is expressed in the text; it reveals identity and degree of attachment security (Fivush, Booker, and Graci, 2017). Analysis of linguistic usage is essential and provides a powerful means to observe the unconscious state-of-mind of the speaker; however, researchers must not forget that narratives are produced after the actual event consequently they may never accurately capture the intensity of the trauma or loss (Dykas, Woodhouse, Cassidy, and Waters, 2006; Main et al., 2003). Despite this limitation, narratives of trauma and loss often have their own unique linguistic characteristics. For example, sexually abused children speak very differently about stressful events compared to narratives about their sexual abuse. The sexual abuse narratives often lack resolution, causal connections, coherence, elaboration, and structure: factors that compromise the essential need to enhance meaning and provide resolution (Mossige, Jensen, Gulbrandsen, Reichelt, and Tjersland, 2005).

Coherence is a key component in narrative analysis (Main et al., 2003). It is the primary process when examining the speaker's ability to create order in a trauma narrative (Fivish et al., 2017). Creating coherence is ultimately the responsibility of the speaker and involves a dual process of self-reflection and an awareness of the listener (Angere, 2008; Main et al., 2003). It reveals individual identity as well as the simultaneous construction of identity (Kraus, 2006). Coherence includes chronological ordering, context ordering which involves placing an event appropriately in space and time, and thematic coherence that incorporates an ability to elaborate and draw connections between events within the narrative and across narratives over time (Fivish et al., 2017). Conceptual organizational coherence reveals the state-of-mind of the speaker who discloses trauma memories; however, it is also essential to determine the degree of narrative cohesion (connectedness) because this illuminates the degree of fragmentation in trauma narratives (Crespo and Fernandez-Lansac, 2016). Study findings that evaluate coherence and cohesion suggest that very low levels across an interview or narrative indicate a pervasive global collapse and an extremely unintegrated state-of-mind in the speaker (Main et al., 2003; Speranza, Nicolais, Vergano, and Dazzi, 2017).

Beyond coherence and cohesion, some of the key factors examined in trauma narratives include "(a) fragmentation or disorganization, (b) length, (c) emotional and sensory/perceptual aspects, (d) temporal context, and (e) references to the self" (Crespo and Fernandez-Lansac, 2016, p. 150). Disorganization (lack of cohesion and coherence) is evidenced in repetitions, unconscious merging of information, and failure to sustain a connection of thoughts and information (Crespo and Fernandez-Lansac, 2016; Main et al., 2003). This form of narrative is strongly associated with psychological difficulties, anxiety, and dissociative symptoms (Mundorf and Paivio, 2011; O'Kearney, Hunt and Wallace, 2011). Temporal organization/disorganization within the narrative reveals a preoccupation with past trauma and loss, including tense confusion indicating that the past adversity still grips the mind of the speaker/writer (Main et al., 2003; Mundorf and Paivio, 2011).

Memory fragmentation or amnestic gaps of memory may also appear in trauma and loss narratives (Ono, Devilly, and Shum, 2016). Autobiographical memory deficits emerge in the form of difficulty recounting events, overgeneralizing memory recall, or overt lack of memory. Autobiographical memory deficits are strongly associated with PTSD and depression (Ono et al., 2016). Unlike individuals with PTSD, individuals with depression tend to recount more negative events with less memory impairment (Ono et al., 2016). Lack of causal connection of words as well as an inability to incorporate reflective connections (i.e., because, realize) suggest greater trauma-related symptoms, in particular avoidance (O'Kearney et al., 2011). Excessive use of emotional words and a fixation on internal states indicate increased distress (Mundorf and Paivio, 2011). Narratives that describe the violent loss of a significant other are often filled with fragmentation (Currier and Neimeyer, 2006). Impaired memory and an inability to produce a coherent narrative that holds a sense of meaning all reveal the devastating effects of these painful losses. Observing narrative changes over time reveals the grieving process, including the degree of dissociation and disorganization in the speaker (Currier and Neimeyer, 2006).

In a group of individuals with PTSD, their narrative accounts of non-trauma based topics included greater use of singular pronouns, which was indicative of more intrusive re-experiencing (Papini, Yoon, Rubin, Lopez-Castro, and Hien, 2015). Avoidance was manifested in fewer death and trauma word usage, and hyperarousal symptoms were indicated by minimal use of anxiety words (Papini et al., 2015). Genocide testimonials also reveal speaker states-of-mind (Ng, Ahishakiye, Miller, and Meyerowitz, 2015). Survivors of the Rwandan genocide suffered intense loss and horrific violence (rape, torture, mutilation). As well, they witnessed family and friends brutally attacked and murdered. Six years after the genocide, over 80 percent of the survivors had elevated PTSD symptoms (Ng et al., 2015). In the narratives of their genocide experiences, sensory/perceptual descriptions were associated with higher rates of mental health problems, as well as a predictor for PTSD. Descriptions of body states were related to intrusion, hyperarousal, and avoidance symptoms. Sensory processing also manifested unique trauma-related responses; for example, hearing was associated with hyperarousal and touching with avoidance. Increased word count (hyper-verbalizing) was associated with hyperarousal symptoms. As well, tactile language was strongly related to PTSD six years later (Ng et al., 2015). Individuals with trauma histories and a diagnosis of PTSD not only reveal difficulties in how they describe the traumatic event but also include details that capture the content of the event. Without actual content it is not possible to truly assess trauma narratives (Jaeger, Lindblom, Parker-Guilbert, and Zoellner, 2014). In contrast, a positive marker for adaptation in highly traumatized individuals is increased description of sadness; it indicates more emotional processing and less avoidance (Ng et al., 2015). The process of providing a narrative description of traumatic experiences indirectly helps the speaker who provides the narrative as well as offering an opportunity to share experiences about those individuals who did not survive (Ng et al., 2015).

Other specific factors are also identified in trauma and loss narratives. For example, women with PTSD who were abused by their intimate partners recounted memories of the abuse with more present tense verbs, more intrusive memories, a sense of reliving the experience, and significant absorption and immersion during the narrative recounting (Crespo and Fernandez-Lansac, 2016; Fernandez-Lansac and Crespo, 2017). When heightened anxiety was present during the trauma disclosure, more negative emotional tone and less perceptual detail typified these speakers. More "I" pronouns also indicated more PTSD arousal severity, whereas, a decrease in details indicated more PTSD avoidance symptoms (Fernandez-Lansac and Crespo, 2017; Pulverman, Lorenz, and Meston, 2015). Less specificity in recounting autobiographical memories of trauma often indicates mild impairment in memory encoding, possibly as a result of the traumatic event. This memory loss is typical of traumatic events in general and is readily manifested in narrative accounts (Billoux, Voltzenlogel, Telmon, Birmes, and Arbus, 2017). Narratives from individuals exposed to violent traumatic events reveal trauma-related difficulties via reductions in psychological content (less emotional thoughts and desires), and increased themes of vengeance that are directed outwardly or inwardly (Pasupathi, Wainryb, Bourne, and Posada, 2017).

Although slightly different from trauma and loss narratives, depression narratives share some similarities. In a study that examined professional poets and prose writers with depression, more cognitive distortions were embedded into their work compared to their non-depressed counterparts (Thomas and Duke, 2007). Specifically, seven cognitive distortions were evaluated: (1) arbitrary inferences (forming conclusions without supportive evidence), (2) selective abstraction (over-emphasizing some aspects and ignoring other details), (3) overgeneralization (forming a general rule based on a single incident), (4) magnification (distortion or exaggeration of a routine event), (5) minimization (reducing importance of significant event), (6) personalization (assuming personal responsibility for an event), and (7) dichotomous thinking (all or none/black or white thinking) (Wedding, 2000). In this study, depressed poets engaged in the most cognitive distortions in their writing; these distortions revealed the depth of their depression and the severity of their mental illness (Thomas and Duke, 2000).

Despite the fact that psychological distress remains present, the act of expressing adversity via writing or narrative discourse tends to decrease negative symptoms, especially when sufficient time is allotted and an engaged and empathetic listener is present (Hamby, Taylor, Grych, and Banyard, 2016). Certainly, the immediate act of emotional disclosure of trauma is associated with increased negative feelings. For most individuals who share a trauma or loss narrative, while expressing these events, they experience both increased arousal in the sympathetic nervous system and greater pain (Creech, Smith, Grimes, and Meagher, 2011). Compared to individuals without trauma history, individuals with a trauma history tend to exhibit diminished tolerance for pain; they are unable to modulate it. The act of producing trauma narratives exposes their struggle to manage both physical and emotional pain (Creech et al., 2011). Paradoxically, producing trauma narratives ultimately offers opportunities to discover meaning from lived experiences and to understand these experiences with a deeper sense of self-awareness; it is an opportunity for the making of a self as well as the healing of the self (Wang, Song, and Koh, 2017).

CONCLUSION

Attachment representations form during infancy and they often remain stable throughout the lifespan (Sroufe et al., 2005). Internal models of attachment experiences influence emotional regulation, cognitive processing, memory formations, and intimate and working relationships. Attachment stability and the transmission to subsequent generations also influences trauma transmission (Dalgaard, Todd, Daniel, and Montgomery, 2016). Research studies have demonstrated that these attachment representations can be modified, especially within long-term therapeutic relationships (Saunders et al., 2011). Child-parent psychotherapy can modify attachment formations between parents and children; ideally both can gain more attachment security (Guild, Toth, Handley, Rogosch, and Cicchetti, 2017). Although attachment representations can be modified, some attachment classifications are more resistant to change. For example, individuals with strong avoidance tendencies are more likely to reject therapeutic interventions and to disengage in romantic relationships. By entering into these relationships their attachment orientation may be challenged, which is often too distressing for dismissing individuals (Dozier, 1990). A history of trauma and loss that remains unresolved also hampers trust, which often decreases successful interactions with support systems and health-care providers. This lack of trust may ultimately compromise their health status (Green et al., 2012).

Attachment security is strongly associated with enhanced achievement and more creative output (Elliot and Reis, 2003). Secure/autonomous caregivers promote child self-regulation, including an increased ability to explore frightening stimuli without increased fear or trepidation (Coppola, Ponzetti, Aureli, and Vaughn, 2016). The ability to explore attachment-related experiences is clearly evidenced in narrative discourse. Characteristics of attachment representations remain similar in children and adults. The language structure and the degree of coherence reveal attachment security, avoidance/dismissing, ambivalent/preoccupied, and disorganized/unresolved states-of-mind (Kelly, 2015). Attachment status also influences memory retrieval, memory difficulties, attentional processes, mentalization abilities, reflective functioning, and emotional regulatory abilities (Kelly, 2015; Jessee, Mangelsdorf, Wong, Schoppe-Sullivan, and Brown, 2016). Regardless of age, narratives are a powerful means to assess attachment strategies (Kelly, 2015).

The value of understanding attachment strategies is clearly evident; however, the use of this form of analysis for forensic purposes remains questionable (Granqvist et al., 2017). For example, infant disorganized attachment does not equal infant maltreatment. Parental insensitivity as well as strategies to decrease stressful activation (dismissing) does not always reach levels of reportable maltreatment (Granqvist et al., 2017). Understanding attachment strategies does provide strong predictive factors for treatment protocol outcomes as well as expectant difficulties during treatment (Walczak, Esbjorn, and Breinholst, 2017). Attachment theory continues to gain substantial research support and it is built on a solid foundation of empirical evidence. Future studies will continue to yield new insights associated with the biological, psychological, and social need to form secure attachment relationships throughout development.

Chapter 8

Trauma and Loss

CRITERIA FOR A PTSD DIAGNOSIS

According to Criterion A in the DSM-5 PTSD diagnosis, exposure to a traumatic event includes

> (1) Directly experiencing the traumatic event(s); (2) Witnessing, in person, the event(s) as it occurred to others; (3) Learning that the traumatic event(s) occurred to a close family member or close friend. In cases of actual or threatened death of a family member or friend, the event(s) must have been violent or accidental; (4) Experiencing repeated or extreme exposure to aversive details of the traumatic event(s) (e.g., first responders collecting human remains; police officers repeatedly exposed to details of child abuse); (APA, 2013, p. 271)

Criterion A has received robust examination, including prevalence rates for each form of traumatic event. In a national survey sample, Kilpatrick et al. (2013) identified the following **DSM-5 Criterion A** prevalence rates: natural disaster (50.5%), accident/fire (48.3%), exposure to hazardous chemicals (16.7%), combat or warzone exposure (7.8%), physical or sexual assault (53.1%), witness physical/sexual assault (33.2%), witness dead bodies/parts unexpectedly (22.6%), accidental or violent deaths among close friends or family members such as homicide, drunk driving, suicide, drug-overdose, disaster, accident-related deaths (13.5%), threat or injury to family/close friend due to violence/accident/disaster (51.8%), and work/secondary exposure (11.5%).

Once a traumatic event(s) is recognized as meeting PTSD Criterion A then four other symptom criteria must be identified and met (APA, 2013). In Criterion B one or more symptoms must reside within the *re-experiencing* grouping such as intrusive memories of the event, recurring nightmares, flashbacks of the event, intense or prolonged psychological reactivity, and significant physiologic reactivity to an internal or external cue that represents the traumatic event. In Criterion C, the *avoidance* cluster, one or more of the following must be present, whether immediately following the event or a delayed response after the event: avoiding reminders such as memories, thoughts, feelings, situations, people, and/or objects. Two or more *negative alterations in mood and cognition* are required in Criterion D. In this grouping, an inability to remember a portion of the traumatic event due to dissociative amnesia may cause increased distress. Compromised well-being is caused by persistent and intense negative feelings and beliefs about the self, others, or the world, and/or distorted blame about the cause of the traumatic event. Negative emotions (terror, fear, anger, guilt, shame) may persist. A significant loss of interest or participation in previous activities and/or feelings of detachment or estrangement from others may compromise functioning. Lastly, an inability to feel positive emotions (happiness, satisfaction, love for others) may intensify negative alterations in mood and cognition. In Criterion E, two (or more) marked *hyperarousal* symptoms must be present. These include irritable behavior and angry outbursts, reckless or self-destructive behavior, hypervigilance (constant scanning for danger), an exaggerated startle response (especially in non-threatening environments), difficulty concentrating on daily activities, and significant sleep disturbances.

All symptoms in the four clusters must continue to exist for at least one month following the traumatic event, although the symptoms may emerge six or more months later (delayed onset). Another essential factor in PTSD diagnosis is that the symptoms cause significant impairment in functioning across work/school, family, and social settings (APA, 2013). *Dissociative symptoms* of depersonalization (feeling detached from self or existing in a dream state) and derealization (perceptual experience that the world is dreamlike) may also coexist with the other PTSD symptoms. When these symptoms exist the PTSD diagnosis is given a dissociative specifier to account for the dissociative symptom profile (APA, 2013; Elhai et al., 2012). Dissociative symptoms are included in the PTSD diagnosis as a result of solid research evidence that supports the relationship between peritraumatic dissociation, a condition that occurs immediately following a traumatic event and subsequent development of PTSD (Elhai et al., 2012). Some individuals are able to derive initial symptom relief from peritraumatic dissociation; they may experience more initial PTSD symptoms but later report increased rates of post-traumatic growth (McCaslin et al., 2009). Once a diagnosis of PTSD with the dissociation specifier is given trauma symptoms have usually intensified (Gil et al., 2016; McCanlies, Sarkisian, Andrew, Burchfiel, and Violanti, 2017).

Although all criteria must be met to receive a diagnosis, several symptoms tend to dominate the symptom profile. Hyperarousal and detachment symptoms are strongly associated with a diagnosis of PTSD (Holowka, Marx, Kaloupek, and Keane, 2012). Intrusive memories and sleep disturbances, although less frequently reported as factors that cause excessive distress, are consistently identified as variables that increase symptom intensity. Panic attacks and the fear of trauma reminders that will provoke panic attacks also intensify avoidance behavior, which further exacerbates PTSD (Pfaltz, Michael, Meyer, and Wilhelm, 2013). Lastly, many other psychiatric comorbid disorders complicate the trauma-related symptom profile, as well as treatment success (Holowka et al., 2012).

The new World Health Organization's International Classification of Diseases (ICD-11) (WHO, 2017), has decreased the number of categories in PTSD compared to the DSM-5 and the ICD-10. This new revision proposes three core factors: re-experiencing of the traumatic event (upsetting dreams, reliving the trauma, amnesia for the traumatic event), avoidance of thoughts and behaviors related to the traumatic event (avoidance of internal and/or external reminders), and an ongoing sense of threat (hypervigilance, exaggerated startle response). Like the DSM-5, exposure to a traumatic event of a threatening or horrific nature is required and symptoms must persist for several weeks and cause impairment in daily functioning (Hyland, Brewin, and Maercker, 2017; WHO, 2017). This new ICD-11 may alter future prevalence rates according to a study that compared DSM-5, ICD-10, and the proposed ICD-11 PTSD diagnostic criteria (Wisco et al., 2016). The reduction to three criteria may reduce the number of individuals who would receive a diagnosis of PTSD. Changes in the ICD-11 may negatively influence service availability and may diminish clinical attention that currently addresses the full spectrum of symptoms listed in the ICD-10 and DSM-5 (Wisco et al., 2016).

PREVALENCE RATES OF TRAUMA AND PTSD

Rates of traumatic event exposure and a diagnosis of PTSD vary radically between studies. This discrepancy can be observed across multiple studies. For example, Yule (2001) reported that 39.1 percent of the population was exposed to a traumatic event but only 9.2 percent received a diagnosis of PTSD. A similar pattern was observed in children, although they display a different PTSD symptom profile compared to adults (Alisic et al., 2014; Yule, 2001). In a national survey, 89.7 percent of the sample was exposed to a traumatic event, with the greater majority exposed to multiple traumatic events (Kilpatrick et al., 2013). In this survey, 8.3 percent had a lifetime diagnosis of PTSD, whereas, 4.7 percent and 3.8 percent met criteria during the past twelve months and past six months respectively. In the Elhai et al. study, 4.3–7.4 percent were diagnosed with PTSD based on the DSM-IV criteria, with a non-significant decrease in prevalence rates when applying the DSM-5 criteria (Elhai et al., 2012). Perrin et al. (2014) found that PTSD was identified in 5 percent of a trauma-exposed sample. In the Lukaschek et al. study, high exposure rates were reported but only 1.7 percent received a PTSD diagnosis and 8.8 percent had a partial diagnosis (Lukaschek et al., 2013). In a national epidemiology study, 6.4 percent of the sample had PTSD; this sample also had elevated rates of mood, anxiety, substance use disorders, and suicide attempts (Pietrzak, Goldstein, Southwick, and Grant, 2011). When primary care physicians assessed PTSD, a higher percentage was reported, with 23 percent of the patients in an urban care facility receiving a diagnosis of PTSD (Liebschutz et al., 2007).

A diagnosis of PTSD and the persistence of symptoms across time are typically contingent on the type of trauma. For example, participants with a full PTSD diagnosis were exposed to accidents, nonsexual assault by a known assailant, combat/war experiences, life-threatening illnesses, and/or interpersonal conflicts (Lukaschek et al., 2013). Those with partial PTSD were exposed to a slightly different array of traumatic events that included accidents, sexual or nonsexual assaults by a known assailant, life-threatening illness, death of relatives, and/or interpersonal conflicts (Lukaschek et al., 2013). In general, individuals who experience non-intentional traumatic events present with symptom abatement; whereas, intentional trauma-exposed individuals have increased PTSD symptoms (Forbes et al., 2014; Morina Wicherts, Lobbrecht, and Priebe, 2014; Santiago et al., 2013). This pattern is also evident in samples of children and adolescents. For example, 32.9 percent of girls exposed to interpersonal trauma were diagnosed with PTSD, a much higher rate compared to non-intentional trauma exposure (Alisic et al., 2014). Although non-intentional trauma is associated with lower rates of PTSD, individuals who are diagnosed with PTSD-related physical diseases have the least likelihood of PTSD remission. This pattern may be associated with increased difficulties managing comorbid disorders that are related to trauma exposure (Morina et al., 2014).

The trajectory of PTSD symptomatology varies greatly; however, there is a general pattern that exists. Typically, stress symptoms evoked by natural disasters, accidents, assaults, or terrorism general dissipate over time, especially during the first year post-exposure (Birkeland, Hansen, Blix, Solberg, and Heir, 2017). Initially, after one month post-exposure there are more individuals who experience symptoms from non-intentional trauma compared to intentional trauma; however, this pattern rapidly changes after three months, six months, and one-year post-trauma. The intentional trauma category steadily increases from 11.8 percent to 23.3 percent with PTSD. Across five studies, 37.1 percent of individuals exposed to intentional trauma had PTSD, and 39.1 percent of this group had a chronic lifetime course of PTSD (Santiago et al., 2013). Similarly, in a longitudinal study of Vietnam veterans (Magruder et al., 2016), 3.9 percent of frontline veterans and 1.16 percent of non-frontline veterans had PTSD and they continued to suffer PTSD twenty years later. In this study, another 6.5 percent of frontline soldiers and 3.29 percent of non-frontline soldiers developed late onset PTSD. The greater majority who received an initial diagnosis of PTSD had early or late recovery; however, a substantial number first developed PTSD decades after combat exposure (Magruder et al., 2016).

In the survey by Perrin et al. (2014) and Kilpatrick et al. (2013) the majority of individuals who met criteria for DSM-5 PTSD had more than one traumatic event. Each event contributes its own symptom distribution and severity; collectively multiple traumatic events produce an array of trauma-related symptoms. Similar to ACE study findings that suggest four or more childhood adversities are associated with increased pathology, adults who are exposed to four or more traumatic events typically receive a diagnosis of PTSD. They also have greater functional impairment and morbidity (Karam et al., 2013). For example, exposure to a hurricane may activate arousal, re-experiencing, and negative beliefs about the world whereas exposure to physical or sexual assault may intensify symptoms of arousal, avoidance, and negative beliefs about the self. Added together, the individual who experienced both these traumatic events meets the criteria for PTSD even though each traumatic event has a different set of responses and may not fully meet PTSD diagnostic criteria.

As stated above, multiple exposures to traumatic events increase the likelihood of PTSD. According to Kilpatrick et al. (2013), the highest PTSD probability was associated with prior childhood trauma and repeated exposure to interpersonal violence or military combat. In a large sample of military veterans who served after the September 11th World Trade Center attacks, the combination of childhood physical assault and exposure to accidents/disasters significantly increased a diagnosis of PTSD as well as comorbid disorders of depression and substance abuse (Dedert et al., 2009). Increased combat exposure alone did not account for severity of PTSD symptoms; however, the cumulative effects of childhood abuse, adult physical assault, and medical/unexpected death accounted for PTSD severity (Dedert et al., 2009). Given these findings, research investigation should explore PTSD symptoms relative to one or multiple events and how type of trauma event may exacerbate responses to other events. Likewise, it is important to determine whether a new trauma exposure reactivates previous experiences and further compounds PTSD symptoms (Kilpatrick et al., 2013). Collectively, these findings support the dose-effect theory; PTSD is more likely to exist as a result of cumulative exposure (Kilpatrick et al., 2013; Perrin et al., 2014).

LOSS AND BEREAVEMENT

A significant source of complicated grief is the loss of a parent during childhood. Attachment relationships are essential during development and these significant relationships persist throughout the lifespan. Even when adults are no longer dependent on their attachment figures for survival, the loss of a parent increases risk for complicated grief (Nickerson, Bryant, Aderka, Hinton, and Hoffmann, 2013). For children, they are also at increased risk for psychopathology, especially depression (Heim, Shugart, Craighead, and Nemeroff, 2010). When a parent is lost during childhood, the child and surviving parent are both thrown into bereavement; this process may compromise the ability to provide caregiving to the child (Nickerson et al., 2013). Inadequate parenting due to grief reactions increases the child's risk for mood, anxiety, substance use, intermittent explosive disorder, and sometimes PTSD. This pattern is more pronounced when the child is very young. The early death of a parent is associated with adult anxiety, depression, and substance use disorders. These findings demonstrate the importance of attachment figures and that the loss of a parent disrupts attachment processes and healthy development (Nickerson et al., 2013; Heim et al., 2010).

Pregnancy loss can provoke PTSD symptoms, especially when core beliefs are disrupted (Krosch and Shakespeare-Finch, 2017). Typically, bereaved women experience depressed mood, anxiety, irritability, sleep disturbances, disordered eating, as well as an intense longing for the baby. Often these women do not receive the emotional support or understanding that is offered to most bereaved people (Krosch and Shakespeare-Finch, 2017). The majority of people assume that because the baby was never alive in an extrauterine environment, it never really existed; however, for the grieving parents, this baby had a full imaginary future that never transpired (Ayers, Rados, and Balouch, 2015). Approximately 3 percent of women report PTSD after a traumatic birth (Ayers et al., 2015). Factors that increase PTSD symptoms after traumatic births include distrust in medical professionals, lack of social support, and intense fear of childbirth (Dikmen-Yildiz, Ayers, and Phillips, 2018). Mothers who experience stillbirths are equally at risk for trauma-related symptoms and they are more likely to raise disorganized attached infants that are born after the experience of a stillbirth (Hughes, Turton, Hopper, and McGauley, 2001). These mothers exhibit higher levels of depression and intrusive thoughts during pregnancy and their intrusive thoughts persist when their infants are twelve months old (Hughes, Turton, McGauley, and Fonagy, 2006). Likewise, midwives who care for these women are also vulnerable to trauma-related symptoms. Cumulative perinatal traumatic births in the careers of midwives are associated with increased negative worldview beliefs and greater rates of burnout and these symptom rates increase in midwives who also have their own history of childhood adversity (Sheen, Spiby, and Slade, 2015).

Loss due to mass violence is associated with higher rates of persistent grief. This form of loss profoundly disrupts worldview beliefs, undermines a sense of self-efficacy, and intensifies PTSD symptoms (Smith, Abeyta, Hughes, and Jones, 2015). Persistent grief shares some features with PTSD but it is also a separate response. It is a failure to integrate the loss of loved ones and return to daily functioning (Bonanno and Mancini, 2012). The intensity of mass violence increases the likelihood of overwhelming cognitive and emotional processing of loss. The personal loss of a loved one plus the loss in a belief that the world is safe are factors that increase grief and PTSD (Smith et al., 2015). The complexity of this loss is clearly identified in second-generation Holocaust survivors. Even without prior personal direct history of trauma, second-generation offspring reveal limited ability to positively adapt to trauma when they are exposed to it. They are also less likely to cultivate post-traumatic growth states (Dekel, Mandl, and Solomon, 2013).

Suicide is one of the top ten leading causes of death across all age groups and across all countries and cultures (Young et al., 2012). One suicide death typically involves at least six significant others (family and friends) who are directly affected by the death. Often these bereaved individuals struggle alone, they feel misunderstood, and they are often alienated from their social support systems. Family or friends often feel awkward and provide well-meaning advice to bereaved individuals; this often intensifies alienation and discomfort (Feigelman, Jordan, McIntosh, and Feigelman, 2012). Many bereaved individuals feel stigmatized by others (Young et al., 2012). Beliefs about suicide that are driven by religious or cultural values may necessitate that burial rituals take place outside of religious practices. Often suicide-bereaved individuals interpret social responses more negatively, perhaps due to unresolved feelings of guilt or self-blame. Likewise, social constraints may actually exacerbate distress and contribute to feelings of guilt (Groff, Ruzek, Bongar, and Cordova, 2016). Consequently, PTSD and depression may increase via negative social responses and increased avoidance behavior to disclose the loss (Young et al., 2012). PTSD symptoms are heightened by feelings of disbelief, preoccupation about the deceased, ruminating thoughts related to what provoked the suicide, increased anxiety, hypervigilance, withdrawal, and despair. Further, in the aftermath of the loss many suicide-bereaved individuals are themselves at increased risk for suicide. The suicide-bereavement process is typically more complicated and takes much longer than the grieving processes due to other forms of loss (Young et al., 2012).

Loss by homicide also increases the likelihood for complicated grief, depression, anxiety, and PTSD (McDevitt-Murphy, Neimeyer, Burke, Williams, and Lawson, 2012). In violent communities, homicide rates are extremely high. Within these communities there is a strong possibility that complicated grief and trauma-related symptoms will persist years after the homicide, and this pattern is stronger among younger survivors as compared to older adults (McDevitt-Murphy et al., 2012). In general, violent losses by homicide, suicide, or accident intensify grief and PTSD symptoms (Currier, Holland, and Neimeyer, 2006). A sense of unrealness persists; efforts to accept the irreversibility of the loss are challenging for bereaved individuals who lost a loved one in a violent manner (Boelen, de Keijser, and Smid, 2015). Negative feelings of self, other, and the world are pronounced which intensifies avoidance behavior, as well as symptoms of anxiety and depression. Catastrophic fears often dominate the thoughts of these bereaved individuals. Compared to bereaved individuals whose loss was due to non-violent factors, distress associated with images of violence and the irreversible loss caused by these acts intensifies both the grieving process and recovery from the traumatic event (Boelen et al., 2015; Currier et al., 2006).

SEXUAL ASSAULT AND PREVALENCE RATES

Perrin et al. (2014) found that individuals with sexual assault histories have increased risk for PTSD, followed by factors such as preexisting mental illness, substance abuse, personality disorders, and insufficient coping strategies. Sexual assault occurs in approximately 13 percent to 26 percent of women in the United States. Approximately half of these women develop PTSD following rape (New et al., 2009). This is even more pronounced when the assaults are aggressive and extremely violent (Weiss et al., 2017). This statistic is even higher for women in South Africa, with over 40 percent of women raped in their lifetime (Mgoqi-Mbalo, Zhang, and Ntuli, 2017). For those women who were raped and yet did not develop PTSD, underlying resilience factors ensured non-PTSD symptom responses (Mgoqi et al., 2017). Positive adaptation was associated with physiologic, social, and/or psychological variables that alter chronic stress response signaling. Unfortunately, the PTSD group faired much worse. The rape was usually more severe (choked, punched/kicked, use of weapon), they lacked sufficient social support, and they often struggled with physical and psychological symptoms (depression, anxiety) for years post-exposure (Mgoqi-Mbalo et al., 2017; New et al., 2009; Ponce-Garcia, Madewell, and Brown, 2016).

Both male and female sexual assault victims manifest similar patterns of trauma-related symptoms and comorbid disorders such as adverse health, increased anxiety, and depression (Millegan, Wang, LeardMann, Miletich, and Street, 2016). Not only do they have increased trauma-related symptoms but they also have poorer sexual self-esteem and they are more vulnerable to subsequent sexual assault victimization (Krahe and Berger, 2017). Transgender (gender non-conforming) individuals report even higher incidents of sexual assault compared to cisgender (male/female) individuals and they also suffer high rates of PTSD symptoms (Lindsay et al., 2016). When alcohol use by the victims and perpetrators is part of the violent sexual assault, more self-blame and negative social reactions intensify PTSD symptoms. These factors complicate treatment as well as increase PTSD severity (Peter-Hagene and Ullman, 2015).

INTERPERSONAL VIOLENCE AND PREVALENCE RATES

Similar to sexual abuse and assault, interpersonal (and community) violence has devastating effects on the victims as well as the perpetrators (Kuijpers, van der Knaap, and Winkel, 2012; Okuda et al., 2015). Both victims and perpetrators often struggle with similar disorders (depression, anxiety, personality disorders, substance use), as well as similar early abuse histories (Kessler et al., 2001; Kessler, Molnar, Feurer, and Appelbaum, 2010). Male perpetrators are usually associated with low income and younger age, whereas, female perpetrators typically have a long history of victimization (Okuda et al., 2015). Both genders experience increased adverse childhood experiences, low levels of social support, and alcohol abuse. Personality disorders such as borderline, histrionic, dependent, and narcissistic are associated with increased levels of interpersonal violence. These personality disorders are generally marked by increased negative affect, poor emotional regulation, and poor interpersonal communication skills. Patterns of intrusive memories, emotional numbing, and avoidance symptoms often occur, which have deleterious effects on parent/child, marital, and family dynamics. These responses diminish responsiveness within the family, which further exacerbates violent interpersonal incidents (Birkley, Eckhardt, and Dykstra, 2016).

Interpersonal violence profoundly harms individuals, families, and society. Decreasing victimization and perpetration will greatly enhance well-being across all levels (Okuda et al., 2015). The primary source of adult interpersonal (and community) violence is violent behavior against children (Nandi et al., 2017). The intergenerational transmission of violence is a strong factor in PTSD, depression, and appetitive aggression (proactive violence associated with thrill, appeal, or fascination) (Nandi et al., 2017). Victims and perpetrators often trade roles repeatedly, which increases the likelihood that interpersonal violence will persist (Kuijpers et al., 2012). Efforts to avoid distressing painful feelings often include emotional avoidance, which intensifies emotional dysregulation, and recurrent violence (Fiorillo, Papa, and Follette, 2013). A lack of safety and increased threat all increase PTSD symptoms, whereas, providing emotion regulation skill training may diminish future interpersonal violence.

NATURAL DISASTERS

Natural disasters are increasing in number worldwide as global warming accelerates (U.S. Global Change Research Program, 2016). In 2015, about 150 major natural disasters occurred worldwide (Huber, 2015). Children and adolescents suffer the most during these events with estimates that 100 million children are exposed to a natural disaster each year (flood, hurricane, tornado, wildfires, drought) (United Nations Office for Disaster Risk Reduction, 2011). One of the major factors associated with trauma-related disorders involves disruptions in functioning such as loss of a home, community, and daily routine. The loss of functioning strongly influences subjective negative perceptions related to natural disasters regardless of the severity of the disaster (Hizli, Taskintuna, Isikli, Kilic, and Zieli, 2009). In general, older children suffer more trauma-related symptoms after a disaster, in part because they are more cognitively mature and have greater ability to understand the severity and consequences of the disaster (Chen and Wu, 2017). Adolescents manifest a unique response that reflects their normative developmental stage; natural disasters are experienced as an assault on their self, especially a loss of personal integrity and control (Weems, Russell, Neill, Berman, and Scott, 2016). They suffer existential anxiety regarding human mortality and the awareness that they fundamental lack control over their destiny. In an adolescent population, natural disasters intensify existential anxiety, which increases levels of PTSD and depression (Weems et al., 2016).

In a meta-analysis study conducted by Lai and colleagues (2017), children exposed to natural disasters were grouped into three trajectories: (1) resilience, (2) recovery, and (3) chronic (Lai, Lewis, Livings, La Greca, and Esnard, 2017). By clustering children into three trajectories clearer symptom profiles are identified compared to evaluating the average symptom profile across the entire sample. The resilience group was the largest group, followed by the recovery group, who manifested symptoms immediately following the natural disaster but then they returned to baseline levels of functioning (Lai et al., 2017). Those in the resilient group tended to suffer less loss and they had more remote exposure to the natural disaster (Chen and Wu, 2017). The chronic group was the smallest; factors that accounted for this chronic trajectory included female gender, greater disaster exposure, negative coping strategies, and lack of social support. Less than 5 percent of the sample was classified in the delayed chronic group; however, these children were initially evaluated with sub-threshold PTSD symptoms. Given the time markers used to evaluate children exposed to a natural disaster, a different pattern may operate, especially if children were evaluated several weeks after the disaster. Their symptoms may have intensified to clinical levels before they resolved (Lai et al., 2017). It is important to note that most children remained in the group in which they were initially placed based on immediate aftermath symptoms; although a small proportion of the children manifested either post-traumatic growth or greater difficulties (Chen and Wu, 2017).

Natural disaster exposure that is compounded by previous experiences of mass terrorist events can increase the likelihood of PTSD and major depression (Bromet et al., 2017). This was found in a study that examined individuals who directly experienced the terrorist attack on the World Trade Center and years later were in the path of Hurricane Sandy (Bromet et al., 2017; Lowe, Sampson, Gruebner, and Galea, 2016). More than 100 lives were lost and 100,000 homes were destroyed by this hurricane; specific factors that increased psychopathology included extensive damage to the home and possessions, extreme concern about gasoline shortages (Bromet et al., 2017), and unemployment (Lowe et al., 2016). The increased prevalence of psychopathology in this group of trauma survivors illustrates the *stress sensitization theory*; it postulates that accrued trauma exposure increases vulnerability to trauma-related symptoms (Kessler et al., 2012).

TERRORIST ATTACKS

Exposure to terrorism is a growing form of trauma with its own unique set of horrific consequences (Melinder, Augusti, Matre, and Endestad, 2015). The indiscriminate killing and wounding of innocent people shocks close loved ones as well as the society at large; in its wake many victims and bystanders suffer PTSD, depression, and deficits in cognitive processing (Blanchard, Rowell, Kuhn, Rogers, and Wittrock, 2005). The horror of these events is even worse when children are targeted; the surviving children suffer protracted psychological and physiologic symptoms, as well as diminished achievement in school and everyday activities (Melinder et al., 2015). In a sample of children and adolescents who were directly exposed to the World Trade Center attack, approximately 10.5 percent suffered severe trauma-related symptoms. Milder disturbances were found in approximately 40 percent of the sample; a finding that indicates that many children recovered from the effects of this mass trauma despite some lingering trauma symptoms (Guffanti et al., 2016).

The dose effect of mass violence directly influences trauma-related responses; factors such as media exposure and learning about details from others add to the dose response (Wilson, 2014). The dose response is also based on prior exposure to traumatic events and emotion regulation abilities (Orcutt, Bonanno, Hannan, and Miron, 2014). For example, the dose response can be magnified when children and their mothers are subjected to ongoing violence such as continual rocket attack (Pat-Horenczyk et al., 2017). In the Pat-Horenczyk et al. study, many mothers and their children demonstrated resilience; however, a significant proportion manifested high chronic clinical distress. In this study, PTSD in mothers strongly predicted PTSD in their children. Due to increased distress and fear responses in the mothers they were unable to provide sensitive caregiving required to create secure attachment in their children (Pat-Horenczyk et al., 2017). Following mass violence, many survivors struggle with feelings of shame and guilt (Aakvaag, Thoresen, Wentzel-Larsen, Roysamb, and Dyb, 2017). They replay possibilities related to how they might have averted the situation. When survivors suffer intense feelings of shame (global devaluing of the self) and guilt (regret about certain behaviors), PTSD symptoms tend to persist. These emotions are psychologically painful which may intensify PTSD symptoms. In general, individuals with chronic PTSD have greater direct shooting exposure as well as more avoidant coping strategies and poorer emotional regulation prior to the pre-shooting event (Orcutt et al., 2014).

The combination of multiple factors such as prior trauma exposure, emotional responses, and emotional regulation all contribute to chronic trauma-related symptoms. This was evidenced in a longitudinal study that examined World Trade Center survivors. A decade after the World Trade Center attacks, 13.7 percent of the male survivors and 24.1 percent of female survivors still had PTSD (Bowler et al., 2017). Despite these different gender prevalence rates, gender was not a predictive factor in a study conducted by Bowler and colleagues (2017). Factors that predicted chronic PTSD included being younger at the time of the attack, unemployment during the course of the ten years post-trauma, less education, higher direct exposure during the attack, less social support, and an inability to receive mental health treatment all increased the probability of sustaining PTSD. Some of the reasons cited for not seeking treatment included males opting to manage their own symptoms and females lacking sufficient funds to afford mental health care

(Bowler et al., 2017). A similar prevalence rate (16.1%) for chronic PTSD was found in World Trade Center responders; among this group all had functional impairments (Clouston, Guralnik, Kotov, Bromet, and Luft, 2017). Functional impairments include slowed walking, difficulties getting out of a chair, and difficulty maintaining balance. These are indicators of aging and are also associated with neurological disorders, cardiovascular disorders, diabetes, and cognitive decline. Sadly, the World Trade Center responders with PTSD appear to be aging faster than their peers (Clouston et al., 2017). These findings gathered from the World Trade Center Health Registry offer a complex array of interacting factors that sustain PTSD; these factors continue to increase risk and diminish well-being a decade after the event (Bowler et al., 2017; Clouston et al., 2017).

In general, exposure to terror attacks has devastating effects immediately after the event, with many continuing to suffer years after the event. Trauma-related symptoms that persist include sleep disturbances and somatic complaints (Gronli et al., 2017; Bugge et al., 2017). Surprisingly, in the Bugge et al. study (2017), non-injured survivors suffered more somatic complaints compared to their hospitalized injured counterparts, a finding that may indicate lack of trauma-related treatment for these non-injured victims (Bugge et al., 2017). A similar result was found with students who experienced mass murder on their campuses. Compared to students who perceived that they had resources to draw upon, students who perceived a loss of resources such as no access to medical or mental health services experienced more distress, especially if they had previous histories of trauma and depression (Felix, Dowdy, and Green, 2018).

FORCED RESETTLEMENT, POLITICAL IMPRISONMENT, AND VIOLENT ENVIRONMENTS

Trauma victims who are forced to re-settle are often at increased risk for PTSD. The loss of personal resources (financial, home, community) intensifies symptoms of depression, hopelessness, and helplessness (Hall et al., 2008). Terrorist activities that necessitate relocation intensify loss experiences. Not only are external personal resources lost but also these victims experience intense loss of faith in human goodness; their belief that humans coexist with a set of shared values is challenged. This was evident in multiple studies that examined victims relocated in Palestine and Israel (Hall et al., 2008). As well, responders to the September 11th World Trade Center terrorist attacks fared much worse when they lost jobs, homes, and friends/family members. Not only were they exposed to a life-threatening event, they also had further adverse life events such as divorce, event-related job losses, and illnesses associated with recovery work. Even a decade later, many struggled with unexpected life adversity that exacerbated their PTSD symptoms (Maslow et al., 2015). These cumulative losses, especially for older victims, intensify PTSD duration and the potential for recovery (Hall et al., 2008; Hobfoll, Canetti-Nisim, and Johnson, 2006).

Social capital describes individual investment, access to resources, and the utilization of these resources; social capital is strongly associated with connections to family, friends, and community. Forced relocation disrupts social capital; a sense of belonging is lost which intensifies alienation and social estrangement (Lin, 2001). Greater loneliness and being disenfranchised from the norms of the community ultimately lead to greater PTSD symptoms. These conditions were fully demonstrated in the forced relocation from Gush Katif in Israel (Dekel and Tuval-Mashiach, 2012). These people lost their daily life routine and family networks. They lost homes, jobs, and infrastructure. Their values and beliefs were threatened and the expression of anger was rendered ineffectual. In this group, once they were relocated the formation of new attachments slowly emerged, although recovery never reached pre-relocation connectiveness (Dekel and Tuval-Mashiach, 2012). This pattern is even worse in the American Indian population who reside on government protected reservation lands. Even after a lifetime of relocation, a substantially larger prevalence rate of PTSD exists. Compared to a lifetime prevalence of PTSD in 7 to 8 percent of the population in the United States (Elhai et al., 2012), 28.3 percent of indigenous people who reside on reservations have chronic PTSD (Beals et al., 2013).

Living within a country or community that is fraught with violence and political/military occupation has devastating effects. Palestinian communities have struggled under these conditions for over sixty years (Hobfoll, Hall, and Canetti, 2012). The negative cumulative traumatic effects for the Palestinian people are evidenced in their living conditions; they are overcrowded with poor health services. There is a high rate of poor health status, increased psychological distress, and 10 percent of the children have stunted growth. A similar decline in physical and psychological health is found in the Bedouin veterans of the Israeli defense force (Caspi, Saroff, Suleiman, and Klein, 2008). In a study that examined war-affected children, children who were highly exposed to trauma manifested multiple symptoms, including PTSD and depression, and these symptoms remained stable and severe (Kangaslampi, Puanmaki, Qouta, Diab, and Peltonen, 2016). Mass casualty studies reinforce the need for interventions such as providing a sense of self and community via connectedness and safety and helping install hope (Hobfoll et al., 2007; Hobfoll et al., 2012). Ultimately, encouraging social support enhances community healing and builds trust and a sense of belonging, whereas, deterioration of social support intensifies psychological and physical disease

(Kaniasty, 2012). Unfortunately, psychological distress can actually erode social support that may have previously been available. Traumatized victims need more social support but their distress may alienate those who are trying to help (Shallcross, Aribisi, Polusny, Kramer, and Erbes, 2016).

The act of torture is another form of violence that is inflicted on individuals and their communities. Throughout the world, acts of torture are perpetrated on civilians, prisoners of war, or within organized groups such as the military, gangs, cults, etc. International agreement on the definition of torture includes "intentionally inflicting severe pain or suffering on another for the purposes such as obtaining information or confession, or punishing, intimidating or coercing someone" (Amnesty International, 2014, p. 8). To be categorized as torture, the perpetrator must have some form of official approval or be in a position of authority. Any form of torture is considered illegal under the Geneva Conventions and the Convention of Crime; however, torture often persists despite these international laws (Amnesty International, 2014). Although it is impossible to gather accurate statistics, systematic torture is practiced in at least three quarters of the countries in the world and sporadically in the majority of countries (Amnesty International, 2014). The psychological effect of torture persists long after the torture stops and is frequently transmitted to the next generation (Campbell, 2007). Treating the victims and their families is challenging; they require medical and mental health services as well as legal aid services. Because the nature of torture is often culturally rooted it also requires greater sensitivity from health care workers, especially if they are unfamiliar with the cultural nature of torture (Campbell, 2007). The negative effects of torture strongly predict PTSD and depression (Steel et al., 2009). The horror of torture and the mental illnesses that follow frequently extend beyond the bounds of individuals and families; entire communities and societies are influenced by these horrendous acts (Campbell, 2007).

When refugees flee from violence and political upheaval they often arrive traumatized and overwhelmed (Johnson and Thompson, 2008; Idemudia, 2017). This population is the most vulnerable to torture and assault because they lack protection from any government (Campbell, 2007). Many of these refugees have suffered torture, including rape and sexual assault (men and women equally), witnessing family members being tortured, as well as suffering burns, threats, and deprivation (Lerner, Bonanno, Keatley, Joscelyne, and Keller, 2016). Generally, refugees have experienced cumulative trauma in their country of origin, during their migration to another country, and post-arrival in their new country; they often arrive with symptoms of PTSD and depression (Nickerson, Schick, Schnyder, Bryant, and Morina, 2017; Rasmussen, Crager, Baser, Chu, and Gany, 2012). As was evident in a study that examined Ivorian refugees, two years after the sociopolitical crisis, 90 percent of the sample had clinical levels of PTSD, poor quality of life, and increased somatic symptoms (Kounou et al., 2017). In a study that examined gender differences in refugees from Iraq, Iran, and Sri Lanka, females experienced more PTSD and anxiety symptoms in response to interpersonal violence; whereas, males struggled with PTSD, anxiety, and depression associated with non-interpersonal trauma exposure such as lack of food, water, health care access, and being close to dying (Haldane and Nickerson, 2016). This gender pattern may be related to cultural and social-role norms. The cultural values of these refugees require that the male's duty is to function as the head of the household and to care for his family; failure to do so intensifies trauma-related symptoms (Haldane and Nickerson, 2016).

Refugee children are frequently exposed to forced displacement, traumatic loss, bereavement, separation, and community/domestic violence (Betancourt et al., 2012). They have high rates of PTSD, anxiety, somatization, dissociative symptoms, phobic disorders, and traumatic grief (Betancourt et al., 2012, 2017). This pattern is even more pronounced when child refugees flee unaccompanied by an adult. They often experience the loss of a family member or friend while fleeing; not surprisingly, there is a high prevalence of PTSD in these unaccompanied children (Pfeiffer and Goldbeck, 2017). Refugee children also have greater academic problems and behavioral difficulties but they do not have increased risk for criminal behavior or substance use (Betancourt et al., 2012, 2017). These children present with a complex trauma profile and require substantial medical and mental health support; however, this support is often in short supply. A multipronged intervention is needed at the community, family, school, and peer support level (Betancnourt et al., 2012). Including cultural healing practices to these displaced children and their families may help ameliorate their high PTSD symptoms. Dancing, prayers, and other indigenous rituals may reduce somatic symptoms and psychological distress (Kounou et al., 2017).

During the post-migration phase, refugee populations often struggle during the process of seeking legal documentation. They often have intense fears of deportation during the process, along with struggles during the acculturation phase (Betancourt et al., 2017). They are at high risk for suicidal ideation or suicidal actions during the post-migration phase (Lerner et al., 2016). A loss of self often follows when the refugees are not able to adequately protect themselves or their families once they have migrated to their new country (Haldane and Nickerson, 2016). Border guards and police officers further traumatize many of these refugees. For example, many Zimbabwean refugees that arrived in South Africa reported rape and sexual harassment. Many suffered insomnia, poverty, homelessness, disruptions in family life, sexual and physical abuse, sociocultural disorientation, anxiety, and PTSD (Idemudia, 2017).

Likewise, detention and deportation practices intensify trauma-related symptoms and increase family distress (Rojas-Flores, Clements, Koo, and London, 2017). Many children born to immigrants in the United States have parents who are undocumented. Forced parent-child separation increases distress in children; they manifest more physical and mental health disorders as well as poorer academic achievement (Finkelhor, Ormrod, and Turner, 2009). Children of detained or deported parents suffer high rates of PTSD, along with increased poverty and loss of family support (Rojas-Flores et al., 2017). Families that live with the threat of deportation often reside in high-risk neighborhoods (Garcini et al., 2017). They struggle with material deprivation, confinement/extortion, bodily injury, and witnessing loved ones injured. Many traumatic experiences such as domestic violence and assault (sexual and nonsexual) are not reported because of fear of deportation. They live with elevated distress and greater rates of PTSD (Garcini et al., 2017).

Worldwide, high rates of individuals are political prisoners, and this rate remains stable overtime (McNeely et al., 2015). Recently released political prisoners manifest greater trauma-related symptoms; however, most appear to recover relatively quickly and do not present differently from non-imprisoned men. A closer examination reveals that trauma-related stress does remain present despite outward functional success. Examining the effects of physical, emotional, and sexual abuse while imprisoned may yield insight beyond evaluating post-release functioning such as successes associated with return to family, community, and employment (McNeely et al., 2015). For example, in a longitudinal study, prisoner of war veterans exhibited persistent dissociative processing and intrusive memories. These veterans struggled with memories of torture, humiliation, and deprivation while imprisoned and the dissociative processing to numb and distance from these memories generalized across all aspects of their life (Zerach, Greene, Ginzburg, and Solomon, 2014). Prisoner of war veterans also experience profound loneliness, largely due to feelings that their experiences are not readily understood or shared by others. They feel isolated experientially and are unable to communicate the depth of their psychic pain. These factors intensify psychological loneliness (Stein and Tuval-Mashiach, 2015).

SYMPTOM PATTERNS AND PERSISTENCE

Beyond high exposure rates (Birkeland et al., 2017), including exposure to past and present intentional/assaultive violence (Gul and Karanci, 2017), studies have demonstrated consistent factors associated with chronic PTSD symptoms. For example, a combination of factors such as female gender, low social support, and high neuroticism tend to predict PTSD chronicity (Birkeland et al., 2017; Ozer, Best, Lipsey, and Weiss, 2003). Low social support has been repeatedly identified as a factor that increases both PTSD and depression after natural disasters such as tornadoes (Paul et al., 2015). Along with low social support, the profound experience of betrayal by a caregiver who fails to protect children from harm intensifies trauma-related symptoms as well as promotes self-blame (Babcock and DePrince, 2012). Self-blame operates as a way to feel control in situations when the child is rendered helpless, such as during sexual or physical abuse. This self-blame strategy often persists into adulthood such as during interpersonal violent assaults (Babcock and DePrince, 2012). Although most factors are consistently associated with increased risk, contradictory study findings examining the personality trait of neuroticism suggests that, as a single factor, it is not a trait that intensifies PTSD (Engelhard, van den Hout, and Lommen, 2009).

Gender is a complex factor that influences PTSD severity, chronicity, and symptom patterns (Wolf et al., 2018). Female gender significantly increases the likelihood of chronic PTSD (Birkeland et al., 2017; Elhai et al., 2012; Kilpatrick et al., 2013; Lai et al., 2017; Lind et al., 2017; Perrin et al., 2014; Pietrzak et al., 2011). This prevalence pattern is also evident in children and adolescents (Alisic et al., 2014), although gender effects do differ across development and based on trauma type. For example, young boys between one to five years of age have higher rates of victimization; whereas, girls between eleven and seventeen have higher rates (OVC, 2017). When investigating the effects of sexual assault, more males manifest trauma-related symptoms and females manifest more sexual distress (Ruiz, 2016). Compared to males, victimized females appraise events in general, and safety specifically, as more negative, which intensifies PTSD symptoms, especially when cumulative trauma is accounted for in the assessment (Kucharska, 2017). This negative appraisal may be related to increased exposure to violence in females as well as almost double the prevalence rate for PTSD (Padmanabhanunni, Campell, and Pretorious, 2017). Males tend to dampen their bias toward negative appraisal by employing more emotional numbing as well as increased substance use (Galatzer-Levy, Nickerson, Litz, and Marmar, 2013). Transgender individuals experience more sexual assault as well as more PTSD symptoms compared to cisgender individuals (Lindsay et al., 2016). Cultural norms associated with gender role expectations also influence PTSD, anxiety, and depression symptoms; for example, men are often more distressed during non-intentional traumatic events because they experience a decreased ability to provide for their families (Haldane and Nickerson, 2016).

Other factors associated with persistent PTSD include intentional/deliberate rumination and a fatalistic coping orientation (Gul and Karanci, 2017). Beliefs that trauma exposure is a violation to core beliefs about the self and the world can instigate significant and pervasive negative beliefs (Park, Mills, and Edmondson, 2017). The *Shattered Assumptions Theory* describes the violation of core beliefs and a loss of optimism in the world and the self (Schuler and Boals, 2016). The destructive nature of trauma provokes trauma-based assumptions that are incongruent with optimistic assumptions. These trauma-assumptions include the notion that people are not trustworthy and the world is dangerous, consequently shattered negative assumptions intensify PTSD symptoms (Schuler and Boals, 2016). For example, in a longitudinal study that examined individuals exposed to the Oslo bombings, not only were the above factors contributors to persistent PTSD, but efforts to suppress negative emotions and cognitions were equally maladaptive over time (Birkeland et al., 2017). A similar pattern was found in survivors of domestic violence. A high incidence of domestic violence (over 30%) (Devries et al., 2013) is associated with higher rates of PTSD and depression (Salcioglu, Urhan, Pirinccioglu, and Aydin, 2017). Ruminating anticipatory fears and a sense of helplessness mark these disorders. Because domestic violent assaults tend to reoccur, victims of domestic violence often perceive a world that is dangerous and that intimate partners are untrustworthy (Salcioglu et al., 2017).

Individual self-concepts are greatly altered after a violent assaultive attack, especially sexual assault (Keshet and Gilboa-Schechtman, 2017). Self-concept influences perceptions about competence and identity (Foa and Rothbaum, 2001). Violent assaults challenge perceptions of self-competence. When victims are forced into submission, overpowered, and attacked they are vulnerable to acquiring beliefs that they are unlovable, inferior, weak, and unworthy. This assault is not only physical but also an assault on a positive self-concept. A loss of self-competence may compromise disclosure and efforts to seek help. This deficit interferes with essential post-assault needs; victims of violent assaults need support to re-evaluate their maladaptive cognitions and to repair a positive self-concept (Keshet and Gilboa-Schechtman, 2017).

In general, an inability to manage negative emotions indicates an inability to regulate trauma-related emotions and behaviors. An inability to adopt appropriate strategies to manage negative emotions often leads to heightened emotional behavior (O'Bryan, McLeish, Kraemer, and Fleming, 2015). Poor emotional regulation may also increase substance use, especially in individuals with histories of early childhood maltreatment (Mandavia et al., 2016). When difficulties regulating negative emotions are dispositional in nature then trauma-related symptoms increase. This is evident in individuals with a neurotic personality; neuroticism is characterized by a bias toward more negative appraisals in all situations (Polusny et al., 2017). Many individuals are also more physiologically reactive to stress, which influences cognitive perceptions that situations are more negative and intense. For individuals who are biologically sensitive and possess a neurotic disposition, further emotional regulation difficulties arise due to poor emotional self-destructive coping strategies such as alcohol/drug abuse, driving intoxicated, gambling, and aggression (Lusk, Sadeh, Wolf, and Miller, 2017). These factors associated with emotional dysregulation often increase vulnerability for major depression and chronic distress after exposure to traumatic events (Polusny et al., 2017).

Another factor associated with increased trauma symptoms is peritraumatic dissociation. A subsequent diagnosis of PTSD is strongly associated with the initial onset of peritraumatic dissociation after exposure to a traumatic event (Lanius et al., 2010). Usually, peritraumatic dissociation persists and is later reclassified as a dissociative disorder; this indicates an inability to manage intense mental and emotional pain, such as shame. This pattern was demonstrated in a study that examined a sample of Latino youth who were exposed to childhood abuse (Vasquez, de Arellano, Reid-Quinones, Bridges, and Rheingold, 2012).

PTSD is likely to persist in individuals who reside in neighborhoods and communities that are marked by a lack of social order and chaos (Monson, Paquet, Daniel, Brunet, and Caron, 2016). Social chaos is often present in communities with abandoned buildings, noise, graffiti, broken windows, litter, and other signs of neglect. These external signs reflect community indifference, which promotes more drug use, panhandling, and violent criminal behavior. Individuals who are attracted to violence often reside in these communities (Nandi et al., 2017). The generational transmission of social chaos is demonstrated by robust findings indicating childhood exposure to violence is a strong predictor for appetitive aggression, a form of aggression that is marked by pleasure derived from hearing sounds of screaming and witnessing pain in others (Nandi et al., 2017). The suffering of others does not thwart perpetrators who display appetitive aggression; they are intrinsically motivated by it (Weierstall and Elbert, 2011). Not surprising, appetitive aggression is highly prevalent in communities with social chaos (Nandi et al., 2017; Weierstall and Elbert, 2011). Increased rates of PTSD are also evident in communities with racial discrimination (Polanco-Roman, Danies, and Anglin, 2016); discriminatory behaviors further intensify social chaos (Monson et al., 2016). The physical chaos, especially factors such as profound overcrowding, limited resources (health care, food, clothing), higher incidence of crime, and limited opportunities for recreational or wellness activities are also evident in refugee camps. The deprivation evident in refugee camps is associated with higher rates of depression and anxiety, although, unlike neighborhoods and communities that are marked by physical and social chaos, many refugee camps sustain strong values of family cohesion and stable ethnic identity, factors that promote social order and resilience (Aitcheson, Abu-Bader, Howell, Khalil, and Elbedour, 2017).

Trauma-related guilt intensifies PTSD symptoms (Held, Owens, Monroe, and Chard, 2017). This form of state guilt, as opposed to trait guilt, is directly associated with a specific traumatic event. Unlike traumatic shame that leads to a belief that the core self is defective, trauma-related guilt is a negative evaluation of behavior during the event (Kubany et al., 1995). Trauma-related guilt has features such as beliefs that one violated personal and moral standards of behavior, belief that one was responsible for the traumatic event, or that the event was preventable. Many victims experience tonic immobility, a physiologic condition in which volitional movement and vocal expression is suppressed or diminished. Unfortunately, tonic immobility intensifies feelings of guilt (TeBockhorst, O'Halloran, and Nyline, 2015). Trauma-related guilt intensifies PTSD and depression symptoms and occurs when cognitive, somatic, and affective forms of guilt are intense, persistent, and maladaptive (Browne, Trim, Myers, and Norman, 2015). Likewise, when shame drives negative beliefs about the self and guilt propels negative thoughts about the world then PTSD symptoms are further amplified; the combination of shame and guilt is often more distressing than the associated symptoms of PTSD-related anxiety and depression (Beck et al., 2015).

Traumatic events may violate moral beliefs and values (Jordan, Eisen, Bolton, Nash, and Litz, 2017). For example, transgressive acts intensify violations of core values, beliefs, and expectations. These experiences become moral injuries that complicate PTSD healing; they often increase re-experiencing, avoidance, and numbing behavior and intensify feelings of shame, guilt, disorientation, burnout, and despair (Currier, Holland, Rojas-Flores, Herrera, and Foy, 2015; Eisen et al., 2017). A combination of PTSD and ongoing awareness of a moral injury strongly increases suicidal thoughts and behaviors (Bryan, Bryan, Roberge, Leifker, and Rozek, 2018). Moral injuries often lead to intense feelings of embitterment. The sudden loss or injury of others may increase embittered feelings associated with a sense of injustice, wrongdoing by a perpetrator or terrorist organization, and being cheated by others. Embitterment hampers the bereavement process or trauma recovery process and can increase depression, anxiety, grief, and trauma-related symptoms (Chae, Huh, and Choi, 2018). Moral injury may be provoked by acts of perpetration such as committing or allowing acts of inappropriate or disproportionate violence or by acts of betrayal by a trusted other (Litz et al., 2009). When moral injuries evoke feelings of embitterment, the desire to right wrongs and redress the situation may persist for years and be transmitted intergenerationally. The legacy of moral injury may define a sense of self and an entire community or culture as evidenced in communities or nations that preserve the memories of those lost due to genocide or hate crimes (Lehrner and Yehuda, 2018).

Betrayal trauma involves victim perpetration by someone trusted (Freyd, DePrince, and Gleaves, 2012). Betrayal trauma in adulthood increases hypervigilance whereas during childhood it is associated with increased dissociation (Freyd et al., 2012). Incidents of high betrayal trauma also increase anxiety and intensify distrust (Bernstein, Delker, Knight, and Freyd, 2015). As well, it is associated with delayed disclosure and increased depression symptoms (Marriott, Lewis, and Gobin, 2016). Study findings have demonstrated that delayed disclosure is increased in individuals who experienced childhood rape by someone known, compared to those who were older and raped by a stranger (Smith et al., 2000). An inability to disclose trauma is associated with increased trauma-related symptoms (Thomson and Jaque, 2017a; Ullman, 2007; Vrana and Lauterbach, 1994). High betrayal trauma that involves physical and emotional abuse plus witnessing violence is related to more cumulative trauma, PTSD, major depressive disorder, and hallucinations (Martin, Van Ryzin, and Dishion, 2016); whereas, high betrayal involving sexual and emotional abuse is associated with hallucinations but not PTSD or major depressive disorder (Martin et al., 2016). In a study that examined active duty Marines, betrayal trauma and moral injury was associated with increased PTSD symptoms that were mediated by anger. On the other hand, in the Marine sample, the perpetration of moral injury increased PTSD symptoms, as well as marginal guilt and shame feelings (Jordan et al., 2017). Betrayal trauma can also extend beyond the individual level to organizations. When assumptions exist that specific institutions are safe (i.e., schools, hospitals), then failure to respond effectively increases distress (Tamaian, Lest, and Mutschler, 2017). This is strongly evident in individuals who experience sexual and violent assaults; feelings of betrayal and isolation are more likely when health services are not provided or when individuals are victimized within these organizations (Smith and Freyd, 2013). In a study that examined betrayal experiences on college campuses, individuals suffered increased symptoms of anxiety, dissociation, trauma-related sexual symptoms, and sexual dysfunction. The lack of action by the institutions added to the harm these students suffered (Smith and Freyd, 2013). The results of these studies indicate the need to assess for experiences of perpetration and betrayal at the individual and institutional level and not just the traditional feelings of fear and horror that are associated with danger-based traumatic events. These studies demonstrate the need to address moral injury and betrayal trauma; they must be treated in order to reduce PTSD symptoms (Jordan et al., 2017; Litz et al., 2009).

High levels of state-anger significantly increase PTSD symptoms in both men and women (Asmundson, LeBouthillier, Parkerson, and Horswill, 2016) and compromise PTSD healing (Kaczkurkin, Asnaani, Zhong, and Foa, 2016). Unregulated anger, a marker of poor emotion regulation, intensifies impulsivity, especially for individuals who are diagnosed with PTSD (Contractor, Armour, Wang, Forbes, and Elhai, 2015; Kaczkurkin et al., 2016). For example, compared to low-anger PTSD individuals, high-anger PTSD individuals exhibit more violent behavior (Novaco and Chemtob, 2015). Violent aggressive behavior may be expressed as either proactive (unprovoked) or reactive (response to being provoked). Cumulative trauma, greater exposure to violence, and a diagnosis of PTSD are associated with unregulated violent aggressive state-anger (Marsee and Frick, 2007; Nandi, 2017). This profile is strongly evident in prison populations and juvenile offenders; although maltreated juvenile offenders tend to engage in more reactive aggression compared to proactive aggression (Stimmel, Cruise, Ford, and Weiss, 2014). A similar pattern of violent anger is found in combat veterans with PTSD and major depressive disorder. This anger response is often related to heightened physiologic arousal and poor emotional regulation. For example, approximately 40 percent of the combat sample periodically desired to inflict harm on others (Gonzalez, Novaco, Reger, and Gahm, 2016). For people who are forced to re-locate, anger is frequently directed at authority figures that imposed relocation or impeded resettlement. Anger often escalates when inadequate arrangements are implemented following relocation. In all samples, unregulated anger intensifies feelings of disenfranchisement, which further increases trauma-related symptoms (Dekel and Mashiach, 2012). Consequently, treating individuals with high state-anger and PTSD raises unique clinical challenges. For example, some individuals manage their anger with alcohol and substance use, which further compromises PTSD resolution. Sometimes women with high levels of state-anger and assault-related PTSD demonstrate less fearful responses; their reactions often interfere with traditional fear-based treatment approaches to resolve PTSD (Foa, Riggs, Massie, and Yarczower, 1995).

Because the diagnosis of PTSD involves avoidance of previous activities, a high proportion of patients withdraw from physical activity, which further exacerbates PTSD and depression symptoms (de Assis et al., 2008). Engaging in sport or other physical forms of exercise enhances mental health and well-being and the loss of these activities increases poor quality of life (de Assis et al., 2008; Johnston et al., 2015). Individuals who avoid situations and activities are often extremely sensitive to anxiety. Their efforts to reduce anxiety involve avoidance behavior; however, this prolongs the presence of PTSD and anxiety symptoms (Brandt et al., 2015; de Assis et al., 2008). Avoidance of sexual activities is also related to a diagnosis of PTSD, especially in women, although both men and women with PTSD claim diminished sexual satisfaction (Breyer et al., 2016). In an even more negative trajectory, avoidance behavior is often associated with a failure or unwillingness to report assaults in general, and sexual assault in particular. This behavior decreases access to legal and professional resources and tends to intensify PTSD symptom severity and persistence. Unlike avoidance behavior, individuals with hyperarousal and re-experiencing symptoms are more likely to seek help and report assaults (Walsh and Bruce, 2014).

COMORBID DISORDERS

Comorbid disorders, including suicide, are commonly associated with chronic PTSD (Kessler, 2000; Pietrzak et al., 2011). Evidence indicates that trauma exposure increases the likelihood of acquiring comorbid disorders more than genetic inheritance (Brown et al., 2014). This high correlation indicates the heterogeneity of PTSD (Byllesby, Durham, Forbes, Armour, and Elhai, 2016; Laugharne, Lillee, and Janca, 2010). For example, patients who receive a PTSD diagnosis frequently have serious somatic disorders such as chronic pain, irritable bowel syndrome, cardiovascular disease, immune dysfunction, somatization disorder, and metabolic syndrome (Brown et al., 2014; Liebschutz et al., 2007; Mellon, Gautam, Hammamieh, and Jett, 2018). Psychiatric illnesses include depression, anxiety, dysthymia, and eating disorders (Brown et al., 2014; Mellon et al., 2018). These somatic and psychiatric disorders intensify PTSD symptom severity and duration. This was evidenced in a study that examined intense physical pain. It was associated with increased PTSD (Vaughan, Miles, Eisenman, and Meredith, 2016), as well as dissociation (Bob, 2008) and maladaptive beliefs that life stress is unmanageable and uncontrollable (Vaughan et al., 2016). Bartoszek and colleagues found that chronic pain was associated with increased avoidance, numbing, and hyperarousal symptoms (Bartoszek, Hannan, Kamm, Pamp, and Maieritsch, 2017). Based on robust research investigating comorbidity with PTSD, it is believed that exposure to even one traumatic event increases the likelihood of greater physical health symptoms in the general population (Perez, Abrams, Lopez-Martinez, and Asumundson, 2012). The influence of stress at a cellular level suggests that all these trauma-related and comorbid symptoms are connected to mitochondrial dysfunction (Mellon et al., 2018).

The investigation of specific populations illustrates similar comorbid physical and mental health concerns. For example, in a combat veteran sample, those with chronic PTSD had increased risk for osteoarthritis, diabetes, heart disease, obesity, depression, and elevated lipid levels, and these comorbid illnesses increased with aging (David, Woodward, Esquenazi, and Mellman, 2004). They were also more likely to struggle with substance use disorders, in particular, alcohol dependence (Berenz, Roberson-Nay, Latendresse, Mezuk, and Gardner, 2017; David et al., 2004). In a firefighter sample, increased rates of musculoskeletal, neurological, gastrointestinal, and cardiorespiratory symptoms were associated with increased PTSD (Milligan-Saville et al., 2017).

SPECIFIC COMORBID DISORDERS

Sustaining traumatic brain injury from combat, physical assault (childhood and/or adulthood), or domestic violence compromises functioning; this impairment may persist for a lifetime depending on the severity of the brain injury (Gagnon and DePrince, 2017; Jackson et al., 2016). When major depression is also present, individuals report more difficulty functioning, as well as higher symptom intensity associated with the traumatic brain injury. A diagnosis of PTSD further intensifies symptom complications and is typically the primary factor limiting psychosocial functioning (Jackson et al., 2016). In addition, many victims suffer chronic or residual injuries to the head, neck, and face such as deformities to the face, mouth, and throat (Weaver and Resick, 2014). The intensity of these injuries increases body image distress, which further exacerbates PTSD avoidance behavior. Adding to this complicated profile, many brain-injured victims have great difficulty disclosing the event, which further intensifies trauma-related symptoms (Pielmaier and Maercker, 2011). Dysfunctional disclosure includes a reluctance to think or speak about these events, strong urges to speak about them, and/or physical and emotional reactions while disclosing the events. These dysfunctional disclosure responses indicate greater difficulty engaging in interpersonal relationships, which further intensifies PTSD symptom severity. Efforts to improve functioning must collectively focus on PTSD, traumatic brain injury, residual injuries to head, neck, and face, dysfunctional disclosure, as well as depression (Jackson et al., 2016; Pielmaier and Maercker, 2011; Weaver and Resick, 2014).

Sleep disorders are common among those exposed to violent traumatic events, and even more so with PTSD samples (Gronli et al., 2017; van Wyk, Thomas, Solms, and Lipinska, 2016). The hyperarousal symptoms, in particular heightened activation of the sympathetic branch of the autonomic nervous system and the noradrenergic system, reduce sleep onset, duration, and quality. Many suffer from constant nightmares, while others have extremely disrupted sleep architecture (disruptions in REM sleep patterns) (van Wyk et al., 2016). Unlike primary insomnia that is not related to PTSD, disrupted sleep in PTSD patients is typified by more variability across nights and inconsistent symptom patterns (Straus, Drummond, Nappi, Jenkins, and Norman, 2015). Sleep disturbance and poor sleep quality also erode the ability to emotionally regulate; a more negative view of self, others and the world intensifies with sleep deprivation. As well, sleep deprivation or poor sleep quality compromise cognitive functioning and psychomotor functioning (Haynes et al., 2017). These factors also intensify PTSD symptoms and diminish healing (Pickett, Barbaro, and Mello, 2016).

In a military sample, active duty military individuals with PTSD actually suffer profound insomnia, and when they manage to fall asleep they are tortured by nightmares (Pruiksma et al., 2016). Among military veterans, both perceived sleep quality and the efficiency/duration of sleep were problematic for veterans. Poor perceived sleep quality was associated with a diagnosis of PTSD and depression; whereas, the efficiency/duration of sleep was only associated with PTSD (Babson, Blonigen, Boden, Drescher, and Bonn-Miller, 2012). Although men and women both suffer sleep disturbances related to PTSD, longer sleep-onset latency in men but not women predicted greater PTSD symptoms. Both men and women had disrupted nocturnal sleep patterns associated with nightmares (Kobayashi and Delahanty, 2013). Poor sleep is also associated with increased physical pain. In a combat veteran sample, the combination of both poor sleep and physical pain was strongly associated with PTSD symptoms as well as increased aggressive behavior (LaMotte et al., 2017).

Eating disorders and trauma exposure are significantly related (Lejonclou, Nilsson, and Homqvist, 2014). Substantial research findings demonstrate the association of PTSD and becoming overweight or obese over time in women. As well, increased body-mass indices elevate the risk for metabolic disorders (Kubzankyet al., 2014). Most in-patient eating disordered patients endorse trauma exposure. In general, non-intentional trauma exposure and less exposure rates are associated with less severe eating disordered symptoms. Individuals with a diagnosis of PTSD are often vulnerable to emotional eating behaviors as a means to manage intense emotional pain. In this group, many gain abdominal fat, which increases their vulnerability to metabolic disorders (diabetes, cardiovascular disease, obesity) (Talbot, Maguen, Epel, Metzler, and Neylan, 2013). Because this disorder is associated with trauma exposure and it is difficult to treat, including trauma-related psychological and emotional regulation skills may improve treatment practices (Lejonclou et al., 2014).

Substance use and addiction are strongly associated with trauma exposure (Debell et al., 2014; Okuda et al., 2015). Smoking and alcohol consumption are the first and third highest contributors to morbidity and mortality in the United States respectively (Mokdad, Marks, Stroup, and Gerberding, 2004). Alcohol abuse is directly associated with PTSD avoidance, numbing, and hyperarousal symptom clusters (Debell et al., 2014). Interpersonal violence increases this risk, and the use of alcohol actually increases rates of interpersonal perpetration (Peter-Hagene and Ullman, 2015). In a military study, men who were sexually assaulted had a higher risk for smoking relapse while females who were sexually assaulted turned to alcohol use (Seelig et al., 2017). The use of cannabis hampers treatment and intensifies PTSD symptoms, in particular more severe avoidance, numbing, and hyperarousal (Bonn-Miller, Boden, Vujanovic, and Drescher, 2013). As well, substance use is believed to operate as an avoidance strategy to dampen painful trauma-related emotions and intrusive thoughts. Over time the actual trauma triggers activate a desire to use substances. Trauma cues then become embedded with addiction craving, which makes the healing of the substance abuse disorder and PTSD more complicated (Zambrano-Vazquez et al., 2017).

COMPLEX TRAUMA

In the upcoming World Health Organization International Classification of Diseases (ICD-11), a new disorder, Complex Post-traumatic Stress Disorder (CPTSD), will be introduced (Hyland, Shevlin et al., 2017). This new disorder will capture the usual PTSD symptoms as well as disturbances in the self (affect dysregulation, negative self-concepts, and disturbed relationships) that are associated with cumulative developmental trauma and maltreatment. CPTSD will hopefully incorporate the traditional PTSD comorbid disorders, along with the neurological deficits caused by cumulative traumatic exposure. To receive a diagnosis of CPTSD, recent exposure to a traumatic event is not required; this will accommodate the multiple maltreatment factors that are described in the ACE study (Litvin, Kaminski, and Riggs, 2017). Ultimately, the ICD-11 will require three PTSD symptom clusters (re-experiencing, avoidance, and heightened threat response) plus three additional clusters of severe and pervasive affect dysregulation, negative self-concept, and disturbances in relationships. In total CPTSD will require six symptom clusters to be met to receive a diagnosis (Litvin et al., 2017). One of the major advantages of CPTSD is its ability to incorporate adult fears of relationship closeness and abandonment and general difficulties with emotional regulation, common features that are also found in Borderline Personality Disorder (van Dijke, Hopman, and Ford, 2018).

One of the questions raised by researchers comparing both PTSD and CPTSD disorders is the ability to discriminate individuals who are placed in either diagnostic category. For example, the study conducted by Wolf and colleagues (2015) suggests that a diagnosis of PTSD accurately accounts for all individuals who are placed in the CPTSD category. In the Wolf study, receiving a diagnosis of CPTSD failed to distinguish individuals with histories of early childhood abuse histories from individuals who were exposed to trauma during adult years. Opposite results were found by Hyland and colleagues; a strong association between CPTSD and multiple forms of childhood interpersonal trauma was evident (Hyland, Murphy et al., 2017). Future studies need to be conducted to explore how the two diagnoses function and influence treatment (Wolf et al., 2015).

Children and adolescents who are exposed to maltreatment, family violence, and/or multiple losses of significant caregivers not only suffer developmentally but they are at increased risk for developing PTSD (Cook et al., 2005) and CPTSD (Hyland, Murphy et al., 2017; Stolbach et al., 2013). Prior to the ICD-11 proposal for CPTSD, researchers strongly recommended a DSM-5 diagnosis of Developmental Trauma Disorder; this disorder was designed to capture the complex nature of trauma exposure within the family and community during childhood (Stolbach et al., 2013). Many adults with a history of childhood maltreatment receive a diagnosis of PTSD; however, this diagnosis fails to capture the full array of difficulties in functioning. This was evident in a study that investigated female juvenile offenders with a history of sexual abuse, four or more psychiatric diagnoses, and a high rate of PTSD (Dixon, Howie, and Starling, 2005). A similar pattern was found in a sample of juveniles placed in compulsory residential care (Leenarts, Bermeiren, van de Ven, Lodewijks, Doreleijers, and Lindauer, 2013). They have a substantial history of early onset interpersonal trauma (physical, sexual, emotional abuse, and increased exposure to violence) and higher rates of PTSD and other mental disorders. In these two samples, the combination of PTSD and other mental disorders is associated with increased disruptive behavior such as running away and risky sexual activities; behaviors that increase the probability for delinquency (Leenarts et al., 2013).

CPTSD can be transmitted generationally when parents are still struggling with their own PTSD. For example, maternal PTSD is significantly associated with impaired infant neurobiological development. Neurobiological alterations in infants increase the likelihood of more trauma-related symptoms when exposed to trauma (Koen et al., 2017). The cumulative effect of multiple traumatic events during development diminishes the capacity to self-regulate under stress, especially in relational situations (Cook et al., 2005). These negative effects are even more pronounced when several factors converge such as inadequate mothering, poor cognitive capacities in the child, and manifestations of high neuroticism in middle childhood (Qouta, Punamaki, Montgomery, and Sarraj, 2007). Children and adolescents who are subjected to these negative developmental factors often receive multiple diagnoses such as attention-deficit/hyperactivity disorder (ADHD), oppositional defiant disorder (OPD), conduct disorder, anxiety disorders, mood disorders, eating disorders, sleep disorders, separation anxiety disorders, and/or communication disorders (Cook et al., 2005). Of note, all these disorders are encapsulated in the proposed CPTSD; collectively they reflect the complex array of trauma symptoms that are associated with disruptions in attachment relationships and the resulting deficits in emotional/behavioral regulatory capacities.

Lower IQ scores across all four domains (perceptual reasoning, working memory, processing speed, and verbal comprehension) are associated in high trauma exposed children and adolescents (Kira, Lewandowski, Somers, Yoon, and Chiodo, 2012). In a study that examined Palestinian adolescents who were exposed to high levels of traumatic and stressful experiences, lower cognitive functioning, in conjunction with neuroticism (trait anxiety) were strongly associated with higher rates of PTSD (Qouta et al., 2007). In the research study by Kira et al. (2012), cumulative trauma, especially deprivation of resources, was related to lower cognitive abilities in a sample of minority and refugee adolescents. The Kira study (2012) demonstrated how trauma type influenced intellectual functioning. Sexual abuse negatively influenced perceptual reasoning and working memory while survival trauma diminished processing speed. Abandonment trauma had the most negative effect on perceptual reasoning, working memory, and processing speed. Surprisingly, parental involvement in war or combat was associated with higher intellectual functioning in adolescents; this may stem from emotional numbing or avoidance strategies employed to manage the distress of a parental figure's potential danger (Kira et al., 2012).

Although seldom included in trauma sampling, severely injured or ill children and adolescents also meet a diagnosis for PTSD as well as presenting with a complex array of trauma symptoms (Saxe, Vanderbilt, and Zukerman, 2003). Intricate medical interventions often overwhelm the child and family. Not surprising, both the injured/ill child and family members are often diagnosed with PTSD, a condition that makes it more difficult to manage trauma-related symptoms (Morris, Lee, and Delahanty, 2013; Saxe et al., 2003). Parents of severely injured or ill children who develop PTSD symptoms often have prior psychosocial difficulties such as anxiety and depression disorders as well as problems managing their children's behavioral problems (Muscara et al., 2017). Consequently, when assessing children, adolescents, and their parents, a simple PTSD diagnosis may not be sufficient to capture the pervasive disruptions in self-regulation; whereas, CPTSD may be a more accurate diagnosis for this population (Cook et al., 2005; Felitti et al., 1998). In all age groups, sudden onset disabilities such as spinal cord injuries are also associated with PTSD, as well as more enduring post-trauma depression (Kunz, Joseph, Geyh, and Peter, 2017). Managing chronic pain may increase post-trauma depression in both adults and children. Although these are life-altering events, once the initial diagnosis and condition is accepted, post-traumatic growth experiences are often possible (Kunz et al., 2017); however, if multiple trauma exposures occur before a sudden illness or injury, more intense trauma-related symptoms manifest, including more difficulty recovering (Briere et al., 2017). Another medical group that is often ignored in research studies is the severely mentally ill population (Starnino, 2016). A high percentage of mentally ill patients (90%) report trauma histories, and PTSD symptoms tend to increase the severity of mental illness (O'Hare, Shen, and Sherrer, 2015; Rosenberg, Mueser, Jankowski, and Hamblen, 2002). Patients with severe mental illnesses such as schizophrenia spectrum disorders and mood disorders often struggle with their symptoms with minimal attention given to their underlying PTSD symptoms (Grubaugh, Zinzow, Paul, Egede, and Frueh, 2011). Increased rates of negative appraisal of self and others, self-harm behaviors, and suicide attempts are highly associated with mental illness and trauma exposure (O'Hare et al., 2015). Despite these negative factors, when physically or mentally ill patients endorse strong spiritual beliefs and/or paranormal experiences, especially when they are regarded as positive and benevolent, a reduction in trauma-related symptoms occurs (Starnino, 2016). Unfortunately, when patients suffer a spiritual crisis, often precipitated by new or worsening psychotic or physical episodes, trauma-related symptoms worsen (Starnino, 2016).

Cumulative developmental trauma profoundly alters neurological and physiologic maturation; these alterations severely constrain optimal development. Behavioral changes are evident well into adulthood. For example, 32 percent of women who were physically abused as children were revictimized in romantic and dating relationships compared to 18 percent of women who were not physically abused as a child but experienced violent adult romantic relationships (Gover, Kaukinen, and Fox, 2008). In general, a history of child abuse is strongly associated with poor emotional regulation and adult revictimization, especially interpersonal violence. In addition, higher rates of trauma-related symptoms emerge (Lilly, London, and Bridgett, 2014).

SUICIDE

Suicidal ideation and attempts are associated with a diagnosis of PTSD, regardless of types of trauma exposure. In a study that investigated a general population sample, individuals with PTSD who were exposed to childhood maltreatment had the highest rates of suicidal ideation (52%) and suicidal attempts (37%). Assaultive violence and peacekeeping trauma were the next highest risk factors for suicidal ideation (41.1–50.7%) and suicide attempts (20.3–27.8%) (LeBouthillier, McMillan, Thibodeau, and Asmundson, 2015). In a military sample that examined Iraq and Afghanistan veterans, suicidal rates were high (Department of Veterans Affairs, 2016). Factors that increase suicidal ideation and attempts in this population include depression, PTSD, increased somatic complaints, sexual assault during deployment, and traumatic brain injury (Gradus, King, Galatzer-Levy, and Street, 2017). Likewise, veterans with four or more ACEs as well as PTSD have increased rates of suicidal ideation (23%) and suicidal actions (24%) (Carroll, Currier, McCormick, and Drescher, 2017). Beyond greater childhood adversity exposure, multiple trauma exposures across the lifespan increase the likelihood for suicidal ideation/attempts, in part, because feelings of hopelessness, defeat, or entrapment may intensify. As well, a history of physical (Norman et al., 2012) and sexual abuse (Devries et al., 2014) increases suicidal ideation and suicide attempts. Not surprising, a history of childhood abuse among incarcerated women strongly predicts suicidal ideation or actions. They also have early onset substance abuse, higher rates of mental illness, more traumatic exposure, and low self-esteem; these factors are strongly associated with early child abuse (Chen and Gueta, 2017; Salina, Figge, Ram, and Jason, 2017). The relationship between physical/sexual abuse and suicide risk is also evident in a sample of firefighters; a population that typically manifests lower rates of psychological distress, despite higher rates of completed suicides (Hom et al., 2017).

Recurrent experiences of pain and fear may actually increase habituation to thoughts of death and suicide, as evidenced by many individuals who attempt suicide following a traumatic event. A history of childhood maltreatment, multiple traumatic events, and PTSD may diminish the effects of suicidal deterrents (LeBouthillier et al., 2015). In conjunction with cumulative traumatic events, an inability to tolerate mental pain often intensifies dissociative processing, which leads to an insensitivity to bodily cues and increases suicidal ideation (Levinger, Somer, and Holden, (2015). Psychological and spiritual pain also increases suicidal ideation (Raines et al., 2017). These factors significantly influence the current epidemic of suicides among U. S. military veterans (Department of Veterans Affairs, 2016). Veterans consistently endorse struggles with spirituality and religious faith; this struggle is evident in their struggle to find meaning and a connection with God or the divine (Raines et al., 2017).

The majority (75%) of worldwide suicides take place in low and middle-income countries (Vawda, Milburn, Steyn, and Zhang, 2017). Adolescents worldwide are one of the highest risk groups. Risk increases among this population when factors such as contact with the police, alcohol use, depression, physical health concerns, anger, perceived stress, and feelings of hopelessness are present. Countries such as South Africa struggle with high rates of adolescent suicide, with 23.53 percent of middle school children reporting thoughts of killing themselves (Vawda et al., 2017). In general, regardless of country of origin or age, individuals who have profound feelings of detachment and estrangement are at the highest risk for suicidal ideation (Davis,

Witte, and Weathers, 2014). An inability to recall important aspects of the trauma, persistent negative beliefs, diminished interest, and feelings of alienation add to suicidal attempts and ideation (Legarreta et al., 2015). Study results support the interpersonal theory of suicide, a model that proposes that increased suicidal ideation and risk for completed suicide are associated with feelings of thwarted belongingness, perceived burden to others, and fearlessness of death (Van Orden et al., 2010).

CULTURAL DIFFERENCES

Cultural factors are also associated with PTSD rates; in particular, cultural beliefs positively or negatively influence reporting rates and treatment outcomes. Many cultures discourage reporting childhood maltreatment as well as adult assaults (Foynes, Platt, Hall, and Freyd, 2014). For example, in a Latino culture, many victims develop PTSD due to higher exposure and severity of symptoms and yet these victims adhere to fixed cultural beliefs not to disrupt family dynamics and family obligations. An inability to shift views about self and others after an intentional traumatic event may deter reporting. These fixed beliefs prohibit integration of traumatic experiences, which intensifies PTSD symptoms (Vasquez et al., 2012; Marquis et al., 2016). Mental health workers, medical professionals, and law enforcement workers can explore the victim's beliefs, validate their experiences, build rapport, and foster trust. This may help shift cognitive processing and help balance reporting incidents and treatment outcomes (Marquis et al., 2016).

Abuse reporting statistics may be skewed based on under-reporting in specific cultural groups. For example, in a study that examined Asian children, there was a higher proportion of Asian female children who failed to disclose sexual abuse perpetrated by a close family member, even though these same children reported physical abuse (Foynes et al., 2014). A similar pattern was demonstrated in a Latino sample (Ullman and Filipas, 2005). Although often under-reported, when targeted assessment of Latino youth was conducted, a higher rate of cumulative trauma and increased psychiatric disorders was evident (Suarez-Morales, Mena, Schlaudt, and Santisteban, 2017). Both these cultures value interpersonal harmony within the family unit and exert efforts to preserve the family and group's moral reputation, values that may compromise reporting. Ethnicity rates often differ after major traumatic events. For example, after Hurricane Katrina, trauma-related symptoms and depression rates were significantly higher in African American groups compared to their Caucasian counterparts; this finding persisted after socio-demographic, cumulative trauma, and social support was statistically accounted for in the analyses (Ali, Farrell, Forde, Stockton, and Ward, 2017).

Racial discrimination and segregation were powerful contributing factors in this study (Ali et al., 2017).

Patterns of under-reporting of PTSD also extend to populations with disabilities. For example, in a study that examined extremely mentally ill patients, PTSD was associated with physical abuse or the unexpected death of a close loved one. Inviting this population to express the nature of their subjective distress helped clarify the source of distress, even though the severity of their mental illness often obfuscated trauma-related symptoms (O'Hare, Shen, and Sherrer, 2013). A higher incidence rate for trauma exposure is repeatedly reported in the deaf community compared to the general population (Schild and Dalenberg, 2012). Members of the deaf community, especially ethnic minority deaf people, had the highest exposure rate of sexual abuse and a higher percentage diagnosed with PTSD. Within this study, many of these deaf participants with a diagnosis of PTSD also had learning disabilities, ADHD, and language deficits (Schild and Dalenberg, 2012). Treatment outcomes are enhanced when practitioners are aware of the specific needs of diverse populations. For example, dealing with the aftermath of trauma for a deaf individual requires treatment from practitioners who can sign and who are aware of the culture in a deaf community (Anderson, Craig, and Ziedonis, 2017).

Adding to reporting difficulties associated with diversity is the variations related to how PTSD symptoms are described. For example, in Latino communities from the Caribbean, "ataques de nervios" is an attack of the nervous system (Guarnaccia, Martinez, Ramirez, and Canino, 2005). Symptoms such as anxiety, crying, depression, heart palpitations, stomachaches, dizziness, self-injurious behavior, and suicidal ideation are all implied when someone reports an ataques de nervios. Recognizing these symptoms within a cultural context may help identify individuals in need of treatment (Guarnaccia et al., 2005). Often natural disasters focus attention on these culture-bound disorders; however, there is strong evidence that childhood maltreatment, in particular, peer and family violence intensifies the likelihood of experiencing one or more ataques de nervios (Rubens, Felix, Bernberg, and Canino, 2014).

In general, studies that examine cultural differences seldom examine the effects of trauma exposure, including when trauma is perpetrated (Bojahr and van Emmerik, 2016). For example, in a study that examined former drug cartel soldiers in Rio de Janeiro, trauma-related psychopathology (especially PTSD and depression) was associated with extremely elevated past trauma exposure. These soldiers are often recruited into the drug cartel with the enticement of making money and gaining status. In this sample, individuals who were perpetrators of one or more traumatic events suffered more intrusion symptoms and higher overall PTSD. They also suffered more childhood and adult victimization and they struggled to manage distressing feelings of perpetrating crimes against others (Bojahr and van Emmerik, 2016). Sadly, a high homicide rate is reported each year in Brazil, with many homicide victims only nineteen years old (United Nations Office on Drugs and Crime, 2012).

These cultural-based studies reinforce the need to expand knowledge and counter assumptions that may be derived from results gathered in more homogenous samples. Continued research is needed to examine different populations based on geographic region, ethnicity, disability (physical and/or mental), gender, age, trauma type, and complex trauma. Today, it is paramount that investigations are conducted on the effects of trauma in low and middle-income countries and communities. Approximately 90 percent of injury-related deaths caused by intentional and non-intentional trauma occur in these low and middle-income countries (Wyatt et al., 2017). For example, efforts to address trauma-related needs in South Africa are increasing; however, the majority of countries in Africa remain under investigated. Likewise, many research studies fail to gather information within low and middle-income communities in upper-income countries, especially in ethnically diverse communities (Suarez-Morales et al., 2017). This failure extends to exploring the effects of systemic racism in North American communities that have long histories of slavery, racial segregation, and racial discrimination (Carter and Muchow, 2017). Despite this deficit, research is beginning to offer a more diverse lens on PTSD. For example, Myers and colleagues (2015) and Hall-Clark and colleagues (2017) investigated low SES African American and Latino/as communities. High levels of discrimination, greater trauma exposure, more prevalence of fear, guilt, numbing, anxiety, and depression, and a higher burden of chronic stress were found in these two communities (Hall-Clark et al., 2017; Myers et al., 2015). Surprisingly, despite these high adversity rates, only a small percentage of individuals in both communities received a PTSD diagnosis. This apparent increased resilience in these communities may actually be due to low reporting rates and minimal interaction with mental health professionals (Myers et al., 2015).

SECONDARY TRAUMATIZATION

Secondary traumatization has been identified in multiple population samples. This form of trauma often describes reactions of individuals who live in close proximity to victims of violent trauma. These victims indirectly transmit their distress to those living or working near them (Galovski and Lyons, 2004). The contagion theory suggests that the process of acquiring PTSD symptoms from a trauma-exposed close loved one with PTSD is partially related to an inability to differentiate self from other (Figley, 1986). Self-differentiation describes a process of distinguishing thoughts and feelings that are separate from an emotionally close other (Lahav, Levin, Bensimon, Kanat-Maymon, and Solomon, 2017). High self-differentiation reflects an individual's ability to remain autonomous while sustaining close feelings; whereas, low self-differentiation is often a loss of a sense of self-autonomy as well as extreme efforts to please another. Similarly, family members who have a strong capacity for emotional empathy are more vulnerable to emotional contagion. The ability to cognitively empathize (i.e., observer can imagine the psychological perspective of the other) with a partner who suffers PTSD may initially comfort the survivor; however, emotional empathy (i.e., experience the same feelings as the other) often intensifies suffering for the survivor and the family member (Dekel, Siegel, Fridkin, and Svetlitzky, 2018). These study findings suggest that low self-differentiation and high affective empathy may be related to secondary traumatization in partners of former prisoner of war veterans. The horrific experiences of veterans, including prisoner of war veterans, may be transmitted to the partner and both experience trauma-related symptoms (Lahav et al., 2017).

In a study investigating Vietnam veteran families, wives suffered the most and this was associated with PTSD and alcoholism in the veteran, which led to feelings of demoralization. Both male and female offspring experienced the demoralization of their mothers; however, they did not manifest significant troubling internalizing or externalizing behavior (Yager, Gerszberg, and Dohrenwend, 2016). This study finding differed from previous studies that demonstrated greater externalizing behavior in boys and internalizing behavior in females (Achenbach, Howell, Quay, Conners, and Bates, 1991). Children of ex-prisoner of war parents also manifest secondary trauma symptoms; they tend to resort to emotional cutoff behaviors (isolation from others), less differentiation from the parent and the self, and/or dysregulated emotional reactivity (Zerach, 2015; Zerach and Solomon, 2016). Surprisingly, the wives are not negatively affected if the former prisoner of war veterans have fewer PTSD avoidance symptoms and are able to recount exposure details (Zerach and Solomon, 2016). Sadly, this response pattern was not found in their children. Even forty years after the war, these ex-prisoners of war veterans continued to revisit their PTSD onto their adult children (Zerach, 2015).

Children of Holocaust survivors have been examined repeatedly in an effort to understand the second-generation transmission of trauma. Many offspring report elevated symptoms of depression, anxiety, and personality disorders (Shmotkin, Shrira, Goldberg, and Palgi, 2011). These offspring frequently perceive the world as less favorable; consequently they are often preoccupied by potential threats (Shrira, 2015). They remain hypervigilant and acquire beliefs that they are incompetent to meet the threatening demands of the world. Despite this pervasive pattern, many offspring actively engage in positive perceptions of self-competency despite heightened awareness of potential threats of annihilation (Shrira, 2015). Even with more resilience, offspring of Holocaust survivors have lower tolerance in stressful situations; the horror visited upon the Holocaust survivors continues to reverberate generationally (Shmotkin et al., 2011). A similar transmission was found in a study that examined the effects of forced starvation and genocide in the Ukraine in 1932–1933. The survivors, adult children, and grandchildren all report more physical health difficulties and more difficulties with psychological and social processing (Bezo and Maggi, 2018). These intergenerational perceptions and experiences demonstrate the long lasting effects of trauma (Bezo and Maggi, 2018; Shmotkin et al., 2011)).

Parents of children who were sexually abused by non-family members are often diagnosed with PTSD as well (van Delft, Finkenauer, Tybur, and Lamers-Winkelman, 2016). The shock to their core values erodes their ability to manage the secondary trauma-related symptoms (van Delft et al., 2016). Parental distress makes it challenging for them to regulate their intense emotions, which further complicates the child's ability to regulate emotions (Langevin et al., 2016). This is most problematic for sexually abused preschool children who are still forming emotion regulation skills. Sadly, this is exacerbated when mothers or fathers have their own history of childhood sexual abuse. Maternal history of childhood sexual abuse as well as parental emotional distress actually predicts their children's emotional dysregulation; these factors are the major contributors to emotional under-regulation (tantrums, impulsivity, overexcitability) in sexually abused preschool children (Langevin et al., 2016). Some of these dysregulating behaviors manifest when mothers struggle with extreme feelings of disgust. A visceral reaction to avoid the noxious sexual abuse stimuli is mobilized; however, the avoidance is one of avoiding the child. For parents, the knowledge that their child was a victim of childhood sexual abuse is often intolerable and feelings of disgust and rage make it more difficult to manage their secondary trauma symptoms (van Delft et al., 2016).

Medical professionals and mental health workers are also vulnerable to secondary traumatization, and this increases with cumulative exposure to distressed family members (Coleman, Delahanty, Schwartz, Murani, and Brondolo, 2016; Cohen and Collens, 2013). They witness the aftermath of highly disturbing events such as victims of violent crime, accidents, or natural disasters. Interacting with distraught family members intensifies negative cognitions about the world. Witnessing inconsolable loss may challenge medical professionals' sense of efficacy and erode their ability to recover. With cumulative exposure to distressed family members, medical professionals are vulnerable to acquiring trauma-related symptoms and depression (Coleman et al., 2016). Efforts to detach and distance sometimes collapse as feelings of empathy and compassion increase (Cohen and Collens, 2013). The strain of managing these highly emotional situations as well as treating these critically ill patients may undermine physicians' and nurses' moral beliefs and values, especially when they are required to provide care for a high volume of patients and the care is viewed as ineffectual (Austin, Saylor, and Finley, 2017).

Terms such as vicarious trauma, compassion fatigue, and secondary traumatization describe trauma-related symptoms acquired from cumulative exposure to distressed individuals (Ahern, Galea, Resnick, and Vlahov, 2004; Palm, Polusny, and Follette, 2004). Mental health professionals who treat trauma survivors are often vulnerable to long-term changes in their worldview of self and others (Cohen and Collens, 2013). Sometimes these views reflect the negative beliefs of their PTSD patients, although some practitioners may shift their views to conform to notions of post-traumatic growth. In general, the shift to post-traumatic growth is often contingent on patient post-traumatic growth. If patients continue to falter, the likelihood of mental health workers adopting negative views is greater; however, practitioners who work long-term with patients generally have more opportunity to experience post-traumatic growth compared to short-term therapy treatments (Cohen and Collens, 2013). Practitioners who derive compassion satisfaction from their work are less likely to suffer burnout, despite the fact that they may experience secondary traumatization. Unfortunately, when negative affect becomes pronounced these mental health workers have greater risk for compassion fatigue, burnout, and secondary traumatization (Craigie et al., 2016).

Compassion fatigue increases in populations who work in the field alongside war and torture victims. It is associated with constant exposure to extreme emotional pain (Kjellenberg, Nilsson, Daukantaite, and Cardena, 2014). These workers include those who have direct contact with victims as well as the journalists who report these atrocities (Browne, Evangeli, and Greenberg, 2012). Volunteers that offer aid after natural disasters or mass trauma are equally vulnerable to acquiring secondary PTSD, especially if they have poor psychosocial support and lower levels of self-esteem (Thormar et al., 2016). Field workers such as refugee resettlement workers are also at increased risk for burnout and secondary traumatization, especially when they engage in behaviors such as self-blame, behavioral disengagement, humor, self-distraction, venting, and substance use. Likewise, increased emotional intelligence in these workers may intensify their distress, which increases burnout risk (Akinsulure-Smith, Espinosa, Chu, and Hallock, 2018). Another population that is at high risk for burnout and secondary trauma are teachers who work in situations where they witness innocent children harmed. These atrocities assault their moral view of the world (Currier Holland, Rojas-Flores et al., 2015). Collectively, these workers witness the results of extreme human evil. They frequently manage their distress with dissociative distancing and depersonalization; however, this coping strategy increases burnout and emotional exhaustion (Ager et al., 2012). Years of working in the field frequently leads to resignation to human evil, which is associated with increased distress (Ager et al., 2012), and for some increased post-trauma survivor guilt (Browne et al., 2012). Surprisingly, in the study by Kjellenberg and colleagues (2014), fear of death decreased for many field workers, but for those who had increased fear of death they exhibited higher levels of depersonalization and diminished level of functioning. Despite years of working with torture victims, many workers derive meaning from their work and endorse markers of post-traumatic growth (Kjellenberg et al., 2014). A cohesive team and strong social support help reduce these chronic stressors (Ager et al., 2012). As well, compassion fatigue may be diminished when workers maintain their professional ethical code. The strength of resilience associated with operating within an ethics code actually distinguishes professional from volunteer caregivers who work in the field (Avieli, Ben-David, and Levy, 2016).

Workers such as firefighters and police officers are exposed to situations that are potentially highly traumatic. The major difference with this population, compared to health care professionals, is that they are well trained to manage potentially traumatic situations (Kehl, Knuth, Hulse, and Schmidt, 2015; Marchand, Nadeau, Beaulieu-Prevost, Boyer, and Martin, 2015). Typically, they have a deep sense of belonging to the organization (Armstrong, Shakespeare-Finch, and Shochet, 2016; Shakespeare-Finch and Daley, 2017). They are given support from members in their profession including an infrastructure within the organization that offers mental health services to those who request help. No differences in trauma-related symptoms are found between men and women, although workers with more experience tend to manage stress more effectively (Marchand et al., 2015). Similar to other populations, predictors of PTSD or secondary trauma include greater exposure to traumatic events during the past year (more than six traumatic events as well as peritraumatic suffering) (Lee, Lee, Kim, Jeon, and Sim, 2017), especially when it is related to cumulative daily operational stress in the workplace (Armstrong et al., 2016). Other factors include the presence of family psychiatric history, neurotic personalities, trait dissociation, personal past trauma, and threat to a partner's life (Marchand et al., 2015). Other risk factors for trauma-related symptoms are emotional coping strategies versus task-oriented strategies, intensity of depression and dissociation post-trauma, and heightened emotional and physical reactions during and after the event (Marchand et al., 2015).

Vicarious trauma is associated with populations that are not directly involved in trauma. They see the effects of trauma via media images. Highly distressing media images, exposure frequency, and emotional reactivity are all predictive of PTSD symptoms even though no direct trauma exposure occurred (Yeung et al., 2018). In a recent study, an investigation was conducted to understand media exposure, in particular, patterns of identification with a victim. In this study, identification was described as individuals who view the event as if the self suffered the traumatic event or when they identify with feelings of friends or family members of the victim (Mash, Ursano, Benevides, and Fullerton, 2017). Greater total identification was associated with both PTSD and depression symptoms. When identifying with the victim as if it were the self, or relating to feelings of the family member, more PTSD symptoms emerge; however, when the self-identification is removed then only depression symptoms emerge. This study demonstrates the nature of vicarious trauma for individuals who strongly identify with victims, despite no personal association beyond media reports (Mash et al., 2017).

CONCLUSION

In general, insufficient attention is given to assessing PTSD, especially as more time elapses from the traumatic event(s) (Kessler, 2000; Liebschutz et al., 2007). Lack of medical awareness is even more pronounced in many countries around the world, especially those in the midst of political unrest or military conflicts (Kessler, 2000). Predicting PTSD involves assessing multiple factors prior to a traumatic event, during the event, and responses following it. There is a vast array of factors that increase PTSD vulnerability, which makes it extremely difficult to accurately predict individual trajectories following a traumatic event. Applying more complex statistical algorithms may increase predictive accuracy; however, gathering information on all factors is a limiting element in any predictive analysis (Karstoft et al., 2015). This predictive challenge is fully amplified in a cross-national study that demonstrated a discrepancy between prevalence rates of PTSD and low versus high vulnerability index countries. Surprisingly, low vulnerability countries had higher rates of PTSD (Duckers, Alisic, and Brewin, 2016a). This study demonstrated the essential need to evaluate vulnerability and resilience factors that range from the individual to the country level (McNally, 2018).

Trauma-related symptoms and PTSD often have a trajectory pattern that is high immediately following the traumatic event with gradual dissipation over time (Kilpatrick et al., 2013; Morina et al., 2014). However, some individuals acquire PTSD much later (Magruder et al., 2016). This delayed onset pattern is often associated with higher educational level, a cumulating effect of new or recurrent traumatic events, and a diminished social support system (Smid, van der Velden, Gersons, and Kleber, 2012). Other individuals do not recover and struggle with chronic PTSD. Unfortunately this group also experiences many other illnesses associated with PTSD (Kilpatrick et al., 2013; Morina et al., 2014). Likewise, individuals who are exposed to multiple traumatic events and who experience more severe trauma-related symptoms, including trauma-related diseases, are more likely to struggle with everyday stressful events (Morina et al., 2014; Suliman et al., 2009). The economic costs to care for individuals with cumulative trauma, late onset PTSD, and/or chronic PTSD are great, especially when adequate trauma-based treatment is not provided (Ferry et al., 2015).

The experience of severe trauma exposure is complicated by a host of factors immediately following a violent traumatic event. For example, traumatized individuals are often faced with police investigations and medical examinations (Risan, Binder, and Milne, 2016). Providing these individuals with a relational rapport that evokes feelings of safety and compassion can greatly assist the mobilization of regulatory coping strategies. These emotional and physiologic regulatory processes can buffer distress. Recommendations for police investigators and medical professionals include offering interview techniques that can promote self-regulation in the traumatized individual (Risan et al., 2016). Comorbid diseases and disorders also complicate treatment. Studies indicate that diseases such as anemia, arthritis, asthma, back pain, chronic pain, diabetes, eczema, kidney disease, lung disease, and ulcers have some relationship with chronic stress or PTSD (Otis, Keane, and Kerns, 2003; Weisberg et al., 2002). Medically unexplained symptoms are pervasive in individuals with cumulative trauma, which complicates treatment and psychological distress (van der Westhuizen, Williams, Stein, and Sorsdahl, 2017). Robust study findings identify the significant negative dosing effect of cumulative trauma, regardless if it is intentional or non-intentional trauma exposure (Morina et al., 2014; Roelofs and Spinhoven, 2007).

Chapter 9

Neurobiological and Psychophysiological Effects of Childhood Adversity, Trauma, and Loss Experiences

HOMEOSTASIS AND ALLOSTASIS

Homeostasis, also referred to as *homeodynamics,* is the regulatory equilibrium that is maintained in all physiologic functioning. Temperature, heart rate, blood pressure, blood sugar levels, oxygen saturation, respiratory rate, and other physiologic processes all fluctuate within a range that is considered normative; these ranges vary slightly depending on the age and gender of the individual (Sherwood, 2010). When these physiologic systems operate outside the homeostatic range then stress symptoms manifest, such as fever, fainting, shivering, panting, etc. These stress symptoms alert the body to mobilize an immune response in an effort to restore homeostasis. Unlike internal or external physiologic stress caused by bacteria, viruses, or exogenous irritants, psychological stress that is perceived as threatening mobilizes even more primitive brain structures in an effort to restore equilibrium. Regardless whether the stress trigger is internally or externally activated, physiologic adaptation is essential for survival. This process is ultimately normative; all biological systems must accommodate and adapt to stress (Baumann and Turpin, 2010; Sherwood, 2010).

Under threat (internal or external), the physiologic systems can increase or decrease responses to meet the demands of the situation; this expansion in regulatory homeodynamic equilibrium is termed *allostasis* (Danese and McEwen, 2012). Allostasis enables more extreme adaptation required to sustain life. For example, blood pressure and cardiovascular rates can increase, whereas, digestion can diminish. The autonomic nervous system (ANS) adjusts to ensure that striated muscles get more blood supply required to fight or flee (Berntson and Cacioppo, 2007). Brain regions also respond, with greater activation in networks that detect environmental threats (Danese and McEwen, 2012). These detecting regions include the amygdala, thalamus, and sensory cortices. Once detected, regions such as the hippocampus and prefrontal cortex must interpret the level of threat. These regions can inhibit amygdala signaling, which will calm the physiologic responses or they will allow the stress response to be fully mobilized. If the hippocampus and prefrontal cortex do not inhibit amygdala activation, then the amygdala sends rapid signals to the locus coeruleus, which releases high levels of norepinephrine required to enhance alertness and attention directed toward the environmental threat (van der Kolk, 2014). Concurrently, the hypothalamus not only accommodates ANS alterations, but also sends signals via several pathways (or axis). The hypothalamus-pituitary-adrenal (HPA) axis supports the increased metabolic demands required to meet the external threat and the hypothalamus-pituitary-thyroid (HPT) axis activates the neuroendocrine and immune systems. Regardless of the nature of the stressor, the neurobiological and physiologic systems trigger an inflammatory response to ensure that an immune response will manage any potential infection caused by tissue damage or pathogen invasion. This inflammatory response is strongly linked to the sympathetic branch of the ANS; high sympathetic activation, coupled with amygdala threat detection, greatly increases inflammation (Danese and McEwen, 2012). After the threat is quelled then the neurobiological and physiologic systems will return to homeodynamic equilibrium, a function that is strongly associated with increased parasympathetic activation (Berntson and Cacioppo, 2007).

Under conditions of chronic or repeated stress, especially during early development, a shift from homeodynamic (homeostasis) to allostasis must be sustained (Danese and McEwen, 2012). Living under long-term conditions such as war or ongoing community violence exceeds the physiologic and neurobiological responses to an acute single traumatic event. The prolonged state of survival required when living in conditions of constant threat and stress impair the ability to recover (Pat-Horenczyk et al., 2017). Specifically, prolonged allostasis has detrimental consequences, especially in the three stress systems: endocrine system, immune system, and the nervous system (central and autonomic). The *allostatic load* (overload) on the neurobiological and physiologic systems leads to structural and functional abnormalities in all these systems (McEwen, Eiland, Hunter, and Miller, 2012). Once alterations transpire in these stress systems, then vulnerability for age-related diseases increase, such as cardiovascular disease, metabolic disorders, and autoimmune disorders. More rapid aging also occurs, including a shortened life span. This is due to genetic alterations and erosion in telomere lengths (Puterman et al., 2016). These deleterious consequences are all associated with excessive allostatic demands (often termed the allostatic debt) that emerge with aging (Danese and McEwen, 2012). The allostatic debt is sadly extended to the next generation. Women who suffer chronic childhood maltreatment transmit allostatic alterations into the brains and stress systems of their fetuses (Meaney, 2001, 2010; Blackmore et al., 2016). For example, these prenatally stressed newborns have smaller intracranial volume (Mood et al., 2017). The stress systems of the infants are primed for conditions of ongoing stress. Even when they are reared as children in optimal conditions their stress systems can only be modified and not reversed (Thomson, 2004, 2007).

Other models have been formulated to describe allostatic loading. *Endophenotype* measures brain functioning at multiple systems levels (Kropotov, 2009). For example, assessments such as neurophysiologic, biochemical, endocrine, neuroanatomical, and neuropsychological tests all reveal behavior changes and diseases associated with chronic trauma exposure. An endophenotype assessment can ultimately demonstrate a "neural signature" of complex trauma. *Equifinality* is a concept that defines how a single disorder emerges from different developmental pathways and *multifinality* describes different outcomes from a single source (Cicchetti and Rogosch, 2002; Curtis and Cicchetti, 2003). Including information derived from equifinality, multifinality, and endophenotype concepts increases a more complex understanding about the effects of trauma, especially early trauma, on the individual (Howard, 2012). This "neural signature" may guide more specific protocols for effective treatment; in particular, it incorporates the effects of early adversity, chronic exposure, and cumulative trauma (Howard, 2012).

EARLY ALTERATIONS IN NEURODEVELOPMENT

Adverse childhood experiences lead to disrupted neurodevelopment, which cascades into social, cognitive, and emotional impairment that ultimately manifests in poor health and early mortality (Felitti and Anda, 2010). During early development, especially prenatal development and into the first three years of life, the rapidly maturing central nervous system (CNS) and ANS require optimal conditions to mature. Adequate nutrition and minimal stress foster growth; lack of nutrition, or poor nutrition, along with ongoing or episodic stressors elicit modifications in the structures and functioning of the CNS and ANS (Thomson, 2004, 2007). Because brain growth is experience-dependent, this critical period is highly sensitive to environmental assaults on neurodevelopment (Schore, 1994, 2003). Experiences during this early period are ultimately "biologically embedded" and directly affect health, well-being, learning, and behavior over the lifetime (Hertzman, 2012). Although the earliest years in development are considered a critical period, a second critical period occurs during adolescence. Both developmental phases are marked by accelerated growth and maturation; during these rapid changes greater vulnerability to environmental adversity is also present (Spear, 2000; Sturman and Moghaddam, 2011). These two developmental periods are associated with the greatest neurobiological alterations; however, adversity throughout childhood increases risk for allostatic loading and subsequent neurobiological damage that often persist into later life (Felitti and Anda, 2010).

Catecholamine System and HPA Axis

Early stress, including prenatal stress, causes increased activation of the catecholamine system (dopamine, norepinephrine, epinephrine, cortisol), especially norepinephrine, an essential neurotransmitter required to activate the sympathetic nervous system as well as the orienting/alerting system that is regulated by the locus coeruleus (Danese and McEwen, 2012; Vermetten and Bremner, 2002). These responses are all monitored by the HPA stress axis. This stress axis operates as a feedback system; once cortisol and glucocorticoids are released from the adrenal and pituitary glands respectively then signals are sent to the hypothalamus to halt the stress response. However, due to chronic early stress, this feedback system is altered. There is either a blunting of cortisol release or the cortisol fails to shut off the stress axis (Danese and McEwen, 2012). Both heightened (hypercortisolism) and blunted (hypocortisolism) responses demonstrate severe damage to the stress axis (De Bellis, Baum et al., 1999).

Genes directly regulate the activity of corticotrophin-releasing hormone (CRH) as well as the HPA axis (Tyrka, Price, Gelernter, Schepker, Anderson, and Carpenter, 2009). CRH receptors are found in widely distributed regions of the brain such as the pituitary, amygdala, hippocampus, locus coeruleus, solitary tract, striatum, cerebellum, and multiple locations throughout the cortex. Early exposure to childhood abuse alters the genetic influence of CRHR1 and FKBP5 SNPs at the CRH receptor sites. These genetic alterations increase the likelihood of developing depression and anxiety disorders during adulthood (Gillespie, Phifer, Bradley, and Ressler, 2009; Heim et al., 2010). During childhood, the neurotoxic effects from excessive CRH and glucocorticoid profusion directly alter reactivity responses in the HPA axis and multiple regulating cortical and subcortical regions (i.e., hippocampus, amygdala, periaqueductal gray, anterior cingulate, prefrontal cortex) (Tyrka et al., 2009).

Hippocampus and Glucocorticoids

An indicator that a stress response is intense and prolonged can be found within the hippocampus; typically there is evidence of overexpression of glucocorticoid receptors. As well, there is a loss of pyramidal hippocampal neurons, which disrupts memory encoding and retrieval (Baumann and Turpin, 2010). Because the hippocampus regulates the HPA axis, when alterations transpire such as decreased hippocampal volume, diminished regulation of the HPA axis occurs (Heim et al., 2010). A cascading effect transpires; alterations in the hippocampus and the HPA axis then provoke changes in the entire neuroendocrine system (Danese and McEwen, 2012). These changes indicate a lifelong predisposition for stress-related syndromes and greater vulnerability to substance abuse (Wei et al., 2012; Zuiden et al., 2012). As well, risk for substance abuse and psychosis is associated with alterations in the hippocampal subfield structure, the subiculum. Collectively, these changes alter the dopaminergic responses to stress and increase dysregulation in the HPA axis (De Bellis et al., 2012).

Brain Volume

Alterations to brain structures are significantly evident in children exposed to extreme childhood maltreatment. Smaller intracranial and brain volume are present, such as in the corpus callosum and prefrontal cortex. Enlarged right and left ventricles further reflect decreased brain volume in these maltreated children (De Bellis, Keshavan et al., 1999). Exposure to early maltreatment has also been associated with epileptiform EEG abnormalities as well as reduced volume in the left neocortex and hippocampus (Vermetten and Bremner, 2002; Teicher, Anderson, and Polcari, 2012; Teicher, Tomoda, and Andersen, 2006; Teicher et al., 2003). A paradoxical pattern of increased volume in the amygdala in maltreated children often results in smaller volume in adulthood. Regardless of amygdala volume, greater reactivity is evident in both maltreated children and adults. Increased PTSD symptoms typically emerge in this population, especially when amygdala dysregulation co-exists with compromised regulatory functions in the hippocampus (Baumann and Turpin, 2010; Danese and McEwen, 2012).

Childhood emotional maltreatment often leads to reductions in the medial prefrontal cortex volume; this indicates a pattern of sustained inhibition of growth and structural damage as a consequence to early pervasive emotional abuse (van Harmelen et al., 2010). The effects associated with deficits in the medial prefrontal cortex include diminished emotional and ANS regulation as well as increased emotional sensitivity (van Harmelen et al., 2010). Likewise, alterations in the volume of the cerebellar vermis significantly compromises regulation, in particular, there is decreased glucocorticoid receptor proliferation, which negatively influences connectivity in the stress networks, especially in the limbic regions (Teicher et al., 2003).

Connectivity

Intense childhood maltreatment is associated with an underactive default mode network in patients who are later diagnosed with PTSD (Bluhm et al., 2009). This network is associated with self-referential thinking as well as tasks that require reflection. In the PTSD patient group, less activation was found in the default network as well as poorer connectivity. Underactive or disrupted connectivity exists between the posterior cingulate cortex and the precuneus and between the amygdala and the hippocampus/parahippocampal gyrus. This lack of connectivity and under-activity in these regions helps explain symptom patterns in patients with PTSD and anxiety disorders (Bluhm et al., 2009).

Dysfunctions in the salience network leads to diminished reward sensitivity in maltreated individuals (Marusak, Etkin, and Thomason, 2015). The insula is a key region in the salience network; the lack of adequate connectivity between this region and the anterior cingulate and default mode network is associated with a compromised ability to process and integrate external stimuli and internal mental events. This leads to emotional misappraisal and inaccurate emotional cueing, deficits that intensify poor conflict resolution and self-regulation (Marusak et al., 2015). Unfortunately, when insula signaling demands increase for trauma-exposed individuals, reward sensitivity diminishes proportionately. Consequently, these individuals are subjectively more distressed in conflict situations, a factor that can intensify anxiety and depressive symptoms over time (Marusak et al., 2015).

A similar lack of connectivity between the amygdala and default mode network pattern is found in patients with early childhood onset depression, a disorder that has strong associations with maternal history of depression (Luking et al., 2011). Maternal depression is often a pervasive disorder and is regarded as one of the childhood adversity factors in the ACE assessment (Felitti and Anda, 2010). Consequently, future studies that investigate neurological alterations should differentiate individuals with depression and childhood adversity compared to individuals with adult-onset depression and no childhood adversity. There may be different neurological factors that influence depression symptom formations (Heim, Plotsky, and Nemeroff, 2004). For example, helplessness, a symptom that may be associated with depression or depression and a history of childhood adversity, is associated with alterations in limbic forebrain (amygdala, hippocampus, parahippocampus) structures as well as alterations in connectivity between the midbrain and hypothalamus (i.e., HPA axis). This passive collapsing behavior results from a significant lack of metabolic resources, including hypo-responsiveness in the glucocorticoid receptors, blunted HPA feedback loops, and a decoupling connectivity within prefrontal regions that are essential for executive functioning (Shumake, Conejo-Jimenez, Gonzalez-Pardo, and Gonzalez-Lima, 2004).

Early childhood adversity also compromises executive networks, with study findings suggesting abnormalities in prefrontal cortical connectivity, including decreased volume in the orbital frontal cortex (Danese and McEwen, 2012). These abnormalities are associated with increased symptoms of attention-deficit-hyperactivity disorder and problem-solving difficulties. Coupled with smaller hippocampus volume, poor activation and connectivity in the medial prefrontal cortex and the anterior cingulate are associated with a failure to extinguish fear responses, leading to a heightened re-experiencing of traumatic events (Bremner, Elzinga, Schmahl, and Vermetten, 2008).

Neuroendocrine Immune System

The immune system undergoes changes as a result of chronic childhood adversity. Prolonged pro-inflammatory cytokine secretion increases inflammation levels and limits protection from infection. As a result, these children are more vulnerable to disease, including autoimmune diseases that often appear in adulthood (Danese and McEwen, 2012). In individuals with chronic stress and PTSD, changes occur in the hypothalamic-pituitary-thyroid axis, in particular, baseline levels of triiodothyronine (T3), total thyroxine (T4), thyroxine-binding globulin (TBG), and thyrotropin (TSH) are increased (Vermetten and Bremner, 2002). When chronic stress persists throughout childhood, sex hormones, growth hormones, and pancreatic insulin are all inhibited, which compromises adolescent development and increases vulnerability to future disease (Baumann and Turpin, 2010). As well, cumulative and chronic stress undermines cardiovascular and autoimmune systems plus the psychological protective factor of self-esteem. Studies have demonstrated that strong self-esteem buffers inflammatory responses; individuals with poor self-esteem and a history of maltreatment have more difficulties reducing stress-related inflammatory activation (O'Donnell, Brydon, Wright, and Steptoe, 2008).

Autonomic Nervous System

The ANS is a dynamic system that regulates physiologic responses to internal and external events. Although inadequate in individuals with stress-related disorders, the ANS directly influences stress coping systems (Berntson and Cacioppo, 2007). In PTSD and dissociative disorders, the ANS is biased toward more sympathetic and adrenal (sympatho-adrenal) activation (PTSD) or more parasympathetic vagal responsivity (dissociation). In general, sympatho-adrenal activation is driven by a tight interaction with the external environment, it requires high levels of energy, and sensory feedback is primarily exteroceptive in nature; whereas, more vagal engagement is dominated by a disengagement with the environment, requires lower levels of energy, and relies on proprioceptive and interoceptive feedback (Recordati, 2003). Similar to PTSD, personality disordered patients (i.e., borderline and histrionic) demonstrate more sympathetic arousal in response to a stressor, whereas, dissociative patients display a blunted sympathetic response (Schmahl, Elzinga, and Bremner, 2002). When extreme sympatho-adrenal or vagal activation is required then normal behaviors such as feeding, hydration, micturition, and defecation are greatly reduced. These extreme stress demands hamper physiologic self-regulation and increase prevalence rates of physical and mental disorders (Recordati, 2003). For example, disruptions in vagal tone are significantly associated with poor self-esteem (Martens, Greenberg, Allen, Hayes, Schimel, and Johns, 2010), increased psychological defensiveness, and social anxiety (Movius and Allen, 2005).

When examining the ANS and the influence of childhood maltreatment, massive dysregulation is evident. For example, living in communities with high levels of violence alters physiologic hyperarousal responses. This is evidenced in an adolescent sample. Rather than becoming physiologically desensitized to repeated exposure to violence, they became physiologically hypersensitized to aggressive behavior and threat (Gaylord-Harden, Bai, and Simic, 2017). As well, exposure to interpersonal violence diminishes vagal tone responsiveness, especially when toxic levels of shame are induced. In shame-prone individuals reminders of these painful experiences actually increases sympathetic arousal. In these shame-prone individuals, vagal regulation is greatly reduced compared to those who are exposed to interpersonal violence but do not suffer toxic levels of shame (Freed and D'Andrea, 2015).

Individuals who are exposed to trauma or who are diagnosed with PTSD often have great difficulty returning to optimal physiologic regulation, and this is exacerbated when cognitive appraisals of threat are high and they are unable to diminish these threat appraisals (Kibler, 2018). This prolonged alteration demonstrates a profound sympathetic dysregulation that can then lead to functional somatic disorders such as irritable bowel syndrome, chronic fatigue, chronic pain, or fibromyalgia (Afari et al., 2014). Likewise, it is strongly associated with increased cardiovascular disease (Kibler, 2009). To counter this negative trajectory, studies indicate that, immediately after a traumatic event, ANS responses can be re-regulated via the administration of beta-blockers (medications that block beta-adrenergic receptors). Without beta-blocker support, hyperarousal of the sympathetic nervous system persists long after the traumatic event ends. This medication also helps inhibit the consolidation of new trauma memories; this is accomplished by blocking beta-adrenergic receptors in the amygdala (Meli et al., 2017).

Diminished vagal tone of the parasympathetic branch of the ANS demonstrates low heart rate variability. It is a marker of physiologic and behavioral dysregulation (Geisler and Kubiak, 2009) and is evident in individuals with anxiety disorders (Pittig, Arch, Lam, and Craske, 2013). Young healthy adults typically display optimal heart rate variability; however, for those with PTSD, low heart rate variability is associated with increased cardiovascular difficulties, in particular, orthostatic hypotension (Oddone et al., 2015). This is a result of inadequate sympathetic vasoconstriction, which leads to decreased blood pressure causing dizziness and fainting, As well, low heart rate variability caused by PTSD increases risk for osteoarthritis, Alzheimer's disease, some cancers, arrhythmias, and cardiovascular disease (Dekker et al., 2000; Kiecolt-Glaser, McGuire, Robles, and Glaser, 2002). Sleep disruptions in PTSD patients are often associated with decreased parasympathetic control (as opposed to increased sympathetic tone) and lower heart rate variability (Rissling et al., 2016). When disease progresses, extreme physical frailty is marked by greatly diminished heart rate variability; this indicates severe disruptions in cardiac autonomic control (Varadhan et al., 2009). With diminished physiologic self-regulation, low heart rate variability is also associated with a compromised pursuit of goals and diminished self-esteem (Geisler and Kubiak, 2009).

Genetics, Methylation, and Telomeres

Genetic inheritance is shaped by environmental interactions. For example, early stress has long lasting effects, in part because of alterations in DNA methylation. Methylation is known to mediate the interactions between genes and environment; individual differences emerge despite experiencing similar conditions (Meaney, 2010). Methylation is the chemical process of altering DNA molecules via adding methyl groups to a specific nucleotide (cytosine). This process adds information to the DNA molecule without changing the specific sequence of the gene; consequently gene expression is altered (Szyf and Bick, 2013). Activating or deactivating DNA methylation may actually operate as a form of genomic memory. The early experiences are encoded into epigenetic patterns that shape subsequent development (Lutz et al., 2017); this genomic memory is transmitted to subsequent generations via DNA methylation expression in the unborn fetuses (Franklin et al., 2010).

Profound methylation changes occur in regulatory regions in the brain during the first year of life when mothers suffer heightened stress (Essex et al., 2013). These changes result because the regulatory regions of the brain are saturated with DNA methylation sites. A similar pattern occurs when fathers are under intense stress during the preschool years of the child. When both early maternal and parental stress is high even more DNA methylation changes transpire. Because neuronal development is prolific in these early years, the effects of parental stress substantially alters the child's genome; whereas, later developmental periods are less influenced by parental stress

(Essex et al., 2013). Studies demonstrate early adverse environments influence specific methylation processes in the kappa opioid and serotonergic systems (i.e., serotonin transporter [5HTTLPR] linked polymorphic region); these alterations increase vulnerability for disorders such as PTSD and unresolved trauma and loss (Beach, Brody, Todorov, Gunter, and Philibert, 2010; Lutz et al., 2017). Levels of methylation vary when accounting for interactions with short or long 5HTT alleles. Greater methylation on long alleles increases the likelihood of unresolved loss/trauma whereas the opposite is true for short allele interactions (van IJzendoorn, Caspers, Bakermans-Kranenburg, Beach and Philibert, 2010). In those with histories of childhood maltreatment, less methylation activation on short 5HTT alleles may serve as genetic protection against more pathology (van IJzendoorn et al., 2010).

Gene-environment interactions have also been demonstrated in children exposed to extreme stress at the level of glucocorticoid receptor genes (NR3C1) and nerve growth factor (NGFI-A) (Romens, McDonald, Svaren, and Pollak, 2015). When specific forms of abuse are experienced repeatedly, specifically childhood sexual abuse, and to a lesser degree, childhood neglect, physical abuse, and emotional abuse, increased methylation of the glucocorticoid receptor gene (NR3C1) is evidenced (Perroud et al., 2011). Changes in methylation of the glucocorticoid receptor gene lead to permanent alterations in the HPA axis. These alterations are strongly associated with adulthood psychopathology, such as borderline personality disorder and major depressive disorder (Perroud et al., 2011). As well, genes that are associated with the HPA axis are strong candidates for PTSD susceptibility (Yehuda, 2001; Yehuda, Golier, Halligan, Meaney, and Bierer, 2004; Yehuda, Golier, Yang, and Tischler, 2004). One of these genes, FKBP5, directly interacts with glucocorticoid receptor regulation and sensitivity, in particular attenuated cortisol response to stress (Buchmann et al., 2014). Like previous studies that demonstrate alterations in the stress axis, the FKBP5 stress-related gene is altered by childhood adversity causing more PTSD symptoms in adulthood (Binder et al., 2008; Reul et al., 2015). This particular study finding indicates that PTSD may be strongly associated with early maltreatment coupled with an adult traumatic event. In a meta-analysis (Lind et al., 2017), a strong candidate for PTSD vulnerability, especially in females is the 'C' allele of rs2267735. This allele interacts within the ADCYAP1R1 gene of the PACAP receptor. The PACAP is critical in regulating central and peripheral stress responses via modulation of the HPA axis through CRH activation. Chronic and/or unpredictable stress increases genetic activation in PACAP within the bed nucleus of the stria terminalis (BNST), which is considered part of the extended amygdala. Activation in this region increases the stress response within the HPA axis and decreases activity in the hippocampus. The results of this meta-analysis demonstrate that PTSD is moderately heritable, especially in females (Lind et al., 2017).

Suicide risk in traumatized individuals is associated with methylation of the spindle and kinetochore-associated complex subunit 2 gene (SKA2) (Sadeh et al., 2016). The neurobiological effects of PTSD on this gene manifest as bilateral reductions of cortical thickness in the fronto-polar gyrus, superior frontal gyrus, right orbitofrontal cortex, and right inferior frontal gyrus. As well, the combination of reduced cortical thickness in these regions along with increased methylation at the SKA2 gene increases the likelihood of suicidal thoughts and behaviors (Sadeh et al., 2016). In an early study, low levels of monoamine oxidase A (MAOA) expression was associated with conduct disorder and antisocial behavior; however, this behavior only emerged when the individual was reared in adverse maltreating childhood conditions (Caspi et al., 2002; Widom and Brzustowicz, 2006)). Genetic deficiencies in MAOA activity lead to deficits in serotonin, dopamine, and norepinephrine systems. Deficits in these neurotransmitters diminish the regulation of aggression; consequently, when children with MAOA genetic insufficiencies are maltreated there is less ability to maintain adequate neurotransmitter levels essential to regulate the stressors of their childhood environment (Caspi et al., 2002). Interpersonal violence and substance use/dependence also have genetic influences (Palmer et al., 2016). In the Palmer et al. study, a genetic bias to acquire a substance use disorder increased the risk for more domestic and interpersonal violence (Palmer et al., 2016). In the Afifi et al. study, the genetic inheritance for specific personality traits influenced partner selection, partner interactions, and interpersonal violence (Afifi, Asmundson, Taylor, and Jang, 2010).

Aging is also influenced by a gene-environment interaction. Telomeres are caps on the ends of chromosomes. With normal aging these DNA-protein protected structures begin to shorten; however, genetic factors and environmental stress cause more rapid degradation of the telomere lengths. With shortened telomeres, risk for age-related disorders such as cardiovascular, pulmonary, or Alzheimer's disease increases (Puterman et al., 2016). Childhood adversity (including prenatal stress) is the greatest predictor for telomere damage, although adult adversity also alters telomere length (Puterman et al., 2016).

Stress Neuropeptides and Endogenous Opioids

Neuropeptides are influential neuromodulators. One of the key anxiolytic neuropeptides is Neuropeptide-Y (NPY); it is expressed in multiple regions in the CNS as well as peripherally in the platelets in the blood, the sympathetic nervous system ganglia, and the adrenal medulla (Enman, Sabban, McGonigle, and Van Bockstaele, 2015). In trauma-exposed individuals, NPY is diminished (Morgan et al., 2003); however, in highly resilient individuals, under stress conditions, more NPY is expressed, which promotes feelings of self-confidence and self-efficacy (Morgan et al., 2002). Lower levels of NPY or genetic variants in NPY are associated with increased depression, anxiety, PTSD, and suicidality (Enman et al., 2015; Vermetten and Bremner, 2002). Increased levels of NPY may underlie resilience in individuals who are exposed to similar childhood adversity. For example, in some individuals, early stressful environments enhance cognitive adaptations and improve executive functioning (Mittal et al., 2015; Pagli et al., 2017). Oxytocin may also increase resilience. It functions as a neuropeptide and a neurotransmitter and is an integral component in the HPA axis, the ANS, hippocampus, amygdala, and hypothalamus. Study findings demonstrate higher levels of oxytocin are associated with empathy and resilience; whereas, lower levels indicate an increased likelihood of PTSD, lack of empathy, and poor resilience (Palgi, Klein, and Shamay-Tsoory, 2017).

Resilience is also influenced by endogenous opioids; they enhance social interactions and well-being. Alterations in the kappa opioid signaling, especially in the anterior insula, are strongly associated with childhood adversity, depression, and suicide (Lutz et al., 2017; Vermetten and Bremner, 2002). These alterations are the result of DNA methylation in the glucocorticoid and kappa opioid receptors. When kappa opioids are decreased in the anterior insula, greater clinical trauma symptomatology manifests, including deficits in social emotional regulation. These results indicate that the kappa opioid may be responsible for encoding social experiences during early childhood, in particular, alterations due to childhood adversity (Lutz et al., 2017).

POSTTRAUMATIC STRESS DISORDER

Adults exposed to trauma who develop PTSD symptoms differ from those who do not develop PTSD, although both trauma-exposed groups display increased neurological activation to negative stimuli (New et al., 2009). For example, trauma-exposed individuals with PTSD have greater difficulty attenuating negative emotional responses. The non-PTSD trauma-exposed individuals are able to increase activation in sensorimotor networks (supplementary motor area) during negative stimuli, suggesting that they can access more empathy while focusing on negative stimuli. This difference may allow them to optimally sustain and regulate their negative emotional experiences via more perspective-taking strategies, including emotional modulation that occurs in the anterior cingulate, prefrontal cortex, and supplementary motor area (New et al., 2009).

Another hallmark feature of adult PTSD is an alteration in response inhibition processes (Aupperle, 2016). Optimal functioning results through a process of inhibiting responses that are no longer needed in any given situation. During tasks that involve attentional complexity, response inhibition and the ability to monitor responses and outcomes is engaged via activation in regions within the dorsal prefrontal cortex, medial prefrontal cortex, and anterior cingulate (Chambers, Garavan, and Bellgrove, 2009). In PTSD patients, these regions are hypo-activated. As well, increased activation occurs in the amygdala and insula, which compromises response inhibition and intensifies emotional responses. Ultimately, during low cognitive demands, PTSD individuals have deficits in disengaging the default mode network and during increased cognitive demand they have more deficits modulating processing of information within the executive control network and salience network. Collectively, these alterations suggest decreased response inhibition and poor neural flexibility in PTSD patients (Aupperle, 2016).

Researchers speculate that the default mode network (DMN) is intricately associated with PTSD symptoms (Daniels, Bluhm, and Lanius, 2013). The DMN is one of the main resting state networks in the brain and is comprised of midline frontal and parietal structures as well as medial and lateral temporal, lateral parietal, insula, and thalamus regions (Spreng, Mar, and Kinm, 2009). The DMN is actively involved in autobiographical memory formation and storage; one of the primary tasks is internal focus such as thinking about the self (self-referential, emotional awareness) and others (theory of mind, moral reasoning, empathy). This network is involved in remembering the past and thinking about the future (Beaty, 2015; Mayseless et al., 2015). The DMN also plays a significant role in processing pain, as well as perceiving pain in others (Jackson et al., 2005). It is speculated that abnormalities in the DMN as well as impaired interconnectivity between the DMN and regions such as the amygdala and the prefrontal cortex may be related to PTSD symptoms (Daniels et al., 2013). For example, timing failures to suppress or engage DMN in resting and active states may result in attentional and behavioral problems, more dissociative processing, and diminished emotional regulation (Daniels et al., 2013; Hassabis, Kumaran, Vann, and Maguire, 2007).

Persistent rumination about trauma and loss experiences is related to increased symptoms of depression, anxiety, and PTSD (Buchholz et al., 2016), as well as sleep disorders (sleep disturbances and daytime sleepiness) (Borders, Rothman, and McAndrew, 2015). In a study that examined women with PTSD and trait rumination behaviors, increased activity in the right inferior orbital frontal cortex was found (Buchholz et al., 2016). This region is considered part of the ventral medial prefrontal cortex, with reciprocal connections to the amygdala. This activation pattern suggests biased attention toward negative emotional stimuli as well as an inability to inhibit them. Disruptions in functioning in this region compromise decision-making and emotional regulation; faulty retrieval of emotional information within the working memory system exacerbates these problems. Failures in this process lead to negative rumination that persists over time and impedes PTSD healing (Buccholz et al., 2016). A similar finding is identified in adults who struggled with chronic embitterment, a form of rumination that is biased toward the moral injury caused by a traumatic event and the desire to seek retribution (Linden and Rottern, 2018). This form of embittered rumination is associated with increased activation in the precuneus and uncinate fasciculus, regions engaged in episodic memory retrieval. This neural activation pattern intensifies trauma-related preoccupation (Kuhn et al., 2018).

Other neurological alterations in adult PTSD groups include hyper-responsivity in the amygdala and hypo-responsivity in the medial prefrontal cortex, especially during cognitive emotional tasks (Shin et al., 2006). PTSD groups have diminished volume and neural functional connectivity in the hippocampus (Bremner, 2006; Shin et al., 2006). Chronic stress in adulthood inhibits dendritic growth in the prefrontal cortex, which has a cascading effect associated with poor amygdala regulation and enhanced norepinephrine activation (Arnsten, Raskind, Taylor, and Connor, 2015). Alterations in the anterior cingulate, basal ganglia, and insula (key regions for emotional and physiologic integration and processing) are also identified (Liberzon and Martis, 2006). These changes are associated with impaired top-down regulation and poor cognitive functioning.

Similar to childhood adversity, adult HPA axis functioning is altered during traumatic exposure (Yehuda, 2006). The HPA axis is a dynamic system that regulates multiple physiologic responses such as circadian rhythm patterns, tonic cortisol secretion, cortisol response during stress, as well as ongoing interactions with the neuroendocrine system in general. Likewise, compared to individuals who are able to successfully find resolution for past trauma and loss experiences, adults who remain unresolved have disruptions in the serotonin system and higher levels of methylation of the long 5HTT promoter gene variant (van IJzendoorn, Caspers et al., 2010). Chronic stress-induced activation of serotonin leads to decreased serotonin receptor density in forebrain regions as well as the hippocampus and amygdala. A dysfunctional serotonergic system ultimately hampers emotional and behavioral regulation (Vermetten and Bremner, 2002). For example, when serotonin activation is altered, individuals are unable to discriminate between safety and danger; fear is increased which compromises adequate appraisal of danger and safety. This inability to manage fear signals is a significant symptom in PTSD (Foilb and Christianson, 2016), anxiety, depression, and impulsivity disorders (Vermetten and Bremner, 2002). Changes in the HPA axis and serotonergic system directly influence systems that regulate sleep, aggression, and suicidality (Vermetten and Bremner, 2002). Further studies are needed to identify neurological alterations that endure after traumatic exposure; the complexity of emotional and behavioral responses is shaped by these alterations (Yehuda, 2006).

CONCLUSION

Alterations to early forming neurobiological systems, due to childhood maltreatment, increase the risk for physical and psychological disorders. Early maltreatment is associated with early age of onset of disorders, more severe course of these disorders, and poorer response to treatment (Teicher et al., 2012). Environmental stress at any age, and even more so in early development, can influence the genome via DNA methylation. Central and peripheral neurobiological systems are all vulnerable during early development, Changes are embedded into the genome and influence both risk and resilience factors (Szyf and Bick, 2013). These changes indicate the multifinality nature of a single overwhelming event during development and how it generates multiple pathological disorders (Curtis and Cicchetti, 2003). Biologically, the single event may intensify latent vulnerability for other disorders (Bosma, 2006).

Individuals who are exposed to extreme stress and psychological trauma are more likely to suffer functional somatic syndromes such as irritable bowel syndrome, chronic fatigue, pain, fibromyalgia, and temporomandibular disorder (Otis et al., 2003). Early maltreatment is also associated with migraine headaches. Physical and emotional abuse as well as emotional neglect are all strongly related to earlier age of migraine onset; they cause debilitating pain and loss of function (Tietjen et al., 2009). Chronic pain is associated with fear and avoidance, anxiety sensitivity, and catastrophic thoughts (Otis et al., 2003). Because approximately one-third of patients examined in health centers report distress of one or several of these functional somatic disorders, it raises concern that physicians may not be addressing the underlying trauma that causes these disorders (Afari et al., 2014). This somatic distress pattern is intensified in individuals exposed to combat and for those given a diagnosis of PTSD (Afari et al., 2014; Otis et al., 2003).

Individuals with functional somatic syndromes may struggle to return to a physiologic baseline once the hyperarousal stress system is mobilized. They manifest dysregulation of the ANS, which negatively influences cognitive processing and behavioral coping strategies (Afari et al., 2014). Initially, during therapeutic trauma recovery, patients are at increased risk for heightened psychological and physiologic symptoms. Remembering painful abuse often overwhelms the central and ANSs and in extreme cases, transient symptoms of pseudo-frontotemporal dementia-like syndromes may emerge, such as extreme spatial disorganization, loss of procedural motor functioning, and an inability to perform daily activities (Cohen and Brody, 2015). Transient dysregulated cortical and subcortical connectivity typically abate as trauma-recovery therapy progresses, although these extreme conditions may be alarming for patients, family members, and practitioners (Cohen and Brody, 2015). However, without adequate treatment, the deleterious effect of trauma increases somatic and psychological symptoms and impairs function and well-being. Hope to return to a homeodynamic balance is lost; there is now a shift to a permanent allostatic balance (Danese and McEwen, 2012). Individuals who suffer a complex array of psychological and physiologic trauma-based symptoms have a lived experience that is now infiltrated by unresolved trauma. Sadly, their perspective is one that is rooted in trauma.

Chapter 10

Shame

Shame, like guilt, embarrassment, and pride, is considered a "self-conscious emotion" (Tangney, Stuewig, and Mashek, 2007). Shame signals a threat to social structures; it operates as a moral emotion and sustains social values (Freed and D'Andrea, 2015; Kemeny, Gruenewald, and Dickerson, 2004). Feelings of shame are associated with self-reflection and self-evaluation; fundamentally the self is regarded as flawed, incompetent, and inferior (Cook, 2001). Like all emotional states, shame influences behavioral responses to external events, and these responses can achieve positive or negative results. Generally, shame interferes negatively with exploration and engagement in activities such as flow or creative experiences that provide enjoyment, pleasure or meaning (Eusanio et al., 2014; Thomson and Jaque, 2013, 2018c). It may be a momentary interruption or a protracted disengagement. Repeated exposure to shaming experiences may influence an internalization process of self-identity. The self then becomes shame-based; literally the self is created by these repeated shaming experiences (Tangney et al., 2007). Behavioral indicators of shame include withdrawal behavior, avoidance, attacking the self, or attacking others (Nathanson, 1992). These behaviors are also accompanied by feelings of fear, distress, anger, and disgust. Shame influences cognitive beliefs associated with personal attractiveness, seeing and being seen, desires and fears of closeness, sense of sexuality, competitive comparisons, dependence and independence, and sense of personal size, strength, ability, and skills (Cook, 2001). Shame also influences physiologic responses that then intensify cognitive beliefs and behavioral responses (Cook, 2001). Shaming experiences can provoke shame states; however, when shame is internalized into self-identity shame is then regarded as a trait (del Rosario and White, 2006). Trait shame is often described as shame-prone or shame-based. Individuals with internalized shame are much more likely to be triggered into shaming experiences and this trait often underlies other psychopathological disorders.

Shame is a self-directed evaluation of defectiveness that is initiated by perceptions of negative opinions of others (Tangney et al., 2007). The action tendency is one of hiding which increases self-oriented distress and diminishes empathic connections with others (Ketelaar and Au, 2003). The inward focus precludes cognitive and emotional resources to evaluate others, consequently the egocentric focus on the "bad self" blocks awareness of others' suffering (Tangney et al., 2007). Shame-prone individuals are biased toward expressions of anger and hostility, including blaming others. These behavioral responses significantly compromise relationships with others, and may increase the perpetration of psychological abuse (Tangney and Dearing, 2002). Shame-proneness may increase externalizing behavior in children, high-risk behavior in adolescents, and substance abuse in adulthood. Unlike guilt, shame is associated with increased breaches of moral behavior. Shame-proneness increases vulnerability to many psychiatric illnesses such as depression, eating disorders, suicidal ideation, PTSD, and dissociation (Tangney et al., 2007). Given the fact that shame is a social self-conscious emotion, research findings demonstrate a strong association between shame-proneness and social anxiety, generalized anxiety, and obsessive-compulsive disorder (Fergus, Valentiner, McGrath, and Jencius, 2010). Likewise shame-proneness is associated with a compromised immune system, increased sympathetic activation, and cardiovascular disease (Tangney et al., 2007).

SOCIAL AND PSYCHOLOGICAL CONCEPTS OF SHAME

The *social self-preservation theory* suggests that shame is an adaptive response within social groupings. Individuals with low-status who face social threat must cower and withdraw to appease high-status members of the group (Dickerson, Gable, Irwin, Aziz, and Kemeny, 2009; Dickerson, Gruenewald, and Kemeny, 2004). Shame postural behaviors such as collapsing, eye contact aversion, low hanging head, and stilling all indicate submissive behavior in response to threat or failure (Dickerson, 2008; Dickerson, Mycek, and Zaldivar, 2008; Tracy and Matsumoto, 2008). According to Atkinson (1964), shame influences avoidance behavior in achievement situations. His *expectancy-value theory of achievement motivation* describes a process of approaching a situation with anticipated success or withdrawing from a situation with anticipated failure. Success increases pride whereas failure increases shame. Along with success, self-efficacy is increased which further encourages expectancies of success (Turner and Schallert, 2001). With expectations of accomplishment, shame may not deter approach behavior, rather it may signal a need to re-evaluate and modify goal strategies. When shame operates in this manner it is associated with increased resilience (Turner and Schallert, 2001); however, individuals with toxic levels of trait shame usually lack this resilience (Cook, 2001).

Shame-prone individuals struggle to move toward goals, even when they identify strong values and express a desire to adhere to their values (Silfver, Helkama, Lonnqvist, and Verkasalo, 2008). In these individuals, shame undermines emotional regulation and increases vulnerability for depression and anxiety. Some compensatory strategies that shame-prone individuals adopt are to work and play alone and to work longer at tasks without seeking help (Chao, Cheng, and Chiou, 2011). The nature of their shame tends to evoke passive avoidance and active independence in social situations. This self-sufficiency behavior may stave off threats to the social self as well as to repair shame that may have been provoked in previous situations. One danger in this strategy is that an exaggerated sense of self-sufficiency may form, which diminishes relationships with friends and family (Chao et al., 2011).

Coping strategies in individuals who are shame-prone tend to be influenced by behaviors to avoid failure and embarrassment. Fear of failing increases anxiety, which then intensifies the anticipation of potential shaming experiences (Partridge and Wiggins, 2008). Fear of failure is associated with fears of self-diminishment. Shame-prone individuals fear they will demonstrate a lack of ability or talent, waste time and effort, or lose the interest of others. Driven by intense feelings of embarrassment and shame, they are uncertain about a future self. Shame-based individuals also struggle with persistent feelings of not being worthy or valued even when success is achieved (Conroy, Poczwardowski, and Henschen, 2001). Perfectionism may intensify fear of failure, which further increases shame (Stoeber, Kempe, and Keogh, 2008); perfectionistic-prone individuals typically suffer persistent states of shame (Stoeber et al., 2007). Perfectionism and shame also increase negative self-concept; this was demonstrated in a mediation study that examined dancers (Eusanio et al., 2014). In another study shame mediated maladaptive perfectionism and depression (Ashby, Rice, and Martin, 2006). Future research is needed to differentiate individuals who are prone to perfectionism versus shame, especially because maladaptive perfectionism is strongly related to shame.

In order to manage these fears or to address shaming situations one of four defensive coping strategies may be mobilized. They have different outcomes and different behavioral manifestations (Cook, 2001; Elison and Partridge, 2012). These strategies, as outlined in *Nathanson's Compass of Shame* (1992), include withdrawal, attack-self, avoidance, and attack-other. The withdrawal style engages behaviors of cowering and retreating from social threats. This style increases anxiety and amplifies a cognitive self-focused belief of being a failure and incompetent. The attack-self style also includes beliefs that the self is bad; however, this style is expressed as anger directed toward the self. This coping style fails to acknowledge feelings of shame, in part, because individuals who engage in this coping style tend to criticize the self with disparaging and self-deprecating remarks. They believe that these criticisms are accurate. Efforts to please others while angrily attacking the self are ultimately failed attempts to control shame. The third coping style is avoidance. This strategy includes denial and minimization; it is designed to distract from the painful feelings of shame. Individuals who engage in this form of coping also fail to recognize their feelings of shame. Lastly, the attack-other style is outwardly directed anger and blame. This strategy also fails to acknowledge shame; all attack-other behavior is directed toward externalizing shame in an effort to protect the self. The attack-other coping strategy is strongly associated with both physically and psychologically aggressive behavior; this pattern is increased in individuals with histories of traumatic exposure (Schoenleber, Sippel, Jakupcak, and Tull, 2015).

Disgust is different than shame, although it is also deeply interconnected. Disgust is ultimately a rejection or revulsion response and is designed to distance individuals from noxious stimuli (Badour and Feldner, 2016). It is a basic emotion that is both a visceral and cognitive feeling. It is difficult to change because it is linked with efforts to move away from contaminating properties of the stimulus (Bomyea and Allard, 2017). In interpersonal contexts, disgust, like guilt and shame, is a moral emotion that is related to aversion of attachment relationships and close connections with others (Bomyea and Allard, 2017). When an individual acts in a manner that others view as disgusting, that individual may feel guilt. In this situation, guilt is not pathological; however, if these feelings persist and intensify feelings of self-blame, disgust, and shame then guilt can become pathological (Bomyea and Allard, 2017). Individuals who believe they are disgusting are generally shame-prone and biased toward attack-self behavior. Self-forgiveness is not possible for these individuals, even though their distress is extremely high (Rangganadhan and Todorov, 2010).

Experiences of humiliation are often hidden by shame; humiliation involves feelings that someone has exposed the "naked-self" which makes the humiliated individual vulnerable to attack (Tomkins, 1963). Engaging in shame behavior helps displace an internalized memory of humiliation (Dorahy, 2017). It shifts the focus to a flawed self rather than grappling with the hurt inflicted by another. Strategies to manage both shame and humiliation often include dissociation. Efforts to compartmentalize and distance are reinforced by dissociative processes; however, this strategy further compromises a sense of an integrated self. Rage directed at the self or others may then be provoked by intense feelings of humiliation or shame (Dorahy, 2017).

NEUROBIOLOGY OF SHAME

The influence of shame on the stress systems and the autonomic nervous system are significant. In interpersonal violence victims with PTSD, unlike fear and anxiety, shame is directly associated with decreased parasympathetic deactivation at baseline testing, and during recovery shame is associated with the most delayed return to baseline (Freed and D'Andrea, 2015). This finding suggests that shame-prone individuals have greater difficulty recovering from the effects of trauma and shame reminders. In another study, shame was directly related to increased sympathetic activation, which indicates diminished parasympathetic regulation (Rohleder, Chen, Wolf, and Miller, 2008). During moments of shame, bodily freeze responses are activated. In a freeze response, signals from the amygdala to the periaqueductal gray region initiate a freeze response and the physical immobility is accompanied by a slowing of the heart rate (bradycardia) (Roelofs, Hagenaars, and Stins, 2010). Under threat situations, bradycardia is the physiologic response to immediate attentive reactivity (Azevedo et al., 2005). It is part of the freeze response. These studies indicate a profile of autonomic inflexibility and increased difficulty regulating emotional and physiologic responses (Thayer and Lane, 2000).

Shame is associated with increased release of cortisol, especially when negative social evaluations are directed at individuals (Dickerson, 2008; Dickerson, Mycek, and Zaldivar, 2008). The experience of social-evaluative threat that provokes shame directly involves the stress systems (Dickerson, 2008). Cortisol levels are elevated in individuals who are exposed to social evaluation, suggesting perceptual experiences of social threat (Rohleder, Beulen, Chen, Wolf, and Kirschbaum, 2007). This is evident in individuals who experience chronic shame; they have elevated inflammation and sympathetic activation in their ANS. Chronic shame is also associated with increased glucocorticoid sensitivity (Rohleder et al., 2008). Studies that investigate inflammatory processes demonstrate that pro-inflammatory cytokine tumor necrosis factor-alpha increases during social-evaluative threat (Dickerson et al., 2009). As well, glucocorticoids are insufficient to shut down the inflammatory response (Dickerson et al., 2009).

The negative effects of chronic shame that are provoked under social threats to the self via social evaluation or rejection have significant deleterious effects on psychological and physiologic well-being. Shame-proneness is both an emotional and physiologic stress activator. Shame-related cognitive and affective states are strong predictors of immunological-related disease (Dickerson et al., 2004). Although shame is a normal socially rooted emotion, when it is chronic or toxic it poses great danger to the health of the individual (Cook, 2001).

CHILDHOOD MALTREATMENT AND SHAME

Attachment figures are the most significant figures in early childhood. When these important figures provoke feelings of shame in small children and they fail to adequately repair shaming experiences, then small children form shame-based memories that reinforce beliefs that their social self is unattractive, worthless, or flawed (Matos, Pinto-Gouveia, and Costa, 2013). Once shame memories are deeply encoded, they become internalized sources of threat and often persist into adulthood. When these shaming experiences are intensely destructive to the social self they may even become traumatic shame memories (Matos and Pinto-Gouveia, 2010). They are recorded into autobiographical memories; hence recall of early childhood and adolescence will provoke the return of shame-based memories. They operate as traumatic memories because they are emotionally and physiologically dysregulating and are experienced as an assault on the self (Matos and Pinto-Gouveia, 2010).

Managing shame memories that are rooted in early attachment experiences includes brooding rumination, efforts to suppress thoughts and memories, and engaging in dissociative processing. Like PTSD memories, they are intrusive, and avoidance behaviors are exerted to minimize emotional dysregulation resulting from these traumatic shame memories (Matos et al., 2013; Pinto-Gouveia and Matos, 2011). Over time, these attachment-based shame memories, coupled with maladaptive emotional regulating strategies, lead to depressive and anxiety symptoms. Attachment figures as well as significant others such as mentors, teachers, and coaches have the power to positively or negatively shape self-identity in young children. Through repeated shaming experiences these children regard themselves as unlovable, unworthy, undesirable, and defective. These beliefs are internalized as indelible beliefs about the self (Pinto-Gouveia and Matos, 2011; Matos et al., 2013).

Psychological child maltreatment is often referred to as emotional abuse or neglect. This form of maltreatment involves rejection, neglect, and/or isolation. Study findings indicate that psychological maltreatment is associated with the onset of depression in adulthood (Bifulco et al., 2002). Likewise, psychological maltreatment increases shame responses, which further intensifies depressive symptoms, as well as bipolar disorder in some individuals (Fowke, Ross, and Ashcroft, 2012; Webb, Heisler, Call, Chickering, and

Colburn, 2007). Parental criticism, family conflict, and poor family cohesion foster shame-prone dispositions in adulthood (Tangeny and Dearing, 2002). Parental disgust that is directed at the child, withdrawal of love, and disciplinary approaches that include messages of rejection all intensify shame-proneness (Tangeny and Dearing, 2002). Similarly, child neglect increases childhood depression and strongly influences the formation of a shame-prone personality (Bennett, Sullivan, and Lewis, 2010). Neglect involves deprivation of warmth, attention, and positivity from parents, which diminishes the formation of positive self-representations (Toth, Cicchetti, Macfie, and Emde, 1997). Childhood neglect influences the formation of cognitive beliefs that are hallmark features in shame and depression diagnoses; these enduring global negative beliefs increase behaviors of withdrawal, isolation, and hiding the damaged self (Bennett et al., 2010).

Following a history of childhood sexual abuse, victims who develop persistent and severe shame-proneness have greater difficulty recovering from PTSD (Feiring and Taska, 2005). They tend to respond poorly to treatment, perhaps due to efforts to hide or withdraw from shame-based memories. Longitudinally, victims who manifest high levels of shame immediately following episodes of childhood sexual abuse frequently display toxic levels of shame years later and this pattern is even more pronounced when intense feelings of shame persist one year post sexual abuse exposure (Feiring and Taska, 2005). Combined with childhood sexual abuse other factors contributing to sustained levels of high shame include parental hostility, rejection, and psychological maltreatment. For example, experiencing ongoing verbal humiliation intensifies shame and often prohibits disclosure of childhood sexual abuse (Negrao, Bonanno, Noll, Putnam, and Trickett, 2005). Shame memories form as a result of these experiences and they are marked by a failure to transfer painful experiences into a meaningful resolution of the trauma (Feiring and Taska, 2005). Consequently, treatment recommendations for victims with childhood sexual abuse histories must include addressing shame-based negative self-appraisals in order to reduce PTSD symptom severity (Ginzburg et al., 2009).

Developmental trauma influences the formation of a defective sense of self. Over time, managing these maladaptive feelings of shame increases risk for psychopathology (Schimmenti, 2012). For example, children with histories of physical abuse demonstrate less pride upon successfully completing tasks and more intense shame following a failed task (Deblinger and Runyon, 2005). Likewise, increased exposure to bullying and the resulting psychological distress is strongly mediated by shame (Strom, Aakvaag, Birkeland, Felix, and Thoresen, 2018). These shame-based negative learning experiences diminish academic achievement and hamper efforts to explore and engage. Ultimately, shame-proneness, which persists into adulthood, is strongly related to early assaults to the developing self (Deblinger and Runyon, 2005).

PTSD AND SHAME

Shame and PTSD are strongly linked, even though PTSD is typically associated with intense fear (Vasquez et al., 2012). Shame is an internalized belief that the self is bad, weak, and powerless. During a traumatic event feelings of being rendered powerless are prototypical. For example, exposure to interpersonal trauma is fertile ground to provoke feelings of shame (La Bash and Papa, 2014). Interpersonal partner violence induces high levels of shame in both the perpetrator and the victim. This shared experience of shame intensifies PTSD symptoms and may reinforce subsequent interpersonal partner violence based on the attack-other coping strategy that some adopt to manage toxic levels of shame (Hundt and Holohan, 2012). This emotional response leads to negative socio-cognitive PTSD symptoms (APA, 2013; La Bash and Papa, 2014). In a sample of sexually assaulted victims, the more severe the sexual assault the more intense the distress, including symptoms of depression and PTSD. With increased shame, these individuals have more difficulty disclosing the sexual assault as well as the psychopathology that follows the traumatic event (DeCou, Cole, Lynch, Wong, and Matthews, 2017). The event is recorded as a traumatic shame memory that intensifies distress (Matos and Pinto-Gouveia, 2010). The ubiquitous nature of this form of shame-based traumatic exposure has led researchers to propose the term post-traumatic shame rather than PTSD. These traumatic events shape perceptions that the self is now flawed (Wilson, Drozdek, and Turkovic, 2006).

Guilt, as well as shame, is often evoked in the aftermath of terror (Aakvaag et al., 2017). Individuals who experience heightened shame often ruminate about their actions after the mass terror event. They negatively appraise themselves as flawed, which is why the event was not stopped, or they feel shame because others witnessed their fear and behaviors such as immobility or fleeing from the scene. They were not the heroes that they imagined they might be. The horror of mass terror is then compounded by painful feelings of guilt and shame, which then intensifies trauma-related symptoms (Aakvaag et al., 2017).

PTSD symptoms and aggression are strongly associated with shame and guilt; however, unlike guilt, shame is associated with verbal and physical aggression as well as PTSD in a veteran sample (Crocker, Haller, Norman, and Angkaw, 2016). Shame reactions of attacking the self or others increase acts of violence including physical aggression, domestic/intimate partner violence, familial homicide, and sexual assault (Velotti, Elison and Garofalo, 2014). Shame-proneness is also associated with higher frequency of revictimization in women who were abused in childhood. Perhaps their feelings of unworthiness increased vulnerability to further victimization in adulthood (Kessler and Bieschke, 1999).

Trauma-related disgust such as feelings evoked after childhood sexual abuse or rape often provokes efforts to reject the body; this feeling is even more distressing for parents who feel that their child is disgusting after being victimized (van Delft et al., 2016). Highly traumatized polyvictimized individuals typically manifest heightened fear responses during a traumatic event, and after the event many also develop disgust along with their fear reactions. The added feelings of disgust increase PTSD symptoms, especially more intense emotional reactivity (Bomyea and Allard, 2017). The *law of contagion* is a belief that contamination spreads and will infect others who are near the noxious stimuli (Rozin, Millman, and Nemeroff, 1986). Contagion fears intensify beliefs that permanent contamination is inevitable; this fear makes it even worse for victims and may activate specific phobias and obsessive-compulsive behaviors (Mason and Richardson, 2012).

Shame, disgust, and guilt are complex social emotions that operate in individuals with PTSD (Budden, 2009). The fear-based model of PTSD does not do justice to the profound social emotions that are also activated during traumatic events. In particular, intentional interpersonal assaults are fundamentally an attack on the self. This attack alters core beliefs and reinforces negative self-evaluations of a negative, inferior self (Budden, 2009). Currently the DSM-5 and the ICD-10 include alterations to self-concept; the diagnosis of PTSD recognizes that the social self was attacked (APA, 2013). Robust research demonstrates the association between shame and PTSD; the need to clinically address shame in order to effectively treat PTSD is essential (Saraiya and Lopez-Castro, 2016).

SHAME AND DISSOCIATION

Shame is also significantly related to dissociative processes. The intensely painful response of shame, one that carries the belief that the self is unworthy, may evoke dissociation in an effort to numb psychic pain (Vasquez et al., 2012). Researchers have posited that shame-proneness may actually be a diathesis for dissociation (Talbot, Talbot, and Tu, 2004). For example, shame is more intense in a population of dissociative identity disorder patients; in particular, they manifest more shame-based attack-self, withdrawal, and avoidance compared to other clinical and non-clinical groups (Dyer et al., 2017). Shame-based attack-self behaviors are associated with increased state shame as well as a history of complex trauma and general mental illness disorders (Dyer et al., 2017). Beyond attack-self behavior, shame-proneness and a current dissociative disorder are strongly associated with relationship disconnections; interpersonal relationships are hampered when both shame and dissociation co-occur (Dorahy, 2010).

Betrayal trauma directly influences both shame and dissociation. The experience of betrayal by someone trusted, close, and depended upon intensifies trauma-related symptoms such as dissociation, depression, anxiety, avoidance, and intrusion (Freyd et al., 2012; Goldsmith, Freyd, and DePrince, 2012). For female victims of high-betrayal trauma, shame and dissociation are significantly evident (Platt and Freyd, 2015). Surprisingly, more trauma exposure intensifies shame and dissociation but not fear responses. Likewise, more trauma exposure and high betrayal is associated with more negative appraisals about traumatic events as well as more severe depression, dissociation, and PTSD symptoms (Martin, Cromer, DePrince, and Freyd, 2013). These findings suggest that complex emotional responses emerge in high-betrayal individuals and that they experience more intense harm to their sense of an integrated and valued self (Platt and Freyd, 2015; Smith and Freyd, 2013).

EATING DISORDERS

Shame and eating disorders are strongly associated, especially body shame (Gilbert, 2002). In patients with anorexia high levels of pride coexist with high levels of body shame (Goss and Allan, 2009). These patients pride themselves in their ability to exert great will-power to restrict food. This pride is countered by crippling negative appraisals about the social self. Eating disordered patients present with internal shame-based beliefs that the self is unworthy, inferior, unattractive, and should be the subject of intense self-criticism (Gilbert, 2002). They also adopt an external shame orientation, one that is built around the notion that others perceive them as flawed. Literally, the external other reflects the internal beliefs held by the patient. External shame orientation reinforces a need to withdraw and to hide; perceptions of rejection from the social group push the shame-based individual into more isolation (Gilbert, 2002). Shame-proneness increases attentional bias to detect threats associated with body shaming such as heightened sensitivity to comments or looks associated with size, shape, or weight. Comments often lead to catastrophic thoughts and further rumination, which then intensifies sensitivity to threat cues. This vicious cycle exacerbates disordered eating behaviors and intensifies eating disorder symptoms (Goss and Allan, 2009). For example, efforts to conceal the body, hide eating disordered behavior, and to destroy the object of shame (the embodied self) are all part of eating disorder symptoms; they are rooted in shame-based beliefs of a flawed self. Compensatory rebellion and restriction reinforce feelings of pride; however, for eating disordered patients, these opposing feelings become part of the same two-sided coin. They are trapped by both intense pride and shame (Goss and Allen, 2009).

Body shame is a specific form of shame. Attention is directed toward a perceived body flaw and this becomes amplified into a full attack on the social self. Media images and ideal body shapes influence body objectification and body shame (Dakanalis et al., 2014). Increased body surveillance intensifies body shame, social anxiety, and disordered eating. Altered perceptions of physical appearance become the beacon of negative self-identity (Troop and Redshaw, 2012). When this occurs, body shame operates as if it was an attack on the social self (Goss and Allen, 2009). This perceptual bias is strongly evident in anorexic disordered patients (Troop and Redshaw, 2012). Anticipated shaming experiences such as weight gain intensifies the shame cycle and provokes maladaptive shame-based regulatory behaviors. Negative self-reflection and rumination dominate in these individuals. As a result of their shame-based thoughts and perceptions, many individuals are no longer able to accurately assess body shape and body size; they perceive a much larger and more distorted physical sense of self (Troop and Redshaw, 2012).

CONCLUSION

Shame operates on a continuum ranging from normal to pathological (Cook, 2001). Optimally, shame influences socially appropriate behavior and may serve as a motivating factor to enhance achievement (Turner and Schallert, 2001). When shame is used as a positive motivating factor increased productivity results. Leaders who are aware of the positive effects of shame may use it as a tool to increase organizational performance and encourage professional development (Sauer and Ropo, 2006). Because shame is a social emotion, recruiting this emotional response is not a manipulation of others, rather it is employed to increase motivation, establish promotional goals, build self-efficacy, and promote shared social values (Gilbert, 2000; Turner and Schallert, 2001). Shame is an integral emotion to maintain social rank; higher ranked individuals have greater power to inflict shame on lower ranked members but they can also instill feelings of pride when individuals are promoted within the social group (Gilbert, 2000). On the other hand, pathological levels of shame intensify symptoms in disorders such as PTSD, anxiety, dissociation, depression, and personality disorders (Cook, 2001; Vikan, Hassel, Rugset, Johansen, and Moen, 2010). Shame, like creativity, is a complex social response that can lead to positive or negative outcomes. It is a significant emotion that shapes human interactions.

Researchers have suggested that maladaptive management of shame regulation may actually lead to personality pathology (Schoenleber and Berenbaum, 2012). Individuals with shame aversion and shame-proneness manifest withdrawal, avoidance, attack-self, and attack-other behavior.

Individuals with high shame-proneness may also adopt a unique array of strategies beyond the four already discussed. For example, efforts to prevent shame may occur via escaping into fantasy worlds. Unfortunately engaging in fantasy may offer relief from shame-based memories; however, shame may also increase ruminating brooding, which makes shame more intense (Thomson and Jaque, 2015). Preventing shame may also be achieved by forming dependent relationships with figures manifesting power and control; this strategy may intensify personality pathology such as a dependent personality disorder. Escaping from potentially shaming experiences may increase social withdrawal (avoidant personality disorder). As stated above, adopting aggressive (verbal or physical) behavior toward the self or others may serve to distract individuals from feelings of shame (Schoenleber and Berenbaum, 2012). These maladaptive regulation strategies are also behaviors that present in personality disordered individuals.

Despite robust research findings that indicate significant pathology associated with shame, especially in shame-prone individuals, many individuals are able to recover from intensely shameful experiences (Birrer and Morgan, 2010). Essentially, the damaged social self must be rebuilt (van Vliet, 2008). Encouragement to socialize and connect with others via talking with others, entering a therapeutic relationship, or engaging in spiritual practices directly challenge shame-based beliefs and offer opportunities to rebuild. Efforts to re-focus away from the brooding self-absorption that is a hallmark of shame-proneness provide opportunities to develop new skills, which can enhance self-esteem (Birrer and Morgan, 2010). Learning to accept the shame-based traumatic memories, understanding how they were formed, and practicing skills such as compassion to self and others reduces the negative appraisals of self (Fredrickson, 2004). This new perspective promotes changes in how meaning can be constructed, including increased resilience in subsequent potentially shaming experiences (van Vliet, 2008).

Chapter 11

Dissociation

Dissociative processing has long been associated with responses to traumatic events, whether it occurs in the initial onset during a traumatic event (peritraumatic dissociation), transiently emerging under stressful situations, or completely fragmenting a sense of self in all avenues of daily life. Although the onset of dissociative pathology results from trauma exposure, some forms of dissociative absorption are enhanced by a greater ability to engage in fantasy (Thomson and Jaque, 2011). In fact, the ability to create multiple selves to manage the complexity of daily life could be regarded as an extremely creative survival response. Many dissociative disordered patients have actually acknowledged that they value their creative abilities (Lynn and Rhue, 1988; Somer, 2002). In the context of this chapter, dissociation is generally regarded as a trauma response, one that interferes with daily functioning; however, it can also be understood as a unique adaptive strategy.

Dissociation has been defined as "disruptions of and/or discontinuity in the normal integration of consciousness, memory, identity, emotion, perception, body representation, motor control, and behavior" (APA, 2013, p. 291). It operates on a continuum with normal absorption residing within the healthy range and integrative pathological failures operating at the opposite end of the continuum. These failures cause significant disruptions in emotional recognition and processing, body representations, motor control, behavior organization and mobilization, memory retrieval and memory errors, and identity diffusion (Butler, 2006; Giesbrecht, Geraerts, and Merckelbach, 2007). Dissociation may manifest as an absence of memory of expectable experiences (amnesia), distortion of expectable perceptions (depersonalization/derealization), absence of memory and identity (dissociative fugue), and/or intrusion into expectable experiences of self-identities (dissociative identities) (Karpel and Jerram, 2015; MacDonald, 2008). Dissociative symptoms are often transient states that vary in degree of severity across time (Maaranen et al., 2008); although when dissociative states become pervasive they become dissociative traits (Kruger and Mace, 2002). Symptoms of dissociation operate as their own diagnosis in the DSM-5, plus they are part of a PTSD and Borderline Personality Disorder diagnosis. The inclusion of dissociation as a specifier for PTSD demonstrates the strong association between dissociation and trauma exposure (APA, 2013), however, dissociation is also associated with multiple disorders that may be unrelated to trauma exposure (i.e., bipolar disorder, schizophrenia, agoraphobia, social phobia, obsessive-compulsive disorder, and major depressive disorder (McKinnon et al., 2016).

Dissociation, although operating on a continuum, is also multidimensional, with many dissociative processes existing in isolation of the other dissociative processes. Some of the dissociative factors include disengagement, depersonalization, derealization, emotional constriction, memory disturbance, and identity disturbance; these factors can be evaluated at clinical and non-clinical levels of disturbance, thus they can be used to differentiate normative from pathological dissociation (Briere, 2002; Briere, Weathers, and Runtz, 2005). The model of multidimensional dissociative processing followings the model that explains complex trauma or cumulative trauma (Briere, Dietrich, and Semple, 2016). Consequently, dissociation research studies may report symptom complexity and comorbidity that are associated with cumulative trauma and cumulative risk for mental and physical disorders (Briere et al., 2016).

Differentiating individuals with the extreme form of dissociation, dissociative identity disorder (DID) (APA, 2013), from those individuals with PTSD and a dissociative specifier can sometimes be difficult because there are many overlapping symptoms (DePrince, Huntjens, and Dorahy, 2015). In most cases, both groups suffer extreme interpersonal abuse. One indicator that differentiates the DID patient population is a sense of alienation; they feel separate from others, disconnected from others, disconnected from a sense of self, and intense feelings of loneliness and emptiness (DePrince et al., 2015). Highly dissociative disordered patients typically have numerous comorbid disorders (i.e., depression, anxiety, personality disorders, substance abuse, PTSD, suicidality), which make their level of functioning low and treatment challenging and costly (Brand et al., 2013).

In a longitudinal study, persistent symptoms of dissociation and PTSD intrusion symptoms in ex-prisoners of war were associated with subjective feelings of loss of emotional control and detachment to reactions to captivity (Zerach et al., 2014). This symptom profile was not typical of veterans who were not held captive. The experience of being rendered helpless, along with systematic torture, deprivation, and humiliation while held as a prisoner of war persisted as intrusive flashbacks. For this ex-prisoner of war population, dissociative processing operated as a means to distance and numb these painful memories (Zerach et al., 2014).

DISSOCIATION AND COGNITIVE PROCESSING

Dissociation is strongly associated with memory deficits, especially for individuals with a trauma history. Many highly dissociative individuals with PTSD have memory intrusions; however, these intrusions manifest as perceptual sensations. Although autobiographical memories may be impaired, perceptual intrusions tend to be stronger, suggesting that somatic memories may be more rapidly retrieved during traumatic priming situations (Dorahy, Peck, and Huntjens, 2016). On the other hand, high dissociators exhibit difficulties in cognitive memory tasks. They tend to perseverate which diminishes memory task functioning and they display difficulties with cognitive tasks such as associative processing, context-dependent verbal content processing, visuospatial working memory access, and executive control during memory retrieval (Amrhein, Hengmith, Maragkos, and Hennig-Fast, 2008). These deficits were identified in a study that examined musicians; in particular, working memory deficits significantly hampered their performance ability (Swart, 2014). Despite efforts to concentrate, the dissociative processing reduced their attentional responses and limited effective learning (Swart, van Niekerk, and Hartman, 2010).

Distractability and processing slowness also compromise cognitive functioning in dissociative individuals (Guralnik, Giesbrecht, Knutelska, Sirroff, and Simeon, 2007). These mild cognitive deficits may be associated with impaired hippocampal function that is often evidenced in dissociative and PTSD patients (Amrhein et al., 2008). Although seemingly contradictory, findings indicate that high dissociators are better able to divide attention (de Ruiter, Phaf, Veltman, Kok, and van Dyck, 2003). For example, they can direct attention toward both emotional negative valence and letter detecting simultaneously. This capacity reflects the need of dissociative-prone individuals to continually monitor threat while also attending to non-threating stimulus (de Ruiter et al., 2003). There is also evidence that high dissociators express incongruent emotions; for example, they will describe a positive feeling for a negative memory, their memories are often visually incoherent, and/or they are filled with contradictory feelings of pride and shame (Sutin and Stockdale, 2011).

Multiple studies have demonstrated that hypnotizability and fantasy proneness are related to dissociation; fundamentally all involve high states of absorption (Terhune, Cardena, and Lindren, 2011). For example, hypnotizability is strongly associated with severe dissociative disorders. Repeated studies support the theory that hypnosis is a diathesis for pathological dissociation (Dell, 2017). Studies that examine the relationship between fantasy proneness and dissociation yield contradictory findings. Currently, it is hypothesized that fantasy proneness and dissociation are fundamentally different, including how absorption is employed. For example, in a psychobiological study that investigated patients with DID, low fantasy scores were reported (Reinders, Willemsen, Vos, den Boer, and Nijenhuis, 2012). Other studies have demonstrated moderate levels of fantasy proneness in patients with depersonalization (Levin et al., 2004). Some of the complications associated with findings that link fantasy and dissociation may be rooted in the conceptual notion that fantasy is uni-dimensional. Studies indicate that fantasy proneness is a more complex concept, especially when it is related to dissociation. For example, fantasy proneness has been dimensionalized into two different components, with dissociative absorption and fantasy related to psychopathology and daydreaming fantasies related to non-pathological dimensions of fantasy (Allen, Fultz, Huntoon, and Brethour, 2002; Klinger et al., 2009). The controversial link between fantasy and dissociation has raised an ongoing debate; specifically researchers posit that dissociation is related to fantasy (*fantasy-dissociation model*) or trauma (*trauma-dissociation model*) (Dalenberg et al., 2012). Growing research findings demonstrate a more complex relationship between fantasy, trauma, and dissociation (Giesbrecht, Merckelbach, and Geraerts, 2007; Dalenberg et al., 2012; Thomson and Jaque, 2011). The complexity of dissociative cognitive processing ultimately requires the need for multifactorial models (Briere, 2006; Lynn et al., 2014).

Because dissociation is fundamentally a disorder marked by lack of integration, difficulties such as recognizing emotions in the self and others are often prevalent (Elzinga, Bermond, and van Dyck, 2002). These difficulties do not reach the severity of alexithymia but there are overlapping features in dissociative disordered individuals (Simeon, Giesbrecht, Knutelska, Smith, and Smith, 2009; Tolmunen et al., 2010). Dissociative patients also tend to perceive themselves as more alone in the world. Perhaps as a compensation for their distress, they endorse more supernatural beliefs and experiences. They struggle with more amnesia and trance-like states, as evidenced in a study that observed perceptual processing in a group of dissociative patients (Pica, Beere, Lovinger, and Dush, 2001). The combination of internal emotional distress and external stress intensifies dissociative processing in individuals who are prone to dissociate. A vicious cycle of external stress incites internal distress which precipitates more dissociative processing which further increases internal distress and inhibits adaptive strategies to manage external stress (Soffer-Dudek and Shahar, 2014–2015). Under these conditions, escape may only reside in increased supernatural beliefs or trance-like states (Pica et al., 2001).

Beyond the commonly understood emotions of fear and anger that may increase dissociation, social self-conscious emotions are also deeply associated with dissociation. Shame and shame proneness, especially intense shame-based memories of childhood adversity and adult traumatic events, are strongly associated with dissociative processing (Dorahy, 2010, 2017; Thomson and Jaque, 2013). Dissociation, depression, and the shared features of brooding and thought suppression are all related to shame (Matos et al., 2013). Surprisingly, the relationship between shame and traumatic memories with attachment figures is not influenced by dissociative processing; perhaps because attachment-based shaming experiences are encoded differently than other traumatic memories (Matos et al., 2013). Similar to shame, feelings of guilt (a subjective feeling of hurting another) evoke strong states of dissociation; for example, intolerable guilt may provoke transient states of depersonalization and derealization (Rugens and Terhune, 2013).

PERITRAUMATIC DISSOCIATION

Peritraumatic dissociation is defined as the initial onset of dissociative symptoms during exposure to a traumatic event (Lanius et al., 2010). These include alterations in perceptions and disengagement from emotions. Typically, peritraumatic dissociative states manifest as depersonalization, derealization, temporal-spatial distortions, and for some individuals, gaps in memory encoding (Thompson-Hollands, Jun, and Sloan, 2017). When individuals report peritraumatic dissociation it usually predicts a subsequent diagnosis of PTSD (Lanius et al., 2010). These individuals rely on the distancing and numbing effects of dissociation to manage overwhelming trauma. Specifically, during traumatic exposure individuals who manifest more peritraumatic dissociation immediately following the traumatic event initially present with reduced PTSD symptoms; however, this reverses as time passes (Gil et al., 2016). Prolonged dissociation tends to consolidate PTSD symptoms, in part because of the inability to integrate memories and emotions. This condition also alters beliefs about the self; specifically more negative beliefs about the self are cultivated (Thompson-Hollands et al., 2017). This association between peritraumatic dissociation and PTSD was found in Israeli civilians who had direct contact with the Israel-Hamas war in 2014 (Gil et al., 2016), as well as in the general population (Thompson-Hollands et al., 2017). In a sample of Latino youth, peritraumatic dissociation, shame, and lifetime number or traumatic events were strong predictors of a future PTSD diagnosis (Vasquez et al., 2012). A similar pattern was found in traumatized detained youth. Peritraumatic dissociation also predicted a continuation of dissociative symptoms that were comorbid with PTSD (Bennett, Modrowski, Kerig, and Chaplo, 2015).

DEPERSONALIZATION/DEREALIZATION

Depersonalization/derealization disorder manifests as either transient or persistent symptoms that include feeling detached or estranged from oneself and/or the world. Future references in this chapter will only include the term depersonalization, although derealization is often implied as a variant of depersonalization. Perceptual alterations such as being an outside observer of one's mental processes and body (or body parts), sensations of numbness, and feeling a loss of self-agency are hallmark symptoms of depersonalization (APA, 2013). Reality testing remains intact despite the intense level of distress that is experienced (Mula, Pini, and Cassano, 2007). Individuals with this form of dissociation are often intensely self-focused; they continually focus on the distress of their symptoms. This bias toward self-focus inevitably intensifies depersonalization (Lawrence et al., 2007), especially when accompanied by deficits in mindfulness or metacognitive appraisals (Matthias et al., 2007; Michal et al., 2007). General prevalence rates for depersonalization range between 1.9 percent and 2.4 percent; these rates suggest that it is a significant contributor to impairment (Michal et al., 2009). Lifetime prevalence rates are even higher, ranging from 26 percent to 74 percent (Hunter, Sierra, and David, 2007). There is also a high prevalence rate of panic disorder in individuals with depersonalization disorder, with estimates ranging from 7.8 percent to 82.6 percent (Hunter et al., 2004). High levels of depersonalization are evident in patients with Borderline Personality Disorder. Efforts to detach from painful memories and feelings may intensify depersonalization states in these patients (Sar, Alioglu, and Akyuz, 2017).

Study findings indicate that anxiety and panic disorder are strong predictors of depersonalization; these results suggest that depersonalization may be one of many ways that anxiety is expressed (Hunter et al., 2004; Lee, Kwok, Hunter, Richards, and David, 2012). Although anxiety, as well as depression, is clearly identified in patients with depersonalization disorder, depersonalization also remains a separate diagnosis with its own symptom profile (Michal, Wiltink, Till, Wild, Blettner, and Beutel, 2011; Sierra, Medfor, Wyatt, and David, 2012). Childhood adversity is inconsistently identified as a significant predictor of depersonalization (Lee et al., 2012; Michal et al., 2009). However, childhood emotional abuse and neglect are strongly associated with depersonalization symptoms (Thomson and Jaque, 2018). Depression and somatic symptoms such as hypertension, diabetes mellitus, chronic pulmonary disease, and chronic pain are all associated with depersonalization (Michal et al., 2009). Auditory hallucinations, absorption, and self-focused attention are also associated with depersonalization (Perona-Garcelan et al., 2011, 2012). Because of the symptom profile of depersonalization, patients often manifest harm-avoidant temperaments (Simeon, Guralnik, Knutelska, and Schmeidler, 2002) and many manifest self-awareness impairments (Sierra and David, 2011). Despite subjective perceptions of detachment from a sense of self and emotional states, individuals who have high depersonalization symptoms actually engage in more emotion-oriented coping strategies and respond with more emotional overexcitability (Thomson and Jaque, 2018). The bias toward more emotional attention may further increase anxiety which then provokes more numbing sensations that are characteristic of depersonalization (Thomson and Jaque, 2018).

ATTACHMENT, CHILDHOOD ADVERSITY, AND DISSOCIATION

Young children exposed to childhood adversity are at greater risk for childhood dissociation; however, when these children are also raised by mothers who strongly dissociate greater dissociative symptoms are predicted in their children (Hagan, Hulette, and Lieberman, 2015). Because children follow parental behavior under stress, maltreated children are more readily primed to imitate maternal dissociative behaviors under stress. In general, exposure to physical and sexual abuse is associated with increased dissociation, although comorbid diagnosis of depression may be more strongly linked with sexual abuse whereas anxiety is generally associated with physical abuse (Boysan, Goldsmith, Cavus, Kayri, and Keskin, 2009). Other studies have identified a significant relationship between childhood emotional neglect by a parent and later emotional abuse by an intimate partner that increases pathological levels of dissociation, although all forms of childhood maltreatment are associated to a lesser extent with dissociation (Kruger and Fletcher, 2017). Because dissociation is fundamentally a failure to integrate a sense of self, a discontinuity of conscious awareness may influence medical assessment; dissociative patients are poor reporters of their symptoms, including the intensity and longevity of symptoms. This characteristic increases the need for medical practitioners to better understand this disorder, especially when they are assessing and treating children, adolescents, and adults who have histories of childhood maltreatment (Weber, 2008).

Disorganized attachment is strongly associated with dissociative processing. Disorganized infant behavior, adult unresolved mourning, and global disorganization in adults and children are identified by a collapse in organized coherent regulatory strategies. Studies have demonstrated that infants who are classified as disorganized have a significantly increased probability of being diagnosed with a dissociative disorder in adolescence (Carlson, 1998; Ogawa, Sroufe, Weinfield, Carlson, and Egeland, 1997). Maltreated preschool-aged children with a classification of disorganized attachment as infants also have higher rates of dissociation (Macfie, Cicchetti, and Toth, 2001). In dissociative children, maltreatment may be mild or severe but in every instance caregiver insensitivity is present (Lyons-Ruth, 2003). For example, parental frightened or frightening behavior has been identified as a source of infant disorganization and later dissociative processing (Abrams, Rifkin, and Hesse, 2006). Evidence derived from attachment self-report studies suggests that fearful attachment is associated with dissociation (Sandberg, 2010). Likewise, studies have demonstrated that disorganized attachment acts as a mediator between severe childhood abuse and dissociation (Byun, Brumariu, and Lyons-Ruth, 2016; Liotti, 2006). In adulthood, attachment studies identify a strong association between a classification of unresolved/global cannot classify and dissociation (Thomson and Jaque, 2012b, 2012c, 2014).

Dissociation may also operate as a protective factor during interpersonal violent incidents that involve parents or intimate partners. Depersonalization, derealization, amnesia, and flashbacks often accompany violent victimization. In a study that examined men who committed acts of intimate interpersonal violence (LaMotte and Murphy, 2017), 22 percent identified at least one instance of dissociative perpetration. Within this group, 71.6 percent reported multiple instances of dissociative perpetration. Because dissociation involves the breakdown of integrative processes, internal and external stimuli are not recognized, poorly recognized, or are not processed. Dissociative attentional avoidance diminishes opportunities to experience negative emotions and helps reduce the awareness of external cues that trigger them. This strategy intensifies depersonalization, which may then increase violent actions (LaMotte and Murphy, 2017). There is some indication that dissociative perpetration involves a disrupted ANS; the synergistic sympathetic and parasympathetic regulation is lost; consequently vagal tone (parasympathetic) may intensify dissociative processing as well as decrease arousal signals via slowing heart rate during the violent assault (Schauer and Ebert, 2010).

A history of childhood sexual abuse perpetrated by a family member often intensifies fear of abandonment in adulthood; this fear moderates the relationship between intimate partner violence and severity of dissociation (Zerubavel, Messman-Moore, DiLillo, and Gratz, 2018). In a study that examined small preschool children who were sexually abused by a family member, increased dissociative symptoms were often accompanied by pronounced sleep problems. Once again a vicious cycle is spawned; sleep deprivation then increases dissociative symptoms in these young children (Hebert et al., 2017). Homeless and unstably housed women typically have high prevalence rates of dissociation; they also have higher rates of childhood sexual abuse and childhood and adult exposure to physical violence (Young, Shumway, Flentje, and Riley, 2017). Sadly, dissociative processes also increase their risk for more violent victimization in the future (Young et al., 2017). In a study that examined violent offenders, compared to non-offenders, violent offenders had higher levels of disorganized attachment histories, childhood maltreatment, and dissociation (Baker and Beech, 2004). In a juvenile delinquent sample, childhood trauma perpetrated by a family member was strongly associated with dissociation (Plattner et al., 2003). In a psychopathic (antisocial) population, childhood abuse histories predicted impulsive and irresponsible lifestyle behaviors, but not dissociation (Poythress, Skeem, and Lilienfeld, 2006).

DISSOCIATION, PTSD, AND OTHER PSYCHIATRIC DISORDERS

The relationship between PTSD and pathological levels of dissociation is fully recognized in the DSM-5 and the ICD-10. Robust research has demonstrated this association in individuals exposed to trauma. The vicarious relationship between PTSD and dissociation that manifests in the spouse of a survivor is less researched (Weinberg, Besser, Ataria, and Neria, 2016). In one study, a bi-directional association between the survivor and spouse was indicated, both demonstrated increased dissociation and trauma-related symptoms in a similar trajectory (Weinberg et al., 2016). In attachment relationships, the transmission of dissociation and PTSD symptoms between caregiver and child has received significant attention. This dyadic relationship often shares dissociative cueing; one member of the dyad often provokes dissociative responses in the other member of the dyad (Hagan et al., 2015).

Patients diagnosed with panic disorder and agoraphobia display higher levels of dissociation (Briere, Scott, and Weathers, 2005; Pfaltz et al., 2013). Specifically, this panic disorder profile is associated with depersonalization disorder (Mendoza et al., 2011). For patients with panic disorder and agoraphobia, reminders of previous panic episodes induce extreme terror, which provokes avoidant behavior and dissociative processing as a means to decrease their panic (Pfaltz et al., 2013). The negative consequence is that dissociative processing intensifies feelings of estrangement from self and others even though a panic attack is diminished (Pfaltz et al., 2013). In one study (Ural, Belli, Akbudak, and Tabo, 2015) 19 percent of patients with panic disorder had a history of childhood trauma as well as comorbid dissociative disorders, especially dissociative disorder not otherwise specified, dissociative amnesia, and depersonalization. Childhood emotional abuse was the most significant predictor for both panic and dissociative disorders in this study (Ural et al., 2015). This prevalence rate is similar to prevalence rates (18%) in samples of patients with at least one comorbid dissociative disorder diagnosis and obsessive-compulsive disorder (Belli, Ural, Vardar, Yesilyurt, and Oncu, 2012).

Other disorders also involve dissociative processing. For example, burnout shares many features with chronic PTSD, especially emotional exhaustion (Boudoukha, Ouagazzal, and Goutaudier, 2017). Burnout is also associated with secondary trauma related to betrayal and moral injuries (Currier, Holland, Rojas-Flores et al., 2015). The combination of PTSD and burnout also indicates greater dissociative symptoms (Boudoukha et al., 2017). Conversely, persistent dissociation that is trauma related also intensifies and prolongs PTSD symptoms (Briere et al., 2005). Depression, PTSD, and dissociation are all related; they compound the risk of suicidality, especially in patients with a dissociative diagnosis (Foote, Smolin, Neft, and Lipschitz, 2008). Depersonalization and Type-D personality (negative affect and social inhibition) are also strongly associated with increased suicide behavior (Michal et al., 2010).

Dissociative responses, especially during stressful situations, are significantly identified in patients diagnosed with Borderline Personality Disorder (Brunner, Parzer, Schmitt, and Resch, 2004; Laddis, Dell, and Korzekwa, 2017; Stiglmayr et al., 2008), as well as in patients with other personality disorders, anxiety disorders, and/or mood disorders. In these patient populations, dissociation is associated with significant impairment (Johnson, Cohen, Kasen, and Brook, 2006). Dissociation is also evident in patients with the bulimic form of eating disorders (Hallings-Pott, Waller, Watson, and Scragg, 2005). Both anorexia and bulimia are associated with a history of childhood abuse, especially childhood emotional neglect and abuse (Pignatelli et al., 2017). Unlike anorexia, binge-eating symptoms are strongly associated with dissociative processing (Palmisano et al., 2018). Under stress, depersonalization is a significant feature of social anxiety; both social anxiety and depersonalization disorders interact and intensify symptoms (Michal et al., 2005). Psychotic and catatonia symptoms may also manifest in severe dissociation; likewise, dissociation is often present in patients diagnosed with a psychotic disorder (Moskowitz, Barker-Collo, and Ellson, 2005; Ross and Browning, 2016). Given the high risk of a dissociative diagnosis, along with other comorbid disorders, treatment protocols are needed to address these complex dissociative symptoms and risk factors (Hagenaars, van Minnen, and Hoogduin, 2010).

SELF-INJURIOUS/DELIBERATE SELF-HARM BEHAVIOR

Symptoms associated with dissociation and trauma exposure often include self-injurious behavior, also known as deliberate self-harm. These behaviors involve self-focused bodily harm that is not suicidal in intention. The frequency and severity of self-harm may range from occasional to frequent and from mild to extremely dangerous behaviors (Carlson, McDade-Montez, Armstrong, Dalenberg, and Loewenstein, 2013). The rate of self-injurious behavior is approximately 5 percent to 15 percent of the population, with young adults, adolescents, and clinical populations comprising the majority of this distribution (Dixon-Gordon, Tull, and Gratz, 2014; Nock and Favazza, 2009). Higher rates of self-harm are evident in men (48%) compared to women (33%) (Nobakht and Dale, 2017). In a study by Briere and Eadie (2016), despite a diagnosis of PTSD and depression, dissociation proved to be the dominant factor that predicted self-injurious behavior. This finding reinforces the notion that inflicting pain is a means of disrupting the numbing effects of dissociation (Briere and Eadie, 2016; Nobakht and Dale, 2017). The dissociative process of intense absorption also influences self-injurious behavior; during a dissociative absorbed state, inflicting self-harm becomes the entire preoccupation of self-injurious individuals (Karpel and Jerram, 2015).

Deliberate self-harm may reduce emotional distress, including the distress of dissociation, especially when maladaptive cognitive beliefs about the self are elevated and self-awareness is experienced as aversive (Armey and Crowther, 2008; Viana, Dixon, Berenz, and Espil, 2017). As well, greater reactivity to interoceptive somatic cues, heightened anxiety, and inadequate emotion regulation may intensify PTSD avoidance behavior and deliberate self-harm (Viana et al., 2017). In males, deliberate self-harm is strongly related to emotional dysregulation, and this behavioral response is greater in males with a history of childhood physical abuse (Gratz and Chapman, 2011). In the Gratz and Chapman study (2011), deliberate self-harm was also associated with blunted emotional intensity. This finding was surprising; however, the researchers did not examine dissociative processing, a factor that may explain the finding of increased self-harm and poor emotion regulation despite diminished emotional intensity (Ford and Gomez, 2015).

Dissociation, along with emotional dysregulation, may operate as a mediator between childhood maltreatment and adolescent and adult self-injurious behavior (Ford, and Gomez, 2015). In a different study, dissociation and PTSD mediated the effects between psychological trauma (childhood sexual abuse and violence) and self-injurious behavior (Ford and Gomez, 2015a). Likewise, in a sample of juvenile offenders, childhood sexual abuse predicted PTSD and self-injurious behavior; combining emotional dysregulation and dissociation in the analysis increased the rate of self-injurious behavior for juvenile offenders who were exposed to sexual abuse (Chaplo, Ferig, Bennett, and Modrowski, 2015). Although dissociation is a major factor associated with deliberate self-harm, other factors such as younger age, increased previous suicide attempts, emotional dysregulation, and alexithymia (inability to identify and express feelings verbally) add to the risk of deliberate self-harm

(Bedi, Muller, and Classen, 2014). Likewise, a history of self-harm increases the likelihood of suicide attempts or completion (Morgan et al., 2017).

NEUROBIOLOGY AND DISSOCIATION

Dissociation impairs attention, executive functioning, memory, and social cognition. These symptoms are primarily linked to functional disconnections between three major networks: the central executive network, the default mode network, and the salience network (McKinnon et al., 2016; Tursich et al., 2015). Specifically, there is an uncoupling of connections to the central executive network and the default mode network (McKinnon, 2016). In the salience network, the insula has been identified as a key source for dissociative symptoms. As well, sensory disruptions in dissociation are evidenced at the level of the thalamus (Schauer and Elbert, 2010), while disruptions in bodily states operate in neural networks such as the insula, parietal lobe, middle frontal gyrus, superior temporal gyrus, and precuneus (Lanius et al., 2005). Neuroimaging of depersonalization patients reveals a very specific activation/deactivation pattern. They have increased prefrontal activation as well as reduced arousal in the insula and limbic related areas during exposure to both aversive and arousing emotional stimuli (Sierra and David, 2011). This neural pattern offers explanations for the emotional numbing and distancing described by depersonalization patients (Erwin et al., 2007; Medford et al., 2006).

Brain imaging has demonstrated differences between dissociative patients listening to a neutral script (engagement of higher cortical structures) compared to listening to a traumatic memory script (more limbic activation). These differences in neurological recruitment reinforce the *cortico-limbic inhibition model of trauma-related dissociative disorders* (Reinders, Willemsen, Vos, den Boer, and Nijenhuis, 2012). Effort to suppress unwanted trauma memories, a common practice in dissociative patients, involves activation in multiple regions in the brain compared to non-dissociative individuals (i.e., frontal areas, cingulate cortex, intraparietal sulcus, precuneus, fusiform gyrus, lingual gyrus, occipital gyrus, and parahippocampal gyrus). In the dissociative patients, more multimodal somatosensory regions are activated which indicates efforts to suppress the sensory and emotional content of trauma-related scripts (Reinder et al., 2012). Likewise, the caudate nucleus is more activated than the hippocampus during the trauma-memory script; this pattern is often present during recall of stressful situations. Perhaps dissociative patients engage the caudate nucleus and hippocampus to process spatial information and not autobiographical information. This response bias may inhibit a fight-flight-freeze response that is typically provoked during trauma reminders (Reinder et al., 2012). It may also serve to decrease the encoding process of autobiographical memory. Minimizing traumatic memories may also be served by increasing speed in attentional and working memory systems; this enables rapid detection of trauma cues in order to mobilize dissociative strategies needed to preempt the emergence of trauma memories (MacDonald, 2008).

Dissociative symptoms are associated with blunted functioning in the HPA axis as well as blunted cortisol and norepinephrine levels, which indicate disruptions in the ANS, and immune systems as well (Quevedo, Johnson, Loman, LaFlavor, and Gunnar, 2012; Stanton et al., 2001). Other study findings indicate the opposite results; elevated cortisol levels in dissociative patients who are under stress were observed. However, the researchers noted that there was great variance in cortisol response, in part because dissociation severity is transient, which may account for some individuals exhibiting heightened levels of cortisol (Bob et al., 2008; Giesbrecht, Smeets, Merckelbach, and Jelicic, 2007). At the ANS level, dissociative identity disordered patients exhibit more variance in both the sympathetic and parasympathetic branches of the ANS. This variance was displayed in a study that examined ANS responses during and following the Adult Attachment Interview. Dissociative identity disordered patients manifested more emotional dysregulation after speaking about past attachment, loss, and trauma experiences (Farina, Speranza, Imperatori, Quintilliani, and Marca, 2015). Similarly, increased arousal and distress was observed in high dissociators when exposed to highly emotional video fragments, they had greater sympathetic activation while watching the video fragments (Giesbrecht, Geraerts et al., 2007).

Depersonalization disorder is strongly associated with anxiety disorders; however, unlike anxiety-disordered patients who respond with greater ANS activation, depersonalization patients manifest decreased sympathetic arousal (Sierra, Senior, Phillips, and David, 2006). The diminished ANS response during threatening or unpleasant stimuli indicates impairment in the normal physiologic processing of threat (Giesbrecht, Merckelbach, van Oorsouw, and Simeon, 2010; Sierra et al., 2006). Disruptions in the ANS system are commonly associated with symptoms of orthostatic intolerance and dizziness (vestibular and ANS imbalance). Patients with depersonalization disorder report a higher incidence of dizziness (Tschan, Wiltink, Adler, Beutel, and Michal, 2013). In depersonalization patients, the atypical stress activating pattern in the ANS and HPA axis suggest that a disconnection in the sensory-limbic system causes this specific symptom profile (Mula et al., 2007). Unlike PTSD patients, depersonalization patients have lower basal norepinephrine levels and there is lack of interaction between norepinephrine and cortisol (Simeon, Guralnik, Knutelska, Yehuda, and Schmeidler, 2003).

In general, dissociative symptom intensity is associated with increased endogenous opioid responses, which further demonstrates paradoxical stress responses in dissociative patients (Simeon and Knutelska, 2005). This finding is reinforced in opioid antagonist studies; when patients are given opioid antagonist medication their dissociation decreases (Simeon and Knutelska, 2005). At the genetic level, the COMT Val158Met polymorphism allele is associated with stress-induced activation of opioids. It is also associated with higher levels of dissociation in individuals with childhood abuse histories (Savitz et al., 2008). This genetic association may explain the opioid response in dissociative patients. Collectively, these physiologic and neurobiological alterations may shed some light on why dissociative patients, and depersonalization patients specifically, have poorer prognosis and higher chronicity of symptoms (Mula et al., 2007).

DISSOCIATIVE COMPLEXITY

Given the multifactorial nature of trauma type, trauma-related symptoms, and multidimensional dissociative processes, Briere and colleagues recommend that dissociation should be investigated as dissociative complexity (2016). Approaching dissociation as a complex multifactorial process expands studies that investigate etiological origins. Although trauma is strongly associated with dissociation, other factors influence dissociation (Goodman et al., 2003). For example, dissociation can be deliberately induced as a way to manage stress or it can spontaneously emerge under stress. During military survival training, 88 to 96 percent of the trainees experience some form of dissociation (Morgan et al., 2001). The majority experience spontaneous dissociation which is associated with diminished coping behavior under stress; however, a subset of individuals are able to deliberately compartmentalize and distance somatic responses which enhances their coping abilities (Morgan and Taylor, 2013). This adaptive capacity to dissociate under performance stress is also recognized in athletes and performing artists (Thomson et al., 2009; Thomson and Jaque, 2012a; Thomson, Kibarska, and Jaque, 2011).

Dissociative complexity can be determined by examining a dissociative profile in individuals with PTSD. Study findings indicate that many individuals with the dissociative form of PTSD have other dissociative processing dimensions beyond the DSM-5 criterion for depersonalization/derealization (Mullerova, Hansen, Contractor, Elhai, and Armour, 2016). As well, dissociative diversity is more likely found in samples that examine individuals who are incarcerated, female gender, and groups that are exposed to more cumulative trauma (Briere et al., 2016). In the study by Mullerova and colleagues (2016), cumulative trauma, male gender, anxiety, and being employed were all predictive factors for complex dissociative profiles. Increased suicidality and substance abuse were also comorbid factors associated with complex dissociation (Briere et al., 2016). Study findings that address racial minorities indicate that multidimensional dissociative strategies are significantly present and that they may operate as defensive structures to manage the added stress of living and working as a minority (Mullerova et al., 2016). This was more pronounced when racial discrimination was included as a factor (Polanco-Roman et al., 2016).

Studies that investigate pathological dissociation have yielded similar profiles as those found when examining factors associated with complex (multidimensional) dissociation. As well, these studies have identified other factors associated with pathological dissociation. For example, in a study that investigated a sample of adolescents, pathological dissociation was associated with female gender, economic vulnerability, second-generation war refugee status, as well as a history of emotional abuse by peers (Gusic, Cardena, Bengtsson, and Sondergaard, 2016). The strongest factors that predicted pathological dissociation were emotional abuse by peers or others and cumulative trauma exposure, with four or more trauma types increasing the potential for PTSD-related dissociation (Gusic et al., 2016). In female rape survivors, pathological dissociation and depression was associated with somatic symptoms; whereas, for women who were raped and also had childhood sexual and/or physical abuse, only pathological dissociation predicted somatic symptoms (Scioli-Salter et al., 2016).

Individuals with complex pathological dissociation manifest more symptoms and they are more severe. They also have more cumulative trauma exposure. In general, this population can be effectively treated but it takes much longer and requires both in-patient and outpatient treatment to achieve stability (Jepsen, Langeland, Sexton, and Heir, 2014). Despite these positive results, patients with early histories of childhood abuse who also suffer complex dissociative disorders struggle to manage dissociation; after treatment, dissociative symptoms tend to persist but at a less severe level (Jepsen et al., 2014).

CONCLUSION

Non-pathological levels of dissociation are normal states within all individuals; the danger in research studies is to over- or under-pathologize dissociation, especially when it is examined from a psychological and psychiatric model. Adopting a sociocultural perspective expands understanding about the nature of the self and how compartmentalized or altered states are examined. Applying an integrative model removes the binary focus that currently dominates dissociative research, including the ongoing discussion regarding whether DID is iatrogenic or a real disorder (Seligman and Kirmayer, 2008).

A lack of understanding related to dissociation strongly influences the rate and prevalence of diagnosing dissociative disorders; consequently dissociation is often under-reported. When clinicians understand dissociation the rates of dissociation are actually quite high. For example, in a study that examined dissociative disorders in a psychiatric outpatient clinic, approximately 29 percent of patients met criteria for a dissociative disorder, with many reporting histories of childhood abuse (Foote, Smolin, Kaplan, Legatt, and Lipschitz, 2006). An even higher rate (34.9%) of patients was identified in a psychiatric emergency ward; these patients had higher rates of psychogenic amnesia, flashback experiences, and childhood adversity (Sar et al., 2007). In a general population sample, 3.4 percent of the sample met criteria for a dissociative diagnosis, a rate that is high considering that this sample was gathered as a non-dissociative patient population (Maaranen et al., 2005).

Neurobiological studies have yielded important consistent findings. Understanding dissociation at a neurobiological level is important, especially because dissociative processing operates within many disorders such as PTSD, psychotic spectrum illnesses, anxiety, and mood disorders (McKinnon et al., 2016). When dissociation is present, the prognosis for recovery is worse and the burden of suffering is intensified (Price, Kearns, Houry, and Rothbaum, 2014). This poor prognosis is intensified when dissociative individuals are exposed to a traumatic event such as the World Trade Center Disaster. Along with dissociation, they frequently display high levels of guilt and shame (Simeon, Greenberg, Nelson, Schmeidler, and Hollander, 2005). Given these findings, the need for further understanding about dissociation remains strong, especially when dissociative processing is understood as a complex psychological construct that is mobilized as an adaptive strategy under conditions of stress.

Section III

RESILIENCE

Chapter 12

Regulation and Resilience
Psychosocial and Biological

SELF-REGULATION

Self-regulation is the ability to adapt to the changing environment while striving to attain goals. It is the ability to regulate internal physiologic responses that reside outside of conscious awareness and manage psychological responses that are initiated by a consciously aware self (Vohs and Baumeister, 2004). Self-regulation increases as the higher cortical structures in the brain mature; however, even in young children a sense of self must be perceived in order to begin acquiring self-regulatory abilities (Schore, 1994). Self-regulation is both learned (behavioral) and dispositional (temperament) (Rothbart, Ellis, and Posner, 2004; Rothbart and Sheese, 2007). In great part, individual reactivity is contingent on temperament, although habituation and sensitization can emerge depending on the intensity of external and internal events. The temperament of an individual can either intensify reactivity (behavioral inhibition/withdrawal) or mute reactivity (behavioral approach) (Cloninger, 1994; Miskovic and Schmidt, 2012). According to Rothbart and colleagues, temperament can influence reactivity in four ways: (1) heighten activation directed toward negative aversive stimuli, (2) increase positive extraverted reactivity, (3) mobilize effortful behavioral inhibition, and (4) flexibly shift focus and attention to accommodate immediate needs (Rothbart et al., 2004). Whether physiologic processes drive temperament or if physiologic responses follow temperament is not known; however, optimal self-regulation is associated with dynamic physiologic ANS responsiveness as evidenced by greater heart rate variability (Segerstrom and Nes, 2007). Enhanced heart rate variability increases strength, effort, and stamina (Segerstrom and Nes, 2007). All reactive processes, whether optimal or sub-optimal, influence self-regulation. However, it is important to note that regulatory responses that are optimal for individual temperaments may not always produce optimal behaviors under taxing situations; some temperamental behaviors are more problematic in situations that require complex or extreme responses (Rothbart and Sheese, 2007).

RESILIENCE

Resilience has been described as the capacity to withstand or recover from significant challenges or adversities (Kaye-Tzadok and Davidson-Arad, 2016). Resilience cannot be evaluated unless an individual is exposed to an adverse event that threatens physiologic and psychological development and stability. To determine resilience, evidence of the mobilization of a dynamic process of adaptability must occur. According to Bonanno (2004) resilience is not part of recovery. Recovery describes a trajectory in which normal functioning temporarily collapses following a significant loss or trauma that is then followed by a return to psychological equilibrium, whereas, resilience is the ability to maintain psychological stability during these events. Measuring resilience requires assessing multiple domains of functioning such as biological, developmental, behavioral, educational, social, employment, emotional, and physiologic (Curtis and Cicchetti, 2003; Kaye-Tzadok and Davidson-Arad, 2016). Examining resilience is much more than investigating risk and protective factors. This narrow approach focuses on individual differences and causal pathways; whereas, resilience investigates a complex interaction of psychosocial and biological factors that operate as resistance to adversity (Rutter, 2006).

The notion that resilience is either extreme lack of feeling (pathological) or exceptional abilities is not accurate. The majority of individuals exposed to trauma are able to function despite adversity; it is a common response with only a small percentage developing PTSD (Bonanno and Mancini, 2012; Masten, 2001). Resilient individuals may suffer initial feelings of horror and overwhelm but they quickly adapt and are able to successfully maintain functioning (Aitcheson et al., 2017; Bonanno and Burton, 2013). To claim that someone is resilient necessitates that they function well across six of eight categories: employment, absence of homelessness history, education, social activity, absence of psychiatric disorder, absence of substance abuse, absence of self-reported violence, and absence of criminal record for violence (McGloin and Widow, 2001). Assessing resilience in children requires a slightly different set of criteria. First the child meets expectations of positive adaptation, and second, they must experience exposure to significant trauma or loss (Masten and Obradovic, 2006). The challenge of assessing resilience in children is related to limitations in measuring neurobiological changes.

These changes may not manifest as overt behavioral or physiologic responses until later in development (Masten and Obradovi, 2006; Teicher et al., 2006).

The *salutogenic model* describes health and disease on a continuum. This model helps situate resilience and PTSD along this continuum. According to Antonovsky (1996), it is essential that researchers examine all factors along the continuum; hence investigating promotive and protective factors becomes as important as investigating risk factors for pathology. This model encourages researchers to view the adaptive process of an individual as one that is nested within a complex fabric of micro- and macro-relationships (Masten, 2004; Hobfoll, 2001). It also recommends investigating population samples that are relatively symptom-free. Many recent studies have followed these recommendations and have identified heterogeneity among mass terror attack samples (Hobfoll et al., 2009). For example, the investigation of children and adolescents who were directly exposed to the World Trade Center attack determined four classes of responses. Approximately 49.4 percent of the sample was identified as resilient (no trauma-related symptoms), 21.5 percent and 18.6 percent were clustered in the two intermediate groups (minimal to some trauma-related symptoms), and 10.5 percent of the sample had severe PTSD symptoms (Guffanti et al., 2016). In a military sample a similar pattern was found; 76 percent of the soldiers manifested a resilient trajectory, 15 percent had a delayed onset of PTSD, and 8 percent of the sample was evaluated on a chronic distress trajectory (Polusny et al., 2017). Likewise, childhood adversity has a curvilinear trajectory; no adversity and high adversity are detrimental to resilience whereas some childhood adversity actually operates as a form or inoculation to stress (Mittal et al., 2015). These studies demonstrate the appropriateness of applying the salutogenic model to PTSD investigations.

SELF-REGULATION AND RESILIENCE THEORIES

Theories regarding successful adaptation to traumatic stress exposure that extend beyond the medical model are essential for understanding human resilience (Benight, 2012). These theories will also propel more theory-driven research that will enable more integrative approaches to promote human adaptation under conditions that are extreme and troubling. There are major theories that have been advanced; however, most of these theories remain isolated with minimal overlap in study protocol and study measures. The key theories that were identified by Benight (2012) include (1) Social Cognitive Theory, (2) Self-Regulation Shift Theory, (3) Terror Management Theory, (4) Transactional Theory of Stress and Coping, (5) Conservation of Resources Theory, (6) Social Support Theory, (7) Attachment Theory, (8)

Information Processing Theories of Trauma Responses, (9) Stress-Diathesis Model, and (10) Kindling Theory. They all provide valuable approaches to appraise post-traumatic stress as well as resilience and adaptation.

Social cognitive theory postulates a bi-directional interactive response that links the environment, the person, and behavior (Bandura, 1997). The primary emphasis is self-regulation; a feedback process that integrates internal and external stimuli that informs optimal adaptation. It is an ongoing process of physiologic and cognitive evaluation and appraisal. Via self-evaluation, perceptions rooted in a sense of self-efficacy shape behavior, beliefs, and motivation. Along with ongoing self-evaluation, persistence and an ability to adjust appraisal and behavior are critical factors in attaining goals (Benight, 2012; Benight and Bandura, 2004). When this appraisal process influences effective adaptive responses then self-efficacy increases along with enhanced motivation to determine appropriate goals and to achieve these goals. Under stressful and traumatic conditions, the self-regulatory capacity is greatly challenged; however, with adequate internal and external resources adaptation is possible (Benight and Bandura, 2004). This model also incorporates social support as a resource for adaptation. With adequate social support, trauma-related emotions and avoidance behavior are better regulated which leads to better health outcomes (McAndrew et al., 2017). The social cognitive theory also incorporates cognitive emotion regulation strategies such as problem solving, acceptance, and positive refocusing (Kaczkurkin et al., 2017). Some of the negative cognitive emotion strategies include rumination, catastrophizing, and self-blame. These negative strategies are evident in individuals with a PTSD diagnosis. They struggle with cognitive emotion regulation strategies, manifest difficulties shifting negative emotions, and consequently employ greater avoidance strategies (APA, 2013). These negative emotions reinforce negative beliefs such as the world is dangerous and I am not strong enough to change things, which diminishes a sense of self-efficacy. When these negative beliefs persist they become maladaptive and increase PTSD symptom severity (Kaczkurkin et al., 2017).

The *self-regulation shift theory* builds from the primary concept of social cognitive theory. It attempts to describe the non-linear moments of state shifts and the key factors that perturb a stable state into a different state (Benight, Shoji, and Delahanty, 2017). When a system is perturbed sufficiently, equilibrium is destabilized. Major events such as traumatic exposure or moments of awe are powerful forces that destabilize self-regulation equilibrium. Four key concepts are embedded in self-regulation shift theory (Benight et al., 2017; Lewis and Granic, 2000): (1) humans are self-aware dynamic living systems that continually monitor and adapt to internal and external conditions and respond to these changing conditions via complex feedback/feedforward systems, (2) dynamic systems respond in a series of nonlinear patterns of organize-disorganize-reorganize shifts that are directed by responses to internal and external demands, (3) traumatic exposure provokes intense biopsychosocial coping responses to adapt to the perceived level of disequilibrium; self-efficacy beliefs are challenged during these extreme demands, and (4) all humans have a critical coping capacity threshold and once that is exceeded a fundamental shift must take place. When the critical threshold is exceeded a dissonance occurs between perceived self-efficacy and coping demands required during the traumatic event. These conditions often challenge self-determination concepts, especially when the individual is psychologically overwhelmed and responds chaotically. In part, the self-regulation shift theory attempts to provide a psychosocial explanation that matches the biological theory of allostasis (Danese and McEwen, 2012). It also includes the essential social cognitive factors of self-determination, self-efficacy, goal selection, goal attainment, and goal alterations: all factors that influence self-regulatory behaviors (Maes and Karoly, 2005).

Terror management theory builds on the notion that self-awareness includes an awareness of death, as well as recognizing feelings of death anxiety (Greenberg, Pyszczynski, and Solomon, 1986). The need for terror management is rooted in an awareness that the human condition is driven to survive despite inevitable death. This awareness necessitates engaging in anxiety-buffering strategies to reduce death anxiety. Strategies include embedding oneself within a cultural worldview that provides an expansion of existence and heightens personal value. Holding a positive view of the self and cultivating strong attachment relationships shifts the focus away from the terror of inevitable death (Pyszczynski and Kesebir, 2011). Proximal terror management strategies involve not thinking about death by actively suppressing these thoughts or accepting a belief that the self is invulnerable. Distal terror management requires the individual to focus on meaning, value, and security. This strategy requires a faith in the community, interpersonal relationships, and the world as a whole (Chatard et al., 2012). However, traumatic exposure challenges these anxiety-buffering strategies (Pyszczynski and Kesebir, 2011). For example, when exposed to war-trauma and struggling with PTSD, individuals are no longer able to engage in proximal terror management and the anxiety-buffering strategies fail (Chatard et al., 2012). Traumatic exposure can alter a view of the self and the world so that the self is no longer invulnerable and the world is no longer benevolent and safe. These alterations may lead to ongoing PTSD; however, helping the individual re-establish anxiety-buffering strategies may mitigate the severity of PTSD symptoms (Benight, 2012; Chatard et al., 2012; Vail, Morgan, and Kahle, 2018).

Transactional theory of stress and coping identifies the interaction between the environment and the individual during stressful situations (Lazarus and

Folkman, 1984). This approach examines coping strategies, physiologic responses, and cognitive appraisals of the stressful event. These responses are dynamic efforts to manage both the internal and external changes that ensue. Lazarus and Folkman describe two forms of appraisal in this theory (1984). Primary appraisal involves assessment of the well-being of the individual; fundamentally it is a harm/threat appraisal that informs the assessment of the challenges that accompany the stressor. Secondary appraisal expands the assessment to resources that surround the individual during the stressor. These resources include physical, social, psychological, and material factors that can be employed to assist the individual during threat/harm. Assessing the interaction of all these factors necessitates robust study designs; this theory still requires much more investigation to fully evaluate all these complex interactions (Benight, 2012).

The *conservation of resources theory* adopts the perspective that both the environment and the individual are predictive factors during a stressful situation (Hobfoll et al., 2007). This theory elaborates on deficit concepts under stress such as the threat or actual loss of resources (family, home, finances) and an insufficient gain of resources after the traumatic event. This theory has direct application to disaster and terrorism events and provides a model to investigate how individuals and communities are faltering or thriving (Hobfoll et al., 2006).

The *social support theory* addresses the role others play under stressful situations (Yule, 2001). Robust research has demonstrated how social support can enhance or diminish coping strategies. It is also an interactive model that examines the influence of social support on PTSD symptoms, PTSD recovery, post-traumatic growth, and other comorbid disorders such as depression, anxiety, and substance use that are associated with stress, loneliness, alienation, and coping (Benight, 2012; Paul et al., 2015). Social support theory includes a sense of belonging at the workplace and within the community. When individuals feel that they belong to a group, social support is implicitly understood and augments resilience within the individuals in the organization (Shakespeare-Finch and Daley, 2017). Although this theory provides robust research findings that demonstrate the positive effects of social support and how it enhances resilience and self-regulation, individuals with PTSD are often unable to acknowledge or accept social support. The nature of their disorder actually increases alienation from others (Brancu et al., 2014; Shallcross, Aribisi, Polusny, Kramer, and Erbes, 2016). Recommendations for future research in social support theory should address this discrepancy within PTSD populations.

Information processing theories of trauma responses proposes that traumatic adaptation is fundamentally a cognitive process of assimilation and accommodation. Horowtiz (1976) proposed that the natural unconscious process of integrating traumatic events is one of pendulation between avoidance and assimilation until the event is fully internalized. PTSD is ultimately the failure of this natural process to integrate the traumatic event. Although Horowtiz focused on the cognitive process, the emotional integration of the event was embedded within his theory. Other theorists have disambiguated these two concepts and addressed either the emotional integration (Foa and Rothbaum, 1998) or the cognitive integration (Ehlers and Clark, 2000) of the traumatic event.

The *stress-diathesis model* is another term for an epigenetic approach to examining PTSD (Benight, 2012). This model focuses on the biological vulnerabilities to stress and how these influence adaptation. It focuses on individual differences that emerge under similar stress conditions. For example, studies that employ this model identify biological differences in samples with and without PTSD. Substantial research studies incorporate this model; currently they are expanding to include the psychosocial influences on biological adaptation, as well as innate genetic predispositions. An example of this expanded design is evident in a study that predicted child social competence despite unresponsive parenting. It demonstrated a strong genetic influence on resilience; despite parental inadequacies, children who inherited sociability and sensitivity traits fared better (van Ryzin et al., 2015). Another study identified genetically resilient individuals who manifested stronger neurological reward circuit activation, even during exposure to stress stimuli. The expectation of rewards increased optimism in these individuals (Vythilingam et al., 2009). Genetic resilience is also demonstrated at the ANS level. Infants with strong vagal tone who were exposed to prenatal cocaine had a more resilient developmental trajectory compared to infants who suffered the same level of cocaine exposure but who had weak vagal tone (Sheinkopf et al., 2007). The stress-diathesis model has also been implemented to predict vulnerability in individuals prior to a traumatic event, such as military studies that examine pre- and post-deployment status (Schmahl et al., 2002). Findings demonstrate an even stronger relationship between genetic vulnerability for PTSD compared to genetic resilience, which further reinforces the role of environmental factors associated with resilience (Wolf et al., 2018).

The *kindling model* is fundamentally a neurobiological approach. The concept of allostasis and allostatic load is a derivative of this model (Danese and McEwen, 2012). This model postulates that early adversity alters the developing stress systems and increases vulnerability for adapting to future adversity. The ACE study provided robust findings that reinforce this model (Felitti et al., 1998). Ultimately, when early trauma reaches a critical threshold, the neurobiological system is sensitized to future traumatic events. The physiologic and psychological processing is primed for more adversity (Benight, 2012). These neurological changes (i.e., gene expression, epigenetic regulation) are fundamentally dynamic responses to environmental demands (internal and external). Although early childhood trauma generally compromises resilience, habituation and adaptation via neural plasticity can occur over time, which dampens the kindling response and enhances resilience in traumatized individuals (Benight, 2012; McEwen, Gray, and Nasca, 2015).

Attachment theory, and in particular, secure attachment behaviors and states of mind are directly associated with resilience and adaptation (Bowlby, 1988). Internal working models of security extends into self-identity as well as interpersonal relationships with attachment figures and important others. Secure attachment is marked by a strong sense of autonomy, high coherence of self-image, and flexible collaboration with others (Ferrajao et al., 2017; Main et al., 2003). Secure attachment internalized models are embedded into optimal neurological and psychological self-regulation and resilience. (See chapter 7 for details on attachment)

COPING STRATEGIES: A COMPONENT OF SELF-REGULATION

Cultivating optimal coping strategies under stressful conditions greatly reduces distress and increases a sense of well-being. Coping strategies imply an ability to adapt to changing environmental situations by altering cognitive or behavioral efforts (Lazarus and Folkman, 1984). Coping strategies inform how individuals confront and recover from adversity, including exposure to trauma, injury, illness, bereavement, and chronic disorders such as pain (Karoly and Ruehlman, 2006). They also influence treatment compliance including dietary, exercise, and medication intervention (Karoly and Ruehlman, 2006). There are many ways to differentiate coping strategies; most of the research conducted on coping strategies grew from the early psychoanalytic defense structures and their association to personality traits and temperament (Cosway, Endler, Sadler, and Deary, 2000; Moos and Holahan, 2003). The simplest coping model is built on temperament traits that bias individuals to move toward/approach or withdraw/avoid novelty or threat (Creech, Benzer, Liebsack, Proctor, and Taft, 2013). Approach coping involves attempts to change a situation and/or how the situation is assessed so that it is less threatening. Avoidant coping is an effort to turn away from the stressor via distraction or denial. These two types of coping can be applied within military, family, and community settings. Unlike avoidant coping, approach coping is strongly associated with resilience and fewer trauma-related symptoms (Creech et al., 2013).

Active coping is a variation on approach coping; it is identified as one of the most adaptive strategies available. For example, in a treatment program for breast cancer survivors, women were given psychoeducational skills based on active adaptive coping, problem-focused coping, positive reappraisal, plus creating and maintaining social networks that provide friendship, encouragement, and camaraderie (Pat-Horenczyk et al., 2015). The outcome of the study demonstrated that these skills enhanced post-traumatic growth, even though they did not decrease post-traumatic distress about receiving the diagnosis and the subsequent treatment that was required (Pat-Horenczyk et al., 2015). Active coping strategies also contribute to diminished dissociative processing, especially among racial minority individuals who suffer cumulative trauma as well as racial discrimination (Polanco-Roman et al., 2016). Active coping under extreme situations is often described as courage (Hannah, Sweeney, and Lester, 2007). The combination of risk, fear, purpose, and action are implied in acts of courage. Traits such as self-efficacy, moral values, conscientiousness, and strong self and group identity all interact to foster courageous actions. Not only is this behavior active coping, it also indicates a mindset biased toward courageous actions (Hannah et al., 2007). Likewise, prosocial behavior, specifically engaging in behaviors that will help others during extremely stressful situations such as natural disasters or mass violence serves to enhance well-being; whereas, an inability to engage in prosocial behavior is associated with declining well-being and increased pathology (Qin et al., 2016).

Inherent within active coping is a key factor, self-efficacy (Samuelson, Bartel, Valdez, and Jordan, 2017). Even when an appraisal of the situation seems dire, a sense of positive self-efficacy shifts cognitive and somatic perceptions and promotes action-oriented behavior. Individuals who possess strong beliefs that they can meet the demands of any given challenge are driven by positive self-efficacy beliefs. When obstacles arise, a sense of self-efficacy motivates them to explore alternate solutions in an effort to succeed (Bandura, 1997; Samuelson et al., 2017). Via their general beliefs in self-efficacy they perceive positive social support options and draw upon them as resources after the traumatic event (Smith, Felix, Benight, and Jones, 2017). If they experience PTSD symptoms, individuals with higher coping self-efficacy seek treatment and recover faster than their low self-efficacy counterparts (Bosmans, van der Knaap, and van der Velden, 2016). Of note, individuals with high levels of self-efficacy may initially manifest severe PTSD symptoms after a traumatic event (i.e., Hurricane Katrina); however, they also report the strongest post-traumatic growth one year later (Cieslak et al., 2009). Strong self-efficacy that operates as a coping strategy enhances the management of stressful situations as well as augments recovery from exposure to traumatic events.

Similar to self-efficacy, and an essential ingredient in active coping, is personal growth initiatives. When exposed to trauma most people experience varying trauma-related symptoms. For those who possess cognitive and behavioral skills that include the belief that change can occur, then efforts to actively plan and set goals are mobilized (Robitscheck et al., 2012). They possess a sense of agency and an adaptive mindset that serves to directly confront distress. They also possess a sense of optimism and hope that positive change can develop; in fact, they may have stronger neurological reward circuits that promote greater reward expectations (Vythilingam et al., 2009). Personal growth initiatives are strongly associated with lower levels of trauma-related symptoms, more life satisfaction, and higher frequency of post-traumatic growth (Gunty et al., 2011). The capacity to initiate personal growth functions as a dispositional trait; however, it can also be taught and nurtured in settings that encourage self-agency and self-efficacy (Blackie, Jayawickreme, Forgeard, and Jayawickreme, 2015).

Coping strategies can also be divided into task-oriented, emotion-oriented, and avoidant-oriented approaches (Endler and Parker, 1990). Task-oriented can be described as problem-focused coping. The individual assesses the problem and searches for task-relevant solutions. Problem-focused strategies necessitate cognitive appraisals of the situation. These appraisals are effective when the perceived challenge is matched by personal and interpersonal coping resources as well as an ability to positively reframe the situation and satisfactorily accept solutions that are provided (Yeung, Lu, Wong, and Huynh, 2016). By implication, a task-oriented focus includes repression of negative emotions; however, some individuals may simply avoid distressing feelings rather than actively suppress them (Coifman, Bonanno, Ray, and Gross, 2007). Although not ideal during daily living, the ability to repress negative feelings while managing traumatic or loss experiences is associated with fewer health or psychopathology symptoms. This task-oriented or problem-focused approach has positive outcomes under stress; it enhances psychological well-being and physical health (Cosway et al., 2000; Taylor and Stanton, 2007).

Emotion-oriented coping includes individual behaviors such as focusing on the feelings that are evoked under stressful situations and the fears that may follow in the aftermath (Cosway et al., 2000). Emotion-oriented coping may be beneficial under certain circumstances, especially when effective emotional processing and expression are facilitated. However, emotion-oriented coping can equally cloud judgment and intensify stressful situations (Endler and Parker, 1990). Generally, emotion-oriented coping is associated with increased anxiety, depression, dissociation, suicidal ideation, and somatic symptoms. It is often viewed as a passive form of coping that involves rumination, self-blame, and resignation (McWilliams, Cox, and Enns, 2003; Moss and Holahan, 2003). However, when emotion-oriented focus is subdivided into positive and negative emotions a different pattern emerges (Britt, Adler,

Sawhney, and Bliese, 2017). Positive emotion-focused coping includes accepting the reality of the uncontrollable nature of the situation, trying to find positive meaning associated with the situation, and maintaining a sense of humor. Similar to task-oriented coping, positive emotion-oriented coping involves strategies such as positively reframing the situation and reappraising the demands incurred by the situation. Negative emotion-oriented coping often involves self-blame and negative rumination about feelings of fear, shame, or guilt. Regardless of emotional valence, emotion-oriented coping can be positive or negative depending on individual emotional regulatory capacity; in particular, regulatory abilities enhance or suppress emotional expression depending on the demands of a situation (Bonanno, Papa, Lalande, Westphal, and Cifman, 2004). This regulatory capacity indicates an emotional flexibility that is shaped by biological and cognitive processes. However, when individuals have poor self-regulatory abilities emotion-oriented coping is strongly associated with increased psychopathology such as elevated depression, anger, and impulsivity (Myers, Flemin, Lancman, Perrine, and Lancman, 2013).

Avoidant-oriented coping is generally regarded as a poor coping strategy and is associated with increased rates of PTSD as well as worse mental health outcomes (McAndrew et al., 2017). Avoidant-oriented coping involves denial, minimizing the importance of the situation, distraction, procrastination, and social diversions. All these tactics involve distancing from the stressful situation (Endler and Parker, 1990). Depending on the situation, avoidance behavior may be an appropriate interim strategy. For example, avoiding situations that increase stress may be prudent when individuals are ill or unprepared. Social diversion may actually increase social support that then bolsters resources to manage adversity (Cosway et al., 2000). Compared to emotion-oriented coping, avoidant-oriented coping is associated with less psychopathology. Although this strategy is less desirable compared to task-oriented coping, contextual factors and timing may determine when it is appropriate.

RESILIENCE FACTORS THAT INFLUENCE COPING STRATEGIES

Identity associated with an organization or culture promotes resilience. Specifically, national, ethnic, or group (military, profession) identity can operate as effective coping resources (Aitcheson et al., 2017; McAndrew et al., 2017). For example, in a combat sample, a strong sense of unit cohesion served to reduce avoidant coping strategies and promoted greater resilience within solders based in the Army National Guard and Army Reserve (McAndrew et al., 2017). In a study that examined African American adolescents, stronger racial identity (personal and racial centrality) as well as a deep belief in racial ideology was associated with higher achievement motivation beliefs. For these adolescents, a sense of racial belonging served as a protective factor and promoted resilience (Butler-Barnes et al., 2017). Ethnic identity and resilience were also evident in a study that examined Palestinian adolescents living in Gaza. A strong sense of their Muslim Arab identity, as well as deep connections with a cohesive family unit enhanced resilience despite the fact that they witnessed horrific trauma and lived in conditions of extreme poverty and overcrowding (Aitcheson et al., 2017). These living conditions did not increase anxiety in the adolescents studied nor depression or PTSD. In general, the highly resilient adolescents had an optimistic view of their work and they possessed strong self-regulation skills (Aitcheson et al., 2017).

Shared assumptions among low-resource countries can also promote resilience. For example, exposure to trauma in low-income high conflict countries results in lower PTSD rates compared to PTSD rates in countries with high resources (greater wealth and health care and longer life expectancy). In low-income countries, both men and women who are exposed to traumatic events tend to fair better in mental health status compared to samples from high-income countries (Duckers and Oliff, 2017). Perhaps trauma-related mental health problems are less stigmatized in poorly resourced countries; hence they receive more community support and acceptance (Duckers and Brewin, 2016). As well, high-resource countries are culturally more individualistic-oriented, which promotes higher expectations about life opportunities and more emotional dissonance when expectations are not met (Duckers, Alisic, and Brewin, 2016a; Duckers and Brewin, 2016). The vulnerability paradox in these low-resource compared to high-resource countries demonstrates the dynamic nature of the traditionally identified protective factors such as notions that increased resources and less cumulative stress should reduce trauma-related symptoms (Duckers and Oliff, 2017).

Optimism is a powerful resilience factor (Lee, Aldwin, and Spiro III, 2017). This dispositional trait promotes positive appraisals and buffers negative assumptions during traumatic events (Vieselmeyer, Holguin, and Mezulis, 2017). Optimism is an important predictor of psychological and physical health, especially for those held captive as prisoners of war. To sustain a belief that a favorable outcome will inevitably result indicates a strong dispositional trait that promotes well-being (Lee et al., 2017). Another example of effective dispositional optimism is observed in women exposed to missile and rocket attacks in the Middle East. Dispositional optimism is identified as a strong predictor for lower levels of generalized anxiety and dissociation. It also enhances higher levels of self-esteem despite enduring extreme exposure to violence (Weinberg, Besser, Zeiger-Hill, and Neria, 2015). Optimism is also associated with a personality trait known as self-enhancement (Bonanno, Rennicke, and Dekel, 2005). Individuals who manifest high levels of self-enhancement are biased toward overly positive and often unrealistic self-serving beliefs. For example, after the September 11th attack on the World Trade Center, high self-enhanced individuals were able to sustain their positive self-enhancing beliefs as well as optimal functioning. They sustained this belief despite concerns and disbelief expressed by those who were socially close to them. This resilience trait enabled them to cope with the horrific events of this mass attack (Bonanno et al., 2005).

Although optimism (and self-enhancement beliefs) buffers trauma-related symptoms; individuals who are rated high in optimism still manifest intrusions and anxious arousal after a traumatic event (Birkeland, Blix, Solberg, and Heir, 2017). The initial insult of severe traumatic events such as mass violence is challenging to manage, even for the most optimistic individuals. One of the traits that counters distress is an increased ability to generate positive vivid images of the future (Blackwell et al., 2013). When optimism influences the generation of a positive future then PTSD symptoms are reduced; this is even stronger when problem-solving coping, a sense of self-efficacy, and mastery are present (Gil and Weinberg, 2015). Optimistic individuals seek achievable goals that are consistent with reality; they focus on the most important needs that appear in the present moment and identify strategic plans to address these needs (Shigemoto and Poyrazli, 2013). They are able to disengage from goals that are unattainable and set new goals. This strategy applies to managing career and academic trajectories as well as health needs (Rasmussen, Wrosch, Scheier, and Carver, 2006). Optimistic-oriented people also tend to draw upon positive emotions to appraise situations. Unlike negative emotional arousal, positive emotions are associated with accelerated cardiovascular recovery, a physiologic feature of resilience (Tugade and Fredrickson, 2004). The dispositional trait of optimism in conjunction with adaptive coping strategies significantly enhances trauma recovery (Gil and Weinberg, 2015).

A variant of optimism is perceptions of life expectancy (Avidor, Palgi, and Solomon, 2017). When individuals perceive a long life as well as an extended sense of self in the future, these beliefs buffer extensive trauma histories and ameliorate the effects of ongoing trauma in the present. This life expectancy orientation is especially true for those in the second half of their life. Despite living in combat zones and war, these individuals manifest less trauma-related symptoms in comparison with the same aged adults who do not harbor beliefs of a long life. Perceptions of impending death differ among these two groupings (Avidor et al., 2017). The acceptance of death, as well as a belief that the world is ultimately morally just directly enhances resilience after the loss of a close loved one; whereas, fear of death and dependency on the person who died increases the likelihood for chronic grief (Bonanno et al., 2002). Reducing fear of death enhances creative explorations, especially when individuals believe that their cultural community values creativity (Routledge and Arndt, 2009).

In students, faculty, and staff who were directly exposed to a campus mass shooting, the combination of psychologically adaptive skills along with expressions of gratitude influenced a reduction in trauma-related symptoms and encouraged post-traumatic growth. For those who endorsed higher resilience and gratitude during and immediately following the mass shooting, they also endorsed less post-traumatic growth simply because their initial level of functioning remained high under stress. Although gratitude is considered a dispositional trait, it can be cultivated after a traumatic event. By encouraging reappraisal and cognitive restructuring many individuals can find a sense of gratitude (Vieselmeyer et al., 2017).

Mindfulness, also a dispositional trait, reflects resilience in an individual. The innate ability to operate with self-awareness indicates a capacity to adapt to new situations via observing, internally or externally communicating during the situation, acting with awareness, inhibiting actions if it is more appropriate, and working without judgment and biased assessments (Hanley, Garland, and Tedeschi, 2017). Dispositional mindfulness encourages reframing the situation and deriving meaning from all situations regardless if they are negative or positive (Garland, Farb, Goldwin, and Fredrickson, 2015). Mindfulness can facilitate positive rumination and reappraisal, which promotes deeper personal connection and core belief changes (Garland et al., 2015).

Creative thinking enhances optimal coping strategies as well as increases a sense of resilience (Metzl, 2009). The ability to generate multiple ideas when seeking solutions for problems, the emotional, cognitive and behavioral flexibility to adapt to new conditions, the capacity to generate original solutions and elaborate on these solutions, and the desire to resume flow activities post trauma all augment resilience (Metzl, 2009). Creative personality features add to resilience. Openness to experience, as well as increased tolerance to manage frustration, enhances optimal coping strategies and encourages more creative flexibility (Metzl and Morrell, 2008). Creativity in mental health workers is also a resilience factor, as evidenced during Hurricane Katrina. Mental health workers who continued to engage creative flexibility during the natural disaster were better able to sustain resilience and continue working with individuals who were equally struggling under the conditions associated with the natural disaster. The capacity to express trauma experiences through an artistic medium helped restore optimism and hope in these workers (Gregerson, 2007). These and other studies consistently demonstrate positive links between creativity and resilience.

The passion to engage in an activity or a career propels intrinsically motivated individuals to exert substantial effort to obtain skills to succeed (Vallerand et al., 2003). When passion operates harmoniously, as opposed to obsessively, it promotes happiness (hedonic), personal growth (eudaemonic), and provides meaning in life (Philippe, Vallerand, and Lavigne, 2009). It also increases creative achievement and innovation despite external or internal challenges that may impede progress (Luh and Lu, 2012). The ability to engage harmonious passion despite adversity promotes resilience. Harmonious passion also increases flow experiences (Luh and Lu, 2012). The love for the activity nullifies the extrinsic pressures to succeed, even though success is welcomed and appreciated.

VICARIOUS RESILIENCE

Trauma workers can develop a form of vicarious resilience (Killian, Hernandez-Wolfe, Engstrom, and Gangsei, 2017). With adequate trauma training and repeated exposure to trauma survivors' resilience and recovery process, mental health workers can also acquire an increased capacity for resourcefulness, increased self-awareness, and greater hope. Resilient clients manifest abilities to change life goals and perspectives, and to ascribe meaning to their experiences. By listening and remaining present to the survivor's process of healing, mental health workers may also build tolerance to manage stress and to sustain hope and optimism (Killian et al., 2017). For example, advocates for victims of sexual assault and domestic violence may experience vicarious resilience. These advocates and workers are provided organizational support, substantial training, and opportunities to facilitate aid to victims. Not only do these workers gain vicarious resilience, they may also experience compassion satisfaction (as opposed to compassion fatigue and burnout). They may derive gratification and pleasure from their work and from the meaningful interactions with the victims (Frey, Beesley, Abbott, and Kendrick, 2017).

CONCLUSION

Self-regulatory behaviors are an integral component in resilience (Anderson, Winett, and Wojcik, 2007). The ability to effectively self-regulate emotional and behavioral responses enhances self-efficacy and well-being. For example, this capacity is directly related to lifestyle choices such as healthy food selection and eating behaviors (Anderson et al., 2007), as well as fitness regimes and engaging in social support during physical activities (Anderson, Wojcik, Winett, and Williams, 2006; Crombie, Brellenthin, Hillard, and

Koltyn, 2018). Optimal self-regulation also informs how individuals manage information regarding health risks and genetic predispositions. It informs cognitive schemas and coping strategies that are mobilized in an effort to deal with health threats as well as health promotion (Bandura, 2005; Marteau and Weinman, 2006).

Resilience research demonstrates that individuals who are exposed to traumatic or loss events do not always suffer trauma-related symptoms, nor do they need to recover from these symptoms (Masten, 2002). Studies have demonstrated that the majority of individuals manifest resilient behavior (i.e., 65% in the study by Bonanno, Galea, Bucciarelli, and Vlhav, 2006). These findings are robust in adult samples; however, investigating resilience in maltreated children demands more complex assessment (Cicchetti, 2013; Sameroff and Rosenblum, 2006). As well, adult samples with a history of childhood abuse and neglect have much lower rates of resilience. In one study, only 22 percent were deemed resilient, with more females compared to males considered resilient despite childhood adversity (McGloin and Widom, 2001). In samples of maltreated children, despite being deemed resilient based on the current resilience criteria, many of these children were more depressed and anxious compared to children with low adversity histories (Luthar, 1991). Factors such as genetics, parenting, and environmental conditions directly interact with trauma-related symptoms. Sometimes biological changes are not evident until adolescence or adulthood; hence assessing the child as resilient may be inaccurate given the high likelihood that symptoms may not emerge until later in development (Danese and McEwen, 2012; Spear, 2000). Risk factors in children include poor parenting, antisocial peers, economic hardships, and low-resource communities. These factors directly influence child development and diminish resilience (Cicchetti, 2013; Sameroff and Rosenblum, 2006). Sadly, even when children possess multiple resilience factors, which buffer the negative effects of childhood abuse and neglect, exposure to chronic violence and high levels of daily stress eventually erodes resilience and increases trauma-related symptoms. This further demonstrates the dose effect of trauma, even on the most resilient individuals (Fincham, Altes, Stein, and Seedat, 2009).

Currently, it is recommended that research in resilience should not focus on a few dominant factors. Multiple independent predictors influence resilience and should be analyzed via methods that probe for complexity (Bonanno, Westphal, and Mancini, 2011). Some of the multiple independent factors include personality traits, demographic variables, degree of exposure (i.e., proximal, distal, single, multiple, duration), social and economic resources, past and current stress, beliefs and values, emotional bias, and regulatory ability (Bonanno et al., 2011). In general, resilience encompasses many conceptual models; however, the three major explorations include determining personality trait stability, evaluation of a positive outcome, and identifying dynamic interactive processes (Everall, Altrows, and Paulson, 2006). These three approaches, although often overlapping, guide current resilience research. Key points that are included in resilience research include the examination of a complex array of behavioral tendencies and personality traits such as extraversion, high self-esteem, assertiveness, and internal locus of control (Agaibi and Wilson, 2005). Resilience is associated with cognitive and behavioral flexibility, humor, affect regulation, energy, and a form of transcendent detachment. As discussed above, resilience is not a unitary concept nor is it a guarantee that traumatic exposure will not present challenges and pain. What is evident is a tendency toward psychological immunity to psychopathology after exposure to traumatic events; resilient individuals have a stable trajectory after adversity (Agaibi and Wilson, 2005).

Chapter 13

Hardiness and Post-traumatic Growth

Compared to resilience, which by definition indicates that minimal trauma-related symptoms were experienced, some individuals do manifest post-traumatic stress symptoms that are followed by an ability to turn adversity into post-traumatic growth opportunities (Kaye-Tzadok and Davidson-Arad, 2016; Maddi, Harvey, Khoshaba, Fazel, and Resurreccion, 2009). The exposure to traumatic events, although challenging, may provide opportunities for psychological growth in some individuals. The growth is a response to distress; without experiencing the trauma-related distress, no endorsement of growth is possible (Dekel, Ein-Dor, and Solomon, 2012). Growth may also be associated with biological adaptations to stress, which then enhances subjective beliefs of more resilience to stress (Lehrner and Yehuda, 2018).

HARDINESS

Hardiness is generally regarded as a personality construct, rather than a psychosocial process of growth. Research studies have demonstrated that hardiness involves attitudes of commitment, control, and challenge (Maddi et al., 2009). Hardy individuals actively embrace adversity experiences rather than withdrawing. They believe that their actions and efforts will provoke positive outcomes; they value challenging opportunities so that they can experience existential courage during times of adversity. Individuals with a hardy personality believe hard work and courage can transform stressful situations into growth opportunities. The hardiness personality construct influences attitudes and efforts in school and work settings; it promotes task-oriented strategies and diminishes avoidant-oriented strategies (Maddi et al., 2009). Hardy individuals demonstrate a robust desire to move toward a better future as well as accept obstacles and failings from their past. They are able to appraise threatening situations as less adverse and accept that life is naturally associated with challenges and stress (Bonanno, 2004; Maddi, 2006).

Hardiness shares features with resilience; however, it also encapsulates a superior capacity to tolerate stress and perform successfully in highly demanding situations. These characteristics are evident in individuals who are selected to serve in the military Special Forces (Bartone, Roland, Picano, and Williams, 2008). Their psychological hardiness includes a strong sense of commitment and control under challenging conditions. They are also emotionally stable and likeable; traits that ensure cooperation while working in small autonomous groups (Bartone et al., 2008). Hardiness traits are equally evident in caregivers of older disabled adults (Clark, 2002). Unlike non-hardy individuals who suffer depression and fatigue, the hardy caregivers demonstrate high levels of resilience with no fatigue or depression. Most of the hardy caregiver individuals have a substantial history of family hardiness, a finding that suggests some degree of heritability (Clark, 2002). Unfortunately, possessing hardiness does not buffer illness. Hardy individuals may approach treatment with more commitment and accept the challenges presented by an illness; however, they are equally vulnerable to succumbing to illness (Klag and Bradley, 2004; Sinclair and Tetrick, 2000).

Hardy individuals also manifest superior abilities to manage terror, including the terror of death (Florian, Mikulincer, and Hirschberger, 2001). They are able to sustain an awareness of mortality without sacrificing moral values. An effort to manage terror does not involve distraction for hardy individuals; they cope with the terror of death and continue to seek solutions to resolve threatening conditions (Florian et al., 2001). One factor that defines hardy individuals is their appraisal bias. They appraise situations as less threatening and trust their abilities to flexibly adapt to unexpected demands (Delahaij, Gaillard, and van Dam, 2010). In addition, hardiness personality is a strong predictor that individuals will engage in problem-solving coping strategies; they will not employ denial, avoidance, or emotion-oriented coping strategies (Delahaij et al., 2010; Maddi, Harvey, Khoshaba, Lu, Persico, and Brow, 2006). In less life-threatening situations, hardy individuals demonstrate high commitment and an abiding faith that they have sufficient control to manage all situations. This control and commitment ensures success (Sheard, 2009). This is evident in a population of university students who achieve academic success. Highly committed hardy students typically have higher grade point averages, especially in their final year of university (Sheard, 2009; Sinclair and Tetrick, 2000). Of note, hardiness traits may not manifest in normal daily activities, but under conditions of high demand or challenge hardiness is revealed via task-oriented coping strategies and the presence of strong self-efficacy (Delahaij et al., 2010). These responses are evident in diverse populations such as military, student, and caregiver samples. Hardiness is generally regarded as a personality trait, although some aspects of hardiness can be trained and promoted (Bartone et al., 2008).

POST-TRAUMATIC GROWTH

Post-traumatic growth is defined as "the positive psychological change that occurs as a result of struggling with highly challenging life circumstances" (Calhoun and Tedeschi, 2001, p. 158). Not surprising, when individuals initially manifest heightened trauma-related symptoms they also have the possibility to endorse post-traumatic growth later. When a core sense of self is threatened during a traumatic event it often intensifies the threat; however, the central wounding of the self becomes fertile ground to later realize post-traumatic growth (Johnson and Boals, 2015). *Event centrality* is a term that describes the extent to which an event is integrated into individual identity (Bernsten and Rubin, 2006). Positive event centrality occurs when the event is regarded as positive and leads to post-traumatic growth; whereas, negative event centrality increases maladaptive PTSD symptoms, depression, and dissociation (Bernard, Whittles, Kertz, and Burke, 2015). Because event centrality is associated with identity formation, the long-term effects of event centrality on post-traumatic growth may not remain stable (Blix, Birkeland, Hansen, and Heir, 2015). This lack of stability may be associated with changing perceptions and appraisals of the traumatic event, especially if the trajectory of events becomes increasingly more challenging as a result of the traumatic event.

Post-traumatic growth may also be evidenced in some individuals who experience heightened peritraumatic dissociation, a symptom typically associated with persistent PTSD. These individuals may succeed in acquiring post-traumatic growth because they had to struggle to overcome the alienating symptoms of dissociation along with other trauma-related symptoms (McCaslin et al., 2009). This effort highlights the fact that post-traumatic growth does not occur when mild trauma-related symptoms manifest (Wilson et al., 2016). Likewise, individuals high in resilience are less likely to endorse post-traumatic growth (Levin, Laufer, Stein, Hamama-Raz, and Solomon, 2009). Studies have demonstrated that post-traumatic growth will emerge in survivors who have a number of traumatic events, and that these experiences intrude into their daily life. Rather than avoiding examining their traumatic experiences they optimistically re-evaluate them and this eventually leads to post-traumatic growth (Shigemoto and Poyrazli, 2013). Despite significant distress by a traumatic event(s), post-traumatic growth is fostered by factors such as perceived social support, conscientiousness, and openness to experience (Chopko et al., 2018; Gul and Karanci, 2017). Although these factors typically lead to post-traumatic growth, some individuals successfully achieve positive change by facilitating cognitive avoidance; they actively shift their attention away from distressing PTSD symptoms, including engaging in problem-solving task-oriented coping strategies that may be directed away from the task of processing trauma symptoms (Chopko, Palmieri, and Adams, 2018).

Post-traumatic growth is based on observations of individuals who describe changes after traumatic events; they experience a need to re-examine and re-formulate beliefs about self and the world (Pat-Horenczyk, 2015). These changes in belief are examples of secondary control; literally individuals change their belief or orientation to accommodate the new demands of the existing reality. Primary control, unlike secondary control, describes the original beliefs about the self, including a sense of self-efficacy and an internalized locus of control (Chang, Chua, and Toh, 1997). The scope of a traumatic event necessitates changes to primary control beliefs, which influences secondary control beliefs. These secondary control beliefs are the key factors in post-traumatic growth. For example, this process of shifting primary control to secondary control was evident in survivors of the Wenchaun earthquake. Secondary control was a major ingredient in successfully navigating this extreme natural disaster (Ying et al., 2014). Despite loss and suffering, achieving post-traumatic growth increases appreciation of life, including interpersonal relationships, personal strength, and existential/spiritual meaning (Kaye-Tzadok and Davidson-Arad, 2016; Tedeschi, Cann, Taku, Senol-Durak, and Calhoun, 2017).

The Post-traumatic Growth Inventory (PTGI) (Tedeschi and Calhoun, 1995, 1996) is one of the most widely used instruments in the traumatic growth field (Tedeschi et al., 2017). The original PTGI scale evaluated personal strength, relating to others, new possibilities, and appreciation of life. Cognitive processing such as deliberate rumination and reflection about the traumatic event, changes in schemas, positive refocusing, and construction of new narratives are all indicators of post-traumatic growth (Kaye-Tzadok and Davison-Arad, 2016; Taku, Cann, Tedeschi, and Calhoun, 2015). Recently, spiritual and existential changes were added to the instrument in an effort to capture alterations in spiritual beliefs and existential meaning that emerge from traumatic experiences (Tedeschi et al., 2017). These growth factors are prominent across different cultures and genders.

Although post-traumatic growth is generally associated with diminished PTSD, many people may still suffer intense distress despite greater growth. Given these conflicting findings, a *Janus-face model* has been proposed. This model suggests that either constructive growth follows a traumatic event or an illusory sense of growth is endorsed; however, illusory growth usually dissipates over time (Pat-Hoernczyk et al., 2015). The illusory sense of growth is founded on denial and a lack of coping, which may explain the co-occurrence of post-traumatic growth and PTSD symptoms (Zoellner and Maercker, 2006). Illusory growth is also marked by avoidance of feelings, endorsement of thriving, and then collapsing into intense struggles (Chen and Wu, 2017). In this Janus model, unlike illusory growth, constructive growth should increase self-transformation over time, along with diminishing denial and promoting active adaptive coping strategies (Zoellner and Maercker, 2006). Although constructive growth emerges, many still acknowledge that they continue to struggle despite identifying clear indicators of post-traumatic growth (Pat-Horenczyk et al., 2016).

FACTORS CONTRIBUTING TO POST-TRAUMATIC GROWTH

Individuals who tend to endorse post-traumatic growth demonstrate specific strengths prior to the traumatic event. For example, in a study that examined a sample prior to and following a major earthquake, individuals who had higher mental health status fared much better post-earthquake compared to those struggling with psychopathology before the earthquake (Marshall, Frazier, Frankfurt, and Kuijer, 2015). Similar findings were revealed in a study that examined Syrian refugees in Jordan. Refugees who manifested post-traumatic growth had a higher income status prior to the Syrian crisis and they were affiliated with nongovernment organizations that offered resources and information (Rizkalla and Segal, 2018). Well-being and post-traumatic growth in these refugees was also related to an absence of psychosis and affective disorders. In general, they had better mental health prior to the crisis and this persisted when they were evaluated as refugees (Rizkalla and Segal, 2018).

Pre-trauma cognitive abilities to ruminate about an event as well as distract from a stressful situation also predict more post-traumatic growth after a traumatic episode (Su and Chen, 2015). Although rumination tends to intensify negative feelings, when rumination is conceptualized as two different facets (*automatic/intrusive rumination versus deliberate rumination*) then a different picture emerges (Lindstrom, Cann, Calhoun, and Tedeschi, 2013). Automatic rumination has a brooding quality that indicates a passive inability to inhibit thoughts about negative situations (Garcia, Duque, and Cova, 2017). Deliberate rumination demonstrates an ability to direct attention toward distressing thoughts and feelings as well as distract from them. There is a volitional control over these thought patterns (Hanley et al., 2017; Lindstrom et al., 2013). This form of rumination has a reflective quality and aids in reframing cognitive appraisals, core beliefs, and behaviors (Garcia et al., 2017).

Deliberate rumination is a key trait in people who recover from traumatic events with even more purpose and meaning (Su and Chen, 2015); whereas, intrusive or brooding rumination perpetuates PTSD symptoms (Garcia et al., 2017; Zhou, Wu, Fu, and An, 2015). Along with deliberate rumination, factors that interact with deliberate rumination and promote growth post-trauma include distraction and social support; they are influential in challenging and altering core beliefs (Taku et al., 2015).

Relational patterns directly and indirectly influence post-traumatic growth. For example, sibling order influences the likelihood of acquiring post-traumatic growth (Kaye-Tzadok and Davidson-Arad, 2016). The eldest or middle child demonstrates greater growth than the youngest sibling. This finding may be related to efforts to find meaning in the midst of adversity. For example, older children will often protect younger siblings from sexual or physical abuse incurred by parental figures. This indirectly enhances their sense of purpose and efficacy, factors that increase post-traumatic growth (Kaye-Tzadok and Davidson-Arad, 2016). Marital couples are also able to co-create post-traumatic growth (Canevello, Michels, and Hilaire, 2016). Greater growth can occur when they share a traumatic event, as well as share in the process of responding to the trauma, actively listening to each other's needs, and perceiving that they receive support from each other. Although traumatic events may rupture marriages, for some the event provides a deeper bonding experience, one that enhances meaning and optimism (Canevello et al., 2016). When supportive dyadic coping (supportive responsive behaviors of a spouse during trauma reminders) and common dyadic coping (collaborative interactions between partners in response to reminders of trauma) are experienced, PTSD symptoms significantly decrease in the traumatized partner (Lambert, Hasbun, Engh, and Holzer, 2015). This relational growth operates slightly differently than individual growth. Recognizing and valuing social complexity, including the ever-shifting changes that manifest because of social contexts, promotes behavioral adaptation and shifting perspectives (Nalipay et al., 2016). Couples, families, societies, and cultures that manifest flexible adaptation during intentional and non-intentional traumatic events are able to adjust beliefs about the social complexity of the self and world; they accommodate to the changes provoked by the traumatic event(s) and have greater potential to achieve post-traumatic growth (Nalipay et al., 2016).

Engaging in ritual and spiritual ceremonies offers communities an opportunity to recover from shared traumatic events (Esala and Taing, 2017). By focusing on the larger social values, a deeper sense of community and belonging can be nurtured. For example, Eastern cultures value an integrated mind-body relationship as well as a sense of a collective whole (Nalipay, Bernardo, and Mordeno, 2016). These fundamental Eastern cultural and spiritual beliefs deeply influence recovery from natural disasters. In general, many people with strong spiritual beliefs are able to find meaning in adverse situations (Currier, Holland, and Drescher, 2015). They often draw upon daily spiritual practices and incorporate positive religious coping strategies such as prayer and forgiveness. When these spiritual beliefs are operational prior to a traumatic event, they tend to buffer the negative intensity of the subjective appraisal; however, when these beliefs are fragile then the traumatic event often overwhelms these coping strategies (Currier, Holland, and Drescher, 2015; Farley, 2007). Likewise, victims and perpetrators who struggle with moral injuries often experience symptom relief when they draw upon their strong religious and spiritual beliefs; however, moral injuries are intensified when individuals struggle with their religious or spiritual beliefs (Evans et al., 2018). Collectively, when trauma survivors are able to sustain religious or spiritual beliefs, they can derive support from those who participate in shared ritual ceremonies and testimonial events. They are also able to generate stronger existential meaning from these experiences (Esala and Taing, 2017). In addition, reading or listening to adversity stories supports empathic growth. The ability to generate imagery while listening or reading increases empathy for those who suffered (Johnson, Cushman, Borden, and McCune, 2013). The nature of these rituals, stories, and testimonies reflect embedded cultural beliefs and their inherent healing values.

Post-traumatic growth is also facilitated by modified or completely altered appraisals of the situation (Yeung et al., 2016). This is evident when people perceive negative events as manageable challenges. They meet the challenge with coping strategies that can address the situation; they also manifest a willingness to accept the challenge, express their emotional responses openly, and positively reframe the events. Some of the positive reframing may be driven by religious beliefs; ultimately they cultivate meaning from the negative event (Yeung et al., 2016). For example, mindfulness practices help facilitate positive reappraisal during post-traumatic coping (Hanley et al., 2017); although severe PTSD symptoms accompanied by maladaptive thinking are only minimally altered by mindfulness practices (Shipherd and Salters-Pedneault, 2018). Essentially, regular contemplative practices increase self-awareness and self-regulation via a heightened capacity to observe, describe, act with awareness, and restrain from judgmental reactions (Hanley et al., 2017). For many individuals, mindfulness is a dispositional trait that is enhanced by formal practice. This provides greater resilience as well as augments post-traumatic growth. It facilitates adaptation of core beliefs in order to accommodate traumatic experiences and to influence enhanced meaning post-trauma (Hanley et al., 2017).

Engaging in creative expression offers an active means to deliberately ruminate/reflect on traumatic events. Many individuals who endorse post-traumatic growth perceive greater inner access to their creativity. A sense of inspiration and motivation may become an antidote and response to traumatic events (Forgeard, 2013). Exposure to extreme traumatic events dramatically changes perceptions and beliefs and the act of capturing these experiences via a creative medium may enhance growth. Grappling with changes that follow a traumatic event, including the array of emotions that are provoked often requires accommodation of previous cognitive beliefs and altering them to match the experience (Gordon et al., 2016). Although traumatic events are not typically associated with experiences of awe, both share immediacy along with profound alterations of perceptions (Chirico, Glaveanu, Cipresso, Riva, and Gaggioli, 2018; Gordon et al., 2016). These indelible experiences expand mental maps. Individuals who are oriented toward creative expression are usually more open to experience and demonstrate idea generating fluency, flexibility, and originality. Awe-inspiring experiences involve complex emotional responses and require an ability to tolerate ambiguity and uncertainty (Chirico et al., 2018). Awe, including the horrific power of trauma, is experienced as either positive or negative. When individual core beliefs and mental models are challenged, accommodation and adaptation to these changes must transpire; often post-traumatic growth is possible as cognitive schemas are amended (Gordon et al., 2016). Creative expressiveness may be promoted as a result of these potentially transcendent experiences (Chirico et al., 2018). After exposure to these intensely life-altering experiences, participating in creative programs that cultivate a sense of connectedness enhances recovery. This is achieved by working collaboratively and by instilling feelings of importance, meaning, and value (Oliver, Collin, Burns, and Nicholas, 2006).

SECONDARY GROWTH

Secondary growth is a conceptual model that accounts for individuals who are raised around someone with PTSD or who work professionally with someone with PTSD (Zerach, 2015). Witnessing and sharing in the process of the survivor who recovers from trauma-related symptoms and exhibits behaviors of post-traumatic growth may be transmitted to those in close relationship with the survivor. In order to acquire secondary growth the individual must also experience secondary traumatization prior to displaying growth behaviors (Zerach, 2015). This acquisition of secondary growth often emerges in children or spouses of partners who experience extreme trauma such as prisoner of war survivors. Evaluating post-traumatic growth requires assessment of values and beliefs pre-trauma, then examining trauma-related symptoms immediately following the trauma, followed by an assessment of coping strategies post-trauma (Zerach, 2015). In a study investigating Israeli children of ex-prisoner of war veterans, the adult children initially manifested elevated symptoms of secondary trauma, which transformed into significantly higher levels of secondary growth compared to adult children who were raised by parents with no trauma exposure. Factors that influenced this secondary growth included higher education, personality traits of extraversion and openness to experience, and initially more severe symptoms of secondary traumatization (Zerach, 2015). The participants who achieved secondary growth expressed a positive outlook on their experiences growing up with their fathers, despite that fact that their fathers manifested emotional difficulties following their prisoner of war experiences. Witnessing their fathers struggle to adapt and find meaning were significant factors that influenced their secondary growth (Zerach, 2015).

In the Israeli study, the two personality traits of extraversion and openness to experience also supported their ability to remain engaged and open to their family's struggles and successes. For those who did not achieve this secondary growth, personality traits such as neuroticism were more pervasive (Zerach, 2015). The two personality traits that predicted secondary growth indicate potential resilience in these individuals, especially because extraversion includes features of optimism, positive affect, high energy, assertiveness, and social ability, while openness to experience involves seeking new experiences, willingness to explore ideas, and a curiosity about internal and external sensations (McCrae and Costa, 1987). Personality traits directly and indirectly influence coping strategies thus they are an integral component of symptoms of PTSD as well as post-traumatic growth (Tedeschi and Calhoun, 1995).

POST-TRAUMATIC GROWTH AND RETALIATORY RESPONSES

Although post-traumatic growth is possible, many individuals actually endorse more psychological distress that manifests as more rigid political attitudes and support for more retaliatory violence. These attitudes and beliefs may translate into positive personal benefits when individuals act according to their beliefs (Hobfoll et al., 2007). This post-traumatic growth response does not resemble the assumption of altruism that springs from traumatic experiences (Tedeschi et al., 2017). For some people, feelings of embitterment emerge in reaction to injustices or humiliation (Linden and Rotter, 2018). This feeling is deeply unpleasant and often provokes a demand for restitution. The impulse to defend one's rights regardless of potential self-harm is driven by feelings of embitterment. In this state, ruminative thoughts regarding being wronged and a desire for retribution to right the wrong may dominate. These thoughts may be painful as well as rewarding, which lends an addictive quality to them (Linden and Rotter, 2018). When they persist, embitterment may become chronic. Once it is chronic, the ruminating behavior constrains feelings of hope and effective problem-solving; it is no longer a vehicle for growth (Dunn and Senky, 2018).

CONCLUSION

Factors that influence post-traumatic growth are not unique. These factors are involved during any change in perception that involves a sense of personal growth (Silverstein, Lee, Witte, and Weathers, 2017). Three major factors that promote growth following adversity are meaning making through actions that are inherent in specific careers (helping others, creative professions), coping strategies that involve reasoning and reappraisal (gaining a deeper understanding about the self and the abuser), and spirituality (commitment to religious practices and community). These three conditions transcend age, gender, and culture (Grossman et al., 2006). These conditions can be seen in all individuals who achieve post-traumatic growth. For example, in families with children diagnosed with cancer many factors associated with post-traumatic growth emerge, specifically religious coping, strong family ties, and a good relationship with the oncologist (Wilson et al., 2016). Without these factors, specifically individuals and families who lack financial and psychosocial resources, more trauma-related symptoms and minimal or no post-traumatic growth results (Wilson et al., 2016).

When investigating hardiness and post-traumatic growth, accounting for different traumatic events may influence outcome results. For example, study findings suggest that it is more difficult to achieve post-traumatic growth after sexual assault. These victims tend to report high levels of distress and significant prolonged alterations in sexual functioning (Steenkamp, Dickstein, Salters-Pedneault, Hofmann, and Litz, 2012). A much higher frequency of adult sexual assault victims have past histories of childhood sexual abuse; these early experiences may compromise self-efficacy and an internalized locus of control (Walsh, Blaustein, Knight, Spinazzola, and van der Kolk, 2007). Likewise, institutional betrayal trauma adds to difficulties recovering from sexual assault, which diminishes the potential for post-traumatic growth (Smith and Freyd, 2013). This specific form of trauma is also associated with more negative social support and maladaptive coping strategies (i.e., isolation, anger, avoidance, numbing); a feedback loop is created between these factors, which intensifies trauma-related symptoms over time (Ullman and Relyea, 2016). Given the difficulties recovering from sexual assault, facilitating post-traumatic growth during treatment requires increased attention directed toward adaptive coping strategies so that sexual assault victims can seek and accept positive social support (Ullman and Relyea, 2016).

The dose effect of cumulative trauma also influences post-traumatic growth. A curvilinear path is often present, with the resolution of some traumatic distress influencing post-traumatic growth but higher rates of exposure and more severe symptoms leading to PTSD (Achterhof et al., 2018). Likewise, acquiring post-traumatic growth after the loss of a significant loved one may fail. This was evident in a study that examined bereaved parents; a significant factor associated with a failure to achieve post-traumatic growth in this sample was being a bereaved father who lost an older child. They were more vulnerable to feelings of intense grief and guilt (Albuquerque et al., 2018). As well, stigmatized populations such as members of the LGBTQ community are at greater disadvantage to experience post-traumatic growth. Helping address perceptions of social stigma may increase post-traumatic growth for this population (Cardenas et al., 2018). Based on study findings, the challenges of achieving post-traumatic growth remain; however, in the future more attention directed toward factors that promote post-traumatic growth may increase positive reappraisals of traumatic experiences. They may positively influence perceptions of the self and the world (Cardenas et al., 2018).

Chapter 14

Constricting and Fostering Creative Resilience

A Complex Relationship

Individual beliefs and values are shaped by early experience. Positive and negative childhood and adult experiences may serve to constrain or enrich creative expression. These experiences may reinforce dispositional personality traits as well as bias personality trait expression (Achterhof et al., 2018). For example, individuals who are predisposed to negative cognitions prior to a traumatic event are more likely to suffer greater trauma-related symptoms (Su and Chen, 2018). These negative cognitions are risk factors for developing PTSD after trauma exposure. They are also factors that constrain creative exploration and cripple self-efficacy (Su and Chen, 2018). Conversely, the resulting trauma symptoms and negative beliefs can be transformed into creative life-choices; these choices can infuse individuals with a sense of meaning and value (Grossman et al., 2006). How these experiences are integrated into perceptions about the self and the world influence individual creative output and resilience (Collishaw et al., 2007). Altered perceptions derived from adversity may offer novel insights into the human condition. Cognitive and perceptual dissonance may be captured within creative expression, regardless of the domain (arts, sciences, humanities, politics, and economics) (Muth, Hesslinger, and Carbon, 2018). As well, the creative products can propel the receiver into a state of semantic instability; literally, assumptions are challenged including means to derive meaning when presented with a novel experience (Muth et al., 2018). The trajectory of creative productivity is not a linear path; rather it is a complex path (Achterhof et al., 2018; Mittal et al., 2015). Consequently, adversity exposure may operate as a creative constraint or it may promote new creative expressions.

CONSTRICTION OF CREATIVITY

Constricting creative expression, and by association, resilience, occurs frequently. Multiple factors are associated with this constriction. For example, childhood adversity has long-term influences on resilience. Poor parenting, bullying, poverty, and low community resources all significantly compromise development, including the capacity to engage in creative activities (Sameroff and Rosenblum, 2006). These childhood risk factors disrupt self-regulatory capacities and increase psychopathology. Likewise, infants and children with temperaments that are classified as "difficult" have greater challenges in learning how to self-regulate; they require more sensitive and attuned parenting compared to children classified with less difficult temperaments (Straight et al., 2008). The temperament of the child combined with the quality of parenting influences academic competence, social skill acquisition, and emotional regulation. Optimal development, as well as creative engagement, are significantly constrained when children have difficult temperaments and are raised by insensitive caregivers (Stright et al., 2008).

Fear, rather than anger or happiness, dampens creative engagement and creative output (Lee, Chang, and Choi, 2017). Fear of parental authoritarian behavior negatively influences creativity in children. This form of parenting is marked by excessive control and judgment, high standards that must be met, and harsh punishment if these standards are not met (Fearon, Copeland, and Saxon, 2013). In general, fear evokes uncertainty. It influences appraisal uncertainty as well as heightened doubt during the creative process; in fact, fear implicitly biases individuals against creativity (Lee et al., 2017). As well, higher levels of stress decrease the quality of creative output; however, it does not reduce originality of ideas (Lovelace and Hunter, 2013). Another form of fear, the fear of death, also constrains creative output. According to the *terror management theory*, fear of mortality increases anxiety, which then initiates denial processes to reduce mortality anxiety (Arndt, Greenberg, Solomon, Pyszczynski, and Schimel, 1999). Engaging creatively may actually operate as an antidote to fear of death; it may be one way to manage terror. When fear provokes feelings of guilt, social connections are further diminished as a result of biased perceptions about self and others. Loss of social connections and intense feelings of guilt are substantial creative deterrents. Not surprising, when feelings of fear, anxiety, and guilt exist concurrently, creative exploration is muted (Arndt et al., 1999).

The term creative mortification has been proposed to capture an unwillingness to engage in some form of creative activity due to a general dissatisfaction with the process, as well as negative perceptions about the actual creative performance (Beghetto, 2014). Creative mortification is ultimately a form of shame, an experience that intensifies desires to hide from social scrutiny (Thomson and Jaque, 2013, 2015). Although every creative person is vulnerable to a shaming event, creative mortification responses are more frequent among younger individuals who have less experience in the creative field. This is intensified if they believe that their creative ability is a finite fixed factor. Often the experience of creative mortification provokes avoidant behavior, which further constricts creative output (Beghetto, 2014).

Perfectionism reduces creative exploration and well-being; it cripples creativity when it dominates behavioral responses. When high personal standards are shaped by perfectionistic ideals, a corresponding increase in psychopathology often emerges (Shafran and Mansell, 2000). Standard definitions of perfectionism indicate behaviors such as placing demands on self and others to perform at higher quality levels than needed or expected in a situation (Hewitt and Flett, 2004). Perfectionism influences unrealistic goal setting, intensifies critical self-evaluation, and increases shame (Eusanio, Thomson, and Jaque, 2014; Sagar and Stoeber, 2009). Fear of failure may motivate perfectionistic tendencies; however, perfectionism may also diminish engagement in tasks (i.e., procrastination, premature termination of a task, avoidance). It is believed that perfectionism develops from exposure to overly critical or demanding parents, teachers, or coaches. Perfectionistic tendencies worsen when expectations and standards of performance are excessively high and approval is absent, inconsistent, or conditional. If parents, teachers, or coaches are perfectionistic then they serve as models for perfectionistic attitudes and behaviors, which further intensify the acquisition of excessive perfectionism (Hewitt and Flett, 2004; Shafran and Mansell, 2000). Ultimately, heightened perfectionism leads to increased distress, including mental illnesses such as anxiety and eating disorders (Penniment and Egan, 2012).

How individuals manage stress directly relates to creative output. Children who have difficulty regulating behavior and emotions often display disruptive behaviors while engaging in creative projects. These negative behaviors and affects strongly diminish creative achievement (Butcher and Niec, 2005). A personal history or family member with a history of severe mental illness may intensify difficulties managing stress. Highly creative people are typically over-represented in samples that examine bipolar or schizophrenia disorders (Kyaga et al., 2011). A high degree of psychopathology generally constrains creative achievement. For example, depressive symptoms are significantly associated with deficits in creative thinking, including divergent thinking, cognitive flexibility, and tolerance for ambiguity (Liknaitzky, Smillie, and Allen, 2018). Another constraint to creativity is disrupted sleep and insomnia. Many individuals who report ongoing sleep disorders exhibit increased daytime dysfunction and poorer stress management (Ram-Vlasov et al., 2016; van Wyk, Thomas, Solms, and Lipinska, 2016). Of note, when working on a creative project, many individuals report difficulty sleeping; however, this is a transient state that is actually associated with increased creative engagement (Preti and Vellante, 2007; Ram-Vlasov, Tzischinsky, Green, and Shocat, 2016).

Creative deviance may not constrict output but it does move creative responses on a trajectory that may violate accepted moral norms and values (Gutworth and Hunter, 2017). Creative deviance/malevolence is often associated with traits such as narcissism (self-love, grandiosity, lack of empathy, entitlement, and sense of superiority), psychopathy (impulsivity, lack of remorse, unreliability, and callousness), and Machiavellianism (manipulative self-serving behaviors) (Kapoor, 2015). The production of products or actions that spring from negative malevolent creativity is generally associated with psychopathic traits, although narcissism and Machiavellianism traits may drive the creation of either benevolent or malevolent products (Kapoor, 2015). For all creative individuals, when a situation is ambiguous, there is a tendency to adapt a more malleable view of moral standards. The desire to produce novel products may increase desires to justify unethical or socially deviant behaviors (Gutworth and Hunter, 2017). This process holds true for creative individuals who generally produce benevolent works as well as for individuals who engage in malevolent creative enterprises (Cropley et al., 2008). Because creative expression tends to move toward some degree of deviance, organizations (corporate, political, academic, scientific, artistic) should provide a more flexible approach to establishing ethical standards and policies. Inevitably, encouraging exploration and autonomy implies a looser adherence to rules. When standards are too constrictive and rigid, creative output will diminish within these organizations (Gutworth and Hunter, 2017).

FOSTERING CREATIVE RESILIENCE

Constraints to creativity are palpable and powerful; however, factors that promote a creative mindset and creative productivity are equally powerful (Hannah et al., 2007). A combination of character traits, coupled with optimal developmental experiences strongly influence effective creative nurturance (Elliot and Reis, 2003). Likewise, skills to foster creative resilience can be readily trained and acquired. Creative resilience factors seldom operate in isolation; a complex network of interactive feedforward and feedback loops are engaged at micro and macro levels (Achterhof et al., 2018). For example, a passion to create something may motivate prolonged problem-solving efforts. This fosters self-efficacy, which increases optimism that then fuels a sense of hope (Hannah et al., 2007). Even workplace constraints can be transformed when individuals acquire a creative mindset; it influences a way of life. A creative mindset strongly informs relational interactions as well as academic and workplace behaviors (Achterhof et al., 2018). The factors listed below fundamentally overlap and interact; although for purposes of this section they are isolated for further examination.

Attachment and Parenting

Early attachment experiences and parenting approaches may foster or constrict childhood creative development and this may persist into adulthood (Bolwby, 1988). Optimal creative development occurs within an environment of sensitive caregiving. Sensitive caregiving involves mothers or fathers who are receptive to their children's needs and who modulate their responses in an effort to provide support to their children (Cantero, Alfonso-Benlliure, and Melero, 2016). When sensitive caregiving persists then secure attachment experiences are integrated into a sense of self and other (Bolwby, 1988; Belsky and Pasco-Fearon, 2008). These experiences help strengthen self-esteem and encourage exploration, as well as enhancing creativity in children (Cantero et al., 2016). Helping establish attachment security in children directly optimizes sensory seeking exploration and creative engagement (Elliot and Reis, 2003; Jerome and Liss, 2005). It also promotes higher positive moods, better emotion regulation, and more constructive coping (Kerns et al., 2007; Steele, Steele, and Croft, 2008). This process can be witnessed in interactions between sensitive parents and infants and children who are distressed. Attuned and congruent emotive vocal communication between the caregiver and child not only offers soothing and safety but also fosters emotional creative expressivity in the offspring (Milligan, Atkinson, Trehub, Benoit, and Poulton, 2003).

As well, caregivers that adopt an authoritative approach to parenting facilitate creative potential. Authoritative parenting provides children with opportunities to explore activities that are supported and encouraged by parents (Fearon et al., 2013). These parents offer respect and imbue confidence in their children. When parenting is dominated by authoritarian behaviors of hostility, rejection, punishment, minimal respect, and no autonomy, then children fair much worse creatively. They fail to explore their creative abilities; their fear of failure and punishment constrains their creative abilities (Fearon et al., 2013). Creative autonomy develops when children are allowed to follow their own motivational desires. Parental support enables children and adolescents to pursue their goals and this is enhanced when parental behavior involves a sense of self-regulation/control. These parents are able to manage their own emotional responses. They do not impose psychological control over their children rather they model flexible adaptive regulation (Ren, Li, and Zhang, 2017). Parental self-regulation also increases autonomous motivation in the child as well as reinforces more creative ideational fluidity, flexibility, and originality (Ren et al., 2017).

Engaging in Creative Expression

Engaging in creative activities during childhood and adolescents can enhance a sense of identity and self-efficacy. Optimal creative experiences during childhood tend to continue into adulthood; they become stable personality traits that shape a creative personality (Karwowski, 2016). With greater self-efficacy and stronger sense of identity, confidence is enhanced during challenging situations, including adverse situations. These factors are evident in young artists who are perceived as "odd" or "eccentric" (Day, 2002). In early childhood these "odd" children are often marginalized or even bullied but by middle school years and adolescence these creative children elevate their oddity into an identity that embraces both their creativity and their bizarreness. As adult artists they often include these experiences into their artwork, which may enrich their creative work (Day, 2002).

Engaging in the creative arts also promotes healing from natural disasters in children. In an intervention study that investigated expressive arts activities following a tornado, children who engaged in creative expression demonstrated increased self-awareness and self-understanding. These gains in personal awareness persisted long after the trauma-related symptoms abated (Davis, 2010). In a general population study, adversity-induced distress frequently promoted intrusive deliberate rumination; however, directing these deliberate ruminations into creative activities facilitated positive interpersonal relationships and increased creative output. Many in this sample reported that engaging in creativity promoted post-traumatic growth and dissipated trauma-related symptoms (Forgeard, 2013).

Artistic expression of loss, death, and traumatic experiences can transform despair into meaning; this applies to the creator of the work as well as those who draw meaning and value while listening or watching the artistic work (Mangione and Keady, 2007). A shared sense of understanding is nurtured among those engaged in the creative expression as well as the audiences who receive it. Optimal positive transformation of these painful life experiences may be further enhanced when creative work actually presents the transformational process via the creation of characters engaged in the traumatic situation or songs that recount this process. For example, in a study that examined the transformative effects of Bruce Springsteen's music, listeners identified the quality of relationships portrayed in the songs as healing. Recognition of trust, a sense of spirituality, and a visceral experience of catharsis were embedded in the songs and communicated to the listeners (Mangione and Keady, 2007).

The inclusion of creative expression in the treatment of PTSD is effective and healing. For example, PTSD typically involves visceral flashbacks that are experienced with full sensory intensity (APA, 2013). These flashbacks are disruptive and painful; however, they also reveal the reality that traumatic events are processed with strong symbolic representation. When symbolization of trauma is intense, engaging in modalities that enable non-verbal expression often helps alleviate distressing symptoms. These symbolic representations may also be powerful elements that are captured in the production of artistic works (Miller and Johnson, 2012). Working creatively with these traumatic visceral intrusions requires appropriate pacing and distancing; when managed effectively symbolic representations of the traumatic event can facilitate creative expression and creative productivity. This is evident in a study that examined the role creativity played following Hurricane Katrina. Creative thinking that involved flexibility and originality predicted more extraverted behavior and life satisfaction as well as diminished trauma-related symptoms (Metzl, 2009). These creative factors were even stronger among African American survivors compared to European American survivors. Creative thinking enhanced coping strategies, and when it was employed in art-making more spontaneous healing and post-traumatic growth resulted (Metzl, 2009). Future research is still needed to determine how creative ability influences trauma-related symptoms and healing. Whether the individual is already predisposed with heightened imaginative abilities prior to the traumatic event or if the traumatic event provoked imaginative engagement is unknown.

Paranormal Beliefs

Under stress, many individuals have greater access to paranormal beliefs. Their usual rational thinking diminishes and more anomalous thoughts and experiences are possible. Accessing more disparate concepts may actually encourage more creative expression and exploration (Lasikiewicz, 2016). These beliefs greatly reduce anxiety and promote a sense of control, especially when residing in environments that may in fact be dangerous and violent (Irwin, 2000; Watt et al., 2006). This process is clearly manifested in some children who suffered childhood abuse (Perkins and Allen, 2006). Paranormal beliefs often persist into adulthood, especially as paranormal experiences accumulate such as out of body experiences or premonitions. Future studies are still needed to determine how these beliefs operate during creative demands and the role they play in managing anxiety and stress (Watt et al., 2006). This line of research may also offer insight about a wider population; in particular, these beliefs and experiences are present in a high proportion of individuals without histories of adversity (Watt et al., 2006).

Meditation, Compassion, and Mindfulness

Meditation practices are well-documented methods to reduce anxiety and increase well-being, including creativity (Muller, Gerasimova, and Ritter, 2016). Mindfulness meditation involves a process of redirecting attention to awareness of breath, physical sensations, and the environment. When attention wanders practitioners are encouraged to re-direct their attention back to their body and environment (Bishop et al., 2004). Concentrative meditation, a common practice in most religions, in particular, Buddhism, requires practitioners to consciously focus on one object or thought. When attention wanders then practitioners recognize their distraction and return their focus back to the object or thought (Muller et al., 2016; Wallace and Shapiro, 2006). Concentrative meditation is a controlled practice; whereas, mindfulness meditation enhances awareness of the impermanence of everything that exists, including thoughts and feelings. Individuals who deliberately practice meditation have decreased inflammatory responses, which enhance physical well-being (Stellar et al., 2015). Findings have demonstrated increased activation in the left anterior region of the brain, a region that is associated with positive emotions as well as decreased inflammatory responses (Davidson et al., 2003). Recently, Muller and colleagues (2016) demonstrated a strong association following a session of meditation and creativity. Both mindfulness and concentrative meditation increased creative performance; however, only concentrative meditation increased cognitive flexibility (Muller et al., 2016). Experienced practitioners are also able to deliberately allow bursts of mind wandering to occur during their mindfulness practices, which further enhance creative originality and achievement (Agnoli, Vanucci, Pelagatti, and Corazza, 2018).

Meditation (i.e., Buddhist meditative practices) increases appraisal of the self with kindness and compassion. It is nonjudgmental regarding inadequacies and failures and increases acceptance of being a member of the human condition (Neff, 2009). This attitude enables exploration without prohibitions (Zabelina and Robinson, 2010). Nurturing self-compassion also enhances creative originality, especially in highly self-judgmental individuals (Zabelina and Robinson, 2010). As well, compassion focused meditative practices and therapeutic treatments are recommended to reduce shame, anxiety, depression, and chronic stress (Lutz, Brefczynski-Lewis, Johnstone, and Davidson, 2008). This form of meditative practice increases activation in limbic regions responsible for self-regulation, empathy, theory of mind, and environmental orientation (Lutz et al., 2008). In addition, adopting compassion meditation increases a deeper understanding about trauma-related symptoms and encourages compassion satisfaction. This was evidenced in a study that examined mental health workers. Compassion satisfaction was directly associated with opportunities to maintain self-care, including during stressful situations that arose in their trauma training (Butler, Carello, and Maguin, 2017).

Psychological mindedness, often referred to as mentalization, metacognition, or theory of mind, is a term that describes psychological abilities to be aware, assess, reflect, and sustain interest in the mental, emotional, and cognitive states of self and other (LeBoutillier and Barry, 2018). Expressing interest is the first step in psychological mindedness; the capacity to reflect on implicit and explicit observations promotes psychological mindedness. This capacity enhances openness to new experiences and fosters creative cognitions and creative associations (LeBoutillier and Barry, 2018). For most individuals, psychological mindedness, compassion, and meditative practices enhance well-being; however, for some individuals who are extremely self-judgmental and fearful of affiliative emotions, these practice forms are difficult and sometimes impossible to endorse (Gilbert, McEwan, Matos, and Rivis, 2011). Alternative approaches may need to be explored for this sector of the population in order to foster creative potential.

Hope, Optimism, and Positive Emotions

Hope is a cognitive belief that success can be derived from a sense of agency in challenging situations (Gilman, Schumm, and Chard, 2012). The ability to direct goals and determine effective planning strategies to meet goals enhances agency, and indirectly installs hope. This process is vitally important during trauma recovery. When individuals are exposed to extreme trauma that evokes profound feelings of hopelessness, helping them regain a sense of agency may promote a state of hope. Hope often represents a shift from negative rumination about adversity to one of positive adaptation (Kaye-Tzadok and Davidson-Arad, 2016). With hope, trauma-related symptoms can begin to dissipate over time and self-agency is strengthened (Gilman et al., 2012). Along with hope, individuals who have a sense of optimism and self-efficacy are more likely to flourish as evidenced in heightened innovative behaviors (Li and Wu, 2011). The combination of optimism and self-efficacy enhances cognitive reappraisal; this is essential during the creative process of producing innovative ideas and engaging in problem-solving explorations. Cognitive, emotional, and behavioral flexibility are evident in optimistic individuals; their bias toward a positive outlook directly influences their adaptability, especially when it is combined with practical problem-solving strategies (Li and Wu, 2011). The interaction of optimism, hope, and self-efficacy ultimately fosters self-agency, including creative acts of courage.

Along with hope, courage, and optimism, nurturing positive emotions promotes health and psychological well-being (Fredrickson, 2004). Joy, interest, contentment, and love all expand a sense of perspective on the self and world. The ability to broaden mindsets as opposed to narrowing them is directly influenced by positive emotional states of being. Positive emotions encourage exploration, expand resource acquisition (internal and external), and increase successful coping. The ability to move readily toward positive emotions is one of the hallmarks of optimism. Studies have demonstrated that activating more positive emotions can be cultivated via meditative practices, as well as consciously choosing a positive view on situations (Tugade and Fredrickson, 2004). With practice these positive mindsets may become courageous mindsets (Hannah et al., 2007). They may function as components that foster creativity.

Constraints that Optimize Creativity

Constraints during the creative process may actually increase creative output and creative originality (Haught, 2015; Haught-Tromp, 2017). Too many options during the creative process can actually overwhelm the process. The paradox of choice reflects this notion; as long as motivation is strong then less options increase exploratory behaviors (Schwartz, 2004). One often under-appreciated constraint is female gender. A longitudinal examination of female career trajectory suggests inconsistent or truncated productivity (Reis, 2002). This assessment is invalidated when other factors are included, in particular, acknowledging creative aspirations and output that includes relationships, family, and parenting. Different aesthetic values and work-related innovations may then be recognized as creative productivity. For example, many women begin their careers with high creative output and then shift to parenting. For most women, the act of parenting is equally regarded as a creative venture. Adopting this assessment approach removes the concept that raising children constrains creativity (Reis, 2002).

Workplace Creativity

Workplace structuring can promote creative output and growth satisfaction (Binyamin and Carmeli, 2017). When workers are placed in low levels of structuring (framework for managing employees) they are able to interact as team members with more ease, which promotes creativity and increases a satisfactory sense of growth. When placed in high levels of structure, work teams have a diminished sense of growth satisfaction despite similar creative output (Binyamin and Carmeli, 2017). Organizational justice within the workplace also influences creative output and growth satisfaction (Hannam and Narayan, 2015). Perceptions of fairness contribute positively to worker performance and satisfaction. For example, distributed justice influences individual perceptions about their input and their output equity. This form of organizational justice is augmented when employees are open to experiences (Simmons, 2011). Procedural justice describes rules and procedures that inform decisions regarding task assignment and outcomes, and interpersonal justice reflects the quality of personal treatment in the work environment. According to Hannam and Narayan (2015), distributed and interpersonal justice processes optimize and mediate intrinsic motivation and creative performance. In addition, within organizations, leaders who offer a sense of inclusiveness promote employee involvement and enhance a sense of safety (Carmeli, Reiter-Palmon, and Ziv, 2010). These leaders are open, accessible, and available; their employees respond with deeper personal investment. They are able to work without fear of negative consequences, which promotes creative exploration and innovation (Carmeli et al., 2010). In these environments a reciprocal relationship is nurtured, one in which the workers and the leadership co-create a sense of genuine care for each other. Similar to secure attachment relationships between caregivers and children, workers are able to increase creative innovation via their freedom to openly express distress and actively seek solutions with their leaders (Binyamin, Friedman, and Carmeli, 2018).

Providing workplace physical environments that encourage creativity also increases worker satisfaction and productivity. For example, ensuring a view of a natural environment, use of natural materials, inclusion of visual detail and spatial complexity, employing warm colors in interior design, and offering less manufactured surface materials all foster worker satisfaction and productivity (McCoy and Evans, 2002). Temperature associated with geographical region is an integral factor in promoting or inhibiting creative invention and innovation (Van de Vliert and Murray, 2018). High productivity tends to cluster in regions that are geographically closer to the north and south poles and nearer the equator. This distribution pattern is associated with higher demands that are required to manage cold or hot temperatures. It necessitates more resources. Not surprising, richer nations compared to poor nations have higher creative output. Creative achievement is strongly associated with both more intense climate demands and more wealth resources to accommodate these demands (Van de Vliert and Murray, 2018).

As well as working within these physical environments, when employees perceive stressors as positive challenges (i.e., time constraints) they are able to generate more ideas; whereas, perceived hindrance challenges (i.e., job insecurity) reduce creative idea generation (Ren and Zhang, 2015). Equally important, an optimal organizational innovation climate in the workplace, such as providing opportunities to work in teams, increasing a sense of autonomy, and ensuring sufficient resources and support are available to the workers are all factors that positively influence intrinsic motivation, idea generation, and idea implementation (Ren and Zhang, 2015). Within the workplace, amplification of positive emotions directly increases job satisfaction (Cote and Morgan, 2002). Negative emotions tend to interfere with job satisfaction; however, the need to suppress these negative emotions actually increases worker intentions to quit their jobs. Providing work environments that encourage the expression of displeasure and facilitating solutions to remedy these problems are directly related to enhancing job satisfaction and job stability (Cote and Morgan, 2002). This practice also fosters optimal stress management within the workplace. Likewise, individual dispositions intensify positive and negative outcomes. For example, individuals who are more pragmatic (create solutions based on threats and opportunities) are able to adapt to stress and increase creative output, whereas, individuals who are ideological or charismatic experience more constraints on their creative output when under stressful conditions (Lovelace and Hunter, 2013). Likewise, pragmatic leaders can readily adapt to changing environments and promote creative output (Lovelace and Hunter, 2013).

Motivation, Passion, and Flow

Individuals who possess traits such as intrinsic motivation, harmonious passion, and dispositional autotelic flow are well situated to engage creatively despite internal and/or external challenges that may constrain their productivity. These traits are often overlapping and are strongly interrelated. Individuals who possess these traits tend to value and perceive organizational justice. They are usually more engaged in their work, which amplifies their belief that fairness in the workplace is vitally important (Hannam and Narayan, 2015). As well, harmonious passion and creative self-efficacy promote creative output via increasing curiosity and imaginative engagement (Puente-Diaz and Cavazos-Arroyo, 2017). With creative self-efficacy, the motivational capacity to identify goals and actively seek them is heightened. One of the components of self-efficacy is the ability to orient toward goals, which helps organize planning strategies and shapes responses to feedback while attempting to achieve these goals (He, Yao, Wang, and Caughron, 2016). This applies across all domains as well as in all creative endeavors. When engaging in a creative project, the cultivation of a clear creative goal is then enhanced by feedback; as a result a sense of failure is diminished. When individuals avoid their goals then feedback becomes negative and reduces creative efforts (He et al., 2016). Positive factors to buffer creative discouragement include curiosity, creative self-efficacy, harmonious passion, persistence, sustained effort, and successful self-beliefs. These are further amplified when people work within environments that encourage and value creative output (Puente-Diaz and Cavazos-Arroyo, 2017).

Beyond strong intrinsic motivation and self-efficacy, opportunities to experience flow within a work setting increases work satisfaction as well as creative well-being (Mihelic and Aleksic, 2017). Currently, organizational enterprises regard creativity as an essential ingredient; hence establishing work environments that promote creativity is advantageous to both the workers and the organization. This is a particularly important factor for Millennial Workers (individuals born after 1980). They find meaning through creative engagement; it is a major motivating factor for their productivity (Espinoza and Ukleja, 2016). Creative productivity is achieved by providing workers with a sense of autonomy and flexibility; key factors in establishing a work-life balance. Workers who are motivated by challenge, especially when they possess the skills to meet these challenges, are able to derive greater satisfaction in their work-life, including experiencing heightened flow states (Mihelic and Aleksic, 2017). Despite engaging in highly pressured environments, these individuals demonstrate traits that are associated with high flow prone individuals. They typically have positive, proactive personality traits, substantial training and experience, a strong sense of control, a capacity to sustain a balanced perspective on situations, demonstrate flexible and adaptive behaviors and cognitions, and they accept perceived social support. These high achieving individuals flourish in careers that offer challenging situations (Sarkar and Fletcher, 2014). They display high achievement desires and actively seek opportunities to fulfill their desires.

Creative skills such as cognitive flexibility, emotional regulation, tolerance for ambiguity, and increased willingness to explore novel situations are fostered when work days, as well as training sessions, include both structured and unstructured activities. The combination of structured and unstructured activities is particularly effective during the training of young athletes and performers (Bowers et al., 2014). These activities enhance flow; performers and athletes learn to perform under stress. They acquire skills to adequately meet the challenges of performance or competition. During the physical activity they are also situated to experience more flow states, and immediately following exercise, they experience increased creative idea generation (Steinberg et al., 1997).

Physical exercise also supports the reduction of trauma-related symptoms, which increases a sense of self-efficacy in individuals exposed to trauma (Powers et al., 2015). According to recent research findings, the positive effect of exercise is associated with greater stress reduction via increased glucocorticoid and HPA axis regulation. These exercise effects influence changes in the GABAergic system, endocannabinoid system, and more regulatory responses initiated by the hippocampal dentate gyrus (Crombie et al., 2018; Reul et al., 2015). As well, exercise positively influences sleep, mood, behavioral changes, and stress resilience. For individuals with PTSD, physical exercise and physical activities that promote flow states are powerfully validating experiences. Typically, individuals with PTSD suffer more dysregulation, including blunted responses in their stress systems. By incorporating physical activity into daily life, these individuals have an opportunity to increase greater feelings of self-efficacy and hope (Crombie et al., 2018). These experiences can then be transferred to workplace environments, especially the confidence that flow states operate when challenging tasks are met via adequate skill acquisition (Crombie et al., 2018; Hallet and Hoffman, 2014).

This pattern is powerfully evident in elite athletes and performers who are trained to master specific skill sets and to implement these skills during competitions or performances (Savage, Collins, and Cruckshank, 2017). Injury, illness, change of a coach or teacher, relational difficulties with significant others, or managing the inevitable blues after a major competition or performance season are all factors that challenge their well-being. Because of the heightened expectations and demands when performing at an elite level, managing these challenging setbacks may cause psychological disorders such as depression or anxiety. When recovery skills are offered and practiced many elite athletes and performers actually return with greater perspective on their talent and profession (Olszewski-Kubilius et al., 2015). Similar to prevalence rates for PTSD versus post-traumatic growth most elite individuals are able to grow after these setbacks (Savage et al., 2017). Factors that enhance recovery from elite level performance challenges include intrinsic motivation, self-belief, focus on tasks and demands, self-awareness, flexible ability to re-appraise and adapt to new situations, and an ability to draw upon social support (Savage et al., 2017).

Creative Courage

Individuals who defy adversity possess resilience and courage. Likewise, defying the force of creative constraints requires the courage to persevere in the face of uncertainty. Courageous acts involve acting in risky situations and demonstrating a willingness to engage in nonconformist behaviors. Individuals who act with courage are often described as possessing integrity, persistence, and vitality (Miller, 2000; Peterson and Seligman, 2004). A courageous mindset involves multiple converging factors such as personality traits of openness to experience and conscientiousness, plus resilience traits such as self-efficacy and a bias to positively appraise situations (Hannah et al., 2007). A strong sense of ethical values and a keen awareness of social forces that interact on personal inner convictions all shape a creative and courageous mindset. These factors, when directed toward innovation and creative expression, promote a sense of personal well-being that can be subjectively experienced as courage, and appraised by others as courageous acts performed by someone with a strong character (Hannah et al., 2007; Miller, 2000).

CONCLUSION

Environments that encourage individual or collective engagement are contingent on providing tasks and goals (Goncalo and Staw, 2006). For collective groups, a sense of cooperation and belonging enhances creative exploration; however, within these groups, individuals must also attend to tasks that demand solitary reflection and individualistic approaches. Ultimately, a fluid application of collectivism and individualism strongly promotes creative idea generation and achievement (Goncalo and Staw, 2006). Likewise, a combination of mindfulness practices, engaging in activities that promote flow experiences, and cognitive flexibility all enhance creativity (Kee and Wang, 2008). Regardless if the individual is a member of a collective group, an employee in an organization, or a leader, all have the potential to share traits that promote creative output. They must cultivate an ability to find meaning in chaos, effectively draw upon available physical and social resources, establish achievable goals, complete them in a timely manner, and engage flexibly in some or all of the nine flow dimensions that promote optimal performance (Simon, 2006).

Creatively engaging in life, despite adversity and hardship, enhances life satisfaction and a sense of happiness. Employment in fields that involves creativity directly reduces negative emotional reactivity and increases well-being (Necka and Hlawacz, 2013). For individuals who experience higher doses of childhood and adult trauma, the residue of terror, worry, and uncertainty may persist (Garfin, Poulin, Blum, and Silver, 2018); however, creatively engaging in life may foster meaning, purpose, and a deeper sense of connection (Thomson and Jaque, 2018b). The psychological legacy of trauma may cast a shadow but patches of light can be found and relished during creative engagement (Garfin et al., 2018; Thomson and Jaque, 2018b). Pursing pleasure through engaging in activities, exploring all aspects of a task, and seeking meaning in these activities enhances a sense of happiness and life satisfaction (Peterson, Park, and Seligman, 2005).

Investigating creativity via an interdisciplinary approach increases opportunities to understand human progress and establish policies to encourage creative innovation (Hennessey and Amabile, 2010). Creativity can be readily trained and the basic embodied cognitive skills (Cramond et al., 2005; Kim, 2011) are transferable to different domains (arts, science, politics, economics, etc.). Applying these skills can positively influence post-traumatic growth; they may also operate as foundational factors associated with resilience. Encouraging children to develop problem-solving skills, fluency of ideas, elaboration of ideas, resistance to premature closure, tolerance for ambiguity, and psychological and physiologic regulation enhances creative innovation and adaptability (Plucker, Beghetto, and Dow, 2004). These skills, if encouraged and practiced, can become dispositional traits that persist throughout adulthood. Even if they are not learned in childhood, they can be acquired in adulthood. Without these skills children and adults are at increased risk for psychopathology, disease, and suicide (Mraz and Runco, 1994). The capacity to engage in creative activities remains despite pronounced pathology associated with cumulative trauma (Thomson and Jaque, 2018b, 2018c). Ultimately, engaging in activities that are meaningful may challenge acts of terrorism (Hobfoll et al., 2007). This same practice may reduce the effects of domestic and community violence that is perpetrated on children and adolescents (Davis, 2010; Grossman et al., 2006; McGllin and Widom, 2001). When meaningful activities are shared, life satisfaction may extend to others. Communities can mobilize to counter domestic, institutional, national, or international terrorism. Engaging in the creative process offers a sense of purpose and hope (Hobfoll et al., 2009). These acts of meaning become fertile ground for individual and societal healing as well as nurturing future generations; adaptive flexibility provides a means to preserve life (Forgeard, 2013; Metzl and Morrell, 2008).

If creativity is practiced regularly it becomes a way of life. It is a skill that can be utilized during ordinary and extraordinary times (Sternberg, 2012). Creative people are not just creative while constructing a product; it is an attitude that informs daily living (Sternberg, 2012). Creativity springs from an open attitude, one that embraces the exploration of new ideas, new approaches, and new possibilities (Florida, 2004). This attitude propels countries and cultures to adapt to change; without openness to new ideas countries and cultures falter. This pattern has long been acknowledged in the United States, a country that was recognized as a land of opportunity and innovation; however, for over a decade researchers have demonstrated that the United States is no longer welcoming new ideas or promoting an education system that strengthens creativity (Florida, 2004; Kim, 2011). In order for countries to flourish, policies must be implemented to promote creativity; the generation of new ideas and the opportunities to develop new products are key elements in nurturing world leaders and world innovators. Creative talent needs to be nurtured by providing adequate pay, working conditions, and work opportunities so that untapped potential is realized. Embracing an attitude of openness and acceptance encourages exploration and installs hope for a better future (Florida, 2004).

Effectively meeting adversity requires mobilization of biological, psychological, and social resources in order to adapt. The trajectory of an individual life is fraught with countless expected and unexpected challenges. The central theme outlined in this book highlights some of the most horrific traumatic events humans suffer, the subsequent trauma-related symptoms that may emerge, as well as the rich resources that reside within our creative nature, whether operating at the everyday creative or eminent creative level. Creativity resides at the heart of human resilience. A society that fosters creativity may also propagate efforts to reduce trauma exposure. In the words of Bruce Perry (2001), "If children are ignored, poorly educated and not protected from violence they will grow into adults that create a reactive, non-creative and violent society . . . All societies reap what they have sown" (p. 231). The fundamental purpose of this book is to encourage a more complex understanding about human resilience. Perpetuating a model that underscores the power of deficits associated with adversity and pathology fails to embrace the diversity associated with resilience. For example, communities that elect to sing and dance in the streets after the devastating destruction of a major hurricane may not be avoiding seeking solutions. Perhaps they are celebrating their connection with their community and reinstalling a sense of hope and vitality (Nicolas, Byer, and Ho, 2015). In order for societies to heal wounds and promote a sense of well-being and meaning, more creative approaches may need to be explored. Even though adversity will always exist within the human condition, embracing the creative resources within us allows us to not only endure but prevail.

References

Aakvaag, H. F., Thoresen, S., Wentzel-Larsen, T., Roysamb, E., & Dyb, G. (2017). Shame and guilt in the aftermath of terror: The Utoya Island Study. *Journal of Traumatic Stress, 27*, 618–621. doi: 10.1002/jts.21957.

Abraham, A., & Windmann, S. (2007). Creative cognition: The diverse operations and the prospect of applying a cognitive neuroscience perspective. *Methods, 42*, 38–48. doi: 10.1016/j.ymeth.2006.12.007.

Abraham, A., Windmann, S., Daum, I., & Gunturkun, O. (2005). Conceptual expansion and creative imagery as a function of psychoticism. *Consciousness and Cognition, 14*, 520–534. doi: 10.1016/j.concog.2004.12.003.

Abrams, K. Y., Rifkin, A., & Hesse, E. (2006). Examining the role of parental frightened/frightening subtypes in predicting disorganized attachment within a brief observational procedure. *Development and Psychopathology, 18*, 345–361. doi: 10.1017/S0954579406060184.

Abtahi, M. M., & Kerns, K. A. (2017). Attachment and emotion regulation in middle childhood: Changes in affect and vagal tone during a social stress task. *Attachment and Human Development, 19*(3), 221–242. doi: 10.1080/14616734.2017.1291696.

Abuhamdeh, S., & Csikszentmihalyi, M. (2012). The importance of challenge for the enjoyment of intrinsically motivated, goal-directed activities. *Personality and Social Psychology, 38*(3), 317–330. doi: 10.1177/0146167211427147.

Acar, S., & Sen, S. (2013). A multilevel meta-analysis of the relationship between creativity and schizotypy. *Psychology of Aesthetics, Creativity, and the Arts, 7*(3), 214–228. doi: 10.1037/a0031975.

Acar, S., Burnett, C., & Cabra, J. F. (2017). Ingredients of creativity: Originality and more. *Creativity Research Journal, 19*(2), 133–144. doi: 10.1080/10400419.2017.1302776.

Achenbach, T. M., Howell, C. T., Quay, H. C., Conners, C. K., & Bates, J. E. (1991). National survey of problems and competencies among four- to sixteen-year-olds: Parents' reports for normative and clinical samples. *Monographs of the Society for Research in Child Development, 56*, 1–131. doi: 10.2307/1166156.

Achterhof, R., Dorahy, M. J., Rowlands, A., Renouf, C., Britt, E., & Carter, J. D. (2018). Predictors of posttraumatic growth 10–11 months after a fatal earthquake. *Psychological Trauma: Theory, Research, Practice, and Policy, 10*(2), 208–215. doi: 10.1037/tra0000286.

Ackerman, C. M. (2009). The essential elements of Dabrowski's Theory of Positive Disintegration and how they are connected. *Roeper Review, 31*(2), 81–95. doi: 10.1080/02783190902737657.

Adshead, G., & Blueglass, K. (2005). Attachment represenatations in mothers with abnormal illness behavior by proxy. *British Journal of Psychiatry, 187*, 328–333.

Afari, N., Ahumada, S. W., Wright, L. J., Mostoufi, S., Golinari, G., Resi, V., & Cuneio, J. G. (2014). Psychological trauma and functional somatic syndromes: A systematic review and meta-analysis. *Psychosomatic Medicine, 76*(1), 2–11. doi: 10.1097/PSY.0000000000000010.

Afifi, T. O., Asmundson, G. J., Taylor, S., & Jang, K. L. (2010). The role of genes and environment in trauma exposure and posttraumatic stress disorder symptoms: A review of twin studies. *Clinical Psychology Review, 30*, 101–112. doi: 10.1016/j.cpr.2009.10.002.

Afifi, T. O., Mather, A., Boman, J., Fleischer, W., Enns, M. W., MacMillan, H., & Sareen, J. (2011). Childhood adversity and personality disorders: Results from a nationally representative population-based study. *Journal of Psychiatric Research, 45*, 814–822. doi: 10.1016/j.jpsychires.2010.11.008.

Agaibi, C. E., & Wilson, J. P. (2005). Trauma, PTSD, and resilience: A review of literature. *Trauma, Violence, and Abuse, 6*(3), 195–216. doi: 10.1177/1524838005277438.

Ager, A., Pasha, E., Yu, G., Duke, T., Eriksson, C., & Cardozo, B. L. (2012). Stress, mental health, and burnout in national humanitarian aid workers in Gulu, Northern Uganda. *Journal of Traumatic Stress, 25*, 713–720. doi: 10.1002/jts.21764.

Agnoli, S., Vanucci, M., Pelagatti, C., & Corazza, G. E. (2018). Exploring the link between mind wandering, mindfulness, and creativity: A multidimensional approach. *Creativity Research Journal, 30*(1), 41–53. doi: 10.1080/10400419.2018.1411423.

Aguiar, N., Mottweilier, C. M., Taylor, M., & Fisher, P. A. (2017). The imaginary companions created by children who have lived in foster care. *Imagination, Cognition and Personality, 36*(4), 340–355. doi: 10.1177/0276236617700590.

Ahern, J., Galea, S., Resnick, H., & Vlahov, D. (2004). Television images and probable posttraumatic stress disorder after September 11: The role of background characteristics, event exposure, and perievent panic. *Journal of Nervous and Mental Disease, 192*, 217–226. doi: 10.1097/01.nmd.0000116465.99830.ca.

Ahmetoglu, G., Harding, X., Akhtar, R., & Chamorro-Premuzic, T. (2015). Predictors of creative achievement: Assessing the impact of entrepreneurial potential, perfectionism, and employee engagement. *Creativity Research Journal, 27*(2), 198–205. doi: 10.1080/10400419.2015.1030293.

Ainley, M., Enger, L., & Kennedy, G. (2008). The elusive experience of 'flow': Qualitative and quantitative indicators. *International Journal of Educational Research, 47*, 109–121. doi: 10.1016/j.ijer.2007.11.0111.

Ainsworth, M. D. S., Blehar, M. C., Waters, E., & Wall, S. (1978). *Patterns of attachment: Assessed in the strange situation and at home.* Hillsdale, NJ: Erlbaum.

Aitcheson, R. J., Abu-Bader, S. H., Howell, M. K., Khalil, D., & Elbedour, S. (2017). Resilience in Palestinian adolescents living in Gaza. *Psychological Trauma: Theory, Research, Practice, and Policy, 9*(1), 36–43. doi: 10.1037/tra0000153.

Akinola, M., & Mendes, W. B. (2008). The dark side of creativity: Biological vulnerable and negative emotions lead to greater artistic creativity. *Personality and Social Psychology Bulletin, 34*(12), 1677–1686. doi: 10.1177/0146167208323933.

Akinsulure-Smith, A. M., Espinosa, A., Chu, R., & Hallock, R. (2018). Secondary traumatic stress and burnout among refugee resettlement workers: The role of coping and emotional intelligence. *Journal of Traumatic Stress, 31*, 202–212. doi: 10.1002/jts.22279.

Albuquerque, S., Narciso, I., & Pereira, M. (2018). Posttraumatic growth in bereaved parents: A multidimensional model of associated factors. *Psychological Trauma: Theory, Research, Practice, and Policy, 10*(2), 199–207. doi: 10.1037/tra0000305.

Alexander, J. M., & Schnick, A. K. (2008). Motivation. In J. A. Plucker & C. M. Callahan (Eds.), *Critical issues and practices in gifted education* (pp. 423–448). Waco, TX: Prufrock Press.

Alexander, P. C. (2009). Childhood trauma, attachment and abuse to multiple partners. *Psychological Trauma: Theory, Research, Practice, and Policy, 1*, 78–88. doi: 10.1037/a0015254.

Ali, J. S., Farrell, A. S., Forde, D. R., Stockton, M., & Ward, K. D. (2017). Race differences in depression vulnerability following Hurricane Katrina. *Psychological Trauma: Theory, Research, Practice, and Policy, 9*(3), 317–324. doi: 10.1037/tra0000217.

Alias, A., Rahman, S., Majid, R. A., & Yassin, S. F. M. (2013). Dabrowski's overexcitabilities profile among gifted students. *Asian Social Science, 9*(16), 120. doi: 10.5539/ass.v9n16p120.

Alisic, E., Zalta, A. K., van Wesel, F., Larsen, S. E., Hafstad, G. S., Hassanpour, K., & Smid, G. E. (2014). Rates of post-traumatic stress disorder in trauma-exposed children and adolescents: Meta-analysis. *British Journal of Psychiatry, 204*, 335–340. doi: 10.1192/bjp.bp.113.131227.

Allen, A. P., & Thomas, K. E. (2011). A dual process account of creative thinking. *Creativity Research Journal, 23*(2), 109–118. doi: 10.1080/10400419.2011.571183.

Allen, J. G., Fultz, J., Huntoon, J., & Brethour, J. R. (2002). Pahtological dissociative taxon membership, absorption, and reported childhood trauma in women with trauma-related disorders. *Journal of Trauma and Dissociation, 3*(1), 89–110.

Alvarez, J. A., Emory, J. A., & Emory, E. (2006). Executive function and the frontal lobes: A meta-analytic review. *Neuropsychology Review, 16*(1), 17–42. doi: 10.1007/s11065-006-9002-x. PMID 16794878.

Amabile, T. M. (1996). *Creativity in context.* Boulder, Colorado: Westview Press.

Amabile, T. M., Barsade, S. G, Mueller, J. S., & Staw, B. M. (2005). Affect and creativity at work. *Administrative Science Quarterly, 50*, 367–403.

American Psychiatric Association (APA). (2013). *Diagnostic and statistical manual of mental disorders* (5th ed.). Washington, DC: American Psychiatric Publishing.

Amnesty International. (2014). *Torture in 2014: 30 years of broken promises.* Retrieved from https://www.amnestyusa.org/files/act1300042014en.pdf.

Amrhein, C., Hengmith, S., Maragkos, M., & Hennig-Fast, K. (2008). Neuropsychological characteristics of highly dissociative healthy individuals. *Journal of Trauma and Dissociation, 9*(4), 525–542. doi: 10.1080/15299730802226332.

Anderson, E. S., Winett, R. A., & Wojcik, J. R. (2007). Self-regulation, self-efficacy, outcome expectations, and social support: Social cognition theory and nutrition behavior. *Annals of Behavioral Medicine, 34*(3), 304–312.

Anderson, E. S., Wojcik, J. R., Winett, R. A., & Williams, D. M. (2006). Social-cognitive determinants of physical activity: The influence of social support, self-efficacy, outcome expectations, and self-regulation among participants in a church-based health promotion study. *Health Psychology, 25*(4), 510–520. doi: 10.1037/0278-6133.25.4.510.

Anderson, M. L., Craig, K. S. W., & Ziedonis, D. M. (2017). Deaf people's help-seeking following trauma: Experiences with and recommendations for the Massachusetts Behavioral Health Care System. *Psychological Trauma: Theory, Research, Practice, and Policy, 9*(2), 239–248. doi: 10.1037/tra0000219.

Andrews-Hanna, J. R., Smallwood, J., & Spreng, R. N. (2014). The default network and self-generated thought: Component processes, dynamic control, and clinical relevance. *Annals of the New York Academy of Sciences, 1316*(1), 29–52. doi: 10.1111/nyas.12360.

Angere, S. (2008). Coherence as a heuristic. *Mind, 117*(465), 1–26. doi: 10.1093/mind/fzn001.

Antonovsky, A. (1996). The salutogenic model as a theory to guide health promotion. *Health Promotion International, 11*, 11–18. doi: 10.1093/heapro/11.1.11.

Arden, R., Chavez, R. S., Grazioplene, R., & Jung, R. E. (2010). Neuroimaging creativity: A psychometric view. *Behavioral Brain Research, 214*, 143–156. doi: 10.1016/j.bbr.2010.05.015.

Armey, M. F., & Crowther, J. H. (2008). A comparison of linear and non-linear models of aversive self-wareness, dissociation, and non-suicidal self-injury. *Journal of Counselting and Clinical Psychology, 76*(1), 9–14. doi: 10.1037/0022-006x.76.1.9.

Armstrong, D. (2012). Contributions of creative cognition and schizotypal symptoms to creative achievement. *Creativity Research Journal, 24*(2–3), 177–190. doi: 10.1080/10400419.2012.677329.

Armstrong, D., Shakespeare-Finch, J., & Shochet, I. (2016). Organizational belongingness mediates the relationship between sources of stress and posttrauma outcomes in firefighters. *Psychological Trauma: Theory, Research, Practice, and Policy, 8*(3), 343–347. doi: 10.1037/tra0000083.

Arnberg, F. K., Hultman, C. M., Michel, P.-O., & Lundin, T. (2012). Social support moderates posttraumatic stress and general distress after disaster. *Journal of Traumatic Stress, 25*, 721–727. doi: 10.1002/jts.21758.

Arndt, J., Greenberg, J., Solomon, S., Pyszcznski, T., & Schimel, J. (1999). Creativity and terror management: Evidence that creative activity increases guilt and social projection following mortality salience. *Journal of Personality and Social Psychology, 77*(1), 19–32.

Arnsten, A. F. T., Raskind, M. A., Taylor, F. B., & Connor, D. F. (2015). The effects of stress exposure on prefrontal cortex: Translating basic research into successful treatments for post-traumatic stress disorder. *Neurobiology of Stress, 1*, 89–99. doi: 10.1016/j.ynstr.2014.10.002.

Asakawa, K. (2004). Flow experience and autotelic personality in Japanese college students: How do they experience challenges in daily life? *Journal of Happiness Studies, 5*, 123–154.

———. (2010). Flow experience, culture, and well-being: How do autotelic Japanese college students feel, behave, and think in their daily lives? *Journal of Happiness, 11*(2), 205–233. doi: 10.1007/s10902-008-9152-3.

Asberg, K., & Renk, K. (2013). Comparing incarcerated and college student women with histories of childhood sexual abuse: The roles of abuse severity, support, and substance use. *Psychological Trauma: Theory, Research, Practice, and Policy, 5*(2), 167–175. doi: 10.1037/a0027162.

Ashby, J. S., Rice, K. G., & Martin, J. L. (2006). Perfectionism, shame, and depressive symptoms. *Journal of Counseling and Development, 84*(2), 148–156.

Asmundson, G. J. G., LeBouthillier, D. M., Parkerson, H. A., & Horswill, S. C. (2016). Trauma-exposed community-dwelling women and men respond similarly to the DAR-5 anger scale: Factor structure invariance and differential item functioning. *Journal of Traumatic Stress, 29*, 214–220. doi: 10.1002/jts.22098.

Assouline, S. G., & Lupkowski-Shoplik, A. (2012). The talent-search model of gifted identification. *Journal of Psychoeducational Assessment, 30*(1), 45–59. doi: 10.1177/0734282911433946.

Aston-Jones, G., & Cohen, J. D. (2005). An integrative theory of locus coeruleus-norepinephrine function: Adaptive gain and optimal performance. *Annual Reviews in Neuroscience, 28,* 403–450. doi: 10.1146/annurev.neuro.28.061604.135709.

Atkinson, J. W. (1964). *An introduction to motivation.* Princeton, NJ: Van Nostrand.

Aupperle, R. L., Stillman, A. N., Simmons, A. N., Flagan, T., Allard, C. B., Thorp, S. R., ... Stein, M. B. (2016). Intimate partner violence PTSD and neural correlates of inhibition. *Journal of Traumatic Stress, 29*, 33–40. doi: 10.1002/jts.22068.

Austin, C. L., Saylor, R., & Finley, P. J. (2017). Moral distress in physicians and nurses: Impact on professional quality of life and turnover. *Psychological Trauma: Theory, Research, Practice, and Policy, 9*(4), 399–406. doi: 10.1037/tra0000201.

Averill, J. R., Chon, K. K., & Hahn, D. W. (2001). Emotions and creativity, East and West. *Asian Journal of Social Psychology, 4,* 165–183.

Avidor, S., Palgi, Y., & Solomon, Z. (2017). Lower subjective life expectancy in later life is a risk factor for posttraumatic stress symptoms among trauma survivors. *Psychological Trauma: Theory, Research, Practice, and Policy, 9*(2), 198–206. doi: 10.1037/tra0000182.

Avieli, H., Ben-David, S., & Levy, I. (2016). Predicting professional quality of life among professional and volunteer caregivers. *Psychological Trauma: Theory, Research, Practice, and Policy, 8*(1), 80–87. doi: 10.1037/tra0000066.

Ayers, L., Beaton, S., & Hunt, H. (1999). The significance of transpersonal experiences, emotional conflict, and cognitive abilities in creativity. *Empirical Studies of the Arts, 17*(1), 73–82.

Ayers, S., Rados, S. N., & Balouch, S. (2015). Narratives of traumatic birth: Quality and changes over time. *Psychological Trauma: Theory, Research, Practice, and Policy, 7*(3), 234–242. doi: 10.1037/a0039044.

Ayman-Nolley, S. (1992). Vygotsky's perspective on the development of imagination and creativity. *Creativity Research Journal, 5*(1), 77–85.

Azevedo, T. M., Volchan, E., Imbiriba, L. A., Rodrigues, E. C., Oliveira, J. M., Oliveira, L. F., ... Vargas, C. D. (2005). A freezing-like posture to pictures of mutilation. *Psychophysiology, 42*, 255–260. doi: 10.1111/j.1469-8986.2005.00287.x.

Baas, M., De Dreu, C. K. W., & Nijstad, B. A. (2008). A meta-analysis of 25 years of mood-creativity research: Hedonic tone, activation, or regulatory focus. *Psychological Bulletin, 134*(6), 779–806. doi: 10.1037/a0012815.

Babcock, R. L., & DePrince, A. P. (2012). Childhood betrayal trauma and self-blame appraisals among survivors of intimate partner violence. *Journal of Trauma and Dissociation, 13*, 526–538. doi: 10.1080/15299732.2012.694842.

Babson, K. A., Blonigen, D. M., Boden, M. T., Drescher, K. D., & Bonn-Miller, M. O. (2012). Sleep quality among U.S. military veterans with PTSD: A factor analysis and structural model of symptoms. *Journal of Traumatic Stress, 25*, 665–674. doi: 10.1002/jts.21757.

Baddeley, A. (2003). Working memory: Looking back and looking forward. *Nature Reviews Neuroscience, 4*(10), 829–839.

Badour, C. L., & Feldner, M. T. (2016). Disgust and imaginal exposure to memories of sexual trauma: Implications for the treatment of posttraumatic stress. *Psychological Trauma: Theory, Research, Practice, and Policy, 8*(3), 267–275. doi: 10.1037/tra0000079.

Baer, J. (2010b). Is creativity domain specific? In J. C. Kaufman & R. J. Sternberg (Eds.), *The Cambridge handbook of creativity* (pp. 321–341). New York, NY: Cambridge University Press. doi: 10.1017/CBO9780511763205.021.

———. (2015). The importance of domain-specific expertise in creativity. *Roeper Review, 37*, 165–178. doi: 10.1080/02783193.2015.1047480.

Baer, J. C., & Martinez, D. (2006). Child maltreatment and insecure attachment: A meta-analysis. *Journal of Reproductive and Infant Psychology, 24*(3), 187–197. doi: 10.1080/0264830600821231.

Bahm, N. I. G., Duschinsky, R., & Hesse, E. (2016). Parental loss of family members within two years of offspring birth predicts elevated absorption scores in college. *Attachment and Human Development, 18*(5), 429–442. doi: 10.1080/14616734.2016.1181096.

Bailey, H. N., Moran, G., & Pederson, D. R. (2007). Childhood maltreatment, complex trauma symptoms, and unresolved attachment in an at-risk sample of adolescent mothers. *Attachment & Human Development, 9*(2), 139–161. doi: 10.1080/14616730701349721.

Bailey, H. N., Tarabulsy, G. M., Moran, G., Pederson, D. R., & Bento, S. (2017). New insight on intergenerational attachment from a relationship-based analysis. *Development and Psychopathology, 29*, 433–448. doi: 10.1017/S0954579417000098.

Baker, E., & Beech, A. R. (2004). Dissociation and variability of adult attachment dimensions and early maladaptive scehmas in sexual and violent offenders. *Journal of Interpersonal Violence, 19*(10), 1119–1136. doi: 10.1177/088620504269091.

Baker, J., & Cote, J. (2003). Resources and commitment as critical factors in the development of "gifted" athletes. *High Ability Studies, 14*(2), 139–140. doi: 10.1080/135813032000163816.

Bakker, A. B. (2005). Flow among music teachers and their students: The crossover of peak experiences. *Journal of Vocational Behavior, 66*, 26–44. doi: 10.1016/j.jvb.2003.11.001.

Bakker, A. B., Oerlemans, W., Demerouti, E., Slot, B. B., & Ali, D. K. (2011). Flow and performance: A study among talented Dutch soccer players. *Psychology of Sport and Exercise, 12*(4), 442–450. doi: 10.1016/j.psychsport.2011.02.003.

Ballen, N., Demers, I., & Bernier, A. (2006). A differential analysis of the subtypes of unresolved states of mind in the Adult Attachment Interview. *Journal of Trauma Practices, 5*(4), 69–93. doi: 10.1300/J189v05n04_04.

Bandura, A. (1997). *Self-efficacy: The exercise of control*. New York, NY: W. H. Freeman & Company.

———. (2005). The primacy of self-regulation in health promotion. *Applied Psychology: An International Review, 54*(2), 245–254.

Barbar, A. E. M., Crippa, J. A. S., & Osorio, F. L. (2014). Performance anxiety in Brazilian musicians: Prevalence and association with psychopathology indicators. *Journal of Affective Disorders, 152–154*, 381−386. doi: 10.1016/j.jad.2013.09.041.

Barnes, T. D., Kubota, Y., Hu, D., Jin, D. Z., & Graybiel, A. M. Activity of striatal neurons reflects dynamic encoding and recoding of procedural memories. *Nature, 437*, 1158−1161. doi: 10.1038/nature0453.

Barone, L. (2003). Developmental protective and risk factors in borderline personality disorder: A study using the Adult Attachment Interview. *Attachment and Human Development, 5*(1), 64–77. doi: 10.1080/1461673031000078634.

Barron, F. (1969/1976). The psychology of creativity. In A. Rothenberg & C. R. Hausman (Eds.), *The creativity question* (pp. 189–200). Durham, NC: Duke University Press.

Bartholomew, K. (1990). Avoidance of intimacy: An attachment perspective. *Journal of Social and Personal Relationships, 7*, 147–178.

Bartholomew, K., & Horowitz, L. (1991). Attachment styles among young adults: A test of a four category model. *Journal of Personality and Social Psychology, 61*, 226–244.

Bartone, P. T., Roland, R. R., Picano, J. J., & Williams, T. J. (2008). Psychological hardiness predicts success in US army Special Forces candidates. *International Journal of Selection and Assessment, 16*(1), 78–81.

Bartoszek, G., Hannan, S. M., Kamm, J., Pamp, B., & Maieritsch, K. P. (2017). Trauma-related pain, re-experiencing symptoms and treatment of posttraumatic stress disorder: A longitudinal study of veterans. *Journal of Traumatic Stress, 30*, 288–295. doi: 10.1037/jts.22183.

Bassett-Jones, N. (2005). The paradox of diversity management, creativity and innovation. *Creativity and Innovation Management, 14*(2), 169–175. doi: 10.1111/j.1467-8691.00337.x.

Batey, M. (2012). The measurement of creativity: From definitional consensus to the introduction of a new heuristic framework. *Creativity Research Journal, 24*(1), 55–65. doi: 10.1080/10400419.2012.649181.

Baumann, N., & Turpin, J.-C. (2010). Neurochemistry of stress: An overview. *Neurochemistry Research, 35*, 1875–1870. doi: 10.1007/s11064-010-0298-9.

Bays, R. B., Zabrucky, K. M., & Foley, M. A. (2015). Imagery induction processes differentially impact imagination inflation. *Imagination, Cognition and Personality, 359*(1), 5–25. doi: 10.1177/0276236615574487.

Beach, S. R. H., Brody, G. H., Todorov, A. A., Gunter, T. D., & Philibert, R. A. (2010). Methylation at SLC6A4 is linked to family history of child abuse: An examination of the Iowa adoptee sample. *American Journal of Medicine and Genetics, 153B*, 710–713.

Beals, J., Manosn, S. M., Croy, C., Klein, S. A., Whitesell, N. R., Mitchell, C. M., & the AI-SUPERPFP Team. (2013). Lifetime prevalence of posttraumatic stress disorder in two American Indian reservation populations. *Journal of Traumatic Stress, 26*, 512–520. doi: 10.1002/jts.21835.

Beaty, R. E. (2015). The neuroscience of musical improvisation. *Neuroscience and Biobehavioral Reviews, 51*, 108–117. doi: 10.1016/j/neruobiorev.2015.01.004.

Beaty, R. E., & Schacter, D. L. (2017). Creativity, self-generated thought, and the brain's default mode network. In M. Karwowski & J. C. Kaufman (Eds.), *The creative self: Effect of beliefs, self-efficacy, mindset, and identity* (pp. 171–183). San Diego, CA: Academic Press.

Bechara, A., & Damasio, A. (2005). The somatic marker hypothesis: A neural theory of economic decision. *Games and Economic Behavior, 52*, 336–372. doi: 10.1016/j.geb.2004.06.010.

Beck, J. G., Reich, C. M., Woodward, M. J., Olsen, S. A., Jones, J. M., & Patton, S. C. (2015). How do negative emotions relate to dysfunctional posttrauma cognitions? An examination of interpersonal trauma survivors. *Psychological Trauma: Theory, Research, Practice, and Policy, 7*(1), 3–10. doi: 10.1037/a0032716.

Bedi, R., Muller, R. T., & Classen, C. C. (2014). Cumulative risk for deliberate self-harm among treatment-seeking women with histories of childhood abuse. *Psychological Trauma: Theory, Research, Practice, and Policy, 6*(6), 600–609. doi: 10.1037/a0033897.

Beghetto, R. A. (2014). Creative mortification: An initial exploration. *Psychology of Aesthetics, Creativity, and the Arts, 8*(3), 266–276. doi: 10.1037/a0036618.

Beghetto, R. A., & Kaufman, J. C. (2015). Promise and pitfalls in differentiating amongst the Cs of creativity. *Creativity Research Journal, 27*(2), 240–241. doi: 10.1080/1040419.2015.1030300.

Beijersbergen, M. D., Bakermans-Kranenburg, M. J., & van IJzendoor, M. H. (2006). The concept of coherence in attachment interviews: Comparing attachment experts, linguists, and non-experts. *Attachment and Human Development, 8*(4), 353–369. doi: 10.1080/14616730601048175.

Beijersbergen, M. D., Bakersmans-Kranenburg, M. J., van IJzendoorn, M. H., & Juffer, F. (2008). Stress regulation in adolescents: Physiological reactivity during the Adult Attachment Interview and conflict interaction. *Child Development, 79*(6), 1707–1720.

Belanger, A.-E., Bernier, A., Simard, V., Bordeleau, S., & Carrier, J. (2015). Attachment and sleep among toddlers: Disentangling attachment security and dependency. *Monographs of the Society for Research in Child Development, 80*(1), 125–140. doi: 10.1111/mono.v80.1/issuetoc.

Belli, H., Ural., C., Vardar, M., Yesiyurt, S., & Oncu, F. (2012). Dissociative symptoms and dissociative disorder comorbidity in patients with obsessive-compulsive disorder. *Comprehensive Psychiatry, 53*, 975–980.

Belsky, J., & Pasco-Fearon, R. M. (2016). Precursors of attachment security. In J. Cassidy & P. Shaver (Eds.), *Handbook of attachment theory and research* (2nd ed., pp. 295–316). New York, NY: Guilford Press.

Benedek, M., Franz, F., Heene, M., & Neubauer, A. C. (2012). Differential effects of cognitive inhibition and intelligence on creativity. *Personality and Individual Differences, 53*, 480–485. doi: 10.1016/j.paid.2012.04.014.

Benight, C. C. (2012). Understanding human adaptation to traumatic stress exposure: Beyond the medical model. *Psychological Trauma: Theory, Research, Practice, and Policy, 4*(1), 1–8. doi: 10.1037/a0026245.

Benight, C. C., & Bandura, A. (2004). Social cognition theory of posttraumatic recovery: The role of perceived self-efficacy. *Behavior Research and Therapy, 42*, 1129–1148. doi: 10.1016/j.brat.2003.08.008.

Benight, C. C., Shoji, K., & Delahanty, D. L. (2017). Self-regulation shift theory: A dynamic systems approach to traumatic stress. *Journal of Traumatic Stress, 30*, 333–342. doi: 10.1002/jts.22208.

Bennett, D. C., Modrowski, C. A., Kerig, P. K., & Chaplo, S. D. (2015). Investigating the dissociative subtype of posttraumatic stress disorder in a sample of traumatized detained youth. *Psychological Trauma: Theory, Research, Practice, and Policy, 7*(5), 465–472. doi: 10.1037/tra0000057.

Bennett, D. S., Sullivan, M. W., & Lewis, M. (2010). Neglected children, shame-proneness, and depressive symptoms. *Child Maltreatment, 15*(4), 305–314. doi: 10.1177/1077559510379634.

Benoit, M., Boutillier, D., Moss, E., Rousseau, C., & Brunet, A. (2010). Emotion regulation strategies as mediators of the association between level of attachment security and PTSD symptoms following trauma in adulthood. *Anxiety, Stress, and Coping, 23*(1), 101–118. doi: 10.1080/10615800802638279.

Berenz, E. C., Roberson-Nay, R., Latendresse, S. J., Mezuk, B., & Gardner, C. O. (2017). Posttraumatic stress disorder and alcohol dependence: Epidemiology and order to onset. *Psychological Trauma: Theory, Research, Practice, and Policy, 6*(4), 485–492. doi: 10.1037/tra0000185.

Bering, J. M. (2006). The folk psychology of souls. *Behavioral and Brain Sciences, 29*(5), 453–498.

Bernard, J. D., Whittles, R. L., Kertz, S. J., & Burke, P. A. (2015). Trauma and event centrality: Valence and incorporaton inot identity influence well-being more than exposure. *Psychological Trauma: Theory, Research, Practice, and Policy, 7*(1), 11–17. doi: 10.1037/a0037331.

Bernard, J. F., & Bandler, R. (1998). Parallel circuits for emotional coping behavior: New pieces in the puzzle. *Journal of Comparative Neurology, 401*, 429–436.

Bernard, R. (2009). Music making, transcendence, flow, and music education. *International Journal of Education and the Arts, 10*(4), 1–21.

Bernardis, P., & Gentilucci, M. (2006). Speech and gesture share the same communication system. *Neuropsychologia, 44*, 178−190. doi: 10.1016/j.neuropsychologia.205.05.007.

Bernier, A., Matte-Gagne, C., Belanger, M.-E., & Whipple, N. (2014). Taking stock of two decades of attachment transmission gap: Broadening the assessment of maternal behavior. *Child Development, 85*(5), 1852–1865. doi: 10.1111/cdev.12236.

Bernstein, L. (1963). Available at: https://leonardbernstein.com/about/ humanitarian/an-artists-response-to-violence.

Bernstein, R. E., Delker, B. C., Knight, J. A., & Freyd, J. J. (2015). Hypervigilance in college students: Associations with betrayal and dissociation and psychometric properties in a Brief Hypervigilance Scale. *Psychological Trauma: Theory, Research, Practice, and Policy, 7*(5), 448–455. doi: 10.1037/tra0000070.

Bernsten, D., & Rubin, D. C. (2006). The Centrality of Event Scale: A measure of integrating a trauma into one's identity and its relation to post-traumatic stress disorder symptoms. *Behavior Research and Therapy, 44*, 219–231. doi: 10.1016/j.brat.2005.01.009.

Berntson, G. G., & Cacioppo, J. T. (2007). Integrative physiology: Homeostasis, allostasis and the orchestration of systemic physiology. In J. T. Cacioppo, L. G. Tassinary, & G. G. Berntson (Eds.), *Handbook of psychophysiology* (3rd ed., pp. 433–452). New York, NY: Cambridge University Press.

Berntson, G. G., Norman, G. J., Hawkley, L. C., & Cacioppo, J. T. (2008). Spirituality and autonomic cardiac control. *Annals of Behavioral Medicine: A Publication of the Society of Behavioral Medicine, 35*(2), 198–208. doi: 10.1007/s12160-008-9027-x.

———. (2008a). Cardiac autonomic balance versus cardiac regulatory capacity. *Psychophysiology, 45*, 643−652. doi: 10.1111/j.1469-8986.2008.00652.x.

Besser, A., & Neira, Y. (2012). When home isn't a safe haven: Insecure attachment orientation, perceived social support, and PTSD symptoms among Israeli evacuees under missile threat. *Psychological Trauma: Theory, Research, Practice, and Policy, 4*(1), 34–46. doi: 10.1037/a0017835.

Betancourt, T. S., Newnham, E. A., Birman, D., Lee, R., Ellis, B. H., & Layne, C. M. (2017). Comparing trauma exposure, mental health needs and survice utilization across clinical samples of refugee, immigrant, and U.S.-origin children. *Journal of Traumatic Stress, 30*, 209−218. doi: 10.1002/jts.22186.

Betancourt, T. S., Newnham, E. A., Layne, C. M., Kim, S., Steinberg, A. M., & Birman, D. (2012). Trauma history and psychopathology in war-affected refugee children referred for trauma-related mental health services in the United States. *Journal of Traumatic Stress, 25*, 682–690. doi: 10.1002/jts.21749.

Bezo, B., & Maggi, S. (2018). Interngenerational perceptions of mass trauma's impact on physical health and well-being. *Psychological Trauma: Theory, Research, Practice, and Policy, 10*(1), 87–94. doi: 10.1037/tra0000284.

Bifulco, A., Moran, P. M., Baines, R., Bunn, A., & Stanford, K. (2002). Exploring psychological abuse in childhood: II. Association with other abuse and adult clinical depression. *Bulletin of the Menninger Clinic, 66*(3), 241–258.

Bigelsen, J., & Schupak, C. (2011). Compulsive fantasy: Proposed evidence of an under-reported syndrome through a systematic study of 90 self-identified non-normative fantasizers. *Consciousness and Cognition, 20*, 1634–1648. doi: 10.1016/j.concog.2011.08.013.

Bille, T., Fjaellegaard, C. B., Frey, B. S., & Steiner, L. (2013). Happiness in the arts–International evidence on artists' job satisfaction. *Economics Letters, 121*, 15–18. doi: 10.1016/j.enconlet.2013.06.016.

Billoux, S., Voltzenlogel, V., Telmon, N., Birmes, P., & Arbus, C. (2017). Peritraumatic assessment of autobiographical memory after exposure to a traumatic event. *Journal of Traumatic Stress, 30*, 666–671. doi: 10.1002/jts/22229.

Binder, E. B., Bradley, R. G., Liu, W., Epstein, M. P., Deveau, T. C., Mercer, K. B., Tang, Y., ... Ressler, K. J. (2008). Association of FKBP5 polymorphisms and childhood abuse with risk of posttraumatic stress disorder symptoms in adults. *Journal of American Medical Association, 299*(11), 1291–1305.

Binyam, G., Friedman, A., & Carmeli, A. (2018). Reciprocal care in hierarchical exchange: Implications for psychological safety and innovative behavior at work. *Psychology of Aesthetics, Creativity, and the Arts, 12*(1), 79–88. doi: 10.1037/aca0000129.

Binyamin, G., & Carmeli, A. (2017). Fostering members' creativity in teams: The role of structuring of human resource management processes. *Psychology of Aesthetics, Creativity, and the Arts, 11*(1), 18–33. doi: 10.1037/aca0000088.

Birkeland, M. S., Blix, I., Solberg, O., & Heir, T. (2017). Does optimism act as a buffer against posttraumatic stress over time? A longitudinal study of the protective role of optimism after the 2011 Oslo bombing. *Psychological Trauma: Theory, Research, Practice, and Policy, 9*(2), 207–213. doi: 10.1037/tra0000188.

Birkeland, M. S., Hansen, M. B., Blix, I., Solberg, O., & Heir, T. (2017). For whom does time heal wounds? Individual differences in stability and change in posttraumatic stress after the 2011 Oslo bombing. *Journal of Traumatic Stress, 30*, 19–26. doi: 10.1002/jts.22158.

Birkley, E. L., Eckhardt, C. I., & Dykstra, R. E. (2016). Posttraumatic stress disorder symptoms, intimate partner violence, and relationship functioning: A meta-analytic review. *Journal of Traumatic Stress, 29*, 397–405. doi: 10.1002/jts.22129.

Birrer, D., & Morgan, G. (2010). Psychological skills training as a way to enhance an athlete's performance in high-intensity sports. *Scandinavian Journal of Medicine and Science in Sports, 20*(Suppl. 2), 78–87. doi: 10.1111/j.1600-0838.2010.01188.x.

Bishop, S. R., Lau, M., Shapiro, S., Carlson, L., Anderson, N. D., Carmody, J., ... Devins, G. (2004). Mindfulness: A proposed operational definition. *Clinical Psychology: Science and Practice, 11*(3), 230–241. doi: 10.1093/clipsy/bph077.

Blackie, L. E. R., Jayawickreme, E., Forgeard, M. J. C., & Jayawickreme, N. (2015). The protective function of personal growth initiative among a genocide-affected population in Rwanda. *Psychological Trauma: Theory, Research, Practice, and Policy, 7*(4), 333–339. doi: 10.1037/tra0000010.

Blackmore, E. R., Putnam, F. W., Pressman, E. K., Rubinow, D. R., Putnam, K. T., Matthieu, M. M., ... O'Connor, T. G. (2016). The effects of trauma history and prenatal affective symptoms on obstetric outcomes. *Journal of Traumatic Stress, 29*, 245–252. doi: 10.1002/jts.22095.

Blackwell, S. E., Rius-Ottenheim, N., Schulte-van Maaren, Y. W. M., Carlier, I. V. E., Middelkoop, V. D., Zitman, F. G., ... Giltay, E. J. (2013). Optimism and mental imagery: A possible marker to promote well-being? *Psychiatry Research, 206*, 56–61. doi: 10.1016/j.psychres.2012.09.04.

Blanchard, E. B., Rowell, D., Kohn, E., Rogers, R., & Wittrock, D. (2005). Posttraumatic stress and depressive symptoms in a college population one year after the September 11 attacks: The effect of proximity. *Behavior Research and Therapy, 43*, 143–150. doi: 10.1016/j.brat.2003.12.004.

Blanchette, D. M., Ramocki, S. P., O'del, J. N., & Casey, M. S. (2005). Aerobic exercise and creative potential: Immediate and residual effects. *Creativity Research Journal, 17*(2 & 3), 257–264.

Blanke, O., & Arzy, S. (2005). The out-of-body experience: Disturbed self-processing at the temporal-parietal junction. *Neuroscientist, 11*(1), 16–24. doi: 10.1177/1073858404270885.

Blix, I., Birkeland, M. S., Hansen, M. B., & Heir, T. (2015). Posttraumatic growth and centraility of event: A longitudinal study in the aftermath of the 2011 Oslo bombing. *Psychological Trauma: Theory, Research, Practice, and Policy, 7*(1), 18–23. doi: 10.1037/tra0000006.

Blood, A. J., & Zatorre, R. J. (2001). Intensely pleasurable responses to music correlate with activity in brain regions implicated in reward and emotion. *Proceedings of the National Academy of Science, 98*, 11818–11823. doi: 10.1037/pnas.191355898.

Bluhm, R. L., Williamson, P. C., Osuch, E. A., Frewen, P. A., Stevens, T. K., Boksman, K., ... Lanius, R. A. (2009). Alterations in default network connectivity in posttraumatic stress disorder related to early-life trauma. *Journal of Psychiatry and Neuroscience, 34*(3), 187–194.

Bob, P. (2008). Pain, dissociation and subliminal self-representations. *Consciousness and Cognition, 17*(1), 355–369. doi: 10.1016/j.concog.2007.12.001.

Bob, P., Fedor-Freybergh, P., Jasova, D., Bizik, G., Susta, M., Pavlat, J., ... Rabach, J. (2008). Dissociative symptoms and neuroendocrine dysregulation in depression. *Medical Science Monitor, 14*(10), CR499–504.

Boelen, P. A., de Keijser, J., & Smid, G. (2015). Cognitive-behavioral variables mediate the impact of violent loss on post-loss psychopathology. *Psychological Trauma: Theory, Research, Practice, and Policy, 7*(4), 382–390. doi: 10.1037/tra0000018.

Boerner, S., & Jobst, J. (2013). Enjoying theatre: The role of visitor's response to the performance. *Psychology of Aesthetics, Creativity, and the Arts, 7*(4), 391–408. doi: 10.1037/a0034570.

Bojahr, L. S., & van Emmerick, A. A. P. (2016). Traumatic events and trauma-related psychopathology in former drug cartel soldiers in Rio de Janeiro: A pilot study. *Psychological Trauma: Theory, Research, Practice, and Policy, 8*(1), 34–40. doi: 10.1037/tra0000021.

Bomyea, J., & Allard, C. B. (2017). Trauma-related disgust in veterans with interpersonal trauma. *Journal of Traumatic Stress, 30*, 149–156. doi: 10.1002/jts.22169.

Bonanno, G. A. (2004). Loss, trauma, and human resilience: Have we underestimated the human capacity to thrive after adverse events? *American Psychologist, 59*(1), 20–28. doi: 10.1037/0003-066X.59.1.20.

Bonanno, G. A., & Burton, C. L. (2013). Regulatory flexibility: An individual differences perspective on coping and emotion regulation. *Perspectives on Psychological Science, 86*(6), 591–612. doi: 10.1177/1745691613504116.

Bonanno, G. A., & Mancini, A. D. (2012). Beyond resilience and PTSD: Mapping the heterogeneity of responses to potential trauma. *Psychological Trauma: Theory, Research, Practice, and Policy, 4*(1), 74–83. doi: 10.1037/a0017829.

Bonanno, G. A., Galea, S., Bucciarelli, A., & Vlahov, D. (2006). Psychological resilience after disaster: New York City in the aftermath of September 11th terror attack. *Psychological Science, 17*(3), 181–186.

Bonanno, G. A., Papa, A., Lalande, K., Westphal, M., & Coifman, K. (2004). The importance of being flexible: The ability to both enhance and suppress emotional expression predicts long-term adjustment. *Psychological Science, 15*(7), 482–487.

Bonanno, G. A., Rennicke, C., & Dekel, S. (2005). Self-enhancement among high-exposure survivors of the September 11th terrorist attack: Resilienc or social maladjustment? *Journal of Personality and Social Psychology, 88*(6), 984–998. doi: 10.1037/0022-3514.88.6.984.

Bonanno, G. A., Westphal, M., & Mancini, A. D. (2011). Resilience to loss and potential trauma. *Annual Review of Clinical Psychology, 7*, 511–535. doi: 10.1146/annurev-clinpsy-032210-104526.

Bonanno, G. A., Wortman, C. B., & Nesse, R. M. (2004). Perspective patterns of resilience and maladjustment during widowhood. *Psychology and Aging, 19*(2), 260–271. doi: 10.1037/0882-7974.19.2.260.

Bonanno, G. A., Wortman, C. B., Lehman, D. R., Tweed, R. G., Haring, M., Sonnega, J., ... Nesse, R. M. (2002). Resilience to loss and chronic grief: A prospective study from preloss to 18-months postloss. *Journal of Personality and Social Psychology, 83*(5), 1150–1164. doi: 10.1037//0022-3514.83.5.1150.

Bonner, B. L., Crow, S. M., & Logue, M. B. (1999). *Fatal child neglect*. In H. Dubowitz (Ed.), *Neglected children: Research, practice, and policy* (pp. 156–173). Thousand Oaks, CA: Sage Publications, Inc.

Bonner, E. T., & Friedman, H. L. (2011). A conceptual clarification of the experience of awe: An interpretative phenomenological analysis. *The Humanistic Psychologist, 39*, 222–235. doi: 10.1080/08873267.2011.593372.

Bonneville-Roussy, A., Lavigne, G. L., & Vallerand, R. J. (2010). When passion leads to excellence: The case of musicians. *Psychology of Music, 39*(1), 123–138. doi: 10.1177/0305735609352441.

Bonn-Miller, M. O., Boden, M. T., Vujanovic, A. A., & Drescher, K. D. (2013). Prospective investigation of the impact of cannabis use disorder on posttraumatic stress disorder symptoms among veterans in residential treatment. *Psychological Trauma: Theory, Research, Practice, and Policy, 5*(2), 193–200. doi: 10.1037/a0026621.

Border, A., Rothman, D. J., & McAndrew, L. M. (2015). Sleep problems may mediate associations between rumination and PTSD and depressive symptoms among IF/OEF veterans. *Psychological Trauma: Theory, Research, Practice, and Policy, 7*(1), 76–84. doi: 10.1037/a0036937.

Borelli, J. L., Somers, J. A., West, J. L., Coffey, J. K., & Shmueli-Goetz, Y. (2016). Shedding light on the specificity of school-aged children's attachment narratives. *Attachment and Human Development, 18*(2), 188–211. doi: 10.1080/14616734.2015.1134605.

Bosma, H. A. (2006). An introduction to developmental psychopathology. *Orientation Scolaire et Professionnelle, 35*, 251–268. doi: 10.4000/osp.1097.

Bosmans, M. W. G., van der Knaap, L. M., & van der Velden, P. G. (2016). The predictive value of trauma-related coping self-efficacy for posttraumatic stress symptoms: Differences between treatment-seeking and non-treatment seeking victims. *Psychological Trauma: Theory, Research, Practice, and Policy, 8*(2), 241–248. doi: 10.1037/tra0000088.

Bouchard, M.-A., Target, M., Lecours, S., Fonagy, P., Tremblay, L.-M., Schacter, A., & Stein, H. (2008). Mentalization in adult attachment narratives: Reflective functioning, mental states, and affect elaboration compared. *Psychoanalytic Psychology, 25*(1), 47–66. doi: 10.1037/0736-9735.25.1.47.

Boudoukha, A. H., Ouagazzi, O., & Goutaudier, N. (2017). When traumatic event exposure characteristics matter: Impact of traumatic event exposure characteristics on posttraumatic and dissociative symptoms. *Psychological Trauma: Theory, Research, Practice, and Policy, 9*(5), 561–566. doi: 10.1037/tra0000243.

Bourgeois-Bougrine, S., Botella, M., Glaveau, V., Guillou, K., De Biasi, P. M., & Lubart, T. (2014). The creativity maze: Exploring creativity in screenplay writing. *Psychology of Aesthetics, Creativity and the Arts, 8*(4), 384–399. doi: 10.1037/a0037839.

Bournelli, P., Makri, A., & Mylonas, K. (2009). Motor creativity and self-concept. *Creativity Research Journal, 21*(1), 104–110. doi: 10.1080/10400410802633657.

Bowers, M. T., Green, B. C., Hemme, F., & Chalip, L. (2014). Assessing the relationship between youth sport participation settings and creativity in adulthood. *Creativity Research Journal, 26*(3), 314–327. doi: 10.1080/10400419.2014.929420.

Bowlby, J. (1988). *A secure base: Parent-child attachment and healthy human development.* New York: Basic Books, Inc.

Bowler, R. M., Adams, S. W., Gocheva, V. V., Li, J., Mergler, D., Brackbill, R., & Cone, J. E. (2017). Posttraumatic stress disorder, gender, and risk factors: World Trade Center Tower survivors 10 to 11 years after the September 11, 2001 attacks. *Journal of Traumatic Stress, 30*, 564–570. doi: 10.1002/jts.22232.

Boysan, M., Goldsmith, R. E., Cavus, H., Kayri, M., & Keskin, S. (2009). Relations among anxiety, depression, and dissociative symptoms: The influence of abuse subtypes. *Journal of Trauma and Dissociation, 10*(1), 83–101. doi: 10.1080/15299730802485185.

Brancu, M., Thompson, N. L., Beckham, J. C., Green, K. T., Calhoun, P. S., Elbogen, E. B., ... Wagner, H. R. (2014). The impact of social support on psychological distress for U.S. Afghanistan/Iraq era veterans with PTSD and other psychiatric diagnoses. *Psychiatry Research, 217*, 86–92. doi: 10.1016/j.psychres.2014.02.025.

Brand, B. L., McNary, S. W., Myrick, A. C., Classen, C. C., Lanius, R., Loewenstein, R. J., ... Putnam, F. W. (2013). A longitudinal naturalistic study of patients with dissociative disorders treated by community clinicians. *Psychological Trauma: Theory, Research, Practice, and Policy, 5*(4), 301–308. doi: 10.1037/a0027654.

Brandt, C. P., Zvolensky, M. J., Vujanovic, A. A., Grover, K. W., Hogan, J., Bakhshaie, J., & Gonzalez, A. (2015). The mediating role of anxiety sensitivity in the relation between avoidant coping and posttraumatic stress among trauma-exposed HIV+ individuals. *Psychological Trauma, Theory, Research, Practice, and Policy, 7*(2), 146–153. doi: 10.1037/a0037236.

Brattico, E., & Pearce, M. (2013). The neuroaesthetics of music. *Psychology of Aesthetics, Creativity and the Arts, 7*(1), 48–61. doi: 10.1037/a0031624.

Bremner, J. D. (2006). The relationship between cognitive and brain changes in posttraumatic stress disorder. *Annals of the New York Academy of Science, 1071,* 80–86. doi: 10.1196/annals.1364.0008.

Bremner, J. D., Elzinga, B., Schmahl, C., & Vermetten, E. (2008). Structural and functional plasticity of the human brain in posttraumatic stress disorder. *Progress in Brain Research, 167,* 171–186. doi: 10.1016/S0079-6123(07)67012-5.

Breyer, B. N., Fang, S. C., Seal., K. H., Ranganathan, G., Marx, B. P., Keane, T. M., & Rosen, R. C. (2016). Sexual health in male and female Iraq and Afghanistan U.S. war veterans with and without PTSD: Findings from the VALOR cohort. *Journal of Traumatic Stress, 29,* 229–236. doi: 10.1002/jts.22097.

Briere, J. (2002). *Multiscale dissociation inventory professional manual.* Odessa, Florida: Psychological Assessment Resources.

———. (2006). Dissociative symptoms and trauma exposure: Specificity, affect dysregulation, and posttraumatic stress. *Journal of Nervous and Mental Disease, 194*(2), 78–82. doi: 10.1097/01.nmd.0000198139.47371.54.

Briere, J., & Eadie, E. M. (2016). Compensatory self-injury: Posttraumatic stress, depression, and the role of dissociation. *Psychological Trauma: Theory, Research, Practice, and Policy, 8*(5), 618–625. doi: 10.1037/tra0000139.

Briere, J., Dias, C. P., Semple, R. J., Scott, C., Bigras, N., & Godbout, N. (2017). Acute stress symptoms in seriously injured patients: Precipitating versus cumulative trauma and the contribution of peritraumatic distress. *Journal of Traumatic Stress, 30,* 381–388. doi: 10.1002/jts.22200.

Briere, J., Dietrich, A., & Semple, R. J. (2016). Dissociative complexity: Antecedents and clinical correlates of a new construct. *Psychological Trauma: Theory, Research, Practice, and Policy, 8*(5), 577–584. doi: 10.1037/tra0000126.

Briere, J., Scott, C., & Weathers, F. (2005). Peritraumatic and persistent dissociation in the presumed etiology of PTSD. *American Journal of Psychiatry, 162*(12), 2295–2301.

Briere, J., Weathers, F. W., & Runtz, M. (2005). Is dissociation a multidimensional construct? Data from the multiscale dissociation inventory. *Journal of Traumatic Stress, 18*(3), 221–231. doi: 10.1002/(ISSN)1573-6598.

Briggs, E. C., Fairbank, J. A., Greeson, J. K. P., Layne, C. M., Steinberg, A. M., Amaya-Jackson, L. M., ... Pynoos, R. S. (2013). Links between child and adolescent trauma exposure and service use histories in a national clinic-referred sample. *Psychological Trauma: Theory, Research, Practice, and Policy, 5*(2), 101–109. doi: 10.1037/a0027312.

Britt, T. W., Adler, A. B., Sawhney, G., & Bliese, P. D. (2017). Coping strategies as moderators of the association between combat exposure and posttraumatic stress disorder symptoms. *Journal of Traumatic Stress, 30,* 491–501. doi: 10.1002/jts.22221.

Bromet, E. J., Clouston, S., Gonzalez, A., Kotov, R., Guerrera, K. M., & Luft, B. J. (2017). Hurricane Sandy exposure and the mental health of World Trade Center responders. *Journal of Traumatic Stress, 30,* 107–114. doi: 10.1002/jts.22178.

Brown, G. L., Gustafsson, H. C., Mills-Koonce, W. R., & Cox, M. J. (2017). Associations between early caregiving and rural, low SES African-American children's representations of attachment relationships. *Attachment and Human Development, 19*(4), 340–363. doi: 10.1080/14616734.2017.1318935.

Brown, J. (2008). The inward path: Mysticism and creativity. *Creativity Research Journal, 20*(4), 365–375. doi: 10.1080/10400410802391348.

Brown, R. C., Berenz, E. C., Aggen, S. H., Knudsen, G. P., Reichborn-Kjennerud, T., Kendler, K. S., & Amstadter, A. B. (2014). Trauma exposure and Axis I psychopathology: A Cotwin control analysis in Norwegian young adults. *Psychological Trauma: Theory, Research, Practice, and Policy, 6*(6), 652–660. doi: 10.1037/a0034326.

Browne, K. C., Trim, R. S., Myers, U., & Norman, S. B. (2015). Trauma-related guilt: Conceptual development and relationship with posttraumatic stress and depressive symptoms. *Journal of Traumatic Stress, 28*, 134–141. doi: 10.1002/jts.21999.

Browne, T., Evangeli, M., & Greenberg, N. (2012). Trauma-related guilt and posttraumatic stress among journalists. *Journal of Traumatic Stress, 25*, 207–210. doi: 10.1002/jts.21678.

Brunner, R., Parzer, P., Schmitt, R., & Resch, F. (2004). Dissociative symptoms in schizophrenia: A comparative analysis of patients with borderline personality disorder and health controls. *Psychopathology, 37*, 281–284. doi: 10.1159/0000081984.

Bryan, C. J., Bryan, A. O., Roberge, E., Leifker, F. R., & Rozek, D. C. (2018). Moral injury, posttraumatic stress disorder, and suicidal behavior among National Guard personnel. *Psychological Trauma: Theory, Research, Practice, and Policy, 10*(1), 36–45. doi: 10.1037/tra0000290.

Buchheim, A., & Mergenthaler, E. (2000). The relationship among attachment representation, emotion-abstraction patterns, and narrative style: A computer-based text analysis of the Adult Attachment Interview. *Psychotherapy Research, 10*(4), 390–407.

Buchholz, K. R., Bruce, S. E., Koucky, E. M., Artime, T. M., Wojtalik, J. A., Brown, W. J., & Sheline, Y. I. (2016). Neural correlates of trait rumination during an emotion interference task in women with PTSD. *Journal of Traumatic Stress, 29*, 317–324. doi: 10.1002/jts.22112.

Buchmann, A. F., Holz, N., Boeker, R., Blomeyer, D., Rietschel, M., Witt, S. H. … Laucht, M. (2014). Moderating role of FKBP5 genotype in the impact of childhood adversity on cortisol stress response during adulthood. *European Neuropsychopharmacology, 24*, 837–845. doi: 10.1016/j.eruoneuro.2013.12.001.

Budden, A. (2009). The role of shame in posttraumatic stress disorder: A proposal for a socio-emotional model for DSM-V. *Social Science and Medicine, 69*, 1032–1039. doi: 10.1016/j.socscimed.2009.07.032.

Bugge, I., Dyb, G., Stensland, S. O., Ekeberg, O., Wentsel-Larsen, T., & Diseth, T. H. (2017). Physical injury complaints: The mediating role of posttraumatic stress symptoms in young survivors of a terror attack. *Journal of Traumatic Stress, 30*, 229–236. doi: 10.1037/jts.22191.

Buisonje, D. R., Ritter, S. M., de Bruin, S., Horst, M.-L., & Meeldijk, A. (2017). Facilitating creative idea selection: The combined effects of self-affirmation, promotion focus and positive affect. *Creativity Research Journal, 29*(2), 174–181. doi: 10.1080/10400419.2017.1303308.

Bunning, S., & Blanke, O. (2005). The out-of-body experience: Precipitating factors and neural correlates. *Progress in Brain Research, 150*, 331–350. doi: 10.1016/S0079-6123(05)50024-4.

Burch, G. S., Pavelis, C., Hemsley, D. R., & Corr, P. J. (2006). Schizotypy and creativity in visual artists. *British Journal of Psychology, 97*, 177–190. doi: 10.1348/000712605X60030.

Busch, H., Hofer, J., Chasiotis, A., & Campos, D. (2013). The achievement flow motive as an element of the autotelic personality: Predicting educational attainment in three cultures. *European Journal of Psychology of Education, 28*(2), 239–254. doi: 10.1007/s10212-012-0112-y.

Butchart, A., Phinney, H. A., Kahane, T., Mian, M., & Furniss, T. (2006). *Preventing child maltreatment: A guide to action and generating evidence*. Geneva: World Health Organization and International Society for Prevention of Child Abuse and Neglect.

Butcher, J. L., & Niec, L. N. (2005). Disruptive behaviors in creativity in childhood: The importance of affect regulation. *Creativity Research Journal, 17*(2 & 3), 181–193.

Butler, L. D. (2006). Normative dissociation. *Psychiatric Clinics of North America, 29*, 45–62.

Butler, L. D., Carello, J., & Maguin, E. (2017). Trauma, stress, and self-care in clinical training: Predictors of burnout, decline in health status, secondary traumatic stress symptoms, and compassion satisfaction. *Psychological Trauma: Theory, Research, Practice, and Policy, 9*(4), 416–424. doi: 10.1037/tra0000187.

Butler-Barnes, S. T., Leath, S., Williams, A., Byrd, C., Carter, R., & Chavous, T. M. (2017). Promoting resilience among African American girls: Racial identity as a protective factor. *Child Development*, e-publ. doi: 10.1111/cdev.12995.

Byllesby, B. M., Durham, T. A., Forbes, D., Armour, C., & Elhai, J. D. (2016). An investigation of PTSD's core dimensions and relations with anxiety and depression. *Psychological Trauma: Theory, Research, Practice, and Policy, 8*(2), 214–217. doi: 10.1037/tra0000081.

Byun, S., Brumariu, L. E., & Lyons-Ruth, K. (2016). Disorganized attachment in young adults as a partial mediator of relations between severity of childhood abuse and dissociation. *Journal of Trauma and Dissociation, 17*(4), 460–479. doi: 10.1080/15299732.2016.1141149.

Cai, W., Ding, C., Tang, Y.-L., Wu, S., & Yang, D. (2014). Effects of social supports on posttraumatic stress disorder symptoms: Moderating role of perceived safety. *Psychological Trauma: Theory, Research, Practice, and Policy, 6*(6), 724–730. doi: 10.1037/a0036342.

Calhoun, L. G., & Tedeschi, R. G. (2001). Posttraumatic growth: The positive lessons of loss: In R. A. Neimeyer (Ed.), *Meaning re-construction and the experience of loss* (pp. 157–172). Washington, DC: American Psychological Association.

Calvo-Merino, B., Jola, C., Glaser, D. E., & Haggard, P. (2008). Towards a sensorimotor aesthetics of performing art. *Consciousness and Cognition, 17*, 911–922. doi: 10.1016/j.concog.2007.11.003.

Campbell, T. A. (2007). Psychological assessment, diagnosis, and treatment of torture survivors: A review. *Clinical Psychology Review, 27*, 628–641. doi: 10.1016/j.cpr.2007.02.003.

Campos, A., & Fuentes, L. (2016). Musical studies and the vividness and clarity of auditory imagery. *Imagination, Cognition and Personality, 36*(1), 75–84. doi: 10.1177/0276236666635985.

Candel, I., & Merckelbach, H. (2003). Fantasy proneness and thought suppression as predictors of the Medical Student Syndrome. *Personality and Individual Differences, 35*, 519–524.

Canevello, A., Michels, V., & Hilaire, N. (2016). Supporting close others' growth after trauma: The role of responsiveness in romantic partners' mutual posttraumatic growth. *Psychological Trauma: Theory, Research, Practice, and Policy, 8*(3), 334–324. doi: 10.1037/tra0000084.

Cantero, M.-J., Alfonso-Benlliure, V., & Melero, R. (2016). Creativity in middle childhood: Influence of perceived maternal sensitivity, self-esteem, and shyness. *Creativity Research Journal, 28*(1), 105–113. doi: 10.1080/10400419.2016.1125246.

Cardenas, M., Barrientos, J., Meyer, I., Gomez, F., Guzman, M., & Bahamondes, J. (2018). Direct and indirect effects of perceived stigma on posttraumatic growth in gay men and lesbian women in Chile. *Journal of Traumatic Stress, 31*, 5–13. doi: 10.1002/jts.22256.

Carlson, E. A. (1998). A prospective longitudinal study of attachment disorganization/disorientation. *Child Development, 69*, 1107–1128.

Carlson, E. A., Sroufe, L. A., & Egeland, B. (2004). The construction of experience: A longitudinal study of representation and behavior. *Child Development, 75*(1), 66–83.

Carlson, E. B., McDade-Montez, E., Armstrong, J., Dalenberg, C., & Loewenstein, R. J. (2013). Development and initial validation of the structured interview for self-destructive behaviors. *Journal of Trauma and Dissociation, 14*, 312–327. doi: 10.1080/15299732.2012.762822.

Carmeli, A., Reiter-Palmon, R., & Ziv, E. (2010). Inclusive leadership and employee involvement in creative tasks in the workplace: The mediating role of psychological safety. *Creativity Research Journal, 22*(3), 250–260. doi: 10.1080/10400419.2010.504654.

Carroll, T. D., Currier, J. M., McCormick, W. H., & Drescher, K. D. (2017). Adverse childhood experiences and risk for suicidal behavior in male Iraq and Afghanistan veterans seeking PTSD treatment. *Psychological Trauma: Theory, Research, Practice, and Policy, 9*(5), 583–586. doi: 10.1037/tra0000250.

Carson, D. K., & Runco, M. A. (1999). Creative problem solving and problem finding in young adults: Interconnections with stress, hassles, and coping abilities. *Journal of Creative Behavior, 33*(3), 167–188.

Carson, S. H. (2011). Creativity and psychopathology: A shared vulnerability model. *Canadian Journal of Psychiatry, 56*(3), 144–153.

Carson, S. H., Peterson, J. B., & Higgins, D. M. (2003). Decreased latent inhibition is associated with increased creative achievement in high-functioning individuals. *Journal of Personality and Social Psychology, 85*(3), 499–506. doi: 10.1037/0022.3514.85.3.499.

Carter, R. T., & Muchow, C. (2017). Construct validity of the Race-Based Traumatic Stress Symptom Scale and tests of measurement equivalence. *Psychological Trauma: Theory, Research, Practice, and Policy, 9*(6), 688–695. doi: 10.1037/tra0000256.

Caspers, K. M., Yucuis, R., Troutman, B., & Spinks, R. (2006). Attachment as an organizer of behavior: Implications for substance abuse problems and willingness to seek treatment. *Substance Abuse, Treatment, Prevention, and Policy, 1,* 32. doi: 10.1186/1747-597X-1-32.

Caspi, A., McClay, J., Moffitt, T. E., Mill, J., Martin, J., Craig, I. W., ... Poulton, R. (2002). Role of genotype in the cycle of violence in maltreated children. *Science, 297*(5582), 851−854.

Caspi, Y., Saroff, O., Suleimani, N., & Klein, E. (2008). Trauma exposure and posttraumatic reactions in a community sample of Bedouin members of the Israel Defense Forces. *Depression and Anxiety, 25,* 700–707.

Cassibba, R., Granqvist, P., Costantini, A., & Gatto, S. (2008). Attachment and god representations among lay Catholics, priests, and religious: A matched comparison study based on the Adult Attachment Interview. *Developmental Psychology, 44*(6), 1753–1763. doi: 10.1037/a0013772.

Centers for Disease Control and Prevention (CDC), National Center for Injury Prevention and Control. (2014). *Understanding child maltreatment: Fact sheet.* Retrieved from https://www.cdc.gov/violenceprevention/pdf/understanding-cm-factsheet.pdf.

Chae, J.-H., Huh, H. J., & Choi, W. J. (2018). Embitterment and bereavement: The Sewol ferry accident example. *Psychological Trauma: Theory, Research, Practice, and Policy, 10*(1), 46–50. doi: 10.1037/tra0000308.

Chambers, C. D., Garavan, H., & Bellgrove, M. A. (2009). Insights into the neural basis of response inhibition from cognitive and clinical neuroscience. *Neuroscience and Biobehavioral Review, 33,* 631–646. doi: 10.1016/j.neubiorev.2008.08.016.

Chang, H. J., & Kuo, C. C. (2009). Overexcitabilities of gifted and talented students and its related research in Taiwan. *Asia-Pacific Journal of Gifted and Talented Education, 1*(1), 41–74.

Chang, W. C., Chua, W. L., & Toh, Y. (1997). The concept of psychological control in the Asian context. In K. Leung, U. Kim, S. Yamaguchi, & Y. Kashima (Eds.), *Progress in Asian social psychology* (Vol. 1, pp. 95–117). Singapore: John Wiley & Sons.

Chao, Y.-H., Cheng, Y.-Y., & Chiou, W.-B. (2011). The psychological consequences of experiencing shame: Self-sufficiency and mood repair. *Motivation and Emotion, 35,* 202–210. doi: 10.1007/s11031-011-9208-y.

Chaplo, S. D., Kerig, P. K., Bennett, D. C., & Morowski, C. A. (2015). The roles of emotion dysregulation and dissociation in the association between sexual abuse and self-injury among juvenile justice-involved youth. *Journal of Trauma and Dissociation, 16,* 272–285. doi: 10.1080/15299732.2015.989647.

Charles, R. E., & Runco, M. A. (2000–2001). Developmental trends in the evaluative and divergent thinking of children. *Creativity Research Journal, 13*(3 & 4), 417–437.

Charyton, C., & Snelbecker, G. E. (2007). Engineers' and musicians' choices of self-descriptive adjectives as potential indicators of creativity by gender and domain. *Psychology of Aesthetics, Creativity, and the Arts, 1*(2), 91–99. doi: 10.1037/1931-3896.1.2.91.

Chatard, A., Pyszczyski, T., Arndt, J., Selimbegovic, L., Konan, P. N. D., & van der Linden, M. (2012). Extent of trauma exposure and PTSD symptom severity as predictors of anxiety-buffering functioning. *Psychological Trauma: Theory, Research, Practice, and Policy, 4*(1), 47–55. doi: 10.1037/a0021085.

Chavez-Eakle, R. A. (2007). From incubation to insight: Working memory and the role of the cerebellum. *Creativity Research Journal, 19*, 31–34.

Chavez-Eakle, R. A., Eakle, A. J., & Cruz-Fuentes, C. (2012). The multiple relations between creativity and personality. *Creativity Research Journal, 24*(1), 76–82. doi: 10.1080/10400419.2012.64923.3.

Chavez-Eakle, R. A., Lara, M. C., & Cruz, C. (2006). Personality: A possible bridge between creativity and psychopathology. *Creativity Research Journal, 18*(1), 27–38.

Chen, G., & Gueta, K. (2017). Lifetime history of suicidal ideation and attempts among incarcerated women in Israel. *Psychological Trauma: Theory, Research, Practice, and Policy, 9*(5), 596–604. doi: 10.1037/tra0000277.

Chen, J., & Wu, X. (2017). Posttraumatic stress symptoms and posttraumatic growth in children and adolescents following an earthquakes: A latent transition analysis. *Journal of Traumatic Stress, 30*, 583–592. doi: 10.1002/jts.22238.

Chen, S. H. A., & Desmond, J. E. (2005). Temproal dynamics of cerebro-cerebellar network recruitment during a cognitive task. *Neuropsychologia, 43*, 1227–1237. doi: 10.1016/j.neuropsychologia.2004.12.015.

Chiesa, M., Cirasola, A., Williams, R., Nassisi, V., & Fonagy, P. (2017). Categorical and dimensional approaches in the evaluation of the relationship between attachment and personality disorders: An empirical study. *Attachment and Human Development, 19*(2), 151–169. doi: 10.1080/14616734.2016.1261915.

Child Abuse Narratives (CAN). (2015). Retrieved from https://www.CANarratives.org.

Child Trends Data Bank. (2016). *Child maltreatment.* Retrieved from http://www.childwelfare.gov.

Child Welfare Department. (2016). Retrieved from https://www.childwelfare.gov/systemwide/laws_policies/statutes/manda.cfm.

Chirico, A., Glaveanu, V. P., Cipresso, P., Riva, G., & Gaggioli, A. (2018). Awe enhances creative thinking: An experimental study. *Creativity Research Journal, 30*(2), 123–131. doi: 10.1080/10400419.2018.1446491.

Chirico, A., Serino, S., Cipresso, P., Gaggioli, A., & Riva, G. (2015). When music "flows". State and trait in musical performance, composition and listening: A systematic review. *Frontiers in Psychology, 6*(906), 1–14. doi: 10.3389/fpsyg.2015.00906.

Chopko, B. A., Palmieri, P. A., & Adams, R. E. (2018). Relationships among traumatic experiences, PTSD, and posttraumatic growth for police officers: A path analysis. *Psychological Trauma: Theory, Research, Practice, and Policy, 10*(2), 183–189. doi: 10.1037/tra0000261.

Christensen, J. F., & Calvo-Merino, B. (2013). Dance as a subject for empirical aesthetics. *Psychology of Aesthetics, Creativity, and the Arts, 7*(1), 76–88. doi: 10.1037/a0031827.

Chua, J. (2015). The role of social support in dance talent development. *Journal for the Education of the Gifted, 38*(2), 169–195. doi: 10.1177/0162353215578281.

Cicchetti, D. (2013). Annual research review: Resilient functioning in maltreated children – Past, present and future. *Journal of Child Psychology and Psychiatry, 54*(4), 402–422. doi: 10.1111/j.1469-7610.2012.02608.x.

Cicchetti, D., & Rogosch, F. A. (2002). A developmental psychopathology perspective on adolescence. *Journal of Consulting and Clinical Psychology, 70*, 6–20.

Cieslak, R., Benight, C., Schmidt, N., Luszczynska, A., Curtin, E., Clark, R. A., & Kissinger, P. (2009). Predicting posttraumatic growth among Hurricane Katrina survivors living with HIV: The role of self-efficacy, social support, and PTSD symptoms. *Anxiety, Stress, and Coping, 22*(4), 449–463. doi: 10.1080/10615800802403815.

Cinzia, D. D., & Vittorio, G. (2009). Neuroaesthetics: A review. *Current Opinion in Neurobiology, 19*, 682–687. doi: 10.1016/j.conb.2009.09.001.

Cirasola, A., Hillman, S., Fonagy, P., & Chiesa, M. (2017). Mapping the road from childhood adversity to personality disorder: The role of unresolved states of mind. *Personality and Mental Health, 11*, 77–90. doi: 10.1002/pmh.1365.

Clark, A. A., & Owens, G. P. (2012). Attachment, personality characteristics, and posttraumatic stress disorder in U. S. veterans of Iraq and Afghanistan. *Journal of Traumatic Stress, 25*, 657–664. doi: 10.1002/jts.21760.

Clark, P. C. (2002). Effects of individual and family hardiness on caregiver depression and fatigue. *Research in Nursing and Health, 25*, 37–48. doi: 10.1002/nur.10014.

Claxton, A. F., Pannells, T. C., & Rhoads, P. A. (2005). Developmental trends in the creativity of school-age children. *Creativity Research Journal, 17*(4), 327–335.

Cloitre, M., Stovall-McClough, C., Zorbas, P., & Charuvastra, A. (2008). Attachment organization, emotion regulation, and expectations of support in a clinical sample of women with childhood abuse history. *Journal of Traumatic Stress, 21*(3), 282–289. doi: 10.1002/jts.20339.

Cloninger, C. R. (1994). Temperament and personality. *Current Opinion in Neurobiology, 4*, 266–273.

Clouston, S. A. P., Guralnik, J. M., Kotov, R., Bromet, E. J., & Luft, B. J. (2017). Functional limitations among responders to the World Trade Center attacks 14 years after the disaster: Implications of chronic posttraumatic stress disorder. *Journal of Traumatic Stress, 30*, 443–452. doi: 10.1002/jts.22219.

Cohen, L. J., & Brody, D. (2015). Frontotemporal dementia-like syndrome following recall of childhood sexual abuse. *Journal of Traumatic Stress, 28*, 240–246. doi: 10.1002/jts.22016.

Cohen, K., & Collens, P. (2013). The impact of trauma work on trauma workers: A metasynthesis on vicarious trauma and vicarious posttraumatic growth. *Psychological Trauma: Theory, Research, Practice, and Policy, 5*(6), 570–580. doi: 10.1037/a0030388.

Coifman, K. G., Bonanno, G. A., Ray, R. D., & Gross, J. J. (2007). Does repressive coping promote resilience? Affective-autonomic response descrepancey during bereavement. *Journal of Personality and Social Psychology, 92*(4), 745–758. doi: 10.1037/0022-3514.92.4.745.

Coleman, J. A., Delahanty, D. L., Schwartz, J., Murani, K., & Brondolo, E. (2016). The moderating impact of interacting with distressed families of decedents on trauma exposure in medical examiner personnel. *Psychological Trauma: Theory, Research, Practice, and Policy, 8*(6), 668–675. doi: 10.1037/tra0000097.

Coleridge, S. T. (1817/1976). Fancy and imagination. In A. Rothenberg & C. R. Hausman (Eds.), *The creativity question* (pp. 61–62). Durham, N.C.: Duke University Press.

Collins, A. L., Sarkisian, N., & Winner, E. (2008). Flow and happiness in later life: An investigation into the role of daily and weekly flow experiences. *Journal of Happiness Studies, 10*(6), 703–719. doi: 10.1007/s10902-008-9116-3.

Collins, M. A., & Amabile, T. M. (1999). Motivation and creativity. In R. J. Sternberg (Ed.), *Handbook of creativity* (pp. 297–312). New York, NY: Cambridge University Press.

Collishaw, S., Pickles, A., Messer, J., Rutter, M., Shearer, C., & Maughan, B. (2007). Resilience to adult psychopathology following childhood maltreatment: Evidence from a community sample. *Child Abuse and Neglect, 31,* 211–229. doi: 10.1016/j.chiabu.2007.02.004.

Conroy, D. E., Poczwardowski, A., & Henschen, K. P. (2001). Evaluative criteria and consequences associated with failure and success for elite athletes and performing artists. *Journal of Applied Sport Psychology, 13*(3), 300–322. doi: 10.1080/104132001753144428.

Contractor, A. A., Armour, C., Wang, Z., Forbes, D., & Elhai, J. D. (2015). The mediating role of anger in the relationship between PTSD symptoms and impulsivity. *Psychological Trauma, Theory, Research, Practice, and Policy, 7*(2), 138–145. doi: 10.1037/a0037112.

Cook, A., Spinazzola, J., Ford, J., Lanktree, C., Blaustein, M., Cloitre, M., … van der Kolk, B. (2005). Complex trauma in children and adolescents. *Psychiatric Annals, 35*(5), 390–398.

Cook, D. R. (2001). *Internalized shame scale: Technical manual.* North Tonawanda, New York: Multi-health Systems, Inc.

Cooper, R. B., & Jayatilaka, B. (2006). Group creativity: The effects of extrinsic, intrinsic, and obligation motivations. *Creativity Research Journal, 18*(2), 153–172.

Copeland, C. T. (2016). Take some time to feel this over: Relations between mood responses, indecision, and creativity. *Creativity Research Journal, 28*(1), 11–15. doi: 10.1080/10400419.2016.1125247.

Coppola, G., Ponzetti, S., Aureli, T., & Vaughn, B. E. (2016). Patterns of emotion regulation at two years of age: Associations with mother's attachment in a fear elicited situation. *Attachment and Human Development, 18*(1), 141–153. doi: 10.1080/14616734.2015.1109676.

Corazzza, G. E. (2016). Potential originality and effectiveness: The dynamic definition of creativity. *Creativity Research Journal, 28*(3), 258–267. doi: 10.1080/10400419.2016.1195627.

Corriveau, K. H., Harris, P. L., Meins, E., Fernhough, C., Arnott, B., Elliot, L., ... de Rosnay, M. (2009). Young children's trust in their mother's claims: Longitudinal links with attachment security in infancy. *Child Development, 80*(3), 750–761. doi: 10.111/j.1467-8624.2009.01295.x.

Corval, R., Belsky, J., Baptista, J., Oliveira, P., Mesquita, A., & Soares, I. (2017). Inhibited attachment disordered behavior in institutionalized preschool children: Links with early and current relational experiences. *Attachment and Human Development, 19*(6), 598–612. doi: 10.1080/14616734.2017.1342172.

Cosway, R., Endler, N. S., Sadler, A. J., & Deary, I. J. (2000). The Coping Inventory for Stressful Situations: Factorial structure and associations with personality traits and psychological health. *Journal of Applied Biobehavioral Research, 5*(2), 121–143.

Cote, S., & Morgan, L. M. (2002). A longitudinal analysis of the association between emotion regulation, job satisfaction, and intentions to quit. *Journal of Organizational Behavior, 23*, 947–962. doi: 10.1002/job.174.

Coubard, O. A., Duretz, S., Lefebrve, V., Lapalus, P., & Ferrufino, L. (2011). Practice of contemporary dance improves cognitive flexibility in aging. *Frontiers in Aging Neuroscience, 3*(13), 1–12. doi: 10.3389/fnagi.2011.000013.

Cox, D. W., Bakker, A. M., & Naifeh, J. A. (2017). Emotion dysregulation and social support in PTSD and depression: A study of trauma-exposed veterans. *Journal of Traumatic Stress, 30*, 545–549. doi: 10.1002/jts.22226.

Crabtree, J., & Green, M. J. (2016). Creative cognition and psychosis vulnerability: What's the difference. *Creativity Research Journal, 28*(1), 24–32. doi: 10.1080/10400419.2015.1030305.

Craig, A. D. (2004). Human feelings: Why are some more aware than others? *Trends in Cognitive Sciences, 8*(6), 239–241. doi: 10.1016/tics.2004.04.004.

Craigie, M., Osseriran-Moisson, R., Hemsworth, D., Aoun, S., Francis, K., Brown, J., ... Rees, C. (2016). The influence of trait-negative affect and compassion satisfaction on compassion fatigue in Australian nurses. *Psychological Trauma: Theory, Research, Practice, and Policy, 8*(1), 89–97. doi: 10.1037/tra0000050.

Cramond, B., Matthews-Morgan, J., & Bandalos, D. (2005). A report on the 40-year follow-up of the Torrance Tests of Creative Thinking: Alive and well in the new millennium. *Gifted Child Quarterly, 49*(4), 283–291.

Creasey, G. (2002). Psychological distress in college-aged women: Links with unresolved/preoccu- pied attachment status and the mediating role of negative mood regulation expectancies. *Attachment & Human Development, 4*(3), 261–277. doi: 10.1080/14616730210167249.

Creech, S. K., Benzer, J. K., Liebsack, B. K., Proctor, S., & Taft, C. T. (2013). Impact of coping style and PTSD on family functioning after deployment in Operation Desert Shield/Storm returnees. *Journal of Traumatic Stress, 26*, 507–511. doi: 10.1002/jts.21823.

Creech, S. K., Smith, J., Grimes, J. S., & Meagher, M. W. (2011). Written emotional disclosure of trauma and trauma history alter pain sensitivity. *The Journal of Pain, 12*(7), 801–810. doi: 10.1016/j.jpain.2011.01.007.

Crespo, M., & Fernandez-Lansac, V. (2016). Memory and narrative of traumatic events: A literature review. *Psychological Trauma: Theory, Research, Practice, and Policy, 8*(2), 149–156. doi: 10.1037/tra0000041.

Crimes Against Children Research Center. (2017). Retrieved from http://www.unh.edu.

Critchley, H. D. (2005). Neural mechanisms of autonomic, affective, and cognitive integration. *Journal of Comparative Neurology, 493*, 154–166. doi: 10.1002/cne.20749.

———. (2012). How emotions are shaped by bodily states. *Emotion Review, 4*(2), 163–168. doi: 10.1177/1754073911430132.

Critchley, H. D., Wiens, S, Rotshtein, P., Ohman, A., & Dolan, R. (2004). Neural systems supporting interoception awareness. *Nature Neuroscience, 7*(2), 189–195.

Crocker, L. D., Haller, M., Norman, S. B., & Angkaw, A. C. (2016). Shame versus trauma-related guilt as mediators of the relationship between PTSD symptoms and aggression among returning veterans. *Psychological Trauma: Theory, Research, Practice, and Policy, 8*(4), 520–527. doi: 10.1037/tra0000151.

Crombie, K. M., Brellenthin, A. G., Hillard, C. J., & Koltyn, K. F. (2018). Psychobiological response to aerobic exercise in individuals with posttraumatic stress disorder. *Journal of Traumatic Stress, 31*, 134–145. doi: 10.1037/jts.22253.

Cropley, A. (2016). The myths of heaven-sent creativity: Toward a perhaps less democratic but more down-to-earth understanding. *Creativity Research Journal, 28*(3), 238–246. doi: 10.1080/10400419.2016.1195614.

Cropley, D. H., Kaufman, J. C., & Cropley, A. J. (2008). Malevolent creativity: A functional model of creativity in terrorism and crime. *Creativity Research Journal, 20*(2), 105–115. doi: 10.1080/1040041080259424.

Cross, E. S., & Ticini, L. F. (2012). Neuroaesthetics and beyond: New horizons in applying the science of the brain to the art of dance. *Phenomenology and Cognitive Science, 11*, 5–16. doi: 10.1007/s11097-010-9190-y.

Cross, T. L. (2014). Social emotional needs: Can the obsessions of gifted students be positive drivers in their development? *Gifted Child Today, 37*(2), 123–125. doi: 10.1177/1076217514520632.

Crowell, J. A., Treboux, D., & Waters, E. (2002). Stability of attachment representations: The transition to marriage. *Developmental Psychology, 38*(4), 467–479. doi: 10.1037//0012-1649.38.4.467.

Csikszentmihalyi, M. (1990). *Flow: The psychology of optimal experience.* New York: Harper & Row.

———. (1996). *Creativity: Flow and the psychology of discovery and invention.* New York: Harper Collins.

———. (1999). Implications of a systems perspective for the study of creativity. In R. J. Sternberg (Ed.), *Handbook of creativity* (pp. 313–335). New York, NY: Cambridge University Press.

Culbertson, R. (1995). Embodied memory, transcendence, and telling: Recounting trauma, re-establishing the self. *New Literary History, 26*(1), 169−195.

Currier, J. M., & Neimeyer, R. A. (2007). Fragmented stories: The narrative integration of violent loss. In E. K. Rynearson (Ed.), *Violent death: Resilience and intervention beyond crisis* (pp. 85–100). New York, NY: Routledge.

Currier, J. M., Holland, J. M., & Allen, D. (2012). Attachment and mental health symptoms among U.S. Afghanistan and Iraq veterans seeking health care services. *Journal of Traumatic Stress, 25*, 633–640. doi: 10.1002/jts.21752.

Currier, J. M., Holland, J. M., & Drescher, K. D. (2015). Spirituality factors in the prediction of outcomes of PTSD treatment for U.S. military veterans. *Journal of Traumatic Stress, 28*, 57–64. doi: 10.1002/jts.21978.

Currier, J. M., Holland, J. M., & Neimeyer, R. A. (2006). Sense-making, grief, and the experience of violent loss: Toward a meditational model. *Death Studies, 30*, 403–428. doi: 10.1080/07481180600614351.

Currier, J. M., Holland, J. M., Rojas-Flores, L., Herrera, S., & Foy, D. (2015). Morally injurious experiences and meaning in Salvadorian teachers exposed to violence. *Psychological Trauma: Theory, Research, Practice, and Policy, 7*(1), 24–33. doi: 10.1037/a0034092.

Curtis, W. J., & Cicchetti, D. (2003). Moving research on resilience into the 21st century: Theoretical and methodological considerations in examining the biological contributors to resilience. *Development and Psychopathology, 15*, 773–800. doi: 10.1017/S0954579403000373.

Dakanalis, A., Clerici, M., Caslini, M., Favagrossa, L., Prunas, A., Volpato, C., ... Zanetti, M. A. (2014). Internalization ofsociocultural standards of beauty and disordered eating behaviors: The role of body surveillance, shame and social anxiety. *Journal of Psychopathology, 20*, 33–37.

Dalebroux, A., Goldstein, T. R., & Winner, E. (2008). Short-term mood repair through art-making: Positive emotion is more effective than venting. *Motivation and Emotion, 32*(4), 288–295. doi: 10.1007/s11031-008-9105-1.

Dalenberg, C. J., Brand, B. L., Gleaves, D. H., Dorahy, M. J., Loewenstein, R. J., Cardena, E., ... Spiegel, D. (2012). Evaluation of the evidence for the trauma and fantasy models of dissociation. *Psychological Bulletin, 138*(3), 550–588. doi: 10.1037/a0027447.

Dalgaard, N. T., Todd, B. K., Daniel, S. I. F., & Montgomery, E. (2016). The transmission of trauma in refugee families: Associations between intra-family trauma communication style, children's attachment security and psychosocial adjustment. *Attachment and Human Development, 18*(1), 69–89. doi: 10.1080/14616734.2015.1113305.

Damasio, A. (1999). *The feeling of what happens: Body and emotion in the making of consciousness*. New York: Harcourt Brace and Company.

Damasio, A. R. (1994). *Descartes' error: Emotion, reason, and the human brain*. New York: G.P. Putnam.

Danese, A., & McEwen, B. S. (2012). Adverse childhood experience, allostasis, allostatic load, and age-related disease. *Physiology and Behavior, 106*, 29–39. doi: 10.1016/j.physbeh.2011.08.019.

Daniels, J. K., Bluhm, R. L., & Lanius, R. A. (2013). Intrinsic network abnormalities in posttraumatic stress disorder: Research directions for the next decade. *Psychological Trauma: Theory, Research, Practice, and Policy, 5*(2), 142–148. doi: 10.1037/a0026946.

Darbor, K. E., Lench, H. C., Davis, W. E., & Hicks, J. A. (2016). Experiencing versus contemplating: Language use during descriptions of awe and wonder. *Cognition and Emotion, 30*(6), 1188–1196. doi: 10.1080/02699931.2015.1042836.

David, D., Woodward, C., Esquenazi, J., & Mellman, T. A. (2004). Comparison of comorbid physical illnesses among veterans with PTSD and veterans with alcohol dependence. *Psychiatric Services, 55*(1), 82–85.

Davidson, R. J., Kabat-Zinn, J., Schumacher, J., Rosenkranz, M., Muller, D., Santorelli, S. F., ... Sheridan, J. F. (2003). Alterations in brain and immune function produced by mindfulness meditation. *Psychosomatic Medicine, 65*, 564–570. doi: 10.1097/01.PSY.0000077505.67574.E3.

Davis, K. M. (2010). Music and the expressive arts with children experiencing trauma. *Journal of Creativity in Mental Health, 5*(2), 125–133.

Davis, M. A. (2009). Understanding the relationship between mood and creativity: A meta-analysis. *Organizational Behavior and Human Decision Processing, 108*, 25–38. doi: 10.1016/j.obhdp.2008.04.001.

Davis, M. T., Witte, T. K., & Weathers, F. W. (2014). Posttraumatic stress disorder and suicide ideation: The role of specific symptoms within the framework of the interpersonal-psychological theory of suicide. *Psychological Trauma: Theory, Research, Practice, and Policy, 6*(6), 610–618. doi: 10.1037/a0033941.

Day, S. X. (2002). "Make it uglier. Make it hurt. Make it real": Narrative construction of the creative writer's identity. *Creativity Research Journal, 14*(1), 127–136.

de Assis, M. A., de Mello, M. F., Scorza, F. A., Cadrobbi, M. P., Schooedl, A. F., da Silva, S. G., ... Arida, R. M. (2008). Evaluation of physical activity habits in patients with posttraumatic stress disorder. *Clinical Science, 64*, 473–478. doi: 10.1590/S1807-59322008000400010.

De Bellis, M. D., Baum, A. S., Birmaher, B., Keshavan, M. S., Eccard, C. H., Boring, A. M., ... Ryan, N. D. (1999). Developmental traumatology Part I: Biological stress systems. *Biological Psychiatry, 45*, 1259–1270.

De Bellis, M. D., Keshavan, M. S., Clark, D. B., Casey, B. J., Giedd, J. N., Boring, A. M., ... Ryan, N. D. (1999). Developmental traumatology Part II: Brain development. *Biological Psychiatry, 45*, 1271–1284.

De Bellis, M. D., Keshavan, M. S., Shifflett, H., Iyengar, S., Beers, S. R., Hall, J., & Moritz, G. (2002). Brain structures in pediatric maltreatment-related posttraumatic stress disorder: A sociodemographically matched study. *Biological Psychiatry, 52*(11), 1066–1078. doi: 10.1016/S00006-3223(02)01459-2.

De Dreu, C. K., Baas, M., & Nijstad, B. A. (2008). Hedonic tone and activation level in the mood-creativity link: Toward a dual pathway of creativity model. *Journal of Personality and Social Psychology, 94*(5), 739–756. doi: 10.1037/0022-3514.94.5.739.

de Gelder, B. (2006). Towards the neurobiology of emotional body language. *Nature Reviews, 7*, 242–249.

de Jesus, S. N., Rus, C. L., Lens, W., & Imaginario, S. (2013). Intrinsic motivation and creativity related to product: A meta-analysis of the studies published between 1990–2010. *Creativity Research Journal, 25*(1), 80–84. doi: 10.1080/10400419.2013.752235.

de Manzano, O., & Ullen, F. (2012). Goal-independent mechanisms for free response generation: Creative and pseudo-random performance share neural substrates. *Neuroimage, 59*, 772–780. doi: 10.1016/jneuroimage.2011.07.016.

de Manzano, O., & Ullen, F. (2012a). Activation and connectivity patterns of the presupplementary and dorsal premotor areas during free improvisation of melodies and rhythms. *Neuroimage, 63*, 271–280. doi: 10.1016/j.neuroimage.2012.06.024.

de Manzano, O., Cervenka, S., Jucaite, A., Hellenas, O., Farde, L., & Ullen, F. (2013). Indivdiual differences in the proneness to have flow experiences are linked to dopamine D2 receptor availability in the dorsal striatum. *Neuroimage, 67*, 1–6. doi: 10.1016/j.neuroimage.2012.10.072.

de Manzano, O., Cervenka, S., Karabanov, A., Farde, L., & Ullen, F. (2010). Thinking outside a less intact box: Thalamic dopamine D2 receptor densities are negatively related to psychometric creativity in healthy individuals. *PLoS ONE, 5*(5), e10670. doi: 10.1371/journal.pone.0010670.

de Manzano, O., Theorell, T., Harmat, L., & Ullen, F. (2010). The psychophysiology of flow during piano playing. *Emotion, 10*, 301–311. doi: 10.1037/a0018432.

de Ruiter, M. B., Phaf, R. H., Veltman, D. J., Kok, A., & van Dyck, R. (2003). Attention as a characteristic of nonclinical dissociation: An event-related potential study. *Neuroimage, 19*, 376–390. doi: 10.1016/S1053-8119(03)00099-5.

Debell, F., Fear, N. T., Head, M., Batt-Rawden, S., Greenberg, N., Wessely, S., & Goodwin, L. (2014). A systematic review of the comorbidity between PTSD and alcohol misuse. *Social Psychoatry and Psychiatric Epidemiology, 49*, 1401–1425. doi: 10.1007/s00127-014-0855-7.

Deblinger, E., & Runyon, M. K. (2005). Understanding and treating feelings of shame in children who have experienced maltreatment. *Child Maltreatment, 10*(4), 364–376. doi: 10.1177559505279306.

Deci, E., & Ryan, R. (1991). A motivational approach to self: Integration in personality. In R. Dienstbier (Ed.), *Nebraska symposium on motivation* (Vol. 38, pp. 237–288). Lincoln: University of Nebraska Press.

Deci, E. L., & Ryan, R. M. (2000). The "what" and "why" of goal pursuits: Human needs and the self-determination of behavior. *Psychological Inquiry, 11*, 227–268. doi: 10.1207/ S15327965PLI1104_01.

DeCou, C. R., Cole, T. T., Lynch, S. M., Wong, M. M., & Matthews, K. C. (2017). Assault-related shame mediates the association between negative social reactions to disclosure or sexual assault and psychological distress. *Psychological Trauma: Theory, Research, Practice, and Policy, 9*(2), 166–172. doi: 10.1037/tra0000186.

Dedert, E. A., Green, K. T., Calhoun, P. S., Yoash-Gantz, R., Taber, K. H., Mumford, M. M., ... Beckham, J. C. (2009). Association of trauma exposure with psychiatric morbidity in military veterans who have served since September 11, 2001. *Journal of Psychiatric Research, 43*, 830–836. doi: 10.1016/j.jpsychires.2009.01.004.

Dekel, R., & Tuval-Mashiach, R. (2012). Multiple losses of social resources following collective trauma: The case of the forced relocation from Gush Katif. *Psychological Trauma: Theory, Research, Practice, and Policy, 4*(1), 56–65. doi: 10.1037/a0019912.

Dekel, S., Ein-Dor, T., & Solomon, Z. (2012). Posttraumatic growth and posttraumatic distress: A longitudinal study. *Psychological Trauma: Theory, Research, Practice, and Policy, 4*(1), 94–101. doi: 10.1037/a 0021865.

Dekel, S., Mandl, C., & Solomon, Z. (2013). Is the Holocaust implicated in posttraumatic growth in second-generation Holocaust survivors? A prospective study. *Journal of Traumatic Stress, 26,* 330–333. doi: 10.1002/jts.21836.

Dekel, R., Siegel, A., Fridkin, S., & Svetlitzky, V. (2018). The double-edged sword: The role of empathy in military veterans' partners distress. *Psychological Trauma: Theory, Research, Practice, and Policy, 10*(2), 216–224. doi: 10.1037/tra0000265.

Dekker, J. M., Crow, R. S., Folsom, A. R. Hannan, P. J., Liao, D., Swenne, C. A., & Schouten, E. G. (2000). Low heart rate variability in a 2-minute rhythm strip predicts risk of coronary heart disease and mortality from several causes: The ARIC Study. *Circulation, 102,* 1239–1244. doi: 10.1161/01.CIR.102.11.1239.

Delahaij, R., Gaillard, A. W. K., & van Dam, K. (2010). Hardiness and the response to stressful situations: Investigating mediating processes. *Personality and Individual Differences, 49,* 386–390. doi: 10.1016/j.paid.2010.04.002.

Del Rosario, P. M., & White, R. M. (2006). The Internalized Shame Scale: Temporal stability, internal consistenvy, and principal components analysis. *Personality and Individual Differences, 41,* 95–103. doi: 10.1016/j.paid.2005.10.026.

Dell, P. F. (2017). Is high hypnotizability a necessary diathesis for pathological dissociation? *Journal of Trauma and Dissociation, 18*(1), 58–87. doi: 10.1080/15299732.2016.1191579.

DeMarco, T. C., Taylor, C. L., & Friedman, R. S. (2015). Reinvestigating the effect of interpersonal sadness on mood-congruency in music preference. *Psychology of Aesthetics, Creativity, and the Arts, 9*(1), 81–90. doi: 10.1037/a0038691.

Deng, L., Wang, L., & Zhao, Y. (2016). How creativity was affected by environmental factors and individual characteristics: A cross-cultural comparison perspective. *Creativity Research Journal, 28*(3), 357–366. doi: 10.1080/10400419.2016.1195615.

Department of Veterans Affairs. (2016). *Suicide among veterans and other Americans: 2001–2014 report.* Retrieved from http://www.mentalhealth.va.gov/docs/2016suicidedatareport.pdf.

DePrince, A. P., Huntjens, R. J. C., & Dorahy, M. J. (2015). Alienation appraisals distinguish adults diagnosed with DID from PTSD. *Psychological Trauma: Theory, Research, Practice, and Policy, 7*(6), 578–582. doi: 10.1037/tra0000069.

Devries, K. M., Mak, J. Y. T., Child, J. C., Falder, G., Bacchus, L. J., Astbury, J., & Watts, C. H. (2017). Childhood sexual abuse and suicidal behavior: A meta-analysis. *Pediatrics, 133,* e1331–e1344. doi: 10.1542/peds.2013.2166.

Devries, K. M., Mak, J. Y. T., Garcia-Moreno, C., Petzold, M., Child, J. C., Falder, G., ... Watts, C. H. (2013). Global health: The global prevalence of intimate partner violence against women. *Science, 340,* 1527–1528. doi: 10.1126/science.124937.

Dickerson, S. S. (2008). Emotional and physiological responses to social-evaluative threat. *Social and Personality Psychology Compass, 2,* 1362–1378. doi: 10.1111/j.1751-9004.2008.00095.x.

Dickerson, S. S., Gable, S. L., Irwin, M. R., Aziz, N., & Kemeny, M. E. (2009). Social-evaluative threat and proinflammatory cytokine regulation: An experimental laboratory investigation. *Psychological Science, 20*(10), 1237–1244. doi: 10.1111/j.1467-9280.2009.02437.x.

Dickerson, S. S., Gruenewald, T. L., & Kemeny, M. E. (2004). When the social self is threatened: Shame, physiology and health. *Journal of Personality, 72*, 1191–1216. doi: 10.1111/j.1467-6494.2004.00295.x.

Dickerson, S. S., Mycek, P. J., & Zaldivar, F. (2008). Negative social evaluation, but not mere social presence, elicits cortisol responses to a laboratory stressor task. *Health Psychology, 27*(1), 116–121. doi: 10.1037/0278-6133.27.1.116.

Diedrich, J., Benedek, M., Jauk, E., & Neubauer, A. C. (2015). Are creative ideas novel and useful? *Psychology of Creativity, Aesthetics, and the Arts, 9*(1), 35–40. doi: 10.1037/a0038688.

Diener, E., & Seligman, M. E. P. (2002). Very happy people. *Psychology Science, 13*(1), 81–84.

Dietrich, A. (2004). Neurocognitive mechanisms underlying the experience of flow. *Consciousness and Cognition, 13*, 746–761. doi: 10.1016/j.concog.2004.07.002.

———. (2007). Who's afraid of a cognitive neuroscience of creativity? *Methods, 42*, 22–27. doi: 10.1016/j.ymeth.2006.12.009.

———. (2008). Imaging the imagination: The trouble with motor imagery. *Methods, 45*, 319–324. doi: 10.1016/j.ymeth.2008.04.004.

Dietrich, A., & Kanso, R. (2010). A review of EEG, ERP, and neuroimaging studies of creativity and insight. *Psychological Bulletin, 136*(5), 822–848. doi: 10.1037/a0019749.

Dijksterhuis, A., & Meurs, T. (2006). Where creativity resides: The generative power of unconscious thought. *Consciousness and Cognition, 15*, 135–146. doi: 10.1016/j.concog.2005.04.007.

Dijkstra, K., Kaschak, M. P., & Zwaan, R. A. (2007). Body posture facilitates retrieval of autobiographical memories. *Cognition, 102*(1), 139–149. doi: 10.1016/j.cognition.2005.12.009.

Dikmen-Yildiz, P., Ayers, S., & Phillips, L. (2018). Longitudinal trajectories of post-traumatic stress disorder (PTSD) after birth and associated risk factors. *Journal of Affective Disorder, 229*, 377–385. doi: 10.1016/j.jad.2017.12.074.

Di Martino, A., Scheres, A., Marguiles, D. S., Kelly, A. M. C., Uddin, L. Q., Shehzad, Z., Biswal, B., ... Milham, M. P. (2008). Functional connectivity of human striatum: A resting state fMRI study. *Cerebral Cortex, 18*, 2735–2747. doi: 10.1093/cercor/bhn041.

Dixon, A., Howie, P., & Starling, J. (2005). Trauma exposure, posttraumatic stress, psychiatric comorbidity in femal juvenile offenders. *Journal of the American Academy of Child and Adolescent Psychiatry, 44*(8), 798–806. doi: 10.1097/01.chi.0000164590.48318.9c.

Dixon-Gordon, K. L., Tull, M. T., & Gratz, K. L. (2014). Self-injurious behaviors in posttraumatic stress disorder: An examination of potential moderators. *Journal of Affective Disorders, 166*, 359–367. doi: 10.1016/j.jad.2014.05.033.

Doinita, N. E., & Maria, N. D. (2015). Attachment and parenting styles. *Procedia-Social and Behavioral Sciences, 203*, 199–204. doi: 10.1016/j.sbspro.2015.08.282.

Dollinger, S. J., Burke, P. A., & Gump, N. W. (2007). Creativity and values. *Creativity Research Journal, 19*(2–3), 91–103.

Domino, G., Short, J., Evans, A., & Romano, P. (2002). Creativity and ego defense mechanisms: Some exploratory empirical evidence. *Creativity Research Journal, 14*(1), 17–25.

Dong, M., Anda, R. F., Dube, S. R., Giles, W. H., & Felitti, V. J. (2003). The relationship of exposure to childhood sexual abuse to other forms of abuse, neglect and household dysfunction during childhood. *Child Abuse and Neglect, 27*, 625–639. doi: 10.1016/S0145-2134(03)00105-4.

Dong, M., Anda, R. F., Felitti, V., Dube, S. R., Williamson, D. F., Thompson, T. J., ... Giles, W. H. (2004). The interrelatedness of multiple forms of childhood abuse, neglect and household dysfunction. *Child Abuse and Neglect, 28*, 771–784. doi: 10.1016/j.chiabu.2004.01.008.

Dong, M., Giles, W. H., Felitti, V. J., Dube, S. R., Williams, J. E., Chapman, D. P., & Anda, R. F. (2004). Insights into causal pathways for ischemic heart disease: Adverse childhood experiences study. *Circulation, 110*, 1761–1766.

Dorahy, M. J. (2010). The impact of dissociation, shame, and guilt on interpersonal relationships in chronically traumatized individuals: A pilot study. *Journal of Traumatic Stress, 23*(5), 653–656. doi: 10.1002/jts.20564.

———. (2017). Shame as a compromise for humiliation and rage in the internal representations of abuse by loved ones: Processes, motivations, and the role of dissociation. *Journal of Trauma and Dissociation, 18*(3), 383–396. doi: 10.1080/15299732.2017.1295422.

Dorahy, M. J., Peck, R. K., & Huntjens, R. J. C. (2016). The impact of dissociation on perceptual priming and intrusions after listening to auditory narratives. *Journal of Trauma and Dissociation, 17*(4), 410–425. doi: 10.1080/15299732.2015.1134746.

Douglas, E. M., & Finkelhor, D. (2005). Child maltreatment fatalities fact sheet. *Crimes Against Children Research Center*. Retrieved from https//www.unh.edu/cccrc.

———. (2005a). Childhood sexual abuse fact sheet. *Crimes Against Children Research Center*. Retrieved from https//www.unh.edu/cccrc.

Dozier, M. (1990). Attachment organization and treatment use for adults with serious psychopathological disorders. *Development and Psychopathology, 2*, 47–60. doi: 10.1017/S095457900000584.

Drapeau, C. W., & DeBrule, D. S. (2013). The relationship of hypomania, creativity and suicidal ideation in undergraduates. *Creativity Research Journal, 25*(1), 75–79. doi: 10.1080/10400419.2013.752231.

Drus, M., Kozbelt, A., & Hughes, R. R. (2014). Creativity, psychopathology, and emotion processing: A liberal response bias for remembering negative information is associated with higher creativity. *Creativity Research Journal, 26*(3), 251–262. doi: 10.1080/10400419.2014.929400.

Du, S., Tao, Y., & Martinez, A. M. (2014). Compound facial expressions of emotion. *Proceedings of the National Academy of Science, 111*(15), E1454–E1462. doi: 10.1073/pnas.1322355111.

Dube, S. R., Felitti, V. J., Dong, M., Chapman, D. P., Giles, W., & Anda, R. F. (2003). Childhood abuse, household dysfunction and the risk of illicit drug use: The Adverse Childhood Experiences Study. *Pediatrics, 111*, 564–572.

Duckers, M. L., & Brewin, C. R. (2016). A paradox in individual versus national mental health vulnerability resource levels associated with higher disorder prevalence? *Journal of Traumatic Stress, 29*, 572–576. doi: 10.1002/jts.22144.

Duckers, M. L., & Oliff, M. (2017). Does the vulnerability paradox in PTSD apply to women and men? An exploratory study. *Journal of Traumatic Stress, 30*, 200–204. doi: 10.1002/jts.22173.

Duckers, M. L., Alisic, E., & Brewin, C. R. (2016a). A vulnerability paradox in the cross-national prevalence of post-traumatic stress disorder. *British Journal of Psychiatry, 209*, 300–305. doi: 10.1192/bjp.bp.115.176628.

Dunn, J. M., & Sensky, T. (2018). Psychological processes in chronic embitterment: The potential contribution of rumination. *Psychological Trauma: Theory, Research, Practice, and Policy, 10*(1), 7–13. doi: 10.1037/tra0000291.

Dunn, L. W., Corn, A. L., & Morelock, M. J. (2004). The relationship between scores on the ICMIC and selected talent domains: An investigation with gifted adolescents. *Gifted Child Quarterly, 48*(2), 133–142.

Dunn, M. G., Tarter, R. E., Mezzich, A. C., Vanyukov, M., Kirisci, L., & Kirillova, G. (2002). Origins and consequences of child neglect in substance abuse families. *Clinical Psychology Review, 22*, 1063–1090.

Dyers, K. F. W., Dorahy, M. J., Corry, M., Black, R., Matheson, L., Coles, H., ... Middleton, W. (2017). Comparing shame in clinical and nonclinical populations: Preliminary findings. *Psychological Trauma: Theory, Research, Practice, and Policy, 9*(2), 173–180. doi: 10.1037/tra0000158.

Dykas, M. J., Woodhouse, S. S., Cassidy, J., & Waters, H. S. (2006). Narrative assessmentof attachment representations: Links between secure base scripts and adolescent attachment. *Attachment and Human Development, 8*(3), 221–240. doi: 10.1080/14616730600856099.

Dykas, M. J., Woodhouse, S. S., Jones, J. D., & Cassidy, J. (2014). Attachment-related biases in adolescents' memory. *Child Development, 85*(6), 2185–2201. doi: 10.1111/cdev.12268.

Edwards, V. J., Holden, G. W., Felitti, V. J., & Anda, R. F. (2003). Relationship between multiple forms of childhood maltreatment and adult mental health in community respondents: Results from the Adverse Childhood Experiences Study. *American Journal of Psychiatry, 160*, 1453–1460.

Ehlers, A., & Clark, D. (2000). A cognitive model of posttraumatic stress disorder. *Behavioral Research and Therapy, 38*, 319–345. doi: 10.1016/S0005-7967(99)00123-0.

Eisenberg, J., & Thompson, W. F. (2011). The effects of competition on improvisers' motivation, stress, and creative performance. *Creativity Research Journal, 23*(2), 129–136. doi: 10.1080/10400419.2011.571185.

Eisenman, R. (2008). Malevolent creativity in criminals. *Creativity Research Journal, 20*(2), 116–119. doi: 10.1080/10400410802059465.

Elhai, J. D., Miller, M. E., Ford, J. D., Biehn, T. L., Palmieri, P. A., & Frueh, B. C. (2012). Posttraumatic Stress Disorder in DSM-5: Estimates of prevalence and symptom structure in a nonclinical sample of college students. *Journal of Anxiety Disorders, 26*, 58–64. doi: 10.1016/j.janxdis.2011.08.013.

Elison, J., & Partridge, J. A. (2012). Relationships between shame-coping, fear of failure, and perfectionism in college athletes. *Journal of Sport Behavior, 35*(1), 19–39.

Ellamil, M., Dobson, C., Beeman, M., & Christoff, K. (2012). Evaluative and generative modes of thought during the creative process. *Neuroimage, 59*, 1783–1794. doi: 10.1016/j.neuroimage.2011.08.008.

Elliot, A. J., & Covington, M. V. (2001). Approach and avoidance motivation. *Educational Psychology Review, 13*(2), 73–92. doi: 10.1040-726X/01/0600-0073$19.50/0.

Elliot, A. J., & Reis, H. T. (2003). Attachment and exploration in adulthood. *Journal of Personality and Social Psychology, 85*(2), 317–331. doi: 10.1037/0022-3514.85.2.317.

Elliot, A. J., & Thrash, T. M. (2001). Achievement goals and the hierarchical model of achievement motivation. *Education Psychology Review, 13*(2), 139–156. doi: 10.1040-726X/01/0600-0139$19.50/0.

———. (2002). Approach-avoidance motivation in personality: Approach and avoidance temperaments and goals. *Journal of Personality and Social Psychology, 82*(5), 804–818. doi: 10.1037//0022-3514.82.5.804.

Ellis, R. J., & Thayer, J. F. (2010). Music and autonomic nervous system (dys)function. *Music Perception: An Interdisciplinary Journal, 27*(4), 317–326. doi: 10.1525/mp.2010.27.4.317.

Elzinga, B. M., Bermond, B., & van Dyck, R. (2002). The relationship between dissociative proneness and alexithymia. *Psychotherapy and Psychosomatics, 71*(2), 104–111. doi: 10.1159/000049353.

Endler, N. S., & Parker, J. D. A. (1990). *Coping inventory for stressful situations: Manual* (2nd ed.). Toronto: Multi-Health Systems.

Engeser, S., & Rheinberg, F. (2008). Flow, performance and moderators of challenge-skill balance. *Motivation and Emotion, 32*, 158–172. doi: 10.1007/s11031-008-9102-4.

Englehard, I. M., van den Hout, M. A., & Lommen, M. J. J. (2009). Individuals high in neuroticism are not more reactive to adverse events. *Personality and Individual Differences, 47*, 697–700. doi: 10.1016/j.paid.2009.05.031.

Enman, N. M., Sabban, E. L., McGonigle, P., & Van Bockstaele, E. J. (2015). Targeting the neuropeptide Y system in stress-related psychiatric disorders. *Neurobiology of Stress, 1*, 33–43. doi: 10.1016/j.ynstr.2014.09.007.

Erez, A., & Isen, A. M. (2002). The influence of positive affect on the components of expectancy motivation. *Journal of Applied Psychology, 87*(6), 1055–1067. doi: 10.1037//0021-9010.87.6.1055.

Ericsson, K. A. (2007). Deliberate practice and the modifiability of body and mind: Toward a science of the structure and acquisition of expert and elite performance. *International Journal of Sport Psychology, 38*(1), 4–34.

———. (2013). Training history, deliberate practice and elite sports performance: An analysis in response to Tucker an Collins review–what makes champions? *British Journal of Sports Medicine, 47*, 533–535.

———. (2014). Why expert performance is special and cannot be extrapolated from studies of performance in the general population: A response to criticism. *Intelligence, 45*, 81–103. doi: 10.1016/j.intell.2013.12.001.

Ericsson, K. A., Roring, R. W., & Nandagopal, K. (2007). Giftedness and evidence for reproducibly superior performance: An account based on the expert performance framework. *High Ability Studies, 18*, 3–56.

Erwin, L., Surguladze, S. A., Giampietro, V. P., Anilkumar, A., Brammer, M. J., Sierra, M., ... Phillips, M. L. (2007). Limibic and prefrontal response to facial emotion expressions in depersonalization. *Neuroreport, 18*(5), 473–477. doi: 10.1097/WNR.obo13e328057deb3.

Esala, J. J., & Taing, S. (2017). Testimony therapy with ritual: A pilot randomized controlled trial. *Journal of Traumatic Stress, 30*, 94–98. doi: 10.1002/jts.22163.

Espinoza, C., & Ukleja, M. (2016). *Managing the millennials: Discover the core competencies for managing today's workforce.* Hoboken, NJ: John Wiley & Sons.

Essex, M., Boyce, W. T., Hertzman, C., Lam, L. L., Armstrong, J. M., Neumann, S. M. A., & Kobor, M. S. (2013). Epigenetic vestiges of early developmental adversity: Childhood stress exposure and DNA methylation in adolescence. *Child Development, 84*(1), 58–75. doi: 10.1111/j.1467-8624.2011.01641.x.

Eusanio, J., Thomson, P., & Jaque, S. V. (2014). Perfectionism, shame, and self-concept in dancers: A mediation analysis. *Journal of Dance Medicine and Science,* 13(3), 106–114.

Evans, G. W., & Kim, P. (2013). Childhood poverty, chronic stress, self-regulation, and coping. *Child Development Perspectives, 7*(1), 43–48. doi: 10.1111/cdep.12013.

Evans, R., Garner, P., & Hong, A. S. (2014). Prevention of violence, abuse and neglect in early childhood: A review of the literature on research, policy and practice. *Early Child Development and Care, 184*(9–10), 1295–1335. doi: 10.1080/03004430.2014.910327.

Evans, W. R., Stanley, M. A., Barrera, T. L., Exline, J. J., Pargament, K. I., & Teng, E. J. (2018). Morally injurious events and psychological distress among veterans: Examining the mediating role of religious and spiritual struggles. *Psychological Trauma, Theory, Research, and Policy, 10*(3), 360–367. doi: 10.1037/tra0000347.

Everall, R. D., Altrows, K. J., & Paulson, B. L. (2006). Creating a future: A study of resilience in suicidal female adolescents. *Journal of Counseling and Development, 84*, 461–470.

Eysenck, H. J. (1997). Creativity and personality. In M. Runco (Ed.), *The creativity research handbook* (Vol. 1, pp. 41–66). Cresskill, New Jersey: Hampton Press.

Eysenck, H. J., & Eysenck, S. B. G. (1991). *The eysenck personality questionnaire-revised.* Sevenoaks: Hodder & Stoughton.

Falk, R. F., Lind, S., Miller, N. B., Piechowski, M. M., & Silverman, L. K. (1999). *The overexcitability questionnaire–two (OEQII): Manual scoring system and questionnaire.* Denver, CO: Institute for the Study of Advanced Development.

Falk, R. F., Manzanero, J. B., & Miller, N. B. (1997). Developmental potential in Venezuelan and American artists: A cross-cultural validity study. *Creativity Research Journal, 10*(2 & 3), 201–206.

Fang, X., Brown, D. S., Florence, C. S., & Mercy, J. A. (2012). The economic burden of child maltreatment in the United States and implications for prevention. *Child Abuse and Neglect, 36,* 156–165. doi: 10.1016/j.chiabu.2011.10.006.

Farina, B., Speranza, A. M., Imperatori, C., Quintilliani, M. I., & Marca, G. D. (2015). Change in heart rate variability after the Adult Attachment Interview in dissociative patients. *Journal of Trauma and Dissociation, 16*, 170–180. doi: 10.1080/15299732.2014.975309.

Farley, Y. R. (2007). Making the connection: Spirituality, trauma and resiliency. *Journal of Religion and Spirituality in Social Work: Social Thought, 1*, 1–15.

Faulkner, Z. E., & Leaver, E. E. (2016). Memories: True or false? Physiological measures may answer the question. *Imagination, Cognition, and Personality, 36*(2), 92–115. doi: 10.1177/0276236616628278.

Faust, M., & Kenett, Y. N. (2014). Rigidity, chaos and integration: Hemispheric interaction and individual differences in metaphor comprehension. *Frontiers in Human Neuroscience, 8*(511), 1–10. doi: 10.3389/fnhum.2014.00511.

Fearon, D. D., Copeland, D., & Saxon, T. F. (2013). The relationship between parenting styles and creativity in a sample of Jamaican children. *Creativity Research Journal, 25*(1), 119–128. doi: 10.1080/10400419.2013.752287.

Fearon, R. M. P., Tomlinson, M., Kumsta, R., Skeen, S., Murray, L., Cooper, P. J., & Morgan, B. (2017). Poverty, early care, and stress reactivity in adolescence: Findings from a prospective, longitudinal study in South Africa. *Development and Psychopathology, 29*, 449–463. doi: 10.1017/S0954579417000104.

Feigelman, W., Jordan, J. R., McIntosh, J. L., & Feigleman, B. (2012). *Devastating losses: How parents cope with the death of a child to suicide or drugs*. New York, NY: Springer.

Feiring, C., & Taska, L. S. (2005). The persistence of shame following sexual abuse: A longitudinal look at risk and recovery. *Child Maltreatment, 10*(4), 337–349. doi: 10.1177/1077559505276686.

Feist, G. J. (1998). A meta-analysis of personality in scientific and artistic creativity. *Personality and Social Psychology Review, 2*(4), 290–309.

Feist, G. J., & Barron, F. X. (2003). Predicting creativity from early to late adulthood: Intellect, potential, and personality. *Journal of Research in Personality, 37*, 62–88. doi: 10.1016/S0092-6566(02)00526-6.

Felitti, V. J., & Anda, R. F. (2010). The relationship of adverse childhood experiences to adult medical disease, psychiatric disorders and sexual behavior: Implications for healthcare. In R. A. Lanius, E. Vermetten, & C. Pain (Eds.), *The impact of early life trauma on health and disease: The hidden epidemic* (pp. 77–87). Cambridge: Cambridge University Press.

Felitti, V. J., Anda, R. F., Nordenberg, D., Williamson, D. F., Spitz, A. M., Edwards, V., . . . Marks, J. S. (1998). Relationship of childhood abuse and household dysfunction to many of the leading causes of death in adults: The Adverse Childhood Experiences (ACE) study. *American Journal of Preventive Medicine, 14*, 245–258.

Felix, E. D., Dowdy, E., & Green, J. G. (2018). University student voices on healing and recovery following a tragedy. *Psychological Trauma: Theory, Research, Practice, and Policy, 10*(1), 76–86. doi: 10.1037/tra0000172.

Feng, Z., Logan, S., Cupchik, G., Ritterfeld, U., & Gaffin, D. (2017). A cross-cultural exploration of imagination as a process-based concept. *Imagination, Cognition, and Personality, 37*(1), 69–94. doi: 10.1177/0276236617712006.

Fergus, T. A., Valentiner, D. P., McGrath, P. B., & Jencius, S. (2010). Shame- and guilt-proneness: Relationships with anxiety disorder symptoms in a clinical sample. *Journal of Anxiety Disorders, 24*, 811–815. doi: 10.1016/j.janxdis.2010.06.002.

Fernandez-Lansac, V., & Crespo, M. (2017). Quality of memories in women abused by their intimate partner: Analysis of traumatic and non-traumatic narratives. *Journal of Traumatic Stress, 30*, 80–87. doi: 10.1002/jts.22154.

Ferrajao, P. C., Badoud, D., & Oliveira, R. A. (2017). Mental strategies as mediators of the link between attachment and PTSD. *Psychological Trauma: Theory, Research, Practice, and Policy, 9*(6), 731–740. doi: 10.1037/tra0000251.

Ferry, F. R., Brady, S. E., Bunting, B. P., Murphy, S. D., Bolton, D., & O'Neill, S. M. (2015). The economic burden of PTSD in Northern Ireland. *Journal of Traumatic Stress, 28*, 191–197. doi: 10.1002/jts.22008.

Figley, C. R. (1986). *Trauma and its wake: Traumatic stress theory, research and intervention.* New York, NY: Brunner/Mazel.

Filipowicz, A. (2006). From positive affect to creativity: The surprising role of surprise. *Creativity Research Journal, 18*(2), 141–152.

Fincham, D. S., Altes, L. K., Stein, D. J., & Seedat, S. (2009). Posttraumatic stress disorder symptoms in adolescents: Risk factors and resilienc moderation. *Comprehensive Psychoatry, 50*, 193–199. doi: 10.1016/j.comppsych.2008.09.001.

Fink, A., Benedeck, M., Grabner, R. H., Staudt, B., & Neubauer, A. C. (2007). Creativity meets neuroscience: Experimental tasks for the neuroscientific study of creative thinking. *Methods, 42*, 68–76. doi: 10.1016/j.ymet.2006.12.001.

Fink, A., Weber, B., Koschutnig, K., Benedek, M., Reishofer, G., Ebner, F., Papousek, I., & Weiss, E. M. (2014). Creativity and schizotypy from the neuroscience perspective. *Cognition, Affect, Behavior and Neuroscience, 14*, 378–387. doi: 10.3758/s13415-013-0210-6.

Finke, R. A. (1996). Imagery, creativity, and emergent structure. *Consciousness and Cognition, 5*, 381–393.

Finkelhor, D. (2017). Screening for adverse childhood experiences: Cautions and suggestions. *Child Abuse and Neglect, (In Press)*, 1–6. doi: 10.1016/j.chiabu.2017.07.016.

Finkelhor, D., Hammer, H., & Sedlak, A. J. (2008). *Sexually assaulted children: National estimates and characteristics.* U.S. Department of Justice, Office of Juvenile Justice and Delinquency Prevention, NISMART Publications, 1–12.

Finkelhor, D., Ormrod, R. K., & Turner, H. A. (2009). Lifetime assessment of polyvictimization in a national sample of children and youth. *Child Abuse and Neglect, 33*, 403–411. doi: 10.1016/j.chiabu.2008.09.012.

Finkelhor, D., Shattuck, A., Turner, H. A., Ormrod, R. K., & Hamby, S. L. (2011). Polyvictimization in developmental context. *Journal of Child & Adolescent Trauma*, 4(4), 291–300.

Fiorillo, D., Papa, A., & Follette, V. M. (2013). The relationship between child physical abuse and victimization in dating relationships: The role of experiential avoidance. *Psychological Trauma: Theory, Research, Practice, and Policy, 5*(6), 562–569. doi: 10.1037/a0030968.

Firth, L., Alderson-Day, B., Woods, N., & Fernyhough, C. (2015). Imaginary companions in childhood: Relations to imagination skills and autobiographical memory in adults. *Creativity Research Journal, 27*(4), 308–313. doi: 10.1080/10400419.2015.1087240.

Fisher, J. E., Mohanty, A., Herrington, J. D., Koven, N. S., Miller, G. A., & Heller, W. (2004). Neuropsychological evidence for dimensional schizotypy: Implications for creativity and psychopathology. *Journal of Research in Personality, 38*(1), 24–31. doi: 10.1016/j.jrp.2003.09.014.

Fivish, R., Booker, J. A., & Graci, M. E. (2017). Ongoing narrative meaning-making within events and across the life span. *Imagination, Cognition and Personality, 37*(2), 127–152. doi: 10.1177/0276236617733824.

Fleming, A. S., Kraemer, G. W., Gonzalez, A., Lovic, V., Rees, S., & Melo, A. (2002). Mothering begets mothering: The transmission of behavior and its neurobiology acros generations. *Pharmacology, Biochemistry and Behavior, 73*, 61–75.

Florian, V., Mikulincer, M., & Hirschberger, G. (2001). An existentialist view on mortality salience effects: Personal hardiness, death-thought accessibility, and cultural worldview defence. *British Journal of Social Psychology, 40*, 437–453.

Florida, R. (October, 2004). Americas looming creativity crisis. *Harvard Business Review*, pp. 1–9. Retrieved from www.hbr.org R0410H.

Foa, E. B., & Rothbaum, B. O. (1998). *Treating the trauma of rape: Cognitive-behavioral therapy for PTSD*. New York, NY: Guilford Press.

Foa, E. B., Riggs, D. S., Massie, E. D., & Yarczower, M. (1995). The impact of fear activation and anger on the efficacy of exposure treatment for post-traumatic stress disorder. *Behavior Therapy, 26*, 487–499. doi: 10.1016/S0005-7894(05)80096-6.

Foilb, A. R., & Christianson, J. P. (2016). Serotonin 2C receptor antagonist improves fear discrimination and subsequent safety signal recall. *Progress in Neuropsychopharmacology and Biological Psychiatry, 65*, 78–84. doi: 10.1016/j.pnpbp.2015.08017.

Foote, B., Smolin, Y., Kaplan, M., Legatt, M. E., & Lipschitz, D. (2006). Prevalance of dissociative disorders in psychiatric outpatients. *American Journal of Psychiatry, 163*(4), 623–629.

Foote, B., Smolin, Y., Neft, D. I., & Lipschitz, D. (2008). Dissociative disorders and suicidality in psychiatric outpatients. *Journal of Nervous and Mental Disease, 196*(1), 29–36. doi: 10.1097/NMD.0b013e31815fa4e7.

Forbes, D., Lockwood, E., Phelps, A., Wade, D., Creamer, M., Bryant, R. A., ... O'Donell, M. (2014). Trauma at the hands of another: Distinguishing PTSD patterns following intimate and nonintimate interpersonal and noninterpersonal trauma in anationally representative sample. *Journal of Clinical Psychiatry, 75*(2), 147–153. doi: 10.4088/JCP.13m08374.

Ford, J. D., & Gomez, J. M. (2015). Self-injury and suicidality: The impact of trauma and dissociation. *Journal of Trauma and Dissociation, 16*, 225–231. doi: 10.1080/15299752.2015.989648.

———. (2105a). The relationship of psychological trauma and dissociative and posttraumatic stress disorders to nonsuicidal self-injury and suicidality: A review. *Journal of Trauma and Dissociation, 16*, 232–271. doi: 10,1080/15299732.2015.989563.

Forgeard, M. J. C. (2013). Perceiving benefits after adversity: The relationship between self-reported posttraumatic growth and creativity. *Psychology of Aesthetics, Creativity, and the Arts, 7*(3), 245–264. doi: 10.1037/a0031223.

Forgeard, M. J. C., & Kaufman, J. C. (2015). Who cares about imagination, creativity, and innovation and why? A review. *Psychology of Aesthetics, Creativity, and the Arts, 10*(3), 250–269. doi: 10.1037/aca000042.

Fornia, G. L., & Frame, M. W. (2001). The social and emotional needs of gifted children: Implications for family counseling. *The Family Journal, 9*(4), 384–390. doi: 10.1177/1066480701094005.

Foster, P. S., Webster, D. G., & Williamson, J. (2003). The psychophysiological differentiation of actual, imagined, and recollected mirth. *Imagination, Cognition, and Personality, 22*(2), 163–180.

Fourie, M. M., Rauch, H. L., Morgan, B. E., Ellis, G. F. R., Jordaan, E. R., & Thomas, K. G. F. (2011). Guilt and pride are heartfelt, but not equally so. *Psychophysiology, 48*, 888–899. doi: 10.1111/j.1469-8986.2010.01157x.

Fowke, A., Ross, S., & Ashcroft, K. (2012). Childhood maltreatment and internalized shame inadults with a diagnosis of bipolar disorder. *Clinical Psychology and Psychotherapy, 19*, 450–457. doi: 10.1002/cpp.752.

Foynes, M. M., Platt, M., Hall, G. C. N., & Freyd, J. J. (2014). The impact of Asian values and victim-perpetrator closeness on the disclosure of emotional, physical, and sexual abuse. *Psychological Trauma: Theory, Research, Practice, and Policy, 6*(2), 134–141. doi: 10.1037/a0032098.

Fraley, R. C., & Bonanno, G. A. (2004). Attachmen and loss: A test of three competing models on the association between attachment related avoidance and adaptation to bereavement. *Personality and Social Psychology, 30*(7), 878–890. doi: 10.1177/0146167204264289.

Franklin, M. S., Moore, K. S., Yip, C.-Y., Jonides, J., Rattray, K., & Moher, J. (2008). The effects of musical training on verbal memory. *Psychology of Music, 36*(3), 1–13. doi: 10.1177/0305735607086044.

Franklin, T. B., Russig, H., Weiss, I. C., Graff, J., Linder, N., Michalon, A., ... Mansuy, I. M. (2010). Epigenetic transmission of the impact of early stress across generations. *Biological Psychiatry, 68*, 408–415. doi: 10.1016/j.biopsych.2010.05.036.

Fredrickson, B. L. (2004). The broaden-and-build theory of positive emotions. *Philosophical Transactions, 359*(1449), 1367–1378. doi: 10.1098/rstb.2004.1512.

Freed, S., & D'Andrea, W. (2015). Autonomic arousal and emotion in victims of interpersonal violence: Shame proneness but not anxiety predicts vagal tone. *Journal of Trauma and Dissociation, 16*, 367–383. doi: 10.1080/15299732.2015.1004771.

Freedberg, D., & Gallese, V. (2007). Motion, emotion and empathy in esthetic experience. *Trends in Cognitive Sciences, 11*(5), 197–203. doi: 10.1016/j.tics.2007.02.003.

Freeman, W. J. (2000). *How brains make up their minds.* New York: Columbia University Press.

Frey, L. L., Beesley, D., Abbott, D., & Kendrick, E. (2017). Vicarious resilience in sexual assault and domestic violence advocates. *Psychological Trauma: Theory, Research, Practice, and Policy, 9*(1), 44–51. doi: 10.1037/tra0000159.

Freyd, J. J., DePrince, A. P., & Gleaves, D. H. (2012). The state of betrayal trauma theory: Reply to McNally–conceptual issues, and further directions. *Memory, 15*(3), 295–311. doi: 10.1080/09658210701256514.

Friedman, B. (2007). An autonomic flexibility-neurovisceral integration model of anxiety and cardiac vagal tone. *Biological Psychology, 74*(2), 185–199.

Friedman, R. S., & Forster, J. (2001). The effects of promotion and prevention cues on creativity. *Journal of Personality and Social Psychology, 81*(6), 1001–1013. doi: 10.1037//0022-3514.81.6.1001.

Fritz, B. S., & Avsec, A. (2007). The experience of flow and subjective well-being of music students. *Horizons of Psychology, 16*(2), 5–17.

Frye, N. (1963). *The educated imagination.* Toronto, Canada: Canadian Broadcasting Organization.

Fryer, M. (2012). Some key issues in creativity research and evaluation as seen from a psychological perspective. *Creativity Research Journal, 24*(1), 24–28. doi: 10.1080/10400419.2012.649236.

Fuchs, G. L., Kumar, V. K., & Porter, J. (2007). Emotional creativity, alexithymia, and styles of creativity. *Creativity Research Journal, 19*(2–3), 233–245. doi: 10.1080/10400410701397313.

Fuller-Thomson, E., & Brennenstuhl, S. (2009). Making a link between childhood physical abuse and cancer: Results from a regional representative survey. *Cancer, 115*, 3341–3350. doi: 10.1002/cncr.24372.

Fuller-Thomson, E., Brennenstuhl, S., & Frank, J. (2010). The association between childhood physical abuse and heart disease in adulthood: Findings from a representative community sample. *Child Abuse and Neglect, 34*, 689–698. doi: 10.1016/j.chiabu.2010.02.005.

Fuller-Thomson, E., Sulman, J., Brennenstuhl, S., & Merchant, M. (2011). Functional somatic syndromes and childhood physical abuse in women: Data from a representative community-based sample. *Journal of Aggression, Maltreatment and Trauma, 20*(4), 445–469. doi: 10.1080/10926771.2011.566035.

Furnham, A., & Bachtiar, V. (2008). Personality and intelligence as predictors of creativity. *Personality and Individual Differences, 45*, 613–617. doi: 10.1016/j.paid.2008.06.023.

Gagnon, K. L., & DePrince, A. P. (2017). Head injury screening and intimate partner violence: A brief review. *Journal of Trauma and Dissociation, 18*(4), 490–506. doi: 10.1080/15299732.2016.1252001.

Gajda, A., Karwowski, M., & Beghetto, R. A. (2017). Creativity and academic achievement: A meta-analysis. *Journal of Educational Psychology, 109*(2), 269–299. doi: 10.1037/edu0000133.

Galatzer-Levy, I. R., Nickerson, A., Litz, B. T., & Marmar, C. R. (2013). Patterns of lifetime PTSD comorbidity: A latent class analysis. *Depression and Anxiety, 30*, 489–496. doi: 10.1002/da.22048.

Gallagher, H. C., Richardson, J., Forbes, D., Harms, L., Gibbs, L. Alkemade, N., … Bryant, R. A. (2016). Mental health following separation in a disaster: Thr role of attachment. *Journal of Traumatic Stress, 29*, 54–64. doi: 10.1002/jts.22071.

Galovski, T., & Lyons, J. A. (2004). Psychological sequelae of combat violence: A review of the impact of PTSD on the veteran's family and possible interventions. *Aggression and Violent Behavior, 9,* 477–501. doi: 10.1016/S1359-1789(03)00045-4.

Garcia, F. E., Duque, A., & Cova, F. (2017). The four faces of rumination to stressful events: A psychometric analysis. *Psychological Trauma: Theory, Research, Practice, and Policy, 9*(6), 758–765. doi: 10.1037/tra0000289.

Garcini, L. M., Pena, J. M., Gutierrez, A. P., Fagundes, C. P., Lemus, H., Lindsay, S., & Klonoff, E. A. (2017). "One scar too many:" The association between traumatic events and psychological distress among undocumented Mexican immigrants. *Journal of Traumatic Stress, 30,* 453–462. doi: 10.1002/jts.22216.

Gardner, H. (1983). *Frames of the mind: The theory of multiple intelligences.* New York: Basic Books.

———. (1993). *Creating minds.* New York, NY: Basic Books.

Garfin, D. R., Poulin, M. J., Blum, S., & Silver, R. C. (2018). Aftermath of terror: A nationwide longitudinal study of posttraumatic stress and worry across the decade following the September 11, 2001 terrorist attacks. *Journal of Traumatic Stress, 31,* 146–156. doi: 10.1002/jts.22262.

Garland, E. L., Farb, N. A. R., Goldwin, P., & Frerickson, B. L. (2015). Mindfulness broadens awareness and builds eudaimonic meaning: A process model of mindful positive emotion regulation. *Psychological Inquiry, 26,* 293–314. doi: 10.1080/1047840X.2015.1064294.

Garrido, S., & Schubert, E. (2011). Individual differences in the enjoyment of negative emotion in music: A literature review and experiment. *Music Perception: An Interdisciplinary Journal, 28*(3), 279–296. doi: 10.1525/mp.2011.28.3.279.

Gaylord-Harden, N. K., Bai, G. J., & Simic, D. (2017). Examining a dual-process model of desensitization and hypersensitization to community violence in African American male adolescents. *Journal of Traumatic Stress, 30,* 463–471. doi: 10.1002/jts.22220.

Gaztambide-Fernandez, R. A., Saifer, A., & Desai, C. (2013). "Talent" and the misrecognition of social advantage in specialized arts education. *Roeper Review, 35,* 124–135. doi: 10.1080/02783193.2013.766964.

Gedaly, L. R., & Leerkes, E. M. (2016). The role of sociodemographic risk and maternal behavior in the prediction of infant attachment disorganization. *Attachment and Human Development, 18*(6), 554–569. doi: 10.1080/14616734.2016.1213306.

Geisler, F. C., & Kubiak, T. (2009). Heart rate variability predicts self-control in goal pursuit. *European Journal of Personality, 23,* 623–633. doi: 10.1002/per.727.

George, J. M., & Zhou, J. (2002). Understanding when bad moods foster creativity and good ones don't: The role of context and clarity of feelings. *Journal of Applied Psychology, 87*(4), 687–697. doi: 10.1037//0021-9010.87.4.687.

Ghacibeh, G. A., Shenker, J. I., Shenal, B., Uthman, B. M., & Heilman, K. M. (2006). Effect of vagus nerve stimulation on creativity and cognitive flexibility. *Epilepsy and Behavior, 8,* 720–725. doi: 10.1016/j.yebeh.2006.03.008.

Gibbs, R. W. (2003). Embodied experience and linguistic meaning. *Brain and Language, 84,* 1–15.

Gibson, C., Folley, B. S., & Park, S. (2009). Enhanced divergent thinking and creativity in musicians: A behavioral and near-infrared spectroscopy study. *Brain and Cognition, 69*, 162–169. doi: 10.1016/j.bandc.2008.07.009.

Giesbrecht, T., & Merckelbach, H. (2006). Dreaming to reduce fantasy? – Fantasy proneness, dissociation, and subjective sleep experiences. *Personality and Individual Differences, 41*(4), 697–706. doi: 10.1016/j.paid.2006.02.015.

Giesbrecht, T., Geraerts, E., & Merckelbach, H. (2007). Dissociation, memory commission errors, and heightened autonomic reactivity. *Psychiatry Research, 150*(3), 277–285. doi: 10.1016/j.psychres.2006.04.016.

Giesbrecht, T., Merckelbach, H., & Geraerts, E. (2007). The dissociative experiences taxon is related to fantasy proneness. *Journal of Nervous and Mental Disease, 195*(9), 769–772. doi: 10.1097/NMD.obo13e318142ce55.

Giesbrecht, T., Merckelbach, H., van Oorsouw, K., & Simeon, D. (2010). Skin conductance and memory fragmentation after exposure to an emotional film clip in depersonalization disorder. *Psychiatry Research, 177*, 342–349. doi: 10.1016/j.psychres.2010.03.010.

Giesbrecht, T., Smeets, T., Merchelbach, H., & Jelicic, M. (2007). Depersonalization experience in undergraduates are related to heightened stress cortisol responses. *Journal of Nervous Mental Disorders, 195*, 282–287. doi: 10.1097/01.nmd.0000253822.60618.60.

Gil, S., & Weinberg, M. (2015). Coping strategies and internal resources of dispositional optimism and mastery as predictors of traumatic exposure and of PTSD symptoms: A prospective study. *Psychological Trauma: Theory, Research, Practice, and Policy, 7*(4), 405–411. doi: 10.1037/tra0000032.

Gil, S., Weinberg, M., Shamai, M., Ron, P., Harel, H., & Or-Chen, K. (2016). Risk factors for DSM-5 Posttraumatic Stress Symptoms (PTSS) among Israeli civilians during the 2014 Israel-Hamas war. *Psychological Trauma: Theory, Research, Practice, and Policy, 8*(1), 49–54. doi: 10.1037/tra0000063.

Gilbert, P. (2000). Anxiety and depression: The role of the evaluation of social rank. *Clinical Psychologyand Psychotherapy, 7*, 174–189.

———. (2002). Body shame: A biopsychosocial conceptualization and overview with treatment implications. In P. Gilbert & J. Miles (Eds.), *Body shame: Conceptualization, research & treatment* (pp. 3–54). Hove, UK: Brunner-Routledge.

Gilbert, P., McEwan, K., Matos, M., & Rivis, A. (2011). Fears of compassion: Development of three self-report measures. *Psychology and Psychotherapy: Theory, Research, and Practice, 84*, 239–255. doi: 10.1348/147608310X526511.

Gill, P., Horgan, J., Hunter, S. J., & Cushenbery, L. D. (2013). Malevolent creativity in terrorists organizations. *Journal of Criminal Behavior, 47*(2), 125–151. doi: 10.1002/jocb.28.

Gillespie, C. F., Phifer, J., Bradley, B., & Ressler, K. J. (2009). Risk and resilience: Genetic and environmental influences on development of the stress response. *Depression and Anxiety, 26*(11), 984–992. doi: 10.1002/da.20605.

Gilman, R., Schumm, J. A., & Chard, K. M. (2012). Hope as a change mechanism in the treatment of posttraumatic stress disorder. *Psychological Trauma: Theory, Research, Practice, and Policy, 4*(3), 270–277. doi: 10.1037/a0024252.

Ginzburg, K., Butler, L. D., Giese-Davis, J., Cavanaugh, C. E., Neri, E., Koopman, C., ... Spiegel, D. (2009). Shame, guilt, and posttraumatic stress disorder in adult survivors of childhood sexual abuse at risk for human immunodeficiency virus: Outcomes of a randomized clinical trial of group psychotherapy treatment. *Journal of Nervous and Mental Disease, 197*(7), 536–542. doi: 10.1097/NMD.0b013e3181ab2ebd.

Gladkevich, A., Korf, J., Kaobyan, V. P., & Melkonyan, K. V. (2006). The peripheral GABAergic system as a target in endocrine disorders. *Autonomic Neuroscience: Basic and Clinical, 124*, 1–8. doi: 10.1016/j.autoneur.2005.11.002.

Glaser, D. (2002). Emotional abuse and neglect (psychological maltreatment): A conceptual framework. *Child Abuse and Neglect, 26*, 697–714.

Gleason, T. R. (2002). Social provisions of real and imaginary relationship in early childhood. *Developmental Psychology, 38*(6), 979–992. doi: 10.1037//0012-1649.38.6.979.

Glimcher, P. W. (2011). Understanding dopamine and reinforcement learning: The dopamine reward prediction error hypothesis. *Proceedings of the National Academy of Science, 108*(3), 15647–15654. doi: 10.1073/pnas.1014269108.

Gluck, J., Ernst, R., & Unger, F. (2002). How creative define creativity: Definitions reflect different types of creativity. *Creativity Research Journal, 14*(1), 55–67.

Godbout, N., Daspe, M.-E., Lussier, Y., Sabourin, S., Dutton, D., & Hebert, M. (2017). Early exposure to violence, relationship violence, and relationship satisfaction in adolescents and emerging adults: The role of romantic attachment. *Psychological Trauma: Theory, Research, Practice, and Policy, 9*(2), 127–137. doi: 10.1037/tra0000136.

Goldsmith, R. E., Freyd, J. J., & DePrince, A. P. (2012). Betrayal trauma: Assumptions with psychological and physical symptoms in young adults. *Journal of Interpersonal Violence, 27*, 547–567. doi: 10.1177/0886260511421672.

Goldstein, A. L., Flett, G. L., Wekerle, C., & Wall, A.-M. (2009). Personality, child maltreatment, and substance use: Examining correlates of deliberate self-harm among university students. *Canadian Journal of Behavioral Science, 41*(4), 241–251. doi: 10.1037/a0014847.

Golland, Y., Keissar, K., & Levit-Binnun, N. (2014). Studying the dynamics of autonomic activity during emotional experience. *Psychophysiology, 51*(11), 1101–1111. doi: 10.1111/psyp.12261.

Goncalo, J. A., & Staw, B. M. (2006). Individualism-collectivism and group creativity. *Organizational Behavior and Human Decision Processes, 100*(1), 96–109. doi: 10.1016/j.obhdp.2005.11.003.

Gonzalez, O. I., Novaco, R. W., Reger, M. A., & Gahm, G. A. (2016). Anger intensification with combat-related PTSD and depression comborbidity. *Psychological Trauma: Theory, Research, Practice, and Policy, 8*(1), 9–16. doi: 10.1037/tra0000042.

Goodman, M., Weiss, D. S., Mitropoulou, V., New, A., Koenigsberg, H., Silverman, J. M., & Siever, L. (2003). The relationship between pathological dissociation, self-injury and childhood trauma in patients with personality disorders using taxometric analyses. *Journal of Trauma and Dissociation, 4*(2), 65–88. doi: 10.1300/J229v04n02_05.

Gordon, A. M., Stellar, J. E., Anderson, C. L., McNeil, G. D., Loew, D., & Keltner, D. (2016). The dark side of the sublime: Distinguishing a threat-based variant of awe. *Journal of Personality and Social Psychology, 113*, 310–328. doi: 10.1037/pspp0000120.

Goss, K., & Allan, S. (2009). Shame, pride and eating disorders. *Clinical Psychology and Psychotherapy, 16*, 303–316. doi: 10.1002/cpp.627.

Gotby, O. V., Lichtenstein, P., Langstrom, N., & Pettersson, E. (2018). Childhood neurodevelopmental disorders and risk of coercive sexual victimization in childhood and adolescence: A population-based prospective twin study. *Journal of Child Psychology and Psychiatry, e-publ.* doi: 10.1111/jcpp.12884.

Gover, A. R., Kaukinen, C., & Fox, K. A. (2008). The relationship between violence in the family of origin and dating violence among college students. *Journal of Interpersonal Violence, 23*, 1667–1693. doi: 10.1177/0886260508314330.

Gow, K., Lang, T., & Chant, D. (2004). Fantasy proneness, paranormal beliefs and personality features in out-of-body experiences. *Contemporary Hypnosis, 21*(3), 107–125. doi: 10.1002/ch.296.

Gradus, J. L., King, M. W., Galatzer-Levy, I., & Street, A. E. (2017). Gender differences in machine learning models of trauma and suicidal ideation in veterans of the Iraq and Afghanistan war. *Journal of Traumatic Stress, 30*, 362–371. doi: 10.1002/jts.22210.

Granqvist, P., Fransson, M., & Hagekull, B. (2009). Disorganized attachment, absorption, and new age spirituality: A mediational model. *Attachment & Human Development, 11*(4), 385–403. doi: 10.1080/14616730903016995.

Granqvist, P., Hagekull, B., & Ivarsson, T. (2012). Disorganized attachment promotes mystical experiences via a propensity for alterations in consciousness (absorption). *International Journal for the Psychology of Religion, 22*(3), 180–197. doi: 10.1080/10508619.2012.670012.

Granqvist, P., Ivarsson, T., Broberg, A. G., & Hagekull, B. (2007). Examining relations among attachment, religiosity, and New Age spirituality using the Adult Attachment Interview. *Developmental Psychology, 43*, 590–601. doi: 10.1037/0012-1649.43.3.590.

Granqvist, P., Sroufe, L. A., Dozier, M., Hesse, E., Steele, M., van IJzendoorn, M., ... Duschinsky, R. (2017). Disorganized attachment in infancy: A review of the phenomenon and its implications for clinicans and policy-makers. *Attachment and Human Development, 19*(6), 534–558. doi: 10.1080/14616734.2017.1354040.

Grasso, D. J., Petitclerc, A., Henry, D. B., McCarthy, K. J., Wakschlag, L. S., & Briggs-Gowan, M. J. (2016). Examining patterns of exposure to family violence in preschool children: A latent class approach. *Journal of Traumatic Stress, 29*, 491–499. doi: 10.1002/jts.22147.

Gratz, K. L., & Chapman, A. L. (2007). The role of emotional responding and childhood maltreatment in the development and maintenance of deliberate self-harm in male undergraduates. *Psychology of Men and Masculinity, 8*(1), 1–14. doi: 10.1037/1524-9220.8.1.1.

Gratz, K. L., & Roemer, L. (2004). Multidimensional assessment of emotion regulation and dysregulation: Development, factor structure, and initial validation of the Difficulties in Emotion Regulation Scale. *Journal of Psychopathology and Behavioral Assessment, 26*(1), 41–54.

Green, B. L., Kaltman, S. I., Chung, J. Y., Holt, M. P., Jackson, S., & Dozier, M. (2012). Attachment and health care relationships in low-income women with trauma histories: A qualitative study. *Journal of Trauma and Dissociation, 13*(2), 190–208. doi: 10.1080/15299732.2012.642761.

Green, M. J., & Williams, L. M. (1999). Schizoptypy and creativity as effects of reduced cognitive inhibition. *Personality and Individual Differences, 27*, 263–276.

Green, M. J., Tzoumakis, S., McIntyre, B., Kariuki, M., Laruens, K. R., Dean, K., ... Carr, V. J. (2017). Childhood maltreatment and early developmental vulnerabilities at age five years. *Child Development*, Online Version of Record. doi: 10.1111/cdev.12928.

Greenberg, J., Pyszczynski, T., & Solomon, S. (1986). The causes and consequences of a need for self-esteem: A terror management theory. In R. F. Baumeister (Ed.), *Public self and private self* (pp. 189–212). New York, NY: Springer-Verlag.

Gregerson, M. B. (2007). Creativity enhances practitioners' resiliency and effectiveness after a hometown disaster. *Professional Psychology: Research and Practice, 38*(6), 596–602. doi: 10.1037/0735-7028.38.6.596.

Griskevicius, V., Cialdini, R. B., & Kenrick, D. T. (2006). Peacocks, Picasso, and parental investment: The effects of romantic motives on creativity. *Journal of Personality and Social Psychology, 91*(1), 63–76. doi: 10.1037/0022.3514.91.1.63.

Groff, E. C., Ruzek, J. I., Bongar, B., & Cordova, M. J. (2016). Social constraints, loss-related factors, depression, and posttraumatic stress in a treatment-seeking suicide bereaved sample. *Psychological Trauma: Theory, Research, Practice, and Policy, 8*(6), 657–660. doi: 10.1037/tra0000128.

Groh, A. M., Fearon, R. M. P., van IJzendoorn, M. H., Bakermans-Kranenburg, M. J., & Roisman, G. I. (2017). Attachment in the early life course: Meta-analytic evidence for its role in socioemotional development. *Chidl Development Perspective, 11*(1), 70–76. doi: 10.1111/cdep.12213.

Groh, A. M., Narayan, A. J., Bakermans-Kranenburg, M. J., Roisman, G. I., Vaughn, B. E., Fearon, R. M. P., & van IJzendoorn, M. H. (2017). Attachment and temperament in the early life course: A meta-analytic review. *Child Development, 88*(3), 770–795. doi: 10.1111/cdev.12677.

Gronli, J., Melinder, A., Ousdal, O. T., Pallesen, S., Endestad, T., & Milde, A. M. (2017). Life threat and sleep disturbances in adolescents: A two-year follow-up of survivors from the 2011 Utoya, Norway, terror attack. *Journal of Traumatic Stress, 30*, 219–228. doi: 10.1002/jts.22196.

Gross, J. J., & Thompson, R. A. (2007). Emotion regulation: Conceptual foundations. In J. J. Gross (Ed.), *Handbook of emotion regulation* (pp. 3–46). New York: Guilford Press.

Grossman, F. K., Sorsoli, L., & Kia-Keating, M. (2006). A gale force wind: Meaning making by male survivors of childhood sexual abuse. *American Journal of Orthopsychiatry, 76*(4), 434–443. doi: 10.1037/0002-9432.76.4.434.

Grubaugh, A., Zinzow, H. M., Paul, L., Egede, L. E., & Frueh, B. C. (2011). Trauma exposure and posttraumatic stress disorder in adults with severe mental illness:

A critical review. *Clinical Psychology Review, 31*, 883–899. doi: 10.1016/j.cpr.2011.04.003.

Gruzelier, J. (2009). The theory of alpha/theta neurofeedback, creative performance enhancement, long distance functional connectivity and psychological integration. *Cognitive Process, 10*(Suppl. 1), S101–S109. doi: 10.1007/s10339-008-0248-5.

———. (2014). EEG-neurofeedback for optimizing performance. II: Creativity, the performing arts and ecological validity. *Neuroscience and Biobehavioral Reviews, 44*, 142–158. doi: 10.1016/j.neurbiorev.2013.11.004.

Grysman, A., & Mansfiled, C. D. (2017). What do we have when we have a narrative? *Imagination, Cognition and Personality, 37*(2), 105–126. doi: 10.1177/0276236617733823.

Guarnaccia, P. J., Martinez, L., Ramirez, R., & Canino, G. (2005). Are ataques de nervios in Puerto Rican children associated with psychiatric disorder? *Journal of American Academy of Child and Adolescent Psychiatry, 44*, 1184–1192. doi: 10.1097/01.chi.000017059.34031.5d.

Guffanti, G., Geronazzo-Alman, L., Fan, B., Durate, C. S., Musa, G. J., & Hoven, C. W. (2016). Homogeneity of severe posttraumatic stress disorder symptom profiles in children and adolescents across gender, age, and traumatic experiences related to 9/11. *Journal of Traumatic Stress, 29*, 430–439. doi: 10.1002/jts.22134.

Guild, D. J., Toth, S. L. Handley, E. D., Rogosch, F. A., & Cicchetti, D. (2017). Attachment security mediates the longitudinal association between child-parent psychotherapy and peer relations for toddlers of depressed mothers. *Delvopment and Psychopathology, 29*, 587–600. doi: 10.1017/S0954579417000207.

Gul, E., & Karanci, A. N. (2017). What determines posttraumatic stress and growth following various traumatic events? A study in a Turkish community sample. *Journal of Traumatic Stress, 30*, 54–62. doi: 10.1002/jts.22161.

Gunty, A. L., Frazier, P. A., Tennen, H., Tomich, P., Tahsiro, T., & Park, C. (2011). Moderators of the relation between perceived and actual posttraumatic growth. *Psychological Trauma: Theory, Research, Practice, and Policy, 3*(1), 61–66. doi: 10.1037/a0020485.

Guralnik, O., Giesbrecht, T., Knutelska, M., Sirroff, B., & Simeon, D. (2007). Cognitive functioning in depersonalization disorder. *Journal of Nervous and Mental Disease, 195*(12), 983–988. doi: 10.1097/NMD.obo13e31815c19cd.

Gusic, S., Cardena, E., Bengtsson, H., & Sondergaard, H. P. (2016). Types of trauma in adolescence and their relation to dissociation: A mixed-methods study. *Psychological Trauma: Theory, Research, Practice, and Policy, 8*(5), 568–576. doi: 10.1037/tra0000099.

Gute, D., & Gute, G. (2015). *How creativity works in the brain*. Washington, DC: National Endowment for the Arts.

Gute, G., Gute, D. S., Nakamura, J., & Csikszentmihalyi, M. (2008). The early lives of highly creative persons: The influence of the complex family. *Creativity Research Journal, 20*(4), 343–357. doi: 10.1080/10400410802391207.

Gutworth, M. B., & Hunter, S. T. (2017). Ethical saliency: Deterring deviance in creative individuals. *Psychology of Aesthetics, Creativity, and the Arts, 11*(4), 428–439. doi: 10.1037/aca.0000093.

Hagan, M. J., Hulette, A. C., & Lieberman, A. (2015). Symptoms of dissociation in a high-risk sample of young children exposed to interpersonal trauma. Prevalence, correlates, and contributors. *Journal of Traumatic Stress, 28*, 258–261. doi: 10.1002/jts.22003.

Hagenaars, M. A., van Minnen, A., & Hoogduin, K. A. L. (2010). The impact of dissociation and depression on the efficacy of prolonged exposure therapy for PTSD. *Behavior Research and Therapy, 48*, 19–27. doi: 10.1016/j.brat.2009.09.001.

Haldane, J., & Nickerson, A. (2016). The impact of interpersonal and noninterpersonal trauma on psychological symptoms in refugees: The moderating role of gender and trauma type. *Journal of Traumatic Stress, 29*, 457–465. doi: 10.1002/jts.22132.

Hall, B. J., Hobfoll, S. E., Palmieri, P. A., Canetti-Nisim, D., Shapira, O., Johnson, R. J., & Galea, S. (2008). The psychological impact of impending forces settler disengagement in Gaza: Trauma and posttraumatic growth. *Journal of Traumatic Stress, 21*(1), 22–29. doi: 10.1002/jts.20301.

Hall, H. K., & Hill, A. P. (2012). Perfectionism, dysfunctional achievement striving and burnout in aspiring athletes: The motivational implications for performing artists. *Theatre, Dance and Performance Training, 3*(2), 216–228. doi: 10.1080/194432927.2012.693534.

Hallam, S. (2002). Musical motivation: Towards a model synthesizing the research. *Music Education Research, 4*(2), 225–244. doi: 10.1080/146138002200001193.9.

Hall-Clark, B. N., Kaczkurkin, A., Asnaani, A., Peterson, A. L., Yarvis, J. S., Borah, E. V., ... Foa, E. B. (2017). Ethnoracial differences in PTSD symptoms and trauma-related cognitions in treatment seeking active duty military personnel for PTSD. *Psychological Trauma: Theory, Research, Practice, and Policy, 9*(6), 741–745. doi: 10.1037/tra0000242.

Haller, C. S., & Courvoisier, D. S. (2010). Personality and thinking style in different creative domains. *Psychology of Aesthetics, Creativity, and the Arts, 4*(3), 149–160. doi: 10.1037/a0017084.

Hallett, M. G., & Hoffman, B. (2014). Performing under pressure: Cultivating the peak performance mindset for workplace excellence. *Counselling Psychology Journal: Practice and Research, 66*(3), 212–230. doi: 10.1037/cpb000009.

Hallings-Pott, C., Waller, G., Watson, D., & Scragg, P. (2005). State dissociation in bulimic eating disorders: An experimental study. *International Journal of Eating Disorders, 38*(1), 37–41.

Hamby, S., Taylor, E., Grych, J., & Banyard, V. (2016). A naturalistic study of narrative: Exploring the choice and impact of adversity versus other narrative topics. *Psychological Trauma: Theory, Research, Practice, and Policy, 8*(4), 477–486. doi: 10.1037/tra0000133.

Hankin, B. L. (2005). Childhood maltreatment and psychopathology: Prospective tests of attachment, cognitive vulnerability, and stress as mediating processes. *Cognitive Therapy and Research, 29*(6), 645–671. doi: 10.1007/s10608-005-9631-z.

Hanley, A. W., Garland, E. L., & Tedeschi, R. G. (2017). Relating dispositional mindfulness, contemplative practice, and positive reappraisal with posttraumatic cognitive coping, stress, and growth. *Psychological Trauma: Theory, Research, Practice, and Policy, 9*(5), 526–536. doi: 10.1037/tra0000208.

Hannah, S. T., Sweeney, P. J., & Lester, P. B. (2007). Toward a courageous mindset: The subjective act and experience of courage. *The Journal of Positive Psychology, 2*(2), 129–135. doi: 10.1080/17439760701228854.

Hannam, K., & Narayan, A. (2015). Intrinsic motivation, organizational justice, and creativity. *Creativity Research Journal, 27*(2), 214–224. doi: 10.10400419.2015.1030307.

Hanrahan, C., & Vergeer, I. (2000–2001). Multiple uses of mental imagery by professional modern dancers. *Imagination, Cognition and Personality, 20*(3), 231–255.

Harari, D., Bakermans-Kranenburg, M. J., de Kloet, C. S., Geuze, E., Vermetten, E., Westenberg, H. G. M., & van IJzendoorn, M. H. (2009). Attachment representations in Dutch veterans with and without deployment-related PTSD. *Attachment & Human Development, 11*(6), 515–536. doi: 10.1080/14616730903282480.

Hardy, L., Barlow, M., Evans, L., Rees, T., Woodman, T., & Warr, C. (2017). Great British medalists: Psychosocial biographies of super-elite and elite athletes from Olympic sports. *Progress in Brain Research, 232*, 1–119. doi: 10.1016/bs.pbr.2017.03.004.

Hargreaves, D. J. (2012). Musical imagination: Perception and production, beauty and creativity. *Psychology of Music, 40*(5), 539–557. doi: 10.1077/0305735612444893.

Harmison, R. J. (2006). Peak performance in sport: Identifying ideal performance states and developing athletes' psychological skills. *Professional Psychology: Research and Practice, 37*(3), 233–243. doi: 10.1037/0735-7028.37.3.233.

Harris, D. J., Reiter-Palmon, R., & Kaufman, J. C. (2013). The effect of emotional intelligence and task type on malevolent creativity. *Psychology of Aesthetics, Creativity, and the Arts, 7*(3), 237–244. doi: 10.1037/a0032139.

Harrison, G. E., & van Haneghan, J. P. (2011). The gifted and the shadow of the night: Dabrowski's overexcitabilities and their correlation to insomnia, death anxiety, and fear of the unknown. *Journal for the Education of the Gifted, 34*(4), 669–697. doi: 10.1177/016235321103400407.

Hartley, K. A., & Plucker, J. A. (2014). Teacher use of creativity-enhancing activities in Chinese and American elementary classrooms. *Creativity Research Journal, 26*(4), 389–399. doi: 10.1080/10400419.2014.961771.

Hartmann, E., Kunzendorf, R. G., Baddour, A., Chapwick, M., Eddins, M., Kruger, C., ... Shannon, R. (2002–2003). Emotion makes daydreams dreamlike, more symbolic. *Imagination, Cognition and Personality, 22*(3), 257–276.

Hass, R. W., Katz-Buonincontro, J., & Reiter-Palmon, R. (2016). Disentangling creative mindsets from creative self-efficacy and creative identity: Do people hold fixed and growth theories of creativity? *Psychology of Aesthetics, Creativity, and the Arts, 10*(4), 436–446. doi: 10.1037/aca0000081.

Hassabis, D., Kumaran, D., & Maguire, E. A. (2007). Using imagination to understand the neural basis of episodic memory. *Journal of Neuroscience, 27*, 14365–14374.

Hassabis, D., Kumaran, D., Vann, S. D., & Macguire, E. A. (2007). Patients with hippocampal amnesia cannot imaging new experiences. *Proceedings of the National Academy of Science, 104*(5), 1726–1731. doi: 10.1073/pnas.0610561104.

Hassandra, M., Goudas, M., & Chroni, S. (2003). Examining factors associated with intrinsic motivation in physical education: A qualitative approach. *Psychology of Sport and Exercise, 4*, 211–223. doi: 10.1016/S1469-0292(02)00006-7.

Haught, C. (2015). The role of constraints in creative sentence production. *Creativity Research Journal, 27*(2), 160–166. doi: 10.1080/10400419.2015.1030308.

Haught-Tromp, C. (2017). The Green Eggs and Ham hypothesis: How constraints facilitate creativity. *Psychology of Aesthetics, Creativity, and the Arts, 11*(1), 10–17. doi: 10.1037/aca 0000061.

Havitz, M. E., & Mannell, R. C. (2005). Enduring involvement, situational involvement and flow in leisure and non-leisure activities. *Journal of Leisure Research, 37*(2), 152–177.

Haydon, K. C., Collins, W. A., Salvatore, J. E., Simpson, J. A., & Roisman, G. I. (2012). Shared and distinctive origins and correlates of adult attachment representations: The developmental organization of romantic functioning. *Child Development, 83*(5), 1689–1702. doi: 10.1111/j.1466-8624.2012.01801.x.

Haynes, P. L., Emert, S. E., Epstein, D., Perkins, S., Parthasarathy, S., & Wilcox, J. (2017). The effect of sleep disorders, sedating medications, and depression on cognitive processing therapy outcomes: A fuzzy set qualitative comparative analysis. *Journal of Traumatic Stress, 30*, 635–645. doi: 10.1002/jts.22233.

He, Y., Yao, X., Wang, S., & Caughron, J. (2016). Linking failure feedback to individual creativity: The moderation role of goal orientation. *Creativity Research Journal, 28*(1), 52–59. doi: 10.1080/10400419.2016.1125248.

Hebert, M., Langevin, R., Guidi, E., Bernard-Bonnin, A. C., & Allard-Dansereau, C. (2017). Sleep problems and dissociation in preschool victims of sexual abuse. *Journal of Trauma and Dissociation, 18*(4), 507–521. doi: 10.1080/15299732.2016.1240739.

Hecker, T., Barnewitz, E., Stenmark, H., & Iversen, V. (2016). Pathological spirit possession as a cultural interpretation of trauma-related symptoms. *Psychological Trauma: Theory, Research, Practice, and Policy, 8*(4), 468–476. doi: 10.1037/tra0000117.

Heffron, K. M., & Ollis, S. (2006). 'Just clicks': An interpretive phenomenological analysis of professional dancers' experience of flow. *Research in Dance Education, 7*(2), 141–159. doi: 10.1080/14647890601029527.

Heidegger, M. (1962). *Being and time*. San Francisco: Harper & Row Publishers, Inc.

Heim, C., Plotsky, P. M., & Nemeroff, C. B. (2004). Importance of studying the contributions of early adverse experience to neurobiological findings in depression. *Neuropsychopharmacology, 29*, 641–648. doi: 10.1038/sj.npp.1300397.

Heim, C., Shugart, M., Craighead, W. E., & Nemeroff, C. B. (2010). Neurobiological and psychiatric consequences of child abuse and neglect. *Developmental Psychobiology, 52*, 671–690. doi: 10.1002/dev.20494.

Held, P., Owens, G. P., Monroe, J. R., & Chard, K. M. (2017). Increased mindfulness skills as predictors of reduced trauma-related guilt in treatment-seeking veterans. *Journal of Traumatic Stress, 30*, 425–431. doi: 10.1002/jts.22209.

Helson, R. (1999). A longitudinal study of creative personality in women. *Creativity Research Journal, 12*(2), 89–101.

Hemlin, S., Allwood, C. M., & Martin, B. R. (2008). Creative knowledge environments. *Creativity Research Journal, 20*(2), 196–210. doi: 10.1080/10400410802060018.

Hennessey, B. A., & Amabile, T. M. (2010). Creativity. *Annual Review of Psychology, 61,* 569–598. doi: 10.1146/annurev.psych.093008.100416.

Hertzman, C. (2012). Putting the concept of biological embedding in historical perspective. *Proceedings of the National Academy of Science, 109*(2), 17160–17167. doi: 10.1073/pnas.1202203109.

Hesse, E. (1996). Discourse, memory, and the Adult Attachmnet Interview: A note with emphasis on the emerging Cannot Classify category. *Infant Mental Health Journal, 17*(1), 4–11.

Hesse, E., & Main, M. (2000). Disorganized infant, child, and adult attachment: Collapse in behavioral and attentional strategies. *Journal of the American Psychoanalytic Association, 48,* 1097−1127.

———. (2006). Frightened, threatening, and dissociative parental behavior in low-risk samples: Description, discussion, and interpretations. *Development and Psychopathology, 18,* 309–343. doi: 10.1017/S0954579406060172.

Hewitt, P. L., & Flett, G. L. (2004). *Multidimensional perfectionism scale technical manual.* Toronto: Multi-Health Systems.

Heylighen, F. (2006). *Characteristics and problems of the gifted: Neural propagation depth and flow motivation as a model of intelligence and creativity* (ECCO working paper 2006-05). Unpublished Manuscript. doi: 10.1.1.143.8307.

Hildyard, K. L., & Wolfe, D. A. (2002). Child neglect: Developmental issues and outcomes. *Child Abuse and Neglect, 26,* 679–695.

Hirao, K., & Kobayashi, R. (2013). Health-related quality of life and sense of coherence among the unemployed with autotelic, average and non-autotelic personalities: A cross-sectional survey in Hiroshima, Japan. *PLoS ONE, 8*(9), e73915. doi: 10.137/journal.pone.0073915.

Hizli, F. G., Taskintuna, N., Isikli, S., Kilic, C., & Zileli, L. (2009). Predictors of posttraumatic stress in children and adolescents. *Children and Youth Services Review, 31,* 394–354. doi: 10.1016/j.childyouth.2008.08.008.

Hobfoll, S. E. (2001). The influence of culture, community, and the nested-self in the stress process: Advancing conservation of resources theory. *Applied Psychology, 50,* 337–421. doi: 10.111/1464.0597.00062.

Hobfoll, S. E., Canetti-Nisim, D., & Johnson, R. J. (2006). Exposure to terrorism, stress-related mental health symptoms, and defensive coping among Jews and Arabs in Israel. *Journal of Counseling and Clinical Psychology, 74*(2), 207–218. doi: 10.1037/0022.006X.74.2.207.

Hobfoll, S. E., Hall, B. J., & Canetti, D. (2012). Political violence, psychological distress, and perceived health: A longitudinal investigation in the Palestinian authority. *Psychological Trauma: Theory, Research, Practice, and Policy, 4*(3), 9–21. doi: 10.1037/a0018743.

Hobfoll, S. E., Hall, B. J., Canetti-Nisim, D., Galea, S., Johnson, R. J., & Palmieri, P. A. (2007). Refining our understanding of traumatic growth in the face of terrorism: Moving from meaning cognitions to doing what is meaningful. *Applied Psychology: An International Review, 56*(3), 345–366. doi: 10.1111/j.1464-0597.2007.00292.x.

Hobfoll, S. E., Palmieri, P. A., Johnson, R. J., Canetti-Nisim, D., Hall, B. J., & Galea, S. (2009). Trajectories of resilience, resistance, and distress during ongoing terrorism: The case of Jews and Arabs in Israel. *Journal of Counseling and Clinical Psychology, 77*(1), 138–148. doi: 10.1037/a0014360.

Hoff, E. V. (2004–2005). A friend living inside me–The forms and functions of imaginary companions. *Imagination, Cognition and Personality, 24*(2), 151–189.

———. (2005). Imaginary companions, creativity, and self-image in middle childhood. *Creativity Research Journal, 17*(2 & 3), 167–180.

Holowka, D. W., Marx, B. P., Kaloupek, D. G., & Keane, T. M. (2012). PTSD symptoms among male Vietnam veterans: Prevalence and associations with diagnostic status. *Psychological Trauma: Theory, Research, Practice, and Policy, 4*(3), 285–292. doi: 10.1037/a0023267.

Holt, R. R. (2002). Quantitative research on the primary process. Method and findings. *Journal of the American Psychoanalytic Association, 50*, 457–482.

Hom, M. A., Matheny, N. L., Stanley, I. H., Rogers, M. L., Cougle, J. R., & Joiner, T. E. (2017). Examining physical and sexual abuse histories as correlates of suicide risk among firefighters. *Journal of Traumatic Stress, 30*, 672–681. doi: 10.1002/jts.22230.

Horowitz, M. J. (1976). *Stress response syndromes*. New York, NY: Aronson.

Horselenberg, R., Merckelbach, H., van Breukelen, G., & Wessel, I. (2004). Individual differences in the accuracy of autobiographical memory. *Clinical Psychology and Psychotherapy, 11*, 168–176. doi: 10.1002/cpp.400.

Houran, R. (2009). The neuropsychological connection between creativity and meditation. *Creativity Research Journal, 21*(2–3), 199–222. doi: 10.1080/10400410902858691.

Howard, C. J. (2012). Neurobiological correlates of partner abusive men: Equifinality in perpetrators of intimate partner violence. *Psychological Trauma: Theory, Research, Practice, and Policy, 4*(3), 330–337. doi: 10.1037/a0024229.

Huba, G. J., Aneshensel, C. S., & Singer, J. L. (1981). Development of scales for three second-order factors of inner experience. *Multivariate Behavioral Research, 16*(2), 181–206. doi: 10.1207/s15327906mbr1602_4.

Huber, C. (2015). *Worst natural disaster of 2015*. Retrieved from http://www.worldvision.org/news-stories-videos/naturaldisasters-2015.

Hughes, P., Turton, P., Hopper, E., & McGauley, G. A. (2001). Disorganized attachment behavior among infants born subsequent to stillbirth. *Jounral of Child Psychology and Psychiatry, 42*(6), 791–801.

Hughes, P., Turton, P., McGauley, G. A., & Fonagy, P. (2006). Factors that predict infant disorganization in mothers classified as U in pregnancy. *Attachment and Human Development, 8*(2), 113–122. doi: 10.1080/14616730600785660.

Hund, A. R., & Espelage, D. L. (2006). Childhood emotional abuse and disordered eating among undergraduate females: Mediating influence of alexithymia and distress. *Child Abuse and Neglect, 30*, 393–407.

Hundt, N. E., & Holohan, D. R. (2012). The role of shame in distinguishing perpetrators of intimate partner iolence in U.S. veterans. *Journal of Traumatic Stress, 25*, 191–197. doi: 10.1003/jts.21688.

Hunter, E. C., Sierra, M., & David, A. S. (2004). The epidemiology of depersonalisation and derealisation: A systematic review. *Social Psychiatry and Psychiatric Epidemiology, 39*, 9–18.

Hunter, J., & Csikszentmihalyi, M. (2008). The phenomenology of body-mind: The contrasting cases of flow in sports and contemplation. *Anthropology of Consciousness, 11*(3–4), 5–24. doi: 10.1525/ac.2000.11.3-4.5.

Hunter, P. G., Schellenberg, E. G., & Schimmack, U. S. (2010). Feelings and perceptions of happiness and sadness induced by music: Similarities, differences, and mixed emotions. *Psychology of Aesthetics, Creativity, and the Arts, 4*(1), 47–56. doi: 10.1037/a0016873.

Hunter, S. T., Bedell, K. E., & Mumford, M. D. (2007). Climate for creativity: A quantitative review. *Creativity Research Journal, 19*(1), 69–90.

Hunter, S. T., Bedell-Avers, K. E., Hunsicker, C. M., Mumford, M. D., & Ligon, G. S. (2008). Applying multiple knowledge structures in creative thought: Effects of idea generation and problem solving. *Creative Research Journal, 20*(2), 137–154. doi: 10.1080/10400410802088779.

Hyland, P., Brwein, C. R., & Maercker, A. (2017). Predictive validity of ICD-II PTSD as measured by the Impact of Event Scale-Revised: A 15-year prospective study of political prisoners. *Journal of Traumatic Stress, 30*, 125–132. doi: 10.1002/jts.22171.

Hyland, P., Murphy, J., Shevlin, M., Vallieres, F., McElroy, E., Elklit, A., … Cloitre, M. (2017). Variation in post-traumatic response: The role of trauma type in predicting ID-11 PTSD and CPTSD symptoms. *Social Psychiatry and Psychiatric Epidemiology, 52*(6), 727–736. doi: 10.1007/s00127-017-1350-8.

Hyland, P., Shevlin, M., Elklit, A., Murphy, J., Vallieres, F., Garvert, D. W., & Cloitre, M. (2017). An assessment of the construct validity of the ICD-11 proposal for complex posttraumatic stress disorder. *Psychological Trauma: Theory, Research, Practice, and Policy, 9*(1), 1–9. doi: 10.1037/tra0000114.

Iacoboni, M. (2009). Neurobiology of imitation. *Current Opinions in Neurobiology, 19*, 661–665. doi: 10.1016/j.conb.2009.09.008.

Idemudia, E. S. (2017). Trauma and PTSS of Zimbabwean refugees in South Africa: A summary of published articles. *Psychological Trauma: Theory, Research, Practice, and Policy, 9*(3), 252–257. doi: 10.1037/tra0000214.

Ilgen, D. R., Nebeker, D. M., & Pritchard, R. D. (1981). Expectancy theory measures: An empirical comparison in an experimental situation. *Organizational Behavior and Human Performance, 28*, 189–223.

Irwin, H. J. (1990). Fantasy proneness and paranormal beliefs. *Psychological Reports, 66*, 655–658.

———. (2000). Belief in the paranormal and a sense of control over life. *European Journal of Parapsychology, 15*, 68–78.

Isaksen, S. G., Lauer, K. J., & Wilson, G. V. (2003). An examination of the relationship between personality type and cognitive style. *Creativity Research Journal, 15*(4), 343–354.

Isen, A. M., & Reeve, J. (2005). The influence of positive affect on intrinsic and extrinsic motivation: Facilitating enjoyment of play, responsible work behavior, and self-control. *Motivation and Emotion, 29*(4), 297–325. doi: 10.1007/s11031-006-9019-8.

Ishimura, I., & Kodama, M. (2009). Flow experiences in everyday activities of Japanese college students: Autotelic people and time management. *Japanese Psychological Review, 51*(1), 47–54. doi: 10.1111/j.1468-5884.2009.00387.x.

Itzhaky, L., Stein, J. Y., Levin, Y., & Solomon, A. (2017). Posttraumatic stress symptoms and marital adjustment among Israeli combat veterans: The role of loneliness and attachment. *Psychological Trauma: Theory, Research, Practice, and Policy, 9*(6), 655–662. doi: 10.1037/tra0000259.

Ivcevic, Z. (2007). Artistic and everyday creativity: An act-frequency approach. *Journal of Creative Behavior, 41*(4), 271–290.

Ivcevic, Z., & Brackett, M. A. (2015). Predicting creativity: Interactive effects of openness to experience and emotion regulation ability. *Psychology of Aesthetics, Creativity, and the Arts, 9*(4), 480–487. doi: 10.1037/a0039826.

Ivcevic, Z., & Mayer, J. D. (2006–2007). Creative types and personality. *Imagination, Cognition and Personality, 26*(1–2), 65–86.

Ivcevic, Z., Mayer, J. D., & Brackett, M. A. (2007). Emotional intelligence and emotional creativity. *Journal of Personality, 75*(2), 199–236. doi: 10.1111/j.1467-6494.2007.00437.x.

Jackson, C. E., Green, J. D., Bovin, M. J., Vasterling, J. J., Holowka, D. W., Ranganathan, G., ... Marx, B. P. (2016). Mild traumatic brain injury, PTSD, and psychosocial functioning among male and female U.S. OEF/OIF veterans. *Journal of Traumatic Stress, 29*, 309–316. doi: 10.1002/jts.22110.

Jackson, P. L., & Decety, J. (2004). Motor cognition: A new paradigm to study self-other interactions. *Current Opinion in Neurobiology, 14*, 259–263.

Jackson, P. L., Meltzoff, A. N., & Decety, J. (2005). How do we perceive the pain of others? A window into the neural processes involved in empathy. *Neuroimage, 24*, 771–779. doi: 10.1016/j.neuroimage.2004.09.006.

Jackson, S. A., & Eklund, R. C. (2002). Assessing flow in physical activity: The Flow State Scale-2 and Dispositional Flow Scale-2. *Journal of Sport and Exercise Psychology, 24*, 133–150.

———. (2004). *The flow scales manual.* Morgantown, WV: Fitness Information Technology, Inc.

Jackson, S. A., Kimiecik, J. C., Ford, S. K., & Marsh, H. W. (1998). Psychological correlates of flow in sport. *Journal of Sport and Exercise Psychology, 20*(4), 358–378.

Jackson, S. A., Martin, A., & Eklund, R. C. (2008). Long and short measures of flow: The construct validity of the FSS-2, DFS-2, and new brief counterparts. *Journal of Sport and Exercise Psychology, 30*, 561–587.

Jackson, S. A., Thomas, P. R., Marsh, H. W., & Smethurst, C. J. (2001). Relationship between flow, self-concept, psychological skills, and performance. *Journal of Applied Sport Psychology, 13*(2), 129–153. doi: 10.1080/104132001753149865.

Jacobvitz, D., Curran, M., & Moller, N. (2002). Measurement of adult attachment: The place of self-report and interview methodologies. *Attachment and Human Development, 4*, 207–215. doi: 10.1080/ 14616730210154225.

Jaeger, J., Lindblom, K. M., Parker-Guilbert, K., & Zoellner, L. A. (2014). Trauma narratives: It's what you say, not how you say it. *Psychological Trauma: Theory, Research, Practice, and Policy, 6*(5), 473–481. doi: 10.1037/a0035239.

Jakobson, L. S., Cuddy, L. L., & Kilgour, A. R. (2003). Time tagging: A key to musician's superior memory. *Music Perception, 20*(3), 307–313.

James, K., & Drown, D. (2008). Whether "malevolent" or "negative" creativity is relevant to terrorism prevention: Lessons from 9/11 and hazardous material trucking. *Creativity Research Journal, 20*(2), 120–127. doi: 10.1080/10400410802059648.

James, K., Brodersen, M., & Eisenberg, J. (2004). Workplace affect and workplace creativity: A review and preliminary model. *Human Performance, 17*(2), 169–194.

Jaussi, K. S., & Randel, A. E. (2014). Where to look? Creative self-efficacy, knowledge retrieval, and incremental and radical creativity. *Creativity Research Journal, 26*(4), 400–410. doi: 10.1080/10400419.2014.961772.

Jeffers, C. S. (2009). On empathy: The mirror neuron system and art education. *International Journal of Education and the Arts, 10*(15), 1–17.

Jefferson, J. G., Cohen, P., Kasen, S., & Brook, J. S. (2006). Dissociative disorders among adults in the community impaired functioning, and axis I and II comorboidity. *Journal of Psychiatric Research, 40*, 131–140. doi: 10.1016/j.jpsychires.2005.03.003.

Jepsen, E. K. K., Langeland, W., Sexton, H., & Heir, T. (2014). Inpatient treatment for early sexually abused adults: A naturalistic 12-month follow-up study. *Psychological Trauma: Theory, Research, Practice, and Policy, 6*(2), 142–151. doi: 10.1037/a0031646.

Jerome, E. M., & Liss, M. (2005). Relationship between sensory processing style, adult attachment, and coping. *Personality and Individual Differences, 38*, 1341–1352. doi: 10.1016/j.paid.2004.08.016.

Jessee, A., Mangelsdorf, S. C., Wong, M. S., Schoppe-Sullivan, S. J., & Brown, G. L. (2016). Structure of reflective functioning and adult attachment scales: Overlap and distinctions. *Attachment and Human Development, 18*(2), 176–187. doi: 10.1080/14616734.2015.1132240.

Johnson, D. R., Cushman, G. K., Borden, L. A., & McCune, M. S. (2013). Potentiating empathic growth: Generating imagery while reading fiction increases empathy and prosocial behavior. *Psychology of Aesthetics, Creativity, and the Arts, 7*(3), 306–312. doi: 10.1037/a0033261.

Johnson, H., & Thompson, A. (2008). The development and maintenance of posttraumatic stress disorder (PTSD) in civilian adult survivors of war trauma and torture: A review. *Clinical Psychology Review, 28*, 36–47. doi: 10.1016/j.cpr.2007.01.017.

Johnson, S. F., & Boals, A. (2015). Refining our ability to measure posttraumatic growth. *Psychological Trauma: Theory, Research, Practice, and Policy, 7*(5), 422–429. doi: 10.1037/tra0000013.

Johnson, S. L., Tharp, J. A., & Holmes, M. K. (2015). Understanding creativity in Bipolar I Disorder. *Psychology of Aesthetics, Creativity, and the Arts, 9*(3), 319–327. doi: 10.1037/a0038852.

Johnston, J. M., Minami, T., Greenwald, D., Li, C., Reinhardt, K., & Khalsa, S. B. S. (2015). Yoga for military service personnel with PTSD: A single arm study.

Psychological Trauma: Theory, Research, Practice, and Policy, 7(6), 555–562. doi: 10.1037/tra0000051.

Johnston, M. A. (1999). Influences of adult attachment exploration. *Psychological Reports, 84*, 31–34.

Jola, C., Davis, A., & Haggard, P. (2011). Proprioceptive integration and body representation: Insights into dancers' expertise. *Experimental Brain Research, 213*(2–3), 257–265. doi: 10.1007/s00221-011-2743-7.

Jones, L. M., Mitchell, K. J., & Turner, H. A. (2015). Victim reports of bystander reactions to in-person and online peer harassment: A national survey of adolescents. *Journal of Youth and Adolescents, 44*(12), 2308–2320. doi: 10.1007/s10964-015-0342-9.

Jones, M. E., Roy, M. M., & Verkuilen, J. (2014). The relationship between reflective rumination and musical ability. *Psychology of Aesthetics, Creativity and the Arts, 8*(2), 219–226. doi: 10.1037/a0035634.

Jordan, A. H., Eisen, E., Bolton, E., Nash, W. P., & Litz, B. T. (2017). Distinguishing war-related PTSD resulting from perpetration- and betrayal-based morally injurious events. *Psychological Trauma: Theory, Research, Practice, and Policy, 9*(6), 627–634. doi: 10.1037/tra0000249.

Joy, S. P. (2008). Personality and creativity in art and writing: Innovation, motivation, psychoticism, and (mal)adjustment. *Creativity Research Journal, 20*(3), 262–277. doi: 10.1080/10400410802278693.

Julmi, C., & Scherm, E. (2015). The domain-specificity of creativity: Insights from new phenomenology. *Creativity Research Journal, 27*(2), 151–152. doi: 10.1080/10400419.2015.1030310.

Jung, C. G. (1923). *Psychological types* (H. B Baynes, Trans.). New York: Harcourt Brace.

Kaczkurkin, A. N., Asnaani, A., Zhong, J., & Foa, E. B. (2016). The moderating effect of state anger on treatment outcome in female adolescents with PTSD. *Journal of Traumatic Stress, 29*, 325–331. doi: 10.1002/jts.22116.

Kaczkurkin, A. N., Zang, Y., Gay, N. G., Peterson, A. L. Yarvis, J. S., Borah, E. V., … The STONG STAR Consortium. (2017). Cognitive emotion regulation strategies associated with the DSM-5 posttraumatic stress disorder criteria. *Journal of Traumatic Stress, 30*, 343–350. doi: 10.1002/jts.22202.

Kaess, M., Parzer, P., Mattern, M., Plener, P. L., Bifulco, A., Resch, F., & Brunner, R. (2013). Adverse childhood experiences and their impact on frequency, severity, and the individual function of nonsuicidal self-injury in youth. *Psychiatry Research, 206*, 265–272. doi: 10.1016/j.psychres.2012.10.012.

Kangaslampi, S., Punamaki, R.-J., Qouta, S., Diab, M., & Peltonen, K. (2016). Psychosocial group intervention among war-affected children: An analysis of changes in posttraumatic cognitions. *Journal of Traumatic Stress, 29*, 546–555. doi: 10.1002/jts.22140.

Kaniasty, K. (2012). Predicting social psychological well-being following trauma: The role of postdisaster social support. *Psychological Trauma: Theory, Research, Practice, and Policy, 4*(1), 22–33. doi: 10.1037/a 0021412.

Kapoor, H. (2015). The creative side of the dark triad. *Creativity Research Journal, 27*(1), 58–67. doi: 10.1080.10400419.2014.961775.

Kapoor, H., & Khan, A. (2016). The measurement of negative creativity: Metrics and relationships. *Creativity Research Journal, 28*(4), 407–416. doi: 10.1080/10400419.2016.1229977.

Karabanov, A., Cervenka, S., de Manzano, O., Forssberg, H., Farde, L., & Ullen, F. (2010). Dopamine D2 receptor density in the limbic striatum is related to implicit but not explicit movement sequence learning. *Proceedings of the National Academy of Sciences, 107*(16), 7574–7579. doi: 10.1073/pnas.0911805107.

Karam, E. G., Freidman, M. J., Hill, E. D., Kessler, R. C., McLaughlin, K. A., Petukhova, … Koenen, K. C. (2014). Cumulative traumas and risk thresholds: 12-month PTSD in the World Mental Health (WMH) surveys. *Depression and Anxiety, 31*, 130–142. doi: 10.1002/da.22169.

Karavasilis, L., Doyle, A. B., & Markiewicz, D. (2003). Associations between parenting syle and attachment to mother in middle childhood and adolescence. *International Journal of Behavioral Development, 27*(2), 153–164. doi: 10.1080/01650250244000155.

Karoly, P., & Ruehlman, L. S. (2006). Psychological "resilience" and its correlates in chronic pain: Findings from a national community sample. *Pain, 123,* 90–97. doi: 10.1016/j.pain.2006.02.014.

Karpel, M. G., & Jerram, M. W. (2015). Levels of dissociation and nonsucidal self-injury: A quartile risk model. *Journal of Trauma and Dissociation, 16,* 303–321. doi: 10.1080/15299732.2015.989645.

Karstoft, K.-I., Galatzer-Levy, I. R., Statnikov, A., Li, Z., Shalev, A. Y., & For Members of the Jerusalem Trauma Outreach and Prevention Study (J-TOPS) group. (2015). Bridging a translational gap: Using machine learning to improve the prediction of PTSD. *BioMed Central Psychiatry, 15*(30), 2–7. doi: 10.1186/s12888-015-0399-8.

Karwowski, M. (2016). The dynamics of creative self-concept: Changes and reciprocal relations between creative self-efficacy and creative personal identity. *Creativity Research Journal, 28*(1), 99–104. doi: 10.1080/1040419.2016.1125264.

Karwowski, M., & Kaufman, J. C. (Eds.). (2017). *The creative self: Effect of belief, self-efficacy, mindset, and identity*. San Diego, CA: Academic Press.

Kasof, J., Chen, C., Himsel, A., & Greenberger, E. (2007). Values and creativity. *Creativity Research Journal, 19*(2–3), 105–122.

Kattenstroth, J.-C., Kalish, T., Holt, S., Tegenthoff, M., & Dinse, H. R. (2013). Six months of dance intervention enhances postural, sensorimotor, and cognitive performance in elderly without affecting cardio-respiratory functions. *Frontiers in Aging Neuroscience, 5*(5), 1–16. doi: 10.3389/fnagi.2013.00005.

Kattenstroth, J.-C., Kolankowska, I., Kalisch, T., & Dinse, H. R. (2010). Superior sensory, motor, and cognitive performance in elderly individuals with multi-year dancing activities. *Frontiers in Aging Neuroscience, 2*(31), 1–9. doi: 10.3389/fnagi2010.00031.

Kaufman, J. C. (2001). The Sylvia Plath effect: Mental illness in eminent creative writers. *Journal of Creative Behavior, 35*(1), 37–50.

———. (2003). The cost of the muse: Poets die young. *Death Studies, 27*, 813–821. doi: 10.1080/0748180390233407.

———. (2005). The door that leads into madness: Eastern European poets and mental illness. *Creativity Research Journal, 17*(1), 99–103.

Kaufmann, G. (2003). Expanding the mood-creativity equation. *Creativity Research Journal, 15*(2–3), 131–135.

Kaufmann, G., & Vosberg, S. K. (1997). "Paradoxical" mood effects on creative problem-solving. *Cognition and Emotion, 11*(2), 151–170.

———. (2002). The effects on early and late idea production. *Creativity Research Journal, 14*(3–4), 317–330.

Kaufman, J. C., & Baer, J. (2012). Beyond new and appropriate: Who decides what is creative? *Creativity Research Journal, 24*(1), 83–91. doi: 10.1080/10400419.2012.649237.

Kaufman, J. C., & Beghetto, R. A. (2009). Beyond big and little: The Four C Model of Creativity. *Review of General Psychology, 13*(1), 1–12. doi: 10.1037/a0013688.

Kaufman, J. C., & Beghetto, R. A. (2013). Do people recognize the Four Cs? Examining layperson conceptions of creativity. *Psychology of Aesthetics, Creativity, and the Arts*, 7(3), 229–236. doi: 10.1037/a0033295.

Kaufman, J. C., Bromley, M. L., & Cole, J. C. (2006–2007). Insane, poetic, lovable: Creativity and endorsement of the "mad-genius" stereotype. *Imagination, Cognition and Personality, 26*(1–2), 149–161.

Kaufman, J. C., Plucker, J. A., & Russell, C. M. (2012). Identifying and assessing creativity as a component of giftedness. *Journal of Psychoeducational Assessment, 30*(1), 60–73. doi: 10.1177/0734282911428196.

Kaufman, J. C., Pumaccahua, T. T., & Holt, R. E. (2013). Personality and creativity in realistic, investigative, artistic, social and enterprising college majors. *Personality and Individual Differences, 54*, 913–917. doi: 10.1016/j.paid.2013.01.013.

Kawabata, M., & Mallett, C. J. (2011). Flow experience in physical activity: Examination of the internal structure of flow from a process-related perspective. *Motivation and Emotion, 35*, 393–402. doi: 10.1007/s11031-011-9221-1.

Kaye-Tzadok, A., & Davidson-Arad, B. (2016). Posttraumatic growth among women survivors of childhood sexual abuse: Its relation to cognitive strategies, posttraumatic symptoms, and resilience. *Psychological Trauma: Theory, Research Practice, and Policy, 8*(5), 550–558. doi: 10.1037/tra00000103.

Kee, Y. H., & Wang, C. K. J. (2008). Relationship between mindfulness, flow dispositions and mental skills adoption: A cluster analytic approach. *Psychology of Sport and Exercise, 9*, 393–411. doi: 10.1016/j.psychsport.2007.07.001.

Keeler, J. R., Roth, E. A., Neuser, B. L., Spitsbergen, J. M., Waters, D. J. M., & Vianney, J.-M. (2015). The neurochemistry and social flow of singing: Bonding and oxytocin. *Frontiers in Human Neuroscience, 9*, 518. doi: 10.3389/fnhum.2015.00518.

Kehl, D., Knuth, D., Hulse, L., & Schmidt, S. (2015). Predictors of postevent distress and growth among firefighters after work-related emergencies–A cross-national study. *Psychological Trauma: Theory, Research, Practice, and Policy, 7*(3), 203–211. doi: 10.1037/a0037954.

Keller, J., & Bless, H. (2008). Flow and regulatory compatibility: An experimental approach to the flow model of intrinsic motivation. *Personality and Social Psychology Bulletin, 34*(2), 196–209. doi: 10.1177/0146167207310026.

Kelly, K. R. (2015). Insecure attachment representations and child personal narrative structure: Implications for delayed discourse in preschool-age children. *Attachment and Human Development, 17*(5), 448–471. doi: 10.1080/14616734.2015.1076011.

Keltner, D., & Haidt, J. (2003). Approaching awe, a moral, spiritual, and aesthetic emotion. *Cognition and Emotion, 17*(2), 297–314. doi: 10.1080/02699930244000318.

Kemeny, M. E., Gruenewald, T. L., & Dickerson, S. S. (2004). Shame as the emotional response to threat to the social self: Implications for behavior, physiology, and health. *Psychological Inquiry, 15*(2), 153–160.

Kerns, K. A., Abraham, M. M., Schlegelmilch, A., & Morgan, T. A. (2007). Mother-child attachment in later middle childhood: Assessment approaches and associations with mood and emotion regulation. *Attachment and Human Development, 9*(1), 33–53. doi: 10.1080/14616730601151144l.

Keshet, H., & Gilboa-Schechtman, E. (2017). Symptoms and beyond: Self-concept among sexually assaulted women. *Psychological Trauma: Theory, Research, Practice, and Policy, 9*(5), 545–552. doi: 10.1037/tra0000222.

Kessler, B. L., & Bieschke, K. J. (1999). A retrospective analysis of shame, dissociation, and adult victimization in survivors of childhood sexual abuse. *Journal of Counseling Psychology, 46*(3), 335–341. doi: 10.1037/0022-0167.46.3.335.

Kessler, R. C., McLaughlin, K. A., Green, J. G., Gruber, M. J., Sampson, N. A., Zaslavsky, A. M., ... Williams, D. R. (2010). Childhood adversities and adult psychopathology in the WHO World Mental Health surveys. *British Journal of Psychiatry, 197*, 378–385. doi: 10.1192/bjp.bp.110.080499.

Kessler, R. C., McLaughlin, K. A., Koenen, K. C., Petukhova, M., Hill, E. D., & WHO World Mental Health Survey Consortium. (2012). The importance of secondary trauma exposure for post-disaster mental disorder. *Epidemiology and Psychiatric Sciences, 21*, 35–45. doi: 10.1017/S2045796011000758.

Kessler, R. C., Molnar, B. E., Feurer, I. D., & Appelbaum, M. (2001). Patterns and mental health predictors of domestic violence in the United States: Results from the National Comorbidity Survey. *International Journal of Law and Psychiatry, 24*, 487–504. doi: 10.1016/S0160-2527(01)00080-2.

Ketelaar, T., & Au, W. T. (2003). The effects of feelings of guilt on the behavior of uncooperative indivdiuals in repeated social bargaining games: An affect-as-information interpretation of the role of emotion in social interacaion. *Cognition and Emotion, 17*, 429–453.

Kharkhurin, A. V. (2014). Creativity. 4 in 1: Four-criterion construct of creativity. *Creativity Research Journal, 26*(3), 338–352. doi: 10.1080/10400419.2014.929424.

Kibler, J. L. (2009). Posttraumatic stress and cardiovascular disease risk. *Journal of Trauma and Dissociation, 10*, 135–150. doi: 10.1080/15299730802624577.

———. (2018). An extension of the perseverative cognitive hypothesis to posttraumatic stress disorder symptomatology: Cardiovascular recovery in relation to posttraumatic stress disorder severity and cognitive appraisals of stress. *Journal of Traumatic Stress, 31*, 25–34. doi: 10.1002/jts.22522.

Kiecolt-Glaser, J. K., McGuire, L., Robles, T. F., & Glase, R. (2002). Emotions, morbidity, and mortality: New perspectives from psychoneuroimmunology. *Annual Review of Psychology, 53*, 83–107. doi: 10.1146/annurev.psych.53.1009901.135217.

Killian, K., Hernandez-Wolfe, P., Engstrom, D., & Gangsei, D. (2017). Development of the vicarious resilience scale (VRS): A measure of positive effects of working with trauma survivors. *Psychological Trauma: Theory, Research, Practice, and Policy, 9*(1), 23–31. doi: 10.1037/tra0000199.

Kilpatrick, D. G., Resnick, H. S., Milanak, M., Miller, M. W., Keyes, K. M., & Friedman, M. J. (2013). National estimates of exposure to traumatic events and PTSD prevalence using DSM-IV and DSM-5 criteria. *Journal of Traumatic Stress, 26*, 537–547. doi: 10.1002/jts.21848.

Kim, J. (2015). Physical activity benefits creativity: Squeezing a ball for enhancing creativity. *Creativity Research Journal, 27*(4), 328–333. doi: 10.1080/10400419.2015.1087258.

Kim, K. H. (2008). Underachievement and creativity: Are gifted underachievers highly creative? *Creativity Research Journal, 20*(2), 234–242. doi: 10.1080/10400410802060232.

———. (2011). The creativity crisis: The decrease in creative thinking scores on the Torrance Tests of Creative Thinking. *Creativity Research Journal, 23*(4), 285–295. doi: 10.1080/10400419.2011.627805.

Kimbell, R. (2000). Creativity in crisis. *Journal of Design and Technology Education, 5*(3), 206–211.

Kira, I., Lewandowski, L., Somers, C. L., Yoon, J. S., & Chiodo, L. (2012). The effects of trauma types, cumulative trauma, and PTSD on IQ in two highly traumatized adolescent groups. *Psychological Trauma: Theory, Research, Practice, and Policy, 4*(1), 128–139. doi: 10.1037/a0022121.

Kirchner, J. M., Bloom, A. J., & Skutnick-Henley, P. (2008). The relationship between performance anxiety and flow. *Medical Problems of Performing Artists, 23*(2), 59–65.

Kirschenbaum, R. J. (1998). The creativity classification system: An assessment theory. *Roeper Review, 21*(1), 20–26.

Kjellenberg, E., Nilsson, F., Daukantaite, D., & Cardena, E. (2014). Transformative narratives: The impact of working with war and torture survivors. *Psychological Trauma: Theory, Research, Practice, and Policy, 6*(2), 120–128. doi: 10.1037/a0031966.

Klag, S., & Bradley, G. (2004). The role of hardiness in stress and illness: An exploration of the effect of negative affectivity and gender. *British Journal of Health Psychology, 9*, 137–161.

Klasen, M., Weber, R., Kircher, T. T. J., Mathiak, K. A., & Mathiak, K. (2012). Neural contributions to flow experiences during video game playing. *Social Cognition and Affective Neuroscience, 7*, 485–495. doi: 10.1093/scan/nsr021.

Kleiger, R., Stein, P. K., & Bigger, T. (2005). Heart rate variability: Measurement and clinical utility. *Annals of Noninvasive Electrocardiology, 10*(1), 88–101.

Klein, B. D., Rossin, D., Guo, Y. M., & Ro, Y. K. (2010). An examination of the effects of flow on learning in a graduate-level introductory operations management course. *Journal of Education for Business, 85*(5), 292–298. doi: 10.1080/08832320903449600.

Klest, B. (2012). Childhood trauma, poverty, and adult victimization. *Psychological Trauma: Theory, Research, Practice, and Policy, 4*(3), 245–251. doi: 10.1037/a0024468.

Klinger, E., Henning, V. R., & Janssen, J. M. (2009). Fantasy-proneness dimensionalized: Dissociative component is related to psychopathology, daydreaming as such is not. *Journal of Research in Personality, 43*, 506–510. doi: 10.1016/j.jrp.2008.12017.

Ko, Y.-G., & Kim, J.-Y. (2008). Scientific geniuses' psychopathology as a moderator in the relation between creative contribution types and eminence. *Creativity Research Journal, 20*(3), 251–261. doi: 10.1080/10400410802278677.

Kobayashi, I., & Delahanty, D. L. (2013). Gender differences in subjective sleep after trauma and the development of posttraumatic stress disorder symptoms: A pilot study. *Journal of Traumatic Stress, 26*, 467–474. doi: 10.1002/jts.21828.

Kochanska, G., & Kim, S. (2013). Early attachment organization with both parents and future behavior problems: From infancy to middle childhood. *Child Development, 84*(1), 283–296. doi: 10.1111/j.1467-8624.2012.01852x.

Kochanska, G., Barry, R. A., Stellern, S. A., & O'Bleness, J. J. (2009). Early attachment organization moderates the parent-child mutually coercive pathway to children's antisocial conduct. *Child Development, 80*, 1288–1300.

Koechlin, E., & Summerfield, C. (2007). An information theoretical approach to prefrontal executive function. *Trends in Cognitive Sciences, 11*(6), 229–235. doi: 10.1016/j.tics.2007.04.005.

Koen, N., Brittain, K., Donald, K. A., Barnett, W., Koopowitz, S., Mare, K., ... Stein, D. J. (2017). Maternal posttraumatic stress disorder and infant developmental outcomes in a South African birth cohort study. *Psychological Trauma: Theory, Research, Practice, and Policy, 9*(3), 292–300. doi: 10.1037/tra0000234.

Konecni, V. (2005). The aesthetic trinity: Awe, being moved, thrills. *Bulletin of Psychology and the Arts, 5*(2), 27–44.

Kosslyn, S. M. (2005). Mental images and the brain. *Cognitive Neuropsychology, 22*(3/4), 333–347. doi: 10.1080/02643290442000130.

Kounou, K. B., Brodard, F., Gnassingbe, A., Foli, A. A. D., Sager, J. C., Schmitt, L., & Bui, E. (2017). Posttraumatic stress, somatization, and quality of life among Ivorian refugees. *Journal of Traumatic Stress, 30*, 682–689. doi: 10.1002/jts.22244.

Kowal, J., & Fortier, M. S. (1999). Motivational determinants of flow: Contributions from self-determination theory. *The Journal of Social Psychology, 139*(3), 355–368. doi: 10.1080/00224549909598391.

Krahe, B., & Berger, A. (2017). Longitudinal pathways of sexual victimization, sexual self-esteem, and depression in women and men. *Psychological Trauma: Theory, Research, Practice, and Policy, 9*(2), 147–155. doi: 10.1037/tra0000198.

Krampe, R. T., & Ericsson, K. A. (1996). Maintaining excellence: Deliberate practice and elite performance in young and older pianists. *Journal of Experimental Psychology: General, 125*(4), 331–359. doi: 10.1037/0096-3445.125.4.331.

Krasnow, D. H., & Wilmerding, M. V. (2015). *Motor learning and control for dance: Principles and practices for performers and teachers*. Champaign, IL: Human Kinetics.

Krasnow, D., Mainwaring, L., & Kerr, G. (1999). Injury, stress, and perfectionism in young dancers and gymnasts. *Journal of Dance Medicine & Science, 3*(2), 51–58.

Krause, W. (2006). The narrative negotiation of identity and belonging. *Narrative Inuqiry, 16*(1), 103–111.

Kreibig, S. D., Gendolla, G. H. E., & Scherer, K. R. (2012). Goal relevance and goal conduciveness appraisals lead to differential autonomic reactivity in emotional responding to performance feedback. *Biological Psychology, 91*, 365–375. doi: 10.1016/j.biopsycho.2012.08.007.

Kring, A. M., Smith, D. A., & Neale, J. M. (1994). Individual differences in dispositional expressiveness: Development and validation of the Emotional Expressivity Scale. *Journal of Personality and Social Psychology, 66*(5), 934–949.

Kristensen, T. (2004). The physical context of creativity. *Creativity and Innovation Management, 13*(2), 89–96.

Kropotov, J. D. (2009). *Quantitative EEG, event-related potentials and neurotherapy*. San Diego, CA: Academic Press.

Krosch, D. J., & Shakespeare-Finch, J. (2017). Grief, traumatic stress, and posttraumatic growth in women who have experienced pregnancy loss. *Psychological Trauma: Theory, Research, Practice, and Policy, 9*(4), 425–435. doi: 10.1037/tra0000183.

Kruger, C., & Fletcher, L. (2017). Predicting a dissociative disorder from type of childhood maltreatment and abuser-abused relational tie. *Journal of Trauma and Dissociation, 18*(3), 356–372. doi: 10.1080/15299732.2017.1295420.

Kruger, C., & Mace, C. J. (2002). Psychometric validation of the State Scale of Dissociation (SSD). *Psychology and Psychotherapy: Theory, Research and Practice, 75*, 33–51.

Kubany, E. S., Abueg, F. R., Owens, J. A., Brennan, J. M., Kaplan, A. S., & Watson, S. B. (1995). Initial examination of a multidimensional model of trauma-related guilt: Applications to combat veterans and battered women. *Journal of Psychopathology and Behavioral Assessment, 17*, 353–376. doi: 10.1007/BF02229056.

Kubzansky, L. D., Bordelois, P., Jun, H. J., Roberts, A. L., Cerda, M., Blueston, N., & Koenen, K. C. (2014). The weight of traumatic stress: A prospective study of posttraumatic stress symptoms and weight status in women. *Journal of the American Medical Association Psychiatry, 7*(1), 44–51. doi: 10.1001/jamapsychiatry.2013.2798.

Kucharska, J. (2017). Sex differences in the appraisal of traumatic events and psychopathology. *Psychological Trauma: Theory, Research, Practice, and Policy, 9*(5), 575–582. doi: 10.1037/tra0000244.

Kuhn, S., Duzel, S., Dreweliers, J., Gerstorf, D., Lindenberger, U., & Gallinat, J. (2018). Psychological and neural correlates of embitterment in old age. *Psychological Trauma: Theory, Research, Practice, and Policy, 10*(1), 51–57. doi: 10.1037/tra0000287.

Kuijpers, K. F., van der Knaap, L. M., & Winkel, F. W. (2012). PTSD symptoms as risk factors for intimate partner violence revictimization and the mediating role of victims' violen behavior. *Journal of Traumatic Stress, 25*, 179–186. doi: 10.1002/jts.21676.

Kuipers, G. S., van Loenhout, Z., van der Ark, A., & Bekker, M. H. J. (2016). Attachment insecutiry, mentalization and their relation to symptoms in eating disorder patients. *Attachment and Human Development, 18*(3), 250–272. doi: 10.1080/14616734.2015.1136660.

Kunz, S., Joseph, S., Geyh, S., & Peter, C. (2017). Posttraumatic growth and adjustment to spinal cord injury: Moderated by posttraumatic depression? *Psychological Trauma: Theory, Research, Practice, and Policy, 9*(4), 434–444. doi: 10.1037/tra0000164.

Kyaga, S., Landen, M., Boman, M., Hultman, C. M., Langstrom, N., & Lichtenstein, P. (2013). Mental illness, suicide, and creativity: 40-year prospective total population study. *Journal of Psychiatric Research, 47*, 83–90. doi: 10.1016/j.jpsychires.2012.09.010.

Kyaga, S., Lichtenstein, P., Boman, M., Hultman, C., Langstrom, N., & Landen, M. (2011). Creativity and mental disorder: Family study of 300,000 people with severe mental disorder. *The British Journal of Psychiatry, 199*, 373–379. doi: 10.1192/bjp.bp.110.085316.

La Bash, H., & Papa, A. (2014). Shame and PTSD symptoms. *Psychological Trauma: Theory, Research, Practice, and Policy, 6*(2), 159–166. doi: 10.1037/a0032637.

Lacaille, N., Koestner, R., & Gaudreau, P. (2007). On the value of intrinsic rather than traditional achievement goals for performing artists: A short-term prospective study. *International Journal of Music Education, 25*(3), 245–257.

Lack, S. A., Kumar, V. K., & Arevalo, S. (2003). Fantasy proneness, creativity capacity, and styles of creativity. *Perceptual and Motor Skills, 96*, 19–24.

Laddis, A., Dell. P. F., & Korzekwa, M. (2017). Comparing the symptoms and mechanisms of "dissociation" in dissociative identity disorder and borderline personality disorder. *Journal of Trauma and Dissociation, 18*(2), 139–173. doi: 10.1080/15299732.2016.1194358.

Lahav, Y., Kanat-Maymon, Y., & Solomon, Z. (2016). Secondary traumatization and attachment among wives of former POWs: A longitudinal study. *Attachment and Human Development, 18*(2), 141–153. doi: 10.1080/14616734.2015.1121502.

Lahav, Y., Levin, Y., Bensimon, M., Kanat-Maymon, Y., & Solomon, Z. (2017). Secondary traumatization and differentiation among wives of former POWs: A reciprocal association. *Journal of Traumatic Stress, 30*, 399–408. doi: 10.1002/jts.22204.

Lai, B. S., Lewis, R., Livings, M. S., La Greca, A. M., & Esnard, A.-M. (2017). Posttraumatic stress symptom trajectory among children after disaster exposure: A review. *Journal of Traumatic Stress, 30*, 571–582. doi: 10.1002/jts.22242.

Laible, D., Panfile, T., & Makariev, D. (2008). The quality and frequency of mother-toddler conflict: Links with attachment and temperament. *Child Development, 79*(2), 426–443.

Lambert, J. E., Hasbun, A., Engh, R., & Holzer, J. (2015). Veteran PTSS and spouse relationship quality: The importance of dyadic coping. *Psychological Trauma: Theory, Research, Practice, and Policy, 7*(5), 493–499. doi: 10.1037/tra0000036.

LaMotte, A. D., & Murphy, C. M. (2017). Trauma, posttraumatic stress disorder symptoms, and dissociative experiences during men's intimate partner violence perpetration. *Psychological Trauma: Theory, Research, Practice, and Policy, 9*(5), 567–54. doi: 10.1037/tra0000205.

LaMotte, A. D., Taft, C. T., Weatherill, R. P., Casement, M. D., Creech, S. K., Milberg, W. P., ... McGlinchey, R. E. (2017). Sleep problems and physical pain as moderators of the relationship between PTSD symptoms and aggression in returning veterans. *Psychological Trauma: Theory, Research, Practice, and Policy, 9*(1), 11–116. doi: 10.1037/tra0000178.

Langens, T. A. (2003). Daydreaming mediates between goal commitment and goal attainment in individuals high in achievement motivation. *Imagination, Cognition and Personality, 22*(2), 103–115.

Langevin, R., Hebert, M., Allard-Dansereau, C., & Bernard-Bonnin, A. C. (2016). Emotional regulation in sexually abused preschoolers: The contribution of parental factors. *Journal of Traumatic Stress, 29*, 180–184. doi: 10.1002/jts.22082.

Lanius, R. A., Vermetten, E., Loewenstein, R. J., Brand, B., Schmahl, C., Bremner, J. D., & Spiegel, D. (2010). Emotion modulation in PTSD: Clinical and neurobiological evidence for dissociative subtype. *American Journal of Psychiatry, 167*, 640–647.

Lanius, R. A., Williamson, P. C., Bluhm, R. L., Densmore, M., Boksman, K., Neufeld, R. W., ... Menon, R. S. (2005). Functional connectivity of dissociative responses in posttraumaticstress disorder: A functional magnetic, resonance imaging investigation. *Biological Psychiatry, 57*, 873–884. doi: 10.1016/j.biopsych.2005.01.011.

Lasikiewicz, N. (2016). Perceived stress, thinking style, and paranormal belief. *Imagination, Cognition, and Personality, 35*(3), 306–320. doi: 10.1177/0276236615595235.

Lassri, D., & Shahar, G. (2012). Self-criticism mediates the link between childhood emotional maltreatment and young adults' romantic relationships. *Journal of Social and Clinical Psychology, 31*(3), 289–311. doi: 10.1521/jscp.2012.31.3.289.

Lassri, D., Luyten, P., Cohen, G., & Shahar, G. (2016). The effect of childhood emotional maltreatment on romantic relationships in young adulthood: A double mediation model involving self-criticism and attachment. *Psychological Trauma: Theory, Research, Practice, and Policy, 8*(4), 504–511. doi: 10.1037/tra0000134.

Laugharne, J., Lillee, A., & Janca, A. (2010). Role of psychological trauma in the cause and treatment of anxiety and depression. *Current Opinions in Psychiatry, 23*, 25–29. doi: 10.1097/YCO.0b013e3283345dc5.

Lawrence, E. J., Shaw, P., Baker, D., Patel, M., Sierra-Siegert, M., Medford, N., & Daivd, A. S. (2007). Empathy and enduring depersonalization: The role of self-related processes. *Social Neuroscince, 2*(3–4), 292–306. doi: 10.1080/17470910391794.

Lazar, S. W., Kerr, C. E., Wasserman, R. H., Gray, J. R., Greve, D. N., Treadway, M. T., ... Fischl, B. (2005). Meditation experience is associated with increased cortical thickness. *Neuroreport, 16*(17), 1893–1897.

Lazarus, R. S., & Folkman, S. (1984). *Stress, appraisal and coping*. New York, NY: Springer.

LeBoutillier, N., & Barry, R. (2018). Psychological mindedness: Personality and creative cognition. *Creativity Research Journal, 30*(1), 78–84. doi: 10.1080/10400419.2018.1411440.

LeBoutillier, N., & Marks, D. F. (2003). Mental imagery and creativity: A meta-analytic review study. *British Journal of Psychology, 94*, 29–44.

LeBoutillier, N., Barry, R., & Westley, D. (2016). Creativity and the measurement of subclinical psychopathology in the general population: Schizotypy, psychoticism, and hypomania. *Psychology of Aesthetics, Creativity, and the Arts, 10*(2), 240–247. doi: 10.1037/aca0000047.

LeBouthillier, D. M., McMillan, K. A., Thibodeau, M. A., & Asmundson, G. J. (2015). Types and number of traumas associated with suicidal ideation and suicide attempts in PTSD: Findings from a U.S. nationally representative sample. *Journal of Traumatic Stress, 28*, 183–190. doi: 10.1002/jts.22010.

Leder, H. (2013). Next steps in neuroaesthetics: Which process and processing stages to study? *Psychology of Aesthetics, Creativity, and the Arts, 7*(1), 27–37. doi: 10.1037/a0031585.

LeDoux, J. E. (1996). *The emotional brain: The mysterious underpinnings of emotional life.* New York: Simon & Schuster.

———. (2002). *Synaptic self: How our brains become who we are.* New York: Viking.

Lee, H., Aldwin, C. M., & Spiro III, A. (2017). Does combat exposure affect well-being in later life? The V A normative aging study. *Psychological Trauma: Theory, Research, Practice, and Policy, 9*(6), 672–678. doi: 10.1037/tra0000282.

Lee, J. E. C., Phinney, B., Watkins, K., & Zamorski, M. A. (2016). Psychosocial pathways linking adverse childhood experiences to mental health in recently deployed Canadian military service members. *Journal of Traumatic Stress, 29*, 124–131. doi: 10.1002/jts.22085.

Lee, J. H., Lee, D., Kim, J., Jeon, K., & Sim, M. (2017). Duty-related trauma exposure and posttraumatic stress symptoms in professional firefighters. *Journal of Traumatic Stress, 30*, 133–141. doi: 10.1002/jts.22180.

Lee, S. A., & Dow, G. T. (2011). Malevolent creativity: Does personality influence malicious divergent thinking. *Creativity Research Journal, 23*(2), 73–82. doi: 10.1080/10400419.2011.57119.

Lee, S.-Y, & Min, J. (2016). The profiles of creative potential and personality characteristic of adult professionals. *Creativity Research Journal, 28*(3), 298–309. doi: 10.1080/10400419.2016.1195634.

Lee, W. E., Kwok, C. H., Hunter, E. C. M., Richards, M., & David, A. S. (2012). Prevalance and childhood antecedents of depersonalization syndrome in a UK birth cohort. *Social Psychiatry and Psychiatric Epidemiology, 47*, 253–261. doi: 10.1007/s00127-010-0327-7.

Lee, Y. S., Chang, J. Y., & Choi, J. N. (2017). Why reject creative ideas? Fear as a driver of implicit bias against creativity. *Creativity Research Journal, 29*(3), 225–235. doi: 10.1080/10400419.2017.1360061.

Leenarts, L. E. W., Vermeiren, R. R. J. M., van de Ven, P. M., Lodewijks, H. P. B., Doreleijers, T. A., & Lindauer, R. J. L. (2013). Relationship between interpersonal trauma, symptoms of posttraumatic stress disorder, and other mental health problems in girls in compulsory residential care. *Journal of Traumatic Stress, 26*, 526–529. doi: 10.1002/jts.21831.

Leerkes, E. M., Gedaly, L. R., Zhou, N., Calkins, S., Henrich, V. C., & Smolen, A. (2017). Further evidence of the limited role of candidate genes in relation to infant-mother attachment outcomes. *Attachment and Human Development, 19*(1), 76–105. doi: 10.1080/14616734.2016.1253759.

Legarreta, M., Graham, J., North, L., Bueler, C. E., McGlade, E., & Yurgelun-Todd, D. (2015). DSM-5 posttraumatic stress disorder symptoms associated with suicide behaviors in veterans. *Psychological Trauma: Theory, Research, Practice, and Policy, 7*(3), 277–285. doi: 10.1037/tra0000026.

Lehrner, A., & Yehuda, R. (2018). Trauma across generations and paths to adaptation resilience. *Psychological Trauma: Theory, Research, Practice, and Policy, 10*(1), 22–29. doi: 10.1037/tra0000302.

Lejonclou, A., Nilsson, D., & Homqvist, R. (2014). Variants of potentially traumatizing life events in eating disorder patients. *Psychological Trauma: Theory, Research, Practice, and Policy, 6*(6), 661–667. doi: 10.1037/a0034926.

Lemons, G. (2011). Diverse perspectives of creativity testing: Controversial issues when used for inclusion into gifted programs. *Journal for the Education of the Gifted, 34*(5), 742–772. doi: 10.1177/0162353211417221.

Lerner, E., Bonanno, G. A., Keatley, E., Joscelune, A., & Keller, A. S. (2016). Predictors of suicidal ideation in treatment-seeking surivors of torture. *Psychological Trauma: Theory, Research, Practice, and Policy, 8*(1), 17–24. doi: 10.1027/tra0000040.

Leube, D. T., Knoblich, G., Erb, M., Grodd, W., Bartels, M., & Kircher, T. T. J. (2003). The neural correlates of perceiving one's own movements. *Neuroimage, 20*, 2084–2090. doi: 10.1016/j.neuroimage.2003.07.033.

Levey, E. J., Gelaye, B., Bain, P., Rondon, M. B., Borba, C. P. C., Henderson, D. C., & Williams, M. A. (2017). A systematic review of randomized controlled trials of interventions designed to decrease child abuse in high risk families. *Child Abuse and Neglect, 65*, 48–57. doi: 10.1016/j.chiabu.2017.01.004.

Levin, R., & Fireman, G. (2001–2002). The relation of fantasy-proneness, psychological absorption and imaginative involvement to nightmare prevalence and nightmare distress. *Imagination, Cognition and Personality, 21*(2), 111–129.

Levin, R., & Spei, E. (2003). Relationship of purported measures of pathological and nonpathological dissociation to self-reported psychological distress and fantasy immersion. *Assessment, 11*(2), 160–168. doi: 10.1177/1073191103256377.

Levin, R., Simeon, D., & Guralnick, O. (2004). Role of fantasy proneness, imaginative involvement, and psychological absorption in depersonalization disorder. *Journal of Nervous and Mental Disease, 192*(1), 69–71. doi: 10.1097/01.nmd.0000106003.46153.54.

Levin, S. Z., Laufer, A., Stein, E., Hamama-Raz, Y., & Solomon, Z. (2009). Examining the relationship between resilience and posttraumatic growth. *Journal of Traumatic Stress, 22*(4), 282–286. doi: 10.1002/jts.20409.

Levinger, S., Somer, E., & Holden, R. R. (2015). The importance of mental pain and physical dissociation in youth suicidality. *Journal of Trauma and Dissociation, 15*, 322–339. doi: 10.1080/15299732.2015.989644.

Lewis, M. D., & Granic, I. (Eds.). (2000). *Emotion, development, and self-organization: Dynamic systems approaches to emotional development*. New York: Cambridge University Press.

Li, C.-H., & Wu, J.-J. (2011). The structural relationships between optimism and innovative behavior: Understanding potential antecedents and mediating effects. *Creativity Research Journal, 23*(2), 119–128. doi: 10.1080/10400419.2011.571184.

Li, W., Yang, W., Li, W., Li, Y., Wei, D., Li, H., … Zhang, Q. (2015). Brain structure and resting – State functional connectivity in university professors with high academic achievement. *Creativity Research Journal, 27*(2), 139–150. doi: 10.1080/10400419.2015.1030311.

Liberzon, I., & Martis, B. (2006). Neuroimaging studies of emotional response in PTSD. *Annals of the New York Academy of Science, 1071*, 87–109. doi: 10.1196/annals.1364.009.

Liebschutz, J., Saltz, R., Brower, V., Keane, T. M., Lloyd-Travaglini, C., Averbuch, T., & Samet, J. H. (2007). PTSD in urban primary care: High prevalence and low physician recognition. *General Internal Medicine, 22*, 719–726. doi: 10.1007/s11606-007-0161-0.

Liknaitzky, P., Smillie, L. D., & Allen, N. B. (2018). The low and narrow: A preliminary test of the association between depressive symptoms and deficits in producing divergent inferences. *Creativity Research Journal, 30*(1), 67–77. doi: 10.1080/10400419.2018.1411459.

Lilly, M. M., London, M. J., & Bridgett, D. J. (2014). Using SEM to examine emotion regulation and revictimization in predicting PTSD symptoms among childhood abuse survivors. *Psychological Trauma: Theory, Research, Practice, and Policy, 6*(6), 644–651. doi: 10.1037/a0036460.

Lim, S., & Smith, J. (2008). The structural relationships of parenting style, creativity personality, and loneliness. *Creativity Research Journal, 20*(4), 412–419. doi: 10.1080/10400410802391868.

Limont, W., Dreszer-Drogorob, J., Bedynksa, S., Sliwinska, K., & Jastrzebska, D. (2014). "Old wine in new bottles"? Relationships between overexcitabilities, the Big Five personality traits and giftedness in adolescents. *Personality and Individual Differences, 69*, 199–204. doi: 10.1016/j.paid.2014.06.003.

Lin, J.-S., Chang, W.-S., & Liang, C. (2015). The imagination constructs with science students: Interplay among social climate, intrinsic motivation, and personality traits. *Imagination, Cognition, and Personality, 34*(4), 340–359. doi: 10.1177/0276236615572589.

Lin, N. (2001). *Social capital: A theory of social structure and action*. New York, NY: Cambridge University Press.

Lind, M. J., Aggen, S. H., Kendler, K. S., York, T. P., & Amstadter, A. B. (2016). An epidemiologic study of childhood sexual abuse and adult sleep disturbances. *Psychological Trauma: Theory, Research, Practice, and Policy, 8*(2), 198–205. doi: 10.1037/tra000080.

Lind, M. J., Marraccini, M. E., Sheerin, C. M., Bountress, K., Bacanu, S.-A., Amstadter, A. B., & Nugent, N. R. (2017). Association of posttraumatic stress disorder with rs2267735 in the ADCYAP1R1 gene: A meat-analysis. *Journal of Traumatic Stress, 30*, 389–398. doi: 10.1002/jts.22211.

Lindell, A. K. (2011). Lateral thinkers are not so laterally minded: Hemispheric asymmetry, interaction, and creativity. *Laterality, 16*(4), 479–498. doi: 10.1080/1357650X.2010.497813.

Linden, M., & Rotter, M. (2018). Spectrum of embitterment manifestations. *Psychological Trauma: Theory, Research, Practice, and Policy, 10*(1), 1–6. doi: 10.1037/tra0000307.

Lindsay, J. A., Keo-Meier, C., Hudson, S., Walder, A., Martin, L. A., & Kauth, M. R. (2016). Mental health of transgender veterans of the Iraq and Afghanistan conflicts who experienced military sexual trauma. *Journal of Traumatic Stress, 29*, 563–567. doi: 10.1002/jts.22146.

Lindstrom, C. M., Cann, A., Calhoun, L. G., & Tedeschi, R. (2013). The relationship of core belief challenge, rumination, disclosure, and sociocultural elements to posttraumatic growth. *Psychological Trauma: Theory, Research, Practice, and Policy, 5*(1), 50–55. doi: 10.1037/a0022030.

Liotti, G. (2006). A model of dissociation based on attachment theory and research. *Journal of Trauma and Dissociation, 7*(4), 55–73. doi: 10.1300/J229v07n04_04.

Litvin, J. M., Kaminski, P. L., & Riggs, S. A. (2017). The complex trauma inventory: A self-report measure of posttraumatic stress disorder and complex posttraumatic stress disorder. *Journal of Traumatic Stress, 30*, 602–613. doi: 10.1002/jts.22231.

Litz, B. T., Stein, N., Delaney, E., Lebowitz, L., Nash, W. P., Silva, C., & Maguen, S. (2009). Moral injury and moral repair in war veterans: A preliminary model and intervention strategy. *Clinical Psychology Review, 29*, 695–706. doi: 10.1016/j.cpr.2009.07.003.

Loggia, M. L., Modli, J. S., & Bushnell, M. C. (2008). Empathy hurts: Compassion for another increases both sensory and affective components of pain perception. *Pain, 136*(1–2), 168–176. doi: 10.1016/j.pain.2007.07.017.

Long, H. (2014). An empirical review of research methodologies and methods in creativity studies (2003–2012). *Creativity Research Journal, 26*(4), 427–438. doi: 10.1080/10400419.2014.961781.

Lotze, M., Scheler, G., Tan, H.-R. M., Braun, C., & Birbaumer, N. (2003). The musician's brain: Functional imaging of amateurs and professionals during performance and imagery. *Neuroimage, 20*, 1817–1829. doi: 10.1016/j.neuroimage.2003.07.018.

Lovelace, J. B., & Hunter, S. T. (2013). Charismatic, ideological, and pragmatic leaders' influences on subordinate creative performance across the creative process. *Creativity Research Journal, 25*(1), 59–74. doi: 10.1080/10400419.2013.752228.

Lovelace, K. J., Manz, C. C., & Alves, J. C. (2007). Work stress and leadership development: The role of self-leadership, shared leadership, physical fitness and flow in managing demands and increasing job control. *Human Resource Management Review, 17*, 374–387. doi: 10.1016/j.hrmr.2007.08.001.

Lowe, S. R., Sampson, L., Gruebner, O., & Galea, S. (2016). Community unemployment and disaster-related stressors shape risk for posttraumatic stress in the longer-term aftermath of Hurricane Sandy. *Journal of Traumatic Stress, 29*, 440–447. doi: 10.1002/jts.22126.

Lubart, T. L. (1994). Creativity. In R. J. Sternberg (Ed.), *Thinking and problem solving* (pp. 290–332). San Diego: Academic Press.

———. (2001). Models of the creative process: Past, present and future. *Creativity Research Journal, 13*(3–4), 295–308. doi: 10.1207/S15326934CRJ1334_07.

Luby, J. L., Barch, D. M., Belden, A., Gaffrey, M. S., Tillman, R., Babb, C., ... Botteron, K. N. (2012). Maternal support in early childhood predicts larger hippocampal volumes at school age. *Proceedings of the National Academy of Science, 109*(8), 2854–2859. doi: 10.1073/pnas.1118003109.

Ludwig, A. M. (1998). Method and madness in the arts and sciences. *Creativity Research Journal, 11*(2), 93–101.

Lueger-Schuster, B., Knefel, M. Gluck, T. M., Jagsch, R., Kantor, V., & Weindl, D. (2018). Child abuse and neglect in institutional settings, cumulative lifetime traumatization, and psychopathological long-term correlates in adult survivors: The Vienna Institutional Abuse Study. *Child Abuse and Neglect, 76*, 488–501. doi: 10.1016/j.chiabu.2017.12.009.

Luh, D.-B., & Lu, C.-C. (2012). From cognitive style to creativity achievement: The mediating role of passion. *Psychology of Aesthetics, Creativity, and the Arts, 6*(3), 282–288. doi: 10.1037/a0026868.

Lukaschek, K., Kruse, J., Emeny, R. T., Lacruz, M. E., von Eisenhart Rothe, A., & Ladwig, K.-H. (2013). Lifetime traumatic experiences and their impact on PTSD: A general population study. *Social Psychiatry and Psychiatric Epidemiology, 48*, 525–532. doi: 10.1007/a00127-012-0585-7.

Luking, K. R., Repovs, G., Belden, A. C., Gaffrey, M. S., Botteron, K. N., Luby, J. L., & Barch, D. M. (2011). Functional connectivity of the amygdala in early-childhood-onset depression. *Journal of American Academy of Child and Adolescent Psychiatry, 50*(10), 1027–1041.

Lusk, J. D., Sadeh, N., Wolf, E. J., & Miller, M. W. (2017). Reckless self-destructive behavior and PTSD in veterans: The mediating role of new adverse events. *Journal of Traumatic Stress, 30*, 270–278. doi: 10.1037/jts.22182.

Luthar, S. S. (1991). Vulnerability and resilience: A study of high-risk adolescents. *Child Development, 62*(3), 600–616.

Lutz, A., Brefczynski-Lewis, J., Johnstone, T., & Davidson, R. J. (2008). Regulation of the neural circuitry of emotion by compassion meditation: Effects of meditative expertise. *PLoS ONE, 3*(3), e1897. doi: 10.1371/journal.pone.0001897.

Lutz, P.-E., Gross, J. A., Dhir, S. K., Maussion, G., Yang, J., Bramoulle, A., ... Turecki, G. (2017). Epigenetic regulation of the kappa opioid receptor by child abuse. *Biological Psychiatry, e-publ.* doi: 10.1016/j.biopsych.2017.07.012.

Lynn, S. J., & Rhue, J. W. (1988). Fantasy proneness: Hypnosis, developmental antecedents and psychopathology. *American Psychologist, 43*(1), 35–40.

Lynn, S. J., Lilienfeld, S. O., Merckelbach, H., Giesbrecht, T., McNally, R. J., Loftus, E. F., ... Malaktaris, A. (2014). The trauma model of dissociation: Inconvenient truths and stubborn fictions. Comment on Dalenberg et al. (2012). *Psychological Bulletin, 140*(3), 896–910. doi: 10.1037/a0035570.

Lyons-Ruth, K. (2003). Dissociation and the parent-infant dialogue: A longitudinal perspective from attachment research. *Journal of the American Psychoanalytic Association, 51*(3), 883–911.

Lyons-Ruth, K., Yellin, C., Melnick, S., & Atwood, G. (2003). Childhood experiences of trauma and loss have different relations to maternal unresolved and hostile-helpless states of mind on the AAI. *Attachment and Human Development, 5*(4), 330–352. doi: 10.1080/14616730310001633410.

———. (2005). Expanding the concept of unresolved mental states: Hostile/helpless states of mind on the Adult Attachment Interview are associated with disrupted mother-infant communication and infant disorganization. *Development and Psychopathology, 17*, 1–23. doi: 10.1017/S09545794050017.

Maaranen, P., Tanskanen, A., Hintikka, J., Honkalampi, K., Haatainen, K., Koivumaa-Honkanen, H., & Viinamaki, H. (2008). The course of dissociation in the general population: A 3-year follou-up study. *Comprehensive Psychiatry, 49*, 269–274. doi: 10.1016/j.comppsych.2007.04.010.

Maaranen, P., Tanskanen, A., Honkalampi, K., Haatainen, K., Hintikka, J., & Viinamaki, H. (2005). Factors associated with pathological dissociation in the general population. *Australian and New Zealand Journal of Psychiatry, 39*, 387–394.

MacArthur, L. J. (2011). Behind closed doors: Emotional abuse in the music studio. In A. Williamon, D. Edwards, & L. Bartel (Eds.), *Proceedings of the International Symposium on Performance Science* (pp. 387–392). Utrecht, The Netherlands: European.

MacDonald, K. (2008). Dissociative disorders unclear? Think 'rainbows from pain blows.' *Current Psychiatry, 7*(5), 73–82.

Macfie, J., Cicchetti, D., & Toth, S. L. (2001). The development of dissociation in maltreated preschool-aged children. *Development and Psychopathology, 13*, 233–254.

Maddi, S. R. (2006). Hardiness: The courage to grow from stresses. *Journal of Positive Psychology, 1*(3), 160–168. doi: 10.1080/17439760600619609.

Maddi, S. R., Harvey, R. H., Khoshaba, D. H., Fazel, M., & Resurreccion, N. (2009). The personality construct of hardiness, IV: Expressed in positive cognitions and emotions concerning oneself and developmentally relevant activities. *Journal of Humanistic Psychology, 49*(3), 292–305. doi: 10.1177/0022167809331860.

Maddi, S. R., Harvey, R. H., Khoshaba, D. M., Lu, J. L. Persico, M., & Brow, M. (2006). The personality construct of hardiness, III: Relationships with repression, innovativeness, authoritarianism, and performance. *Journal of Personality, 74*(2), 575–598. doi: 10.1111/j.1467-6494.2006.00385.x.

Madigan, S., Bakermans-Kranenburg, M. J., van IJzendoorn, M. H., Moran, G., Pederson, D. R., & Benoit, D. (2006). Unresolved states of mind, anomalous parental behavior, and disorganized attachment: A review and meta-analysis of a transmission gap. *Attachment and Human Development, 8*(2), 89–111. doi: 10.1080/14616730600774458.

Maes, S., & Karoly, P. (2005). Self-regulation assessment and intervention in physical health and illness: A review. *Applied Psychology: An International Review, 54*(2), 267–299.

Mageau, G. A., Vallerand, R. J., Charest, J., Salvy, S.-J., Lacaille, N., Boufford, T., & Koestner, R. (2009). On the development of harmonious and obsessive passion: The role of autonomy support, activity specialization, and identification with the activity. *Journal of Personality, 77*(3), 601–646. doi: 10.1111/j.1467-6494.2009.00559.x.

Magruder, K. M., Goldberg, J., Forsberg, C. W., Friedman, M. J., Litz, B. T., Vaccarino, V., ... Smith, N. L. (2016). Long-term trajectories of PTSD in Vietnam-era veterans: The course and consequences of PTSD in twins. *Journal of Traumatic Stress, 29*, 5–16. doi: 10.1002/jts.22075.

Maier, M. A., Bernier, A., Pekrun, R., Zimmermann, P., Strasser, K., & Grossmann, K. E. (2005). Attachment state of mind and perceptual processing of emotional stimuli. *Attachment and Human Development, 7*, 67–81. doi: 10.1080/14616730500039606.

Main, M. (2000). The organized categories of infant, child and adult attachment: Flexible vs. inflexible attention under attachment-related stress. *Journal of the American Psychoanalytic Association, 48*(4), 1055–1096.

Main, M., Goldwyn, R., & Hesse, E. (2003). *Adult attachment scoring and classification systems.* Unpublished manuscript, University of California at Berkeley.

Maltby, J., Day, L., McCutcheon, L. E., Houran, J., & Ashe, D. (2006). Extreme celebrity worship, fantasy proneness and dissociation: Developing the measurement and understanding of celebrity worship within a clinical personality context. *Personality and Individual Differences, 40*(2), 273–283. doi: 10.1016/j.paid.2005.07.004.

Mandavia, A., Robinson, G. G. N., Bradley, B., Ressler, K. J., & Powers, A. (2016). Exposure to childhood abuse and later substance use: Indirect effects of emotion dysregulation and exposure to trauma. *Journal of Traumatic Stress, 29*, 422–429. doi: 10.1002/jts.22131.

Mangione, L., & Keady, S. (2007). "Spirit in the Night" to "Mary's Place": Loss, death, and the transformative power of relationship. *Psychology of Aesthetics, Creativity, and the Arts, 1*(4), 179–190. doi: 10.1037/1931.3896.1.4.179.

Marchand, A., Nadeau, C., Beaulieu-Prevost, D., Boyer, R., & Martin, M. (2015). Predictors of posttraumatic stress disorder among police officers: A prospective study. *Psychological Trauma: Theory, Research, Practice, and Policy, 7*(3), 212–221. doi: 10.1037/ta0038780.

Marcusson-Clavertz, D., Gusic, S., Bengtsson, H., Jacobsen, H., & Cardena, E. (2017). The relation of dissociation and mind wandering to unresolved/disorganized attachment: An experimental sampling study. *Attachment and Human Development, 19*(2), 170–190. doi: 10.1080/14616734.2016.1261914.

Marinelli, R., Bindi, R., Marchi, S., Castellani, E., Carli, G., & Santarcangelo, E. (2012). Hypnotizability-related differences in written language. *International Journal of Clinical and Experimental Hypnosis, 60*(1), 54–66. doi: 10.1080/00207144.2011.622196.

Marques, L., Eustis, E. H., Dixon, L., Valentine, S. E., Borba, C. P. C., Kaysen, D., & Wiltsey-Stirman, S. (2016). Delivering cognitive processing therapy in a community health setting: The influence of Latino culture and community violence on posttraumatic change. *Psychological Trauma: Theory, Research, Practice, and Policy, 8*(1), 98–106. doi: 10.1037/tra0000044.

Marriott, B. R., Lewis, C. C., & Gobin, R. L. (2016). Disclosing traumatic experiences: Correlates, context, and consequences. *Psychological Trauma: Theory, Research, Practice, and Policy, 8*(2), 141–148. doi: 10.1037/tra0000058.

Marsee, M. A., & Frick, P. J. (2007). Exploring the cognitive and emotional correlates to proactive and reactive aggression in a sample of detained girls. *Journal of Abnormal Child Psychology, 35*, 969–981. doi: 10.1007/s10802-007-9147-y.

Marshall, E. M., Frazier, P., Frankfurt, S., & Kuijer, R. G. (2015). Trajectories of posttraumatic growth and depreciation after two major earthquakes. *Psychological Trauma: Theory, Research, Practice, and Policy, 7*(2), 112–121. doi: 10.1037tra0000005.

Marteau, T. M., & Weinman, J. (2006). Self-regulation and the behavioral response to DNA risk information: A theoretical analysis and framework for future research. *Social Science and Medicine, 62*, 1360–1368. doi: 10.1016/j.soscimed.2005.08.005.

Martens, A., Greenberg, J., Allen, J. J. B., Hayes, J., Schimel, J., & Johns, M. (2010). Self-esteem and autonomic physiology: Self-esteem levels predict cardiac vagal tone. *Journal of Research in Personality, 44*, 573–584. doi: 10.1016/j.jrp.2010.07.001.

Martin, A. J., & Jackson, S. A. (2008). Brief approaches to assessing task absorption and enhanced subjective experience: Examining 'short' and 'core' flow in diverse performance domains. *Motivation and Emotion, 32*(3), 141–157. doi: 10.1007/s11031-008-9094-0.

Martin, C. G., Cromer, L. D., DePrince, A. P., & Freyd, J. J. (2013). The role of cumulative trauma, betrayal, and appraisals in understanding trauma symptomatology. *Psychological Trauma: Theory, Research, Practice, and Policy, 5*(2), 110–118. doi: 10.1037/a0025686.

Martin, C. G., Van Ryzin, M. J., & Dishion, T. J. (2016). Profiles of childhood trauma: Betrayal, frequency, and psychological distress in late adolescence. *Psychological Trauma: Theory, Research, Practice, and Policy, 8*(2), 206–1213. doi: 10.1037/tra0000005.

Martin, C. T., Ric, A., & Hristovski, R. (2015). Creativity and emergence of specific dance movements using instructional constraint. *Psychology of Aesthetics, Creativity, and the Arts, 9*(1), 65–74. doi: 10.1037/a0038706.

Martin, J. J., & Cutler, K. (2002). An exploratory study of flow and motivation in theatre actors. *Journal of Applied Sport Psychology, 14*, 344–352. doi: 10.1080/10413200290103608.

Martin, J., Raby, K. L., Labella, M. H., & Roisman, G. I. (2017). Childhood abuse and neglect, attachment states of mind and non-suicidal self-injury. *Attachment and Human Development, 19*(5), 425–446. doi: 10.1080/14616734.2017.1330832.

Martindale, C. (2001). Oscillations and analogies: Thomas Young MD, FRS, Genius. *American Psychologist, 56*(4), 342–345. doi: 10.1037//0003-066X.56.4.342.

———. (2007). Recent trends in the psychological study of aesthetics, creativity, and the arts. *Empirical Studies of the Arts, 25*(2), 121–141.

Martinsen, O. L. (2011). The creative personality: A synthesis and development of the creative person profile. *Creativity Research Journal, 23*(3), 185–202. doi: 10.1080/10400419.2011.5956565.

Marusak, H. A., Etkin, A., & Thomason, M. E. (2015). Disrupted insula-based neural circuit organization and conflict interference in trauma-exposed youth. *Neuroimage: Clinical, 8*, 516–525. doi: 10.1016/j.nicl.2015.04.007.

Mash, H. B. H., Ursano, R. J., Benevides, K. N., & Fullerton, C. S. (2017). Identification with terrorist victims of the Washington, DC sniper attacks: Posttraumatic Stress and depression. *Journal of Traumatic Stress, 29,* 41–48. doi: 10.1002/jts.22069.

Maslow, C. B., Caramanica, K., Welch, A. E., Stellman, S. D., Brackbill, R. M., & Farfel, M. R. (2015). Trajectories of scores on a screening instrument for PTSD among World Trade Center rescue, recovery, and clean-up workers. *Journal of Traumatic Stress, 28,* 198–205. doi: 10.1002/jts.22011.

Mason, E., & Richardson, R. (2012). Treating disgust in anxiety disorders. *Clinical Psychology: Science and Practice, 19,* 180–194. doi: 10.1111/j.1468.2850.2012.01282.x.

Masten, A. S. (2001). Ordinary magic: Resilience processes in development. *American Psychologist, 56*(3), 227–238. doi: 10.1037//0003-066X.56.3.227.

———. (2004). Regulatory processes, risk, and resilience in adolescent development. *Annals of the New York Academy of Sciences, 1021,* 310–319. doi: 10.1196/annals.1308.036.

Masten, A. S., & Obradovic, J. (2006). Competence and resilience in development. *Annals of the New York Academy of Science, 1094,* 13–27. doi: 10.1196/annals.1376.003.

Matare, J. (2009). Creativity or musical intelligence? A comparative study of improvisation/improvisation performance by European and African musicians. *Thinking Skills and Creativity, 4,* 194–203. doi: 10.1016/j.tsc.2009.09.005.

Matos, M., & Pinto-Gouveia, J. (2010). Shame as a traumatic memory. *Clinical Psychology and Psychotherapy, 17*(4), 299–312. doi: 10.1002/cpp.659.

Matos, M., Pinto-Gouveia, J., & Costa, V. (2013). Understanding the importance of attachment in shame traumatic memory relation to depression: The impact of emotion regulation processes. *Clinical Psychology and Psychotherapy, 20,* 149–165. doi: 10.1002/cpp.786.

Matthias, M., Beutel, M. E., Jordan, J., Zimmermann, M., Wolters, S., & Heidenreich, T. (2007). Depersonalization, mindfulness, and childhood trauma. *Journal of Nervous and Mental Disease, 195*(8), 693–696. doi: 10.1097/NMD.obo13e31811f4492.

Mattingly, M. J., & Walsh, W. A. (2010). Rural families with a child abuse report are more likely headed by a single parent and endure economic and family stress. *Casey Institute Report Brief, 10,* 1–4. Retrieved from https://www. www.carsey-institute.unh.edu.

Maxwell, H., Tasca, G. A., Grenon, R., Faye, M., Ritchie, K., Bissada, H., & Balfour, L. (2017). The role of coherence of mind and reflective funtionsing inunderstanding binge-eating disorder and co-morbid overwight. *Attachment and Human Development, 19*(4), 407–424. doi: 10.1080/14616734.2017.1318934.

Mayer, J. D., Perkins, D. M., Caruso, D. R., & Salovey, P. (2001). Emotional intelligence and giftedness. *Roeper Review, 23*(3), 131–137. doi: 10.1080/02783190109554084.

Mayseless, N., Eran, A., & Shamay-Tsoory, S. G. (2015). Generating original ideas: The neural underpinning of originality. *Neuroimage, 116,* 232–239. doi: 10.1016.neuroimage.2015.05.030.

Mayseless, N., Uzefovsky, F., Shalev, I., Ebstein, R. P., & Shamay-Tsoory, S. G. (2013). The association between creativity and 7R polymorphism in the dopamine receptor D4 gene (DRD4). *Frontiers in Human Neuroscience, 7*(502), 1–7. doi: 10.3389/fnhum.2013.00502.

McAdams, D. P., & Olson, B. D. (2010). Personality development: Continuity and change over the life course. *Annual Review of Psychology, 61*, 517–542. doi: 10.1146/annurev.psych.093008.100507.

McAdams, D. P., & Pals, J. L. (2006). A new Big Five: Fundamental principles for an integrative science of personality. *American Psychologist, 61*(3), 204–217. doi: 10.1037/0003-066X.61.3.204.

McAndrew, L. M., Markowitz, S., Lu, S.-E., Borders, A., Rothman, D., & Quigley, K. S. (2017). Resilience during war: Better unit cohesion and reductions in avoidant coping are associated with better mental health function after combat deployment. *Psychological Trauma: Theory, Research, Practice, and Policy, 9*(1), 52–61. doi: 10.1037/tra0000152.

McCanlies, E. C., Sarkisian, K., Andrew, M. E., Burchfiel, C. M., & Violanti, J. M. (2017). Association of peritraumatic dissociation with symptoms of depression and posttraumatic stress disorder. *Psychological Trauma: Theory, Research, Practice, and Policy, 9*(4), 479–484. doi: 10.1037/tra0000215.

McCaslin, S. E., de Zoysa, P., Butler, L. D., Hart, S., Marmar, C. R., Metzler, T. J., & Koopman, C. (2009). The relationship of posttraumatic growth to peritraumatic reactions and posttraumatic stress among Sri Lankan university students. *Journal of Traumatic Stress, 22*(4), 334–339. doi: 10.1002/jts.20426.

McCoy, J. M., & Evans, G. W. (2002). The potential role of the physical environment in fostering creativity. *Creativity Research Journal, 14*(3 & 4), 409–426.

McCrae, R. R. (2007). Aesthetic chills as a universal marker of openness to experience. *Motivation and Emotion, 31*, 5–11. doi: 10.1007/s11031-007-9053-1.

McCrae, R. R., & Costa, P. C., Jr. (1987). Validation of the five-factor model across instruments and observers. *Journal of Personality and Social Psychology, 52*, 81–90.

McDevitt-Murphy, M. E., Neimeyer, R. A., Burke, L. A., Williams, J. L., & Lawson, K. (2012). The toll of traumatic loss in African Americans bereaved by homicide. *Psychological Trauma: Theory, Research, Practice, and Policy, 4*(3), 303–311. doi: 10.1037/a0024911.

McEwen, B. S., Eiland, L., Hunter, R. G., & Miller, M. M. (2012). Stress and anxiety: Structural plasticity and epigenetic regulation as a consequence of stress. *Neuropharmacology, 62*, 3–12.

McEwen, B. S., Gray, J. D., & Nasca, C. (2015). Recognizing resilience: Learning from the effects of stress on the brain. *Neurobiology of Stress, 1*, 1–11. doi: 10.1016/j.ynstr.2014.09.001.

McGloin, J. M., & Widom, C. S. (2001). Resilience among abused and neglected children grown up. *Development and Psychopathology, 13*(4), 1021–1038.

McKay, A. S., Karwowski, M., & Kaufman, J. C. (2017). Measuring the muses: Validating the Kaufman Domains of Creativity Scale (K-DOCS). *Psychology of Aesthetics, Creativity, and the Arts, 11*(2), 216–230. doi: 10.1037/aca0000074.

McKerracher, A. (2016). Understanding creativity, one metaphor at a time. *Creativity Research Journal, 28*(4), 417–425. doi: 10.1080/10400419.2016.1229982.

McKinnon, M. C., Boyd, J. E., Frewin, P. A., Lanius, U. F., Jetly, R., Richardson, J. D., & Lanius, R. A. (2016). A review of the relation between dissociation, memory, executive functioning and social cognition in military members and civilians with neuropsychiatric conditions. *Neuropsychologia, 90*, 210–234. doi: 10.1016/j.neuropsychologia.2016.07.017.

McNally, R. J. (2018). Resolving the vulnerability paradox in the cross-national prevalence of postttaumatic stress disorder. *Journal of Anxiety Disorders, 54*, 33–35. doi: 10.1016/j.janxdis.2018.01.005.

McNeely, C., Barber, B. K., Spellings, C., Belli, R., Giacaman, R., Arafat, C., … Mallouh, M. A. (2015). Political imprisonment and adult functioning: A life event history analysis of Palestinians. *Journal of Traumatic Stress, 28*, 223–231. doi: 10.1002/jts.22015.

McPherson, M., & Limb, C. J. (2013). Difficulties in the neuroscience of creativity: Jazz improvisation and the scientific method. *Annals of the New York Academy of Sciences, 1303*, 80–83. doi: 10.1111/nyas.12174.

McWilliams, L. A., Cox, B. J., & Enns, M. W. (2003). Use of the Coping Inventory for Stressful Situations in a clinically depressed sample: Factor structure, personality correlates, and predictions of distress. *Journal of Clinical Psychology, 59*(12), 1371–1385. doi: 10.1002/jclp.10228.

Meaney, M. J. (2001). Maternal care, gene expression, and the transmission of individual differences in stress reactivity across generations. *Annual Review of Neuroscience, 24*, 1161–1192.

———. (2010). Epigenetics and the biological definition of gene-environment interactions. *Child Development*, 81, 41–79.

Medeiros, K. E., Partlow, P. J., & Mumford, M. D. (2014). Not too much, not too little: The influence of constraints on creative problem solving. *Psychology of Aesthetics, Creativity, and the Arts, 8*(2), 198–210. doi: 10.1037//a0036210.

Medford, N., Brierley, B., Brammer, M., Bullmaore, E. T., David, A. S., & Phillips, M. L. (2006). Emotional memory in depersonalization disorder: A functional MRI study. *Psychiatry Research: Neuroimaging, 148*, 93–102. doi: 10.1016/j.psychresns.2006.05.007.

Meister, I. G., Krings, T., Foltys, H., Boroojerdi, B., Uller, M., Topper, R., & Thron, A. (2004). Playing piano in the mind–an fMRI study of music imagery and performance in pianists. *Cognitive Brain Research, 19*, 219–228. doi: 10.1016/j.cogbrainres.2003.12.005.

Melendez, J. C., Alfonso-Benlliure, V., Mayordomo, T., & Sales, A. (2016). Is age just a number? Cognitive reserve as a predictor of divergent thinking in late adulthood. *Creativity Research Journal, 28*(4), 435–441. doi: 10.1080/10400419.2016.1229983.

Meli, L., Chang, B. P., Shimbo, D., Swan, B. W., Edmondson, D., & Sumner, J. A. (2017). Beta-blocker administration during emergency department evaluation for acute coronary syndrome is associated with lower posttraumatic stress symptoms 1-month later. *Journal of Traumatic Stress, 30*, 313–317. doi: 10.1037/jts.22195.

Melinder, A., Augusti, E.-M., Matre, M., & Endestad, T. (2015). Associations between executive functions and long-term stress reactions after extreme trauma: A two-year follow-up of the Utoya survivors. *Psychological Trauma: Theory, Research, Practice, and Policy, 7*(6), 583–590. doi: 10.1037/tra0000048.

Mellon, S. H., Gautam, A., Hammamieh, R., & Jett, M. (2018). Metabolism, metabolomics, and inflammation in Post-Traumatic Stress Disorder, Biological Pychiatry, e-publ. doi: 10.1016/j.biopsych.2018.02.007.

Mendaglio, S., & Tillier, W. (2006). Dabrowski's Theory of Positive Disintegration and giftedness: Overexcitability research findings. *Journal for the Education of the Gifted, 30*(1), 68–87.

Mendoza, L., Navines, R., Crippa, J. A., Fagundo, A. B., Gutierrez, F., Nardi, A. E., … Martin-Santos, R. (2011). Depersonalization and personality in panic disorder. *Comprehensive Psychiatry, 52*, 413–419. doi: 10.1016/j.comppsych.2010.09.002.

Meneely, J., & Portillo, M. (2005). The adaptable mind in design: Relating personality, cognitive style, and creative performance. *Creativity Research Journal, 17*(2 & 3), 155–166.

Mennin, D. S., Heimberg, R. G., Turk, C. L., & Fresco, D. M. (2002). Applying an emotion regulation framework to integrative approaches to generalized anxiety disorder. *Clinical Psychology: Science and Practice, 9*(1), 85–90. doi: 10.1093/clipsy.9.1.85.

Menon, V., & Levitin, D. J. (2005). The rewards of music listening: Response and physiological connectivity of the mesolimbic system. *Neuroimage, 28*, 175–184. doi: 10.1016/j.neuroimage.2005.05.053.

Merckelbach, H. (2004). Telling a good story: Fantasy proneness and the quality of fabricated memories. *Personality and Individual Differences, 37*(7), 1371–1382. doi: 10.1016/j.paid.2004.01.007.

Merckelbach, H., & van de Ven, V. (2001). Another white Christmas: Fantasy proneness and reports of 'hallucinatory experiences' in undergraduate students. *Journal of Behavior Therapy and Experimental Psychiatry, 32*, 137–144.

Merriam Webster Dictionary and Thesaurus. http://www.merriam-webster.com.

Merritt, R. D., & Waldo, T. G. (2000). MMPI code types and the fantasy prone personality. *Assessment, 7*(1), 87–95.

Messman-Moore, T. L., & Long, P. J. (2003). The role of childhood sexual abuse sequelae in the sexual revictimization of women: An empirical review and theoretical reformulation. *Clinical Psychology Review, 23*, 537–571. doi: 10.1016/S0272-7358(02)00203-9.

Metzl, E. S. (2009). The role of creative thinking in resilience after Hurrican Katrina. *Psychology of Aesthetics, Creativity, and the Arts, 3*(2), 112–123. doi: 10.1037/a0013479.

Metzl, E. S., & Morrell, M. A. (2008). The role of creativity in models of resilience: Theoretical explorations and practical applications. *Journal of Creativity in Mental Health, 3*(3), 303–318. doi: 10.1080/15401380802385228.

Metzler, M., Merrick, M. T., Klevens, J., Ports, K. A., & Ford, D. C. (2017). Adverse childhood experiences and life opportunities: Shifting the narrative. *Children and Youth Services Review, 72*, 141–149. doi: 10.1016/j.childyouth.2016.10.021.

Mgoqi-Mbalo, N., Zhang, M., & Ntuli, S. (2017). Risk factors for PTSD and depression in female survivors of rape. *Psychological Trauma: Theory, Research, Practice, and Policy, 9*(3), 301–308. doi: 10.1037/tra0000228.

Michal, M., Beutel, M. E., Jordan, J., Zimmerman, M., Wolters, S., & Heidenreich, T. (2007). Depersonalizatio, mindfulness, and childhood trauma. *Journal of Nervous and Mental Disease, 195*, 693–696. doi: 10.1097/NMD.0b013e31811f4492.

Michal, M., Kaufhold, J., Grabhorn, R., Krakow, K., Overbeck, G., & Heidenreich, T. (2005). Depersonalization and social anxiety. *Journal of Nervous and Mental Disease, 193*(9), 629–632.

Michal, M., Wiltnik, J., Subic-Wrana, C., Zwerenz, R., Tuin, I., Lichy, M., ... Beutel, M. E. (2009). Prevalence, correlates, and predictors of depersonalization experiences in the German population. *Journal of Nervous and Mental Disease, 197*, 499–506. doi: 10.1097/NMD.0b013e3181aacd94.

Michal, M., Wiltink, J., Till, Y., Wild, P. S., Blettner, M., & Beutel, M. (2011). Distinctiveness and overlap of depersonalization with anxiety and depression in a community sample: Results from the Gutenberg Heart Study. *Psychiatry Research, 188*, 264–268. doi: 10.1016/j.psychres.2010.11.004.

Michal, M., Wiltink, J., Till, Y., Wild, P. S., Munzel, T., Blankenberg, S., & Beutel, M. E. (2010). Type-D personality and depersonalization are associated with suicidal ideation in the German generation population aged 35–74: Results from the Gutneberg Heart Study. *Journal of Affective Disorders, 125*, 227–233. doi: 10.1016/j.jad.2010.02.108.

Michalica, K., & Hunt, H. (2013). Creativity, schizoptypicality, and mystical experiences: An empirical study. *Creativity Research Journal, 25*(3), 266–279. doi: 10.1080/10400419.2013.813780.

Middleton, W., Stavropoulos, P. Dorahy. M. J., Kruger, C., Lews-Fernandez, R., Martinez-Taboas, A., ... Brand, B. (2014). Institutional abuse and societal silence: An emerging problem. *Australian and New Zealand Journal of Psychiatry, 48*(1), 22–25. doi: 10.1177/0004867413514640.

Middlewood, B. L., Gallegos, J., & Gasper, K. (2016). Embracing the unusual: Feeling tired and happy is associated with greater acceptance of atypical ideas. *Creativity Research Journal, 28*(3), 310–317. doi: 10.1080/10400419.2016.1195639.

Mihelic, K. K., & Aleksic, D. (2017). "Dear employer, let me introduce myself" – Flow, satisfaction with work-life balance and millennials' creativity. *Creativity Research Journal, 29*(4), 397–408. doi: 10.1080/10400419.2017.1376503.

Mika, E. (2005). Theory of Positive Disintegration as a model of personality development for exceptional individuals. In N. L. Hafenstein, B. Kutrumbos, & J. Delisle (Eds.), *Perspectives in gifted education: Complexities of emotional development, spirituality and hope* (vol. 3) (pp. 4–32). Publication Institute for the Development of Gifted Education, Ricks Center for Gifted Children: University of Denver, CO.

Mikulincer, M., & Shaver, P. R. (2007). *Attachment in adulthood: Structure, dynamics, and change.* New York, NY: Guilford Press.

Mikulincer, M., & Sheffi, E. (2000). Adult attachment style and cognitive reactions to positive affect: A test of mental categorization and creative problem solving. *Motivation and Emotion, 24*(3), 149–174.

Mikulincer, M., Gillath, O., & Shaver, P. R. (2002). Activation of the attachment system in adulthood: Threat-related primes increase the accessibility of mental representations of attachment figures. *Journal of Personality and Social Psychology, 83*, 881–895. doi: 10.1037//0022-3514.83.4.881.

Milevsky, A., Schlechter, M., Netter, S., & Keehn, D. (2007). Maternal and paternal parenting styles in adolescent associations with self-esteem, depression and life-satisfaction. *Journal of Child and Family Studies, 16*, 39–47. doi: 10.1007/s10826-006-9066-5.

Millegan, J., Wang, L., LeardMann, C. A., Miltech, D., & Street, A. E. (2016). Sexual trauma and adverse health and occupational outcomes among men serving in the U.S. military. *Journal of Traumatic Stress, 29*, 132–140. doi: 10.1002/jts.22081.

Miller, E. M., & Cohen, L. M. (2012). Engendering talent in others: Expanding domains of giftedness and creativity. *Roeper Review, 34*, 104–113. doi: 10.1080/02783193.2012.660684.

Miller, N. B., Falk, R. F., & Huang, Y. (2009). Gender identity and the overexcitability profiles of gifted college students. *Roeper Review, 31*, 161–169. doi: 10.1080/02783190902993920.

Miller, R. J., & Johnson, D. R. (2012). The capacity for symbolization in posttraumatic stress disorder. *Psychological Trauma: Theory, Research, Practice, and Policy, 4*(1), 112–116. doi: 10.1037/a0021580.

Miller, W. (2000). *The mystery of courage*. Cambridge, MA: Harvard University Press.

Miller-Graff, L. E., & Cheng, P. (2017). Consequences of violence across the lifespan: Mental health and sleep quality in pregnant women. *Psychological Trauma: Theory, Research, Practice, and Policy, 9*(5), 587–595. doi: 10.1037/tra0000252.

Miller-Graff, L. E., & Howell, K. H. (2015). Posttraumatic stress symptom trajectory among children exposed to violence. *Journal of Traumatic Stress, 28*, 17–24. doi: 10.1002/jts.1989.

Milletich, R. J., Kelley, M. L., Doane, A. N., & Pearson, M. R. (2010). Exposure to interparental violence and childhood physical and emotional abuse as related to physical aggression in undergraduate dating relationships. *Journal of Family Violence, 25*, 627–637. doi: 10.1007/s10896-010-9319-3.

Milligan, K., Atkinson, L., Trehub, S. E., Benoit, D., & Poulton, L. (2003). Maternal attachment and the communication of emotion through song. *Infant Behavior and Development, 26*, 1–13.

Milligan-Saville, J. S., Paterson, H. M., Harkness, E. L., Marsh, A. M., Dobson, M., Kemp, R. J., ... Harvey, S. B. (2017). The amplification of common somatic symptoms by posttraumatic stress disorder in firefighters. *Journal of Traumatic Stress, 30*, 142–148. doi: 10.1002/jts.22166.

Mills, M. J., & Fullagar, C. J. (2008). Motivation and flow: Toward an understanding of the dynamics of the relation in architecture students. *The Journal of Psychology: Interdisciplinary and Applied, 142*(5), 533–556. doi: 10.3200/JRLP.142.5.533-556.

Milton, J., Small, S. L., & Solodkin, A. (2008). Imaging motor imagery: Methodological issues related to expertise. *Methods, 45*, 336–341. doi: 10.1016/j.ymeth.2008.05.002.

Miskovic, V., & Schmidt, L. A. (2012). New directions in the study of individual differences in temperament: A brain-body approach to understanding fearful and fearless children. *Monographs of the Society for Research in Child Development, 77*(2), 28–38.

Mitchell, K. J. (2016). The role of technology in youth harassment victimization. U.S. Department of Justice, Office of Justice Programs, 1–12. Retrieved from https://www.ncjrs.gov/pd les1/nij/grants/249003.pdf.

Mitchell, K. J., Hamby, S. L., Turner, H. A., Shattuck, A., & Jones, L. M. (2015). Weapon involvement in the victimization of children. *Pediatrics, 136*(1), 1–10. doi: 10.1542/peds.2014-3966.

Mitchell, K. J., Jones, L. M., Turner, H. A., Shattuck, A., & Wolak, J. (2016). The role of technology in peer harassment: Does it amplify harm to youth? *Psychology of Violence, 6*(2), 193–204. doi: 10.1037/a0039317.

Mittal, C., & Griskevicius, V. (2014). Sense of control under uncertainty depends on people's childhood environment: A life history theory approach. *Journal of Personality and Social Psychology, 107*(4), 621–637. doi: 10.1037/a0037398.

Mittal, C., Griskevicius, V., Simpson, J. A., Sung, S., & Young, E. S. (2015). Cognitive adaptations to stressful environments: When childhood adversity enhances adult executive functioning. *Journal of Personality and Social Psychology, 109*(4), 604–621. doi: 10.1037/pspi000028.

Mokdad, A. H., Marks, J. S., Stroup, D. F., & Gerberding, J. L. (2004). Actual causes of death in the United States, 2000. *Journal of the American Medical Society, 291*, 1238–1245. doi: 10.1001/jama.291.10.1238.

Molnar-Szakacs, I., & Overy, K. (2006). Music and mirror neurons: From motion to 'e'motion. *Social Cognition and Affective Neuroscience, 1*, 235–241. doi: 10.1093/scan/ns1029.

Moneta, G. B. (2004). The flow experience across cultures. *Journal of Happiness Studies, 5*, 115–121.

Monson, E., Paquet, C., Daniel, M., Brunet, A., & Caron, J. (2016). Place and posttraumatic stress disorder. *Journal of Traumatic Stress, 29*, 293–300. doi: 10.1002/jts.22108.

Montero, B. (2006). Proprioception as an aesthetic sense. *Journal of Aesthetics and Art Criticism, 64*(2), 231–242.

Montgomery, D., Hodges, P. A., & Kaufman, J. S. (2004). An exploratory study of the relationship between mood states and creativity self-perceptions. *Creativity Research Journal, 16*(2 & 3), 341–344.

Moog, N. K., Entringer, S., Rasmussen, J. M., Styner, M., Gilmore, J. H., Kathermann, N., ... Buss, C. (2017). Intergenerational effect of maternal exposure to childhood maltreatment on newborn brain anatomy. *Biological Psychiatry, e-publ.* doi: 10.1016/j.biopsych.2017.017.009.

Moore, D. W., Bhadelia, R. A., Billings, R. L., Fulwiler, C., Heilman, K. M., Rood, K. M. J., & Gansler, D. A. (2009). Hemispheric connectivity and the visual-spatial divergent-thinking component of creativity. *Brain and Cognition, 70*, 267–272. doi: 10.1016/j.bande.2009.02.011.

Moore, M. (2007). Golgi tendon organs: Neuroscience update with relevance to stretching and proprioception in dancers. *Journal of Dance Medicine and Science, 11*(3), 85–92.

Moos, R. H., & Holahan, C. J. (2003). Dispositional and contextual perspectives on coping: Toward an integrative framework. *Journal of Clinical Psychology, 59*(12), 1387–1403. doi: 10.1002/jclp.10229.

Morelock, M. (1996). On the nature of giftedness and talent: Imposing order on chaos. *Roeper Review, 19*(1), 4–12. doi: 10.1080/02783199609553774.

Morgan, C. A., 3rd, & Taylor, M. K. (2013). Spontaneous and deliberate dissociative states in military personnel: Are such states helpful? *Journal of Traumatic Stress, 26*, 492–497. doi: 10.1002/jts.21843.

Morgan, C. A., 3rd, Hazlett, G., Wang, S., Richardson, E. G., Schnurr, P., & Southwick, S. M. (2001). Symptoms of dissociation in humans experiencing acute, uncontrollable stress: A prospective investigation. *American Journal of Psychiatry, 158*, 1239–1247. doi: 10.1176/appi.ajp.158.8.1239.

Morgan, C. A., 3rd, Rasmusson, A. M., Wang, S., Hoyt, G., Hauger, R. L., & Hazlett, G. (2002). Neuropeptide-Y, cortisol, and subjective distress in humans exposed to acute stress: Replication and extension of previous report. *Biological Psychiatry, 52*(2), 136–142.

Morgan, C. A., 3rd, Rasmusson, A. M., Winters B., Haugher R. L., Morgan, J., Hazlett, G., & Southwick, S. (2003). Trauma exposure rather than posttraumatic stress disorder is associated with reduced baseline plasma neuropeptide-Y levels. *Biological Psychiatry, 54*, 1087–1091. doi: 10.1016/S0006-3223(03)00433-5.

Morgan, C., Carr, M. J., Green, J., Chew-Graham, C. A., Kapur, N., & Ashcroft, D. M. (2017). Incidence, clinical management, and mortality risk following self harm among children and adolescents. *British Medical Journal, 359*, j4351, e-publ. doi: 10.1136/bmj.j4351.

Morina, N., Wicherts, J. M., Lobbrecht, J., & Priebe, S. (2014). Remission from posttraumatic stress disorder in adults: A systematic review and meta-analysis of long term outcome studies. *Clinical Psychology Review, 34*, 249–255. doi: 10.1016/j.cpr.2014.03.002.

Morinville, A., Miranda, D., & Gaudreau, P. (2013). Music listening motivation is associated with global happiness in Canadian late adolescents. *Psychology of Aesthetics, Creativity, and the Arts, 7*(4), 384–390. doi: 10.1037/a0034495.

Morris, A., Lee, T., & Delahanty, D. (2013). Interactive relationships between parent and child event appraisals and child PTSD symptoms after an injury. *Psychological Trauma: Theory, Research, Practice, and Policy, 5*(6), 554–561. doi: 10.1037/a0029894.

Mosing, M. A., Magnusson, P. K. E., Pedersen, N. L., Nakamura, J., Madison, G., & Ullen, F. (2012). Heritability of proneness for psychological flow experiences. *Personality and Individual Differences, 53*, 699–704. doi: 10.1016/j.paid.2012.05.035.

Mosing, M. A., Pedersen, N. L., Cesarini, D., Johannesson, M., Magnusson, P. K. E., Nakamura, J., … Ullen, F. (2012). Genetic and environmental influences on the relationship between flow proneness, locus of control and behavioral inhibition. *PLoS ONE, 7*(11), e47958. doi: 10.1371/joural.pone.0047958.

Moskowitz, A., Barker-Collo, S., & Ellson, L. (2005). Replication of dissociation-psychosis link in New Zealand students and inmates. *Journal of Nervous and Mental Disease, 193*(11), 722–727. doi: 10.1097/01.nmd.0000185895.47704.62.

Moss, R. H., & Holahan, C. J. (2003). Dispositional and contextual perspectives on coping: Toward an integrative framework. *Journal of Clinical Psychology, 59*(12), 1387–1403. doi: 10.1002/jclp.10229.

Mossige, S., Jensen, T. K., Gulbrandsen, W., Reichelt, S., & Tjersland, O. A. (2005). Children's narratives of sexual abuse: What characterizes them and how do they contribute to meaning-making? *Narrative Inquiry, 15*(2), 377–404.

Movius, H. L., & Allen, J. J. B. (2005). Cardiac vagal tone, defensiveness, and motivational style. *Biological Psychology, 68*, 147–162. doi: 10.1016/j.biopsycho.2004.03.019.

Mraz, W., & Runco, M. A. (1994). Suicide ideation and creative problem solving. *Suicide and Life-Threatening Behavior, 24*(1), 38–47.

Mula, M., Pini, S., & Cassano, G. B. (2007). The neurobiology and clinical significance of depersonalization in mood and anxiety disorders: A critical reappraisal. *Journal of Affective Disorders, 99*, 91–99. doi: 10.1016/j.jad.2006.08.025.

Muller, B. C. N., Gerasimova, A., & Ritter, S. M. (2016). Concentrative meditation influences creativity by increasing cognitive flexibility. *Psychology of Aesthetics, Creativity, and the Arts, 10*(3), 278–286. doi: 10.1037/a0040335.

Mullerova, J., Hansen, M., Contractor, A. A., Elhai, J. D., & Armour, C. (2016). Dissociative features in posttraumatic stress disorder: A latent profile analysis. *Psychological Trauma: Theory, Research, Practice, and Policy, 8*(5), 601–608. doi: 10.1037/tra0000148.

Mumford, M. D. (2003). Where have we been, where are we going? Taking stock in creativity research. *Creativity Research Journal, 15*(2–3), 107–120. doi: 10.1080/10400419.2003.9651403.

Mumford, M. D., Mobley, M. I., Uhlman, C. E., Reiter-Pamon, R., & Doares, L. (1991). Process analytic models of creative capacities. *Creativity Research Journal, 4*, 91–122.

Mundorf, E. S., & Paivio, S. C. (2011). Narrative quality and disturbance pre- and post- emotion-focused therapy for child abuse trauma. *Journal of Traumatic Stress, 24*(6), 643–650. doi: 10.1002/jts.20707.

Murphy, A., Steele, M., Dube, S. R., Bate, J., Bonuck, K., Meissner, P., Goldman, H., & Steele, H. (2014). Adverse Childhood Experiences (ACEs) questionnaire and Adult Attachment Interview (AAI): Implications for parent child relationships. *Child Abuse and Neglect, 38*, 224–233. doi: 10.1016/j.chiabu.2013.09.004.

Musacchia, G., Sams, M., Skoe, E., & Kraus, N. (2007). Musicians have enhanced subcortical auditory and audiovisual processing of speech and music. *Proceedings of the National Academy of Science, 104*(40), 15894–15898. doi: 10.1073/pnas.0701498104.

Muscara, F., McCarthy, M. C., Thompson, E. J., Heaney, C.-M., Hearps, S. J., Rayner, M., Burke, K., Nicholson, J. M., & Anderson, V. A. (2017). Psychosocial, demographic, and illness-related factors associated with acute traumatic stress responses in parents with children with a serious illness or injury. *Journal of Traumatic Stress, 30*, 237–244. doi: 10.1037/jts.22193.

Muth, C., Hesslinger, V. M., & Carbon, C.-C. (2018). Variants of semantic instability (Selns) in the arts: A classification study based on experiential reports. *Psychology of Aesthetcis, Creativity, and the Arts, 12*(1), 11–23. doi: 10.1037/aca0000113.

Myers, H. F., Wyatt, G. E., Ullman, J. B., Loch, T. B., Chin, D., Prause, N., ... Liu, H. (2015). Cumulative burden of lifetime adversities: Trauma and mental health in low-SES African Americans and Latino/as. *Psychological Trauma: Theory, Research, Practice, and Policy, 7*(3), 243–251. doi: 10.1037/a0039077.

Myers, L., Fleming, M., Lancman, M., Perrine, K., & Lancman, M. (2013). Stress coping strategies in patients with psychogenic non-epileptic seizures and how they relate to trauma symptoms, alexithymia, anger and mood. *Seizure, 22*, 634–639. doi: 10.1016/j.seizure.2013.04.018.

Nadal, M., & Skov, M. (2013). Introduction to the special issue: Toward an interdisciplinary neuroaesthetics. *Psychology of Aesthetics, Creativity and the Arts, 7*(1), 1–12. doi: 10.1037/a00318482.

Nalipay, M. J., Bernardo, A. B. I., & Mordeno, I. G. (2016). Social complexity beliefs predict posttraumatic growth in survivors of a natural disaster. *Psychological Trauma: Theory, Research, Practice, and Policy, 8*(5), 559–567. doi: 10.1037/tra0000154.

Nandi, C., Elbert, T., Bambonye, M., Weierstall, R., Reichert, M., Zeller, A., & Crombach, A. (2017). Predicting domestic and community violence by soldiers living in a conflict region. *Psychological Trauma: Theory, Research, Practice, and Policy, 9*(6), 663–671. doi: 10.1037/tra0000262.

Nathanson, D. L. (1992). *Shame and pride: Affect, sex, and the birth of the self.* New York: W. W. Norton & Company.

Naylor, J. C., Pritchard, R. D., & Ilgen, D. R. (1980). *A theory of behavior organization.* New York: Academic Press.

Necka, E., & Hlawcz, T. (2013). Who has an artistic temperament? Relationships between creativity and temperament among artists and bank officers. *Creativity Research Journal, 25*(2), 182–188. doi: 10.1080/10400419.2013.783744.

Neff, K. D. (2009). The role of self-compassion in development: A healthier way to relate to oneself. *Human Development, 52*, 211–214. doi: 10.1159/000215071.

Negrao, C., Bonanno, G. A., Noll, J. G., Putnam, F. W., & Trickett, P. K. (2005). Shame, humiliation, and childhood sexual abuse: Distinct contributions and emotional coherence. *Child Maltreatment, 10*(4), 350–363. doi: 10.1177/1077559505279366.

Neihart, M. (1998). Creativity, the arts, and madness. *Roeper Review, 21*(1), 47–50.

———. (1999). The impact of giftedness on psychological well-being: What does the empirical literature say? *Roeper Review, 22*(1), 10–17.

Nelson, B., & Rawlings, D. (2007). Its own reward: A phenomenological study of artistic creativity. *Journal of Phenomenological Psychology, 38*, 217–255. doi: 10.1163/156916207X234284.

Nelson, B., & Rawlings, D. (2009). How does it feel? The development of the Experience of Creativity Questionnaire. *Creativity Research Journal, 21*(1), 43–53. doi: 10.1080/10400410802633442.

———. (2010). Relating schizotypy and personality to the phenomenology of creativity. *Schizophrenia Bulletin, 36*(2), 388–399. doi: 10.1093/schbul/sbn098.

Nemiro, J. E. (2002). The creative process in virtual teams. *Creativity Research Journal, 14*(1), 69–83.

Nettle, D., & Clegg, H. (2006). Schizotypy, creativity and mating success in humans. *Proceedings of the Royal Society of Biological Sciences, 273*, 611–615. doi: 10.1098/rsp.2005.3349.

Nevarez, M. D., Yee, H. M., & Waldinger, R. J. (2017). Friendship in war: camaraderie and prevention of posttraumatic stress disorder prevention. *Journal of Traumatic Stress, 30*, 512–520. doi: 10.1002/jts.22224.

New, A. S., Fan, J., Murrough, J. W., Liu, X., Liebman, R. E., Guise, K. G., ... Charney, D. S. (2009). A functional magnetic resonance imaging study of deliberate emotion regulation in resilience and Posttraumatic Stress Disorder. *Biological Psychiatry, 66*, 656–664. doi: 10.1016/j.biopsych.2009.05.020.

Newman, B. M., & Newman, P. R. (2015). *Development through the life: A psychosocial approach* (12th ed.). Stamford, CT: Cengage Learning.

Newman, S. D., Carpenter, P. A., Varma, S., & Just, M. A. (2003). Frontal and parietal participation in problem solving in the Tower of London: fMRI and computational modeling of planning and high-level perception. *Neuropsychologia, 41*, 1668–1682.

Ng, L. C., Ahishakiye, N., Miller, D. E., & Meyerowitz, B. E. (2015). Narrative characteristics of genocide testimonies predict posttraumatic stress disorder symptoms years later. *Psychological Trauma: Theory, Research, Practice, and Policy, 7*(3), 303–311. doi: 10.1037/tra0000024.

Nickerson, A., Bryant, R. A., Aderka, I. M., Hinton, D. E., & Hofman, S. G. (2013). The impacts of parental loss and adverse parenting on mental health: Findings from the National Comorbidity Survey-Replication. *Psychological Trauma: Theory, Research, Practice, and Policy, 5*(2), 119–127. doi: 10.1037/a0025695.

Nickerson, A., Schick, M., Schnyder, U., Bryant, R. A., & Morina, N. (2017). Comorbidity of posttraumatic stress disorder and depression in tortured, treatment-seeking refugees. *Journal of Traumatic Stress, 30*, 409–415. doi: 10.1002/jts.22205.

Nicolas, G., Byer, K., & Ho, K. (2015). Implementing culturally sensitive and sustainable mental health programs internationally: Lessons from Haiti. *International Journal of Culture and Mental Health, 8*(4), 446–457. doi: 10.1080/17542863.2014.996237.

Niedenthal, P. M., Brauer, M., Robin, L., & Innes-Ker, A. H. (2002). Adult attachment and the perception of facial expression of emotions. *Journal of Personality and Social Psychology, 82*(3), 419–433. doi: 10.1037//0022-3514.82.3.419.

Nobakht, H. N., & Dale, K. Y. (2017). The prevalence of deliberate self-harm and its relationship to trauma and dissociation among Iranian young adults. *Journal of Trauma and Dissociation, 18*(4), 601–623. doi: 10.1080/15299732.2016.1246397.

Nock, M. K., & Favazza, A. R. (2009). Nonsuicidal self-injury: Definition and classification. In M. K. Nock (Ed.), *Understanding nonsuicidal self-injury: Origins, assessment, and treatment* (pp. 9–18). Washington, DC. American Psychological Association.

Norman, R. E., Byambaa, M., De, R., Butchart, A., Scott, J., & Vos, T. (2012). The long-term health consequences of child physical abuse, emotional abuse, and neglect: A systematic review and meta-analysis. *PLoS ONE Medicine, 9*(11), e1001349. doi: 10.1371/journal.pmed.1001349.

Novaco, R. W., & Chemtob, C. M. (2015). Violence associated with combat-related posttraumatic stress disorder: The importance of anger. *Psychological Trauma: Theory, Research, Practice, and Policy, 7*(5), 485–492. doi: 10.1037/tra0000067.

Nusbaum, E. C., & Silvia, P. J. (2011). Are intelligence and creativity really so different? Fluid intelligence, executive processes, and strategy use in divergent thinking. *Intelligence, 39*, 36–45. doi: 10.1016/j.intell.2010.11.002.

Nusbaum, E. C., Silvia, P. J., Beaty, R. E., Burgin, C. J., Hodges, D. A., & Kwapil, T. R. (2014). Listening between the notes: Aesthetic chills in everyday music listening. *Psychology of Aesthetics, Creativity, and the Arts, 8*(1), 104–109. doi: 10.1037/a0034867.

Nyberg, L., Eriksson, J., Larsson, A., & Marklund, P. (2006). Learning by doing versus learning by thinking: An fMRI study of motor and mental training. *Neuropsychologia, 44*, 711–717. doi: 10.1016/j.neuropsychologia.2005.08.006.

Nye, E. C., Katzman, J., Bell, J. B., Kilpatrick, J., Brainard, M., & Haaland, K. Y. (2008). Attachment organization in Vietnam combat veterans with posttraumatic stress disorder. *Attachment and Human Development, 10*(1), 41–57. doi: 10.1080/14616730701868613.

———. (2009). Attachment representation and suicidal ideation in Vietnam combat veterans with posttraumatic stress disorder. *Archives of Suicide Research, 13*, 195–199. doi: 10.1080/13811110902835213.

O'Brian, E. M., McLeish, A. C., Kraemer, K. M., & Fleming, J. B. (2015). Emotion regulation difficulties and posttraumatic stress disorder symptom cluster severity among trauma-exposed college students. *Psychological Trauma: Theory, Research, Practice, and Policy, 7*(2), 131–137. doi: 10.1037/a0037764.

O'Donnell, K., Brydon, L., Wright, C. E., & Steptoe, A. (2008). Self-esteem levels and cardiovascular and inflammatory responses to acute stress. *Brain, Behavior, and Immunity, 22*, 1241–1247. doi: 10.1016/j.bbi.2008.06.012.

O'Hare, T., Shen, C., & Sherrer, M. (2013). Trauma and posttraumatic stress symptoms in people with severe mental illness: Examining alternative measures of trauma. *Psychological Trauma: Theory, Research, Practice, and Policy, 5*(6), 529–535. doi: 10.1037/a0030796.

———. (2015). Lifetime abuse and self-harm in people with severe mental illness: A structural equation model. *Psychological Trauma: Theory, Research, Practice, and Policy, 7*(4), 348–355. doi: 10.1037/tra0000016.

O'Kearney, R., Hunt, A., & Wallace, N. (2011). Integration and organization of trauma memories and posttraumatic symptoms. *Journal of Traumatic Stress, 24*(6), 716–725. doi: 10.1002/jts.20690.

Obsuth, I., Hennighausen, K., Brumariu, L. E., & Lyons-Ruth, K. (2014). Disorganized behavior in adolescent-parent interaction: Relations to attachment state of mind, partner abuse and psychopathology. *Child Development, 85*(1), 370–387. doi: 10.1111/cdev.12113.

Oddone, A. E., Dennis, P. A., Calhoun, P. S., Watkins, L. L., Sherwood, A., Dedert, E. A., Green, K. T., ... Beckham, J. C. (2015). Orthostatic hypotension in young adults with and without posttraumatic stress disorder. *Psychological Trauma: Theory, Research, Practice, and Policy, 7*(3), 239–233. doi: 10.1037/a0036716.

Office for Victims of Crime (OVC). (2016). *2016 NCVRW resource guide: Youth victimization fact sheet.* Retrieved from https://www.ovc.ncjrs.gov/ncvrw2016/fact_sheet.

———. (2017). *2017 NCVRW resource guide: Youth victimization fact sheet.* Retrieved from https://www.ovc.ncjrs.gov/ncvrw2017/fact_sheet.

Ogawa, J. R., Sroufe, L. A., Weinfield, N. S., Carlson, E. A., & Egeland, B. (1997). Development and the fragmented self: Longitudinal study of dissociative symptomatology in a nonclinical sample. *Development and Psychopathology, 9*, 855–879.

Ogle, C. M., Rubin, D. C., & Rubin, I. C. (2015). The relation between insecure attachment and posttraumatic stress: Early life versus adult trauma. *Psychological Trauma: Theory, Research, Practice, and Policy, 7*(4), 324–332. doi: 10.1037/tra0000015.

———. (2016). Maladaptive trauma appraisals mediate the relation between attachment anxiety and PTSD symptom severity. *Psychological Trauma: Theory, Research, Practice, and Policy, 8*(3), 301–309. doi: 10.1037/tra0000112.

Okuda, M., Olfson, M., Wang, S., Rubio, J. M., Xu, Y., & Blanco, C. (2015). Correlates of intimate partner violence perpetration: Results from a National Epidemiologic Survey. *Journal of Traumatic Stress, 28*, 49–56. doi: 10.1002/jts.21986.

Oliver, K. G., Collin, P., Burns, J., & Nicholas, J. (2006). Building resilience in young people through meaningful participation. *Australian e-Journal for the Adancement of Mental Health, 5*(1), 1–7. www.auseinet.com/journal/vol5iss1/oliver.pdf.

Olszewski-Kubilius, P., Subotnik, R. F., & Worrell, F. (2015). Antecedent and concurrent psychosocial skills that support levels of achievement within talent domains. *High Ability Studies, 26*(2), 195–210. doi: 10.13598139.2015.1095077.

Ono, M., Devilly, G. J., & Shum, D. H. (2016). A meta-analytic review of overgeneral memory: The role of trauma history, mood, and the presence of posttraumatic stress disorder. *Psychological Trauma: Theory, Research, Practice, and Policy, 8*(2), 157–164. doi: 10.1037/tra0000027.

Orcutt, H. K., Bonanno, G. A., Hannon, S. M., & Miron, L. R. (2014). Prospective trajectories of posttraumatic stress in college women following a campus mass shooting. *Journal of Traumatic Stress, 27*, 249–256. doi: 10.1002/jts.21914.

Oreck, B. A., Owen, S. V., & Baum, S. M. (2003). Validity, reliability, and equity issues in an observational talent assessment process in the performing arts. *Journal for the Education of the Gifted, 27*(1), 62–94.

Ornstein, R. E. (1997). *The right mind: Making sense of the hemispheres.* San Diego: Harcourt Brace & Company.

Otis, J. D., Keane, T. M., & Kerns, R. D. (2003). An examination of the relationship between chronic pain and post-traumatic stress disorder. *Journal of Rehabiliatation Research and Development, 40*(5), 397–406.

Overby, L. Y., Hall, C., & Haslam, I. (1997–1998). A comparison of imagery used by dance teachers, figure skating coaches, and soccer coaches. *Imagination, Cognition and Personality, 17*(4), 323–337.

Ozer, E. J., Best, S. R., Lipsey, T. L., & Weiss, D. S. (2003). Predictors of posttraumatic stress disorder and symptoms in adults: A meta-analysis. *Psychological Bulletin, 129*, 52–73. doi: 10.1037/0033-2909.129.1.52.

Padmanabhanunni, A., Campbell, J., & Pretorius, T. B. (2017). Gendered role of appraisals of safety in psychological outcome in relation to trauma. *Psychological Trauma: Theory, Research, Practice, and Policy, 9*(5), 518–525. doi: 10.1037/tra0000167.

Pagona, B., & Costas, M. (2008). The development of motor creativity in elementary school children and its retention. *Creativity Research Journal, 20*(1), 72–80. doi: 10.1080/10400410701842078.

Paletz, S. B. F., Peng, K., & Li, S. (2011). In the world or in the head: External and internal implicit theories of creativity. *Creativity Research Journal, 23*(2), 83–98. doi: 10.1080/10400419.2011.571181.

Palgi, S., Klein, E., & Shamay-Tsoory, S. (2017). The role of oxytocin in empathy in PTSD. *Psychological Trauma: Theory, Research, Practice, and Policy, 9*(1), 70–75. doi: 10.1037/tra0000142.

Palm, K. M., Polusny, M. A., & Follette, V. M. (2004). Vicarious traumatization: Potential hazards and interventions for disaster and trauma workers. *Prehospital and Disaster Medicine, 19*, 73–78. doi: 10.1017/S1049023X00001503.

Palmer, R. H. C., Nugent, N. R., Brick, L. A., Bidwell, C. L., McGreary, J. E., Keller, M. C., & Knopik, V. S. (2016). Evidence of shared genome-wide additive genetic effects on interpersonal trauma exposure and generalized vulnerability to drug dependence in a population of substance users. *Journal of Traumatic Stress, 29*, 197–204. doi: 10.1002/jts.22103.

Palmisano, G. L., Innamorati, M., Susca, G., Traetta, D., Sarracino, D., & Vanerlinden, J. (2018). Childhood traumatic experiences and dissociative phenomena in eating disorders: Level and association with the severity of binge eting symptoms. *Journal of Trauma and Dissociation, 19*(1), 88–107. doi: 10.1080/15299732.2017.1304490.

Panksepp, J. (1998). *Affective neuroscience: The foundations of human and animal emotions.* New York: Oxford Press.

———. (2003). At the interface of the affective, behavioral, and cognitive neurosciences: Decoding the emotional feelings of the brain. *Brain and Cognition, 52*, 4–14. doi: 10.1016/S0278-2626(03)00003-4.

Papini, S., Yoon, P., Rubin, M., Lopez-Castro, T., & Hien, D. A. (2015). Linguistic characteristics in a non-trauma-related narrative task are associated with PTSD diagnosis and symptom severity. *Psychological Trauma: Theory, Research, Practice, and Policy, 7*(3), 295–302. doi: 10.1037/tra0000019.

Pappa, I., Szekely, E., Mileva-Seitz, V. R., Luijk, M. P. C. M., Bakermans-Kranenburg, M. J., van IJzendoorn, M. H., & Tiemeier, H. (2015). Beyond the usual suspects: A multidimensional genetic exploration of infant attachment disorganization and security. *Attachment and Human Development, 17*(3), 288–301. doi: 10.1080/14616734.2015.1037316.

Paret, L., Bailey, H. N., Roche, J., Bureau, J.-F., & Moran, G. (2015). Preschool ambivalent attachment associated with a lack of vagal withdrawl in response to stress. *Attachment and Human Development, 17*(1), 65–82. doi: 10.1080/14616734.2014.967786.

Park, C. L., Mills, M. A., & Edmondson, D. (2012). PTSD as meaning violation: Testing a cognitive worldview perspective. *Psychological Trauma: Theory, Research, Practice, and Policy, 4*(1), 66–73. doi: 10.1037/a0018792.

Park, H. R. P., Kirk, I. J., & Waldie, K. E. (2015). Neural correlates of creative thinking and schizotypy. *Neuropsychologia, 73*, 94–107. doi: 10.1016/j.neuropsychologia.2015.05.007.

Parra, A. (2006). "Seeing and feeling ghosts": Absorption, fantasy proneness, and healthy schizotypy as predictors of crisis apparition experiences. *The Journal of Parapsychology, 70*(2), 357–372.

Partridge, J. A., & Wiggins, M. S. (2008). Coping styles for trait shame and anxiety intensity and direction in competitive athletes. *Psychological Reports, 103*, 703–712. doi: 10.2466/PRO.103.3.703-712.

Pasupathi, M., Wainryb, C., Bourne, S., & Posada, R. (2017). Narrative construction of morality in adolescence among typically developing and violence-exposed youth. *Imagination, Cognition and Personality, 37*(2), 178–198. doi: 10.1177/0276236617733826.

Pates, J., Karageorghis, C. I., Fryer, R., & Maynard, L. (2003). Effects of asynchronous music on flow states and shooting performance among netball players. *Psychology of Sport and Exercise, 4*(4), 415–427. doi: 10.1016/S1469-0292(02)000039-0.

Pat-Horenczyk, R., Cohen, S., Ziv, Y., Achituv, M., Brickman, S., Blanchard, T., & Brom, D. (2017). Stability and change in posttraumatic distress: A 7-year follow-up study of mothers and young children exposed to cumulative trauma. *Journal of Traumatic Stress, 30*, 115–124. doi: 10.1002/jts.22177.

Pat-Horenczyk, R., Perry, S., Hamama-Raz, Y., Ziv, Y., Schramm-Yavin, S., & Stemmer, S. M. (2015). Posttraumatic growth in breast cancer survivors: Constructive and illusory aspects. *Journal of Traumatic Stress, 28*, 214–222. doi: 10.1002/jts.22014.

Pat-Horenczyk, R., Saltzman, L. Y., Hamama-Raz, Y., Perry, S., Ziv, Y., Ginat-Frolich, R., & Stemmer, S. M. (2016). Stability and transitions in posttraumatic growth trajectories among cancer patients: LCA and LTA analyses. *Psychological Trauma: Theory, Research, Practice, and Policy, 8*(5), 541–549. doi: 10.1037/tra0000094.

Patston, L. L., Kirk, I. J., Rolfe, M., H. S., Corballis, M. C., & Tippett, L. J. (2007). The unusual symmetry of musicians: Musicians have equilateral interhemispheric transfer for visual information. *Neuropsychologia, 45*, 2059–2065. doi: 10.1016/j.neuropsychologia.2007.02.001.

Paul, L. A., Felton, J. W., Adams, Z. W., Welsh, K., Miller, S., & Ruggiero, K. J. (2015). Mental health among adolescents exposed to a tornado: The influence of social support and its interactions with sociodemographic characteristics and disaster exposure. *Journal of Traumatic Stress, 28*, 232–239. doi: 10.1002/jts.22012.

Pavlik, K., & Nordin-Bates, S. (2016). Imagery in dance: A literature review. *Journal of Dance Medicine and Science, 20*(2), 51–63. doi: 10.12678/1089-313x.20.2.51.

Peifer, C., Schulz, A., Schachinger, H., Bauman, N., & Antoni, C. H. (2014). The relation of flow-experience and physiological arousal under stress–can u shape it? *Journal of Experimental Social Psychology, 53*, 62–69. doi: 10.1016/j.jesp.2014.01.009.

Peilloux, A., & Botella, M. (2016). Ecological and dynamical study of the creative process and affects of scientific students working in groups. *Creativity Research Journal, 28*(2), 165–170. doi: 10.1080/10400419.2016.1162549.

Pekala, R. J., Angelini, F., & Kumar, V. K. (2001). The importance of fantasy-proneness in dissociation: A replication study. *Contemporary Hypnosis, 18*(4), 204–214.

Pennestri, A.-H., Moss, E., O'Donnell, K., Lecompte, V., Bouvette-Turcot, A.-A., Atkinson, L., ... Gaudreau, H. (2015). Establishment and consolidation of the slee-wake cycle as a function of attachment pattern. *Attachment and Human Development, 17*(1), 23–42. doi: 10.1080/14616734.2014.953963.

Penniment, K. J., & Egan, S. J. (2012). Perfectionism and learning experiences in dance class as risk factors for eating disorders in dancers. *European Eating Disorders Review, 20*(1), 13–22.

Perez, L. G., Abrams, M. P., Lopez-Marinez, A. E., & Asmundson, G. J. G. (2012). Trauma exposure and health: The role of depressive and hyperarousal symptoms. *Journal of Traumatic Stress, 25*, 641–648. doi: 10.1002/jts.21762.

Perkins, S. L., & Allen, R. (2006). Childhood physical abuse and differential development of paranormal belief systems. *Journal of Nervous and Mental Disease, 194*(5), 349–355. doi: 10.1097/01.nmd.0000217832.85665.c5.

Perona-Garcelan, S., Carrascoso-Lopez, F., Garcia-Montes, J. M., Vallina-Fernandez, O., Perez-Alvarez, M., Ductor-Recuerda, M. J., ... Gomez-Gomez, M. T. (2011). Depersonalization as a mediator in the relationship between self-focused attention and auditory hallucinations. *Journal of Trauma and Dissociation, 12*, 535–548. doi: 10.1080/15299732.2011.602181.

Perona-Garcelan, S., Garcia-Montes, J. M., Ductor-Recuerda, M. J., Vallina-Fernandez, O., Cuevas-Yust, C., Perez-Alvarez, M., ... Gomez-Gomez, M. T. (2012). Relationship of metacognition, absorption, and depersonalization in patients with auditory hallucinations. *British Journal of Clinical Psychology, 51*, 100–118. doi: 10.1111/j.2044-8260.2011.02015.x.

Perrin, M., Vandeleur, C. L., Castelao, E., Rothen, S., Glaus, J., Vollenweider, P., & Preisig, M. (2014). Determinants of the development of post-trraumtic stress disorder, in the general population. *Social Psychiatry and Psychiatric Epidemiology, 49*, 447–457. doi: 10.1007/s00127-013-0762-3.

Perrone, K. M., Ksiazak, T. M., Wright, S. L., Vannatter, A., Crane, A. L., & Tanney, A. (2010). Multigenerational giftedness: Perceptions of giftedness across three generations. *Journal for the Education of the Gifted, 33*(4), 606–627.

Perroud, N., Paoloni-Giacobino, A., Prada, P., Olie, E., Salzmann, A., Nicastro, R., ... Malafosse, A. (2011). Increased methylation of glucocorticoid receptor gene

(NR3C1) in adults with a history of childhood maltreatment: A link with the severity and type of trauma. *Translational Psychiatry, 1*(e59), 1–9. doi: 10.1038/tp.2011.60.

Perry, B. D. (2001). Violence and childhood: How persisting fear can alter the developing child's brain. In D. Schetky & E. P. Benedek (Eds.), *Textbook of child and adolescent forensic psychiatry* (pp. 221–238). Washington, DC: American Psychiatric Press, Inc.

Perryman Group. (2014). *Suffer the little children: An assessment of the economic costs of child maltreatment.* Retrieved from http://perrymangroup.com/special-reports/chlld-abuse-study/.

Perry-Smith, J. E., & Shalley, C. E. (2003). The social side of creativity: A static and dynamic social network perspective. *Academy of Management Review, 28*(1), 89–106.

Peter-Hagene, L. C., & Ullman, S. E. (2015). Sexual assault-characteristics effects on PTSD and psychological mediators: A cluster-analysis approach to sexual assault type. *Psychological Trauma: Theory, Research, Practice, and Policy, 7*(2), 162–170. doi: 10.1037/a0037304.

Peterson, C., & Seligman, M. (2004). *Character strengths and virtues.* New York: Oxford University Press.

Peterson, C., Park, N., & Seligman, M. E. P. (2005). Orientation to happiness and life satisfaction: The full life versus the empty life. *Journal of Happiness Studies, 6*, 25–41. doi: 10.1007/s10902-004-1278-z.

Peterson, R. J., & Greenleaf, C. A. (2014). Exploring flow among NCAA division 1 and intramural athletes. *Imagination, Cognition and Personality, 33*(4), 421–440. doi: 10.2190/IC.33.4.g.

Pfaltz, M. C., Michael, T., Meyer, A. H., & Wilhelm, F. H. (2013). Reexperiencing symptoms, dissociation, and avoidance behaviors in daily life of patients with PTSD and patients with panic disorder with agoraphobia. *Journal of Traumatic Stress, 26*, 443–450. doi: 10.1002/jts.21822.

Pfeiffer, E., & Goldbeck, L. (2017). Evaluation of a trauma-focused group intervention for unaccompanied young refugees: A pilot study. *Journal of Traumatic Stress, 30,* 531–536. doi: 10.1002/jts.22218.

Pfeiffer, S. I. (2012). Current perspectives on the identification and assessment of gifted students. *Journal of Psychoeducational Assessment, 30*(1), 3–9. doi: 10.1177/0734282911428192.

Phelps, J. L., Belsky, J., & Crnic, K. (1998). Earned security, daily stress, and parenting: A comparison of five alternative models. *Development and Psychopathology, 10*, 21–38.

Philippe, F. L., Vallerand, R. J., & Lavigne, G. L. (2009). Passion does make a difference in people's lives: A look at well-being in passionate and non-passionate individuals. *Applied Psychology: Health and Well-Being, 1*(1), 3–22. doi: 10.1111/j.1758-0854.2008.01003.x.

Pica, M., Beere, D., Lovinger, S., & Dush, D. (2001). The response of dissociative patients on the Thematic Apperception Test. *Journal of Clinical Psychology, 57*(7), 847–864.

Pickett, S. M., Barbaro, N., & Mello, D. (2016). Relationship between subjective sleep disturbance, sleep quality, and emotion regulation difficulties in a sample of college students reporting trauma exposure. *Psychological Trauma: Theory, Research, Practice, and Policy, 8*(1), 25–33. doi: 10.1037/tra0000064.

Piechowski, M. M., & Cunningham, K. (1985). Patterns of overexcitability in a group of artists. *Journal of Creative Behavior, 19*(3), 153–174. doi: 10.1002/j.2162-6057.1985.tb00655.x.

Piechowski, M. M., Silverman, L., Cunningham, K., & Falk, R. F. (1982). A comparison of intellectually gifted and artists on five dimensions of mental functioning.

Piffer, D., & Hur, Y.-M. (2014). Heritability of creative achievement. *Creativity Research Journal, 26*(2), 151–157. doi: 10.1080/10400419.2014.901068.

Pielmaier, L., & Maercker, A. (2011). Psychological adaptation to life-threatening injury in dyads: The role of dysfunctional disclosure of trauma. *European Journal of Psychotraumatology, 2*(8749), 1–12. doi: 10.3402/ejpt.v2i0.8749.

Pietrek, C., Elbert, T., Weierstall, R., Muller, O., & Rockstroh, B. (2013). Childhood adversities in relation to psychiatric disorders. *Psychiatry Research, 206*, 103–110. doi: 10.1016/j.psychres.2012.11.003.

Pietrzak, R. H., Goldstein, R. B., Southwick, S. M., & Grant, B. F. (2011). Prevalence and Axis I commorbidity of full and partial posttraumatic stress disorder in the United States: Results from Wave 2 of the National Epidemiologic Survey on alcohol and related conditions. *Journal of Anxiety Disorder, 25*, 456–465. doi: 10.1016/j.janxdis.2010.11.010.

Pignatelli, A. M., Wampers, M., Loriedo, C., Bionid, M., & Vanderlinden, J. (2017). Childhood neglect in eating disorders: A systematic review and metaanalysis. *Journal of Trauma and Dissociation, 18*(1), 100–115. doi: 10.1080/15299732.2016.1198951.

Piirto, J. (1995). Deeper and broader: The pyramid of talent development in the context of giftedness construct. *The Education Forum, 59*(4), 363–370. doi: 10.1080/00131729509335068.

———. (1998). *Understanding those who create*, 2nd Ed. Scottsdale, AZ: Gifted Potential Press, Inc.

Piirto, J., & Fraas, J. (2012). A mixed-methods comparison of vocational and identified-gifted high school students on the overexcitability questionnaire. *Journal for the Education of the Gifted, 35*(1), 3–34. doi: 10.1177/0162353211433792.

Pinheiro, I. R., & Cruz, R. M. (2014). Mapping creativity: Creativity measurements network analysis. *Creativity Research Journal, 26*(3), 263–275. doi: 10.1080/10400419.2014.929404.

Pinho, A. L., de Manzano, O., Fransson, P., Eriksson, H., & Ullen, F. (2014). Connecting to create: Expertise in musical improvisation is associated with increased functional connectivity between premotor and prefrontal areas. *Journal of Neuroscience, 34*(18), 6156–6163. doi: 10.1523/JNEUROSCI.4769.13.2014.

Pinto-Gouveia, J., & Matos, M. (2011). Can shame memories become a key to identity? The centrality of shame memories predicts psychopathology. *Applied Cognitive Psychology, 25*, 281–290. doi: 10.1002/acp.1689.

Pittig, A., Arch, J., Lam, C. W. R., & Craske, M. G. (2013). Heart rate and heart rate variability in panic, social anxiety, obsessive-compulsive and generalized anxiety disorders at baseline and in response to relaxation and hyperventilation. *International Journal of Psychophysiology, 87*, 19–27. doi: 10.1016/j.ijpsycho.2012.10.012.

Platt, M. G., & Freyd, J. J. (2015). Betray my trust, shame on me: Shame, dissociation, fear, and betrayal trauma. *Psychological Trauma: Theory, Research, Practice, and Policy, 7*(4), 398–404. doi: 10.1037/tra0000022.

Plattner, B., Silvermann, M. A., Redlich, A., Carrion, V. G., Feucht, M., Friedrich, M. H., & Steiner, H. (2003). Pathways to dissociation: Intrafamilial versus extrafamilial trauma in juvenile delinquents. *Journal of Nervous and Mental Disease, 191*(12), 781–788.

Plucker, J. A., Beghetto, R. A., & Dow, G. T. (2004). Why isn't creativity more important to educational psychologists? Potential pitfalls, and future directions in creativity research. *Educational Psychologist, 39*(2), 83–96. doi: 10.1207/s15326985ep3902_1.

Polanco-Roman, L., Danies, A., & Anglin, D. M. (2016). Racial discrimination as race-based trauma, coping strategies, and dissociative symptoms among emerging adults. *Psychological Trauma: Theory, Research, Practice, and Policy, 8*(5), 609–617. doi: 10.1037/tra0000125.

Polner, B., Nagy, H., Takats, A., & Keri, S. (2015). Kiss of the muse for the chosen ones: De novo schizotypal traits and lifetime creative achievement are related to changes in divergent thinking during dopaminergic therapy in Parkinson's Disease. *Psychology of Aesthetics, Creativity, and the Arts, 9*(3), 328–339. doi: 10.1037/a0039303.

Polusny, M. A., Erbes, C. R., Kramer, M. D., Thuras, P., DeGarmo, D., Koffel, E., … Arbisi, P. A. (2017). Resilience and posttraumatic stress disorder symptoms in National Guard soldiers deployed to Iraq: A prospective study of latent class trajectory and their predictors. *Journal of Traumatic Stress, 30*, 351–361. doi: 10.1002/jts.22199.

Ponce-Garcia, E., Madewell, A. N., & Brown, M. E. (2016). Resilience in men and women experiencing sexual assault or traumatic stress: Validation and replication of the scale of protective factors. *Journal of Traumatic Stress, 29*, 537–545. doi: 10.1002/jts.22148.

Porges, S. (1995). Cardiac vagal tone: A physiological index of stress. *Neuroscience and Biobehavioral Reviews, 19*(2), 225–233.

Power, R. A., Steinberg, S., Bjornsdottir, G., Rietveld, C., Abdellaoui, A., Nivard, M. M., Johnannesson, M., … Stefansson, K. (2015). Polygenic risk scores for schizophrenia and bipolar disorder predict creativity. *Nature Neuroscience, 18*, 953–955. doi: 10.1038/nn.4040.

Powers, M. B., Medina, J. L., Burns, S., Kauffman, B. K., Monfils, M., Asmundson, G. J. G., Diamond, A., … Smits, J. A. J. (2015). Exercise augmentation of exposure therapy for PTSD: Rationale and pilot efficacy data. *Cognitive Behavior Therapy, 44*(4), 314–327. doi: 10.1080/16506073.2015.1012740.

Poythress, N. G., Skeem, J. L., & Lilienfeld, S. O. (2006). Associations among early abuse, dissociation, and psychopathology in an offender sample. *Journal of Abnormal Psychology, 115*(2), 288–297. doi: 10.1037/002-843X.115.2.288.

Prabhu, V., Sutton, C., & Sauser, W. (2008). Creativity and certain personality traits: Understanding the mediating effects of intrinsic motivation. *Creativity Research Journal, 20*(1), 53–66. doi: 10.1080/10400410701841955.

Pradham, M., & Aujla, I. (2014). The relationship between passion and the psychological well-being of professional dancers. *Journal of Dance Medicine and Science, 18*(1), 37–44. doi: 10.12678/1089-313X.18.1.37.

Preckel, F., Holling, H., & Wiese, M. (2006). Relationship of intelligence and creativity in gifted and non-gifted students: An investigation of threshold theory. *Personality and Individual Differences, 40,* 159–170. doi: 10.1016/j.paid.2005.06.022.

Preti, A., & Miotto, P. (1999). Suicide among eminent artists. *Psychological Reports, 84,* 291–301.

Preti, A., & Vellante, M. (2007). Creativity and psychopathology: Higher rates of psychosis proneness and nonright-handedness among creative artists compared to same age and gender peers. *Journal of Nervous and Mental Disease, 195*(10), 837–845. doi: 10.1097/NMD.06013e3181568180.

Price, M., Kearns, M., Houry, D., & Rothbaum, B. O. (2014). Emergency department predictors of posttraumatic stress reduction for trauma-exposed individuals with and without an early intervention. *Journal of Consulting and Clinical Psychology, 82,* 336–341. doi: 10.1037/a0035537.

Pruiksma, K. E., Taylor, D. J., Wachen, J. S., Mintz, J., Young-McCaughan, S., Peterson, A. L., ... Resnick, P. A. (2016). Residual sleep disturbances following PTSD treatment in active duty military personnel. *Psychological Trauma: Theory, Research, Practice, and Policy, 8*(6), 697–701. doi: 10.1037/tra0000150.

Pryor, J., Hurtado, S., Saenz, V., Londholm, J., Korn, W., & Mahoney, K. (2006). *The American freshman.* Los Angeles: UCLA Higher Education Research Institute.

Puente-Diaz, R., & Cavazos-Arroyo, J. (2017). Creative self-efficacy: The influence of affective states and social persuasion as antecedents and imagination and divergent thinking as consequences. *Creativity Research Journal, 29*(3), 304–312. doi: 10.1080/10400419.2017.1360067.

Pulverman, C. S., Lorenz, T. A., & Meston, C. M. (2015). Linguistic changes in expressive writing predict psychological outcomes in women with history of childhood sexual abuse and adult sexual dysfunction. *Psychological Trauma: Theory, Research, Practice, and Policy, 7*(1), 50–57. doi: 10.1037/a0036462.

Punamaki, R.-L., Diab, S. Y., Isosavi, S., Kuiitinen, S., & Qouta, S. R. (2018). Maternal pre- and postnatal mental health and infant development in war conditions: The Gaza Infant Study. *Psychological Trauma: Theory, Reserch, Practice, and Policy, 10*(2), 144–153. doi: 10.1037/tra0000275.

Puryear, J. S., Kettler, T., & Rinn, A. N. (2016). Relationships of personality to differential conceptions of creativity: A systemic review. *Psychology of Aesthetics, Creativity, and the Arts, 11*(1), 59–68. doi: 10.1037/aca0000079.

Puterman, E., Gemmill, A., Karasek, D., Weir, D., Adler, N. E., Prather, A. A., & Epel, E. S. (2016). Lifespan adversity and later adulthood telomere length in the nationally representative US health and retirement study. *Proceedings of the National Academy of Science, 113*(42), E6335–E6342. doi: 10.1073/pnas.1525602113.

Putnam, K. T., Harris, W. W., & Putnam, F. W. (2013). Synergistic childhood adversities and complex adult psychopathology. *Journal of Traumatic Stress, 26*, 435–442. doi: 10.1002/jts.21833.

Pyszczynski, T., & Kesebir, P. (2011). Anxiety buffer disruption theory: A terror management account of posttraumatic stress disorder. *Anxiety, Stress, and Coping: An International Journal, 24*, 3–26. doi: 10.1080/10615806.2010.517524.

Qin, Y., Zhou, Y., Fan, F., Chen, S., Huang, R., Cai, R., & Peng, T. (2016). Developmental trajectories and predictors of prosocial behavior among adolescents exposed to the 2008 Wenchuan earthquake. *Journal of Traumatic Stress, 29*, 80–87. doi: 10.1002/jts.22064.

Qouta, S., Punamaki, R.-L., Montgomery, E., & Sarraj, E. E. (2007). Predictors of psychological distress and positive resources among Palestinian adolescents: Trauma, child and mothering characteristics. *Child Abuse and Neglect, 31*, 699–717. doi: 10.1016.j.chiabu.2005.07007.

Quevedo, K., Johnson, A. E., Loman, M. L., LaFavor, T. L., & Gunnar, M. (2012). The con- fluence of adverse early experience and puberty on the cortisol awakening response. *International Journal of Behavioral Develpoment, 36*, 19–28. doi: 10.1177/0165025411406860.

Rabb, N., Nissel, J., Alecci, A., Madid, L., Ambrosoli, J., & Winner, E. (2016). Truths about beauty and goodness: Disgust affects moral but not aesthetic judgments. *Psychology of Aesthetics, Creativity, and the Arts, 10*(4), 492–500. doi: 10.1037//aca0000051.

Raby, K. L., Labella, M. H., Martin, J., Carlson, E. A., & Roisman, G. I. (2017). Childhood abuse and neglect and insecure attachment states of mind in adulthood: Prospective, longitudinal evidence from a high-risk sample. *Development and Psychopathology, 29*, 347–363. doi: 10.1017/S0954579417000037.

Raines, A. M., Currier, J., McManus, E. S., Walton, J. L., Uddo, M., & Franklin, C. L. (2017). Spiritual struggle and suicide in veterans seeking PTSD treatment. *Psychological Trauma: Theory, Research, Practice, and Policy, 9*(6), 746–749. doi: 10.1037/tra0000239.

Ram-Vlasov, N., Tzischinsky, O., Green, A., & Shochat, T. (2016). Creativity and habitual sleep patterns among art students and social sciences undergraduate students. *Psychology of Aesthetics, Creativity, and the Arts, 10*(3), 270–277. doi: 10.1037/aca0000062.

Randell, K. A., O'Malley, D., & Dowd, M. D. (2015). Association of parental adverse childhood experiences and current child adversity. *Pediatrics, 169*(8), 786–787.

Rangganadhan, A. R., & Todorov, N. (2010). Personality and self-forgiveness: The role of shame, guilt, empathy and conciliatory behavior. *Journal of Social and Clinical Psychology, 29*(1), 1–22. doi: 10.1521/jscp.2010.29.1.1.

Rasmussen, A., & Rasmussen, P. (2015). Conceptions of student talent in the context of talent development. *International Journal of Qualitative Studies in Education, 28*(4), 476–495. doi: 10.1080/09518398.2014.916013.

Rasmussen, A., Crager, M., Baser, R. E., Chu, T., & Gany, F. (2012). Onset of posttraumatic stress disorder and major depression among refugees and voluntary migrants to the United States. *Journal of Traumatic Stress, 25*, 705–712. doi: 10.1002/jts.21763.

Rasmussen, H. N., Wrosch, C., Scheier, M. F., & Carver, C. S. (2006). Self-regulation processes and health: The importance of optimism and goal adjustment. *Journal of Personality, 74*(6), 7121–1748. doi: 10.1111/j.1467-6494.2006.00426.x.

Rathunde, K. (2000). Broadening and narrowing in the creative process: A commentary on Fredrickson's "Broaden-and-Build" model. *Prevention and Treatment, 3*, Article 6c. doi: 10.1037//1522-3736.3.1.36c.

Rauschenberger, S., & Lynn, S. J. (2002–2003). Fantasy-proneness, negative affect and psychopathology. *Imagination, Cognition and Personality, 22*(3), 239–255.

Rawlings, D., & Locarnini, A. (2008). Dimensional schizoptypy, autism, and unusual word associations in artists and scientists. *Journal of Research in Personality, 42*, 465–471. doi: 10.1016/j.jrp.2007.06.005.

Razumnikova, O. M., & Volf, N. V. (2015). Creativity-related hemispheric selective processing: Correlations on global and local levels of attentional set. *Creativity Research Journal, 27*(4), 394–399. doi: 10.1080/10400419.2015.1087272.

Razunmnikova, O. M., Kovtun, L. T., & Krivoshchekov, S. G. (2013). Cardiorespiratory response to hypoxia in persons with different levels of creativity. *Human Physiology, 39*(4), 105–111. doi: 10.1134/S0362119713020138.

Recordati, G. (2003). A thermodynamic model of the sympathetic and parasympathetic nervous system. *Autonomic Neuroscience: Basic and Clinical, 103*, 1–12.

Rees, T., Hardy, L., Gullich, A., Albernethy, B., Cote, J., Woodman, T., … Warr, C. (2016). The great British Medalists Project: A review of current knowledge on the development of the world's best sporting talent. *Sports Medicine, 46*, 1041–1058. doi: 10.1007/s40279-016-0476-2.

Reinders, S. (1992). The experience of artistic creativity: A phenomenological psychological analysis. *Dissertation Abstracts International, 52*, 4512.

Reinders, A. A. T. S., Willemsen, A. T. M., Vos, H. P. J., den Boer, J. A., & Nijenhuis, E. S. (2012). Fact or factitious? A psychobiological study of authentic and simulated dissociative identity states. *PLoS ONE, 7*(6), e39279. doi: 10.1371/journal.pone.0039279.

Reis, S. M. (2002). Toward a theory of creativity in diverse creative women. *Creativity Research Journal, 14*(3 & 4), 305–316.

Reiter-Palmon, R., Illies, M. Y., Buboltz, C. Cross, L. K., & Nimps, T. (2009). Creativity and domain specificity: The effect of task type on multiple indexes of creative problem-solving. *Psychology of Creativity, Aesthetics, and the Arts, 3*(2), 73–80. doi: 10.1037/a0013410.

Ren, F., & Zhang, J. (2015). Job stressors, organizational innovation climate, and employees' innovative behavior. *Creativity Research Journal, 27*(1), 16–23. doi: 10.1080/10400419.2015.992659.

Ren, F., Li, Y., & Zhang, J. (2017). Perceived parental control and Chinese middle school adolescents' creativity: The mediating role of autonomous motivation.

Psychology of Aesthetics, Creativity, and the Arts, 11(1), 34–42. doi: 10.1037/aca.0000078.

Renzulli, J. S. (1978). What makes giftedness? Reexamining a definition. *Phi Delta Kappan, 60*, 180–184, 261.

———. (2002). Emerging conceptions of giftedness: Building a bridge to the new century. *Exceptionality, 10*(2), 67–75.

———. (2005). The three-ring definition of giftedness: A developmental model for promoting creative productivity. In R. J. Sternberg & J. E. Davidson (Eds.), *Conceptions of giftedness* (2nd ed., pp. 246–279). New York: NY: Cambridge University Press.

Reul, J. M. H. M., Collins, A., Saliba, R. S. Mifsud, K. R., Carter, S. D., Gutierrez-Mecinas, M., ... Linthorst, A. C. E. (2015). Glucocorticoids, epigenetic control and stress resilience. *Neurobiology of Stress, 1*, 44–59. doi: 10.1016/j.ynstr.2014.10.001.

Rhodes, M. (1961). An analysis of creativity. *Phi Delta Kappan, 42*, 305–310.

Rhue, J. W., & Lynn, S. J. (1987). Fantasy proneness: Developmental antecedents. *Journal of Personality, 55*(1), 121–137.

Riber, K. (2016). Attachment organization in Arabic-speaking refugees with post traumatic disorder. *Attachment and Human Development, 18*(2), 154–175. doi: 10.1080/14616734.2015.1124442.

Richards, D. A., & Schat, A. C. H. (2010). Attachment at (not to) work: Applying attachment theory to explain individual behavior in organizations. *Journal of Applied Psychology, 96*(1), 169–182. doi: 10.1037/a0020372.

Richards, R. (1993). Everyday creativity, eminent creativity, and psychopathology. *Psychological Inquiry, 4*(3), 212–217.

Riem, M. M. E., Bakermans-Kranenburg, M. J., & van IJzendoorn, M. H. (2016). Intranasal administration of oxytocin modulates behavioral and amygdala responses to infant crying in females with insecure attachment representations. *Attachment and Human Development, 18*(3), 213–234. doi: 10.1080/14616734.2016.1149872.

Riggs, K. (2006). Foundations for flow: A philosophical model for studio instruction. *Philosophy of Music Education Review, 14*(2), 175–191. doi: 10.1353/pme.2007.0008.

Riggs, S. A., Paulson, A., Tunnell, E., Sahl, G., Atkinson, H., & Ross, C. A. (2007). Attachment, personality, and psychopathology among adult inpatients: Self-reported romantic attachment style versus Adult Attachment Interveiw states of mind. *Development and Psychopathology, 19*, 263–291. doi: 10.1017/S0954579407070149.

Rinn, A. N., Mendaglio, S., Rudasill, K. M., & McQueen, K. S. (2010). Examining the relationship between the overexcitabilities and self-concepts of gifted adolescents via multivariate cluster analysis. *Gifted Child Quarterly, 54*(1), 3–17. doi: 10.1177/0016986209352682.

Rip, B., Fortin, S., & Vallerand, R. J. (2006). The relationship between passion and injury in dance students. *Journal of Dance Medicine and Science, 10*(1 & 2), 14–20.

Risan, P., Binder, P.-E., & Milne, R. (2016). Regulating and coping with distress during police interviews of traumatized individuals. *Psychological Trauma: Theory, Research, Practice, and Policy, 8*(6), 736–744. doi: 10.1037/tra0000119.

Rissling, M. B., Dennis, P. A., Watkins, L. L., Calhoun, P. S., Dennis, M. F., Beckham, J. C., ... Ulmer, C. S. (2016). Circadian contrasts in heart rate variability associated with posttraumatic stress disorder symptoms in a young adult cohort. *Journal of Traumatic Stress, 29*, 415–421. doi: 10.1002/jts.22125.

Rizkalla, N., & Segal, S. P. (2018). Well-being and posttraumatic growth among Syrian refugees in Jordan. *Journal of Traumatic Stress, 31*, 213–222. doi: 10.1002/jts.22281.

Rizzolatti, G., & Craighero, L. (2004). The mirror-neuron system. *Annual Review of Neuroscience, 27*, 169–192. doi: 10.1146/annurev.neuro.27.070203.144230.

Robb, A., & Davies, M. (2015). 'Being inside the story': A phenomenology of onstage experience and the implications of flow. *About Performance, 13*, 45–67.

Robitschek, C., Ashton, M. W., Spering, C. C., Geiger, N., Byers, D., Christian Schotts, G., & Thoen, M. A. (2012). Development and psychometric evaluation of the Personal Growth Initiative Scale-II. *Journal of Counseling Psychology, 59*(2), 274–287. doi: 10.1037/a0027310.

Rochman, D., & Diamond, G. M. (2008). From unresolved anger to sadness: Identifying physiological correlates. *Journal of Counseling Psychology, 55*(1), 96–105. doi: 10.1037/0022-0167.55.1.96.

Roelofs, K., & Spinhoven, P. (2007). Trauma and medically unexplained symptoms: Towards an integration of cognitive and neuro-biological accounts. *Clinical Psychology Review, 27*, 798–820. doi: 10.1016/j.cpr.2007.07.004.

Roelofs, K., Hagenaars, M. A., & Stins, J. (2010). Facing freeze: Social threat induces bodily freeze in humans. *Psychological Science, 21*(11), 1575–1581. doi: 10.1177/0956797610384746.

Rohleder, N., Beulen, S. E., Chen, E., Wolf, J. M., & Kirschbaum, C. (2007). Stress on the dance floor: The cortisol stress response to social-evaluative threat in competitive ballroom dancers. *Personality and Social Psychology Bulletin, 33*(1), 69–84. doi: 10.1177/0146167206293986.

Rohleder, N., Chen, E., Wolf, J. M., & Miller, G. E. (2008). The psychobiology of trait shame in young women: Exteding the social self preservation theory. *Health Psychology, 27*(5), 523–532. doi: 10.1037/0278-6133.27.5.523.

Roisman, G. I. (2009). Adult attachment: Toward a rapprochement of methodological cultures. *Current Directions in Psychological Science, 18*(2), 122–126.

Roisman, G. L., Fortuna, K., & Holland, A. (2006). An experimental manipulation of retrospectively defined earned and continuous attachment security. *Child Development, 77*(1), 59–71.

Roisman, G. I., Holland, A., Fortuna, K., Fraley, R. C., Clausell, E., & Clarke, A. (2007). The Adult Attachment Interview and self-reports of attachment style: An empirical rapprochement. *Journal of Personality and Social Psychology, 92*, 678–697. doi: 10.1037/0022-3514.92.4.678.

Roisman, G. I., Padron, E., Sroufe, L. A., & Egeland, B. (2002). Earned-secrue attachment status in retrospect and prospect. *Child Development, 73*(4), 1204–1219.

Roisman, G. I., Rogosch, F. A., Cicchetti, D., Groh, A. M., Haltigan, J. D., Haydon, K. C., ... Steele, R. D. (2017). Attachment states of mind and inferred childhood experiences in maltreated and comparison adolescents from low-income families. *Development and Psychopathology, 29*, 337–345. doi: 10.1017/S0954579417000025.

Roisman, G. I., Tsai, J. L., & Chiang, K.-H. S. (2004). The emotional integration of childhood experience: Physiological, facial, expressive, and self-reported emotional response during the Adult Attachment Interview. *Developmental Psychology, 40*(5), 776–789. doi: 10.1037/0012-1649.40.5.776.

Rojas-Flores, L., Clenents, M. L., Koo, J. H., & London, J. (2017). Trauma and psychological distress in Latino citizen children following parental detention and deportation. *Psychological Trauma: Theory, Research, Practice, and Policy, 9*(3), 352–361. doi: 10.1037/tra0000177.

Romens, S. E., McDonald, J., Svaren, J., & Pollak, S. D. (2015). Associations between early life stress and gene methylation in children. *Child Development, 86*(1), 303–309. doi: 10.1111/cdev.12270.

Root-Bernstein, M., & Root-Bernstein, R. (2006). Imaginary worldplay in childhood and maturity and its impact on adult creativity. *Creativity Research Journal, 18*(4), 405–425.

Rosenberg, S., Mueser, K., Jankowski, M. K., & Hamblen, J. (2002). Trauma exposure and PTSD in people with severe mental illness. *PTSD Research Quatrerly, 13*(3), 1–3.

Ross, C. A., & Brwoning, E. (2016). The relationship between catatonia and dissociation: A preliminary investigation. *Journal of Trauma and Dissociation, 17*(4), 426–434. doi: 10.1080/15299732.2016.1136858.

Ross, S. R., & Keiser, H. N. (2014). Autotelic personality through a five-factor lens: Individual differences in flow-propensity. *Personality and Individual Differences, 59*, 3–8. doi: 10.106/j.paid.2013.09.029.

Rostan, S. M. (1997). A study of young artists: The development of artistic talent and creativity. *Creativity Research Journal, 10*(2–3), 175–192.

Rostan, S. M., Pariser, D., & Gruber, H. E. (2002). A cross-cultural study of the development of artistic talent, creativity and giftedness. *High Ability Studies, 13*, 125–155. doi: 10.1080/1359813022000048789.

Rothbart, M. K., & Sheese, B. E. (2007). Temperament and emotion regulation. In J. J. Gross (Ed.), *Handbook of emotion regulation* (pp. 331–350). New York: Guilford Press.

Rothbart, M. K., Ellis, L. K., & Posner, M. I. (2004). Temperament and self-regulation. In R. F. Baumeister & K. D. Vohs (Eds.), *Handbook of self-regulation: Research, theory, and Application* (pp. 357–370). NYC, NY: The Guilford Press.

Rothenberg, A. (1990). *Creativity and madness: New findings and old stereotypes.* Baltimore: John Hopkins University Press.

Routledge, C. D., & Arndt, J. (2009). Creative terror management: Creativity as a facilitator of cultural exploration after mortality salience. *Personality and Social Psychology Bulletin, 35*(4), 493–505. doi: 10.1177/0146167208329629.

Rozin, P., Millman, L., & Nemeroff, C. (1986). Operations of the laws of sympathetic magic in disgust and other domains. *Journal of Personality and Social Psychology, 50*, 703–712. doi: 10.1037/0022-3514.50.4.703.

Rubens, S. L., Felix, E. D., Vernberg, E. M., & Canino, G. (2014). The role of peers in the relation between hurricane exposure and Ataques de Nervios among Puerto Rican adolescents. *Psychological Trauma: Theory, Research, Practice, and Policy, 6*(6), 716–723. doi: 10.1037/a0036701.

Rudd, M., Vohs, K. D., & Aaker, J. (2012). Awe expands people's perception of time, alters decision making, and enhances well-being. *Psychological Science, 23*(10), 1130–1136. doi: 10.1177/0956797612438731.

Rugens, A., & Terhune, D. B. (2013). Guilt by dissociation: Gulit primes augment the relationship between dissociative tendencies and state dissociation. *Psychiatric Research, 206*, 114–116. doi: 10.1016/j.psychres.2012.09.010.

Ruiz, E. (2016). Trauma symptoms in a diverse population of sexually abused children. *Psychological Trauma: Theory, Research, Practice, and Policy, 8*(6), 680–687. doi: 10.1037/tra00000160.

Runco, M. A. (2004). Creativity. *Annual Review of Psychology, 55*, 657–687.

———. (2015). Meta-creativity: Being creative about creativity. *Creativity Research Journal, 27*(3), 295–298. doi: 10.1080/10400419.20115.1065134.

Russ, S. W., & Wallace, C. E. (2013). Pretend play and creative processes. *American Journal of Play, 6*(1), 136–148.

Rutter, I. M. (2006). Implications of resilience concepts for scientific understanding. *Annals of the New York Academy of Science, 1094*, 1–12. doi: 10.1196/1nn1ls.1376.002.

Ryan, R. M. (2007). Motivation and emotion: A new look and approach for two emerging fields. *Motivation and Emotion, 31*, 1–3. doi: 10.1007/s11031-007-9055-z.

Sadeh, N., Spielberg, J. M., Logue, M. W., Wolf, E. J., Smith, A. K., Lusk, J., … Miller, M. W. (2016). SKA2 methylation is associated with decreased prefrontal cortical thickness and greater PTSD severity among trauma-exposed veterans. *Molecular Psychiatry, 21*(3), 357–363. doi: 10.1038/mp.2015.134.

Sadler-Smith, E. (2015). Wallas' four-stage model of the creative process: More than meets the eye? *Creativity Research Journal, 27*(4), 342–352. doi: 10.1080/10400419.2015.1087277.

Sagar, S. S., & Stoeber, J. (2009). Perfectionism, fear of failure, and affective response to success and failure: The central role of fear of experiencing shame and embarrassment. *Journal of Sport and exercise Psychology, 31*(5), 602–627.

Salcioglu, E., Urhan, S., Pirinccioglu, S., & Aydin, S. (2017). Anticipatory feat and helplessness predict PTSD and depression in domestic violence survivors. *Psychological Trauma: Theory, Research, Practice, and Policy, 9*(1), 117–125. doi: 10.1037/tra0000200.

Salimpoor, V. N., & Zatorre, R. J. (2013). Neural interactions that give rise to musical pleasure. *Psychology of Aesthetics, Creativity, and the Arts, 7*(1), 62–75. doi: 10.1037/a0031819.

Salimpoor, V. N., Benovoy, M., Larcher, K., Dager, A., & Zatoore, R. J. (2011). Anatomically distinct dopamine release during anticipation and experience of peak emotion to music. *Nature Neuroscience, 14*, 257–262. doi: 10.1038/nn.2726.

Salimpoor, V. N., Benovoy, M., Longo, G., Cooperstock, J. R., & Zatorre, R. J. (2009). The rewarding aspects of music listening are related to degree of emotional arousal. *PloS ONE, 4*, e7487. doi: 10.137/journal.pone.0007487.

Salina, D. D., Figge, C., Ram, D., & Jason, L. A. (2017). Rates of traumatization and psychopathology in criminal justice-involved women. *Journal of Trauma and Dissociation, 18*(2), 174–188. doi: 10.1080/15299732.2016.1207745.

Sameroff, A. J., & Rosenblum, K. L. (2006). Psychosocial contraints on the development of resilience. *Annals of the New York Academy of Science, 1094*, 116–124. doi: 10.1196/annals.1376.010.

Samuelson, K. W., Bartel, A., Valdez, R., & Jordan, J. T. (2017). PTSD symptoms and perception of cognitive problems: The roles of posttraumatic cognitions and trauma coping self-efficacy. *Psychological Trauma: Theory, Research, Practice, and Policy, 9*(5), 537–544. doi: 10.1037/tra0000210.

Sanchez-Bernardos, M. L., & Avia, M. D. (2004). Personality correlates of fantasy proneness among adolescents. *Personality and Individual Differences, 37*, 1969–1079.

———. (2006). The relationship between fantasy proneness and schizotypy in adolescents. *Journal of Nervous and Mental Disease, 194*(6), 411–414. doi: 10.1097/01.nmd.0000222406.16820.13.

Sanchez-Bernardos, M. L., Lloreda, M. J. H., Avia, M. D., & Bragado-Alvarez, C. (2015). Fantasy proneness and personality profiles. *Imagination, Cognition and Personality, 34*(4), 327–339. doi: 10.1177/0276236615572584.

Sandberg, D. A. (2010). Adult attachment as a predictor of posttraumatic stress and dissociation. *Journal of Trauma and Dissociation, 11*, 203–307. doi: 10.1080/15299731003780937.

Santiago, P. N., Ursano, R. J., Gray, C. L., Pynoos, R. S., Spiegel, D., Lewis-Fernandez, R., ... Fullerton, C. S. (2013). A systematic review of PTSD prevalence and trajectories in DSM-5 defined trauma exposed populations: Intentional and nonintentional traumatic events. *PLoS ONE, 8*(4), e59236, 1–5. doi: 10.1371/journal.pone.0059236.

Sar, V., Alioglu, F., & Akyuz, G. (2017). Depersonalization and derealization in self-report and clinical interview: The spectrum of borderline personality disorder, dissociative disorder, and healthy controls. *Journal of Trauma and Dissociation, 18*(4), 490–506. doi: 10.1080/15299732.2016.1240737.

Sar, V., Koyuncu, A., Ozturk, E., Yargic, L. I., Kundakci, T., Yazici, A., ... Aksut, D. (2007). Dissociative disorders in the psychiatric emergency ward. *General Hospital Psychiatry, 29*, 45–50. doi: 10.1016/j.genhosppsych.2006.10.009.

Saraiya, T., & Lopez-Castro, T. (2016). Ashamed and afraid: A scoping review of the role of shame in post-traumatic stress disorder (PTSD). *Journal of Clinical Medicine, 5*(11), 94. doi: 10.3390/jcm5110094.

Sarkar, M., & Fletcher, D. (2014). Ordinary magic, extraordinary performance: Psychological resilience and thriving in high achievers. *Sport, Exercise, and Performance Psychology, 3*(1), 46–60. doi: 10.1037/spy0000003.

Sauer, E., & Ropo, A. (2006). Leadership and the driving force of shame: A social constructionist analysis of narrative. In W. J. Zerbie, N. M. Ashkanasy, & C. E. J. Hartel (Eds.), *Research on emotion in organizations* (Vol. 2, pp. 57–80). London: Emerald Group Publishing Ltd. doi: 10.1016/S1746-9791(06)02003-7.

Saunders, R., Jacobvitz, D., Zaccagnino, M., Beverung, L. M., & Hazen, N. (2011). Pathwasy to earned-security: The role of alternative support figures. *Attachment and Human Development, 13*(4), 403–420. doi: 10.1080/14616734.2011.584405.

Savage, J., Collins, D., & Cruckshank, A. (2017). Exploring trauma in the development of talent: What are they, what do they do, and what do they require? *Journal of Applied Sport Psychology, 29*, 101–117. doi: 10.1080/10413200.2016.1194910.

Savitz, J. B., van der Merwe, L., Newman, T. K., Solms, M., Stein, D. J., & Ramesar, R. S. (2008). The relationship between childhood abuse and dissociation. Is it influenced by catechol-0-methyltransferase (COMT) activity? *International Journal of Neuropsychopharmacology, 11*, 149–161. doi: 10.1017/S1461145707007900.

Sawyer, R. K. (2000). Improvisational cultures: Collaborative emergence and creativity in improvisation. *Mind, Culture, and Activity, 7*(3), 180–185. doi: 10.1207/515327884MCA0703_05.

———. (2006). *Explaining creativity: The science of human innovation*. New York: Oxford University Press.

———. (2011). The cognitive neuroscience of creativity: A critical review. *Creativity Research Journal, 23*(2), 137–154. doi: 10.1080/10400419.2011.571191.

Sawyer, R. K., & DeZutter, S. (2009). Distributed creativity: How collective creations emerge from collaboration. *Psychology of Aesthetics, Creativity and the Arts, 3*(2), 81–92. doi: 10.1037/a0013282.

Saxe, G., Vanderbilt, D., & Zukerman, B. (2003). Traumatic stress in injured and ill children. *PTSD Research Quarterly, 14*(2), 1–8.

Scharf, M., Mayseless, O., & Kivenson-Baron, I. (2004). Adolescents' attachment representations and developmental tasks in emerging adulthood. *Developmental Psychology, 40*(3), 430–444. doi: 10.1037/0012.1649.40.3.430.

Schauer, M., & Ebert, T. (2010). Dissociation following traumatic stress: Etiology and treatment. *Zeitschrift fur Psychologie, 218*, 109–127.

Schild, S., & Dalenberg, C. J. (2012). Trauma exposure and traumatic symptoms in deaf adults. *Psychological Trauma: Theory, Research, Practice, and Policy, 4*(1), 117–127. doi: 10.1037/a0021578.

Schilling, M. (2005). A "small-world" network model of cognitive insight. *Creativity Research Journal, 17*(2–3), 131–154.

Schimmack, U., & Diener, E. (2010). Affect intensity: Separating intensity and frequency in repeatedly measured affect. *Journal of Personality and Social Psychology, 73*(6), 1313–1329.

Schimmenti, A. (2012). Unveiling the hidden self: Developmental trauma and pathological shame. *Psychodynamic Practice: Individuals, Groups and Organizations, 18*(2), 195–211. doi: 10.1080/14753634.2012.664873.

Schimmenti, A., Di Carlo, G., Passanis, A., & Caretti, V. (2015). Abuse in childhood and psychopathic traits in a sample of violent offenders. *Psychological Trauma: Theory, Research, Practice, and Policy, 7*(4), 340–347. doi: 10.1037/tra0000023.

Schlaug, G., Forgeard, M., Zhu, L., Norton, A., Norton, A., & Winner, E. (2009). Training-induced neuroplasticity in young children. *Annals of New York Academy of Science, 1169*, 205–208. doi: 10.1111/j.1749-6632.2009.04842.x.

Schlaug, G., Norton, A., Overy, K., & Winner, E. (2005). Effects of music training on the child's brain and cognitive development. *Annals of New York Academy of Science, 1060*, 219–230. doi: 10.1196/annals.1360.015.

Schlesinger, J. (2009). Creative mythoconceptions: A closer look at the evidence for the "Mad Genius" hypothesis. *Psychology of Aesthetics, Creativity, and the Arts, 3*(2), 62–72. doi: 10.1037/a0013975.

Schmahl, C. G., Elzinga, B. M., & Bremner, J. D. (2002). Individual differences in psychophysiological reactivity in adults with childhood abuse. *Clinical Psychology and Psychotherapy, 9*(4), 271–276. doi: 10.1002/cpp.325.

Schnitker, S. A., Porter, T. J., Emmons, R. A., & Barrett, J. L. (2012). Attachment predicts adolescent conversions at young life religious summer camps. *International Journal for the Psychology of Religion, 22*(3), 198–215. doi: 10.1080/10508619.2012.670024.

Schoenleber, M., & Berenbaum, H. (2012). Shame regulation in personality pathology. *Journal of Abnormal Psychology, 121*(2), 433–446. doi: 10.1037/a0025281.

Schoenleber, M., Sippel, L. M., Jakupcak, M., & Tull, M. T. (2015). Role of trait shame in the association between posttraumatic stress and aggression among men with a history of interpersonal trauma. *Psychological Trauma: Theory, Research, Practice, and Policy, 7*(1), 43–49. doi: 10.1037/a0037434.

Schoenmaker, C., Juffer, F., van IJzendoorn, M. H., Linting, M., van der Voort, A., & Bakermans-Kranenburg, M. J. (2015). From maternal sensitivity in infancy to adult attachment representations: A longitudinal adoption study with secure base scripts. *Attachment and Human Development, 17*(3), 241–256. doi: 10.1080/14616734.2015.1037315.

Schore, A. N. (1994). *Affect regulation and the origin of the self: The neurobiology of emotional development*. Hillsdale, NJ: L. Erlbaum Associates.

———. (2003). *Affect regulation and the repair of the self*. New York: W.W. Norton & Company.

Schottenbauer, M. A., Klimes-Dougan, B., Rodriguex, B. F., Arnkoff, D. B., Glass, C. R., & LaSalle, V. H. (2006). Attachment and affective resolution following a stressful event: General and religious coping as possible mediators. *Mental Health, Religion and Culture, 9*(5), 448–471. doi: 10.1080/136949670500440684.

Schuldberg, D. (2000–2001). Creativity and psychopathology: Categories, dimensions, and dynamics. *Creativity Research Journal, 13*(1), 105–110.

Schuler, E. R., & Boals, A. (2016). Shattering world assumptions: A perspective view of the impact of adverse events on world assumptions. *Psychological Trauma: Theory, Research, Practice, and Policy, 8*(3), 259–266. doi: 10.1037/tra0000073.

Schupak, C., & Rosenthal, J. (2009). Excessive daydreaming: A case history and discussion of mind wandering and high fantasy proneness. *Consciousness and Cognition, 18*(1), 290–292. doi: 10.1016/j.concog.2008.10.002.

Schurtz, D. R., Blincoe, S., Smith, R. H., Powell, C. A. J., Combs, D. J. Y., & Kim, S. H. (2012). Exploring the social aspects of goose bumps and their role in awe and envy. *Motivation and Emotion, 36*, 205–217. doi: 10.1007/s11031-011-9243-8.

Schwartz, B. (2004). *The paradox of choice: Why less is more*. New York, NY: HarperCollins.

Schwartz, S. H. (1992). Universals in the content and structure of values: Theoretical advances and empirical tests in 20 countries. In M. P. Zanna (Ed.), *Advances in Experimental social psychology* (Vol. 25, pp. 1–26). San Diego, CA: Academic Press.

Schwartz, S. H., & Bardi, A. (2001). Value hierarchies across cultures: Taking a similarities perspective. *Journal of Cross-Cultural Psychology, 32*, 268–290.

Scibinetti, P., Tocci, N., & Pesce, C. (2011). Motor creativity and creative thinking in children: The diverging role of inhibition. *Creativity Research Journal, 23*(3), 262–272. doi: 10.1080/10400419.2011.595993.

Scioli-Salter, E. R. Johnides, B. D., Mitchell, K. S., Smith, B. N., Resick, P. A., & Rasmusson, A. M. (2016). Depression and dissociation as predictors of physical health symptoms among female rape survivors with posttraumatic stress disorder. *Psychological Trauma: Theory, Research, Practice, and Policy, 8*(5), 585–591. doi: 10.1037/tra0000135.

Sedlak, A. J., Finkelhor, D., & Brick, J. M. (2017). *National estimates of missing children: Updated findings from a survey of parents and other primary caretakers.* U.S. Department of Justice, Office of Justice Programs, Office of Juvenile Justice and Delinquency Prevention. Retrieved from https://www.ncjrs.gov.

Seeley, W. W., Menon, V., Schatzberg, A. F., Keller, J., Glover, G. H., Kenna, H., Reiss, A. L., & Greicius, M. D. (2007). Dissociable intrinsic connectivity networks for salience processing and executive control. *Journal of Neuroscience 27*, 2349–2356.

Seelig, A. D., Rivera, A. C., Powell, T. M., Williams, E. C., Peterson, A. V., Littman, A. J., … Boyoko, E. J. (2017). Patterns of smoking and unhealthy alcohol use following sexual trauma among U.S. service members. *Journal of Traumatic Stress, 30*, 502–511. doi: 10.1002/jts.22214.

Segerstrom, S. C., & Nes, L. S. (2007). Heart rate variability reflects self-regulatory strength, effort, and fatigue. *Psychological Science, 18*(3), 275–281. doi: 10.1111/j.1467-9280.2007.01888.x.

Seidler, R. D., Noll, D. C., & Thiers, G. (2004). Feedforward and feedback processes in motor control. *Neuroimage, 22*, 1775–1783. doi: 10.1016/j.neuroimage.2004.05.003.

Seiler, A., Kohler, S., Ruf-Leuschner, M., & Landolt, M. A. (2016). Adverse childhood experiences, mental health and quality of life of Chilean girls placed in foster care: An exploratory study. *Psychological Trauma: Theory, Research, Practice, and Policy, 8*(2), 180–187. doi: 10.1037/tra0000037.

Selby, E. C., Shaw, E. J., & Houtz, J. C. (2005). The creative personality. *Gifted Child Quarterly, 49*(4), 300–314.

Seligman, R., & Kirmayer, L. J. (2008). Dissociative experienceand cultural neuroscience: Narrative, metaphor and mechanism. *Cultural Medicine and Psychiatry, 32*, 31–64. doi: 10.1007/s11013-007-9077-8.

Seng, J. S., Low, L. M. K., Sperlich, M., Ronis, D., & Liberzon, I. (2009). Prevalence, trauma history, and risk for posttraumatic stress disorder among nullipoarous womein in maternity care. *Obstetrics and Gynecology, 114*(4), 839–847. doi: 10.1097/AOG.0b013e3181b8f8a2.

Sevdalis, V., & Raab, M. (2014). Empathy in sports, exercise, and the performing arts. *Psychology of Sport and Exercise, 15*, 173–179. doi: 10.1016/j.psychsport.2013.10.013.

Sexton, M. B., Davis, M. T., Menke, R., Raggio, G. A., & Muzik, M. (2017). Mother-child interactions at six months postpartum are not predicted by maternal histories of abuse and neglect or maltreatment type. *Psychological Trauma: Theory, Research, Practice, and Policy, 9*(5), 622–626. doi: 10.1037/tra0000272.

Sexton, M. B., Hamilton, L., McGinnis, E. W., Rosenblum, K. L., & Muzik, M. (2015). The roles of resilience and childhood trauma history: Main and moderating effects on postpartum maternal health and functioning. *Journal of Affective Disorders, 174*, 562–568. doi: 10.1016/j.jad.2014.12.036.

Shafran, R., & Mansell, W. (2000). Perfectionism and psychopathology: A review of research and treatment. *Clinical Psychology Review, 21*(6), 879–906.

Shahaeian, A., Peterson, C. C., Slaughter, V., & Wellman, H. M. (2011). Culture and the sequence of steps in Theory of Mind development. *Developmental Psychology, 47*(5), 1239–1247. doi: 10.1037/a0023899.

Shakespeare-Finch, J., & Daley, E. (2017). Workplace belongingness, distress, and resilience in emergency service workers. *Psychological Trauma: Theory, Research, Practice, and Policy, 9*(1), 32–35. doi: 10.1037/tra0000108.

Shallcross, S. L., Arbisi, P. A., Polusny, M. A., Kramer, M. D., & ERbes, C. (2016). Social causation versus social erosion: Comparisons of causal models for relations between support and PTSD symptoms. *Journal of Traumatic Stress, 29*, 167–175. doi: 10.1002/jts.22086.

Sharman, S. J., & Barnier, A. J. (2008). Imagining nice and nasty events in childhood or adulthood: Recent positive events show the most imagination inflation. *Acta Psychologica, 129*(2), 228–233. doi: 10.1016/j.actpsy.2008.06.003.

Shear, K., & Shair, H. (2005). Attachment, loss, and complicated grief. *Developmental Psychobiology, 47*(3), 253–267. doi: 10.1002/dev.20091.

Sheard, M. (2009). Hardiness commitment, gender, and age differentiate university academic performance. *British Journal of Educational Psychology, 79*, 189–204. doi: 10.1348/000709908X304406.

Sheen, K., Spiby, H., & Slade, P. (2015). Exposure to traumatic perinatal experiences and posttraumatic stress symptoms in midwives: Prevalence and association with burnout. *International Journal of Nursing Studies, 52*, 578–587. doi: 10.1016/j.ijnurstu.2014.11.006.

Sheinkopf, S. J., Lagasse, L. L., Lester, B. M., Liu, J., Seifer, R., Bauer, C. R., … Das, A. (2007). Vagal tone as a resilience factor in children with prenatal cocaine exposure. *Development and Psychopathology, 19*, 649–673. doi: 10.1017/S0954579407000338.

Shen, W., Liu, C., Zhang, X., Zhao, X., Zhang, J., Yuan, Y., & Chen, Y. (2013). Right hemisphere dominance of creative insight: An event-related potential study. *Creativity Research Journal, 25*(1), 48–58. doi: 10.1080/10400419.2013.752195.

Sherwood, L. (2010). *Human physiology from cells to systems* (7th ed.). Pacific Grove, CA: Brooks/cole.

Shigemoto, Y., & Poyrazli, S. (2013). Factors related to posttraumatic growth in U.S. and Japanese college students. *Psychological Trauma: Theory, Research, Practice, and Policy, 5*(2), 128–134. doi: 10.1037/a0026647.

Shin, L. M., Rauch, S. L., & Pitman, R. K. (2006). Amygdala, medial prefrontal cortex, and hippocampal function in PTSD. *Annals of the New York Academy of Science, 1071*, 67–79. doi: 10.1196/annals.1364.007.

Shiota, M. N., Keltner, D., & Mossman, A. (2007). The nature of awe: Elicitors, appraisals, and effects on self-concept. *Cognition and Emotion, 21*(5), 944–963. doi: 10.1080/02699930600923668.

Shiota, M. N., Thrash, T. M., Danvers, A. F., & Dombrowski, J. T. (2016). Transcending the self: Awe, elevation, and inspiration. In M. M. Tugade, M. N. Shiota, & L. D. Kirby (Eds.), *Handbook of positive emotions* (pp. 362–377). New York: Guilford Press. Retrieved from http://www.osf.io/preprints/psyarxiv/hkswj.

Shipherd, J. C., & Salters-Pednaeault, K. (2018). Do acceptance and mindfulness moderate the relationship between maladaptive beliefs and posttraumatic distress? *Psychological Trauma: Theory, Research, Practice, and Policy, 10*(1), 95–102. doi: 10.1037/tra0000248.

Shmotkin, D., Shrira, A., Goldberg, S., & Palgi, Y. (2011). Resilience and vulnerability among old Holocaust survivors and their families: An intergenerational overview. *Journal of Intergenerational Relationships, 9*, 7–21. doi: 10.1080/15350770.2011.544202.

Shrira, A. (2015). Transmitting the sum of all fears: Iranian nuclear threat salience among offspring of holocaust survivors. *Psychological Trauma: Theory, Research, Practice, and Policy, 7*(4), 364–371. doi: 10.1037/tra0000029.

Shumake, J., Conejo-Jimenez, N., Gonzalez-Pardo, H., & Gonzalez-Lima, F. (2004). Brain differences in newborn rats predisposed to helpless and depressive behavior. *Brain Research, 1030*, 267–276. doi: 10.1016/j.brainres.2004.10.015.

Siedler, R. D., Noll, D. C., & Thiers, G. (2004). Feedforward and feedback processes in motor control. *Neuroimage, 22*, 1775–1783. doi: 10.1016/j.neuroimage.2004.05.003.

Siegel, J., & Bugg, J. M. (2016). Dissociating divergent thinking and creative achievement by examining attentional flexibility and hypomania. *Psychology of Aesthetics, Creativity, and the Arts, 10*(4), 416–424. doi: 10.1037/zcz0000071.

Sierra, M., & David, A. S. (2011). Depersonalization: A selective impairment of self-awareness. *Consciousness and Cognition, 20*, 99–108. doi: 10.1016/j.concog.2010.10.018.

Sierra, M., Medford, N., Wyatt, G., & David, A. S. (2012). Depersonalization disorder and anxiety: A special relationship? *Psychiatry Research, 197*, 123–127. doi: 10.1016/j.psychres.2011.12.017.

Sierra, M., Senior, C., Phillips, M. L., & David, A. S. (2006). Autonomic response in the perception of disgust and happiness in depersonalization disorder. *Psychiatry Research, 145*, 225–231. doi: 10.1016/j.psychres.2005.05.022.

Silfver, M., Helkama, K., Lonnqvist, J.-E., & Verkasalo, M. (2008). The relation between value priorities and proneness to guilt, shame, and empathy. *Motivation and Emotion, 32*, 69–80. doi: 10.1007/s11031-008-9084-2.

Silverstein, M. W., Lee, D. J., Witte, T. K., & Weathers, F. W. (2017). Is posttraumatic growth trauma-specific? Invariance across trauma- and stressor-exposed groups. *Psychological Trauma: Theory, Research, Practice, and Policy, 9*(5), 553–560. doi: 10.1037/tra0000236.

Silvestrini, N., & Gendolla, G. H. E. (2009). The joint effect of mood, task valence, and task difficulty on effort-related cardiovascular response and facial EMG. *International Journal of Psychophysiology, 73*, 226–234. doi: 10.1016/j.ijpsycho.2009.03.004.

Silvia, P. J. (2008). Another look at creativity and intelligence: Exploring higher-order models and probable confounds. *Personality and Individual Differences, 44*(4), 1012–1021. doi: 10.1016/j.paid.2007.10.027.

Silvia, P. J., & Kimbrel, N. A. (2010). A dimensional analysis of creativity and mental illness. Do anxiety and depression symptoms predict creative cognition, creative accomplishments, and creative self-concepts? *Psychology of Aesthetics, Creativity and the Arts, 4*(1), 2–10. doi: 10.1037/a0016494.

Silvia, P. J., Fayn, K., Nusbaum, E. C., & Beaty, R. E. (2015). Openness to experience and awe response to nature and music: Personality and profound aesthetic experiences. *Psychology of Aesthetics, Creativity, and the Arts, 9*(4), 376–384. doi: 10.1037/aca000028.

Silvia, P. J., Kaufman, J. C., & Pretz, J. E. (2009). Is creativity domain-specific? Latent class models of creative accomplishments and creative self-descriptions. *Psychology of Aesthetics, Creativity, and the Arts, 3*(3), 139–148. doi: 10.1037/a0014940.

Simard, V., Chevelier, V., & Bedard, M.-M. Sleep and attachment in early childhood: A series of meta-analyses. *Attachment and Human Development, 19*(3), 298–321. doi: 10.1080/14616734.2017.1293703.

Simeon, D., & Knutelska, M. (2005). An open trial of naltrexone in the treatment of depersonalization disorder. *Journal of Clinical Psychopharmacology, 25*, 267–270. doi: 10.1097/01.jcp.0000162803.61700.4f.

Simeon, D., Giesbrecht, T., Knutelska, M., Smith, R. J., & Smith, L. (2009). Alexithymia, absorption, and cognitive failues in depersonalization disorder: A comparison to posttraumatic stress disorder and healthy volunteers. *Journal of Nervous and Mental Disease, 197*(7), 492–498. doi: 10.1097/NMD.obo13e3181aaef6b.

Simeon, D., Greenberg, J., Nelson, D., Schmeidler, J., & Hollander, E. (2005). Dissociation and posttraumatic stress 1 year after the World Trade Center Disaster: Follow-up of a longitudinal survey. *Journal of Clinical Psychiatry, 66*(2), 231–237. doi: 10.4088/JCP.v66n0212.

Simeon, D., Guralnik, O., Knutelska, M., & Schmeidler, J. (2002). Personality factors associated with dissociation: Temperament, defenses, and cognitive schemata. *American Journal of Psychiatry, 159*, 489–491.

Simeon, D., Guralnik, O., Kuntelska, M., Yehuda, R., & Schmeidler, J. (2003). Basal norepinephrine in depersonalization disorder. *Psychiatry Research, 121*, 93–97. doi: 10.1016/S0165-1781(03)00205-1.

Simeonova, D. I., Chang, K. D., Strong, C., & Ketter, T. A. (2005). Creativity in familial bipolar disorder. *Journal of Psychiatric Research, 39*, 623–631. doi: 10.1016/j.jpsychires.2005.01.005.

Simmons, A. L. (2011). The influence of openness to experience and organizational justice on creativity. *Creativity Research Journal, 23*(1), 9–23. doi: 10.1080/10400419.2011.545707.

Simmons, A. L., & Ren, R. (2009). The influence of goal orientation and risk in creativity. *Creativity Research Journal, 21*(4), 400–408. doi: 10.1080/10400410903297980.

Simon, L. (2006). Managing creative projects: An empirical synthesis of activities. *International Journal of Project Management, 24*, 116–126. doi: 10.1016/j.ijproman.2005.09.002.

Simonton, D. K. (1999). Creativity from a historiometric perspective. In R. J. Sternberg (Ed.), *Handbook of creativity* (pp. 116–133). New York, NY: Cambridge University Press.

———. (2000). Creativity: Cognitive, personal, developmental, and social aspects. *American Psychologist, 55*(1), 151–158. doi: 10.1037//003.066X.55.1.151.

Sinclair, R. R., & Tetrick, L. E. (2000). Implications of item wording for hardiness structure, relation with neuroticism, and stress buffering. *Journal of Research in Personality, 34*, 1–25. doi: 10.1006/jrpe.1999.2265.

Sitar, A. S., Cerne, M., Aleksic, D., & Mihelic, K. K. (2016). Individual learning styles and creativity. *Creativity Research Journal, 28*(3), 334–341. doi: 10.1080/10400419.2016.1195651.

Smid, G. E., van der Velden, P. G., Gersons, B. P. R., & Kleber, R. J. (2012). Late-onset posttraumatic stress disorder following a disaster: A longitudinal study. *Psychological Trauma: Theory, Research, Practice, and Policy, 4*(3), 312–322. doi: 10.1037/a0023868.

Smith, G. J. W. (2005). How should creativity be defined? *Creativity Research Journal, 17*(2 & 3), 293–295.

———. (2008). The creative personality in search of a theory. *Creativity Research Journal, 20*(4), 383–390. doi: 10.1080/10400410802391645.

Smith, C. P., & Freyd, J. J. (2013). Dangerous safe havens: Institutional betrayal exacerbates sexual trauma. *Journal of Traumatic Stress, 26*, 119–124. doi: 10.1002/jts.21778.

Smith, N., & Harrell, S. (2013). Sexual abuse of children with disabilities: A national snapshot. In *Vera Institute of Justice Bulletin, Center on Victimization and Safety Issue Brief* (pp. 1–12). New York City, New York.

Smith, A. J., Abeyta, A. A., Hughes, M., & Jones, R. T. (2015). Persistent grief in the aftermath of mass violence: The predictive roles of posttraumatic stress symptoms, self-efficacy, and disrupted worldview. *Psychological Trauma: Theory, Research, Practice, and Policy, 7*(2), 179–186. doi: 10.1037/tra0000002.

Smith, A. J., Felix, E. D., Benight, C. C., & Jones, R. T. (2017). Protective factors, coping appraisals, and social barriers predict mental health following community violence: A prospective test of social cognitive theory. *Journal of Traumatic Stress, 30*, 245–253. doi: 10.1037/jts.22197.

Smith, D. W., Letourneau, E. J., Saunders, B. E., Kilpatrick, D. G., Resnick, H. S., & Best, C. L. (2000). Delay in disclosure of childhood rape: Results from a national survey. *Child Abuse and Neglect, 24*(2), 273–287.

Smitt, M. S., & Bird, H. A. (2013). Measuring and enhancing proprioception in musicians and dancers. *Clinical Rheumatology, 32*, 469–473. doi: 10.1007/s10067-013-2193-7.

Snowden, P. L., & Christian, L. G. (1999). Parenting the young gifted child: Supportive behaviors. *Roeper Review, 21*(3), 215–221.

Snyder, F. J., Roberts, Y. H., Crusto, C. A., Connell, C. M., Griffin, A., Finely, M. K., ... Kaufman, J. S. (2012). Exposure to traumatic events and the behavioral health of children enrolled in an early childhood system of care. *Journal of Traumatic Stress, 25,* 700–704. doi: 10.1002/jts. 21756.

Soffer-Dudek, N., & Shahar, G. (2014–2015). Evidence from two longitudinal studies concerning internal distress , external stress, and dissociative trajectories. *Imagination, Cognition, and Personality, 34*(1), 3–24. doi: 10.2190/IC.34.1.b.

Somer, E. (2002). Maladaptive daydreaming: A qualitative inquiry. *Journal of Contemporary Psychotherapy, 32*(2–3), 197–212. doi: 10.1023/A:1020597026919.

Somer, E., Lehrfeld, J., Bigelsen, J., & Jopp, D. S. (2016). Development and validation of the Maladaptive Daydreaming Scale (MDS). *Consciousness and Cognition, 39,* 77–91. doi: 10.1016/j.concog.2015.12.001.

Somer, E., Somer, L., & Jopp, D. S. (2016). Parallel lives: A phenomenological study of the lived experience of maladaptive daydreaming. *Journal of Trauma and Dissociation, 17*(5), 561–576. doi: 10.1080/15299732.2016.1160463.

Sonnby-Borgstrom, M., & Jonsson, P. (2004). Dismissing-avoidant pattern of attachment and mimicry reactions at different levels of information processing. *Scandinavian Journal of Psychology, 45,* 103–113.

Spear, L. P. (2000). The adolescent brain and age-related behavioral manifestations. *Neuroscience and Biobehavioral Reviews, 24,* 417–463.

Speranza, A. M., Nicolais, G., Vergano, C. M., & Dazzi, N. (2017). Emerging criteria for the low-coherence cannot classify category. *Attachment and Human Development, 19*(6), 613–634. doi: 10.1080/14616734.2017.1355396.

Spertus, I. L., Yehuda, R., Wong, C. M., Halligan, S., & Seremetis, S. V. (2003). Childhood emotional abuse and neglect as predictors of psychological and physical symptoms in women presenting to a primary care practice. *Child Abuse and Neglect, 27,* 1247–1258. doi: 10.1016/j.chiabu.2003.05.001.

Springer, K. W., Sheridan, J., Kuo, D., & Carnes, M. (2003). The long-term health outcomes of childhood abuse: An overview and a call to action. *Journal of General Internal Medicine, 18,* 864–870.

Srivastava, S., Childers, M. E., Baek, J. H., Strong, C. M., Hill, S. J., Warsett, K., S., Wang, P. W., ... Ketter, T. A. (2010). Toward interaction of affective and cognitive contributors to creativity in bipolar disorders: A controlled study. *Journal of Affective Disorders, 125,* 27–34. doi: 10.1016/j.jad.2009.12.018.

Sroufe, L. A., Egeland, B., Carlson, E., & Collins, W. A. (2005). *The development of the person: The Minnesota study of risk and adaptation from birth to adulthood.* New York: Guilford Press.

Stams, G.-J. J. M., Juffer, F., & van IJzendoorn, M. H. (2002). Maternal sensitivity, infant temperament, and temperament in early childhood predict adjustment in middle childhood: The case of adopted children and their biologically unrelated parents. *Developmental Psychology, 38*(5), 806–821. doi: 10.1037//0012-1649.38.5.806.

Stanley, J. C., & Benbow, C. P. (1986). Youths who reason exceptionally well mathematically. In R. J. Sternberg & J. E. Davidson (Eds.), *Conceptions of giftedness* (pp. 361–387). New York: Cambridge University Press.

Stansky, M., & Finkelhor, D. (2008). *How many juveniles are involved in prostitution*. Crimes Against Children Research Center. Retrieved from https://www.unh.edu/ccrc.

Stanton, B. R., David, A. S., Cleare, A. J., Sierra, M., Lambert, M. V., Phillips, M. L., ... Young, A. H. (2001). Basal activity of the hypothalamus-pituitary-adrenal axis in patients with depersonalization disorder. *Psychiatry Research, 104*, 85–89.

Starnino, V. R. (2016). When trauma, spirituality, and mental illness intersect: A qualitative case study. *Psychological Trauma: Theory, Research, Practice, and Policy, 8*(3), 375–383. doi: 10.1037/tra0000105.

Steel, Z., Chey, T., Silove, D., Marnane, C., Bryant, R. A., & van Ommeren, M. (2007). Traumatic events with mental health outcomes among populations exposed to mass conflict and displacement: A systematic review and meta-analysis. *Journal of the American Medical Association, 302*(5), 537–549.

Steele, H., Steele, M., & Croft, C. (2008). Early attachment predicts emotion recognition at 6 and 11 years old. *Attachment and Human Development, 10*(4), 379–393. doi: 10.1080/14616730802461409.

Steele, H., Steele, M., & Murphy, A. (2009). Use of the Adult Attachment Interview to measure process and change in psychotherapy. *Psychotherapy Research, 19*(6), 633–743. doi: 10.1080/10503300802609698.

Steenkamp, M. M., Dickstein, B. D., Salters-Pedneault, K., Hofmann, S. G., & Litz, B. T. (2012). Factories of PTSD symptoms following sexual assault: Is resilience the modal outcome? *Journal of Traumatic Stress, 25*, 469–474. doi: 10.1002/jts.21718.

Stein, H., Koontz, A. D., Fonagy, P., Allen, J. G., Fultz, J., Brethour, J. R., ... Evans, R. B. (2002). Adult attachment: What are the underlying dimensions? *Psychology and Psychotherapy: Theory, Research and Practice, 75*, 77–91.

Stein, J. Y., & Tuval-Mashiach, R. (2015). Loneliness and isolation in life-stories of Israeli veterans of combat and captivity. *Psychological Trauma: Theory, Research, Practice, and Policy, 7*(2), 122–130. doi: 10.1037/a0036936.

Steinberg, H., Sykes, E. A., Moss, T., Lowery, S., LeBoutillier, N., & Dewey, A. (1997). Exercise enhances creativity independently of mood. *British Journal of Sports Medicine, 31*, 240–245.

Stellar, J. E., John-Henderson, N., Anderson, C. L., Gordon, A. M., McNeil, G. D., & Keltner, D. (2015). Positive affect and markers of inflammation: Positive emotions predict lower levels of inflammatory cytokines. *Emotion, 15*(2), 129–133. doi: 0.1037/emo0000033.

Sternberg, R. J. (2001). What is the common thread of creativity?: Its dialectical relation to intelligence and wisdom. *American Psychologist, 56*(4), 360–362. doi: 10.1037//0003-066X.56.4.360.

———. (2005). Creativity or creativities? *International Journal of Human-Computer Studies, 63*, 370–382. doi: 10.1016/j.ijhcs.2005.04.003.

———. (2012). The assessment of creativity: An investment-based approach. *Creativity Research Journal, 24*(1), 3–12. doi: 10.1080/10400419.2012.652925.

Sternberg, R. J., & Lubart, T. I. (1992). Buy low and sell high: An investment approach to creativity. *Current Directions in Psychological Science, 1*(1), 1–5.

Stewart, S. H., Buffett-Jerrott, S. E., & Kokaram, R. (2001). Heartbeat awareness and heart rate reactivity in anxiety sensitivity: A further investigation. *Anxiety Disorders, 15,* 535–553. doi: 10.1016/S0887-6185(01)00080-9.

Stiglmayr, C. E., Ebner-Priemer, U. W., Bretz, J., Mohse, M., Lammers, C.-H., ... Bohus, M. (2008). Dissociative symptoms are positively related to stress in borderline personality disorder. *Acta Psychiatrica Scandinavica, 117*(2), 139–147. doi: 10.1111/acp.2008.117.issue-2/issuetoc.

Stimmel, M. A., Cruise, K. R., Ford, J. D., & Weiss, R. A. (2014). Trauma exposure, posttraumatic stress disorder symptomatology, and aggression in male juvenile offenders. *Psychological Trauma: Theory, Research, Practice, and Policy, 6*(2), 184–191. doi: 10.1037/a0032509.

St-Louis, A. C., & Vallerand, R. J. (2015). A successful creative process: The role of passion and emotions. *Creativity Research Journal, 27*(2), 175–187. doi: 10.1080/10400419.2015.1030314.

Stoeber, J., & Otto, K. (2006). Positive conceptions of perfectionism: Approaches, evidence, challenges. *Personality and Social Psychology Review, 10*(4), 295–319. doi: 10.1207/s15327957pspr1004_2.

Stoeber, J., Harris, R. A., & Moon, P. S. (2007). Perfectionism and the experience of pride, shame, and guilt: Comparing healthy perfectionists, unhealthy perfectionists, and non-perfectionists. *Personality and Individual Differences, 43*(1), 131–141. doi: 10.1016/j.paid.2006.11.012.

Stoeber, J., Kempe, T., & Keogh, E. J. (2008). Facets of self-oriented and socially prescribed perfectionism and feelings of pride, shame, and guilt following success and failure. *Personality and Individual Differences, 44*(7), 1506–1516. doi: 10.1016/j.paid.2008.01.007.

Stokes, P. D. (2001). Variability, constraints, and creativity: Shedding light on Claude Monet. *American Psychologist, 56*(4), 355–359. doi: 10.1037/0003.066X.56.4.355.

———. (2007). Using constraints to generate and sustain novelty. *Psychology of Aesthetics, Creativity, and the Arts, 1*(2), 107–113. doi: 10.1037//1931-3896.1.2.107.

Stolbach, B. C., Minshew, R., Rompala, V., Dominguez, R. Z., Gazibara, T., & Finke, R. (2013). Complex trauma exposure and symptoms in urban traumatized children: A preliminary test of proposed criteria for developmental trauma disorder. *Journal of Traumatic Stress, 26,* 483–491. doi: 10.1002/jts.21826.

Stolorow, R. D., Atwood, G. E., & Orange, D. M. (2002). *Worlds of experience: Interweaving philosophical and clinical dimensions in psychoanalysis.* New York: Basic Books.

Stovall-McClough, K. C., & Cloitre, M. (2006). Unresolved attachment, PTSD, and dissociation in women with childhood abuse histories. *Journal of Counseling and Clinical Psychology, 74*(2), 219–228. doi: 10.1037/0022-006X.74.2.219.

Straus, L. D., Drummon, S. P. S., Nappi, C. M., Jenkins, M. M., & Norman, S. B. (2015). Sleep variability in military-related PTSD: A comparison to primary insomnia and healthy controls. *Journal of Traumatic Stress, 28,* 8–16. doi: 10.1002/jts.21982.

Streminger, G. (1980). Hume's theory of imagination. *Hume Studies, 6*(2), 91–118.

Stright, A. D., Gallagher, K. C., & Kelley, K. (2008). Infant temperament moderates relations between maternal parenting in early childhood and children's adjustment in first grade. *Child Development, 79*(1), 186–200.

Stroebe, M., Schut, H., & Stroebe, W. (2005). Attachment in coping with bereavement: A theoretical integration. *Review of General Psychology, 9*(1), 48–66. doi: 10.1037/1089-2680.9.1.48.

Strom, I. F., Aakvaag, H. F., Birkeland, M. S., Felix, E., & Thoresen, S. (2018). The mediating role of shame in the relationship between childhood bullying victimization and adult psychosocial adjustment. *European Journal of Psychotraumatology, 9*, 1418570. doi: 10.1080/20008198.2017.1418570.

Strong, C. M., Nowakowska, C., Santosa, C. M., Wang, P. W., Kraemer, H. C., & Ketter, T. A. (2007). Temperament-creativity relationships in mood disorder patients, healthy controls and highly creative individuals. *Journal of Affective Disorders, 100*, 41–48. doi: 10.1016/j.jad.2006.10.015.

Stupica, B., Brett, B. E., Woodhouse, S. S., & Cassidy, J. (2017). Attachment security priming decreases children's physiological response to threat. *Child Development, e-publ.* doi: 10.1111/cdev.13009.

Sturman, D. A., & Moghaddam, B. (2011). The neurobiology of adolescence: Changes in brain architecture, functional dynamics, and behavioral tendencies. *Neuroscience and Biobehavioral Reviews, 35*, 1704–1712.

Su, Y.-J., & Chen, S.-H. (2015). Emerging posttraumatic growth: A prospective study with pre- and postrauma psychological predictors. *Psychological Trauma: Theory, Research, Practice, and Policy, 7*(2), 103–111. doi: 10.1037tra0000008.

———. (2018). Negative cognitions prior to trauma predict acut posttraumatic stress disorder symptomatology. *Journal of Traumatic Stress, 31*, 14–24. doi: 10.1002/jts.22255.

Suarez-Morales, L., Mena, M., Schlaudt, V. A., & Santisteban, D. A. (2017). Trauma in Hispanic youth with psychiatric symptoms: Investigating gender and family effects. *Psychological Trauma: Theory, Research, Practice, and Policy, 9*(3), 334–343. doi: 10.1037/tra0000216.

Subotnik, R. F., Olszewski-Kubilius, P., & Worrell, F. C. (2011). Rethinking giftedness and gifted education: A proposed direction forward based on psychological science. *Psychological Science in the Public Interest, 12*(1), 3–54. doi: 10.1177/1529100611418056.

Suliman, S., Mkabile, S. G., Fincham, D. S., Ahmed, R., Stein, D. J., & Seedat, S. (2009). Cumulative effect of multiple trauma on symptoms of postttaumatic stress disorder, anxiety, and depression in adolescents. *Comprehensive Psychiatry, 50*, 121–127. doi: 10.1016/j.comppsych.2008.06.006.

Sullivan, P., & Knutson, J. (2000). Maltreatment and disabilities: A population-based epidemiological study. *Child Abuse and Neglect, 24*(10), 1257–1273.

Sullivan, P., & McCarthy, J. (2009). An experiential account of the psychology of art. *Psychology of Aesthetics, Creativity and the Arts, 3*(3), 181–187. doi: 10.1037/a0014292.

Summer, S. A., Mercy, J. A., Saul, J., Motsa-Nzuza, N., Kwesigabo, G., Buluma, R., ... Hills, S. D. (2015). Sexual violence against children and use of social services–Seven countries, 2007–2013. *Morbidity and Mortality Weekly Report, Centers for Disease Control and Prevention, 64*(21), 565–569.

Sutin, A. R., & Stockdale, G. D. (2011). Trait dissociation and the subjective affective, motivational, and phenomenological experience of self-defining memories. *Journal of Personality, 79*(5), 939–964. doi: 10.1111/j.1467-6494.2010.00708.x.

Swami, V., Malpass, F., Harvard, D., Benford, K., Costescu, A., Sofitiki, A., & Taylor, D. (2013). Metalheads: The influence of personality and individual differences on preference for heavy metal. *Psychology of Aesthetics, Creativity, and the Arts, 7*(4), 377–383. doi: 10.1037/a0034493.

Swart, I. (2014). Overcoming adversity: Trauma in the lives of music performers and composers. *Psychology of Music, 42*(3), 386–402. doi: 10.1177/0305735613475371.

Swart, I., van Niekerk, C., & Hartman, W. (2010). Trauma-related dissociation as a factor affecting musicians' memory for music: Some possible solutions. *Australian Journal of Music Education, 2*, 117–134.

Swiatek, M. A. (2007). The talent search model: Past, present, and future. *Gifted Child Quarterly, 51*, 320–329. doi: 10.1177/0016986207306318.

Szechtman, H., Woody, E., Bowers, K. S., & Nahmias, C. (1998). Where the imaginal appears real: A positron emission tomography study of auditory hallucinations. *Procedures of the National Academy of Science, 95*(4), 1956–1960.

Szyf, M., & Bick, J. (2013). DNA methylation: A mechanism for embedding early life experiences into the genome. *Child Development, 84*(1), 49–57. doi: 10.1111/j.1467-8624.2012.01793.x.

Taillieu, T. L., Brownridge, D. A., Sareen, J., & Afifi, T. O. (2016). Childhood emotional maltreatment and mental disorders: Results from a nationally representative adult sample from the United States. *Child Abuse and Neglect, 59*, 1–12. doi: 10.1016/j.chiabu.2016.07.005.

Taku, K., Cann, A., Tedeschi, R. G., & Calhoun, L. G. (2015). Core beliefs by an earthquake correlate with posttraumatic growth. *Psychological Trauma: Theory, Research, Practice, and Policy, 7*(6), 563–569. doi: 10.1037/tra0000054.

Talbot, J. A., Talbot, N. L., & Tu, X. (2004). Shame-proneness as a diathesis for dissociation in women with histories of childhood sexual abuse. *Journal of Traumatic Stress, 17*(5), 445–448.

Talbot, L. S., Maguen, S., Epel, E. S., Metzler, T. J., & Neylan, T. C. (2013). Posttraumatic stress disorder is associated with emotional eating. *Journal of Traumatic Stress, 26*, 521–525. doi: 10.1002/jts.21824.

Tamaian, A., Klest, B., & Mutschler, C. (2017). Patient dissatisfaction and institutional betrayal in the Canadaina medical system: A qualitative study. *Journal of Trauma and Dissociation, 18*(1), 38–57. doi: 10.1080/15299732.2016.1181134.

Tan, A.-G. (2015). Convergent creativity: From Arthur Cropley (1935 -) onwards. *Creativity Research Journal, 27*(3), 271–280. doi: 10.1080/10400419.2015.1063892.

Tan, F. B., & Chou, J. B. (2011). Dimensions of autotelic personality and their effects on perceived playfulness in the context of mobile information and entertainment services. *Australian Journal of Information Systems, 17*(1), 5–22.

Tang, H.-H., & Gero, J. S. (2002). A cognitive method to measure potential creativity in designing. In C. Bento, A. Cardoso & G. Wiggins (Eds.), *Workshop 17 – Creative systems: Approaches to creativity in AI and cognitive science* (pp. 47–54). Lyon, France: ECAI-02.

Tangney, J. P., & Dearing, R. (2002). *Shame and guilt*. New York: Gilford Press.

Tangney, J. P., Stuewig, J., & Mashek, D. J. (2007). Moral emotions and moral behavior. *Annual Review of Psychology, 58*, 345–372. doi: 10.1146/annurev.psyc.56.091103.070145.

Tannenbaum, A. J. (1992). Early signs of giftedness: Research and commentary. In P. Klein & A. Tannenbaum (Eds.), *To be young and gifted* (pp. 104–133). Norwood, NJ: Ablex Publishing Corp.

———. (2003). Nature and nurture of giftedness. In N. Colangelo & G. A. Davis (Eds.), *Handbook of gifted education* (3rd ed., pp. 45–59). New York, NY: Allyn & Bacon.

Taylor, K., Fletcher, I., & Lobban, F. (2015). Exploring the links between the phenomenology of creativity and bipolar disorder. *Journal of Affective Disorders, 174*, 658–664. doi: 10.1016/j.jad.2014.10.040.

Taylor, M., Mottweiler, C. M., Naylor, E. R., & Levernier, J. G. (2015). Imaginary worlds in middle childhood: A qualitative study of two pairs of coordinated paracosms. *Creativity Research Journal, 27*(2), 167–174. doi: 10.1080/10400419.2015.1030318.

Taylor, S. E., Pham, L. B., Rivkin, I. D., & Armor, D. A. (1998). Harnessing the imagination: Mental simulation, self-regulation, and coping. *American Psychologist, 53*(4), 429–439.

Taylor, S., & Stanton, A. L. (2007). Coping resource, coping processes, and mental health. *Annual Review of Clinical Psychology, 3*, 377–401. doi: 10.1146/annurev.clinpsy.3.022806.091520.

TeBockhorst, S. F., O'Halloran, M. S., & Nyline, B. N. (2015). Tonic immobility among survivors of sexual assault. *Psychological Trauma: Theory, Research, Practice, and Policy, 7*(2), 171–178. doi: 10.1037/a0037953.

Tedeschi, R. G., & Calhoun, L. G. (1995). *Trauma and transformation: Growing in the aftermath of suffering*. Thousand Oaks, CA: Sage.

———. (1996). The Posttraumatic Growth Inventory: Measuring the positive legacy of trauma. *Journal of Traumatic Stress, 9*, 455–472. doi: 10.1002/jts.2490090305.

Tedeschi, R. G., Cann, A., Taku, K., Senol-Durak, E., & Calhoun, L. G. (2017). The Posttraumatic Growth Inventory: A revision integrating existential and spiritual change. *Journal of Traumatic Stress, 30*, 11–18. doi: 10.1002/jts.22155.

Teicher, M., Anderson, C. M., & Polcari, A. (2012). Childhood maltreatment is associated with reduced volume in the hippocampal subfields CA3, dentate gyrus and subiculum. *Proceedings of the National Academy of Science, 109*(9), E563–E572. doi: 10.1073/pnas.1115396109.

Teicher, M., Andersen, S. L., Polcari, A., Anderson, C. M., Navalta, C. P., & Kim, D. M. (2003). The neurobilological consequences of early stress and childhood maltreatment. *Neuroscience and Biobehavioral Reviews, 27*, 33–44. doi: 10.1016/S0149-7634(03)000007-1.

Teicher, M., Tomoda, A., & Andersen, S. L. (2006). Neurobiological consequences of early stress and childhood maltreatment: Are results from human and animal studies comparable? *Annals of New York Academy of Science, 1071*, 313–323. doi: 10.1196/annals.1364.024.

Teng, C.-I. (2011). Who are likely to experience flow? Impact to temperament and character on flow. *Personality and Individual Differences, 50*, 863–868. doi: 10.1016/j.paid.2011.01.012.

Teo, A. R., Marsh, H. E., Forsberg, C. W., Nicolaidis, C., Chen, J. I., Newson, J., Saha, S., & Dobscha, S. K. (2018). Loneliness is closely associated with depression outcomes and suicidal ideation among military veterans in primary care. *Journal of Affectie Disorders, 230*, 42–49. doi: 10.1016/j.jad.2018.01.003.

Thalbourne, M. A., Crawley, S. E., & Houran, J. (2003). Temporal lobe lability in the highly Transliminal mind. *Personality and Individual Differences, 35*, 1965–1974. doi: 10.1016/S0191-8869(03)00044-8.

Thayer, J. F., & Lane, R. D. (2000). A model of neurovisceral integration in emotion regulation and dysregulation. *Journal of Affective Disorders, 61*(3), 201–216.

Thayer, J. F., Ahs, F., Fredrikson, M., Sollers III, J. J., & Wager, D. D. (2012). A meta-analysis of heart rate variability and neuroimaging studies: Implications for heart rate variability as a marker of stress and health. *Neuroscience and Biobehavioral Reviews, 36*, 747–756. doi: 10.1016/j.neubiorev.2011.11.009.

Thomas, K. M., & Duke, M. (2007). Depressed writing: Cognitive distortions in the works of depressed and nondepressed poets and writers. *Psychology of Aesthetics, Creativity, and the Arts, 1*(4), 204–218. doi: 10.1037/1931-3896.1.4.204.

Thomas, N. J. T. (1999). Are theories of imagery theories of imagination? An active perception approach to conscious mental content. *Cognitive Science, 23*(2), 207–245.

Thompson-Hollands, J., Jun, J. J., & Sloan, D. M. (2017). The association between peritraumatic dissociation and PTSD symptoms: The mediating role of negative beliefs about the self. *Journal of Traumatic Stress, 30*, 190–194. doi: 10.1002/jts.22179.

Thompson, R., Wiley, T. R. A., Lewis, T., English, D. J., Dubowitz, H., Litrownik, A. J., ... Block, S. (2012). Links between traumatic experiences and expectations about the future in high risk youth. *Psychological Trauma: Theory, Research, Practice, and Policy, 4*(3), 293–302. doi: 10.1037/a0023867.

Thomson, P. (2004). The impact of trauma on the embryo and fetus: An application of the diathesis-stress model and the neurovulnerability-neurotoxicity model. *Journal of Prenatal and Perinatal Psychology and Health, 19*(1), 9–63.

Thomson, P. (2007). Down will come baby: Prenatal development, primitive defenses and gestational dysregulation. *Journal of Trauma and Dissociation, 8*(3), 85–114.

Thomson, P., & Jaque, S. V. (2011). Testimonial theatre-making: Establishing or dissociating the self. *Psychology of Aesthetics, Creativity and the Arts, 5*(3), 229–236.

———. (2011–2012). Anxiety and the influences of flow, trauma, and fantasy experiences on dancers. *Cognition, Imagination and Personality, 32*(2), 165–178. doi: 10.2190/IC.32.2.e.

———. (2011a). Psychophysiological study: Ambulatory measure of the ANS in performing artists. In A. Williamon, D. Edwards, & L. Bartel (Eds.), *Proceedings of the International Symposium on Performance Science* (pp. 149–154). Utrecht, The Netherlands: European Association of Concervatoires (AEC).

———. (2012a). Dancing with the Muses: Dissociation and flow. *Journal of Trauma and Dissociation*, 13(4), 478–489. doi: 10.1080/15299732.2011.652345.

———. (2012b). Dissociation and the Adult Attachment Interview in Artists. *Attachment and Human Development*, 14(2), 145–160.Thomson, P., & Jaque, S. V. (2012c). Holding a mirror up to nature: Psychological vulnerability in actors. *Psychology of Aesthetics, Creativity and the Arts*, 6(4), 361–369.

———. (2013). Exposing shame in dancers and athletes: Shame, trauma, and dissociation in a nonclinical population. *Journal of Trauma and Dissociation*, 14, 439–454. doi: 10.1080/15299732.2012.757714.

———. (2014). Unresolved mourning, supernatural beliefs and dissociation: A mediation analysis. *Attachment and Human Development*, 16(5), 499–514.

———. (2015). Shame and fantasy in athletes and dancers. *Imagination, Cognition, and Personality*, 34(3), 291–305. doi: 10.1177/0276236614568639.

———. (2016a). Overexcitability and optimal flow in talented dancers, singers and athletes. *Roeper Review*, 38(1), 32–39. doi: 10.1080/02783193.2015.1112865.

———. (2016b). Overexcitability: A psychological comparison between dancers, opera singers and athletes. *Roeper Review*, 38(2), 84–92. doi: 10.1080/02783193.2016.1150373.

———. (2016c). Exquisite moments: Achieving optimal flow in three different activity-based groups regardless of early childhood adversity. *American Journal of Play*, 8(3), 346–362.

———. (2016d). Visiting the muses: Creativity, coping and PTSD in talented dancers and athletes. *American Journal of Play*, 8(3), 363–378.

———. (2017). *Creativity and the performing artist: Behind the mask*. San Diego, CA: Academic Press.

———. (2017a). Adverse Childhood Experiences (ACE) and Adult Attachment Interview (AAI) in a non-clinical population. *Child Abuse and Neglect*, 70, 255–263. doi: 10.1016/j.chiabu.2017.06.001.

———. (2018). Depersonalization, adversity, emotionality, and coping with stressful situations. *Journal of Trauma and Dissociation*, 19(2), 143–161. doi: 10.1080/15299732.2017.1329770.

———. (2018a). Attachment and childhood adversity in athletes, actors, dancers, and healthy controls. *International Journal of Sport and Exercise Psychology*, e-publ. doi: 10.1080/1612197X.2017.1349824.

———. (2018b). Childhood adversity and the creative experience in adult professional performing artists. *Frontiers in Psychology*, 9, 111. doi: 10.3389/fpsyg.2018.00111.

———. (2018c). Shame and Anxiety: The mediating role of childhood adversity in dancers. *Journal of Dance Medicine and Science*, 22(2), 100–108. doi: 10.12678/1089-313X.22.2.100.

Thomson, P., Keehn, E. B., & Gumpel, T. P. (2009). Generators and interpreters in a performing arts population: Dissociation, trauma, fantasy proneness, and affective states. *Creativity Research Journal, 21*(1), 72–91. doi: 10.1080/10400410802633533.

Thomson, P., Kibarska, L., & Jacque, S. V. (2011). Comparison of dissociative experiences between rhythmic gymnasts and female dancers. *International Journal of Sport and Exercise Psychology, 9*(3), 238–250.

Thormar, S. B., Sijbrandij, M., Gersons, B. P. R., Van de Schoot, R., Juen, B., Karlsson, T., & Olff, M. (2016). PTSD symptom trajectories in disaster volunteers: The role of self-efficacy, social acknowledgment, and tasks carried out. *Journal of Traumatic Stress, 29,* 17–25. doi: 10.1002/jts.22073.

Thrash, T. M., & Elliot, A. J. (2003). Inspiration as a psychological construct. *Journal of Personality and Social Psychology, 84,* 871–889.

Thrash, T. M., Elliot, A. J., Maruskin, L. A., & Cassidy, S. E. (2010). Inspiration and the pro- motion of well-being: Tests of causality and mediation. *Journal of Personality and Social Psychology, 98,* 488–506.

Tidikis, V., Ash, I. K., & Collier, A. F. (2017). The interaction of emotional valence and arousal on attentional breadth and creative task performance. *Creativity Research Journal, 29*(3), 313–330. doi: 10.1080/10400419.2017.1360068.

Tietjen, G. E., Brandes, J. L., Peterlin, B. L., Eloff, A., Dafer, R. M., Stein, M. R., … Kuder, S. A. (2010). Childhood maltreatment and migraine (Part II): Emotional abuse as a risk factor for headache chronification. *Headache, 50,* 32–41. doi: 10.1111/j.1526-4610.2009.01557.x.

To, M. L., Fisher, C., Ashkanasy, N. M., & Rowe, P. A. (2012). Within-person relationships between mood and creativity. *Journal of Applied Psychology, 97*(3), 599–612. doi: 10.1037/a0026097.

Tolmunen, T., Honkalampi, K., Hintikka, J., Rissanen, M.-L., Maaranen, P., Kylma, J., & Laukkanen, E. (2010). Adolescent dissociation and alexithyia are distinctive but overlapping phenomena. *Psychiatry Research, 176*(1), 40–44. doi: 10.1016/j.psychres.2006.10.029.

Tomkins, S. S. (1963). *Affect, imagery, consciousness. Volume 2: The negative affects.* New York, NY: Springer.

Tomlinson, M., Cooper, P., & Murray, L. (2005). The mother-infant relationship and infant attachment in a South African peri-urban settlement. *Child Development, 76*(5), 1044–1054.

Toth, S. L., Cicchetti, D., Macfie, J., & Emde, R. N. (1997). Representation of self and other in the narratives of neglected, physically abused, and sexually abused preschoolers. *Development and Psychopathology, 9,* 781–796.

Tracy, J. L., & Matsumoto, D. (2008). The spontaneous expression of pride and shame: Evidence for biologically innate nonverbal displays. *Proceedings of the National Academy of Sciences, 105*(33), 11655–11660. doi: 10.1073/pnas.0802686105.

Tranckle, P., & Cushion, C. J. (2006). Rethinking giftedness and talent in sport. *Quest, 58*(2), 265–282. doi: 10.1080/00336297.2006.10491883.

Trapnell, P. D., & Campbell, J. D. (1999). Private self-consciousness and the five-factor model of personality: Distinguishing rumination from reflection. Journal of *Personality and Social Psychology, 76,* 284–304. doi: 10.1037/0022-3514.76.2.284.

Treffinger, D. J., Selby, E. C., & Isaksen, S. G. (2008). Understanding individual problem-solving style: A key to learning and applying creative problem solving. *Learning and Individual Differences, 18*, 390–401. doi: 10.1016/j.lindif.2007.11.007.

Trepanier, S.-G., Fernet, C., Austin, S., Forest, J., & Vallerand, S. J. (2014). Linking job demands and resources to burnout and work engagement: Does passion underlie these differential relationships? *Motivation and Emotion, 38*(3), 353–366.

Trinka, R., Zahradnik, M., & Kuska, M. (2016). Emotional creativity and real-life involvement in different types of creative leisure activities. *Creativity Research Journal, 28*(3), 348–356. doi: 10.1080/10400419.2016.1195653.

Troop, N. A., & Redshaw, C. (2012). General shame and bodily shame in eating disorders: A 2.5 year longitudinal study. *European Eating Disorder Review, 20*, 373–378. doi: 10.1002/erv.2160.

Tsakiris, M., Tajadura-Jimenez, A., & Costantini, M. (2011). Just a heartbeat away from one's body: Interoception sensitivity predicts malleability of body-representations. *Proceedings of the Royal Society Bulletin, 278*, 2470–2476. doi: 10.1098/rspb.2010.2547.

Tschan, R., Wiltink, J., Adler, J., Beutel, M. E., & Michal, M. (2013). Depersonalization experiences are strongly associated with dizziness and vertigo symptoms leading to increased health care consumption in the German general population. *Journal of Nervous and Mental Disease, 201*, 629–635. doi: 10.1097/NMD.0b013e3182982995.

Tugade, M. M., & Fredrickson, B. L. (2004). Resilient individuals use positive emotions to bounce back from negative emotional experiences. *Journal of Personality and Social Psychology, 86*(2), 320–333. doi: 101037/0022-3514.86.2.320.

Turhune, D. B., Cardena, E., & Lindren, M. (2011). Dissociative tendencies and individual differences in high hypnotic suggestibility. *Cognitive Neuropsychiatry, 16*(2), 113–135. doi: 10.1080/13546805.2010.503048.

Turner, J. E., & Schallert, D. L. (2001). Expectancy-value relationships of shame reactions and shame resiliency. *Journal of Educational Psychology, 93*(2), 320–329. doi: 10.1037/0022-0663.93.2.320.

Turner, H. A., Finkelhor, D., & Ormrod, R. K. (2010). Poly-victimization in a national sample of children and youth. *American Journal of Preventive Medicine, 38*(3), 323–330.

Turner, H. A., Finkelhor, D., Shattuck, A., Hamby, S., & Mitchell, K. (2015). Beyond bullying: Aggravating elements of peer victimization episodes. *School Psychology Quarterly, 30*(3), 66–84. doi: 10.1037/spq0000058.

Turner, S., Taillieu, T., Cheung, K., & Afifi, T. O. (2017). The relationship between childhood sexual abuse and mental health outcomes among males: Results from a nationally representative United States sample. *Child Abuse and Neglect, 66*, 64–77. doi: 10.1016/j.chiabu.2017.01.018.

Tursich, M., Ros, T., Frewen, P., Kluetsch, R., Calhoun, V., & Lanius, R. (2015). Distinct intrinsic network connectivity patterns of post-traumatic stress disorder symptom clusters. *Acta Psychiatry Scandinavia, 132*, 29–38. doi: 10.1111/acps.12387.

Tyrka, A. R., Price, L. H., Gelernter, J., Schepker, C., Anderson, G. M., & Carpenter, L. L. (2009). Interaction of childhood maltreatment with the corticotropin-releasing hormone receptor gene: Effects on Hypothalamic-Pituitary-Adrenal axis reactivity. *Biological Psychiatry, 66,* 681–685. doi: 10.1016/j.biopsych.2009.05.012.

U.S. Department of Health and Human Services, Administration on Children, Youth and Families. (2016). *Child maltreatment 2014.* Washington, DC: US Government Printing Office. Retrieved from http://www.acf.hhs.gov/programs/cb/resource/child-maltreatment-2014.

———. (2015). *Child welfare outcomes 2010–2014: Report to Congress.* Washington, DC: US Government Printing Office. Retrieved from https://www.acf.hhs.gov/cb/resource/cwo-10-14.

U.S. Global Change Research Program. (2016). *The impacts of climate change on human health in the United States: A scientific assessment.* Washington, DC: Author.

Ullen, F., de Manzano, O., Almeida, R., Magnusson, P. K., Pedersen, N. L., Nakamura, J., Csikzntmilhaly, M., & Madison, G. (2012). Proneness for psychological flow in everyday life: Associations with personality and intelligence. *Personality and Individual Differences, 52,* 167–172. doi: 10.1016/j.paid.2011.10.003.

Ullman, S. E. (2007). Relationship to perpetrator, disclosure, social reactions, and PTSD symptoms in child sexual abuse survivors. *Journal of Child Sexual Abuse, 16*(1), 19–36. doi: 10.1300/J070v16n01_02.

Ullman, S. E., & Filipas, H. H. (2005). Gender differences in social reactions to abuse disclosure, post-abuse coping and PTSD of child sexual abuse survivors. *Child Abuse and Neglect, 29,* 767–782. doi: 10.1016/j.chiabu.2005.01.005.

Ullman, S. E., & Relyea, M. (2016). Social support, coping, and pottraumatic symptoms in female sexual assault surivors: A longitudinal analysis. *Journal of Traumatic Stress, 29,* 500–506. doi: 10.1002/jts.22143.

Ulrich, M., Keller, J., Hoening, K., Waller, C., & Gron, G. (2014). Neural correlates of experimentally induced flow experiences. *Neuroimage, 86,* 194–2002. doi: 10.106/j.neuroimage.2013.08.019.

United Nations Office for Disaster Risk Reduction (UNISDR). (2011). *UNISDR says young are the largest group affected by disasters.* Brussels, Belgium: Author. Retrieved from http://www.unisdr.org/archive/22742.

United Nations Office on Drugs and Crime. (2012). *World drug report.* Vienna, Austria: United Nations. Retrieved from http://www.unodc.org.

United States Administration for Children & Families. (2005). *Child maltreatment 2003: Reports from the States to the National Child Abuse and Neglect Data Systems – National statistics on child abuse and neglect.* Retrieved from https://www.acf.hhs.gov/cb.

Ural, C., Belli, H., Akbudak, M., & Tabo, A. (2015). Childhood traumatic experiences, dissociative symptoms, and dissociative disorder comorbidity among patients with panic disorder: A preliminary study. *Journal of Trauma and Dissociation, 16,* 463–475. doi: 10.1080/15299732.2015.1019175.

Urban, K. K. (1991). On the development of creativity in children. *Creativity Research Journal, 4*(2), 177–191.

Uzzi, B., & Spiro, J. (2005). Collaboration and creativity: The small world problem. *American Journal of Sociology, 111*(2), 447–504.

Vail, K. E., 3rd, Morgan, A., & Kahle, L. (2018). Self-affirmation attuenuates death-thought accessibility after mortality salience, but not among high posttraumatic stress sample. *Psychological Trauma: Theory, Research, Practice, and Policy, 10*(1), 112–120. doi: 10.1037/tra0000304.

Valdesolo, P., & Graham, J. (2014). Awe, uncertainty, and agency detection. *Psychological Science, 25*(1), 170–178. doi: 10.1177/0956797613501884.

Vallerand, R. J., Blanchard, C., Mageau, G. A., Koestner, R., Ratelle, C., Leonard, M., … Marsolais, J. (2003). Les Passions de l'Ame: On obsessive and harmonious passion. *Journal of Personality and Social Psychology, 85*, 756–767.

Vallerand, R. J., Mageau, G. A., Elliot, A. J., Dumais, A., Demers, M.-A., & Rousseau, F. (2008). Passion and performance attainment in sport. *Psychology of Sport and Exercise, 9*, 373–392. doi: 10.1016/j.psychsport.2007.05.003.

Van Cappellen, P., & Saroglou, V. (2012). Awe activates religious and spiritual feelings and behavioral intentions. *Psychology of Religion and Spirituality, 4*(3), 223–236. doi: 10.1037/a0025986.

Van de Vliert, E., & Murray, D. R. (2018). Climate and creativity: Cold and heat trigger invention and innovation in richer populations. *Creativity Research Journal, 30*(1), 17–28. doi: 10.1080/10400419.2018.1411571.

van Delft, I., Finkenauer, C., Tybur, J. M., & Lamers-Winkelman, F. (2016). Disgusted by sexual abuse: Exploring the association between disgust sensitivity and posttraumatic stress symptoms among mothers of sexually abused children. *Journal of Traumatic Stress, 29*, 237–244. doi: 10.1002/jts.22099.

Van den Broeck, W., Hofmans, J., Cooremans, S., & Staels, E. (2014). Factorial validity and measurement invariance across intelligence levels and gender of the Overexcitabilities Questionnaire–II (OEQ-II). *Psychological Assessment, 26*(1), 55–68. doi: 10.1037/a0034475.

van der Kolk, B. A. (2014). *The body keeps the score: Brain, mind, and body in the healing of trauma.* NYC, NY: Viking.

van der Westhuizen, C., Williams, J. K., Stein, D. J., & Sorsdahl, K. (2017). Assault injury presentation and lifetime psychological trauma in emergency center patients in South Africa: A cross-sectional study. *Psychological Trauma: Theory, Research, Practice, and Policy, 9*(3), 258–266. doi: 10.1037/tra0000223.

van Dijke, A., Hopman, J. A. B., & Ford, J. D. (2018). Affect dysregulation, psychoform dissociation, and adult relational fears mediate the relationship between childhood trauma and complex, posttraumatic stress disorder between childhood traum and complex posttraumatic stress disorder independent of the symptoms of borderline personality disorder. *European Journal of Psychotraumatology, 9*, 1400878. doi: 10.1080/20008198.2017.1400878.

van Ee, E., Kleber, R. J., Jongmans, M. J., Mooren, T. T. M., & Out, D. (2016). Parental PTSD, adverse parenting and child attachment in a refugee sample. *Attachment and Human Development, 18*(3), 273–291. doi: 10.1080/14616734.2016.1148748.

Van Harmelen, A.-L., van Tol, M.-J., van der Wee, N. J. A., Veltman, D. J., Aleman, A., Spinhoven, P., … Elzinga, B. M. (2010). Reduced medial prefrontal cortex volume in adults reporting childhood emotional maltreatment. *Biological Psychiatry, 68*, 832–838. doi: 10.1016/j.biopsych.2010.06.011.

van IJzendoorn, M. H., Caspers, K., Bakermans-Kranenburg, M. J., Beach, S. R. H., & Philibert, R. (2010). Methylation matters: Interaction between methylation density and serotonin transporter genotype predicts unresolved loss or trauma. *Biological Psychiatry, 68*, 405–407. doi: 10.1016/j.biopsych.2010.05.008.

Van Orden, K. A., Witte, T. K., Cukrowicz, K. C., Braithwaite, S. R., Selby, E. A., & Joiner Jr., T. E. (2010). The interpersonal theory of suicide. *Psychological Review, 117*, 575–600. doi: 10.1037/a0018697.

van Ryzin, M. J., Leve, L. D., Neiderhiser, J. M., Shaw, D. S., Natsuaki, M. N., & Reiss, D. (2015). Genetic influences can protect against unresponsive parenting in the prediction of child social competence. *Child Development, 86*, 667–680. doi: 10.1111/cdev.12335.

van Vliet, K. J. (2008). Shame and resilience in adulthood: A grounded theory study. *Journal of Counseling Psychology, 55*(2), 233–245. doi: 10.1037/0022-0167.55.2.233.

van Wyk, M., Thomas, K. G. F., Solms, M., & Lipinska, G. (2016). Prominence of hyperarousal symptoms explains variability of sleep disruption in posttraumatic stress disorder. *Psychological Trauma: Theory, Research, Practice, and Policy, 8*(6), 688–696. doi: 10.1037/tra0000115.

Varadhan, R., Chaves, P. H. M., Lipsitz, L. A., Stein, P. K., Tian, J., Windham, B. G., ... Fried, L. P. (2009). Frailty and impaired cardiac autonomic control: New insights from principal components aggregation of traditional heart rate variability indices. *Journal of Gerontology, 64*(6), 662–667. doi: 10.1093/gerona/glp013.

Vasileva, M., & Petermann, F. (2017). Posttraumatic stress symptoms in preschool children in foster care: The influence of placement and foster family environment. *Journal of Traumatic Stress, 30*, 472–481. doi: 10.1002/jts.22217.

Vasquez, A. D., de Arellano, M. A., Reid-Quinones, K., Bridges, A. J., & Rheingold, A. A. (2012). Peritraumatic dissociation and peritraumatic emotional predictors of PTSD in Latino youth: Results from the Hispanic family study. *Journal of Trauma and Dissociation, 13*, 509–525. doi: 10.1080/15299732.2012.678471.

Vaughan, C. A., Miles, J. N. V., Eisenman, D. P., & Meredith, L. S. (2016). Longitudinal associations among pain, posttraumatic stress disorder symptoms and stress appraisals. *Journal of Traumatic Stress, 29*, 176–179. doi: 10.1002/jts.22083.

Vawda, N. B. M., Milburn, N. G., Steyn, R., & Zhang, M. (2017). The development of a screening tool for the early identification of risk for suicidal behavior among students in a developing country. *Psychological Trauma: Theory, Research, Practice, and Policy, 9*(3), 267–273. doi: 10.1037/tra0000229.

Vellante, M., Zucca, G., Preti, A., Sisti, D., Rocchi, M. B. L., Akiskal, K. K., & Akiskal, H. S. (2011). Creativity and affective temperaments in con-clinical professional artists: An empirical psychometric investigation. *Journal of Affective Disorders, 135*, 28–36. doi: 10.1016/j/jad.2011.06.062.

Velotti, P., Elison, J., & Garofalo, C. (2014). Shame and aggression: Different trajectories and implications. *Aggression and Violent Behavior, 19*, 454–461. doi: 10.1016/j.avb.2014.04.011.

Venables, P. H., & Rector, N. A. (2000). The content and structure of schizotypy: A study using confirmatory factor analysis. *Schizophrenia Bulletin, 26*(3), 587–602.

Venta, A., Hatkevich, C., Mellick, W., Vanwoerden, S., & Sharp, C. (2017). Social cognition mediates the relation between attachment schemas and posttraumatic stress disorder. *Psychological Trauma: Theory, Research, Practice, and Policy, 9*(1), 88–95. doi: 10.1037/tra0000165.

Verhaeghen, P., Joorman, J., & Aikman, S. N. (2014). Creativity, mood, and the examined life: Self-reflective rumination boosts creativity, brooding breeds dysphoria. *Psychology of Aesthetics, Creativity, and the Arts, 8*(2), 211–218. doi: 10.1037/a0035594.

Verhaeghen, P., Khan, R., & Joorman, J. (2005). Why we sing the blues: The relation between self-reflective rumination, mood, and creativity. *Emotion, 5,* 226–232. doi: 10.1037/1528-3542.2.226.

Vermetten, E., & Bremner, J. D. (2002). Circuits and systems in stress II: Applicatios to neurobiology and treatment in posttraumatic stress disorder. *Depression and Anxiety, 16,* 14–38. doi: 10.1002/da.10017.

Vessey, W. B., & Mumford, M. D. (2012). Heuristics as a basis for assessing creative potential: Measures, methods, and contingencies. *Creativity Research Journal, 24*(1), 41–54. doi: 10.1080/10400419.2012.652928.

Viana, A. G., Dixon, L. J., Berenz, E. C., & Espil, F. M. (2017). Trauma and deliberate self-harm among inpatient adolescents: The moderating role of anxiety sensitivity. *Psychological Trauma: Theory, Research, Practice, and Policy, 9*(5), 509–517. doi: 10.1037/tra0000161.

Vickhoff, B., Malmgren, H., Astrom, R., Nyberg, G., Ekstrom, S.-R., Engwall, M., Snygg, J., ... Jornsten, R. (2013). Music structure determines heart rate variability of singers. *Frontiers in Psychology, 4*(334), 1–16. doi: 10.3389/f.psyg.2013.00334.

Vieselmeyer, J., Holguin, J., & Mezulis, A. (2017). The role of resilience and gratitude in posttraumatic stress and growth following a campus shooting. *Psychological Trauma: Theory, Research, Practice, and Policy, 9*(1), 62–69. doi: 10.1037/tra0000149.

Vikan, A., Hassel, A. M., Rugset, A., Johansen, H. E., & Moen, T. (2010). A test of shame in outpatients with emotional disorder. *Nordic Journal of Psychiatry, 64*(3), 196–202. doi: 10.3109/08039480903398177.

Vohs, K. D., & Baumeister, R. F. (2004). Understanding self-regulation. In R. F. Baumeister & K. D. Vohs (Eds.), *Handbook of self-regulation: Research, theory, and application* (pp. 1–9). NYC, NY: The Guilford Press.

von Stumm, S., Chung, A., & Furnham, A. (2011). Creative ability, creative ideation and latent classes of creative achievement: What is the role of personality? *Psychology, Aesthetics, Creativity, and the Arts, 5*(2), 107–114. doi: 10.1037/a0020499.

Vrana, S., & Lauterbach, D. (1994). Prevalence of traumatic events and posttraumatic psychological symptoms in a non-clinical sample of college students. *Journal of Traumatic Stress, 7,* 298–302.

Vroom, V. H. (1964). *Work and environment.* New York: Wiley.

Vythilingam, M., Nelson, E. E., Scaramozza, M., Waldeck, T., Hazlett, G., Southwick, S. M., ... Ernst, M. (2009). Reward circuitry in resilience to severe trauma: An fMRI investigation of resilient special forces soldiers. *Psychiatry Research: Neuroimaging, 172,* 75–77. doi: 10.1016/j.psychresns. 2008.06.008.

Walczak, M., Esbjorn, B. H., & Breinholst, S. (2017). Attachment as a predictor of non response to CBT treatment in children with anxiety disorders. *Attachment and Human Development, 19*(6), 635–653. doi: 10.1080/14616734.2017.1339099.

Waldo, T. G., & Merritt, R. D. (2000). Fantasy proneness, dissociation, and DSM-IV Axis II symptomatology, *Journal of Abnormal Psychology, 109*(3), 555–558. doi: 10.1037//0021.843X.109.3.555.

Wallace, B. A., & Shapiro, S. L. (2006). Mental balance and well-being: Building bridges between Buddhism and western psychology. *American Psychologist, 61*(7), 690–701. doi: 10.1037/0003-066X.61.7.690.

Wallace, C. E., & Russ, S. W. (2015). Pretend play, divergent thinking, and math achievement in girls: A longitudinal study. *Psychology of Aesthetics, Creativity, and the Arts, 9*(3), 296–305. doi: 10.1037/a0039006.

Wallas, G. (1926). *The art of thought.* New York, NY: Harcourt Brace.

———. (1926/1976). Stages in the creative process. In A. Rothenberg & C. R. Hausman (Eds.), *The creativity question* (pp. 69–73). Durham, NC: Duke University Press.

Wallis, P., & Steele, H. (2001). Attachment representations in adolescence: Further evidence from psychiatric settings. *Attachment and Human Development, 3*(3), 259–268. doi: 10.1080/1461673011009687-0.

Walsh, K., Blaustein, M., Knight, W. G., Spinazzola, J., & van der Kolk, B. A. (2007). Resiliency factors in the relationship between childhood sexual abuse and adulthood sexual assault in college-age women. *Journal of Child Sexual Abuse, 16*(1), 1–17. doi: 10.1300/J070v16n01_01.

Walsh, R. M., & Bruce, S. E. (2014). Reporting decisions after sexual assault: The impact of mental health variables. *Psychological Trauma: Theory, Research, Practice, and Policy, 6*(6), 691–699. doi: 10.1037/a0036592.

Walters, E., Merrick, S., Treboux, D., Crowell, J., & Albersheim, L. (2000). Attachment security in infancy and early adulthood: A twenty-year longitudinal study. *Child Development, 71*(3), 684–689.

Wang, F., Willoughby, M., Mills-Koonce, R., & Cox, M. J. (2016). Infant attachment disorganization and moderation pathways to level and change in externalizing behavior during preschool ages. *Attachment and Human Development, 18*(6), 141–153. doi: 10.1080/14616734.2016.1243139.

Wang, Q., Song, Q., & Koh, J. B. K. (2017). Culture, memory, and narratiave self-making. *Imagination, Cognition and Personality, 37*(2), 199–223. doi: 10.1177/0276236617733827.

Ward, M. J., Lee, S. S., & Lipper, E. G. (2000). Failure-to-thrive is associated with disorganized infant-mother attachment and unresolved maternal attachment. *Infant Mental Health Journal, 21*(6), 428–442.

Ward, M. J., Lee, S. S., & Polan, H. J. (2006). Attachment and psychopathology in a community sample. *Attachment & Human Development, 8*(4), 327–340. doi: 10.1080/14616730601048241.

Waters, E., & Deane, K. (1985). Defining and assessing individual differences in attachment relation- ships: Q-methodology and the organization of behavior in infancy and early childhood. *Monographs of the Society for Research in Child Development, 50*, 41–65. doi: 10.2307/3333826.

Waters, H. S., & Waters, E. (2006). The attachment working models concept: Among other things, we build script-like representations of secure base experiences. *Attachment and Human Development, 8*(3), 185–197. doi: 10.1080/14616730600856016.

Watson, E. (2007). Who or what creates? A conceptual framework for social creativity. *Human Resource Development Review, 6*(4), 419–441. doi: 10.1177/1534484307308255.

Watt, C., Watson, S., & Wilson, L. (2007). Cognitive and psychological mediators of anxiety: Evidence from a study of paranormal belief and perceived childhood control. *Personality and Individual Differences, 42*(2), 335–343. doi: 10.1016/j.paid.2006.07.015.

Watts, L. L., Steele, L. M., & Song, H. (2017). Re-examining the relationship between need for cognition and creativity: Predicting creative problem solving across multiple domains. *Creativity Research Journal, 29*(1), 21–28. doi: 10.1080/10400419.2017.1263505.

Weaver, T. L., & Resick, P. A. (2014). Injury dimensions in female victims of intimate partner violence: Expanding the examination of associations with symptoms of posttraumatic stress disorder. *Psychological Trauma: Theory, Research, Practice, and Policy, 6*(6), 683–690. doi: 10.1037/a0036063.

Webb, M., Heisler, D., Call, S., Chickering, S. A., & Colburn, T. A. (2007). Shame, guilt, symptoms of depression, and reported history of psychological maltreatment. *Child Abuse and Neglect, 31*, 1143–1153. doi: 10.1016/j.chiabu.2007.09.003.

Weber, S. (2008). Diagnosis of trauma and abuse-realted dissociative symptoms disorders in children and adolescents. *Journal of Child and Adolescent Psychiatric Nursing, 21*(4), 205–212.

Webster, L., Hackett, R. K., & Joubert, D. (2009). The association of unresolved attachment status and cognitive processes in maltreated adolescents. *Child Abuse Review, 18*, 6–23. doi: 10.1002/car.1053.

Wedding, D. (2000). Cognitive distortions in the poetry of Anne Sexton. *Suicide and Life-Threatening Behavior, 30*, 140–144.

Weems, C. F., Russell, J. D., Neill, E. L., Berman, S. L., & Scott, B. G. (2016). Existential anxiety among adolescents exposed to disaster: Linkages among level of exposure, PTSD, and depression symptoms. *Journal of Traumatic Stress, 29*, 466–473. doi: 10.1002/jts.22128.

Wei, Q., Fentress, H. M., Hoversten, M. T., Zhang, L., Hebda-Bauer, E. K., Watson, S. J., ... Akil, H. (2012). Early-life forebrain glucocorticoid receptor overexpression increases anxiety behavior and cocaine sensitization. *Biological Psychiatry, 71*(3), 224–231. doi: 10.1016/j.biopsych.2011.07.009.

Weierstall, R., & Elbert, T. (2011). The Appetitive Aggression Scale: Development of an instrument for the assessment of human attraction to violence. *European Journal of Psychotraumatology, 2*, 8430. doi: 10.3402/ejpt.v2i0.8430.

Weinberg, M., Besser, A., Ataria, Y., & Neria, Y. (2016). Survivor-spouse dissociation and posttraumatic stress disorder: Personal and dyad relationships. *Journal of Trauma and Dissociation, 17*(4), 448–459. doi: 10.1080/15299732.2016.1130006.

Weinberg, M., Besser, A., Zeigler-Hill, V., & Neria, Y. (2015). Dispositional optimism and self-esteem as competing predictors of acute symptoms of generalized anxiety disorders and dissociative experiences among civilians exposed to wr trauma. *Psychological Trauma: Theory, Research, Practice, and Policy, 7*(1), 34–42. doi: 10.1037/a0035170.

Weinfield, N. S., Whaley, G. J. L., & Egeland, B. (2004). Continuity, discontinuity, and coherence in attachment from infancy to late adolescence: Sequelae of organization and disorganization. *Attachment and Human Development, 6*(1), 73–97. doi: 10.1080/14616730310001659566.

Weinstein, A. A., Deuster, P. A., & Kop, W. J. (2007). Heart rate variability as a predictor of negative mood symptoms induced by exercise withdrawal. *Medicine and Science in Sports and Exercise, 39*(4), 735–741. doi: 10.1249/mss.0b013e31802f590c.

Weisberg, R. W. (2006). *Creativity: Understanding innovation in problem solving, science, invention and the arts.* New Jersey: Wiley and Sons, Inc.

———. (2015). On the usefulness of "value" in the definition of creativity. *Creativity Research Journal, 27*(2), 111–124. doi: 10.1080/10400419.2015.1030320.

Weisberg, R. B., Bruce, S. E., Machan, J. T., Kessler, R. C., Culpepper, L., & Keller, M. B. (2002). Nonpsychiatric illness among primare care patients with trauma histories and posttraumatic stress disorder. *Psychiatric Services, 53*(7), 848–854.

Weiss, N. H., Dixon-Gordon, K. L., Peasant, C., Jaquire, V., Johnson, C., & Sullivan, T. P. (2017). A latent profile analysis of intimate partner victimization and aggression and examination of between-class differences in psychopathology symptoms and risky behavior. *Psychological Trauma: Theory, Research, Practice, and Policy, 9*(3), 370–378. doi: 10.1037/tra0000202.

Wellisch, M., & Brown, J. (2013). Many faces of a gifted personality: Characteristics along a complex gifted spectrum. *Talent Development and Excellence, 5*(2), 43–58.

Welter, M. M., Jaarsveld, S., van Leeuwen, C., & Lachmann, T. (2016). Intelligence and creativity: Over the threshold together? *Creativity Research Journal, 28*(2), 212–218. doi: 10.1080/10400419.2016.1162564.

White, H. A., & Shah, P. (2006). Uninhibited imaginations: Creativity in adults with Attention-Deficit/Hyperactivity Disorder. *Personality and Individual Differences, 40,* 1121–1131. doi: 10.1016/j.paid.2005.11.007.

Whitman, R. D., Holocomb, E., & Zanes, J. (2010). Hemispheric collaboration in creative subjects: Cross-hemisphere priming in a lexical decision task. *Creativity Research Journal, 22*(2), 109–118. doi: 10.1080/10400419.2010.481480.

Widom, C. S., & Brzustowicz, L. M. (2006). MAOA and the "cycle of violence:" Childhood abuse and neglect and antisocial behavior. *Biological Psychiatry, 60*(7), 684–689.

Wilkins, N., Tsao, B., Hertz, M., Davis, R., & Klevens, J. (2014). *Connecting the dots: An overview of the links among multiple forms of violence.* Centers for Disease Control and Prevention, Atlanta, GA: National Center for Injury Prevention and Control. Retrieved from https://www.cdc.gov/violenceprevention.

Williams, H., & Vess, M. (2016). Daydreams and the true self: Daydreaming styles are related to authenticity. *Imagination, Cognition and Personality, 36*(2), 128–149. doi: 10.1177/0276236616646065.

Wills, G. I. (2003). Forty lives in the bebop business: Mental health in a group of eminent jazz musicians. *British Journal of Psychiatry, 183,* 255–259.

Wilson, J. P., Drozdek, B., & Turkovic, S. (2006). Posttraumatic shame and guilt. *Trauma, Violence, & Abuse, 7*(2), 122–141. doi: 10.1177/15248005285914.

Wilson, J. Z., Marin, D., Maxwell, K., Cumming, J., Berger, R., Saini, S., ... Chibnall, J. T. (2016). Association with posttraumatic growth and illness-related burden with psychosocial factors of patient, family, and provider pediatric cancer survivors. *Journal of Traumatic Stress, 29*, 448–456. doi: 10.1002/jts.22123.

Wilson, L. C. (2014). Mass shootings: A meta-analysis of the dose-response relationship. *Journal of Traumatic Stress, 27*, 631–638. doi: 10.1002/jts.21964.

Wilson, S. C., & Barber, T. X. (1983). The fantasy-prone personality: Implications for understanding imagery, hypnosis and parapsychological phenomena. In A. A. Sheikh (Ed.), *Imagery: Current theory, research and application* (pp. 340–387). New York: John Wiley & Sons.

Winner, E. (2000a). The origins and ends of giftedness. *American Psychologist, 55*(1), 159–169. doi: 10.1037/0003-066X.55.1.159.

———. (2000b). Giftedness: Current theory and research. *Current Directions in Psychological Science, 9*(5), 153–156. doi: 10.1111/1467-8721.00082.

Wisco, B. E., Miller, M. W., Wolf, E. J., Kilpatrick, D., Resnick, H. S., Badour, C. L., ... Friedman, M. J. (2016). The impact of proposed changes ti ICD-11 on estimates of PTSD prevalence and comorbidity. *Psychiatry Research, 240*, 226–233. doi: 10.1016/j.psychres.2016.04.043.

Wittmann, B. C., Bunzeck, N., Dolan, R. J., & Duzel, E. (2007). Anticipation of novelty recruits reward system and hippocampus while promoting recollection. *Neuroimage, 38*, 194–202. doi: 10.1016/j.neuroimage.2007.06.038.

Wolak, J., & Finkelhor, D. (2016). *Sextortion: Key findings from an online survey*. Crimes Against Children Research Center. Retrieved from https://www.unh.edu/ccrc/.

Wolak, J., Finkelhor, D., & Sedlak, A. J. (2016). *Child victims of stereotypical kidnapping known to law enforcement in 2011*. Juvenile Justice Bulletin, U.S. Department of Justice, Office of Juvenile Justice and Delinquency Prevention, 1–20. Retrieved from: https://www.ncjrs.gov.

Wolf, E. J., Miller, M. W., Kilpatrick, D., Resnick, H. S., Badour, C. L., Marx, B. P., ... Friedman, M. J. (2015). ICD-11 Complex PTSD in U.S. national and veteran samples: Prevalence and structural associations with PTSD. *Clinical Psychology Science, 3*(2), 215–229. doi: 10.1177/2167702614545480.

Wolf, E. J., Miller, M. W., Sullivan, D. R., Amstadter, A. B., Mitchell, K. S., Goldberg, J., & Magruder, K. M. (2018). A classical twin study of PTSD symptoms and resilience: Evidence for a single spectrum of vulnerability to traumatic stress. *Depression and Anxiety, 35*, 132–139. doi: 10.1002/da.22712.

Wolfradt, U., & Engelmann, S. (2003). Depersonalization, fantasies, and coping behavior in clinical context. *Journal of Clinical Psychology, 59*(10), 1117–1124. doi: 10.1002/jclp.10204.

Woodward, J., & Sikes, P. L. (2015). The creative thinking ability of musicians and nonmusicians. *Psychology of Aesthetics, Creativity, and the Arts, 9*(10), 75–80. doi: 10.1037/a0038177.

World Health Organization (WHO). (2017). *International classification of diseases* (11th ed.). Manuscript in preparation.

Wright, M. O., Crawford, E., & Del Castillo, D. (2009). Childhood emotional maltreatment and later psychological distress among college students: The mediating role of maladaptive schemas. *Child Abuse and Neglect, 33*, 59–68. doi: 10.1016/j.chiabu.2008.12.007.

Wyatt, G. E., Thames, A., Simbayi, L., Stein, D. J., Burns, J., & Maselesele, M. (2017). Trauma and mental health in South Africa: Overview. *Psychological Trauma: Theory, Research, Practice, and Policy, 9*(3), 249–251. doi: 10.1037/tra0000144.

Yager, T. J., Gerszberg, N., & Dohrenwend, B. P. (2016). Secondary traumatization in Vietnam veterans' families. *Journal of Traumatic Stress, 29*, 349–355. doi: 10.1002/jts.22115.

Yehuda, R. (2001). Biology of posttraumatic stress disorder. *Journal of Clinical Psychiatry, 62*(suppl. 17), 41–46.

———. (2006). Adances in understanding neuroendocrine alteration in PTSD and their therapeutic implications. *Annals of the New York Academy of Science, 1071*, 137–166. doi: 10.1196/annals.1364.012.

Yehuda, R., Golier, J. A., Halligan, S. L., Meaney, M., & Bierer, L. M. (2004). The ACTH response to dexamethasone in PTSD. *American Journal of Psychiatry, 161*(8), 1397–1403.

Yehuda, R., Golier, J. A., Yang, R. K., & Tischler, L. (2004). Enhanced sensitivity to glucocorticoids in peripheral mononuclear leukocytes in posttraumatic stress disorder. *Biological Psychiatry, 55*(11), 1110–1116.

Yeung, N. C. Y., Lau, J. T. F., Yu, N. X., Zhang, J., Xu, Z., Choi, K. C., … Lui, W. W. S. (2018). Media exposure related to the 2008 Sichuan Earthquate predicted probable PTSD among Chinese adolescents in Kunming, China: A longitudinal study. *Psychological Trauma: Theory, Research, Practice, and Policy, 10*(2), 253–262. doi: 10.1037/tra0000121.

Yeung, N. C. Y., Lu, Q., Wong, C. C. Y., & Huynh, H. C. (2016). The roles of needs satisfaction, cognitive appraisals, and coping strategies in promoting posttraumatic growth: A stress and coping perspective. *Psychological Trauma: Theory, Research, Practice, and Policy, 8*(3), 284–292. doi: 10.1037/tra0000091.

Ying, L.-H., Lin, C.-D., Wu, X.-C., Chen, C., Greenberger, E., & An, Y.-Y. (2014). Trauma severity and control beliefs as predictors of posttraumatic growth aong adolescent survivors of the Wenchuan earthquake. *Psychological Trauma: Theory, Research, Practice, and Policy, 6*(2), 192–198. doi: 10.1037/a0031964.

Yoon, S., Steigerwald, S., Holmes, M. R., & Perzynski, A. T. (2016). Children's exposure to violence: The underlying effect of posttraumatic stress symptoms on behavior problems. *Journal of Traumatic Stress, 29*, 72–79. doi: 10.1002/jts.22063.

Young, D. A., Shumway, M., Flentje, A., & Riley, E. D. (2017). The relationship between childhood abuse and violent victimization in homeless and marginally housed women: The role of dissociation as a potential mediator. *Psychological Trauma: Theory, Research, Practice, and Policy, 9*(5), 613–621. doi: 10.1037/tra0000288.

Young, I. T., Iglewicz, A., Glorioso, D., Lanouette, N., Seay, K., Ilapakurti, M., & Zisook, S. (2013). Sicide bereavement and complicated grief. *Dialogues in Clinical Neuroscience, 14*(2), 177–186.

Yule, W. (2001). Posttraumatic Stress Disorder in the general population and in children. *Journal of Clinical Psychiatry, 62*(17), 23–28.

Zabelina, D. L., & Robinson, M. D. (2010). Don't be so hard on yourself: Self-compassion facilitates creative originality among self-judgmental individuals. *Creativity Research Journal, 22*(3), 288–293. doi: 10.1080/10400419.2010.503538.

Zabellina, D. L., Felps, D., & Blanton, H. (2013). The motivational influence of self-guides on creative pursuits. *Psychology of Aesthetics, Creativity, and the Arts, 7*(3), 112–118. doi: 10.1037/a0030464.

Zajac, K., & Kobak, R. (2009). Caregiver unresolved loss and abuse and child behavior problems: Intergenerational effects in a high-risk sample. *Development and Psychopathology, 21*, 173–187. doi: 10.1017/S095457940900011X.

Zambrano-Vazquez, L., Levy, H. C., Belleau, E. L., Dworkin, E. R., Sharp, K. M. H., Pittenger, S. L., Schumacher, J. A., & Coffey, S. F. (2017). Using the research domain criteria framework to track domains of change in comorbid PTSD and SUD. *Psychological Trauma: Theory, Research, Practice, and Policy, 9*(6), 679–687. doi: 10.1037/tra0000257.

Zeanah, C. H., Smyke, A. T., Koga, S. F., & Carlson, E. (2005). Attachment in institutionalized and community children in Romania.*Child Development, 76*(5), 1015–1028.

Zegers, M. A. M., Schuengel, C., van IJzendoorn, M. H., & Janssens, J. M. A. M. (2008). Attachment and problem behavior of adolescents during residential treatment. *Attachment and Human Development, 10*(1), 91–103. doi: 10.1080/14616730701868621.

Zeki, S. (1999). *Inner vision: An exploration of art and the brain.* Oxford, England: Oxford University Press.

Zerach, G. (2015). Secondary growth among former prisoner of war's adult children: The result of exposure to stress, secondary traumatization, or personality traits? *Psychological Trauma: Theory, Research, Practice, and Policy, 7*(4), 313–323. doi: 10.1037/tra0000009.

Zerach, G. (2015). Secondary traumatization among ex-POWs' adult children: The mediating role of differentiation of the self. *Psychological Trauma: Theory, Research, Practice, and Policy, 7*(2), 187–194. doi: 10.1037/a0037006.

Zerach, G., & Solomon, Z. (2016). Indirect exposure to captivity is not related to posttraumatic stress symptoms among the spouses and offspring of former prisoners of war. *Journal of Traumatic Stress, 29*, 530–536. doi: 10.1002/jts.22140.

Zerach, G., Greene, T., Ginzburg, K., & Solomon, A. (2014). The relationship between posttraumatic stress disorder and persistent dissociation among ex-prisoner of war: A longitudinal study. *Psychological Trauma: Theory, Research, Practice, and Policy, 6*(2), 99–108. doi: 10.1037a0031599.

Zerubavel, N., Messman-Moore, T. L., DiLillo, D., & Gratz, K. L. (2018). Childhood sexual abuse and fear of abandonment moderate the relation of intimate partner violence to severity of dissociation. *Journal of Trauma and Dissociation, 18*(1), 9–24. doi: 10.1080/15299732.2017.1289491.

Zhang, L., & Sternberg, R. J. (2011). Revisiting the investment theory of creativity. *Creativity Research Journal, 23*(3), 229–238. doi: 10.1080/10400419.2011.595974.

Zhang, S., & Zhang, J. (2017). The association of TPH genes with creative potential. *Psychology of Aesthetics, Creativity, and the Arts, 11*(1), 2–9. doi: 10.1037/aca000073.

Zhang, W., Zhang, Q., Yu, B., & Zhao, L. (2015). Knowledge map of creativity research based on keywords network and co-word analysis, 1992–2011. *Quality and Quantity, 49*, 1023–1038. doi: 10.1007/s11135-014-0032-9.

Zhou, X., Wu, X., Fu, F., & An, Y. (2015). Core beliefs challenge and rumination as predictors of PTSD and PTG among adolescent survivors of the Wenchuan earthquake. *Psychological Trauma: Theory, Research, Practice, and Policy, 7*(4), 391–397. doi: 10.1037/tra0000031.

Zisk, A., Abbott, C. H., Ewing, S. K., Diamond, G. S., & Kobak, R. (2017). The Suicide Narrative Interview: Adolescents' attachment expectations and symptom severity in a clinical sample. *Attachment and Human Development, 19*(5), 447–462. doi: 10.1080/14616734.2016.1269234.

Zoellner, T., & Maercker, A. (2006). Posttraumatic growth in clinical psychology: A critical review and introduction of a two component model. *Clinical Psychology Review, 26*, 626–653. doi: 10.1016/j.cpr.2006.01.008.

Zuiden, M., Geuze, E., Wilemen, H. L., Vermetten, E., Maas, M., Amarouchi, K., … Heijnen, C. J. (2012). Glucocorticoid receptor pathway components predict posttraumatic stress disorder symptom development: A prospective study. *Biological Psychiatry, 71*(4), 309–316. doi: 10.1016/j.biopsych.2011.10.026.

Index

action-oriented neural network, 87–88, 99–100, 104, 117
adverse childhood experience, 183, 217, 224–25, 296;
    adverse childhood experience (ACE) study, 124–26, 136–38, 141–42, 179, 201, 205, 267
affect, 30, 49–50, 61–62, 64, 92–93, 112, 117, 135, 165, 183, 195, 201, 211, 236, 252
aggression, 29, 40, 48, 50, 89, 125, 135, 139, 182–185, 194, 197, 200, 222, 229, 234, 238, 242
allostasis, 203, 215–18, 230, 265, 267
amygdala, 100, 108–9, 113, 118, 216, 218–20, 222, 224, 227–28, 235
anger, 62, 112, 124, 126, 130–31, 153–54, 158, 169, 176, 184–85, 188, 193, 196–97, 203, 205, 228, 231–36, 247, 253, 257, 264, 271, 288, 292, 297
anxiety, 42, 50, 53, 59, 68–72, 92–95, 101, 106, 125–26, 131, 149, 158, 208, 236, 178, 180–84, 190, 192
    Panic, 132, 134, 165, 177, 248, 251
attachment, 135–64;
    Adult Attachment Interview, 137, 142–51, 154–68;
    ambivalent (Preoccupied), 136–37, 149–50, 153–59, 160, 167, 173, 209;
    avoidant (Dismissing), 136–37, 148–51, 153, 155–60, 163–67, 173, 271;
    Disorganized (Unresolved), 9, 11, 92–93, 136–37, 138, 148, 150, 152, 154–63, 172–73, 180–81, 224, 228, 230, 249–51;
    earned security, 143–44, 154–55;
    infant attachment assessment, 139–42;
    insecure, 11, 150, 152–56, 159, 161–67;
    internal working models, 135, 147, 156, 172, 268;
    Secure, 11, 50, 136, 137, 148–51, 153–55, 156, 158–68, 172–73, 186, 268, 295;
    self-report measures and results, 150–54;
    transmission, 123, 137–38, 144–45, 154–57, 172, 184, 194, 209–10, 251
attention-deficit/hyperactivity disorder, 42, 81, 84, 92–94, 202, 207, 216

421

autonomic nervous system (ANS), 88, 100, 111, 166, 168, 199, 215–16, 221, 230, 235–36;
  parasympathetic nervous system, 111–12, 117, 167, 216, 221–23, 235, 250, 255;
  sympathetic nervous system, 111–12, 117–18, 167, 172, 199, 216, 218, 221–25, 235, 250, 255
autotelic, 54, 58, 67–70, 90
awe, 11, 75–78, 88–90, 95–96, 113–16, 264, 286

betrayal, 42, 142, 184, 192, 195–96, 240, 252, 288
bipolar disorder, 36, 82, 93–95, 236, 244, 293
bullying, 115–16, 123, 127–28, 131, 134–35, 137, 237, 292
burnout, 51, 61, 74, 181, 195, 211–21, 240, 252, 275

catecholamine. *See* neurotransmitters
cognition, 15, 20, 40, 44, 47, 60, 73, 81–82, 90, 96–98, 100–101, 105–6, 108, 113, 155, 168, 176, 185, 193, 210, 254, 296, 299;
  coherence, 70, 72, 116, 149–50, 154, 157, 169, 173, 268
  convergent, 21, 25, 32, 36, 86, 94, 98;
  divergent, 21, 24–26, 32, 36–38, 50, 63, 68, 86, 89, 91–94, 98, 101–2, 109, 293
comorbid disorders, 11, 178–79, 183, 186–89, 198–99, 201, 214, 244, 247, 251–52, 266
compassion, 76, 149–50, 211–12, 214, 230, 242, 275
complexity, 16, 18, 32, 41, 52–53, 78, 91, 96, 99, 105, 109, 111, 113–14, 119, 181, 227, 229, 243–44, 246, 256, 276, 284
constraint, 15, 27, 62–64, 74, 76, 105, 181, 291, 293–94

copying strategies, 9, 11, 45, 75, 83, 109, 136, 140, 142, 155, 157, 159, 161, 182, 185–86, 192, 194, 200, 212, 214, 221, 229, 233–34, 238, 249, 256–59, 263, 265–76, 280–285–289, 295–97
cortisol, 148, 155, 167, 218, 224, 228, 235, 255
courage, 279, 292–93, 299, 375
creativity, 4–6, 11, 16–21, 23, 33, 35–39, 44, 47–50, 53–54, 57–59, 62–65, 69, 74–83, 86, 90, 92–95, 98–105, 107–13, 115, 117–19, 241, 274, 285, 293–294–297
creativity models, 17, 25–28, 33;
  component model, 14, 26, 28, 38, 246;
  Consensual Assessment Technique, 5–6, 17–18, 30;
  distributed creativity, 14–15, 17–18, 26–27, 30, 118;
  domain-specific and domain-general, 8–10, 15–16, 18–21, 27, 31, 35–40, 43–44, 46–48, 54–55, 65–66, 77, 87, 98–100, 102, 118, 291;
  four-Cs, 9–11, 21–22;
  four-Ps, 20;
  four-Stage Based model, 12–14, 24–25, 29, 88;
  geneplore model, 5, 13–14, 25–26, 86–88, 98–100;
  investment theory, 11, 23;
  radical and incremental creativity, 16, 28;
  two dimension model. *See* geneplore model
creativity research methods, 15, 18–20, 32, 46, 59–61, 71, 91
culture, 9, 18, 21, 30, 32, 53, 57, 64–65, 70, 74, 79, 107, 135, 148, 181, 194–96, 206–7, 271, 282, 284, 288

dance, 44, 72, 99, 107, 113–14, 163, 165, 170, 177, 198, 201, 233

Index

daydreams, 10, 67, 71–72, 79–81, 83–85, 95–96, 104, 246;
  maladaptive daydream, 70, 72
default mode network, 87, 89, 99–103, 106, 108, 111, 117, 220, 227, 254
depersonalization, 11, 70, 82, 105, 176, 212, 236–37, 244, 246–248–252, 255, 266
depression, 50, 82, 93–95, 127, 101, 116, 125–26, 131, 133, 135, 137, 139–41, 143, 149, 151, 154, 156, 163–64, 166, 168–69, 171, 179–184–185, 187–90, 192–200, 203–4, 207–10, 212–13, 218, 220, 224, 226–27, 229, 232–33, 236–38, 240–41, 244, 247–49, 252–53, 257, 266, 270–72, 280–81, 293
disabilities, 115, 127–28, 133, 203, 207–8
disgust, 62, 210, 222, 231, 234, 237, 239
dissociation, 48, 68, 82, 133, 139, 149, 154, 157, 160, 170, 176, 194, 196, 198, 212, 231–46, 248, 250–58, 270, 272, 281;
  cognitive processing, 233–34;
  comorbid disorders, 239–40;
  peritraumatic dissociation, 164, 176, 194, 212, 235, 247, 281;
  self-injurious behavior, 135, 150, 207, 240–42, 252–53
diversity, 15, 23, 27–28, 31, 46, 54, 75, 114, 207, 256
domestic violence, 123, 125, 129, 131, 135–36, 138–40, 150, 178, 190–91, 193, 199, 225, 238, 275
dopamine, 93, 97, 109–10, 115, 117–18, 219, 225

embitterment, 195, 228, 275–76, 287–88
embodied, 31, 73–74, 78, 82–83, 90, 95, 98, 100, 113, 107–8
emotion, 19, 29, 37–38, 41–43, 45–46, 48, 50, 52, 55, 59–65, 70–71, 74, 77, 83–84, 86, 88–90, 93, 95–96, 98–100, 107–9, 111–14, 119, 123, 126, 128, 135, 141, 147, 150–58, 161, 163–73, 176, 180–84, 186, 192, 193–97, 199–203, 209–13, 217, 220, 227–28, 231–36, 238–55, 262, 264, 267, 270–74, 276, 280, 285–87, 292–93, 295
emotional abuse, 114, 124, 126, 133, 136–39, 142–44, 159, 191, 202, 204, 219, 224, 229, 248, 252, 257
emotion-creativity equation (also mood-creativity equation), 51–54, 63, 38, 65
empathy, 54, 65, 87, 99, 144, 209, 211, 226–27, 285, 294
epigenetics, 69, 90, 156, 168, 223, 267
ethnicity, 120, 132, 134, 139, 194, 206, 208
executive network, 36, 87, 99–101, 103–105–106, 108, 117, 220–21, 226–27, 245, 254
exercise, 25, 64, 76, 197, 268, 291
explicit processing, 91–92, 103–4, 106–7, 109, 114, 116–17, 128, 299

fantasy (also fantasy proneness), 48, 52, 67–71, 79–85, 87, 89–96, 142, 242, 245–46
fatalities, 119–20, 131–34, 192
flow, 10, 11, 54–59, 61, 65–71, 73, 92, 105–6, 112, 117–19, 231, 274–75, 292
forced relocation, 175–76, 188–87, 197
foster care, 120–21, 132–33

gender, 35–36, 43, 45, 47, 60, 90, 110, 116–17, 132, 139–40, 149, 180, 183, 185–86, 190–92, 208, 215, 256–57, 282, 288
genetics, 40, 91, 69, 91, 96, 111, 117, 156, 168, 198, 211–13, 216, 218, 223–26, 265, 267, 276
giftedness, 8, 10–11, 20, 23–55, 69, 81, 83, 85, 95

424 *Index*

glucocorticoids, 206–7, 218–20, 224, 226
guilt, 50, 62, 83–84, 112, 155, 176, 183, 181, 186, 195–96, 208, 220–21, 231–32, 234, 238–39, 247, 258, 271, 289, 292

hardiness, 9–11, 267–69, 279–81, 283, 285, 287, 288–89
heart rate variability, 99–100, 111–12, 119, 222–23, 261
hippocampus, 99, 104, 113, 206, 218, 216, 219–21, 224, 226, 228, 254
homeostasis (homeodynamics), 98–99, 110, 215–16
HPA axis, 204, 216, 218–20, 226, 228–29, 255
hypothalamus, 100, 108–9, 111, 113, 206, 216, 218, 220, 226

illumination. *See* Four-Stage Based Model
imagery, 67, 74–75, 79–80, 86–87, 98, 104, 107, 115, 285
imaginary companion, 72–73, 84–85, 142, 180
imagination, 31, 40, 42–44, 46, 52, 67–74, 79–80, 84–87, 96
immune system, 111, 198, 204, 209, 215, 221, 232, 255
implicit processing, 91–92, 98, 103, 104–7, 109–10, 114, 117
incubation. *See* Four-Stage Based Model
intelligence, 11, 23–26, 29, 35–40, 69, 77, 101, 211
interoception, 95, 106, 108, 116, 222, 253

justice, 58, 129, 143, 183, 195, 239, 287

kidnapping, 117–18, 123, 130–31, 133

latent inhibition, 89, 101–2, 229
loss, 9, 11, 66–68, 71, 80, 119, 138–39, 149–52, 154, 157, 160–62, 168–72, 175–77, 179–182–185, 187–91, 193, 195, 197, 199, 201–3, 205, 207, 209–11, 213, 215, 219, 224, 227–30, 244, 248, 255, 262, 266, 270, 273, 276, 282, 289, 292, 296;
Complicated grief, 168, 170, 180–82, 190, 195, 289

malevolent and benevolent, 4, 16–18, 21, 28–29, 31, 59, 77, 282, 294
maltreatment, 111, 123–26, 131–45, 152–54, 156, 159–60, 163–64, 166, 173, 193, 197, 201–2, 204–7, 213, 219–22, 224–25, 229, 236–37, 249–51, 253, 276
meaning, 9–10, 17, 22, 42, 57, 65, 67, 71–72, 85, 90, 96, 102, 107, 110, 112, 119, 142, 151, 156, 168–70, 172, 181, 205, 212, 231, 242, 265, 271, 274–75, 282, 284–88, 296
meditation, 25, 73, 103–5, 115–17
memory, 25–26, 81, 85–87, 91, 99–101, 103–4, 107, 108–10, 149, 154, 157, 164, 167–73, 176–77, 183, 191, 196, 203, 219, 222–23, 227–28, 234, 236–38, 242–45, 247–48, 255
mental illness, 29, 41–42, 54, 80, 82, 91–92, 94–95, 123–24, 126–27, 131, 137, 139–41, 143–44, 154, 170–71, 182, 186, 189–91, 194, 198, 201–2, 204–5, 207–8, 210, 217–18, 222, 229, 237, 239, 244, 246, 249, 263, 265, 267, 271–72, 293, 295
mindfulness, 57, 61, 68, 248, 274, 285
mirror neurons, 94, 106
mood, 32, 49–54, 61–64, 72, 81, 89, 93–96, 112, 153, 160, 176, 178, 180, 202, 204, 217, 252, 258, 295
moral, 30–31, 59, 62, 99, 126, 183, 195–96, 206, 208–9, 211, 227–28, 231–32, 234, 252, 269, 273, 280, 282, 285, 294

motivation, 11, 18, 23, 29, 31, 36, 39, 43–46, 48, 51–53, 55, 57–61, 62–63, 68–69, 72, 76, 90–91, 103, 241, 264, 272, 286, 295;
    achievement-motivation model, 48, 60;
    expectancy motivation theory, 48, 60, 221, 232;
    extrinsic, 30, 46–48, 57–60, 69, 275;
    intrinsic, 23, 30, 46, 55, 57–60, 63, 67–70, 73, 263, 275;
    self-determination theory, 48, 57, 60, 69, 253, 265;
    synergistic, 46, 47, 58–60
motor cognition, 15, 37, 44, 65, 93–94, 107, 243
music, 9, 44, 48, 61–63, 65, 68, 70, 77, 86–87, 89, 98–99, 102–4, 105, 107–8, 113–14, 118, 245, 296
mystical, 11, 26, 89, 95, 115, 103–4

narratives, 11, 42, 47–48, 86, 149–50, 154, 156–60, 167–73, 282
natural disasters, 158, 172–73, 175, 178–79, 184–85, 192, 207, 210–11, 258, 266, 269, 274, 282, 284
neglect (physical or emotional), 55, 105, 114, 123–24, 126–27, 129–33, 136, 140–44, 152, 154–56, 194, 224, 229, 236–37, 248–49, 252, 276
neuroaesthetics, 11, 100–101, 112–15
neurotransmitters and neuropeptides, 97–98, 109–10, 117, 167, 206, 212–13, 218, 224–26, 228–29, 243, 255–56
novelty, 5, 16–18, 22, 28–30, 46, 48, 53, 57, 69, 110, 116, 119, 268

open to experience, 19, 22–23, 28, 36, 39, 44, 50–52, 65, 67, 69, 72, 77, 79, 81, 89–93, 114, 274, 281, 285–87, 299
optimism, 58, 70, 193, 255, 267, 270, 272–74, 275, 282, 284, 287, 294
organizational justice, 58, 288–89

overexcitability, 29–32, 40, 42, 83, 95, 210, 249
oxytocin, 110, 167, 214, 226

pain, 28, 65, 72, 81, 90, 96, 98, 100, 106, 108, 138, 151, 161, 166, 170, 172, 181, 184, 186, 189, 191, 194, 198, 200–201, 2203, 05, 211, 214, 222, 227, 229–30, 234, 237–39, 245, 248, 253, 268, 277, 287, 296–97
paracosms, 30, 42, 73, 84–85, 96
paranormal, 42, 68–70, 77, 80–82, 84, 89, 142, 154, 161, 204, 287, 297
parenting, 52–53, 123, 135–36, 141, 144, 149, 152, 156–57, 164, 180, 267, 276, 292, 295
passion (obsessive and harmonious), 11, 19, 23, 40, 48–49, 61–62, 67, 73–74, 76, 149–50, 211–12, 214, 242, 275, 294
perfectionism, 39–40, 51, 64, 76, 233, 281, 293
personality, 11, 23, 26, 29–31, 35–43, 47–52, 54, 62, 67, 69–71, 80–82, 84, 89–94, 107, 126, 133, 137, 139, 160, 168, 182–83, 192–93, 201, 209, 222, 224–25, 237, 241–42, 244, 248, 252, 268, 273–74, 276–77, 279–81, 287, 291, 296;
    creative personality profile, 39–40;
    Five-Factor Model (Big Five), 38–39, 49–51, 69;
    Myers-Briggs Type Indicator, 37, 49;
    Three Factor Model (extraversion, neuroticism, psychoticism), p. 37–38, 47, 49–50, 91
physical abuse, 107, 112, 123–28, 130, 133, 137–41, 143, 156–57, 172, 175, 178–79, 182, 188, 190–94, 196–200, 202, 204–8, 210, 212, 222–24, 234–35, 237–38, 241–42, 244, 249–50, 253, 257, 266
physiologic, 10–11, 61–62, 88, 97–99, 101, 103, 105–7, 109, 111–15, 117–19, 136, 138–39, 141, 166–

67, 176, 182, 185, 193, 195, 197, 204, 214–15, 217, 219, 216, 221–23, 225, 228–31, 236, 255–56, 262–64, 266–67, 273
polyvictimization, 111, 119, 123, 131, 134–35, 239
posttraumatic Stress Disorder (PTSD), 125, 131, 133, 135, 139, 140, 143, 152, 154, 156, 158–60, 163–65, 169–71, 175–79, 180–86, 188–206–214, 219–29, 232, 235–37, 239–41, 244–45, 247, 251–53, 255–58, 262–67, 269, 271–73, 281–87, 289, 291, 297;
  Complex PTSD (CPTSD), 189–90, 201–3;
  diagnostic criteria, 163–65;
  intentional and non-intentional, 27, 113, 124, 126, 130, 166, 178–79, 189, 191–92, 200, 208, 214, 239
post-traumatic growth, 164, 176, 181, 185, 203, 211–12, 262, 266, 269–71, 274, 281–83, 285–87, 289, 296;
  event centrality, 72, 269, 2272, 81;
  factors contributing to post-traumatic growth, 271–74;
  Post-traumatic Growth Inventory (PTGI), 270;
  retaliatory responses, 275–76;
  secondary growth, 274–75
pretend play, 73, 85
prisoners of war, 164, 179, 189, 191, 209, 244, 272, 286–87
problem solving, 9, 17, 20–27, 29, 42, 44–45, 47–48, 55, 59, 63, 69, 74–77, 80, 83, 87, 98–99, 101, 103, 117, 138, 143, 159, 165, 269–70, 273–74, 280, 282, 288, 294
psychosis, 94, 96, 101, 155, 207, 219, 283

rape. *See* sexual assault
refugee, 152, 160, 177–79, 182, 189–90, 194, 211, 203, 257, 283

religion, 128, 144, 149, 286
resilience, 10–11, 53–54, 67, 70, 90–91, 111–12, 119, 141–42, 145, 147, 151, 155–56, 158–59, 182, 184, 186, 195, 210, 213, 226, 229–30, 233, 242, 250–51, 259, 262, 264–67, 268–69, 271, 273–77, 279–81, 285, 287, 292–93, 295, 297;
  factors to promote resilience, 259–63;
  salutogenic model, 251, 263;
  vicarious resilience, 263, 275
revictimization, 131, 139, 158, 166, 192, 204
reward network, 88, 100, 102, 106, 109–11, 113–14, 118, 220, 267, 270
risk-taking, 20, 28, 48
rumination (Self-reflection and Brooding), 41, 51, 61, 63–64, 76, 95, 169, 181, 192–93, 227–28, 230–31, 236, 240–42, 247, 264, 271, 274–75, 282–84, 287–88, 296

salience network, 88, 100–101, 111, 220, 227, 254
schizotypy, 69, 79–81, 91–94, 160
self-efficacy, 28, 59–60, 67, 70, 76–77, 181, 210, 226, 232, 257, 264–65, 269–70, 273, 275, 280, 282, 284, 288, 291, 294, 296
self-regulation, 10, 45, 48, 83–84, 89, 103, 140, 152, 156, 172, 214, 220, 222–23, 253, 261, 263–66, 268, 272, 276, 285, 295;
  theories of Self-regulation, 251–56
sensorimotor (sensory-motor), 89–90, 94–95, 103, 104–6, 108, 113, 115, 117, 226
serotonin, 98, 110, 224–25, 228–29
sextortion, 116–17, 128
sex trafficking (also prostitution), 117, 119, 123–24, 125, 129–31, 144
sexual abuse, 60, 115, 124–25, 127–28, 130, 133, 135, 137, 139–40, 143,

156–57, 169, 178, 183, 191, 193, 201, 207, 210, 224, 231, 238, 250, 257, 288
sexual assault, 80, 83, 113, 123, 125, 128, 130–31, 134, 136, 141, 144, 158, 166, 170–71, 175, 178–79, 196, 182–84, 189, 190–92, 196–99, 201–6, 211, 221, 236–39, 249–50, 253, 275, 284, 288–89
shame, 42, 51, 62, 64, 67, 126, 139–40, 155, 165, 176, 186, 194–96, 219–42, 245, 247, 258, 271, 292–93;
  Nathanson's Compass of Shame, 219, 221–22, 233;
  social self-preservation theory, 220, 232
shared vulnerability model, 79
Shattered Assumptions Theory, 181
sleep, 25, 43, 82, 94, 138–39, 143, 152–53, 176–77, 180, 187, 199, 200, 202, 223, 227, 229, 250, 282, 293–94
small-world network model, 63, 65, 76–77
social support, 16, 18, 26, 29, 32, 35, 38, 43–45, 48, 55, 57–62, 64, 75, 77, 81–82, 84–85, 88, 90, 97, 99, 123, 127–28, 131–32, 136, 138, 141, 144, 146, 151–52, 155, 158–59, 162, 164–65, 168, 173, 176, 180–83, 185–86, 188–90, 192, 194–95, 203, 206, 210–13, 217, 222, 225–26, 231–33, 235–36, 239–41, 244, 247, 251–52, 254, 261–63, 264–67, 269, 271, 273, 275–76, 279, 281, 284, 287–89, 292, 294
somatic-marker hypothesis, 61, 65, 96, 108
stress, 41, 42–43, 45, 59, 64, 70, 75–76, 83–84, 87, 89, 92, 99, 110–12, 117–18, 123, 125, 127 128, 131, 133–36, 138–42, 147–48, 150–51, 153–56, 158–73, 176–78, 181–82, 185–86, 188–90, 191–96, 198–99, 201–3, 205, 207–8, 210, 211–16, 217–22, 228–29, 231–32, 235, 238–39, 243, 246, 248–49, 252–58, 263, 267–69, 270–74, 275–76, 279–80, 282–83, 287–89, 292–93, 295, 297;
  Stress Sensitization Theory, 173, 185
substance abuse, 30, 42, 94, 123–24, 126, 136, 139–40, 142, 143, 156, 158, 178–80, 182–83, 190, 192–93, 197–98, 200–201, 205, 211, 219, 225, 232, 244, 256, 262, 266
suicide, 20, 82, 93–94, 127, 131, 137, 139–40, 144, 150, 160, 164, 175, 178, 181–82, 190, 192–95, 198, 204–5, 207, 213, 225–26, 229, 232, 244, 252–54, 256, 270

talent, 11, 20, 23–43, 45, 47, 49–55, 60, 71, 77, 85, 94–95, 233;
  Enrichment Triad Model (also Three-Ring Model), 27, 39;
  identifying, 18–20, 24, 31–35, 37–39, 42, 44–45, 46, 49, 54–55, 61–62, 64, 67, 71, 82, 84, 119;
  mega-model of talent development, 32–33, 44–45;
  nurturing, 40–42, 45, 47, 50, 52–54, 64, 76, 80, 142, 158, 270, 284, 294, 296;
  positive disintegration theory (Dabrowski), 28–29, 40–42, 44, 83, 95;
  pyramid Model, 28, 40;
  scaffolding, 40–41, 52–53;
  talent development model, 26–27, 38;
  talent search model, 27–28, 40
temperament, 47–49, 149, 152, 248–49, 261–62, 268, 280, 292
terror management theory, 265–66, 280, 292
Torrance Tests of Creative Thinking (TTCT), 7–8, 17, 19, 20, 24
torture, 128, 170, 177, 179, 189, 191, 200, 212, 244

transliminal, 104, 111, 117
transmission (of trauma), 123, 125, 137–38, 154, 168, 184, 194, 209–10
trauma, 31, 80, 108, 119, 121, 124–25, 127–28, 133, 135, 140, 142, 144–45, 150–52, 154–65, 168–72, 175–217, 220–21, 224–30, 234–40, 242–46, 251–58, 262–268–270, 272–77, 279, 281–89, 296;
Cumulative trauma, 133, 135, 137, 140, 143–44, 159, 179–81, 188–89, 192, 196–97, 201–6, 210, 212, 214, 217, 221, 244, 256–57, 269, 272, 289;
Secondary traumatization (compassion fatigue, vicarious trauma), 164, 175, 196–201, 208–13, 252, 275, 282, 287
trauma-informed care, 133, 142, 145, 151

unresolved (trauma/loss), 9, 11, 145, 150, 152, 154–62, 172–73, 181, 224, 228, 230, 249–50

useful, 4, 16–18, 28–29, 98, 119

vagal, 112, 155, 167, 221–22, 250, 267
values, 17, 30–31, 35, 39, 44, 46, 54, 57–59, 65, 89, 114, 176, 181, 187–88, 190, 195, 206, 211, 231, 233, 241, 269, 274, 276, 280, 284–86, 294
violence, 9, 117, 123, 125, 127–29, 131, 134–36, 138–42, 144, 149–50, 156, 161, 170, 175, 179, 181–84, 186, 188–97, 199, 200, 202, 204, 207, 216, 222, 225, 235, 238, 250, 253, 262, 269, 272–73, 275–76, 287
interpersonal violence, 133, 144, 171–72, 178–79, 183–84, 190, 192, 199–202, 204, 206, 225, 234–35, 238–39, 250, 282

working memory, 88–89, 91, 99–104, 228, 245, 255

About the Authors

Paula Thomson, PsyD, is Professor in the Department of Kinesiology, California State University, Northridge (CSUN). She is a licensed clinical psychologist, adjunct faculty at Pacifica Graduate Institute, faculty at OperaWorks, and Professor Emeritus and Senior Scholar at York University (Canada). She is Co-Director of the Performance Psychophysiology Laboratory at CSUN, which focuses on research investigating the psychological and physiologic effects of stress on performers, athletes, healthy active individuals and patients with functional disorders. She is co-author of the book *Creativity and the Performing Artist: Behind the Mask*. For over thirty years she has worked professionally in the performing arts, including choreographer at Stratford Shakespearean Festival, Canadian Opera Company, Canadian Stage Company, and Artistic Director/Choreographer for Northern Lights Dance Theatre. She continues to work professionally as a choreographer and dance educator. In 2013, she was named one of the top twenty female professors in California.

S. Victoria Jaque earned her PhD in Exercise Science from the University of Southern California, and is professor and graduate coordinator in both the Department of Kinesiology and Assisted Technology Studies and Human Services at California State University, Northridge (CSUN). She is Co-Director of the Performance Psychophysiology Laboratory at CSUN and co-author of the book *Creativity and the Performing Artist: Behind the Mask*. As an exercise physiologist, she has conducted research in a variety of areas, including the influence of physical activity on the development of peak bone mass in humans and rodents. Her current research focuses on developing a better understanding of how the autonomic nervous system responds to physiologic and psychological stressors in performing artists, athletes, healthy active individuals and patients with functional disorders. She is an active researcher in laboratory and field settings (concert halls, studios).

Printed in Great Britain
by Amazon